Random House
Webster's
Large Print
Thesaurus

RANDOM HOUSE
NEW YORK

Contents

Staff

Project Editor: Enid Pearsons

Editor, First Edition: Laurence Urdang

Editor, Revised Edition: Robert B. Costello

Previous Contributors: Seymour Barofsky, Mary Louise Byrd, Carole Cook, Pamela DeVinne, Robin Fleisig, Wanda Hernandez, Ruth Koenigsberg, Trudy Nelson, Maria Padilla, Julia Penelope

Director of Production: Patricia W. Ehresmann

Editorial Production Services: Jennifer Dowling, Seaside Press

Database Manager: Constance A. Baboukis

Programming Consultant: Paul Hayslett

Designer: Charlotte Staub

Editorial Director: Wendalyn Nichols

Editorial Director Emeritus: Sol Steinmetz

Publisher: Charles Levine

Choosing the Right Word

The *Random House Webster's Large Print Thesaurus* can be a significant help in expanding your vocabulary, allowing you to express yourself with added variety, depth, and interest.

The book has thousands of synonyms to choose from. At each main entry term, the synonyms are arranged (1) by part of speech and (2) by sense, with each sense numbered separately. For example, the entry for **close** has twenty numbered senses divided among three parts of speech—*verb, adjective,* and *noun.*

When you need another word to replace one that isn't quite right, first try to determine the particular sense you need from what you have already written. In the *Thesaurus,* look up the word you want to replace and find the set of synonyms that comes closest to the general meaning you are looking for. If the word you are trying to look up is not listed as a main entry term, try a closely related word. For instance, if there is no entry for **hilarious,** try **amusing** instead, which does have a list of useful and appropriate synonyms.

For the most part, synonyms for a word or for a sense of a word are presented with those closest in meaning given first, continuing to words that are more distantly related. In other cases, the progression may go from the more formal (or academic) to the less formal, and even to the slangy—or vice versa. There is, in each group of synonyms, some sort of underlying organizational principle that the editors hope will be self-evident. Synonyms are never given in a completely random sequence.

Antonyms—words that are opposite in meaning from synonyms—are given at the end of an entry whenever they are thought to be especially appropriate. You will find that the presence of antonyms enhances the usefulness of the *Thesaurus.*

The book also contains Synonym Studies—small essays that clarify distinctions among three or four words that are closely related in meaning. All of these studies include example sentences that illustrate appropriate contexts for the words under discussion.

A Word of Caution

While is it clearly a great advantage to have a variety of synonyms available, both to improve one's writing and to clarify one's thinking, it is also helpful to bear in mind that rarely do two words mean *precisely* the same thing. That is, words have shades of meaning or usage such that one word may be more appropriate to a context than another, even though they may be generally related in meaning. Before choosing a synonym, try to determine what sort of word your context calls for. If you are writing something fairly formal, and you want a synonym for "clothes," you may want a word like "garment," or "apparel," or "attire." If you wish to be deliberately fancy, you can choose "raiment" or "habiliment." But if you choose "duds," or "gear," or "getup," or "threads," you will alter the tone in a way that will jar the reader or listener. Similarly, "duds" may fit a certain context very nicely whereas "habiliment" will sound out of place. It can help to look up unfamiliar synonyms in a good-size dictionary, where the words are likely to be shown in typical contexts that will help guide you in making a choice.

Abbreviations Used in This Book

adj.	adjective	*adv.*	adverb
Ant.	Antonym	*Brit.*	British
conj.	conjunction	*n.*	noun
prep.	preposition	*Syn. Study*	Synonym Study
v.	verb		

New Words
Keeping Up with Vocabulary in the Nineties and Beyond the Millennium

Like dictionaries, thesauruses grow larger over the years, they try to keep pace with the explosive growth of the English vocabulary. But for the thesaurus maker, new terms are troublemakers.

Often, these terms come from the volatile worlds of personal relationships, politics, and other new social phenomena. As such they carry both the fascination and disapproval associated with new fads, new slang, and new ways of using language. In consequence, these terms raise many questions: Do they fit into existing synonym lists? What kinds of people are using them? In what contexts? And, most importantly, what are the guidelines for using them appropriately?

Without the support of a full dictionary entry—with its word origins, usage and subject labels, and definitions—can a thesaurus convey these guidelines? After all, expanding your vocabulary should enrich your powers of expression, not cause you embarassment.

In other words, it is important for the editors of a book of synonyms to determine which new terms belong in a thesaurus at all, where they fit in the existing lists, and what labels and other guidelines can usefully accompany them.

The following terms provide examples of such analysis:

Terms	List under	Comments and Examples
ASAP, *adv.* (as soon as possible; promptly)	IMMEDIATELY 1	Pronounced ($\overline{a}'$sap *or as the initials A-S-A-P*); found esp. in business contexts.
bodice ripper, *n. Slang.* (romance novel)	ROMANCE 1	A pejorative reference to the lurid pictures on the covers of paperback romance novels.
buff, *adj. Slang.* (physically attractive, muscular)	MUSCULAR	A term popular with people in their twenties and thirties.
challenged, *adj.* (deficient; handicapped)	DEFECTIVE	A euphemism, replacing words like *disabled, handicapped,* and *deficient*, the term **challenged**, usually used in combination, reflects a

Terms	List under	Comments and Examples
challenged continued		genuine attempt to avoid negative connotations. However, it has itself become the subject of exaggerated humor, as in *vertically challenged* ("short") and *follicularly challenged* ("bald").
chilling effect, *n.* (discouraging or deterring effect)	DISCOURAGEMENT 2	In legal parlance a *chilling effect* is serious enough to inhibit the exercise of one's constitutional rights.
chump change, *n.* (a small amount of money)	MONEY 3	A slang term used to refer disparagingly to some insignificant cost, payment, etc.

Terms	List under	Comments and Examples
def, *adj.* (superb; outstanding)	EXCELLENT	Current slang term; used primarily by people in their twenties or younger.
to die for, (exceptionally attractive)	BEAUTIFUL, GORGEOUS	An informal adjectival phrase placed following the noun it modifies: *an incredible face, with eyes to die for.*
dis, *v.* (affront, insult)	SLIGHT 5	Slang term.
drop-dead, *adj.* (1. inspiring awe or envy) (2. being the most extreme limit; ultimate)	EXTRAORDINARY; FINAL 1	*A drop-dead beauty of a car. What's the drop-dead date for finishing the renovation?*

Terms	List under	Comments and Examples
du jour, *adj.* (fashionable)	FASHIONABLE, CURRENT 2	Suggests the ephemeral nature of fads: *SUVs are the cars du jour.*
gazillion, *n.* (a large but indeterminate number)	LOT 4	Same sense as *zillion,* but a newer and more forceful term.
finger-pointing, *n.* (accusation; reproach)	BLAME 2	This is used in perfectly standard contexts.
in-your-face, *adj.* (provoking, antagonistic)	DEFIANT	An informal term, but used for effect in standard contexts: *The other side came to the bargaining table with a distinctly in-your-face attitude.*

Terms	List under	Comments and Examples
phat, *adj. Slang.* (great; fine)	WONDERFUL	Probably from a respelling of *fat,* relating to its senses of "lucrative," "prosperous," and "abundant."
poster child, *n.* (exemplar; paragon)	MODEL 2	From the tradition of choosing a child to represent a charitable cause during a fund-raising campaign.
slap on the wrist, *n.* (mild criticism)	CENSURE	Used to describe or denote punishment that the writer or speaker considers insufficient to compensate for an offense or crime.
take-no-prison-ers, *adj.* (zealous; gung-ho)	AGGRESIVE 1, 2	Conveys unyielding single-mindedness: *The hockey team has a take-no-prisoners attitude on the rink.*

A

abandon, *v.* **1.** leave, forsake, desert, relinquish, evacuate, drop, discard, cast off, quit, vacate. **2.** resign, retire, quit, abjure, forswear, withdraw, forgo. **3.** abdicate, waive, give up, yield, surrender, resign, cede, renounce, repudiate. **—Ant.** keep, maintain; pursue.

abandoned, *adj.* **1.** forsaken, left, deserted, relinquished, dropped, discarded, cast off, cast aside, cast out, rejected, demitted, sent down. **2.** unrestrained. **3.** wicked, depraved, unprincipled, sinful, corrupt, licentious, amoral, profligate, vicious, dissolute, shameless; shameful, immoral, incorrigible, impenitent, graceless, irreclaimable, reprobate, demoralized, vice-ridden. **—Ant.** virtuous, honest, good, righteous.

abase, *v.* lower, reduce, humble, degrade, downgrade, demote; disgrace, dishonor, debase, take down, humiliate. **—Ant.** elevate, exalt, honor.

abash, *v.* shame, embarrass, mortify, disconcert, discompose, confound, confuse; cow, humble, humiliate, discountenance, affront.

abate, *v.* **1.** lessen, diminish, reduce, discount, decrease, lower, slow. **2.** deduct, subtract, remit, rebate, allow, discount. **3.** omit, eliminate, disallow. **4.** *(law)* suppress; suspend, extinguish; annul; remove, disallow, nullify, repress. **5.** diminish, lessen, decrease, lower, slow, subside, decline, sink, wane, ebb, slack off, slacken, fade, fade out, fade away. **—Ant.** increase, intensify.

abatement, *n.* **1.**

alleviation, mitigation, lessening, let-up, diminution, decrease, slackening. **2.** suppression, termination, ending, end, cessation. **3.** subsidence, decline, sinking, way, ebb, slack, fade-out, fading. —**Ant.** intensification, increase.

abbreviate, *v.* shorten, abridge, reduce, curtail, cut, contract, compress; crop, dock, pare down, prune, truncate; condense, digest, epitomize, abstract. —**Ant.** lengthen, expand. —**Syn. Study.** See SHORTEN.

abbreviation, *n.* shortening, abridgment, compendium, reduction, curtailment, cut, contraction, compression; truncation; condensation, digest, epitome, brief, essence, heart, core, soul. —**Ant.** lengthening, expansion.

ABC's, *n.* **1.** alphabet, letters of alphabet. **2.** essentials, rudiments, basics, fundamentals, principles, grammar, elements.

abdicate, *v.* renounce, disclaim, disavow, disown, repudiate; resign, retire, quit, relinquish, abandon, surrender, cede, give up, waive. —**Ant.** commit.

abdication, *n.* renunciation, disclaimer, disavowal, repudiation, resignation, retirement, quittance; abandonment, surrender, cession, waiver. —**Ant.** commitment.

abdomen, *n.* **1.** stomach, belly, visceral cavity, viscera, paunch. **2.** *(slang)* pot, guts, gut, potbelly, corporation, alderman, beer-barrel.

abduct, *v.* kidnap, carry off, bear off, capture, carry away, ravish, steal away, run away *or* off with, seize, rape.

abduction, *n.* kidnapping, capture, ravishment, deprehension, seizure, rape.

abductor, *n.* kidnapper, captor, ravisher, seizer, rapist.

abecedarian, *n.* **1.** beginner. —*adj.* **2.** alphabetical. **3.** primary, basic, rudimentary.

aberrant, *adj.* **1.** straying, stray, deviating, deviate, wandering, errant, erring, devious, erratic, rambling, diverging, divergent. **2.** abnormal, irregular, unusual, odd, eccentric, peculiar, exceptional, weird, queer, curious, singular, strange; unconforming, nonconforming, anomalous. **—Ant.** direct.

aberration, *n.* **1.** wandering, straying, deviation, rambling, divergence, departure. **2.** strangeness, abnormality, abnormity, oddness, anomaly, irregularity, eccentricity; peculiarity, curiosity, oddity. **3.** unsoundness, illusion, hallucination, delusion, *lapsus mentis.*

abet, *v.* aid, assist, help, support, back, succor, sustain; countenance, sanction, uphold, second, condone, approve, favor; encourage, promote, conduce, advocate, advance, further, subsidize. **—Ant.** hinder.

abeyance, *n.* suspension, suspense, inactivity, hiatus, recess, deferral, intermission, interregnum, dormancy, quiescence. **—Ant.** operation, action.

abhor, *v.* hate, detest, loathe, abominate, despise, regard with repugnance, execrate, view with horror, shrink from, shudder at, bear malice *or* spleen. **—Ant.** love. **—Syn. Study.** See HATE.

abhorrence, *n.* hate, hatred, loathing, execration, odium, abomination, aversion, repugnance, revulsion, disgust, horror, antipathy, detestation, animosity, enmity. **—Ant.** love.

abhorrent, *adj.* **1.** hating, loathing, loathsome, execrating, execratory, antipathetic, detesting, detestable. **2.** horrible, horrifying, shocking, disgusting, revolting, sickening, nauseating, repugnant, repulsive, odious; hateful, detestable, abominable, invidious. **3.** remote, far, distant, removed. **—Ant.** amiable, lovable.

abide, *v.* **1.** remain, stay, wait, wait for, tarry, sojourn. **2.** dwell, reside, live, inhabit, tenant, stay. **3.** remain, continue, endure, last, persist, persevere, remain steadfast *or* faithful *or* constant, go on, keep on. **4.** stand by, support, second; await *or* accept the consequences of. **5.** await, attend, wait for. **6.** stand one's ground against, await *or* sustain defiantly. **7.** put up with, stand, suffer, brook, allow, tolerate, bear, endure.

ability, *n.* **1.** power, proficiency, expertness, dexterity, capacity, ableness, capability, knack, facility, competency, competence, enablement; puissance, prepotency. **2.** faculty, talent, aptitude, skill, skillfulness, aptness, ingenuity. —**Ant.** inability. —**Syn. Study.** ABILITY, FACULTY, TALENT denote power or capacity to do something. ABILITY is the general word for a natural or acquired capacity to do things; it usually implies doing them well: *a leader of great ability; ability in mathematics.* FACULTY denotes a natural or acquired ability for a particular kind of action: *a faculty for putting people at ease.* TALENT usually denotes an exceptional natural ability or aptitude in a particular field: *a talent for music.*

abject, *adj.* **1.** humiliating, disheartening, debasing, degrading. **2.** contemptible, despicable, scurvy, hateful; base, mean, low, vile, groveling, corrupt; faithless, treacherous, perfidious, dishonorable, inglorious, dishonest, false, fraudulent; disgraceful, ignominious, discreditable. —**Ant.** supercilious; exalted.

able, *adj.* **1.** qualified, fit, fitted, competent, capable, apt. **2.** talented, accomplished, gifted, endowed; skilled, clever, adroit, expert, ingenious, skillful, proficient, versed. —**Ant.** unable, incompetent, inept.

able-bodied, *adj.* well-knit, brawny, burly, sturdy, strapping, powerful, vigorous, red-blooded, robust, vital, lusty.

abnormal, *adj.* nonconforming, nonconformant, irregular, erratic, anomalous, unusual, unnatural, queer, odd, peculiar, aberrant, eccentric, weird, curious, strange, singular, idiosyncratic. **—Ant.** normal, regular.

abnormality, *n.* abnormity, irregularity, unconformity, anomaly, peculiarity, aberrance, idiosyncrasy, singularity, curiosity; malformation, monstrosity. **—Ant.** regularity, normality.

abolish, *v.* suppress, put an end to, cease, void, annul, invalidate, nullify, cancel, revoke, rescind, repeal, eradicate, stamp out, annihilate, extirpate, destroy, do away with, abrogate, obliterate, erase, extinguish, put out, eliminate. **—Ant.** establish.

abolition, *n.* destruction, annihilation, extirpation, abrogation, obliteration, eradication, elimination, extinction; annulment, nullification, invalidation, cancellation, revocation, repeal. **—Ant.** establishment.

abominable, *adj.* detestable, hateful, loathsome, abhorrent, odious, contemptible, despicable, scurvy; horrible, horrifying, disgusting, nauseating, sickening, revolting, repugnant, obnoxious, foul, noxious. **—Ant.** likable, admirable, delightful.

abominate, *v.* abhor, regard with aversion, detest, hate, loathe, execrate, contemn, despise, regard with repugnance, view with horror, shrink from, shudder at, bear malice *or* spleen. **—Ant.** like, love, enjoy.

abomination, *n.* **1.** hatred, loathing, abhorrence, detestation, revulsion, loathsomeness, odiousness, odium; aversion. **2.** vice, sin, impurity, corruption, wickedness, evil, viciousness, depravity, immorality, amorality, profligacy, defilement, pollution, filth.

abortive, *adj.* **1.** failing, unsuccessful, miscarrying, immature, premature. **2.** undeveloped, underdeveloped, rudimentary, primitive. **3.** *(medicine)* abortifacient. **4.** *(pathology)* short, mild, without symptoms. —**Ant.** consummate.

abound, *v.* prevail, teem, swarm, be very prevalent, pour, stream, shower. —**Ant.** want, need, lack.

about, *prep.* **1.** of, concerning, in regard to, respecting, with regard *or* respect *or* reference to, relating *or* relative to. **2.** connected with, in connection with, relating *or* relative to. **3.** near, around, round, not far from, close to. **4.** near, close to, approximately, almost. **5.** around, circling, encircling, inclosing, enclosing, surrounding. **6.** on one's person, having in one's possession. **7.** on the point of, ready, prepared. **8.** here and there, in, on, hither and yon, to and fro, back and forth, hither and thither. —*adv.* **9.** near, approximately, nearly, almost, well-nigh. **10.** nearby, close, not far, around. **11.** on every side, in every direction, all around, everywhere, every place, all over. **12.** half round, reversed, backwards, opposite direction. **13.** to and fro, back and forth, hither and thither, hither and yon, here and there. **14.** in succession, alternately, in rotation.

about-face, *n.* 180° turn, reversal, turnabout, reverse, changeabout, reversion, volte-face.

above, *adv.* **1.** overhead, aloft, on high, atop, on top of. **2.** higher, beyond, over, superior, surpassing. **3.** before, prior, earlier, sooner, previous, first. **4.** in heaven, on high, *in excelsis.* —*prep.* **5.** over, in a higher place than, higher than, superior to.

6. more, greater than, more than, exceeding. **7.** superior to, beyond, surpassing. —*adj.* **8.** supra, said, written, mentioned previously, foregoing, preceding.

aboveboard, *adv.* **1.** in open sight, without tricks, without disguise, openly, overtly, candidly, honestly, frankly, sincerely, guilelessly, unequivocally, unequivocatingly. —*adj.* **2.** open, candid, overt, honest, frank, sincere, guileless, unequivocal, unequivocating. —**Ant.** underhand, treacherous, seditious.

abrade, *v.* wear off, wear down, scrape off; erode, wear away, rub off.

abrasion, *n.* **1.** sore, scrape, cut, scratch. **2.** friction, abrading, rubbing, erosion, wearing down, rubbing off.

abreast, *adv., adj.* side by side, alongside, equal, aligned, in alignment.

abridge, *v.* **1.** condense, digest, scale down, reduce, epitomize, abstract. **2.**

curtail, reduce, lessen, diminish, contract. **3.** deprive, cut off, dispossess, divest. —**Ant.** expand, extend. —**Syn. Study.** See SHORTEN.

abridgment, *n.* **1.** condensation, shortening, digest, epitome, curtailment, reduction, abbreviation, contraction, retrenchment, compression; compendium, synopsis, abstract, abstraction, summary, syllabus, brief, outline, précis. **2.** dispossession, limitation. —**Ant.** expansion, extension, enlargement.

abroad, *adv.* **1.** overseas, beyond the sea, away. **2.** out-of-doors, outside, out of the house. **3.** astir, in circulation, bruited about. **4.** broadly, widely, expansively, at large, everywhere, ubiquitously, in all directions. **5.** untrue, wide of the truth. —**Ant.** here, domestically.

abrogate, *v.* abolish, cancel, annul, repeal, disannul, revoke, rescind, nullify, void, invalidate. **—Ant.** ratify, establish.

abrogation, *n.* abolition, cancellation, annulment, repeal, disannulment, revocation, rescission, nullification, invalidation. **—Ant.** establishment.

abrupt, *adj.* **1.** sudden, unceremonious, short, precipitous, hasty, blunt, curt, brusque, uncomplaisant; rude, rough, discourteous, inconsiderate, boorish. **2.** discontinuous, spasmodic, uneven. **3.** steep, precipitous, acclivitous, craggy. **—Ant.** gradual, slow, deliberate.

abscond, *v.* depart suddenly, depart secretly, steal away, sneak off *or* out, decamp, run away, run off, escape, flee, fly, bolt. **—Ant.** remain.

absence, *n.* **1.** want, lack, need, deficiency, defect. **2.** non-appearance. **—Ant.** presence.

absent, *adj.* **1.** away, out, not in, not present, off. **2.** lacking, missing, not present, away. **—v. 3.** stay away, keep away. **—Ant.** present.

absent-minded, *adj.* forgetful, preoccupied, abstracted, oblivious, inattentive, wandering, withdrawn; musing, in a brown study, dreaming, daydreaming. **—Ant.** attentive.

absolute, *adj.* **1.** complete, whole, entire, perfect, free from imperfection, ideal. **2.** pure, unmixed, unadulterated, sheer, unqualified. **3.** unqualified, utter, total, entire, unconditional, unrestricted, unlimited, unbound, unbounded. **4.** arbitrary, despotic, autocratic, dictatorial, tyrannous, tyrannical, imperious, Nazi, Fascist, Fascistic. **5.** uncompared, categorical, certain, unquestionable, unequivocal. **6.** positive, affirmative, unquestionable, indubitable, certain, sure, unequivocal, unequivocating, firm, definite. **—Ant.** mixed; relative.

absolutely, *adv.* **1.** completely, wholly, entirely, unqualifiedly, definitely, unconditionally. **2.** positively, affirmatively, unquestionably, definitely, unequivocally, indubitably, really, without doubt, beyond doubt.

absolve, *v.* **1.** acquit, exonerate, free from blame, exculpate, excuse, forgive, pardon, clear, release, liberate, set free, free, disentangle, discharge, loose, rid. **2.** set free, loose, release, liberate, exempt. **3.** pardon, excuse, forgive. —**Ant.** blame, censure. —**Syn. Study.** ABSOLVE, ACQUIT, EXONERATE all mean to free from blame. ABSOLVE is a general word for this idea. To ACQUIT is to release from a specific and usu. formal accusation: *The court must acquit the accused if there is insufficient evidence of guilt.* To EXONERATE is to consider a person clear of blame or consequences for an act (even when the act is admitted), or to justify

the person for having done it: *to be exonerated for a crime committed in self-defense.*

absorb, *v.* **1.** swallow, consume, assimilate, amalgamate, devour, engulf, ingurgitate; destroy. **2.** engross, occupy.

abstemious, *adj.* temperate, continent, sober, abstinent, self-denying, ascetic, sparing, austere, stinting, frugal. —**Ant.** greedy, gluttonous, grasping.

abstinence, *n.* **1.** abstemiousness, sobriety, soberness, teetotalism, moderation, temperance. **2.** self-restraint, forbearance, avoidance, self-denial, nonindulgence. —**Ant.** indulgence.

abstract, *adj.* **1.** apart, special, unrelated, separate, isolated. **2.** theoretical, unpractical. **3.** abstruse, difficult, deep, complex, complicated. **4.** *(art)* nonrepresentational, unrealistic, unphotographic. —*n.* **5.** summary, digest, epitome, abridgment, synopsis, compendium, condensation, brief; syllabus, outline, précis; gist, substance. **6.** essence, distillation, condensation, substance; core, heart, idea. —*v.* **7.** draw away, take away, remove, distill; separate, fractionate. **8.** divert, disengage. **9.** steal, purloin, rob, pilfer, shoplift, hijack. **10.** separate, consider apart, isolate, dissociate; disjoin, disunite. **11.** summarize, epitomize, distill, abridge, abbreviate, outline, condense, edit, digest. —**Ant.** concrete; interpolate.

abstruse, *adj.* esoteric, recondite, profound, deep, difficult, knotty, complex, involved, secret, hermetic, orphic. —**Ant.** open, straightforward, obvious.

absurd, *adj.* ridiculous, preposterous, foolish, inane, asinine, stupid, unwise, false, unreasonable, irrational, incongruous, self-contradictory. —**Ant.** sensible, rational. —**Syn.**

Study. ABSURD, RIDICULOUS, PREPOSTEROUS all mean inconsistent with reason or common sense. ABSURD means utterly opposed to truth or reason: *an absurd claim.* RIDICULOUS implies that something is fit only to be laughed at, perhaps contemptuously: *a ridiculous suggestion.* PREPOSTEROUS implies an extreme of foolishness: *a preposterous proposal.*

abundance, *n.* **1.** overflow, plenty, copiousness, fertility, profusion, plenteousness, prodigality, extravagance, oversupply, flood. **2.** fullness, generosity, large-heartedness. **3.** affluence, wealth. —**Ant.** lack, need, paucity.

abundant, *adj.* abounding, teeming, thick, plentiful, plenteous, flowing, copious, profuse, overflowing, rich, replete. —**Ant.** sparse, scarce, poor. —**Syn. Study.** See PLENTIFUL.

abuse, *v.* **1.** misuse, misapply, mistreat, misemploy, misappropriate; desecrate, profane, prostitute; deceive, betray, seduce, subvert. **2.** maltreat, ill-use, injure, harm, hurt. **3.** revile, malign, vilify, vituperate, berate, rate, rail at, upbraid, scold, carp at, inveigh against, reproach; traduce, slander, defame, denounce, asperse, calumniate, disparage; satirize, lampoon. —*n.* **4.** misuse, misapplication, mistreatment, misemployment, misappropriation; desecration, profanation, prostitution; deception, betrayal, seduction, subversion. **5.** censure, adverse criticism, blame, condemnation, hostile condemnation; denunciation, vilification, malignment, vituperation, invective, slander, defamation, aspersion, calumniation, curse, disparagement; contumely, scorn, reproach, opprobrium. **6.** offense, crime, corruption. —**Ant.** esteem; praise, acclaim. —**Syn. Study.** ABUSE,

CENSURE, INVECTIVE all mean strongly expressed disapproval. ABUSE implies an outburst of harsh and scathing words, often against one who is defenseless: *abuse directed against an opponent.* CENSURE implies blame, adverse criticism, or condemnation: *severe censure of her bad judgment.* INVECTIVE applies to strong but formal denunciation in speech or print, often in the public interest: *invective against graft.*

abyss, *n.* chasm, gulf, bottomless pit, abysm, depths, pit, crater, crevasse, shaft, well, hollow, cavity.

academic, *adj.* **1.** college, collegiate, university. **2.** unscientific, literary, lettered, scholastic, unprofessional. **3.** theoretical, unpractical, impractical. **4.** conventional, formal. —**Ant.** illiterate.

accept, *v.* **1.** receive, take. **2.** admit, agree to, accede to, acquiesce in, assent to, approve, allow, concede, acknowledge. **3.** resign oneself to, accommodate oneself to, yield, consent. **4.** believe, acknowledge. **5.** understand, construe, interpret. **6.** receive, acknowledge. —**Ant.** reject.

access, *n.* **1.** fit, seizure, attack, spasm, throe, outburst, eruption, explosion. **2.** entry, entrance, doorway, ingress, entrée, passage, adit, right of entry, admittance, way, way in, route, approach. —*v.* **3.** reach, approach, contact, get, communicate with, go into, enter.

accessory, See Syn. study at ADDITION.

accident, *n.* **1.** mischance, misfortune, disaster, calamity, catastrophe, casualty, mishap, misadventure, contingency. **2.** fortuity, chance. —**Ant.** intent, calculation.

accidental, *adj.* **1.** casual, fortuitous, undesigned, unplanned, contingent. **2.** nonessential, incidental, subsidiary, secondary, dispensable, expendable, adventitious. —**Ant.** planned, designed, essential.

acclaimed, *adj.* notable, distinguished, great, major, famous, honored, famed, renowned, celebrated, prominent, world-renowned, world-famous, stellar, world-class, outstanding, preeminent, premiere.

accolade, *n.* honor, praise, tribute, award, distinction, decoration, laurels, kudos.

accommodate, *v.* **1.** oblige, serve; aid, assist, help, abet. **2.** provide, supply, furnish, minister to. **3.** furnish room for, board, entertain. **4.** make suitable, suit, fit, adapt. **5.** bring into harmony, adjust, reconcile, compose, harmonize. **6.** contain, hold. **7.** conform, agree, concur, assent. —**Ant.** inconvenience, incommode. —**Syn. Study.** See OBLIGE. See also CONTAIN.

accompany, *v.* **1.** go along, attend, join, escort,

convoy, wait on. **2.** coexist with, consort with. **3.** associate with, consider together with, couple with. —**Ant.** desert, abandon, forsake. —**Syn. Study.** ACCOMPANY, ATTEND, CONVOY, ESCORT mean to go along with. To ACCOMPANY is to go as an associate or companion, usu. on equal terms: *My daughter accompanied me on the trip.* ATTEND usu. implies going along as a subordinate, as to render service: *to attend the queen.* To CONVOY is to accompany ships or other vehicles with an armed guard: *to convoy a fleet of merchant vessels.* To ESCORT is to accompany in order to protect, honor, or show courtesy: *to escort a visiting dignitary.*

accomplice, *n.* associate, partner, confederate, accessory.

accomplish, *v.* **1.** fulfill, complete, achieve, execute, do, carry out, perform, finish, attain, consummate, culminate, dispatch, effect, effectuate, perfect, realize.

2. succeed in, be successful with *or* in, triumph over, win over. **3.** equip, supply, furnish, provide. —**Ant.** foil.

accomplishment, *n.* **1.** fulfillment, completion, effecting, execution. **2.** achievement, success, consummation. **3.** attainment, acquirement, acquisition, proficiency. —**Ant.** failure.

accord, *v.* **1.** agree, assent, concur, correspond, be harmonious *or* in harmony, harmonize. **2.** adapt, accommodate, reconcile, suit, fit. **3.** grant, concede, yield, give up *or* in, allow, deign, vouchsafe. —**Ant.** conflict, disagree.

accordingly, *adv.* **1.** correspondingly, conformably, agreeably. **2.** in due course, consequently, hence, therefore, thus, so, wherefore.

account, *n.* **1.** narrative, narration, recital, report, history, chronicle, journal, anecdote, description, story, exposé, tale. **2.** explanation, elucidation. **3.** explication, clearing up, exposition. **4.** reason, consideration, motive, excuse, purpose. **5.** consequence, importance, value, consideration, worth, distinction, repute, reputation. **6.** estimation, judgment, consideration, regard. **7.** profit, advantage, benefit. **8.** statement, ledger, inventory, register, score, book, books. **9.** record, ledger; balance. —*v.* **10.** give an explanation for, explain, elucidate. **11.** make excuse for, give reasons for, answer, reply. **12.** explain, explicate. **13.** cause death *or* capture for. **14.** count, reckon, estimate, consider, regard, judge, deem, rate, assess, hold, see, view, look upon. **15.** assign to, impute to, blame, credit, accuse.

accurate, *adj.* correct, exact, precise, careful, true, unerring. —**Ant.** inaccurate. —**Syn. Study.** See CORRECT.

accuse, *v.* **1.** arraign, indict, charge, incriminate, impeach. **2.** blame, inculpate, charge, involve, point to. —**Ant.** exonerate.

accustomed, *adj.* **1.** customary, habitual, usual, characteristic, familiar, common. **2.** wont, used to, in the habit of. —**Ant.** unused, unaccustomed.

acerbic, *adj.* **1.** sour, acerb, tart, acid, acidy, acidulous, acetose. **2.** sarcastic, mordant, sardonic, ironic, wry, satiric, caustic, biting, scathing, sour, vinegary, vinegarish. —**Ant.** sweet, dulcet, generous, upbeat, Pollyannaish, goody-goody.

ache, *v.* **1.** suffer, hurt, suffer pain. —*n.* **2.** pain, continued *or* dull pain, agony.

achieve, *v.* **1.** carry through, accomplish, consummate, complete, effect, execute, do, perform, realize, reach. **2.** gain, obtain, acquire, procure, secure, get, attain, realize, win. **3.** effect, result. —**Ant.** fail.

achievement, *n.* **1.** exploit, feat, deed. **2.** accomplishment, realization, attainment, consummation. —**Ant.** failure.

acid, *adj.* **1.** vinegary. **2.** sour, tart, biting, ill-natured, ill-tempered, sarcastic, sardonic, scornful. —**Ant.** sweet, mild.

acknowledge, *v.* **1.** admit, confess, own, declare, grant, concede, give in, allow, agree. **2.** realize, recognize. **3.** accept, receive, allow. **4.** appreciate, be grateful for, express gratitude for. **5.** reply to, receive, indorse, admit *or* certify receipt of. —**Syn. Study.** ACKNOWLEDGE, ADMIT, CONFESS agree in the idea of declaring something to be true. ACKNOWLEDGE implies making a statement reluctantly, often about something previously doubted or denied: *to acknowledge one's mistakes.* ADMIT esp. implies acknowledging under pressure: *to admit a charge.* CONFESS usu. means stating somewhat formally an admission of wrongdoing or shortcoming: *to confess guilt; to confess an inability to understand.*

acquaintance, *n.* **1.** associate, companion, friend. **2.** personal knowledge, familiarity. —**Syn. Study.** ACQUAINTANCE, ASSOCIATE, COMPANION, FRIEND refer to a person with whom one is in contact. An ACQUAINTANCE is a person one knows, though not intimately: *a casual acquaintance at school.* An ASSOCIATE is a person who is often in one's company, usu. because of some work or pursuit in common: *a business associate.* A COMPANION is a person who shares one's activities or fortunes; the term usu. suggests a familiar relationship: *a traveling companion; a companion in despair.* A FRIEND is a person with whom one is on intimate terms and for whom one feels a warm affection: *a trusted friend.*

acquiesce, *v.* assent, accede, comply, agree, concur, consent, bow, submit, yield, resign *or* reconcile oneself, rest, be satisfied *or* content (with). —**Ant.** protest, object.

acquire, *n.* **1.** appropriate, gain, win, earn, attain; take over, take possession of, procure, secure, obtain, get. **2.** accomplish, achieve. —**Ant.** forfeit. —**Syn. Study.** See GET.

acquit, *v.* **1.** absolve, exonerate, exculpate, pardon, excuse, forgive. **2.** release *or* discharge, liberate, set free. **3.** settle, pay, fulfill. —**Ant.** convict, condemn. —**Syn. Study.** See ABSOLVE.

acrimonious, *adj.* harsh, bitter, biting, sharp, rancorous, angry, contentious, disputatious, antagonistic, hostile, vitriolic. —**Ant.** peaceful, pacific, irenic, tactful, diplomatic.

act, *n.* **1.** feat, exploit, achievement, transaction, accomplishment, performance. **2.** deed, performance. **3.** decree, edict, law, statute, judgment, resolve, award. **4.** record, deed, enactment, ordinance. **5.** turn, routine, performance, stint. —*v.* **6.** exert energy *or* force, operate, function, perform, do, work. **7.** function, be active, substitute (for). **8.** produce an effect, operate, be efficient *or* effective *or* efficacious. **9.** behave, perform, conduct *or* deport *or* comport oneself. **10.** pretend, sham, dissemble, feign, fake, do imitations, dissimulate, play. **11.** play parts, do imitations *or* impersonations. **12.** represent, impersonate, imitate, play the part of. **13.** feign, counterfeit, fake, imitate. **14.** behave as, play the part of.

action, *n.* **1.** movement, work, performance, moving, working, operation. **2.** deed, act. **3.** *(plural)* conduct, behavior. **4.**

energetic activity. **5.** exertion, energy, effort. **6.** gesture. **7.** mechanism, contrivance, apparatus. **8.** skirmish, brush, affair, encounter, meeting, engagement, conflict, combat, fight, battle. **9.** *(law)* proceeding, process, case, suit, lawsuit. —**Ant.** lethargy, inactivity.

active, *adj.* **1.** acting, moving, working, operative. **2.** busy, energetic, strenuous, vigorous, animated, enterprising, efficient, fervent, earnest, eager, diligent, industrious; engaged, occupied, consumed with. **3.** nimble, sprightly, agile, alert, smart, quick, spirited, brisk, supple, lively. **4.** practical, working, applicable, applied. **5.** *(commerce)* busy, profitable; interest-bearing. **6.** *(medicine)* effective, productive. —**Ant.** inactive, lazy.

actual, *adj.* **1.** true, genuine, real, veritable, palpable, tangible, certain, positive, absolute, sure, categorical, decided, definite, determinate, substantial. **2.** now existing, present, here and now. —**Ant.** unreal, untrue, fake.

acute, *adj.* **1.** pointed, cuspidate, aciform, acicular, acuminate, sharp, sharpened. **2.** intense, poignant, touching; severe, fierce, violent, distressing, crucial, sudden, piercing, penetrating. **3.** sharp, penetrating, perceptive, keen, astute, discerning, intelligent, perspicacious, sharp-witted, shrewd, clever, knowing, wise, sage, sagacious, sapient; smart, bright, ingenious. **4.** sensitive, keen. **5.** alt, high, intense. —**Ant.** blunt.

adapt, *v.* suit, adjust, modify, fit, reconcile, accommodate, prepare, conform, make conformable *or* suitable, qualify, compose. —**Syn. Study.** See ADJUST.

add, *v.* **1.** unite, annex, connect, affix, join; append, attach, supplement, increase, make an addition to, augment, adjoin, tack on. **2.** total, tot, sum, aggregate. —**Ant.** subtract, deduct.

addiction, *n.* dependency, compulsive need, obsession, fixation, habit, craving, appetite, itch, lust, passion, monkey.

addition, *n.* **1.** uniting, adding, joining. **2.** summing up. **3.** increase, increment, enlargement, aggrandizement, accession; supplement, appendix, accessory, adjunct, attachment, addendum, appendage. —**Ant.** deduction, subtraction. —**Syn. Study.** ADDITION, ACCESSORY, ADJUNCT, ATTACHMENT refer to something joined to or used with something else. ADDITION is the general word for anything joined to something previously existing; it carries no implication of size, importance, or kind: *to build an addition to the town library.* An ACCESSORY is a nonessential part or object that makes something more complete,

convenient, or attractive: *clothing accessories; camera accessories.* An ADJUNCT is a subordinate addition that aids or assists but is usu. separate: *a second machine as an adjunct to the first.* An ATTACHMENT is a supplementary part that may be easily connected and removed: *a sewing machine attachment for pleating.*

address, *n.* **1.** discourse, lecture, speech, oration. **2.** location, post office. **3.** residence, domicile, abode, habitation, lodging, dwelling, home quarters, house. **4.** manner, bearing. **5.** skillful management, skill, art, adroitness, cleverness, tact, ingenuity, technique, dexterity, ability. —*v.* **6.** direct (speech or writing to), speak to; accost. **7.** invoke, appeal to, apply to. —**Syn. Study.** See SPEECH.

adequate, *adj.* commensurate, equal, suitable, fit for; satisfactory, competent,

sufficient, enough; capable.
—**Ant.** inadequate,
insufficient.

adhere, *v.* **1.** stick fast,
cleave, cling to, stick,
hold, cohere. **2.** be
devoted, identify, be
attached, be a follower, be
faithful, be true. **3.** hold
closely *or* firmly to.
—**Ant.** separate. —**Syn.
Study.** See STICK.

adherent, *n.* **1.** supporter,
follower, partisan, disciple;
devotee, fan, aficionado.
—*adj.* **2.** clinging,
adhering, sticking,
cleaving. —**Ant.** recreant,
deserter. —**Syn. Study.**
See FOLLOWER.

adjacent, *adj.* near, close,
contiguous, adjoining,
juxtaposed, neighboring,
nearby, touching. —**Ant.**
distant. —**Syn. Study.** See
ADJOINING.

adjoining, *adj.* bordering,
contiguous, adjacent, near
or close *or* next to,
touching. —**Syn. Study.**
ADJOINING, ADJACENT both
mean near or close to
something. ADJOINING
implies touching at a

common point or line:
adjoining rooms. ADJACENT
implies being nearby or
next to something else,
with nothing of the same
sort intervening: *a motel
adjacent to the highway;
the adjacent houses.*

adjourn, *v.* **1.** suspend *(for
a day),* postpone,
interrupt, put off, defer,
delay, prorogue. **2.**
postpone, defer, transfer.
—**Ant.** convene; begin.

adjunct, *n.* **1.** addition,
appendix, supplement,
attachment. **2.** aide,
attaché, subordinate,
accessory. —**Syn. Study.**
See ADDITION.

adjust, *v.* **1.** fit, make
correspondent *or*
conformable to, adapt,
accommodate, suit. **2.**
regulate, set, repair, fix;
change, alter. **3.** arrange,
rectify, reconcile, settle. **4.**
adapt oneself, make
oneself suitable *or* suited
for. —**Syn. Study.** ADJUST,
ADAPT, ALTER imply making
necessary or desirable
changes, as in position,
shape, or the like. To
ADJUST is to make a minor

change, as to move into proper position for use: *to adjust the eyepiece of a telescope.* To ADAPT is to make a change in character, or to make something useful in a new way: *to adapt a method to a new task.* To ALTER is to change the appearance but not the use: *to alter a suit.*

ad-lib, *v.* **1.** improvise, extemporize, make up, invent, throw away, wing it. —*n.* **2.** improvisation, extemporization, invention, throwaway. —*adj.* **3.** improvised, extemporized, extemporaneous, made up, extempore, impromptu, unrehearsed, unpremeditated, spontaneous, off-hand, off-the-cuff, spur-of-the-moment, ad hoc.

administer, *v.* **1.** manage, conduct, control, execute; rule, govern; direct, superintend, oversee, supervise. **2.** dispense, distribute, supply, job, furnish, contribute. **3.** give, dispense, apply, dose, deal out, dole out. **4.**

tender, offer, proffer; impose. **5.** provide aid, contribute assistance. **6.** *(law)* act as executor; act as administrator.

admirable, *adj.* estimable, praiseworthy, fine, rare, excellent. —**Ant.** abhorrent.

admiration, *n.* wonder, awe, pleasure, approbation, delight, esteem; liking, affection, regard. —**Ant.** abhorrence, disgust, hatred.

admire, *v.* esteem; revere, venerate; like, delight in. —**Ant.** detest, hate.

admission, *n.* **1.** entrance, introduction, access, admittance, entrée, ticket, pass, Annie Oakley, key, shibboleth. **2.** confession, acknowledgment, allowance, concession. —**Ant.** rejection.

admit, *v.* **1.** allow to enter, grant *or* afford entrance to, let in, afford access to, receive. **2.** permit, allow, agree to, concede, bear. **3.** acknowledge, own, avow, confess. **4.** permit entrance, give access. **5.**

grant permission, be capable of. **—Ant.** reject. **—Syn. Study.** See ACKNOWLEDGE.

admittance, *n.* **1.** entrance, admission, introduction. **2.** access, reception.

admonish, *v.* **1.** caution, advise, warn, counsel. **2.** rebuke, censure, reprove. **3.** recall to duty, remind, notify, make aware, apprise, acquaint, inform. **—Syn. Study.** See WARN. See also REPRIMAND.

ado, *n.* fuss, stir, flurry, dither, pother, commotion, disturbance, hubbub, upset, uproar, upheaval, turmoil, hurly-burly, ruckus, brouhaha, foofaraw. **—Ant.** calm, serenity, tranquillity.

adolescent, *adj.* **1.** immature, youthful, young. —*n.* **2.** youth, teen-ager, minor. **—Ant.** adult.

adore, *v.* idolize, worship, love; respect, honor, esteem, reverence, revere, venerate, idolize. **—Ant.** abhor, detest, abominate, hate.

adorn, *v.* **1.** embellish, add luster to. **2.** decorate, enhance, beautify, deck, bedeck, ornament, trim, bedizen, array. **—Ant.** disfigure, deface.

adroit, *adj.* expert, ingenious, skillful, dexterous, clever, resourceful, ready, quick, apt, adept. **—Ant.** clumsy, maladroit. **—Syn. Study.** See DEXTEROUS.

adult, *adj.* **1.** mature, grown up, full-grown, ripe, of age. —*n.* **2.** grown-up, man, woman. **—Ant.** immature, adolescent.

advance, *v.* **1.** move *or* set *or* push *or* bring forward, further, forward. **2.** propose, bring to view *or* notice, adduce, propound, offer, allege. **3.** improve, further, forward, promote, strengthen. **4.** promote, elevate, dignify, exalt. **5.** increase, raise the pride of, augment. **6.** update, accelerate, quicken, hasten, speed up, bring forward. **7.** furnish *or* supply on credit, lend, loan. **8.** move *or* go forward, proceed, move on. **9.** improve, progress, make progress, grow, increase, flourish, rise, thrive. **10.** rise, increase, appreciate. —*n.* **11.** moving forward, progress, procedure, way; march, procession. **12.** advancement, promotion, improvement, advance, rise. **13.** overture, proposal, proposition, tender, offer, proffer, offering. **14.** price rise, raise, rise, increase. —*adj.* **15.** going before, preceding, precedent. **16.** beyond, ahead, before; prepublication. **—Ant.** retreat.

advantage, *n.* **1.** favorable opportunity *or* state *or* circumstance *or* means *or* situation, vantage point, superiority, superior condition. **2.** benefit, avail, gain, profit, value; return, dividend; utility, usefulness, expediency, use, service. **3.** superiority, ascendancy, preeminence. **4.** behalf, vantage; privilege, prerogative, convenience, accommodation. —*v.* **5.** be of service to, serve, avail, benefit, profit, help, aid, yield profit *or* gain to. **—Ant.** disadvantage.

—Syn. Study. ADVANTAGE, BENEFIT, PROFIT all mean something that is of use or value. ADVANTAGE is anything that places a person in a favorable or superior position, esp. in coping with competition or difficulties: *It is to your advantage to have traveled widely.* BENEFIT is anything that promotes the welfare or improves the state of a person or group: *The new factory will be a great benefit to our town.* PROFIT is any valuable or useful gain, usually financial, moral, or educational: *profit from trade; profit from experience.*

adventurous, *adj.* daring, bold, audacious, courageous, venturous, venturesome, enterprising, dashing, risk-taking, cutting-edge, daredevil, brash, rash, foolhardy. **—Ant.** timid, tame, docile, cautious, unadventurous.

adversary, *n.* **1.** antagonist, opponent, enemy, foe. **2.**

contestant, litigant, opponent. **3.** Satan, the Devil, the Evil One, the Prince of Darkness, Beelzebub, the Tempter. —**Ant.** ally, compatriot, friend. —**Syn. Study.** ADVERSARY, ANTAGONIST refer to a person, group, or personified force contending against another. ADVERSARY suggests an enemy who fights determinedly, continuously, and relentlessly: *a formidable adversary.* ANTAGONIST suggests one who, in hostile spirit, opposes another, often in a particular contest or struggle: *a duel with an antagonist.*

adverse, *adj.* **1.** antagonistic, contrary, opposite, conflicting, opposed, hostile, against, con, contra, inimical, unfriendly. **2.** unfavorable, unlucky, unfortunate; calamitous, disastrous, catastrophic. **3.** opposite, confronting, opposed, facing, vis-à-vis, face-to-face. —**Ant.** favorable, beneficial.

adversity, *n.* calamity, distress, catastrophe, disaster; bad luck, misfortune, misery, trouble, affliction, wretchedness. —**Ant.** happiness, wealth. —**Syn. Study.** See MISFORTUNE.

advice, *n.* **1.** admonition, warning, caution, counsel, opinion, recommendation, guidance, suggestion, persuasion, urging, exhortation. **2.** communication, information, news, report, intelligence, tidings, word, notice, notification. —**Syn. Study.** ADVICE, COUNSEL refer to opinions offered as worthy bases for thought, conduct, or action. ADVICE is a practical recommendation, generally from a person with relevant knowledge or experience: *Get a lawyer's advice about the purchase.* COUNSEL is weighty and serious advice, given after careful deliberation and consultation: *to seek* *counsel during a personal crisis.*

advisable, *adj.* **1.** expedient, advantageous, politic, proper, fit, suitable, desirable, correct, prudent, sensible, common-sense, judicious. **2.** receptive, open to suggestion *or* advice.

advise, *v.* **1.** give counsel to, counsel, admonish, caution, warn, recommend to. **2.** suggest, recommend. **3.** inform, notify, apprise, acquaint. **4.** take counsel, confer, deliberate, discuss, consult. **5.** give advice, offer counsel.

advocate, *v.* **1.** plead in favor of, support, urge, argue for, speak for, recommend. —*n.* **2.** lawyer, attorney, counselor, counselor-at-law, counsel, barrister, solicitor; intercessor. **3.** defender, vindicator, espouser, upholder, supporter, maintainer, promoter, patron, friend. —**Ant.** oppose; opponent.

aesthete, *n.* dilettante,

connoisseur, virtuoso, expert, discriminator, collector.

affable, *adj.* courteous, urbane, debonair, suave, civil, approachable, polite, friendly, cordial, pleasant, amiable, obliging, gracious; benign, mild, easy, casual, social. —**Ant.** discourteous, boorish, reserved.

affect, *v.* **1.** effect, exert influence on, accomplish, bring about, influence, sway, act on; modify, alter, transform, change. **2.** move, impress, touch, stir, overcome. **3.** pretend, feign, fake, assume, adopt. **4.** imitate, act, mimic. **5.** use, adopt, prefer, choose, select. **6.** profess, pretend. —**Syn. Study.** See PRETEND.

affectation, *n.* pretension, airs, mannerisms, pose, artificiality, pretense, affectedness, unnaturalness, insincerity. —**Ant.** sincerity.

affected, *adj.* assumed, pretended, feigned. —**Ant.** sincere, genuine.

affecting, *adj.* touching,

pathetic, piteous, moving, impressive.

affection, *n.* **1.** attachment, liking, friendliness, amity, fondness, devotion, friendship, tenderness, endearment, heart, love. **2.** feeling, inclination, partiality, proclivity, disposition, predisposition, bent, bias. **3.** (*pathology*) disease, disorder, affliction, malady, ailment, illness, complaint. —**Ant.** abhorrence.

affectionate, *adj.* tender, loving, fond, attentive, attached, devoted, warm, kind, sympathetic. —**Ant.** apathetic.

affectless, *adj* unemotional, unfeeling, remote, numb, dead, distant, passionless, dispassionate, detached, disinterested, indifferent, lukewarm, impersonal, cold, cool, cold-blooded, self-absorbed, impassive, untouchable. —**Ant.** interested, involved, passionate, ardent, excitable, committed.

affirm, *v.* **1.** state, assert, aver, maintain, declare, asseverate, depose, testify, say, pronounce. **2.** establish, confirm, ratify, approve, endorse. —**Ant.** deny. —**Syn. Study.** See DECLARE.

affliction, *n.* **1.** pain, distress, grief, adversity, misfortune, trial, mishap, trouble, tribulation, calamity, catastrophe, disaster. **2.** sickness, loss, calamity, persecution, suffering, misery, woe, depression, wretchedness, heartbreak; plague, scourge, epidemic. —**Ant.** relief. —**Syn. Study.** See MISFORTUNE.

affluent, *adj.* **1.** abounding, rich, wealthy, opulent. **2.** abundant, free-flowing, teeming. —*n.* **3.** tributary, feeder. —**Ant.** poor; scarce.

affront, *n.* **1.** offense, slight, disrespect, insult, impertinence, contumely, scorn, indignity, abuse, outrage, injury. **2.** shame, disgrace, degradation. —*v.* **3.** offend, insult, slight, abuse, outrage. **4.** shame, disgrace, discountenance, confuse, confound, disconcert, abash. **5.** confront, encounter, face, meet. —**Ant.** compliment. —**Syn. Study.** See INSULT.

afraid, *adj.* scared, fearful, alarmed, frightened, terrified, disquieted, shocked, apprehensive, timid, cowardly, pusillanimous, timorous, shy, cautious, overcautious. —**Ant.** bold, sanguine, confident.

age, *n.* **1.** period, life, duration. **2.** maturity, years of discretion. **3.** old age, decline. **4.** era, epoch, time, date, period. —*v.* **5.** grow old, mature, ripen. —**Ant.** youth. —**Syn. Study.** AGE, EPOCH, ERA, PERIOD all refer to an extent of time. AGE usu. implies a considerable extent of time, esp. one associated with a dominant personality, influence, characteristic, or institution: *the age of chivalry.* EPOCH and ERA are often used interchangeably to refer to an extent of time characterized by changed conditions and new undertakings: *an era (or epoch) of invention.* EPOCH sometimes refers esp. to the beginning of an era: *The steam engine marked a new epoch in technology.* A PERIOD usu. has a marked condition or feature: *a period of industrial expansion; the Victorian period.*

aged, *adj.* **1.** old, ancient, decrepit, elderly. **2.** old, of the age of. —**Ant.** young.

aggravate, *v.* worsen, make severe, intensify, heighten, increase, make serious *or* grave. —**Ant.** assuage, improve, better.

aggregate, *adj.* **1.** added, combined, total, complete. —*n.* **2.** sum, mass, assemblage, total, gross, body, amount. —*v.* **3.** bring together, assemble, collect, amass, accumulate, gather. **4.** amount to, add up to. **5.** combine into a mass, form a collection. —**Ant.** particular.

aggressive, *adj.* **1.** pugnacious, attacking, offensive, assaulting, militant, assailing, take-no-prisoners. **2.** energetic, vigorous, pushing, enterprising, assertive, determined, forward. —**Ant.** retiring, bashful, shy.

aghast, *adj.* dismayed, horrified, appalled, horror-struck, undone, stricken, stunned, shocked, agape, dumbfounded, thunderstruck, overwhelmed, jolted, jarred, shaken up, shook-up.

agile, *adj.* quick, light, nimble, sprightly, active, lively, brisk, ready, smart, alert, spry. —**Ant.** awkward.

agitate, *v.* **1.** shake *or* move briskly, disturb, toss, jar. **2.** move to and fro. **3.** disturb, ruffle, stir *or* work up, perturb, excite, fluster. **4.** discuss, debate, controvert, campaign *or* argue for, dispute. **5.** plan, devise; revolve *or* turn over in the mind, cogitate, consider, deliberate. **6.** arouse public interest, ferment, disturb, rouse. —**Ant.** tranquilize.

agitation, *n.* **1.** agitating, shaking, jarring, disturbing. **2.** disturbance, excitement, turmoil, tumult, storm; unrest, disquiet; struggle, conflict; perturbation, flurry, ado, to-do. **3.** urging, persistence; debate, discussion, dispute, argument, campaign. —**Ant.** serenity, calm, tranquility.

agnostic, See Syn. study at ATHEIST.

agony, *n.* **1.** pain, distress, suffering, torment, torture, rack; throe, paroxysm, spasm, seizure, pang; ache. **2.** excitement, suspense, anguish, torment, torture. —**Ant.** comfort.

agree, *v.* **1.** assent, yield, consent, accede, concede, acquiesce, allow, comply. **2.** harmonize, concur, unite, accord, combine. **3.** come to an agreement *or* arrangement *or* understanding, compromise, arrive at a settlement. **4.** accord, correspond, compare favorably, coincide, conform, tally, match, stand up, suit. **5.** be applicable *or* appropriate *or* similar, resemble. **6.** make *or* write a contract *or* bargain, contract, stipulate, bargain. **7.** concede, grant, allow, let, permit. —**Ant.** disagree.

agreement, *n.* **1.** agreeing, being in concord. **2.** bargain, contract, compact, understanding, arrangement, deal. **3.** unanimity, harmony, accord, concord, settlement, treaty, pact, word, conformity, unity, uniformity. —**Ant.** disagreement. —**Syn. Study.** AGREEMENT, BARGAIN, COMPACT, CONTRACT all suggest an arrangement between two or more parties. AGREEMENT ranges in meaning from a mutual understanding to a binding obligation: *an agreement to meet next week; a tariff agreement.* BARGAIN applies particularly to agreements about buying and selling; it suggests haggling: *We made a bargain that I would do the work if they supplied the materials.*

COMPACT applies to treaties or alliances between nations or to solemn personal pledges: *a compact to preserve the peace.* CONTRACT is used esp. in law and business for such agreements as are legally enforceable: *a contract to sell a house.*

aid, *v.* **1.** support, help, succor, assist, serve, abet, back, second; spell, relieve. **2.** promote, facilitate, ease, simplify. **3.** be of help, give help *or* assistance. —*n.* **4.** help, support, succor, assistance, service, furtherance; relief, charity. **5.** assistant, helper, supporter, servant, aide, aide-de-camp. —**Ant.** hinder, obstruct; obstacle, obstruction. —**Syn. Study.** See HELP.

ailing, *adj.* sickly, sick, ill, unwell. —**Ant.** healthy, well.

ailment, *n.* disorder, infirmity, affliction, malady, disease, sickness, complaint, ill, debility, disability, handicap, defect.

aim, *v.* **1.** direct, point, give direction to. **2.** direct, point. **3.** strive, try, purpose. —*n.* **4.** direction, sighting. **5.** target, object, end. **6.** purpose, end, object, goal; intent, intention, reason; design, scheme. —**Syn. Study.** AIM, END, OBJECT all imply something that is the goal of one's efforts. AIM implies a direct effort toward a goal, without diversion from it: *Her aim is to be an astronaut.* END emphasizes the goal as separate from the effort: *unscrupulous means to achieve noble ends.* OBJECT emphasizes the goal of a specific effort: *the object of my research.*

air, *n.* **1.** atmosphere. **2.** breeze, breath, zephyr, wind. **3.** circulation, publication, publicity. **4.** character, complexion, appearance, impression, aspect, look, mien; manner, demeanor, attitude, conduct, carriage, behavior, deportment, bearing. **5.** affectation, haughtiness. —*v.* **6.**

ventilate. **7.** expose, display. —**Syn. Study.** See WIND.

alarm, *n.* **1.** fear, apprehension, fright, consternation, terror, panic, dismay. **2.** alarum, tocsin, distress-signal, siren. —*v.* **3.** terrify, frighten, scare, startle; appall, shock; dismay, daunt. —**Ant.** calm, comfort.

alert, *adj.* **1.** attentive, vigilant, watchful, aware, wary, observant, circumspect, heedful, cautious, on the lookout, on the qui vive. **2.** nimble, brisk, lively, quick, active, agile, sprightly, spirited. —*n.* **3.** vigilance, caution, wariness. **4.** air-raid alarm. —*v.* **5.** prepare for action, warn. —**Ant.** asleep, listless.

alien, *n.* **1.** stranger, foreigner, immigrant. —*adj.* **2.** strange, foreign. **3.** adverse, hostile, opposed, unfriendly, differing, unallied, unconnected, separate. —**Ant.** native, friendly.

—**Syn. Study.** See STRANGER.

alienate, See Syn. study at ESTRANGE.

alive, *adj.* **1.** existing, living, breathing, quick. **2.** unextinguished, operative, functioning. **3.** lively, active, alert. **4.** swarming, thronged, aswarm. —**Ant.** dead.

all-around, *adj.* all-round, adaptable, versatile, many-sided, many-talented, flexible, elastic, well-rounded. —**Ant.** narrow, restricted, limited.

allay, *v.* quiet, appease, moderate, soothe, soften, assuage, alleviate, lighten, lessen, mitigate, mollify, temper, relieve, ease. —**Ant.** aggravate.

allege, *v.* **1.** declare, affirm, attest, state, asseverate, assert, aver. **2.** plead, advance. —**Ant.** deny.

allegiance, *n.* duty, obligation, faithfulness, loyalty, fealty, fidelity; homage. —**Ant.** treason, treachery.

alleviate, *v.* ease, lessen,

diminish, quell, abate, mitigate, lighten, relieve, assuage, allay, mollify. —**Ant.** aggravate, intensify.

alley, *n.* back street, lane, byway, street.

alliance, *n.* **1.** association, coalition, combination, bloc, partnership, affiliation, connection, federation, confederacy, confederation, league, union, treaty, pact, compact. **2.** marriage, intermarriage, relation, relationship. **3.** affinity. —**Syn. Study.** ALLIANCE, LEAGUE, CONFEDERATION, UNION refer to the joining of states for mutual benefit or for the joint exercise of functions. ALLIANCE refers to a combination of states for the promotion of common interests: *a trade alliance.* LEAGUE usu. suggests a closer, more formal combination or a more definite purpose: *The League of Nations was formed to promote world peace.* CONFEDERATION applies to a fairly permanent combination for the exercise in common of certain governmental functions: *a confederation of Canadian provinces.* UNION implies an alliance so close and permanent that the separate states become essentially one: *the union of England and Scotland to form Great Britain.*

allocate, See Syn. study at ASSIGN.

allot, *v.* **1.** divide, distribute, parcel out, apportion, assign, deal out, dole out, mete out, deal, dispense, measure out. **2.** appropriate, allocate, set apart, appoint. **—Syn. Study.** See ASSIGN.

allow, *v.* **1.** let, permit, grant. **2.** grant, yield, cede, relinquish, give. **3.** admit, acknowledge, concede, own, confess. **4.** set apart, abate, deduct, remit. **5.** bear, suffer, tolerate, put up with. **—Ant.** forbid, prohibit; refuse. **—Syn. Study.** ALLOW, PERMIT, LET imply granting or conceding the right of someone to do something. ALLOW suggests passivity or even oversight; it points to the absence of an attempt or intent to hinder: *The baby-sitter allowed the children to run around the house.* PERMIT implies a more positive or willing consent; it is often used of a formal authorization: *Bicycle riding is not permitted in this park.* LET is a familiar, conversational term used in a similar sense: *My parents let me stay up late.*

allowance, *n.* **1.** allotment, stipend. **2.** deduction, discount, rebate, tret. **3.** acceptance, admission, concession, acknowledgment. **4.** sanction, tolerance, leave, permission, license, permit, authorization, authority, approval, approbation, imprimatur, sufferance.

ally, *v.* **1.** unite, unify, join, confederate, combine, connect, league, marry, wed. **2.** associate, relate. **3.** join, unite. **—n. 4.** associate, partner, friend, confederate, aide, accomplice, accessory, assistant, abettor; colleague, coadjutor, auxiliary. —**Ant.** enemy, foe, adversary.

almost, *adv.* nearly, well-nigh, somewhat, toward, towards.

alone, *adj.* apart, lone, lonely, lonesome, single, solitary, desolate, isolated, enisled, unaccompanied, solo. —**Ant.** together, accompanied.

also, *adv.* in addition, too, further, likewise, besides, moreover, furthermore.

alter, *v.* **1.** modify, adjust, change, permute, vary. **2.** castrate, spay. **3.** differ, vary, change. —**Ant.** preserve, keep. —**Syn. Study.** See ADJUST, CHANGE.

alternate, *v.* **1.** reciprocate. **2.** act *or* follow reciprocally, interchange successively. —*adj.* **3.** reciprocal, successive, in turn, one after another. —*n.* **4.** substitute, stand-in.

alternative, *n.* **1.** choice, option, selection, course, other. —*adj.* **2.** mutually exclusive (*choice between two things*). —**Syn. Study.** See CHOICE.

although, *conj.* though, even though, notwithstanding, even if, albeit.

altitude, *n.* height, elevation. —**Syn. Study.** See HEIGHT.

always, *adv.* **1.** all the time, uninterruptedly, perpetually, everlastingly, eternally, forever, continually, ever, evermore, forevermore, unceasingly. **2.** every time. —**Ant.** never.

amateur, *n.* dilettante, tyro, novice, nonprofessional, neophyte, greenhorn. —**Ant.** professional, expert.

amaze, *v.* astound, dumfound, surprise, astonish, stagger; stupefy, bewilder, confuse, perplex, daze.

ambiguous, *adj.* **1.** equivocal, doubtful, dubious, unclear, uncertain, vague, indistinct, indeterminate; deceptive. **2.** difficult, obscure, unclassifiable, anomalous. **3.** puzzling, enigmatic, problematic. —**Ant.** explicit, clear. —**Syn. Study.** AMBIGUOUS, EQUIVOCAL both refer to words or expressions that are not clear in meaning. AMBIGUOUS describes that which is capable of two or more contradictory interpretations, usu. unintentionally so: *an ambiguous line in a poem; an ambiguous smile.* EQUIVOCAL also means susceptible of contradictory interpretations, but usu. by a deliberate intent to mislead or mystify: *an equivocal response to an embarrassing question.*

ambition, *n.* **1.** aspiration, enterprise, yearning, longing. **2.** energy. —**Ant.** satisfaction.

ambitious, *adj.* **1.** aspiring, enterprising. **2.** eager, desirous, emulous. **3.** showy, pretentious, ostentatious. —**Ant.** apathetic; humble. —**Syn. Study.** AMBITIOUS, ENTERPRISING describe a person who wishes to rise above his or her present position or condition. An AMBITIOUS person strives for worldly success; such efforts may be admired or frowned on by others: *an ambitious college graduate; an ambitious social climber.* An ENTERPRISING person is characterized by energy and daring in undertaking projects: *This company needs an enterprising new manager.*

ambivalent, *adj.* undecided, uncertain, equivocal, contradictory, unresolved, dubious, mutable, fence-sitting, vacillating, irresolute, hesitant.

ameliorate, *v.* improve, better, amend, raise, elevate, promote. —**Ant.** aggravate. —**Syn. Study.** See IMPROVE.

amend, revise, alter, emend, change. —**Syn. Study.** AMEND, EMEND both mean to alter, improve, or correct something written. AMEND is the general term, used of any such correction or improvement in details; it may refer to adding, taking away, or changing a character, word, or phrase: *to amend spelling and punctuation in a report; to amend a contract.* EMEND applies specifically to the critical alteration of a text in the process of editing or preparing it for publication; it implies improvement in the direction of greater accuracy: *The scholar emended the text by restoring the original reading.*

amiable, *adj.* **1.** gracious, agreeable, kind-hearted. **2.** kind, friendly, amicable. —**Ant.** hostile.

amid, *prep.* among, amidst, amongst, surrounded by.

amnesty, See Syn. study at PARDON.

among, *prep.* amid, between, surrounded by.

amorous, *adj.* **1.** loving, amatory, tender. **2.** enamored, in love, fond of, ardent, tender, passionate, impassioned, erotic, filled with desire, lustful, libidinous. —**Ant.** indifferent, cold.

ample, *adj.* **1.** large, spacious, extensive, vast, great, capacious, roomy, broad, wide. **2.** liberal, generous, free, abundant, copious, abounding, unrestricted, rich, lavish, inexhaustible, plenteous, plentiful, overflowing, full, bountiful, exuberant. —**Ant.** insufficient, meager, scanty, sparse. —**Syn. Study.** See PLENTIFUL.

amplify, *v.* **1.** enlarge, extend, greaten, expand, widen, broaden, develop, augment, dilate, magnify. **2.** exaggerate, overstate, blow up. —**Ant.** abridge, abbreviate.

amuse, *v.* entertain, divert, please, charm, cheer, enliven. —**Ant.** bore. —**Syn. Study.** AMUSE, DIVERT, ENTERTAIN mean to occupy the attention with something pleasant. That which AMUSES is usu. playful or humorous and pleases the fancy. DIVERT implies turning the attention from serious thoughts or pursuits to something light, amusing, or lively. That which ENTERTAINS usu. does so because of a plan or program that engages the attention by being pleasing and sometimes instructive.

amusing, *adj.* **1.** entertaining, diverting, pleasing, charming, cheering, lively. **2.** comical, comic, droll, risible, laughable, delightful, mirth-provoking, funny, farcical, ludicrous, ridiculous. —**Ant.** boring, tedious. —**Syn. Study.** AMUSING, COMICAL, DROLL describe that which causes mirth. That which is AMUSING is quietly humorous or funny in a gentle, good-humored way: *The baby's attempts to talk were amusing.* That which is COMICAL causes laughter by being incongruous, witty, or ludicrous: *His huge shoes made the clown look comical.* DROLL adds to COMICAL the idea of strangeness or peculiarity, and sometimes that of sly or waggish humor: *a droll imitation.*

ancestral, *adj.* hereditary, inherited, patrimonial.

ancestry, *n.* **1.** pedigree, descent, stock, genealogy. **2.** family, house, race, line, lineage. —**Ant.** posterity, descendants.

ancient, *adj.* **1.** old, primitive. **2.** old, aged, antique, antiquated, old-fashioned, out-of-date; antediluvian, prehistoric, of yore. —**Ant.** new, modern. —**Syn. Study.** ANCIENT, ANTIQUATED, ANTIQUE refer to something dating from the past. ANCIENT implies existence or first occurrence in the distant past: *an ancient custom.* ANTIQUATED connotes something that is outdated or no longer useful: *antiquated methods; antiquated ideas.* ANTIQUE suggests a curious or pleasing quality in something old: *antique furniture.*

anger, *n.* **1.** displeasure, resentment, exasperation, wrath, ire, fury, indignation, rage, choler, bile, spleen. —*v.* **2.** displease, vex, irritate, arouse, nettle, exasperate, infuriate, enrage, incense, madden. —**Ant.** patience. —**Syn. Study.** ANGER, INDIGNATION, RAGE, FURY describe deep and strong feelings aroused by injury, injustice, etc. ANGER is the general term for sudden violent displeasure accompanied by an impulse to retaliate: *insults that provoked a burst of anger.* INDIGNATION, a more formal word, implies deep and justified anger, often directed at something unworthy: *The scandal aroused public indignation.* RAGE is vehement, uncontrolled anger: *rage at being fired from a job.* FURY is rage so great that it resembles insanity: *He smashed his fist against the wall in a drunken fury.*

angry, *adj.* indignant, resentful, irate, incensed, enraged, wrathful, wroth, infuriated, furious, mad, passionate, inflamed; provoked, irritated, nettled, galled, chafed, piqued. —**Ant.** patient, calm.

anguish, *n.* **1.** pain, pang, suffering, distress, agony, torment, torture, rack. —*v.* **2.** agonize, distress, torture. —**Ant.** comfort.

angular, *adj.* **1.** with angles *or* corners. **2.** bony, gaunt, skinny, cadaverous. **3.** awkward, stiff, unbending. —**Ant.** curved; plump; graceful.

animal, *n.* **1.** creature. **2.** beast, brute, monster. —*adj.* **3.** living, sentient. **4.** carnal, fleshly, unspiritual, physical; beastly, brutal. —**Syn. Study.** See CARNAL.

animate, *v.* **1.** vivify, enliven, vitalize, quicken. **2.** invigorate, encourage, inspire, inspirit, hearten, energize, fortify, stimulate, arouse, waken. **3.** refresh, exhilarate, buoy up, excite, fire, heat, urge, provoke, incite, kindle, prompt. —*adj.* **4.** alive, lively, vigorous. —**Ant.** thwart; inanimate, sluggish.

animation, *n.* liveliness, vivacity, spirit, life, vigor, energy; enthusiasm, ardor, exhilaration, cheerfulness, sprightliness, buoyancy, airiness. **—Ant.** sluggishness.

announce, *v.* proclaim, publish, declare, report, set forth, promulgate, publicize. **—Ant.** suppress. **—Syn. Study.** ANNOUNCE, PROCLAIM, PUBLISH mean to communicate something in a formal or public way. TO ANNOUNCE is to give out news, often of something expected in the future: *to announce a lecture series.* TO PROCLAIM is to make a widespread and general announcement of something of public interest: *to proclaim a holiday.* TO PUBLISH is to make public in an official way, now esp. by printing: *to publish a book.*

annoy, *v.* molest, harry, hector, badger, tease, irk, pester, harass, bother, worry, trouble, irritate, chafe, fret, disturb, disquiet. **—Ant.** comfort, soothe. **—Syn. Study.** See BOTHER.

answer, *n.* **1.** reply, response, retort, rejoinder. **2.** solution. **3.** defense, plea. **—v. 4.** reply, make reply *or* response, respond, rejoin. **5.** be responsible *or* liable *or* accountable. **6.** pass, serve, do, suit; suffice, be sufficient. **7.** conform, correspond, be correlated. **8.** reply to, respond to. **9.** serve, suit, satisfy, fulfill. **10.** discharge (a responsibility, debt, etc.). **11.** conform *or* correspond to, be similar *or* equivalent to. **12.** atone for, make amends for. **—Ant.** ask, question; differ. **—Syn. Study.** ANSWER, REPLY, RESPONSE, REJOINDER, RETORT all refer to words used to meet a question, proposal, charge, etc. An ANSWER is something said or written in return: *an answer giving the desired information.* A REPLY is usually somewhat more formal or detailed: *a courteous reply to a letter.* A RESPONSE is often a reaction to an appeal, suggestion, etc.: *an enthusiastic response to a plea for cooperation.* A REJOINDER is a quick, usually clever answer to another person's reply or comment: *a rejoinder that silenced the opposition.* A RETORT is a keen, prompt answer, usually to a charge or criticism: *The false accusation provoked a sharp retort.*

antagonist, *n.* opponent, adversary, rival, competitor, contestant, enemy, foe. —**Ant.** ally, friend. —**Syn. Study.** See ADVERSARY.

anticipate, *v.* **1.** foresee, expect, foretaste, forecast. **2.** expect, await, wait for. **3.** preclude, obviate, prevent. **4.** forestall, antedate. **5.** accelerate, precipitate. —**Ant.** close, terminate; slow.

antipathy, *n.* **1.** repugnance, dislike, aversion, disgust, abhorrence, hatred, detestation, hate, loathing, horror. **2.** contrariety, opposition. —**Ant.** attraction, sympathy, love.

antiquated, See Syn. study at ANCIENT.

antique, *adj.* **1.** ancient, old, archaic, bygone; antediluvian. **2.** early, old. **3.** antiquated, old-fashioned, out-of-date, obsolescent, obsolete, passé, demoded, démodé. —*n.* **4.** objet d'art, bibelot, curio, rarity. —**Ant.** modern, new. —**Syn. Study.** See ANCIENT.

antisocial, *adj.* unfriendly, asocial, unsociable, standoffish, aloof, distant, unapproachable, solitary, reclusive, hermitlike, eremitic, eremitical, withdrawn, misanthropic, sociopathic. —**Ant.** social, sociable, friendly, gregarious.

anxiety, *n.* **1.** apprehension, fear, foreboding; worry. distress, uneasiness, disquietude, disquiet; trouble, pain. **2.** solicitous desire, eagerness. —**Ant.** security, certainty.

anxious, *adj.* concerned, worried, apprehensive, uneasy. —**Ant.** secure, certain, sure, confident.

any, See Syn. study at SOME.

apartment, *n.* compartment, suite *or* set of rooms, flat, tenement.

apathetic, *adj.* unfeeling,

passionless, emotionless,
indifferent, unconcerned,
impassive, stoical, cool,
cold, uninterested,
phlegmatic, dull, lifeless,
flaccid, obtuse, sluggish,
torpid, callous,
cold-blooded, insensible,
soulless. **—Ant.** alert,
emotional, sensitive.

ape, *v.* imitate, mimic,
counterfeit, copy, affect.

apex, *n.* tip, point, vertex,
summit, top, pinnacle,
zenith; acme, climax.

apology, *n.* **1.** excuse, plea,
explanation, reparation. **2.**
defense, justification,
vindication. **3.** poor
substitute, makeshift.

appall, *v.* frighten, horrify,
terrify, dismay; daunt,
shock, petrify. **—Ant.**
reassure, comfort; activate,
innervate.

apparel, *n.* **1.** clothes,
dress, garb, attire, raiment,
costume, garments,
habiliments, vesture,
vestments, robes, rig,
accouterments, trappings,
outfit, equipment. **2.**
aspect, guise. **—v. 3.** dress,
clothe, garb, attire; equip,

rig, outfit, accouter; adorn,
ornament, array, deck out.

apparent, *adj.* **1.** plain,
clear, open, evident,
obvious, conspicuous,
patent, unquestionable,
unmistakable, manifest. **2.**
seeming, ostensible, unreal,
specious, quasi, superficial,
external. **3.** visible, open,
in sight, perceptible,
detectable, discernible. **4.**
entitled. **—Ant.** concealed,
obscure; real. **—Syn.
Study.** APPARENT, EVIDENT,
OBVIOUS all refer to
something easily perceived.
APPARENT applies to that
which can readily be seen
or perceived: *an apparent
effort.* EVIDENT applies to
that which facts or
circumstances make plain:
*Your innocence was
evident.* OBVIOUS applies to
that which is
unquestionable, because of
being completely manifest
or noticeable: *an obvious
change of method.*

apparition, *n.* **1.** specter,
vision, illusion, phantom,
wraith, spirit, sprite, ghost,
phantasm, shade, chimera.
2. appearance, appearing,

manifestation,
phenomenon.

appeal, *n.* **1.** entreaty,
request, petition, prayer,
supplication, invocation.
2. application, suit,
solicitation. **3.** attraction.
—*v.* **4.** entreat, supplicate,
petition, ask, request. **5.**
resort.

appear, *v.* **1.** become
visible, come into sight *or*
view, emerge, crop up,
arise, turn up, see the
light. **2.** have an
appearance, seem, look,
show, have the
appearance. **3.** be obvious
or manifest *or* clear.
—**Ant.** disappear. —**Syn.
Study.** See SEEM.

appearance, *n.* **1.** form,
being, apparition; arrival,
coming, advent. **2.** aspect,
mien, guise, air,
expression, look; manner,
demeanor, presence. **3.**
show, seeming, semblance,
face, pretense, pretext,
colors. —**Syn. Study.**
APPEARANCE, ASPECT, GUISE
refer to the way in which
something outwardly
presents itself to view.
APPEARANCE refers to the

outward look: *the shabby
appearance of the car.*
ASPECT refers to the
appearance at some
particular time or in
special circumstances; it
often has emotional
implications, either
ascribed to the object itself
or felt by the beholder: *In
the dusk the forest had a
terrifying aspect.* GUISE
suggests a misleading
appearance, assumed for
an occasion or a purpose:
an enemy in friendly guise.

appease, *v.* **1.** pacify, quiet,
soothe, calm, placate,
tranquilize, mollify,
alleviate, mitigate, temper,
allay, assuage, ease, abate,
lessen; still, hush, lull;
keep down, quell, subdue.
2. satisfy, fulfill,
propitiate. **3.** conciliate,
propitiate, win over, make
amends, accede to the
demands of, make
favorable. —**Ant.**
aggravate, perturb;
dissatisfy. —**Syn. Study.**
APPEASE, CONCILIATE,
PROPITIATE imply trying to
overcome hostility or win
favor. To APPEASE is to

make anxious overtures and often undue concessions to satisfy someone's demands: *Chamberlain tried to appease Hitler at Munich.* To CONCILIATE is to win over an enemy or opponent by friendly gestures and a willingness to cooperate: *to conciliate an opposing faction.* To PROPITIATE is to soften the anger of a powerful superior who has been offended: *Offerings were made to propitiate the gods.*

appendix, *n.* appendage, supplement, addendum, adjunct, appurtenance, addition, extra; enhancement, corrigendum, excursus.

appetite, *n.* **1.** hunger, desire, longing, craving, thirst. **2.** demand. **3.** propensity, liking, relish, gusto, zest, zeal. —**Ant.** renunciation, anorexia.

appetizing, See Syn. study at PALATABLE.

applause, *n.* hand-clapping, shouting; approval, acclamation, approbation, acclaim, plaudit, laurel. —**Ant.** disapproval, condemnation.

apple-polish, *v.* fawn, toady, flatter, kowtow, truckle, blandish, cajole, honey, sweet-talk, butter up, bootlick, suck up to.

appliance, *n.* **1.** instrument, apparatus, device, tool, appurtenance; adjunct, expedient, means, way, resource. **2.** application, use, practice, exercise.

applicable, *adj.* fit, suitable, suited, relevant, apt, fitting, befitting, proper, apropos, germane, pertinent, pointed. —**Ant.** inept.

application, *n.* **1.** applying, appliance, utilization, use, practice. **2.** usability, utility, relevance, aptness, aptitude, suitability, pertinence. **3.** request, petition, solicitation, appeal. **4.** attention, persistent effort, assiduity, industry, persistence, perseverance. —**Ant.** inattention, laziness. —**Syn. Study.** See EFFORT.

apply, *v.* **1.** lay on, place on *or* upon. **2.** use, employ, put to use, effect, utilize. **3.** devote, prescribe, dedicate, assign, appropriate, allot. **4.** have a bearing, refer, be pertinent, hold true *or* good, be appropriate, impinge. **5.** ask, petition, sue, entreat, solicit, appeal. —**Ant.** neglect.

appoint, *v.* **1.** nominate, assign, name, elect, select, set apart, designate, point out, allot, destine. **2.** constitute, ordain, establish, prescribe, direct, require, command, order, decree, impose *or* insist on. **3.** fix, settle, determine, agree on *or* upon. **4.** equip, rig, outfit, accouter, furnish, supply; apparel; decorate. —**Ant.** dismiss; strip. —**Syn. Study.** See FURNISH.

appointment, *n.* **1.** appointing, designating, designation, place, installation. **2.** office, post, station, sinecure, position. **3.** engagement, agreement, arrangement, assignation, rendezvous, tryst.

apportion, *v.* divide, allot, distribute, assign, allocate, appoint, partition, measure, mete, dole out, deal, dispense, parcel out.

appreciate, *v.* **1.** esteem, prize, value, estimate *or* rate highly. **2.** be aware *or* conscious of, detect. **3.** raise the value of. **4.** rise *or* increase in value. —**Ant.** disparage; scorn. —**Syn. Study.** APPRECIATE, ESTEEM, VALUE, PRIZE imply holding a person or thing in high regard. To APPRECIATE is to exercise wise judgment, delicate perception, and keen insight in realizing worth: *to appreciate fine workmanship.* To ESTEEM is to feel respect combined with a warm, kindly sensation: *to esteem one's former teacher.* To VALUE is to attach importance because of worth or usefulness: *I value your opinion.* To PRIZE is to value highly and cherish: *to prize a collection of rare books.*

apprehension, *n.* **1.** anticipation, anxiety,

misgiving, dread, fear, alarm; worry, uneasiness, suspicion, distrust, mistrust. **2.** understanding, intelligence, reason. **3.** view, opinion, idea, belief, sentiment. **4.** arrest, seizure, capture. —**Ant.** confidence, composure; release.

apprise, *v.* inform, tell, advise, give notice to, acquaint, notify, disclose to.

appropriate, *adj.* **1.** fitting, suitable, suited, apt, befitting, meet, felicitous, proper, opportune, apropos, seemly, due, becoming, germane, pertinent, to the point. **2.** proper, individual, unique, sui generis. —*v.* **3.** set apart, direct, assign, apportion, allocate; adopt, take as one's own. —**Ant.** inappropriate, inept.

approve, *v.* **1.** commend, praise, recommend, appreciate, value, esteem, prize. **2.** sanction, authorize, confirm, endorse, ratify, validate, uphold, support, sustain. —**Ant.** disapprove.

apt, *adj.* **1.** inclined, disposed, prone, liable. **2.** likely. **3.** clever, bright, intelligent, brilliant, ingenious; adroit, handy, dexterous, skillful, expert. **4.** appropriate, suited, pertinent, relevant, fit, fitting, apt, befitting, meet, germane, applicable, apropos, felicitous. —**Ant.** inapt, indisposed, malapropos. —**Syn. Study.** APT, RELEVANT, PERTINENT all refer to something suitable or fitting. APT means to the point and particularly appropriate: *an apt comment.* RELEVANT means pertaining to the matter in hand: *a relevant question.* PERTINENT means directly related to and important to the subject: *pertinent information.*

aptitude, *n.* **1.** tendency, propensity, predilection, proclivity, inclination, bent, gift, genius, talent, knack, faculty. **2.** readiness, intelligence, cleverness, talent; understanding, ability, aptness. **3.** fitness, suitability, applicability.

arbitrary, *adj.* **1.** discretionary. **2.** capricious, uncertain, unreasonable, willful, fanciful, whimsical. **3.** uncontrolled, unlimited, unrestrained; absolute, despotic, dictatorial, totalitarian, tyrannical, imperious, overbearing, peremptory, domineering; Fascistic, undemocratic. —**Ant.** relative.

archaic, *adj.* old, ancient, antiquated, antique, old-fashioned, out-of-date. —**Ant.** modern, up-to-date.

archetype, *n.* model, form, pattern, prototype, example, type, paragon, ideal.

ardent, *adj.* **1.** passionate, glowing, fervent, fervid, intense, eager, sanguine, enthusiastic, zealous; vehement, forceful, impassioned, strenuous. **2.** glowing, flashing, flushed. **3.** hot, burning, fiery. —**Ant.** cool, apathetic.

ardor, *n.* **1.** warmth, fervor, fervency, eagerness, zeal, passion, enthusiasm. **2.** fire, burning, heat, warmth, glow. —**Ant.** indifference.

arduous, *adj.* **1.** laborious, hard, difficult, toilsome, onerous, burdensome, wearisome, exhausting, herculean. **2.** energetic, strenuous; fatiguing. **3.** steep, high, acclivitous. **4.** severe, unendurable. —**Ant.** easy.

argue, *v.* **1.** debate, discuss, reason, plead, hold. **2.** contend, dispute. **3.** reason upon, contest, controvert, debate, discuss, dispute. **4.** maintain, support, contend. **5.** persuade, drive, convince. **6.** show, indicate, prove, imply, infer, betoken, evince, denote. —**Ant.** agree.

argument, *n.* **1.** controversy, dispute, debate, discussion. **2.** reasoning, reason, proof, ground, evidence. **3.** fact, statement; theme, thesis, topic, subject, matter. **4.** summary, abstract, epitome, outline, précis. —**Ant.** agreement. —**Syn.**

Study. ARGUMENT, CONTROVERSY, DISPUTE imply the expression and discussion of differing opinions. An ARGUMENT usu. arises from a disagreement between two persons, each of whom advances facts supporting his or her point of view: *an argument over a debt.* A CONTROVERSY is usu. a public expression of contrary opinions; it may be dignified and of some duration: *a political controversy.* A DISPUTE is an oral contention, usu. brief, and often of an angry or undignified character: *a heated dispute between neighbors.*

arid, *adj.* **1.** dry, moistureless, desert, parched; barren, infertile. **2.** dull, lifeless, uninteresting, dry, empty, jejune. —**Ant.** wet, damp. —**Syn. Study.** See DRY.

aroma, *n.* **1.** perfume, odor, scent, fragrance, bouquet, redolence. **2.** subtle quality, spirit, essence, characteristic, air; suggestion, hint. —**Ant.**

stench. —**Syn. Study.** See PERFUME.

arouse, *v.* **1.** animate, stir, rouse, awaken; inspirit, inspire, excite, incite, provoke, instigate, stimulate, warm, kindle, fire. **2.** awaken, get up, arise. —**Ant.** alleviate, calm, mitigate.

arrange, *v.* **1.** order, place, adjust, array, group, sort, dispose, classify, class, rank, distribute. **2.** settle, determine, establish, adjust. **3.** prepare, plan, contrive, devise, concoct, organize. **4.** *(music)* adapt, adjust. **5.** settle, agree, come to terms. **6.** prepare, adjust, adapt, make preparations *or* plans. —**Ant.** disarrange, disorder, disturb.

array, *v.* **1.** arrange, order, range, marshal, rank, place, dispose, draw up. **2.** clothe, apparel, dress, attire, equip, accouter, rig, outfit; deck, bedeck, ornament, trim, decorate, garnish, adorn. —*n.* **3.** order, arrangement, disposition; allotment. **4.** display, show, exhibit, exhibition, showing, demonstration. **5.** attire, dress, clothes, raiment, apparel, garments; panoply. **—Ant.** disarray.

arrest, *v.* **1.** seize, apprehend, capture, catch, take, trap, take into custody, take prisoner. **2.** catch, fix, secure, rivet, engage, capture, occupy, attract. **3.** stop, check, bring to a standstill, stay, hinder, deter, obstruct, delay, interrupt, restrain, hold, withhold. **—n. 4.** detention, custody, imprisonment, apprehension, capture. **5.** seizure, capture, rape. **6.** stoppage, halt, stay, staying, check, hindrance, obstruction, deterrent, detention, restraint, delay, interruption. **—Ant.** release; activate, animate; continue. **—Syn. Study.** See STOP.

arrival, *n.* **1.** advent, coming. **2.** reaching, attainment. **3.** arriver, comer. **—Ant.** departure.

arrive, *v.* come, reach a point, attain, attain a position of success. **—Ant.** depart; fail.

arrogance, *n.* haughtiness, pride, insolence, disdain, effrontery, superciliousness, scorn, contumely, self-confidence, self-importance, conceit, egotism, hauteur. **—Ant.** humility.

arrogant, *adj.* presumptuous, haughty, imperious, supercilious, assuming, proud, insolent, scornful, contumelious, overbearing, overweening, conceited, egotistic, egotistical. **—Ant.** humble, self-effacing.

art, *n.* **1.** trade, craft; skill, adroitness, dexterity, aptitude, ingenuity, knack, cleverness. **2.** cunning, craft, guile, deceit, duplicity, wiliness, dishonesty, artfulness.

articulate, *adj.* fluent, expressive, eloquent. **—Syn. Study.** See ELOQUENT.

artifice, *n.* **1.** ruse, device, subterfuge, wile, machination, expedient, trick, stratagem. **2.** craft, trickery, guile, deception, deceit, art, cunning, artfulness, fraud, duplicity, double-dealing. **3.** skillful, apt *or* artful contrivance. —**Syn. Study.** See TRICK.

artificial, *adj.* **1.** unreal, inauthentic, fabricated, manmade, fashioned, mock, false, fake, imitation, spurious, ersatz, pretend, counterfeit, simulated, sham, bogus. **2.** affected, put-on, insincere, pretentious, assumed, feigned, deceitful, disingenuous. —**Ant.** real, genuine, authentic.

artisan, See Syn. study at ARTIST.

artist, *n.* **1.** artisan, painter, sculptor, sketcher. **2.** actor, actress, thespian, singer, artiste. **3.** designer, artificer, workman. **4.** trickster, designer, contriver. —**Syn. Study.** ARTIST, ARTISAN both refer to a person having superior skill or ability, or one capable of superior workmanship or performance. An ARTIST is a creative person who is skilled in one of the fine or performing arts: *The concert featured a famous pianist and other noted artists.* An ARTISAN is one who is skilled in a craft or applied art that requires manual dexterity: *carpentry done by skilled artisans.*

artless, *adj.* ingenuous, naive, unsophisticated, natural, simple, guileless, open, frank, plain, unaffected, candid, honest, sincere, true, truthful, trusting, trustful, unsuspicious, unsuspecting; unskillful, rude, crude. —**Ant.** cunning, sly, crafty.

ascend, *v.* **1.** mount, rise, climb *or* go upward, soar, climb, arise. **2.** tower. **3.** climb, mount, scale, go *or* get up. —**Ant.** descend; fall.

ascertain, *v.* determine, establish, define, pinpoint, fix, certify, settle, verify; learn, find out, discover, uncover, get at. —**Ant.** guess, assume. —**Syn. Study.** See LEARN.

ascribe, *v.* attribute, impute, refer, assign,

charge. **—Syn. Study.** See ATTRIBUTE.

ashamed, *adj.* **1.** abashed, humiliated, mortified, shamefaced, embarrassed, confused. **2.** unwilling, restrained. **—Ant.** vain, arrogant; willing.

ask, *v.* **1.** put a question to, interrogate, question, inquire of. **2.** inquire, seek information. **3.** request, solicit, petition, sue, appeal, seek, beseech, implore, beg, supplicate, entreat. **4.** demand, expect, require, exact, call for. **5.** invite, call in. **6.** make inquiry, inquire, question. **7.** request, petition, sue, appeal, pray, beg. **—Ant.** answer; refuse, decline.

askance, *adv.* **1.** sideways, sidewise, obliquely, crookedly, at an angle. **2.** suspiciously, dubiously, doubtfully, skeptically, mistrustfully, critically.

aspect, *n.* **1.** appearance, look, attitude, situation, condition. **2.** countenance, expression, mien, visage; air. **3.** view, viewpoint, point of view, attitude, outlook, prospect, direction, bearing. **—Syn. Study.** See APPEARANCE.

aspire, *v.* desire, long, yearn.

assail, *v.* assault, set *or* fall upon, attack; abuse, impugn, maltreat, asperse, malign. **—Syn. Study.** See ATTACK.

assassinate, *v.* murder, kill, blight, destroy, slay, dispatch.

assault, *n.* **1.** assailing, attack, onslaught, onset, combat, invasion, aggression; threat. **—***v.* **2.** attack, assail, storm, charge, invade; threaten. **—Syn. Study.** See ATTACK.

assemble, *v.* **1.** bring together, gather, congregate, collect, convene, convoke, summon, call, call together. **2.** put together, manufacture, connect, set up. **3.** meet, convene, congregate, gather, gather together, come together. **—Ant.** disperse. **—Syn. Study.** See GATHER.

assembly, *n.* **1.** company,

assemblage, throng, mob, gathering, convention, congress, convocation, meeting, meet. **2.** congress, legislature, parliament, lower house, conclave, synod, council, diet. **—Syn. Study.** See CONVENTION.

assent, *v.* **1.** acquiesce, accede, concur, agree, fall in, consent, admit, yield, allow. —*n.* **2.** agreement, concurrence, acquiescence, consent, allowance, approval, concord, accord, approbation. **—Ant.** refuse, deny, dissent.

assert, *v.* **1.** declare, asseverate, affirm, maintain, aver, say, pronounce, allege, avow. **2.** maintain, defend, uphold, support, vindicate, claim, emphasize. **3.** press, make felt, emphasize. **—Ant.** controvert, contradict, deny. **—Syn. Study.** See DECLARE.

assertion, *n.* allegation, statement, asseveration, avowal, declaration, claim, affirmation, predication, vindication, defense, maintenance, emphasis, support. **—Ant.** denial, contradiction.

asseverate, *v.* affirm, assert, state, insist, aver, declare, hold, maintain, contend, avow, avouch, stress, emphasize. **—Ant.** equivocate, waffle, tergiversate.

assiduous, *adj.* constant, unremitting, continuous, applied, industrious, untiring, tireless, persistent, persisting, devoted, zealous, studious, attentive, diligent, solicitous, sedulous. **—Ant.** random, casual, lazy.

assign, *v.* **1.** distribute, allot, apportion, allocate, measure, appropriate. **2.** appoint, designate, specify; fix, determine, pinpoint. **3.** ascribe, attribute, refer, adduce, allege, advance, show, offer, bring up *or* forward. **—Syn. Study.** ASSIGN, ALLOCATE, ALLOT mean to apportion or measure out. To ASSIGN is to distribute available things, designating them to be given to or reserved for specific persons or

purposes: *to assign duties.*
To ALLOCATE is to earmark
or set aside parts of things
available or expected in
the future, each for a
specific purpose: *to
allocate income to various
types of expenses.* To
ALLOT implies making
restrictions as to amount,
size, purpose, etc., and
then apportioning or
assigning: *to allot spaces
for parking.*

assignment, See Syn. study
at TASK.

assist, *v.* help, support,
aid, sustain, patronize,
befriend, further, second,
abet, back, speed,
promote, serve, succor,
relieve, spell. —**Ant.**
impede, obstruct, hinder.
—**Syn. Study.** See HELP.

associate, *v.* **1.** connect,
link. **2.** join, affiliate, team
up with. **3.** unite,
combine, couple. **4.** unite,
combine. **5.** fraternize,
consort, keep company.
—*n.* **6.** acquaintance,
consort, comrade, fellow,
companion, friend, mate,
peer, compeer, equal. **7.**
confederate, accomplice,

ally, partner, colleague,
fellow. —**Ant.** dissociate,
alienate; adversary,
opponent. —**Syn. Study.**
See ACQUAINTANCE.

association, *n.* **1.**
organization, alliance,
union, guild, society, club,
fraternity, sorority, lodge;
company, corporation,
firm, partnership; set,
coterie, clique, band. **2.**
companionship, intimacy,
fellowship, friendship. **3.**
connection, combination.

assume, *v.* **1.** suppose,
presuppose, take for
granted, infer. **2.**
undertake, take on, take
upon oneself. **3.** pretend,
feign, affect, simulate,
counterfeit, put on. **4.**
appropriate, arrogate,
usurp. —**Syn. Study.** See
PRETEND.

assumption, *n.* **1.**
supposition,
presupposition, assuming,
presumption, taking for
granted; hypothesis,
conjecture, guess,
postulate, theory. **2.**
arrogance, presumption,
effrontery, forwardness,
insolence, hauteur

haughtiness, superciliousness, lordliness, stateliness, pride, conceit.

assurance, *n.* **1.** declaration, avowal, asseveration, averment, deposition. **2.** pledge, warranty, surety, guaranty, oath. **3.** confidence, firmness, trust, certainty. **4.** courage, bravery, self-reliance, self-confidence, intrepidity, sang-froid. **5.** boldness, impudence, presumption, arrogance, effrontery, rudeness, impertinence, nerve, cheek. —**Ant.** denial; distrust, uncertainty; cowardice, diffidence. —**Syn. Study.** See CONFIDENCE.

astonish, *v.* amaze, strike with wonder, surprise, astound, shock, startle; daze, stun, stupefy, confound, stagger, overwhelm.

astringent, *adj.* **1.** *(medical)* contracting, constrictive, styptic, binding. **2.** stern, severe, austere, sharp, harsh, rigorous, hard, unrelenting.

astute, *adj.* keen, shrewd, cunning, artful, crafty, sly, wily, penetrating, eagle-eyed, sharp, quick, perspicacious, ingenious, intelligent, sagacious, discerning. —**Ant.** ingenuous, naive, candid, unsophisticated; dull.

asylum, *n.* **1.** hospital, institute, retreat, sanitarium. **2.** refuge, haven, preserve, reserve, sanctuary, shelter, retreat.

atheist, *n.* agnostic, disbeliever, nonbeliever, infidel, skeptic, doubter, heathen, pagan, gentile. —**Ant.** theist. —**Syn. Study.** ATHEIST, AGNOSTIC, INFIDEL refer to persons not inclined toward religious belief or a particular religious faith. An ATHEIST denies the existence of a deity or of divine beings. An AGNOSTIC believes it is impossible to know whether there is a God without sufficient evidence. An INFIDEL is an unbeliever, esp. one who does not accept Christianity or Islam; the word is usu. applied pejoratively.

atom, *n.* iota, jot, dot, whit, tittle, scintilla, mote; indivisible particle.

atrocious, *adj.* **1.** wicked, cruel, heinous, flagitious, monstrous, felonious, flagrant, grievous, outrageous, diabolical, devilish, infernal, hellish. **2.** bad, tasteless, execrable, detestable, abominable. —**Ant.** kind, benevolent; good, praiseworthy.

attach, *v.* **1.** fasten to, affix, join, cement, connect, subjoin, append, add, tack on, annex. **2.** go with, accompany. **3.** associate, attribute, assign. **4.** attract, charm, endear, enamour, captivate, engage, bind. **5.** adhere, pertain, belong, obtain. —**Ant.** detach, separate; repel.

attachment, *n.* **1.** affection, friendship, regard, admiration, fondness, liking, love, devotion; assiduity, bent, predilection. **2.** tie, fastening, junction, connection. **3.** device, apparatus, adjunct. —**Ant.** detachment, separation. —**Syn. Study.** See ADDITION.

attack, *v.* **1.** assail, assault, molest, threaten, interfere with, storm, charge, oppugn, engage in battle, set upon. **2.** criticize, impugn, censure, blame, abuse. **3.** affect. **4.** begin hostilities. —*n.* **5.** onslaught, assault, offense, onset, encounter, aggression. —**Ant.** defend; defense. —**Syn. Study.** ATTACK, ASSAIL, ASSAULT all mean to set upon someone forcibly, with hostile or violent intent. ATTACK is a general word that applies to the beginning of any planned aggressive action, physical or verbal: *to attack an enemy from ambush; to attack a candidate's record.* ASSAIL implies a vehement, sudden, and usu. repeated attack that aims to weaken an opponent: *assailed by gunfire; assailed by gossip.* ASSAULT implies a violent physical attack involving direct contact; it may also refer to a sudden and violent verbal attack: *an elderly couple assaulted by a mugger; a reputation assaulted by the press.*

attain, *v.* **1.** reach, achieve, accomplish, effect, secure, gain, procure, acquire, get, obtain, win. **2.** arrive at, reach. **—Ant.** fail. **—Syn. Study.** See GAIN.

attempt, *v.* **1.** try, undertake, seek, make an effort, essay. **2.** attack, assault, assail. **—n. 3.** trial, essay, effort, endeavor, enterprise, undertaking. **4.** attack, assault. **—Ant.** accomplish, attain. **—Syn. Study.** See TRY.

attend, *v.* **1.** be present at, frequent. **2.** accompany, go with, escort. **3.** minister to, serve, wait on. **4.** tend, take charge of. **5.** heed, listen to, pay attention to, respect. **6.** be present. **7.** pay attention, pay respect, give heed, listen. **8.** apply oneself. **9.** take care *or* charge. **10.** depend, rely. **11.** wait on, serve, minister. **—Syn. Study.** See ACCOMPANY.

attendant, *n.* **1.** escort, companion, comrade, follower; servant, waiter, valet, footman, lackey, flunky, menial, slave. **2.** attender, frequenter. **3.** concomitant, accompaniment, consequence. **—adj. 4.** present, in attendance, accompanying, concomitant, consequent.

attention, *n.* **1.** attending. **2.** care, consideration, observation, heed, regard, mindfulness, notice, watchfulness, alertness. **3.** civility, courtesy, homage, deference, respect, politeness, regard. **4.** *(plural)* regard, court, courtship, suit, devotion, wooing. **—Ant.** inattention.

attentive, *adj.* **1.** observant, regardful, mindful, heedful, thoughtful, alive, alert, awake, on the qui vive; wary, circumspect, watchful, careful. **2.** polite, courteous, respectful, deferential, assiduous. **—Ant.** inattentive, unwary; discourteous.

attitude, *n.* **1.** position,

disposition, manner, bearing, mien, pose. **2.** position, posture. **—Syn. Study.** See POSITION.

attract, *v.* **1.** draw, cause to approach, magnetize. **2.** draw, invite, allure, win, engage, captivate, endear, enamor, charm. **—Ant.** repel, repulse.

attribute, *v.* **1.** ascribe, impute. **—***n.* **2.** quality, character, characteristic, property, mark; peculiarity, quirk. **—Syn. Study.** ATTRIBUTE, ASCRIBE, IMPUTE mean to assign something to a definite cause or source. Possibly because of an association with *tribute*, ATTRIBUTE often has a complimentary connotation: *to attribute one's success to a friend's encouragement.* ASCRIBE is used in a similar sense, but has a neutral implication: *to ascribe an accident to carelessness.* IMPUTE usu. means to attribute something dishonest or discreditable to a person; it implies blame or accusation: *to impute an error to a new employee.* See also QUALITY.

audacious, *adj.* **1.** bold, daring, spirited, adventurous, fearless, intrepid, brave, courageous, dauntless, venturesome, undaunted, valiant. **2.** reckless, bold, impudent, presumptuous, assuming, unabashed, unashamed, shameless, flagrant, insolent, impertinent, brazen, forward. **—Ant.** cowardly, contumelious, feckless.

augment, *v.* **1.** enlarge, extend, increase, swell, bloat. **2.** increase. **—Ant.** reduce, abate.

aura, *n.* atmosphere, mood, feeling, feel, air, ambiance, climate, character, quality, spirit, overtone, sense, undertone.

austere, *adj.* **1.** harsh, hard, stern, strict, forbidding, severe, formal, stiff, inflexible, rigorous, uncompromising, relentless, stringent, restrictive. **2.** grave, sober, serious. **3.** simple, severe, without ornament, plain.

4. rough, harsh, sour, astringent, acerb, bitter. —**Ant.** soothing, flexible; kind; sweet.

austerity, *n.* severity, harshness, strictness, asceticism, rigor, rigidity, rigorousness, stiffness, inflexibility. —**Ant.** lenience, flexibility.

authentic, *adj.* **1.** reliable, trustworthy, veritable, true, accurate, authoritative. **2.** genuine, real, true, unadulterated, pure, uncorrupted. —**Ant.** unreliable, inaccurate; sham, fraudulent, corrupt.

authoritative, *adj.* **1.** official, conclusive, unquestioned, authentic. **2.** impressive, positive; peremptory, dogmatic, authoritarian, dictatorial, imperious, arrogant, autocratic. —**Ant.** unofficial; servile.

authority, *n.* **1.** control, influence, command, rule, sway, power, supremacy. **2.** expert, adjudicator, arbiter, judge, sovereign. **3.** statute, law, rule, ruling. **4.** warrant, justification, permit, permission, sanction, liberty, authorization. **5.** testimony, witness. —**Syn. Study.** AUTHORITY, CONTROL, INFLUENCE denote a power or right to direct the actions or thoughts of others. AUTHORITY is a power or right, usu. because of rank or office, to issue commands and to punish for violations: *to have authority over subordinates.* CONTROL is either power or influence applied to the complete and successful direction or manipulation of persons or things: *to be in control of a project.* INFLUENCE is a personal and unofficial power derived from deference of others to one's character, ability, or station; it may be exerted unconsciously or may operate through persuasion: *to have influence over one's friends.*

authorize, *v.* **1.** empower, commission, allow, permit, let. **2.** sanction, approve. **3.** establish, entrench. **4.** warrant, justify, legalize,

support, back. —**Ant.**
forbid, prohibit.

automatic, *adj.* **1.**
self-moving, self-acting,
mechanical. **2.**
involuntary,
uncontrollable. —**Ant.**
manual; deliberate,
intentional.

auxiliary, *adj.* **1.**
supporting, helping,
helpful, aiding, assisting,
abetting. **2.** subsidiary,
subordinate, secondary,
ancillary, additional. —*n.*
3. helper, aide, ally,
assistant, confederate.
—**Ant.** chief, main.

available, *adj.* **1.** accessible,
ready, at hand, handy,
usable, of use *or* service,
serviceable; suitable, fit,
appropriate, fitting,
befitting. **2.** valid,
efficacious, profitable,
advantageous. —**Ant.**
unavailable; unbecoming;
invalid, unprofitable.

avaricious, *adj.* greedy,
covetous, grasping,
acquisitive, appetent,
predatory, mercenary,
rapacious, grabby. —**Syn.**
Study. AVARICIOUS,

COVETOUS, GREEDY suggest a
desire to possess more of
something than one needs
or is entitled to. AVARICIOUS
often implies a
pathological, driven
greediness for money or
other valuables and
usually suggests a
concomitant miserliness:
an avaricious usurer.
COVETOUS implies a
powerful and often illicit
desire for the property or
possessions of another:
*The book collector was
covetous of my rare first
edition.* GREEDY, the most
general of these terms,
suggests an uncontrolled
desire for almost anything:
*greedy for knowledge;
greedy for power.*

avenge, *v.* revenge,
vindicate, take vengeance,
exact satisfaction for.
—**Ant.** forgive, pardon.

average, *n.* **1.** mean, mean
proportion, median. **2.**
mediocrity. —*adj.* **3.** mean,
medial, normal,
intermediate, middle;
mediocre, middling,
ordinary, passable,
tolerable, satisfactory. —*v.*

4. reduce to a mean, equate; proportion. **5.** show *or* produce a mean.

averse, *adj.* disinclined, reluctant, unwilling, loath, opposed. —**Ant.** inclined, disposed. —**Syn. Study.** See RELUCTANT.

aversion, *n.* repugnance, disgust, antipathy, loathing, detestation, hate, hatred, abhorrence; dislike, distaste, objection, disinclination, unwillingness, reluctance. —**Ant.** predilection, liking; favor.

avoid, *v.* keep away from *or* clear of, shun, evade, escape, elude, fight shy of, eschew. —**Ant.** confront, face.

await, *v.* **1.** wait for, look for, expect. **2.** attend, be in store for, be ready for. **3.** wait.

aware, *adj.* cognizant *or* conscious (of), informed, mindful, apprised. —**Ant.** unaware, oblivious. —**Syn. Study.** See CONSCIOUS.

awe, *n.* **1.** reverence, respect, veneration; dread, fear, terror. —*v.* **2.** solemnize; daunt, cow, frighten, intimidate. —**Ant.** contempt, irreverence; scorn.

awkward, *adj.* **1.** clumsy, bungling, unskillful, inexpert, gauche, inept, maladroit. **2.** ungraceful, ungainly, unwieldy, unmanageable, coarse, rude, crude, wooden, stiff, constrained, gawky, unrefined, unpolished, rough. **3.** hazardous, dangerous. **4.** trying, embarrassing. —**Ant.** deft, adroit, adept; graceful, refined, polished.

B

babble, *v.* **1.** gibber, blabber, gabble, jabber, bibble-babble, blather, prate, prattle. **2.** talk, chat, gossip, chatter, natter, palaver, gab, jaw, schmooze. —*n.* **3.** nonsense, gibberish, twaddle, prattle, mumbo jumbo, drivel, blather.

back, *n.* **1.** rear, posterior, end. —*v.* **2.** support, sustain, second, aid, abet, favor, assist; countenance, allow, side with, endorse, stand by. **3.** reverse, move *or* push backward. **4.** retire, retreat, withdraw, go backward. —*adj.* **5.** hind, posterior, rear; remote, frontier, unpopulated. —**Ant.** front, fore, face. —**Syn. Study.** BACK, HIND, POSTERIOR, REAR refer to something situated behind something else. BACK means the opposite of front: *a back window.* HIND, and the more formal word POSTERIOR, refer to the rearmost of two or more, often similar objects: *hind wings; posterior lobe.* REAR is used of buildings, conveyances, etc., and in military language it is the opposite of fore: *the rear end of a truck; rear echelon.*

backward, *adv.* **1.** rearward, back foremost, retrogressively, behind. —*adj.* **2.** reversed, returning. **3.** behind, late, slow, tardy, behindhand. **4.** reluctant, hesitant, bashful, wavering, disinclined, timid, retired. **5.** slow, retarded, undeveloped, underdeveloped, ignorant. —**Ant.** forward; precocious.

backwater, *n.* back country, hinterland, outback, back woods, bush, up-country, sticks, boondocks, boonies, middle of nowhere.

bad, *adj.* **1.** evil, wicked, ill, corrupt, base, depraved, unprincipled, immoral, disingenuous, rascally, mischievous, sinful, criminal, dishonest, villainous, baneful; deleterious, pernicious, harmful, hurtful, injurious, detrimental. **2.** defective, worthless, poor, inferior, imperfect; incompetent, ill-qualified, inadequate. **3.** incorrect, faulty. **4.** invalid, unsound. **5.** sick, ill. **6.** regretful, sorry, contrite, wretched, upset. **7.** unfavorable, unfortunate, adverse, unlucky, unhappy. **8.** offensive, disagreeable, painful, mean, abominable. **9.** vile, wretched, shabby, scurvy. **10.** severe, serious. **11.** rotten, decayed. —**Ant.** good.

bag, *n.* **1.** pouch, receptacle, sack, reticule, wallet. **2.** handbag, purse, moneybag. —*v.* **3.** catch, net, trap, entrap, kill.

bailiwick, *n.* domain, field, sphere, purview, territory, province, department, jurisdiction, realm, terrain, precinct.

balance, *n.* **1.** scales. **2.** equilibrium, equilibration, symmetry, equipoise, equality. **3.** poise, composure, self-control, equilibrium, equipoise, self-possession. **4.** counterpoise, equalizer, stabilizer. —*v.* **5.** weigh, compare, equilibrate, estimate, assay. **6.** counterpoise, counterbalance, offset, counteract, neutralize, countervail, compensate, allow for, make up for. **7.** proportion, equalize, square, adjust. —**Syn. Study.** See SYMMETRY.

ball, *n.* **1.** sphere, globe, orb. **2.** bullet, shot, missile, projectile. **3.** dance, assembly, dancing-party.

ban, *v.* **1.** prohibit, interdict, outlaw, forbid, proscribe, taboo. —*n.* **2.** prohibition, interdiction, interdict, taboo, proscription. **3.** anathema, curse, malediction, excommunication, denunciation. —**Ant.**

permit, allow; permission, blessing.

banal, See Syn. study at COMMONPLACE.

band, *n.* **1.** company, party, troop, crew, gang, group; body; clique, coterie, set, society, association, sodality, horde, host, assembly. **2.** strip, fillet, belt, tag, strap, cincture, girdle; *(heraldry)* bend. **3.** cord, fetter, shackle, manacle, bond, chain. —*v.* **4.** unite, confederate. **5.** stripe; mark, tag, identify.

banish, *v.* **1.** exile, expel, expatriate, deport, ostracize, outlaw. **2.** send *or* drive *or* put away, exclude, expel, dismiss, dispel. —**Ant.** admit, receive.

bank, *n.* **1.** pile, heap, embankment, mount, knoll, hillock, hill, tumulus, dike. **2.** slope, shore, acclivity, shoal, ridge. **3.** row, ridge, tier, course. —*v.* **4.** embank, border, bound, rim, edge, dike.

bankrupt, *v.* **1.** impoverish, pauperize, ruin, deplete,

exhaust, drain dry, bleed. —*adj.* **2.** impoverished, pauperized, insolvent, indigent, impecunious, destitute, broke, stone-broke, flat broke, in receivership. **3.** ruined, worn out, jejune, exhausted, spent, broken, wasted.

banter, *n.* **1.** badinage, joking, jesting, pleasantry, persiflage; mockery, ridicule, derision. —*v.* **2.** tease, twit, make fun of; ridicule, deride, mock, jeer, chaff.

bar, *n.* **1.** rod, pole. **2.** obstruction, hindrance, deterrent, stop, impediment, obstacle, barrier, barricade. **3.** ridge, shoal, reef, sand-bunk, bank, sand-bar, shallow. **4.** counter; saloon, pub, café, bistro, nightclub, cocktail lounge. **5.** lawyers, the legal fraternity; tribunal, judgment-seat, court. **6.** stripe, band. —*v.* **7.** hinder, obstruct, deter, stop, impede, barricade, prevent, prohibit, restrain. **8.** exclude, shut out, eliminate, block, except. **—Ant.** suffer, allow, permit.

barbarian, *n.* **1.** savage, philistine, alien, brute, boor, ruffian. —*adj.* **2.** rude, uncivilized, savage, primitive, barbaric, barbarous, rough, crude, coarse, untutored, ignorant, uncultivated, unlettered. **3.** cruel, ferocious, wild, feral, inhuman, brutal, harsh, harsh-sounding, raucous. **—Ant.** cosmopolite; refined, civilized, cultivated; kind.

bare, *adj.* **1.** naked, nude, uncovered, unclothed, undressed, exposed, unprotected, unsheltered, unshielded, open. **2.** unfurnished, undecorated, plain, stark, mean, poor, destitute, meager, unadorned, bald, empty, barren. **3.** simple, sheer, mere, alone, sole, just. **4.** unconcealed, undisguised, unreserved, conspicuous, obvious, glaring, evident, palpable. —*v.* **5.** disclose, denude, lay open, expose. **—Ant.** covered, dressed.

barely, See Syn. study at HARDLY.

bargain, *n.* **1.** compact, agreement, stipulation, arrangement, contract, convention, concord, concordat, treaty, stipulation, transaction. **2.** good purchase, buy. —*v.* **3.** contract, agree, stipulate, covenant, transact. **4.** trade, sell, transfer. **—Syn. Study.** See AGREEMENT.

barren, *adj.* **1.** sterile, unprolific, childless, infecund, unfruitful, infertile, unproductive, poor, bare. **2.** uninteresting, dull, stupid; uninstructive, unsuggestive, ineffectual, ineffective. **—Ant.** fertile; interesting, effectual.

barricade, *n.* **1.** barrier, obstruction, bar. —*v.* **2.** obstruct, block, bar, shut in, stop up, fortify.

barrier, *n.* bar, obstruction, hindrance, barricade, stop, impediment, obstacle, restraint; fence, railing, stockade, palisade, wall; limit, boundary.

barter, *v.* trade, exchange, traffic, bargain; sell.

base, *n.* **1.** bottom, stand, rest, pedestal, understructure, substructure, foot, basis, foundation, ground, groundwork; principle. **2.** fundamental part, ingredient, element. **3.** station, goal, starting-point, point of departure. —*adj.* **4.** (morally) low, despicable, contemptible, mean-spirited, mean, degraded, degrading, selfish, cowardly. **5.** servile, lowly, slavish, menial, beggarly, abject, sordid, ignoble. **6.** poor, inferior, cheap, tawdry, worthless; debased, counterfeit, fake, spurious, shabby, coarse. **7.** unrefined, plebeian, vulgar, lowly, humble, unknown, baseborn; impure, corrupted, corrupt, vile, venal. **8.** scandalous, shameful, disreputable, disgraceful, discreditable, dishonorable, infamous, notorious. —*v.* **9.** found, rest, establish, ground. —**Ant.** top, peak; moral, virtuous; good, valuable; refined, pure; honorable. —**Syn. Study.** BASE, BASIS, FOUNDATION refer to anything upon which a structure is built and upon which it rests. BASE usu. refers to a physical supporting structure: *the base of a statue.* BASIS more often refers to a figurative support: *the basis of a report.* FOUNDATION implies a solid, secure understructure: *the foundation of a skyscraper; the foundation of a theory.*

bashful, *adj.* diffident, shy, abashed, timid, timorous, coy, sheepish, modest, self-effacing, embarrassed, shamefaced, ashamed. —**Ant.** arrogant, immodest.

basics, *n.* fundamentals, essentials, rudiments, principles, grammar, rules, guidelines, ABC's.

basis, *n.* bottom, base, foundation. —**Syn. Study.** See BASE.

batter, *v.* beat, pound,

belabor, smite, pelt; bruise, wound; break, shatter, shiver, smash, destroy, demolish, ruin.

battle, *n.* **1.** action, skirmish, campaign, contest, conflict, engagement, military engagement *or* encounter. **2.** warfare, combat, war, fight. —*v.* **3.** strive, struggle, fight, combat, war, contest, conflict.

beach, *n.* **1.** coast, seashore, littoral, shore, strand, sands, margin, rim. —*v.* **2.** run ashore, strand, put aground.

beam, *n.* **1.** girder. **2.** ray, pencil, streak, gleam, suggestion, hint, glimmer. —*v.* **3.** shine, gleam, glisten, glitter, radiate. **4.** smile, grin.

bear, *v.* **1.** support, hold up, uphold, sustain. **2.** carry, transport, convey, waft; conduct, guide, take. **3.** thrust, drive, force, push, press. **4.** render, give, yield, afford, produce. **5.** transmit, utter, spread, broadcast, advertise, exhibit, show, demonstrate. **6.** sustain, endure, suffer, undergo, tolerate, brook, abide, put up with, stand, stand for, submit to; allow, admit, permit, admit of, hold up under, be capable of. **7.** maintain, keep up, carry on. **8.** entertain, harbor, cherish. **9.** give birth to, bring forth. **10.** confirm, prove. **11.** hold, remain firm. **12.** be patient. **13.** tend, relate, be pertinent, concern, affect, refer. **14.** act, operate, take effect, work, succeed. —**Syn. Study.** BEAR, STAND, ENDURE refer to supporting the burden of something distressing, irksome, or painful. BEAR is the general word and suggests merely being able to put up with something: *She is bearing the disappointment quite well.* STAND is an informal equivalent, but with an implication of stout spirit: *I couldn't stand the pain.* ENDURE implies continued resistance and patience over a long period of time: *to endure torture.*

bearing, *n.* **1.** carriage,

posture, manner, mein, deportment, demeanor, behavior, conduct, air. **2.** relation, connection, dependency, reference, application. **3.** direction, course, aim.

beastly, *adj.* **1.** bestial, animalistic, animal, brutish, brutal, primitive, barbaric, base, inhuman. **2.** unkind, cruel, uncivil, mean, pitiless. **3.** inclement, stormy, severe, disagreeable, miserable.

beat, *v.* **1.** hit, pound, strike, thrash, belabor, batter, knock, thump, drub, maul, baste, pommel, thwack, whack, punch, cudgel, cane, whip, flog, lash, buffet. **2.** break, forge, hammer. **3.** conquer, subdue, overcome, vanquish, overpower, defeat, checkmate. **4.** excel, outdo, surpass. **5.** throb, pulsate. **6.** win, conquer. —*n.* **7.** stroke, blow. **8.** pulsation, throb, tattoo, rhythm. **—Syn. Study.** BEAT, HIT, POUND, STRIKE, THRASH refer to the giving of a blow or blows. BEAT

implies the giving of repeated blows: *to beat a rug.* To HIT is usu. to give a single blow, definitely directed: *to hit a ball.* To POUND is to give heavy and repeated blows, often with the fist: *to pound the table.* To STRIKE is to give one or more forceful blows suddenly or swiftly: *to strike a gong.* To THRASH implies inflicting repeated blows as punishment, to show superior strength, or the like: *to thrash an opponent.*

beautiful, *adj.* handsome, comely, seemly, attractive, lovely, pretty, fair, fine, elegant, beauteous, graceful, pulchritudinous, to die for. **—Ant.** ugly; inelegant, ungraceful. **—Syn. Study.** BEAUTIFUL, HANDSOME, LOVELY, PRETTY refer to a pleasing appearance. BEAUTIFUL is used of a person or thing that gives intense pleasure to the senses; it may refer to a woman but rarely to a man: *a beautiful landscape; a beautiful actress.* HANDSOME often implies stateliness or pleasing proportions and symmetry; it is used of a man and sometimes a woman: *a handsome sofa; a handsome man.* That which is LOVELY is beautiful in a warm and endearing way: *a lovely smile.* PRETTY usu. suggests a moderate beauty in persons or things that are small or feminine: *a pretty blouse; a pretty child.*

beautify, *v.* embellish, adorn, ornament, decorate, bedeck, deck, deck out, dress up, enhance, prettify, glamorize, titivate, cosmeticize. —**Ant.** uglify, despoil, mar, deface, vandalize.

beauty, *n.* **1.** loveliness, pulchritude, elegance, grace, gracefulness, comeliness, seemliness, fairness, attractiveness. **2.** belle. **3.** grace, charm, excellence, attraction. —**Ant.** ugliness; witch; gracelessness.

because, *conj.* as, since, for, inasmuch as, for the reason that.

becoming, *adj.* **1.** attractive, comely, neat, pretty, graceful. **2.** fit, proper, apt, suitable, appropriate, meet, right, correct, decorous, congruous, fitting, seemly. —**Ant.** unbecoming, ugly; unfit, inappropriate, indecorous.

bedevil, *v.* pester, annoy, plague, nag, harass, harry, worry, beleaguer, bother, beset, trouble, vex, torment, try, persecute, hassle.

bedim, *v.* darken, dim, obscure, cloud, becloud. —**Ant.** brighten.

bedlam, *n.* hubbub, din, confusion, racket, noise, clamor, chaos, pandemonium, babel, tumult, uproar, hullabaloo, ruckus, rumpus. —**Ant.** calmness, tranquillity, peace, serenity.

befitting, *adj.* fitting, proper, suitable, seemly, appropriate, becoming, fit, apt. —**Ant.** unbecoming, improper, unsuitable, inappropriate.

beg, *v.* ask for, entreat, pray, crave, implore, beseech, importune, petition, sue, request, supplicate, sue for, solicit.

begin, *v.* **1.** commence, start, initiate, inaugurate, institute, enter upon, set about. **2.** originate, create; arise. —**Ant.** end, conclude, die. —**Syn. Study.** BEGIN, COMMENCE, INITIATE, START (when followed by noun or gerund) refer to setting into motion or progress something that continues for some time. BEGIN is the common term: *to begin knitting a sweater.* COMMENCE is a more formal word, often suggesting a more prolonged or elaborate beginning: *to commence proceedings in court.* INITIATE implies an active and often ingenious first act in a new field: *to initiate a new procedure.* START means to make a first move or to set out on a course of action: *to start paving a street.*

beginning, *n.* **1.** initiation, inauguration, inception, start, commencement, outset, rise, onset, arising, emergence. **2.** source, birth, origin, rise, first cause.

begrudge, *v.* envy, grudge, covet.

beguile, *v.* **1.** mislead, delude, charm, cheat, deceive, befool. **2.** divert, charm, amuse, entertain, cheer, solace.

behave, *v.* conduct oneself, act, deport *or* comport oneself, demean oneself, acquit oneself. —**Ant.** misbehave.

behavior, *n.* demeanor, conduct, manners, deportment, bearing, carriage, mien, air. —**Ant.** misbehavior.

belief, *n.* **1.** opinion, view, tenet, doctrine, dogma, creed. **2.** certainty, conviction, assurance, confidence, persuasion, believing, trust, reliance. **3.** credence, credit, acceptance, assent. —**Syn. Study.** BELIEF, CONVICTION refer to acceptance of or confidence in an alleged fact or body of facts as true or right without positive knowledge or proof. BELIEF is such acceptance in general: *belief in astrology.* CONVICTION is a settled, profound, or earnest belief that something is right: *a conviction that a decision is just.*

belt, *n.* **1.** girth, girdle, cinch, cinture, zone. **2.** band, zone, strip, stripe, stretch. —*v.* **3.** gird, girdle, surround, encircle.

bend, *v.* **1.** curve, crook, bow, deflect, draw, flex. **2.** cause to yield, subdue, persuade, influence, mold, dispose, bias, incline, direct, turn. **3.** stoop, bow. **4.** yield, submit, bow, stoop, kneel, give way, acquiesce, agree. **5.** crook, deflect, deviate, swerve, diverge, incline. —*n.* **6.** curve, crook, bow, rib, elbow, turn, angle, curvature, turning.

beneficial, *adj.* salutary, wholesome, serviceable, useful, favorable, helpful, profitable, advantageous. —**Ant.** unwholesome, unfavorable, disadvantageous.

benefit, See Syn. study at ADVANTAGE

benevolent, *adj.* kind, kindly, well-disposed, kindhearted, humane, tender, tender-hearted, unselfish, generous, liberal, obliging, benign, benignant, charitable, philanthropic, altruistic. —**Ant.** cruel, selfish, egotistical.

bent, *adj.* **1.** curved, crooked, hooked, bowed, flexed, deflected. **2.** determined, set on, resolved, fixed on. —*n.* **3.** inclination, leaning, bias, tendency, propensity, proclivity, disposition, turn, penchant, predilection, partiality, liking, fondness, proneness. —**Ant.** straight; undecided; disinclination.

bequeath, *v.* leave, will, pass on, pass along, devise, legate, hand down, transmit.

beseech, *v.* **1.** implore, beg, entreat, pray, petition, obsecrate, obtest, supplicate, importune, adjure. **2.** solicit, ask, entreat, beg, implore, importune, crave.

beset, *v.* **1.** assail, harass, surround, encompass, encircle, enclose, besiege, beleaguer. **2.** set, bestud, stud, decorate, ornament, embellish, garnish.

besides, *adv.* **1.** moreover, in addition, furthermore, else, otherwise, too, also, yet, further. —*prep.* **2.** over and above, in addition to, except, other than, save, distinct from.

betray, *v.* **1.** deliver, expose, give up, uncover, reveal. **2.** be unfaithful to, be a traitor to, deceive, be disloyal to, disappoint. **3.** show, exhibit, display, manifest, indicate, imply, betoken, evince, expose, uncover, reveal. —**Ant.** protect, safeguard.

better, *adj.* **1.** more good; more useful, more valuable; more suitable, more appropriate, more fit, more applicable. **2.** larger, greater, bigger. —*v.*

3. improve, amend, ameliorate, meliorate, emend; advance, promote; reform, correct, rectify. **4.** improve upon, surpass, exceed. —**Ant.** worse; worsen. —**Syn. Study.** See IMPROVE.

bewilder, *v.* confuse, perplex, puzzle, mystify; confound, nonplus, astonish, daze, stagger, befog, muddle.

bewitch, *v.* throw a spell over, charm, enchant, captivate, transport, enrapture, fascinate, hypnotize.

bias, *n.* **1.** prejudice, inclination, preconception, predilection, prepossession, proclivity, propensity, proneness, partiality, predisposition, bent, leaning, tendency. —*v.* **2.** prejudice, warp, predispose, bend, influence, incline, dispose. —**Ant.** justness, impartiality. —**Syn. Study.** BIAS, PREJUDICE mean a strong inclination of the mind or a preconceived opinion about something or someone. A BIAS may be favorable or unfavorable: *bias in favor of or against an idea.* PREJUDICE implies a preformed judgment even more unreasoning than BIAS, and usu. implies an unfavorable opinion: *prejudice against a race.*

bid, *v.* **1.** command, order, direct, charge, require, enjoin, summon. **2.** greet, wish, say. **3.** offer, propose, tender, proffer. —*n.* **4.** offer, proposal, proffer. —**Ant.** forbid, prohibit, enjoin.

big, *adj.* **1.** large, great, huge, bulky, massive, immense, tremendous, capacious, gigantic, extensive. **2.** pregnant, with child, enceinte. **3.** filled, teeming, overflowing, productive. **4.** important, consequential, haughty, proud, arrogant, pompous, swelling, swollen, inflated, tumid, self-important, conceited, self-sufficient, bombastic, boastful. **5.** generous, big-hearted, kindly. —**Ant.** small; trivial, nugatory.

bigoted, *adj.* intolerant, narrow-minded, closed-minded, narrow, small-minded, illiberal, hidebound, parochial, biased, prejudiced, know-nothing, mean-spirited, —**Ant.** tolerant, broad-minded, open-minded, generous.

bill, *n.* **1.** account, reckoning, score, charges, invoice, statement. **2.** bulletin, handbill, notice, advertisement, broadside, poster, placard, announcement, throwaway, circular. **3.** beak, nib, neb, mandible.

billow, *v.* swell, expand, distend, inflate, bloat, balloon, belly, fill out, puff up, mushroom. —**Ant.** contract, shrink.

bind, *v.* **1.** band, bond, tie, make fast, fasten, secure, gird, attach. **2.** encircle, border; confine, restrain, restrict. **3.** engage, obligate, oblige. **4.** indenture, apprentice. —**Ant.** untie, unbind.

birth, *n.* **1.** act of bearing, bringing forth, parturition.

2. lineage, extraction, parentage, descent, ancestry, line, blood, family, race. **3.** origin, beginning, rise, nativity. —**Ant.** death, end.

bit, *n.* **1.** particle, speck, grain, mite, crumb, iota, jot, atom, scintilla, tittle, whit, fragment. **2.** bridle, curb, control, rein, check, checkrein, restrainer.

bite, *v.* **1.** gnaw, chew, champ; nip, rip, rend, tear. **2.** cut, pierce; sting, burn, cause to smart. **3.** corrode, erode, eat away. **4.** cheat, deceive, defraud, dupe, trick, gull, make a fool of, cozen, outwit, fool, bamboozle, inveigle, mislead, beguile. —*n.* **5.** nip, sting, cut. **6.** food, snack; morsel, mouthful.

bitter, *adj.* **1.** harsh, acrid, biting. **2.** grievous, distasteful, painful, distressing, intense, sore, poignant, sorrowful, calamitous. **3.** piercing, stinging, biting, nipping. **4.** harsh, sarcastic, caustic, cutting, acrimonious, acerbate, severe, stern, sardonic, scornful,

sneering. **5.** fierce, cruel, savage, mean, merciless, ruthless, relentless, virulent, dire. —**Ant.** sweet.

bizarre, See Syn. study at FANTASTIC.

black, *adj.* **1.** dark, dusky, sooty, inky, ebon, sable, swart, swarthy. **2.** soiled, dirty, dingy, dusky, stained. **3.** gloomy, sad, dismal, sullen, hopeless, dark, depressing, doleful, funereal, somber, mournful, forbidding, disastrous, calamitous. **4.** amoral, evil, wicked, sinful, fiendish, inhuman, devilish, diabolic, infernal, monstrous, atrocious, horrible, outrageous, heinous, flagitious, nefarious, treacherous, traitorous, infamous, villainous. **5.** ruined, desolate, empty. —**Ant.** white; clean, pure, undefiled; happy; good, upright.

blackguard, *n.* churl, scoundrel, scamp, rascal, rapscallion, rogue, roué, devil, rake, wastrel, villain. —**Ant.** hero, protagonist.

blame, *v.* **1.** reproach, reprove, reprehend, censure, condemn, find fault, criticize, disapprove. —*n.* **2.** censure, reprehension, condemnation, finger-pointing, stricture, disapproval, disapprobation, reproach, reproof, animadversion. **3.** guilt, culpability, fault, wrong, misdeed, misdoing, shortcoming, sin, defect, reproach. **—Ant.** credit, honor.

blameless, *adj.* irreproachable, guiltless, unimpeachable, faultless, innocent, inculpable, not guilty, undefiled, unsullied, unspotted, spotless, unblemished. **—Ant.** guilty, culpable; sullied, besmirched.

blanch, *v.* whiten, bleach, etiolate, pale, fade. **—Ant.** darken, blacken.

bland, *adj.* **1.** gentle, agreeable, affable, friendly, kindly, mild, amiable; suave, urbane, mild-mannered; complaisant, self-satisfied. **2.** soft, mild, balmy, soothing, nonirritating. **—Ant.** cruel, unfriendly; boorish, crude; irritable, irksome.

blank, *adj.* **1.** unmarked, void, empty, unadorned, undistinguished. **2.** amazed, astonished, nonplussed, astounded, confused, dumfounded, disconcerted. **3.** complete, utter, pure, simple, unadulterated, unmixed; perfect, entire, absolute, unmitigated, unabated, unqualified, mere. —*n.* **4.** space, line, area; form; void, vacancy, emptiness. **—Ant.** distinguished, marked; blasé; impure; significant.

blarney, *n.* **1.** flattery, blandishment, cajolery, honey, sweet talk, soft soap. **2.** nonsense, rubbish, blather, humbug, claptrap, flummery.

blasé, *adj.* **1.** worldly-wise, sophisticated, jaded, knowing, worldly, disillusioned, world-weary. **2.** unconcerned, indifferent, uninterested, unsurprised, nonchalant, cool.

blasphemy, *n.* profanity, cursing, swearing, impiousness, sacrilege. —**Ant.** reverence, piety.

blast, *n.* **1.** wind, squall, gust, gale, blow, storm. **2.** blare, peal, clang. **3.** explosion, outburst, burst, outbreak, discharge. —*v.* **4.** blow, toot, blare. **5.** wither, blight, kill, shrivel. **6.** ruin, destroy, annihilate. **7.** explode, burst, split. —**Syn. Study.** See WIND.

blaze, *n.* **1.** fire, flame, holocaust, inferno; glow, gleam, brightness; outburst. —*v.* **2.** burn, shine, flame, flare up, flicker.

bleach, *v.* **1.** whiten, blanch, etiolate, pale. —*n.* **2.** whitener. —**Ant.** blacken, darken.

blemish, *v.* **1.** stain, sully, spot, taint, injure, tarnish, mar, damage, deface, impair. —*n.* **2.** stain, defect, blot, spot, speck, disfigurement, flaw, taint, fault. —**Ant.** purify; purity, immaculateness. —**Syn. Study.** See DEFECT.

blend, *v.* **1.** mingle, combine, coalesce, mix, intermingle, commingle, amalgamate, unite, compound. —*n.* **2.** mixture, combination, amalgamation. —**Ant.** separate, precipitate. —**Syn. Study.** See MIX.

blind, *adj.* **1.** sightless, stone-blind, purblind. **2.** ignorant, undiscerning, unenlightened, benighted. **3.** irrational, uncritical, indiscriminate, headlong, rash, heedless, careless, thoughtless, unreasoning, inconsiderate. **4.** hidden, concealed, obscure, remote, dim, confused, dark. **5.** closed, dead-end, shut. —*n.* **6.** curtain, shade, blinker, blinder, screen, cover. **7.** hiding place, ambush. **8.** cover, decoy, ruse, stratagem, pretense, pretext. —**Ant.** discerning, enlightened; rational, discriminating; open.

blink, *v.* **1.** wink, nictitate. **2.** flicker, flutter, twinkle. **3.** ignore, overlook, disregard, evade, avoid, condone. —*n.* **4.** wink, twinkle; glance, glimpse, peep, sight.

bliss, *n.* blitheness, happiness, gladness, joy, transport, rapture, ecstasy. —**Ant.** misery, unhappiness, dejection.

blithe, *adj.* joyous, merry, gay, glad, cheerful, happy, mirthful, sprightly, lighthearted, buoyant, lively, animated, elated, vivacious, joyful, blithesome. —**Ant.** unhappy, miserable, cheerless.

block, *n.* **1.** mass. **2.** blockhead, dolt, idiot, imbecile, simpleton, fool, dunce. **3.** mold. **4.** blank. **5.** pulley, tackle, sheave. **6.** obstacle, hindrance, impediment, blocking, blockade, obstruction, stoppage, blockage, jam. —*v.* **7.** mold, shape, form. **8.** obstruct, close, hinder, deter, arrest, stop, blockade, impede, check. —**Ant.** genius; encourage, advance, continue.

bloody, *adj.* **1.** bloodstained, sanguinary, ensanguined, gory. **2.**

murderous, cruel, bloodthirsty, savage, barbarous, ferocious, homicidal, inhuman, ruthless.

bloom, *n.* **1.** flower, blossom, efflorescence. **2.** freshness, glow, flush, vigor, prime. —*v.* **3.** flourish, effloresce; glow.

blot, *n.* **1.** spot, stain, inkstain, erasure, blotting, blotch, obliteration, blur. **2.** blemish, reproach, stain, taint, dishonor, disgrace, spot. —*v.* **3.** spot, stain, bespatter; sully, disfigure, deface. **4.** darken, dim, obscure, eclipse, hide, overshadow. **5.** destroy, annihilate, obliterate, efface, erase, expunge, rub out, cancel, strike out, eliminate.

blow, *n.* **1.** stroke, buffet, thump, thwack, rap, slap, cuff, box, beat, knock. **2.** shock, calamity, reverse, disaster, misfortune, affliction. **3.** attack. **4.** blast, wind, gale, gust. **5.** blossom, flower, bloom. —*v.* **6.** pant, puff, wheeze. **7.** blossom, bloom, flower.

blowhard, *n.* braggart, bragger, boaster, braggadocio, miles gloriosus, blusterer, self-advertiser, self-promoter, blower, vaunter, big-I-am, big mouth, windbag, gasbag. —**Ant.** introvert, milquetoast, shrinking violet.

blue, *n.* **1.** azure, cerulean, sky-blue, sapphire. **2.** prude, censor, pedant. —*adj.* **3.** depressed, dismal, unhappy, morose, gloomy, doleful, melancholy, dispiriting, dispirited, dejected, sad, glum, downcast, crestfallen, despondent. **4.** prudish, moral, rigid, unbending, righteous, puritanical, self-righteous, severe, rigorous. **5.** obscene, lewd, lascivious, licentious, indecent, risqué, ribald, irreverent, scurrilous, suggestive, immoral, amoral. —**Ant.** happy, mirthful.

blueprint, *n.* plan, outline, scheme, design, schema, master plan, ground plan, diagram, program, model, paradigm, game plan, strategy.

bluff, *adj.* **1.** abrupt, unconventional, blunt, direct, frank, open, honest, hearty, rough, crude. **2.** steep, precipitous, abrupt. —*n.* **3.** cliff, headland, hill, bank. **4.** fraud, deceit, lie, dissembling. —*v.* **5.** mislead, defraud, deceive, lie, dissemble, fake. —**Ant.** suave, diplomatic, tactful; gradual; plain.

blunder, *n.* **1.** mistake, error, faux pas, gaffe, lapse, slip, misstep, slipup, miscue, misjudgment, impropriety, solecism, indiscretion, indecorum, bungle, misdoing, boner, howler, blooper, goof, boo-boo, (*Brit.*) clanger. *v.* **2.** bungle, botch, bobble, bumble, muff, flub, fluff, mess up, goof up, louse up, screw up. —**Syn. Study.** See MISTAKE.

blunt, *adj.* **1.** rounded, not sharp, dull. **2.** abrupt, bluff, brusque, curt, short, obtuse, difficult, gruff, uncourtly, uncivil, rough, harsh, uncourteous, discourteous, rude, impolite. **3.** slow, dull, dimwitted, dullwitted, stupid, thick, stolid. —*v.* **4.** dull, obtund. **5.** numb, paralyze, deaden, stupefy, make insensible. —**Ant.** sharp, acute; courteous, civil, polite; quick, alert. —**Syn. Study.** BLUNT, BRUSQUE, CURT characterize manners and speech. BLUNT suggests unnecessary frankness and a lack of regard for the feelings of others: *blunt and tactless remarks.* BRUSQUE connotes a sharpness and abruptness that borders on rudeness: *a brusque denial.* CURT applies esp. to disconcertingly concise language: *a curt reply.*

boast, *v.* **1.** exaggerate, brag, vaunt, swagger, crow. —*n.* **2.** bragging, rodomontade, swaggering, braggadocio. —**Ant.** depreciate, belittle. —**Syn. Study.** BOAST, BRAG imply vocal self-praise or claims to superiority over others. BOAST usu. refers to a particular ability, possession, etc., that may justify a good deal of

pride: *He boasts of his ability as a singer.* BRAG, a more informal term, usu. suggests a more ostentatious and exaggerated boasting but less well-founded: *He brags loudly about his marksmanship.*

bodily, See Syn. study at PHYSICAL.

body, *n.* **1.** carcass, corpse, cadaver. **2.** trunk, torso, substance, matter, bulk, main part; fuselage, hull. **3.** collection, group; company, party, band, coterie, society, clique, set; association, corporation. **4.** consistency, density, substance, thickness. —**Ant.** spirit, soul. —**Syn. Study.** BODY, CARCASS, CORPSE, CADAVER all refer to a physical organism, usu. human or animal. BODY denotes the material substance of a human or animal, either living or dead: *the muscles in a horse's body; the body of an accident victim.* CARCASS means the dead body of an animal, unless applied humorously or contemptuously to the human body: *a sheep's carcass; Save your carcass.* CORPSE usu. refers to the dead body of a human being: *preparing a corpse for burial.* CADAVER refers to a dead body, usu. a human one used for scientific study: *dissection of cadavers in anatomy classes.*

bogus, *adj.* false, sham, counterfeit, inauthentic, bastard, mock, phony, spurious, brummagem, pinchbeck, pseudo. —**Ant.** genuine, real, true, authentic.

bohemian, *adj.* **1.** free-living, free-spirited, unconventional, unconstrained, unorthodox, free and easy, offbeat, eccentric, artistic, arty, recusant. —*n.* **2.** nonconformist, free spirit, maverick, eccentric. —**Ant.** conformist, conservative, straight arrow.

boil, *v.* **1.** seethe, foam, froth, churn, stew, simmer, rage. —*n.* **2.** ebullition. **3.** furuncle, pustule. —**Syn.**

Study. BOIL, SEETHE, SIMMER, STEW are used figuratively to refer to agitated states of emotion. To BOIL suggests being very hot with anger or rage: *He was boiling when the guests arrived late.* To SEETHE is to be deeply stirred, violently agitated, or greatly excited: *a mind seething with conflicting ideas.* To SIMMER means to be at the point of bursting out or boiling over: *to simmer with curiosity; to simmer with anger.* To STEW is an informal term that means to worry, or to be in a restless state of anxiety and excitement: *to stew over one's troubles.*

boisterous, *adj.* rough, noisy, loud, clamorous, roaring, unrestrained, wild, tumultuous, turbulent, violent, impetuous, stormy, tempestuous, uproarious, obstreperous, roistering, vociferous. —**Ant.** calm, serene, pacific.

bold, *adj.* **1.** fearless, courageous, brave, intrepid, daring, dauntless, valorous, valiant, heroic, manly, doughty, undaunted, hardy, spirited, mettlesome, gallant, stout-hearted, resolute. **2.** forward, brazen, brassy, presumptuous, shameless, insolent, impudent, immodest, defiant, overconfident, saucy, pushing. **3.** conspicuous, prominent, obvious, evident. **4.** steep, abrupt, precipitous. **—Ant.** cowardly, timorous, timid; backward, shy; inconspicuous; gradual. **—Syn. Study.** BOLD, BRAZEN, FORWARD, PRESUMPTUOUS refer to behavior or manners that break the rules of propriety. BOLD suggests shamelessness and immodesty: *a bold stare.* BRAZEN suggests the same, together with a defiant manner: *a brazen liar.* FORWARD implies making oneself unduly prominent or bringing oneself to notice with too much assurance: *The forward young man challenged the speaker.* PRESUMPTUOUS implies overconfidence, or taking too much for granted: *It was presumptuous of her to think she could defeat the champion.*

bombastic, *adj.* flowery, pretentious, pompous, turgid, verbose, portentous, loud, brassy. **—Syn. Study.** BOMBASTIC, FLOWERY, PRETENTIOUS all describe a use of language more elaborate than is justified by or appropriate to the content being expressed. BOMBASTIC suggests language with a theatricality or staginess of style far too powerful or declamatory for the meaning or sentiment being expressed: *a bombastic sermon on the evils of gambling.* FLOWERY describes language filled with extravagant images and ornate expressions: *a flowery eulogy.* PRETENTIOUS refers specifically to language that is purposely inflated in an effort to impress: *a pretentious essay filled with obscure literary allusions.*

bond, *n.* **1.** binder, fastener, fastening, band, cord, ligature, ligament, link, rope. **2.** tie, connection, link, attraction, attachment, union. **3.** bondsman, security, ward, promise; promissory note; obligation, contract, compact. **4.** *(pl.)* chains, fetters, captivity, constraint, restriction, bondage; prison, imprisonment. —*v.* **5.** mortgage. **6.** cement, glue.

bondage, *n.* slavery, indenture, servitude, serfdom, thraldom, captivity, imprisonment, confinement. —**Ant.** freedom. —**Syn. Study.** See SLAVERY.

bonhomie, *n.* good humor, good-humoredness, affability, cordiality, geniality, hospitality, warmth, graciousness, heartiness, neighborliness, friendliness, congeniality, sociability. —**Ant.** unfriendliness, surliness, enmity.

bonus, *n.* bounty, premium, reward, honorarium, gift, subsidy; dividend, perquisite. —**Syn. Study.** BONUS, BOUNTY, PREMIUM refer to a gift or an additional payment. A BONUS is a gift to reward performance, paid either by an employer or by a government: *a bonus based on salary; a soldier's bonus.* A BOUNTY is a public reward offered to stimulate interest in a specific purpose or undertaking and to encourage performance: *a bounty for killing wolves.* A PREMIUM is usu. something additional given as an inducement to buy, produce, or the like: *a premium received with a magazine subscription.*

border, *n.* **1.** side, edge, margin; orphrey; periphery, circumference, lip, brim, verge, brink. **2.** frontier, limit, confine, boundary. —*v.* **3.** bound, limit, confine; adjoin. —**Syn. Study.** See BOUNDARY.

bore, *v.* **1.** perforate, drill, pierce. **2.** weary, fatigue, tire, annoy. —*n.* **3.** caliber, hole. **4.** tidal wave, eagre. —**Ant.** amuse.

bosom, *n.* **1.** breast, heart, affection. —*adj.* **2.** intimate, close, confidential.

bother, *v.* **1.** annoy, pester, worry, trouble, plague, tease, harass, vex, harry; molest, disturb. **2.** bewilder, confuse. —**Ant.** solace, comfort. —**Syn. Study.** BOTHER, ANNOY, PLAGUE imply persistent interference with one's comfort or peace of mind. To BOTHER is to cause irritation or weariness, esp. by repeated interruptions in the midst of pressing duties: *Don't bother me while I'm working.* To ANNOY is to cause mild irritation or mental disturbance, as by repetition of an action that displeases: *The dog's constant barking annoyed the neighbors.* To PLAGUE is to trouble or bother, but usu. connotes severe mental distress: *The family was plagued by lack of money.*

bottom, *n.* **1.** base, foot. **2.** underside. **3.** foundation, base, basis, groundwork.

4. seat, buttocks. —*adj.* **5.** fundamental, basic, elementary; undermost, lowest. —**Ant.** top; superficial, superfluous.

bough, *n.* branch, limb, arm, shoot.

bound, *v.* **1.** leap, jump, spring. **2.** rebound, ricochet. —*n.* **3.** *(usually plural)* limit, confine, boundary, verge, border. —*adj.* **4.** constrained; destined for, tending, going. —**Ant.** free.

boundary, *n.* border, frontier, line, line of demarcation, delimitation, circumference, perimeter, division, dividing line, edge. —**Syn.** BOUNDARY, BORDER, FRONTIER refer to that which divides one territory or political unit from another. BOUNDARY most often designates a line on a map; it may be a physical feature, such as a river: *Boundaries are shown in red.* BORDER refers to a political or geographic dividing line; it may also refer to the region adjoining the actual line: *crossing the Mexican* *border.* FRONTIER refers specifically to a border between two countries or the region adjoining this border: *Soldiers guarded the frontier.*

bountiful, See Syn. study at PLENTIFUL.

bounty, *n.* **1.** generosity, munificence, charity, liberality, beneficence. **2.** gift, award, present, benefaction. **3.** reward, premium, bonus. —**Syn. Study.** See BONUS.

bow, *v.* **1.** stoop, bend, buckle, give way. **2.** yield, submit. **3.** subdue, crush, depress, cast down. **4.** curve, bend, inflect. —*n.* **5.** front, forepart, prow.

brace, *n.* **1.** clasp, clamp, vise. **2.** stay, support, prop, strut. **3.** bitstock. **4.** couple, pair. —*v.* **5.** fasten firmly, strengthen, support, back up, fortify, prop, steady. **6.** tighten, tauten, make tense. **7.** stimulate, strengthen, fortify.

brag, *v., n.* boast, rodomontade, bluster.

—**Ant.** depreciate. —**Syn. Study.** See BOAST.

brains, *n.* understanding, intelligence, mind, intellect, sense, reason; capacity. —**Ant.** stupidity.

branch, *n.* **1.** bough, limb, arm, shoot, offshoot. **2.** limb, offshoot, ramification, arm. **3.** section, subdivision, department; member, portion, part; article. **4.** tributary, feeder. —*v.* **5.** divide, subdivide, diverge, ramify.

bravado, *n.* boasting, swaggering, braggadocio, pretense, brag, bluster, bombast. —**Ant.** shame, modesty.

brave, *adj.* **1.** courageous, fearless, gallant, confident, cool, chivalrous, impetuous, dashing, intrepid, daring, dauntless, doughty, bold, valiant, heroic, manly, hard, mettlesome, stout-hearted. **2.** fine, showy, effective, brilliant; gay; debonair. —*n.* **3.** warrior *(esp. American Indian).* —*v.* **4.** face, defy, challenge, dare.

—**Ant.** cowardly, fearful; craven, pusillanimous.

—**Syn. Study.** BRAVE, COURAGEOUS, VALIANT, FEARLESS refer to facing danger or difficulties with moral strength and endurance. BRAVE is a general term that suggests fortitude, daring, and resolve: *a brave pioneer.* COURAGEOUS implies a higher or nobler kind of bravery, esp. as resulting from an inborn quality of mind or spirit: *courageous leaders.* VALIANT implies an inner strength manifested by brave deeds, often in battle: *a valiant knight.* FEARLESS implies unflinching spirit and coolness in the face of danger: *a fearless firefighter.*

bravery, *n.* boldness, courage, intrepidity, daring, prowess, heroism, pluck, gallantry, spirit, audacity, nerve, mettle, fearlessness, spunk, valor. —**Ant.** cowardice.

brawl, *n.* **1.** quarrel, squabble, argument, spat, wrangle, feud, disagreement, dispute, fracas, disturbance, disorder, row, tumult, clamor, rumpus, fray, fight, affray, altercation, melee, riot. —*v.* **2.** quarrel, squabble, argue, wrangle, feud, disagree, dispute, fight, bicker.

brazen, *adj.* **1.** brassy. **2.** bold, forward, shameless, impudent, insolent, immodest, defiant. —**Ant.** shy, diffident, modest. —**Syn. Study.** See BOLD.

breach, *n.* **1.** break, rupture, fracture, crack, gap, fissure, rift, rent, opening, chasm. **2.** infraction, violation, infringement. **3.** alienation, disaffection, falling out, misunderstanding; split, rift, schism, severance, separation; dissension, disagreement, difference, variance, quarrel, dispute. —**Ant.** observance. —**Syn. Study.** BREACH, INFRACTION, VIOLATION all denote an act of breaking or disregarding a legal or moral code. BREACH is most often used of a legal offense, but it may refer to the breaking of any code of conduct: *breach of contract; breach of etiquette.* INFRACTION most often refers to the breaking of clearly formulated rules or laws: *an infraction of regulations.* VIOLATION often suggests a willful, forceful refusal to obey: *done in violation of instructions.*

break, *v.* **1.** fracture, crush, shatter, splinter, shiver, smash, batter, demolish, destroy. **2.** contravene, transgress, disobey, violate, infringe, infract. **3.** dissolve, annul, negate, dismiss. **4.** lacerate, wound, cut, injure, harm, hurt. **5.** interrupt, suspend, disrupt, stop; abbreviate, curtail. **6.** end, overcome. **7.** exceed, outdo, surpass, beat. **8.** disclose, open, unfold, divulge. **9.** ruin, bankrupt, make bankrupt. **10.** impair, weaken, enfeeble, enervate; dispirit. **11.** tame, make obedient. **12.** discharge, degrade, cashier, demote. **13.** shatter, shiver; burst. **14.** dissolve, separate, split. **15.** escape, break loose. **16.** dawn, open, appear. **17.** decline, weaken. —*n.* **18.** disruption, separation, rent, tear, rip, rift, schism, severance, split; breach, gap, fissure, crack, chasm, rupture, fracture. **19.** suspension, stoppage, stop, caesura, hiatus, interruption, lacuna, pause, discontinuity. —**Ant.** repair.

breaker, *n.* wave, comber, surge, whitecap, roller; bore, eagre.

breed, *v.* **1.** beget, bear, bring forth, conceive, give birth to, produce, engender, father, mother. **2.** propagate, procreate, originate, create, beget, occasion, generate. **3.** raise, rear, bring up, nurture; train, educate, discipline, instruct, teach, school. **4.** grow, develop, flourish, arise, rise. —*n.* **5.** race, lineage, strain, family, pedigree, line, extraction, stock, progeny. **6.** sort, kind, species, class, denomination, order, rank, character, nature, description.

breeze, *n.* wind, air, blow, zephyr. —**Ant.** calm. —**Syn. Study.** See WIND.

brevity, *n.* **1.** shortness, briefness. **2.** conciseness, compactness, condensation, succinctness, pithiness; terseness, curtness. —**Ant.** lengthiness. —**Syn. Study.** BREVITY, CONCISENESS refer to the use of few words in speaking. BREVITY emphasizes the short duration of speech: *reduced to extreme brevity.* CONCISENESS emphasizes compactness of expression: *clear in spite of great conciseness.*

bridle, *n.* **1.** curb, restraint, check, control, governor. —*v.* **2.** restrain, check, curb, control, govern. **3.** bristle, ruffle. —**Ant.** freedom; decontrol.

brief, *adj.* **1.** short, short-lived, fleeting, transitory, ephemeral, transient, temporary. **2.** concise, succinct, pithy, condensed, compact,

laconic; curt, short, terse, abrupt. —*n.* **3.** outline, précis, synopsis, summary, epitome, syllabus, abstract, abridgment, conspectus, compendium, breviary. —*v.* **4.** abstract, summarize, outline, epitomize, abridge, abbreviate. —**Ant.** long, tedious, boring. —**Syn. Study.** See SHORT. See also SUMMARY.

bright, *adj.* **1.** radiant, radiating, refulgent, resplendent, effulgent, lucent, lustrous, glowing, beaming, lambent, splendid, brilliant, shining, irradiant, gleaming, luminous; scintillating, sparkling, twinkling, glistening, glistering, shimmering, coruscating, glittering; flashing, flaming, blazing; shiny, sheeny, glossy, burnished; vivid, light, sunny, fulgid, fulgent. **2.** clear, transparent, pellucid, translucent, lucid, limpid, unclouded, crystal, cloudless, lambent. **3.** illustrious, distinguished, glorious, famous, golden, silver. **4.** quick-witted, intelligent, keen, discerning, acute, ingenious, sharp, clever. **5.** lively, animated, cheerful, merry, happy, sprightly, lighthearted, gay, vivacious, genial, pleasant. **6.** favorable, auspicious, propitious, promising, encouraging, inspiriting, inspiring, enlivening, exhilarating. —**Ant.** dull; opaque, dense; undistinguished, ignominious; slow, stupid; laconic, doleful, melancholy; unfavorable, discouraging.

brilliance, *n.* **1.** brightness, splendor, luster, refulgence, effulgence, radiance, brilliancy; sparkle, glitter, glister, gleam. **2.** excellence, distinction, eminence, renown, prominence, preeminence, singularity, fame, illustriousness. —**Ant.** dullness; notoriety. oblivion.

brim, *n.* rim, edge, border; orphrey; periphery, circumference, bound,

brink, lip. —**Ant.** center. —**Syn. Study.** See RIM.

bring, *v.* **1.** take along, conduct, convey, lead, fetch, guide, convoy, accompany, transport, carry. **2.** lead, induce, prevail upon, draw. —**Ant.** remove, withdraw.

brisk, *adj.* **1.** active, lively, energetic, peart, quick, nimble, agile, alert, spry, on the qui vive, spirited, bright, vivacious. **2.** sharp, stimulating, acute. **3.** effervescent, bubbly, bubbling. —**Ant.** slow, lethargic; dull; flat.

brittle, *adj.* fragile, frail, breakable, frangible. —**Ant.** supple, flexible, elastic. —**Syn. Study.** See FRAIL.

broad, *adj.* **1.** wide. **2.** large, extensive, vast, spacious, ample. **3.** diffused, diffuse, open, full. **4.** liberal, large, big, tolerant, open-minded, hospitable. **5.** main, general, chief, important, obvious. **6.** plain, clear, bold, plain-spoken, open, unconfined, free, unrestrained. **7.** rough, coarse, countrified, unrefined, vulgar, indecent, indelicate, gross. **—Ant.** narrow; penurious, stingy; refined, cultivated, decent.

broad-minded, *adj.* tolerant, open, open-minded, liberal, large-minded, progressive, generous-hearted, charitable, forbearing, lenient, live-and-let-live, unbigoted, unparochial, ecumenical. **—Ant.** narrow-minded, bigoted, close-minded.

brood, *n.* **1.** offspring, litter, young, progeny, issue. **2.** breed, kind, sort, line, lineage, stock, family, strain, species, class, order. **—***v.* **3.** incubate, sit. **4.** dwell on, ponder, ruminate over, meditate on. **5.** sit, hatch, set. **6.** rest. **7.** meditate morbidly.

brook, *n.* **1.** stream, rivulet, run, runnel, runlet, streamlet, rill, burn, branch. **—***v.* **2.** bear, suffer, tolerate, allow, stand, endure, abide, put up with, submit to.

brother, *n.* fellow man, fellow countryman, kinsman, associate; sibling.

brownie, *n.* goblin, fairy, elf, pixie, leprechaun, nix, nixie, sprite, imp.

brush, *n.* **1.** encounter, brief encounter, meeting; engagement, affair, contest, collision, action, fight, battle, skirmish, struggle, conflict. **2.** bushes, scrub, thicket, copse, shrubs, bracken, brake.

brusque, *adj.* abrupt, blunt, rough, unceremonious, bluff, gruff, ungracious, uncivil, discourteous, impolite, rude, crude, curt. **—Ant.** courteous, courtly, polished, refined, gentle. **—Syn. Study.** See BLUNT.

brutal, *adj.* **1.** savage, cruel, inhuman, ruthless, pitiless, unfeeling, barbarous, barbarian, uncivilized, ferocious, brutish, barbaric, truculent. **2.** crude, coarse, gross, harsh, rude, rough, uncivil, ungracious, impolite, unmannerly, ungentlemanly, brusque.

3. irrational, unreasoning, brute, unthinking. **4.** bestial, beastly, animal, carnal. —**Ant.** kind, sensitive; artistic; gracious, rational, sensible; human.

brute, *n.* **1.** beast, quadruped. **2.** barbarian. —*adj.* **3.** animal, brutish, irrational, unreasoning. **4.** savage, cruel, brutal. **5.** sensual, carnal. —**Ant.** human; kind; spiritual.

bubbly, *adj.* **1.** frothy, foamy, effervescent, sparkling, spumescent, carbonated. **2.** high-spirited, vivacious, animated, lively, bouncy, effusive, energetic, sprightly, effervescent, sparky, perky, pert, peppy, frisky. —**Ant.** flat, colorless.

building, *n.* edifice, structure, construction, erection.

bulk, *n.* **1.** size, magnitude, mass, volume, dimensions. **2.** greater part, majority, most; body, mass. —*v.* **3.** grow, swell, bulge, expand, enlarge, aggrandize.

bulky, *adj.* massive, ponderous, unwieldy, clumsy, cumbersome; great, big, large, huge, vast. —**Ant.** small, delicate.

bunch, *n.* **1.** cluster; group, lot, bundle, batch, collection. **2.** knob, lump, protuberance.

bundle, *n.* **1.** bunch. **2.** parcel, pack, package, packet.

burden, *n.* **1.** load, weight. **2.** encumbrance, impediment, grievance, trial. **3.** substance, core, point, essence, epitome, central idea, tenor, drift. **4.** refrain, chorus. —*v.* **5.** load, overload, oppress. —**Ant.** disburden.

burlesque, *n.* caricature, parody, travesty, satire, farce, imitation, comedy, spoof, lampoon, sendup, takeoff. —**Syn. Study.** BURLESQUE, CARICATURE, PARODY, TRAVESTY refer to literary or dramatic forms that imitate works or subjects to achieve a humorous or satiric purpose. The characteristic device of BURLESQUE is mockery of serious or trivial subjects through association with their opposites: *a burlesque of high and low life.* CARICATURE, usu. associated with visual arts or with visual effects in literary works, implies exaggeration of characteristic details: *The caricature emphasized his large nose.* PARODY achieves its humor through application of the style or technique of a well-known work or author to unaccustomed subjects: *a parody of Hemingway.* TRAVESTY takes a serious subject and uses a style or language that seems incongruous or absurd: *a travesty of a senator making a speech.*

burn, *v.* **1.** flame. **2.** tingle, be hot, glow. **3.** consume, scorch, sear, singe, char, toast, brown, tan, bronze. —*n.* **4.** brook, rivulet, rill, run, runnel, streamlet, runlet.

burst, *v.* **1.** explode, crack, blow up, split. **2.** rend, tear, break. —*n.* **3.**

explosion. **4.** spurt, outpouring, gust. —**Ant.** implode.

bury, *v.* **1.** inter, entomb, inhume, inearth. **2.** sink. **3.** cover, hide, conceal, secrete, shroud, enshroud. —**Ant.** disinter; rise; uncover.

business, *n.* **1.** occupation, trade, craft, metier, profession, calling, employment, vocation, pursuit. **2.** company, concern, enterprise, corporation, firm, partnership. **3.** affair, matter, concern, transaction. **4.** commerce, trade, traffic. **5.** function, duty, office, position.

busy, *adj.* **1.** engaged, occupied, diligent, industrious, employed, working, assiduous, active, sedulous, hardworking. **2.** active, brisk, bustling, spry, agile, nimble. **3.** officious, meddlesome, prying. —**Ant.** indolent, unoccupied, lazy.

but, *conj.* **1.** however, nevertheless, yet, further, moreover, still. **2.**

excepting, save, except. —*prep.* **3.** excepting, except, save, excluding. —*adv.* **4.** only, just, no more than.

butcher, *n.* **1.** meat dealer. **2.** slaughterer, meat dresser. **3.** murderer, slayer, killer, assassin, cutthroat, thug. —*v.* **4.** kill, slaughter. **5.** slaughter, massacre, murder, kill, assassinate. **6.** bungle, botch, fail in. —**Syn. Study.** See SLAUGHTER.

buy, *v.* **1.** purchase. **2.** hire, bribe, corrupt. —**Ant.** sell.

byword, *n.* **1.** slogan, motto. **2.** proverb, maxim, apothegm, aphorism, saw, adage, saying. **3.** epithet.

C

cabal, See Syn. study at CONSPIRACY.

cabin, *n.* **1.** hut, shanty, shack, cot, cottage, shed, hovel. —*v.* **2.** cramp, confine, enclose, restrict.

cadaver, See Syn. study at BODY

cadaverous, *adj.* **1.** deathly pale, deathly, ghastly, ghostly, ghostlike, spectral, corpselike, pallid, livid. **2.** gaunt, haggard, drawn, withered, shriveled, emaciated, skeletal, wasted, hollow-eyed, scrawny, peaked, wizened. —**Ant.** robust, hearty, healthy.

cagey, *adj.* cunning, clever, shrewd, wily, astute, smart, wise, artful, canny, crafty, foxy, ingenious, sharp, slick, nimble-witted, quick-thinking, quick-witted, sharp-witted, savvy, hip.

cajole, *v.* wheedle, coax, beguile, entice, inveigle, flatter, soft-soap, sweet-talk, blandish.

calamity, *n.* affliction, adversity, ill fortune, misery, bad luck, distress, trouble, evil, hardship, trial, reverse, mischance, mishap, blow, misfortune, disaster, catastrophe, cataclysm. —**Ant.** fortune, blessing, boon. —**Syn. Study.** See DISASTER.

calculate, *v.* **1.** count, figure, reckon, cast, estimate, weigh, deliberate, compute, rate. **2.** suit, adapt, fit, adjust. —**Ant.** assume, guess.

calculation, *n.* **1.** computation, figuring, reckoning, estimate, estimation. **2.** estimate, forecast, expectation, prospect, anticipation. **3.** forethought, planning, circumspection, caution, wariness, foresight, cautiousness, discretion, prudence, deliberation. —**Ant.** guess, assumption.

call, *v.* **1.** cry out. **2.** announce, proclaim. **3.** awaken, waken, rouse, wake up, arouse. **4.** summon, invite, send for. **5.** convoke, convene, call together, assemble, muster. **6.** telephone, ring up. **7.** name, give a name to, label, term, designate, style, dub, christen, entitle,

nominate, denominate. **8.** reckon, consider, estimate, designate. **9.** shout, cry, voice. **10.** visit, stop. —*n.* **11.** shout, cry, outcry. **12.** summons, signal; invitation, bidding; appointment. **13.** need, occasion; demand, claim, requisition.

callous, *adj.* **1.** hard, hardened, inured, indurated. **2.** unfeeling, insensible, blunt, apathetic, unimpressible, indifferent, unsusceptible, obtuse; dull, sluggish, torpid, slow. —**Ant.** soft; sensitive; alert.

calm, *adj.* **1.** still, quiet, smooth, motionless, tranquil, unruffled, mild, peaceful. **2.** tranquil, peaceful, serene, self-possessed, cool, collected, unruffled, composed, undisturbed, sedate, aloof. —*n.* **3.** stillness, serenity, calmness, quiet, smoothness, tranquillity, peacefulness, aloofness, self-possession, composure, repose, equanimity. —*v.* **4.** still, quiet, tranquilize, pacify, smooth, appease, compose; allay, assuage, mollify, soothe, soften. —**Ant.** perturbed; tempestuous; excite, agitate. —**Syn. Study.** CALM, COLLECTED, COMPOSED, COOL imply the absence of agitation. CALM implies an unruffled state in the midst of disturbance all around: *He remained calm throughout the crisis.* COLLECTED implies complete command of one's thoughts, feelings, and behavior, usu. as a result of effort: *The witness was remarkably collected during questioning.* COMPOSED implies inner peace and dignified self-possession: *pale but composed.* COOL implies clarity of judgment and absence of strong feeling or excitement: *cool in the face of danger.*

can, *v.* **1.** know how to, be able to, have the ability *or* power *or* right *or* qualifications *or* means to. —*n.* **2.** tin, container.

cancel, *v.* **1.** cross out, delete, dele, erase, expunge, obliterate, blot out, efface, rub out. **2.** void, annul, countermand, revoke, rescind, counterbalance, compensate for, allow for. —**Ant.** ratify.

candid, *adj.* **1.** frank, open, outspoken, sincere, ingenuous, naive, artless, honest, plain, guileless, straightforward, aboveboard, free, honorable. **2.** impartial, honest, just, fair, unprejudiced, unbiased. **3.** white, clear, pure, unadulterated, lucid, transparent, pellucid, lucent. —**Ant.** concealed, hidden, wily, deceitful; biased, prejudiced; turgid, cloudy, dull, impure. —**Syn. Study.** See FRANK.

candor, *n.* frankness, honesty, forthrightness, directness, candidness, truthfulness, sincerity, openness, outspokenness, bluntness, brusqueness, plain speaking. —**Ant.** evasiveness, deceitfulness.

canon, *n.* **1.** rule, law, standard, formula. **2.** criterion, principle, standard.

cantankerous, *adj.* irritable, irascible, quarrelsome, fractious, cross, crotchety, captious, choleric, foul-tempered, mean-tempered, grumpy, ornery, testy, touchy, peevish, surly, vinegary, vinegarish, petulant, snappish, waspish. —**Ant.** sweet-natured, kindly, gracious.

capable, *adj.* **1.** able, competent, efficient, intelligent, clever, skillful, ingenious, sagacious, gifted, accomplished. **2.** fitted, adapted, suited, qualified. **3.** susceptible, open, admitting, allowing, permitting, permissive. —**Ant.** incapable.

capacious, *adj.* spacious, roomy, ample, large, broad, comprehensive, wide. —**Ant.** confining, narrow.

capacity, *n.* **1.** cubic contents, volume, magnitude, dimensions, amplitude. **2.** ability, power, aptitude, faculty, wit, genius, aptness, bent, forte, leaning, propensity, ableness, talent,

discernment; caliber, cleverness, skill, skillfulness, competency, competence, readiness, capability. **3.** position, relation, function, sphere, area, province; office, post, charge, responsibility. —**Ant.** incapacity, incompetence.

caper, *v.* **1.** gambol, frolic, frisk, play, romp, cavort, rollick. —*n.* **2.** escapade, prank, frolic, lark, antic, adventure, dido, bit of mischief.

capital, *n.* **1.** metropolis, seat. **2.** wealth, principal, investment, worth, resources, assets, stock. —*adj.* **3.** principal, first, important, chief, prime, primary, major, leading, cardinal, essential, vital. **4.** excellent, first-rate, splendid, fine. **5.** large-size, upper case. **6.** fatal, serious. —**Ant.** trivial, unimportant. —**Syn. Study.** CAPITAL, CHIEF, MAJOR, PRINCIPAL apply to a main or leading representative of a kind. CAPITAL may suggest preeminence, importance, or excellence: *a capital idea.* CHIEF often means highest in office or power; it may mean most important: *the chief clerk; the chief problem.* MAJOR refers to someone or something that is greater in number, quantity, or importance: *a major resource; a major poet.* PRINCIPAL refers to the most distinguished, influential, or foremost person or thing: *a principal stockholder; the principal reason.*

capricious, *adj.* wayward, arbitrary, whimsical, whimsied, inconstant, changeable, impulsive, unpredictable, fickle, temperamental, mercurial, volatile, unstable, erratic. —**Ant.** predictable, stable, steady. —**Syn. Study.** See FICKLE.

capsize, *v.* overturn, upset. —**Ant.** right.

captivate, *v.* charm, enthrall, enchant, fascinate, hypnotize, bewitch, enamor, win, catch. —**Ant.** repel, repulse.

captivity, *n.* bondage, servitude, slavery, thralldom, serfdom, subjection; imprisonment, confinement, incarceration. —**Ant.** freedom.

capture, *v.* **1.** seize, take prisoner, catch, arrest, snare, apprehend, grab, nab; imprison, incarcerate. —*n.* **2.** arrest, seizure, apprehension, catch. —**Ant.** release.

carcass, *n.* **1.** body, corpse, cadaver. **2.** framework, skeleton. —**Syn. Study.** See BODY.

care, *n.* **1.** worry, anxiety, concern, solicitude, trouble. **2.** heed, caution, pains, anxiety, regard, attention, vigilance, carefulness, solicitude, circumspection, alertness, watchfulness, wakefulness. **3.** burden, charge, responsibility. —*v.* **4.** have concern *or* regard, be solicitous *or* anxious, worry, be troubled. **5.** like, be inclined *or* disposed *or* interested.

careen, *v.* sway, lurch, lean, heel over, swing, roll,

rock, wobble, reel, weave, waver.

careful, *adj.* **1.** cautious, circumspect, watchful, wakeful, vigilant, guarded, chary, discreet, wary, suspicious, prudent, tactful; trustworthy. **2.** painstaking, meticulous, discerning, exact, thorough, concerned, scrupulous, finical, conscientious, attentive, heedful, thoughtful. —**Ant.** careless. —**Syn. Study.** CAREFUL, CAUTIOUS, DISCREET, WARY imply a watchful guarding against something. CAREFUL implies guarding against mistakes, harm, or bad consequences by paying close attention to details and by being concerned or solicitous: *He was careful not to wake the baby.* CAUTIOUS implies a fear of some unfavorable situation and investigation before acting: *cautious about investments.* DISCREET implies being prudent in speech or action and being trustworthy: *discreet inquiries about his credit rating.* WARY implies a vigilant lookout for a danger suspected or feared: *wary of polite strangers.*

caregiver, *n.* protector, safekeeper, guardian, caretaker, attendant, custodian, warden, patron, nurse.

careless, *adj.* **1.** inattentive, incautious, unwary, unthoughtful, forgetful, remiss, negligent, neglectful, unmindful, heedless, reckless, indiscreet, thoughtless, unconcerned. **2.** negligent, inaccurate, inexact. **3.** unconsidered; inconsiderate. —**Ant.** careful.

careworn, *adj.* drawn, worn, pinched, worn-down, strained, haggard, hollow-eyed, ravaged, woebegone.

cargo, *n.* freight, load, burden, lading.

caricature, *n.* **1.** burlesque, exaggeration, travesty, take-off, parody, farce, satire, lampoon, cartoon. —*v.* **2.** burlesque, exaggerate, travesty, parody, take off, satirize, lampoon. **—Syn. Study.** See BURLESQUE.

carnal, *adj.* **1.** human, temporal, worldly, mundane, earthly, unregenerate, natural, unspiritual. **2.** sensual, fleshly, bodily, animal. **3.** lustful, impure, gross, lecherous, worldly, lascivious, salacious, libidinous, concupiscent, lewd, lubricious, wanton, lubricous. **—Ant.** spiritual, moral, intellectual. **—Syn. Study.** CARNAL, SENSUAL, ANIMAL all refer to the physical rather than the rational or spiritual nature of human beings. CARNAL, although it may refer to any bodily need or urge, most often refers to sexuality: *carnal knowledge; the carnal sin of gluttony.* SENSUAL most often describes the arousal or gratification of erotic urges: *sensual eyes; sensual delights.* ANIMAL may describe any physical appetite, but is sometimes used of sexual appetite:

animal greediness; animal lust.

carriage, *n.* **1.** vehicle, cart, wagon, conveyance; dog-cart, brougham, hansom, victoria, calash, buckboard, carry-all, shay, sulky, surrey. **2.** bearing, manner, mien, deportment, behavior, conduct, demeanor.

carry, *v.* **1.** convey, bear, transport; transmit, transfer, take, bring. **2.** bear, support, sustain, stand, suffer. **3.** lead, impel, drive, conduct, urge. **4.** effect, accomplish, gain, secure, win, capture.

cascade, *n.* **1.** waterfall, falls, cataract, Niagara, downpour, shower, torrent, deluge. **—***v.* **2.** spill, spill over, overflow, fall, flow over, brim over, overbrim, pour, pour down, plummet.

case, *n.* **1.** instance, example, illustration, occurrence. **2.** state, circumstance, situation, condition, contingency; plight, predicament. **3.** patient; action, suit, lawsuit, cause, process, trial. **4.** receptacle, box, container, chest, folder, envelope, sheath. **5.** frame, framework.

cast, *v.* **1.** throw, fling, hurl, deposit, propel, put, toss, pitch, shy, sling, pitch. **2.** throw off, shed, slough, put off, lay aside. **3.** direct, turn, cause to fall, throw, shed, impart. **4.** throw out, send forth, hurl, toss. **5.** throw down, defeat, overwhelm. **6.** part with, lose. **7.** set aside, throw aside, discard, reject, dismiss, disband. **8.** emit, eject, vomit, spew forth, puke. **9.** bestow, confer. **10.** arrange, plan out, allot, apportion, appoint, assign. **11.** mold, form, found. **12.** compute, calculate, reckon; forecast, foretell. **13.** ponder, consider, contrive, devise, plan. **14.** throw. **15.** calculate, add. **16.** consider; plan, scheme. —*n.* **17.** throw, fling, toss. **18.** fortune, lot. **19.** appearance, form, shape, mien, demeanor. **20.** sort, kind, style. **21.** tendency, inclination, turn, bent, trend, air. **22.** turn, twist; warp. **23.** tinge, tint, hue, shade, touch; dash, trace, hint, suggestion. **24.** computation, calculation, addition. **25.** forecast, conjecture, guess.

caste, *n.* rank, class, status, social level, social stratum, standing, place, station, position, estate, echelon, grade.

castle, *n.* **1.** fortress, citadel, stronghold. **2.** palace, chateau, mansion. **3.** (*chess*) rook.

casual, *adj.* **1.** unexpected, fortuitous, unforeseen, chance, accidental. **2.** unpremeditated, offhand, unintentional. **3.** careless, negligent, unconcerned. **4.** irregular, occasional, random. —**Ant.** premeditated, deliberate, calculated; careful; regular, routine.

cataclysm, *n.* **1.** disaster, calamity, catastrophe, debacle, crash, collapse, convulsion, meltdown. **2.** flood, deluge, inundation. —**Syn. Study.** See DISASTER.

catalog, See Syn. study at
LIST.

catalogue, *n.* list, roll,
roster, register, record,
inventory.

catastrophe, *n.* disaster,
mishap, cataclysm,
calamity, misfortune,
mischance; end,
dénouement, finale;
upshot, conclusion,
windup, termination.
—Ant. triumph. **—Syn.
Study.** See DISASTER.

catch, *v.* **1.** capture,
apprehend, arrest. **2.**
ensnare, entrap, deceive,
entangle. **3.** surprise,
detect, take unawares. **4.**
strike, hit. **5.** lay hold of,
grasp, seize, snatch, grip,
entangle, clutch. **6.**
captivate, charm, enchant,
fascinate, win, bewitch.
—n. 7. capture,
apprehension, arrest,
seizure. **8.** ratchet, bolt. **9.**
take. **—Ant.** release.

catchword, *n.* slogan,
catchphrase, byword,
motto, watchword, maxim,
household word, tag line,
battle cry, rallying cry.

cause, *n.* **1.** occasion,
reason, ground, grounds,
basis; motive, determinant,
incitement, inducement. **2.**
purpose, object, aim, end.
—v. 3. bring about, effect,
determine, make, produce,
create, originate, occasion,
give rise to. **—Syn. Study.**
See REASON.

caustic, *adj.* corrosive,
cutting, scathing, stinging,
slashing, mordant, incisive,
keen, acid, trenchant,
sharp, ironic, satiric,
sarcastic, sardonic,
mordacious. **—Ant.**
bland, harmless,
innocuous.

caution, *n.* **1.** prudence,
discretion,
circumspectness,
watchfulness,
circumspection, heed, care,
wariness, heedfulness,
vigilance, forethought,
providence. **2.** warning,
admonition, advice,
injunction, counsel. **—v. 3.**
warn, admonish, advise,
enjoin, counsel, forewarn.
—Ant. carelessness.
—Syn. Study. See WARN.

cautious, *adj.* prudent,
careful, heedful, watchful,
discreet, wary, vigilant,

alert, provident, chary, circumspect, guarded. —**Ant.** careless, heedless, indiscreet. —**Syn. Study.** See CAREFUL.

caveat, *n.* warning, caution, forewarning, notice, notification, admonition, recommendation, suggestion, monition, verbum sapienti *or* verbum sap *or* verbum sat *or* verb. sap., word to the wise, tip, tip-off.

cavity, *n.* hollow, hole, void.

cease, *v.* **1.** stop, desist, stay. **2.** terminate, end, culminate. **3.** discontinue, end. —**Ant.** start, begin; continue, persist.

cede, *v.* yield, resign, surrender, relinquish, abandon, give up; make over, grant, transfer, convey. —**Ant.** persist, maintain.

celebrate, *v.* **1.** commemorate, honor, observe. **2.** proclaim, announce. **3.** praise, extol, laud, glorify, honor, applaud, commend. **4.** solemnize, ritualize.

celebrated, *adj.* famous, renowned, well-known, distinguished, illustrious, eminent, famed. —**Ant.** obscure, unknown. —**Syn. Study.** See FAMOUS.

celebrity, *n.* **1.** fame, renown, celebrityhood, stardom, superstardom, name, acclaim, acclamation, recognition, eminence, distinction, illustriousness, reputation, repute, éclat, notoriety. **2.** notable, big name, personage, star, superstar, luminary, VIP, name, somebody, nabob, big shot, biggie, megastar, celeb. —**Ant.** nobody, nonentity, has-been, wannabe.

celerity, See Syn. study at SPEED.

celestial, *adj.* heavenly, ethereal, empyreal, empyrean, elysian, otherworldly, transcendental, unearthly, divine, paradisial, paradisaic, supernal.

—**Ant.** earthly, mundane, terrestrial.

censure, *n.* **1.** condemnation, reproof, disapproval, disapprobation, blaming, criticism, blame, reproach, reprehension, rebuke, reprimand, stricture, animadversion. —*v.* **2.** criticize, disapprove, condemn, find fault with. **3.** reprove, rebuke, reprimand, reprehend, chide, blame, reproach. —**Ant.** praise, commend. —**Syn. Study.** See ABUSE. See also REPRIMAND.

center, *n.* **1.** middle, midst. **2.** pivot, hub, point, axis. —**Ant.** brim, edge.

ceremony, *n.* rite, ritual, formality, observance. —**Ant.** informality.

certain, *adj.* **1.** confident, sure, assured, convinced, satisfied, indubitable, indisputable, unquestionable, undeniable, incontestable, irrefutable, unquestioned, incontrovertible, absolute, positive, plain, patent, obvious, clear. **2.** sure,

inevitable, infallible, unfailing. **3.** fixed, agreed upon, settled, prescribed, determined, determinate, constant, stated, given. **4.** definite, particular, special, especial. **5.** unfailing, reliable, trustworthy, dependable, trusty. —**Ant.** uncertain; unclear, unsure; unsettled; indefinite; fallible, unreliable.

certainty, *n.* **1.** unquestionableness, inevitability, certitude, assurance, confidence, conviction. **2.** fact, truth. —**Ant.** doubt, uncertainty.

chagrin, *n.* **1.** embarrassment, distress, disconcertion, discomfiture, discomposure, abashment, humiliation, shame, mortification. —*v.* **2.** abash, take aback, discomfit, distress, disconcert, embarrass, shame, humiliate, mortify. —**Syn. Study.** See SHAME.

champion, *n.* **1.** winner, victor, hero. **2.** defender, protector, vindicator. **3.** fighter, warrior. —*v.* **4.** defend, support, maintain,

fight for, advocate.
—**Ant.** loser; oppose.

chance, *n.* **1.** fortune, fate, luck, accident, fortuity. **2.** possibility, contingency, probability. **3.** opportunity, opening, occasion. **4.** risk, hazard, peril, danger, jeopardy. —*v.* **5.** happen, occur, befall, take place. —*adj.* **6.** casual, accidental, fortuitous. —**Ant.** necessity, inevitability; surety.

change, *v.* **1.** alter, make different, turn, transmute, transform, vary, modify. **2.** exchange, substitute, convert, shift, replace; barter, trade, commute. **3.** interchange. —*n.* **4.** variation, alteration, modification, deviation, transformation, transmutation, mutation, conversion, transition. **5.** substitution, exchange. **6.** variety, novelty, innovation, vicissitude. —**Ant.** remain, endure; immutability. —**Syn. Study.** CHANGE, ALTER both mean to make a difference in the state or condition of a thing. To CHANGE is to make a material or radical difference or to substitute one thing for another of the same kind: *to change a lock; to change one's plans.* To ALTER is to make some partial change, as in appearance, but usu. to preserve the identity: *to alter a garment; to alter a contract.*

chaotic, *adj.* confused, upset, tumultuous, turbulent, disordered, unruly, disorderly, anarchic, scattered, disarrayed, higgledy-piggledy.

character, *n.* **1.** individuality, personality. **2.** feature, trait, characteristic. **3.** nature, quality, disposition, mien, constitution, cast. **4.** name, reputation, repute. **5.** status, capacity. **6.** symbol, mark, sign, letter, figure, emblem. —**Syn. Study.** CHARACTER, PERSONALITY refer to the sum of the characteristics possessed by a person. CHARACTER refers esp. to the moral qualities and ethical standards that make up the inner nature of a person: *a man of sterling character*. PERSONALITY refers particularly to outer characteristics, as wittiness or charm, that determine the impression that a person makes upon others: *a pleasing personality*. See also REPUTATION.

characteristic, *adj.* **1.** typical, distinctive, discrete, special, peculiar, singular. —*n.* **2.** feature, quality, trait, peculiarity, mark, attribute, property. —**Syn. Study.** See FEATURE.

charge, *v.* **1.** load, lade, burden, freight. **2.** command, enjoin, exhort, order, urge, bid, require. **3.** impute, ascribe. **4.** blame, accuse, indict, arraign, impeach, inculpate, incriminate, involve, inform against, betray. **5.** attack, assault, set on. —*n.* **6.** load, burden, cargo, freight. **7.** duty, responsibility, commission, office, trust, employment. **8.** care, custody, superintendence, ward, management. **9.** command, injunction, exhortation, order, direction, mandate, instruction, precept. **10.** accusation, indictment, imputation, allegation, crimination, incrimination. **11.** price, cost. **12.** tax, lien, cost, expense, encumbrance, outlay, expenditure, liability, debt. **13.** onset, attack, onslaught, assault, encounter.

charismatic, *adj.* alluring, attractive, fascinating, magnetic, captivating, spellbinding, beguiling, glamorous, entrancing, riveting, bewitching, prepossessing.

charitable, *adj.* **1.** generous, open-handed, liberal, beneficent, benign, kind, benignant, benevolent, bountiful, lavish. **2.** broad-minded, liberal, lenient, considerate, mild, kindly. —**Ant.** mean, stingy; narrow-minded, inconsiderate. —**Syn. Study.** See GENEROUS.

charm, *n.* **1.** attractiveness,

allurement, fascination, enchantment, bewitchment, spell, witchery, magic, sorcery. **2.** trinket, bauble, jewelry; amulet. —*v.* **3.** enchant, fascinate, captivate, catch, entrance, enrapture, transport, delight, please; attract, allure, enamor, bewitch; ravish. **—Ant.** revulsion; disgust.

chart, *n.* map, plan.

charter, *n.* **1.** privilege, immunity, guaranty, warranty. —*v.* **2.** lease, hire, rent, let. **—Syn. Study.** See HIRE.

chary, *adj.* **1.** careful, wary, cautious, circumspect. **2.** shy, bashful, self-effacing. **3.** fastidious, choosy, particular. **4.** sparing, stingy, frugal. **—Ant.** careless.

chaste, *adj.* virtuous, pure, moral, decent, undefiled, modest, continent; clean, elevated, unsullied; unaffected, simple, subdued, neat, straight, honest; refined, classic, elegant. **—Ant.** sinful, impure, immodest;

unrefined, coarse, inelegant.

chasten, *v.* discipline, punish, chastise, restrain, subdue, humble. **—Ant.** indulge, humor.

chattels, See Syn. study at PROPERTY.

cheap, *adj.* **1.** inexpensive, low-priced. **2.** paltry, common, mean, low, lowly, poor, inferior, base. **—Ant.** dear, expensive, costly; exceptional, extraordinary, elegant. **—Syn. Study.** CHEAP, INEXPENSIVE agree in their suggestion of low cost. CHEAP now often suggests shoddiness, inferiority, showy imitation, unworthiness, and the like: *a cheap fabric.* INEXPENSIVE emphasizes lowness of price (although more expensive than CHEAP) and suggests that the value is fully equal to the cost: *an inexpensive dress.* It is often used as an evasion for the more pejorative CHEAP.

cheat, *n.* **1.** fraud, swindle, deception, trick,

imposture, wile, deceit, artifice, chicanery, stratagem, hoax, imposition, snare, trap, pitfall, catch. **2.** swindler, imposter, trickster, sharper, cheater, dodger, charlatan, fraud, fake, phony, mountebank, rogue, knave. —*v.* **3.** deceive, defraud, trick, victimize, mislead, dupe, gudgeon, cog, gull, cozen, outwit, bamboozle, delude, hoodwink, beguile, inveigle, swindle, con; entrap, hoax, ensnare, fool, cajole; dissemble. —**Syn. Study.** CHEAT, DECEIVE, TRICK, VICTIMIZE refer to the use of fraud or artifice to obtain an unfair advantage or gain. CHEAT usu. means to be dishonest in order to make a profit for oneself: *to cheat customers by shortchanging them.* DECEIVE suggests misleading someone by false words or actions: *He deceived his parents about his whereabouts.* TRICK means to mislead by a ruse or stratagem, often of a crafty or dishonorable

kind: *I was tricked into signing the note.* VICTIMIZE means to make a victim of; it connotes a particularly contemptible act: *to victimize a blind person.*

check, *v.* **1.** stop, halt, delay, arrest. **2.** curb, restrain, control, repress, chain, bridle, hinder, hobble, obstruct, curtail. **3.** investigate, verify, assess, test, measure, examine, compare. **4.** agree, correspond. **5.** pause, stop. —*n.* **6.** restraint, curb, bridle, bit, hindrance, obstacle, obstruction, impediment, control, bar, barrier, restriction, damper, interference, deterrent, repression. **7.** rebuff, arrest, stoppage, cessation, repulse, halt. **8.** ticket, receipt, coupon, tag, counterfoil, stub. —**Ant.** continue, advance, foster, support. —**Syn. Study.** CHECK, CURB, RESTRAIN refer to putting a control on movement, progress, action, etc. CHECK implies arresting suddenly, halting or causing to halt by means of drastic action: *to check a movement toward reform.* CURB implies slowing or stopping forward motion: *to curb inflation; to curb a horse.* RESTRAIN implies the use of force to put under control or hold back: *to restrain one's enthusiasm; to restrain unruly spectators.* See also STOP.

cheer, *n.* **1.** encouragement, comfort, solace. **2.** gladness, gaiety, animation, joy, mirth, glee, merriment, cheerfulness. **3.** food, provisions, victuals, repast, viands. —*v.* **4.** gladden, enliven, inspirit, exhilarate, animate, encourage. **5.** shout, applaud, acclaim, salute. —**Ant.** derision; misery; discourage, deride; boo, hiss.

cheerful, *adj.* **1.** cheery, gay, blithe, happy, lively, spirited, sprightly, joyful, joyous, mirthful, buoyant, gleeful, sunny, jolly. **2.** pleasant, bright, gay, winsome, gladdening, cheery, cheering, inspiring, animating. **3.** hearty, robust, ungrudging, generous. —**Ant.** miserable; unpleasant; stingy, mean.

cherish, *v.* **1.** foster, harbor, entertain, humor, encourage, indulge. **2.** nurse, nurture, nourish, support, sustain, comfort. **3.** treasure, cling to, hold dear. —**Ant.** abandon, scorn. —**Syn. Study.** CHERISH, FOSTER, HARBOR imply the giving of affection, care, or shelter. CHERISH suggests regarding or treating something or someone as an object of affection or value: *to cherish a friendship.* FOSTER implies sustaining and nourishing something with care, esp. in order to promote, increase, or strengthen it: *to foster a hope.* HARBOR usu. suggests sheltering someone or entertaining something undesirable: *to harbor a criminal; to harbor a grudge.*

chicanery, *n.* dishonesty, deception, trickery, subterfuge, double-dealing, underhandedness, fraud, fraudulence, rascality, roguery, knavery, dupery, hanky-panky, villainy, dissimulation,

chide, *v.* **1.** scold, fret, fume, chafe. **2.** reprove, rebuke, censure, criticize, scold, admonish, upbraid, reprimand, blame, reprehend. **—Ant.** praise, commend.

chief, *n.* **1.** head, leader, ruler, chieftain, commander. —*adj.* **2.** principal, most important, prime, first, supreme, leading, paramount, great, grand, cardinal, master; vital, essential. **—Ant.** follower, disciple; unimportant, trivial, trifling; secondary. **—Syn. Study.** See CAPITAL.

chiefly, *adv.* mostly, principally, mainly, especially, particularly, eminently. **—Ant.** last, lastly.

childish, *adj.* childlike, puerile, infantile, young, tender; weak, silly, simple, ingenuous, guileless, trusting, confident. **—Ant.**

adult, sophisticated.
—Syn. Study. CHILDISH, INFANTILE, CHILDLIKE refer to characteristics or qualities of childhood. CHILDISH refers to characteristics that are undesirable and unpleasant: *childish selfishness.* INFANTILE usu. carries an even stronger idea of disapproval or scorn: *infantile temper tantrums.* CHILDLIKE refers to those characteristics that are desirable or merely neutral: *childlike innocence.*

childlike, See Syn. study at CHILDISH.

chill, *n.* **1.** cold, coldness, frigidity. **2.** shivering, ague. **3.** depression, damp. —*adj.* **4.** chilly, cool, unfriendly, depressing, discouraging, bleak. —*v.* **5.** cool, freeze; depress, discourage, deject, dishearten. **—Ant.** warm.

chivalrous, *adj* courteous, gallant, noble, courtly, gracious, helpful, thoughtful, considerate, unselfish, attentive, generous, giving, magnanimous, greathearted, benevolent, altruistic, kindhearted, kindly. **—Ant.** selfish, self-centered, ungenerous.

choice, *n.* **1.** selection, choosing, election, option, alternative, preference. **—***adj.* **2.** worthy, excellent, superior, fine, select, rare, uncommon, valuable, precious. **—Syn. Study.**
CHOICE, ALTERNATIVE, OPTION suggest the power of choosing between things. CHOICE implies the opportunity to choose freely: *Her choice for dessert was ice cream.* ALTERNATIVE suggests a chance to choose only one of a limited number of possibilities: *I had the alternative of going to the party or staying home alone.* OPTION emphasizes the right or privilege of choosing: *He had the option of taking the prize money or a gift.*

choose, *v.* select, elect, prefer, pick, cull.

chop, *v.* cut, mince.

chore, See Syn. study at TASK.

chronic, *adj.* **1.** inveterate, constant, habitual, confirmed, hardened. **2.** perpetual, continuous, continuing, unending, never-ending, everlasting. **—Ant.** fleeting, temporary.

chuckle, *v., n.* laugh, giggle, titter. **—Ant.** cry, sob.

chutzpah, *n.* audacity, pluck, self-confidence, self-assertiveness, brashness, boldness, temerity, temerariousness, aggressiveness, hardihood, effrontery, presumption, presumptuousness, brazenness, impudence, impertinence, insolence, nerve, cheek, gall, face, crust, brass. **—Ant.** timidity, modesty, self-effacement.

circle, *n.* **1.** ring, periphery, circumference, perimeter. **2.** ring, circlet, crown. **3.** compass, area, sphere, province, field, region, bounds, circuit. **4.** cycle, period, series. **5.** coterie, set, clique, society, club,

company, class, fraternity.
6. sphere, orb, globe, ball.
—*v.* **7.** surround, encircle,
encompass, round, bound,
include. **8.** orbit, circuit,
revolve. —**Syn. Study.**
CIRCLE, CLUB, COTERIE refer
to restricted social groups.
A CIRCLE is a little group;
in the plural it often
suggests a section of
society interested in one
mode of life, occupation,
etc.: *a sewing circle;
theatrical circles.* CLUB
implies an organized
association with fixed
requirements for
membership: *an athletic
club.* COTERIE suggests a
small and exclusive group
intimately associated
because of similar
backgrounds and interests:
a literary coterie.
circuit, *n.* **1.** course, tour,
journey, revolution, orbit.
2. circumference,
perimeter, periphery,
boundary, compass. **3.**
space, area, region,
compass, range, sphere,
province, district, field.
circuitous, *adj.* indirect,
roundabout, circular,

wandering, meandering,
crooked, devious, deviant,
tortuous, serpentine,
twisting, vagrant, oblique,
errant, circumambulatory,
circumlocutory. —**Ant.**
straight, straightforward,
blunt.
civil, *adj.* polite, courteous,
courtly, gracious,
complaisant, respectful,
deferential, obliging;
affable, urbane, debonair,
chivalrous, gallant, suave;
refined, well-mannered,
well-bred, civilized. —**Ant.**
uncivil, discourteous; rude;
ill-mannered, unrefined.
—**Syn. Study.** CIVIL,
COURTEOUS, POLITE imply
avoidance of rudeness
toward others. CIVIL
suggests only minimal
observance of social
amenities: *a civil reply.*
COURTEOUS implies
respectful, dignified,
sincere, and thoughtful
consideration for others: *a
courteous thank-you note.*
POLITE implies habitual
courtesy, arising from a
consciousness of one's
training and the demands

of good manners: *a polite young man.*

claim, *v.* **1.** demand, require, ask, call for, challenge. **2.** assert, maintain, uphold. —*n.* **3.** demand, request, requirement, requisition, call. **4.** right, title, privilege, pretension.

clamor, *n.* **1.** shouting, uproar, outcry, noise, hullabaloo. **2.** vociferation. —*v.* **3.** vociferate, cry out, shout. **4.** importune, demand noisily. —**Ant.** quiet, serenity, taciturnity. —**Syn. Study.** See NOISE.

clandestine, *adj.* secret, private, concealed, hidden, sly, underhand. —**Ant.** open, candid, aboveboard.

clannish, *adj.* exclusive, exclusionary, exclusory, select, selective, restricted, restrictive, cliquish, cliquey, snobbish, snobby, elite, elect, ethnocentric. —**Ant.** open, unrestricted, all-embracing.

clash, *v.* **1.** clang, crash, clap, dash, clatter, clank. **2.** collide. **3.** conflict, struggle, disagree, interfere, content. —*n.* **4.** collision. **5.** conflict, opposition, disagreement, interference, struggle, contradiction. —**Ant.** harmony, agreement.

clasp, *n.* **1.** brooch, pin, clip, hook, fastening, catch, hasp. **2.** embrace, hug, grasp. —*v.* **3.** clip. **4.** grasp, grip, clutch. **5.** embrace, hug, clutch, grasp, fold.

clean, *adj.* **1.** unsoiled, unstained, clear, unblemished, pure, flawless, spotless, unsullied, neat, immaculate. **2.** pure, purified, unmixed, unadulterated, clarified. **3.** uncontaminated, not radioactive. **4.** clear, readable, legible. **5.** unsullied, undefiled, moral, innocent, upright, honorable, chaste. **6.** neat, trim, shapely, graceful, delicate, light. **7.** adroit, deft, dextrous. **8.** complete, perfect, entire, whole, unabated, unimpaired. —*adv.* **9.** cleanly, neatly. **10.** wholly, completely, perfectly, entirely, altogether, fully, thoroughly, in all respects, out and out. —*v.* **11.** scour, scrub, sweep, brush, wipe, mop, dust, wash, rinse, lave, cleanse, deterge, purify, clear; decontaminate. —**Ant.** dirty, contaminated; radioactive; impure, immoral; clumsy, awkward.

cleanse, *v.* clean. —**Ant.** soil.

clear, *adj.* **1.** unclouded, light, bright, pellucid, limpid, diaphanous, crystalline, transparent, luminous. **2.** bright, shining, lucent. **3.** perceptible, understood, distinct, intelligible, orotund, comprehensible, lucid, plain, perspicuous, conspicuous, obvious. **4.** distinct, evident, plain, obvious, apparent, manifest, palpable, patent, unmistakable, unequivocal, unambiguous, indisputable, undeniable, unquestionable. **5.** convinced, certain, positive, definite, assured, sure. **6.** innocent, pure, not guilty, unsullied, irreproachable, unblemished, clean, unspotted, unadulterated, moral, undefiled, virtuous, immaculate, spotless. **7.** serene, calm, untroubled, fair, cloudless, sunny. **8.** unobstructed, open, free, unimpeded, unhindered, unhampered, unencumbered, unentangled. **9.** smooth, clean, even, regular, unblemished. **10.** emptied, empty, free, rid. **11.** limitless, unlimited, unqualified, unequivocal, boundless, free, open. **12.** net. —*adv.* **13.** clearly. —*v.* **14.** clarify, purify, refine, clean, cleanse. **15.** acquit, absolve, exonerate, vindicate, excuse, justify. **16.** extricate, disentangle, disabuse, rid, disencumber, disengage. **17.** liberate, free, emancipate, set free, disenthrall, loose, unchain, unfetter, let go. —**Ant.** cloudy, dim, obscure; indistinct, unclear; equivocal, doubtful; guilty, culpable; troubled, disturbed, perturbed, obstructed; limited, confined.

clearly, *adv.* definitely, distinctly, evidently, plainly, understandably, obviously, certainly, surely, assuredly, entirely, completely, totally. **—Ant.** confusedly, indefinitely; partly.

cleft, *n.* split, fissure, crack, crevice, cleaving, cleavage, rift, breach, break, fracture, cranny, gap, chasm. **—Ant.** joint, link.

clemency, *n.* mildness, mercy, lenience, leniency, forbearance, compassion, tenderness, kindness, kindliness, gentleness, mercifulness. **—Ant.** severity, austerity, cruelty, mercilessness.

clever, *adj.* **1.** bright, quick, able, apt, smart, intelligent, expert, gifted, talented, ingenious, quick-witted. **2.** skillful, adroit, dextrous, nimble, agile, handy. **—Ant.** dull, slow, dimwitted; clumsy, awkward, maladroit.

climb, *v.* **1.** mount, ascend, scale, surmount. **2.** rise, arise. **—***n.* **3.** ascent, climbing, scaling, rise. **—Ant.** descend; descent.

cloister, *n.* monastery, nunnery, convent, abbey, priory.

close, *v.* **1.** stop, obstruct, shut, block, bar, stop up, clog, choke. **2.** enclose, cover in, shut in. **3.** bring together, join, unite. **4.** end, terminate, finish, conclude, cease, complete. **5.** terminate, conclude, cease, end. **6.** come together, unite, coalesce, join. **7.** grapple, fight. **—***adj.* **8.** shut, tight, closed, fast, confined. **9.** enclosed, shut in. **10.** heavy, unventilated, muggy, oppressive, uncomfortable, dense, thick. **11.** secretive, reticent, taciturn, close-mouthed, silent, uncommunicative, incommunicative, reserved, withdrawn. **12.** parsimonious, stingy, tight, closefisted, penurious, niggardly, miserly, mean. **13.** scarce, rare. **14.**

compact, condensed, dense, thick, solid, compressed, firm. **15.** near, nearby, adjoining, adjacent, neighboring, immediate. **16.** intimate, confidential, attached, dear, devoted. **17.** strict, searching, minute, scrupulous, exact, exacting, accurate, precise, faithful, nice. **18.** intent, fixed, assiduous, intense, concentrated, earnest, constant, unremitting, relentless, unrelenting. —*n.* **19.** end, termination, conclusion. **20.** junction, union, coalescence, joining. —**Ant.** open.

clothes, *n.* clothing, attire, raiment, dress, garments, vesture, habit, costume, garb, vestments, habiliments, accouterments.

cloud, *n.* **1.** fog, haze, mist, vapor. **2.** host, crowd, throng, multitude, swarm, horde, army. —*v.* **3.** becloud, bedim, shadow, overshadow, obscure, shade. —**Ant.** clarify.

cloudy, *adj.* **1.** overcast, shadowy, clouded, murky, lowering, gloomy, cloudy, dismal, depressing, sullen. **2.** obscure, indistinct, dim, blurred, blurry, unclear, befogged, muddled, confused, dark, turbid, muddy, opaque. —**Ant.** clear; distinct.

club, *n.* **1.** stick, cudgel, bludgeon, blackjack, billy; bat. **2.** society, organization, association, circle, set, coterie, clique, fraternity, sorority. —**Syn. Study.** See CIRCLE.

clumsy, *adj.* **1.** awkward, unskillful, ungainly, lumbering, ungraceful, lubberly. **2.** unhandy, maladroit, unskillful, inexpert, bungling, ponderous, heavy, heavy-handed, inept. —**Ant.** adroit, clever, dexterous.

coarse, *adj.* **1.** impure, base, common, inferior, faulty, crude, rude, rough. **2.** indelicate, unpolished, uncivil, impolite, gruff, bluff, boorish, churlish. **3.** gross, broad, indecent, vulgar, crass, ribald, lewd, lascivious, amoral, immoral, dirty. —**Ant.**

pure, refined; civil, civilized, cultivated; decent, decorous.

coast, *n.* shore, seashore, strand, beach, seaside, seacoast, littoral.

coax, *v.* wheedle, cajole, beguile, inveigle, persuade, flatter. —**Ant.** force, bully; deter.

cockeyed, *adj.* **1.** askew, skewed, out of kilter, awry, deviant, crooked, alop, askance, topsy-turvy, oblique, (*Brit.*) wonky. **2.** foolish, silly, whimsical, loony, wacky. **3.** drunk, intoxicated, inebriated, dazed with drink, loaded, plastered.

coeval, See Syn. study at CONTEMPORARY.

cognizant, See Syn. study at CONSCIOUS.

cohere, See Syn. study at STICK.

coherence, *n.* **1.** cohesion, union, connection. **2.** connection, congruity, consistency, correspondence, harmony, harmoniousness, agreement, unity,

rationality. —**Ant.** incoherence.

coincident, See Syn. study at CONTEMPORARY.

cold, *adj.* **1.** chilly, chill, cool, frigid, gelid, frozen, freezing. **2.** dead. **3.** impassionate, unemotional, unenthusiastic, passionless, apathetic, unresponsive, unsympathetic, unaffected, stoical, phlegmatic, unfeeling, unsusceptible, unimpressible, unimpressed, cool, sluggish, torpid, indifferent, cold-blooded, unconcerned, heartless, unperturbed, imperturbable. **4.** polite, formal, reserved, unresponsive, unfriendly, inimical, hostile. **5.** calm, deliberate, depressing, dispiriting, disheartening, uninspiring, spiritless, unaffecting, dull. **6.** faint, weak. **7.** bleak, raw, cutting, nipping, arctic, polar, frosty, icy, wintry, chill, chilly. —*n.* **8.** chill, shivers, ague. —**Ant.** warm, hot.

collect, *v.* gather, assemble, amass, accumulate,

aggregate, scrape together. —**Ant.** strew, broadcast, spread. —**Syn. Study.** See GATHER.

collected, See Syn. study at CALM.

collection, *n.* **1.** set, accumulation, mass, heap, pile, hoard, store, aggregation. **2.** contribution, alms.

colloquial, *adj.* conversational, informal. —**Ant.** formal. —**Syn. Study.** COLLOQUIAL, CONVERSATIONAL, INFORMAL refer to types of speech or to usages that are not on a formal level. COLLOQUIAL is often mistakenly used with a connotation of disapproval, as if it meant "vulgar" or "bad" or "incorrect" usage, whereas it merely describes a casual or familiar style used in speaking and writing: *colloquial expressions.* CONVERSATIONAL refers to a style used in the oral exchange of ideas, opinions, etc.: *The newsletter was written in an easy conversational style.* INFORMAL means without formality, without strict attention to set forms, unceremonious; it describes the ordinary, everyday language of cultivated speakers: *informal English.*

colossal, See Syn. study at GIGANTIC.

column, *n.* pillar, shaft, stele, pilaster.

combat, *v.* **1.** fight, contend, battle, oppose, struggle, contest, war, resist, withstand. —*n.* **2.** fight, skirmish, contest, battle, struggle, conflict, war, brush, affair, encounter, engagement. —**Ant.** support, defend.

combination, *n.* **1.** conjunction, association, union, connection, coalescence, blending. **2.** composite, compound, mixture, amalgamation, amalgam. **3.** alliance, confederacy, federation, union, league, coalition, association, society, club; cartel, combine, monopoly; conspiracy, cabal.

combine, *v.* **1.** unite, join,

conjoin, associate, coalesce, blend, mix, incorporate, involve, compound, amalgamate. —*n.* **2.** combination (def. 3). —**Ant.** dissociate, separate. —**Syn. Study.** See MIX.

comfort, *v.* **1.** soothe, console, relieve, ease, cheer, pacify, calm, solace, gladden, refresh. —*n.* **2.** relief, consolation, solace, encouragement. —**Ant.** agitate, discommode, incommode; discomfort, discouragement. —**Syn. Study.** COMFORT, CONSOLE, SOOTHE imply assuaging sorrow, worry, discomfort, or pain. COMFORT means to lessen someone's grief or distress by giving strength and hope and restoring a cheerful outlook: *to comfort a despairing friend.* CONSOLE, a more formal word, means to make grief or distress seem lighter by means of kindness and thoughtful attentions: *to console a bereaved parent.* SOOTHE means to pacify or calm: *to soothe a crying child.*

comical, *adj.* amusing, humorous, funny, comic, laugh-provoking, silly, droll, risible, playful, clownish, ludic; laughable, ridiculous, ludicrous, absurd, foolish. —**Syn. Study.** See AMUSING.

command, *v.* **1.** order, direct, bid, demand, charge, instruct, enjoin, require. **2.** govern, control, oversee, manage, rule, lead, preside over; dominate, overlook. **3.** exact, compel, secure, demand, require, claim. —*n.* **4.** order, direction, bidding, injunction, charge, mandate, behest, commandment, requisition, requirement, instruction, dictum. **5.** control, mastery, disposal, ascendancy, rule, sway, superintendence, power, management, domination. —**Ant.** obey. —**Syn. Study.** See DIRECT.

commence, *v.* begin, open, start, originate, inaugurate, enter upon *or* into. —**Ant.** end, finish, terminate. —**Syn. Study.** See BEGIN.

commend, *v.* **1.**

recommend, laud, praise, extol, applaud, eulogize. **2.** entrust. **—Ant.** censure, blame; distrust.

commendation, *n.* **1.** recommendation, praise, approval, approbation, applause; medal. **2.** eulogy, encomium, panegyric, praise. **—Ant.** censure, blame.

comment, *n.* **1.** explanation, elucidation, expansion, criticism, critique, note, addendum, annotation, exposition, commentary. **2.** remark, observation, criticism. **—v. 3.** remark, explain, annotate, criticize.

commerce, *n.* **1.** interchange, traffic, trade, dealing, exchange, business. **2.** intercourse, conversation, converse, intimacy.

commercial, *adj.* **1.** mercantile, trafficking. **—n. 2.** advertisement.

common, *adj.* **1.** mutual. **2.** joint, united. **3.** public, communal. **4.** notorious. **5.** widespread, general, ordinary, universal, prevalent, popular. **6.** familiar, usual, customary, frequent, habitual, everyday. **7.** hackneyed, trite, stale, commonplace. **8.** mean, low, mediocre, inferior. **9.** coarse, vulgar, ordinary, undistinguished, ill-bred. **—Ant.** exceptional, singular, extraordinary, separate; unfamiliar, strange. **—Syn. Study.** COMMON, ORDINARY, VULGAR refer, often with derogatory connotations, to what is usual or most often experienced. COMMON applies to what is widespread or unexceptional; it often suggests inferiority or coarseness: *common servants; common cloth.* ORDINARY refers to what is to be expected in the usual order of things; it suggests being average or below average: *a high price for something of such ordinary quality.* VULGAR means belonging to the people or characteristic of common people; it suggests low taste, coarseness, or ill breeding: *vulgar manners;*

vulgar speech. See also GENERAL.

commonplace, *adj.* **1.** ordinary, uninteresting. **2.** trite, hackneyed, common, banal, stereotyped. —*n.* **3.** cliché, bromide. —**Ant.** extraordinary, original. —**Syn. Study.** COMMONPLACE, BANAL, TRITE, HACKNEYED describe words, remarks, and styles of expression that are lifeless and uninteresting. COMMONPLACE characterizes expression that is so ordinary, self-evident, or generally accepted as to be boring or pointless: *a commonplace affirmation of the obvious.* BANAL often suggests an inane or insipid quality: *banal conversation.* TRITE suggests that an expression has lost its force because of excessive repetition: *trite poetic imagery.* HACKNEYED is a stronger word implying that the expression has become meaningless from overuse: *hackneyed metaphors.*

commotion, *n.* **1.** tumult, disturbance, perturbation, agitation, disorder, pother, bustle, ado, turmoil, turbulence, riot, violence. **2.** sedition, insurrection, uprising, revolution. —**Ant.** peace, calm, serenity.

communicate, *v.* **1.** impart, transmit; give, bestow. **2.** divulge, announce, declare, disclose, reveal, make known. —**Ant.** withhold, conceal.

community, *n.* **1.** hamlet, town, village, city. **2.** public, commonwealth, society. **3.** agreement, identity, similarity, likeness. —*adj.* **4.** common, joint, cooperative.

compact, *adj.* **1.** dense, solid, firm, tightly packed, condensed. **2.** concise, pithy, terse, laconic, short, sententious, succinct, brief, pointed, meaningful. —*v.* **3.** condense, consolidate, compress. **4.** stabilize, solidify. —*n.* **5.** covenant, pact, contract, treaty, agreement, bargain, entente, arrangement, convention, concordat. —**Ant.** diverse, dispersed.

—**Syn. Study.** See
AGREEMENT.

companion, *n.* **1.** associate,
comrade, partner, fellow,
mate. **2.** assistant; nurse,
governess. —**Syn. Study.**
See ACQUAINTANCE.

company, *n.* **1.** group,
band, party, troop,
assemblage, body, unit. **2.**
companionship, fellowship,
association, society. **3.**
assembly, gathering,
concourse, crowd, circle,
set, congregation. **4.** firm,
partnership, corporation,
concern, house, syndicate,
association.

compare, *v.* **1.** liken,
contrast. **2.** vie, compete,
equal, resemble.

compartment, *n.* division,
section, apartment, cabin,
roomette.

compass, See Syn. study at
RANGE.

compassion, *n.* sorrow,
pity, sympathy, feeling,
ruth, mercy,
commiseration, kindness,
kindliness, tenderness,
heart, tender-heartedness,
clemency. —**Ant.**
mercilessness, indifference.

—**Syn. Study.** See
SYMPATHY.

compassionate, *adj.*
pitying, sympathetic,
tender, kind, merciful,
tender-hearted, kindly,
clement, gracious,
benignant, gentle. —**Ant.**
merciless, pitiless, harsh,
cruel, mean.

compel, *v.* **1.** force, drive,
coerce, constrain, oblige,
commit, impel, motivate,
necessitate. **2.** subdue,
subject, bend, bow,
overpower. **3.** unite, drive
together, herd. —**Ant.**
coax. —**Syn. Study.**
COMPEL, IMPEL agree in the
idea of forcing someone to
be or do something.
COMPEL implies an external
force; it may be a
persuasive urging from
another person or a
constraining reason or
circumstance: *Bad health
compelled him to resign.*
IMPEL suggests an internal
motivation deriving either
from a moral constraint or
personal feeling: *Guilt
impelled him to offer
money.*

compensate, *v.* **1.**

counterbalance, counterpoise, offset, countervail, make up for. **2.** remunerate, reward, pay, recompense, reimburse. **3.** atone, make amends.

compensation, *n.* **1.** recompense, remuneration, payment, amends, reparation, indemnity, reward. **2.** atonement, requital, satisfaction, indemnification.

compete, *v.* contend, vie, contest, rival, emulate, oppose, dispute, strive, cope, struggle. —**Ant.** support. —**Syn. Study.** COMPETE, CONTEND, CONTEST mean to strive or struggle. COMPETE emphasizes a sense of rivalry and of striving to do one's best: *to compete for a prize.* CONTEND suggests striving in opposition or debate as well as competition: *to contend against obstacles; to contend about minor details.* CONTEST implies struggling to gain or hold something in a formal competition or battle: *to*

contest with the incumbent for the nomination.

competent, *adj.* **1.** fitting, suitable, sufficient, convenient, adequate, qualified, fit, apt, capable, proficient. **2.** permissible, allowable, —**Ant.** incompetent, inapt.

competitor, *n.* opponent, contestant, rival, antagonist. —**Ant.** ally, friend.

complain, *v.* grumble, growl, murmur, whine, moan, bewail, lament, bemoan. —**Syn. Study.** COMPLAIN, GRUMBLE, WHINE are terms for expressing dissatisfaction or discomfort. To COMPLAIN is to protest against or lament a condition or wrong: *to complain about high prices.* To GRUMBLE is to utter surly, ill-natured complaints half to oneself: *to grumble about the service.* To WHINE is to complain in a meanspirited, objectionable way, using a nasal tone; it often suggests persistence: *to whine like a spoiled child.*

complement, *v.* **1.** complete, supplement, add to, round out. —*n.* **2.** supplement. —**Syn. Study.** COMPLEMENT, SUPPLEMENT both mean to make additions to something; a lack or deficiency is implied. To COMPLEMENT means to complete or perfect a whole; it often refers to putting together two things, each of which supplies what is lacking in the other: *Statements from different points of view may complement each other.* To SUPPLEMENT is to add something in order to enhance, extend, or improve a whole: *Some additional remarks supplemented the sales presentation.*

complete, *adj.* **1.** whole, entire, full, intact, unbroken, unimpaired, undivided, one, perfect, developed, unabated, undiminished, fulfilled. **2.** finished, ended, concluded, consummated, done, consummate, perfect, thorough; through-and-through, dyed-in-the-wool. —*v.* **3.** finish, end, conclude, consummate, perfect, accomplish, do, fulfill, achieve, effect, terminate, close. —**Ant.** incomplete; unfinished; begin, commence, initiate. —**Syn. Study.** COMPLETE, ENTIRE, INTACT suggest that there is no lack or defect, nor has any part been removed. COMPLETE implies that a unit has all its parts, fully developed or perfected; it may also mean that a process or purpose has been carried to fulfillment: *a complete explanation; a complete assignment.* ENTIRE describes something having all its elements in an unbroken unity: *an entire book.* INTACT implies that something has remained in its original condition, complete and unimpaired: *a package delivered intact.*

complex, *adj.* **1.** compound, composite, complicated, mixed, mingled. **2.** involved, complicated, intricate, perplexing, tangled. —*n.* **3.** complexus, net, network, complication, web, tangle. —**Ant.** simple; simplex.

compliment, *n.* **1.** praise, commendation, admiration, tribute, honor, eulogy, encomium, panegyric. **2.** regard, respect, civility; flattery. —*v.* **3.** commend, praise, honor, flatter. **4.** congratulate, felicitate. —**Ant.** insult, injury; decry, disparage.

comply, *v.* acquiesce, obey, yield, conform, consent, assent, agree, accede, concede. —**Ant.** refuse.

component, *adj.* **1.** composing, constituent. —*n.* **2.** element, ingredient, part. —**Ant.** complex.

composed, *adj.* calm, tranquil, serene, undisturbed, peaceful, cool, placid, pacific, unruffled, sedate, unperturbed, self-possessed, controlled, imperturbable, quiet. —**Ant.** upset, perturbed, disturbed, disquieted. —**Syn. Study.** See CALM.

composite, *adj., n.*

compound, complex. —**Ant.** divers.

composure, *n.* serenity, calm, calmness, tranquillity, equability, peacefulness, quiet, coolness, equanimity, self-possession. —**Ant.** agitation.

comprehend, *v.* **1.** understand, conceive, know, grasp, see, discern, imagine, perceive. **2.** include, comprise, embrace, take in, embody, contain. —**Syn. Study.** See KNOW, INCLUDE.

comprehensive, *adj.* comprehending, inclusive, broad, wide, large, extensive, sweeping. —**Ant.** limited.

compress, *v.* **1.** condense, squeeze, constrict, contract, press, crowd. —*n.* **2.** pad, bandage. —**Ant.** spread, stretch.

comprise, *v.* include, comprehend, contain, embrace, embody; consist *or* be composed of. —**Ant.** exclude. —**Syn. Study.** See INCLUDE.

compulsory, *adj.* **1.**

compelling, coercive, constraining. **2.** compelled, forced, obligatory, arbitrary, binding, necessary, unavoidable, inescapable, ineluctable. —**Ant.** free, unrestrained, unrestricted.

compute, *v.* reckon, calculate, estimate, count, figure.

comrade, *n.* associate, companion, intimate, friend, fellow, partner, mate, yokefellow, colleague, confrere, cohort, compeer, crony, ally, sidekick, chum, buddy, pal.

conceal, *v.* **1.** hide, secrete, cover, put away, bury, screen. **2.** keep secret, hide, disguise, dissemble. —**Ant.** reveal. —**Syn. Study.** See HIDE

conceit, *n.* **1.** self-esteem, vanity, *amour-propre,* egotism, complacency. **2.** fancy, imagination, whim, notion, vagary; thought, idea, belief, conception. —**Ant.** humility, modesty. —**Syn. Study.** See PRIDE.

conceited, *adj.* vain, proud,

egotistical, self-important, self-satisfied, smug, complacent, self-sufficient. —**Ant.** humble, modest, shy, retiring.

conceive, *v.* **1.** imagine, create, ideate, think. **2.** understand, apprehend, comprehend.

concentrate, *v.* **1.** focus, condense. **2.** intensify, purify, clarify. —**Ant.** dissipate, disperse.

conception, See Syn. study at IDEA.

concern, *v.* **1.** affect, touch, interest, relate to, engage, involve, include. **2.** disquiet, trouble, disturb. —*n.* **3.** business, affair, interest, matter. **4.** solicitude, anxiety, care, worry, burden, responsibility. **5.** relation, bearing, appropriateness, consequence. **6.** firm, company, business, establishment, corporation, partnership, house. —**Ant.** exclude; calm; unconcern, indifference. —**Syn. Study.** CONCERN, CARE, WORRY connote an uneasy and burdened state of mind.

CONCERN implies an anxious sense of interest in or responsibility for something: *concern over a friend's misfortune.* CARE suggests a heaviness of spirit caused by dread, or by the constant pressure of burdensome demands: *Poverty weighed them down with care.* WORRY is a state of agitated uneasiness and restless apprehension: *distracted by worry over investments.*

conciliate, *v.* **1.** placate, win over, soothe, propitiate, appease. **2.** reconcile, pacify. —**Ant.** alienate, antagonize, —**Syn. Study.** See APPEASE.

concise, *adj.* succinct, terse, compact, to the point, crisp, curt, laconic, short. —**Syn. Study.** CONCISE, SUCCINCT, TERSE refer to speech or writing that uses few words to say much. CONCISE implies that unnecessary details or verbiage have been eliminated: *a concise summary of a speech.* SUCCINCT suggests clarity of expression as well as brevity: *praised for her succinct statement of the problem.* TERSE suggests brevity combined with wit or polish to produce particularly effective expression; however, it may also suggest brusqueness: *a terse prose style; offended by a terse reply.*

conciseness, *n.* brevity, laconicism, summary, terseness, pithiness, sententiousness. —**Ant.** diversity. —**Syn. Study.** See BREVITY.

conclusion, *n.* **1.** end, close, termination, completion, ending, finale. **2.** summing up, summation. **3.** result, issue, outcome. **4.** settlement, arrangement, wind-up. **5.** decision, judgment, determination. **6.** deduction, inference. —**Ant.** beginning, commencement.

concur, *v.* **1.** agree, consent, coincide, harmonize. **2.** cooperate, combine, help, conspire, contribute. —**Ant.** disagree.

condemn, *v.* **1.** blame, censure, disapprove. **2.** doom, find guilty, sentence, damn. **—Ant.** liberate, release, exonerate.

condense, *v.* compress, concentrate, consolidate, contract; abridge, epitomize, digest, shorten, abbreviate, reduce, diminish, curtail. **—Ant.** expand.

condescend, *v.* deign, stoop, descend, degrade oneself.

condition, *n.* **1.** state, case, situation, circumstance, conjuncture, circumstances. **2.** requisite, prerequisite, requirement, contingency, consideration, proviso, provision, stipulation, *sine qua non.* **—v. 3.** determine, limit, restrict.

conduct, *n.* **1.** behavior, demeanor, action, actions, deportment, bearing, carriage, mien, manners. **2.** direction, management, execution, guidance, leadership, administration. **3.** guidance, escort, leadership, convoy, guard. **—***v.* **4.** behave, deport, act, bear. **5.** direct, manage, carry on, supervise, regulate, administrate, administer, execute, guide, lead. **6.** lead, guide, escort, convoy.

confederation, *n.* alliance, confederacy, league, federation, union, coalition. **—Syn. Study.** See ALLIANCE.

confer, *v.* **1.** bestow, give, donate, grant, vouchsafe, allow, promise. **2.** compare. **3.** consult together, discuss, deliberate, discourse, parley, converse, advise, talk. **—Syn. Study.** See CONSULT. See also GIVE.

conference, *n.* meeting, interview, parley, colloquy, convention, consultation. **—Syn. Study.** See CONVENTION.

confess, *v.* acknowledge, avow, own, admit, grant, concede; declare, aver, confirm. **—Syn. Study.** See ACKNOWLEDGE.

confidence, *n.* **1.** trust, belief, faith, reliance, dependence. **2.**

self-reliance, assurance, boldness, intrepidity, self-confidence, courage. —**Ant.** distrust, mistrust; modesty. —**Syn. Study.** CONFIDENCE, ASSURANCE both imply a faith in oneself. CONFIDENCE usually implies a firm belief in oneself without a display of arrogance or conceit: *His friends admired his confidence at the party.* ASSURANCE implies even more sureness of one's own abilities, often to the point of offensive boastfulness: *She spoke with assurance but lacked the qualifications for the job.*

confident, *adj.* sure, bold, believing, assured, self-assured, certain, positive, convinced; brave, intrepid. —**Ant.** shy, modest, diffident.

confidential, *adj.* **1.** secret, restricted, private. **2.** familiar, trusted, trusty, trustworthy, faithful, honorable, honest. —**Syn. Study.** See FAMILIAR.

confine, *v.* **1.** enclose, bound, circumscribe, circle, encircle, limit, bind, restrict. **2.** immure, imprison, incarcerate. —*n.* **3.** (*usually plural*) bounds, boundary, perimeter, periphery, limits; frontiers, borders.

confirm, *v.* **1.** make certain *or* sure, assure, corroborate, verify, substantiate, authenticate. **2.** make valid *or* binding, ratify, sanction, approve, validate, bind. **3.** make firm, strengthen, settle, establish, fix, assure.

conflict, *v.* **1.** collide, clash, oppose, vary with, interfere. **2.** contend, fight, combat, battle. —*n.* **3.** battle, struggle, encounter, contest, collision, fight; siege, strife; contention, controversy, opposition, variance. **4.** interference, discord, disunity, disharmony, inconsistency, antagonism. —**Ant.** harmony.

conform, *v.* **1.** comply, yield, agree, assent, harmonize. **2.** tally, agree, correspond, square. **3.** adapt, adjust, accommodate. —**Ant.** disagree, dissent.

confuse, *v.* **1.** jumble, disorder, disarrange, disturb, disarray. **2.** confound, mix, mix up, intermingle, mingle. **3.** perplex, mystify, nonplus, bewilder, astonish, surprise, disarm, shock, disconcert, embarrass, disturb. **4.** disconcert, abash, mortify, shame, confound. —**Ant.** enlighten.

confusion, *n.* **1.** perplexity, embarrassment, surprise, astonishment, shock, bewilderment, distraction. **2.** disorder, disarray, disarrangement, jumble, mess, turmoil, chaos, tumult, furor, commotion, ferment, agitation, stir. **3.** embarrassment, abashment, shamefacedness, shame, mortification. —**Ant.** enlightenment; clarity.

congenial, *adj.* sympathetic, kindred, similar, friendly, favorable, genial; agreeable, pleasing, pleasant, complaisant, suited, adapted, well-suited, suitable, apt, proper. —**Ant.** unsympathetic, disagreeable; unsuitable.

congenital, See Syn. study at INNATE.

congress, *n.* meeting, assembly, conference, council, convention.

conjecture, *n.* **1.** hypothesis, theory, guess, surmise, opinion, supposition, inference, deduction. —*v.* **2.** conclude, suppose, assume, presume, suspect, surmise, hypothesize, theorize, guess. —**Ant.** determine, ascertain. —**Syn. Study.** See GUESS.

conjoin, *v.* associate, unite, join, combine, connect. —**Ant.** disjoin, dissociate.

connect, *v.* join, unite, link, conjoin, couple, associate, combine; cohere. —**Ant.** disconnect, disjoin. —**Syn. Study.** See JOIN.

connection, *n.* **1.** junction, conjunction, union, joining, association, alliance, dependence, interdependence. **2.** link, yoke, connective, bond, tie, coupling. **3.** association, relationship, affiliation, affinity. **4.** circle, set, coterie, acquaintanceship. **5.** relation, relative, kinsman; kin, kith. **—Ant.** disjunction, dissociation.

conquer, *v.* **1.** win, gain. **2.** overcome, subdue, vanquish, overpower, overthrow, subjugate, defeat, master, subject, beat, rout, crush, reduce. **3.** surmount, overcome, overwhelm. **—Ant.** surrender, submit, give up, yield. **—Syn. Study.** See DEFEAT.

conquest, *n.* **1.** captivation, seduction, enchantment. **2.** vanquishment, victory, triumph. **3.** subjugation, overthrow, defeat, mastery, subjection, rout. **—Ant.** surrender. **—Syn. Study.** See VICTORY.

conscientious, *adj.* just, upright, honest, straightforward, incorruptible, faithful, careful, particular, painstaking, scrupulous, exacting, demanding; devoted, dedicated. **—Ant.** dishonest, corrupt, unscrupulous. **—Syn. Study.** See PAINSTAKING.

conscious, *adj.* **1.** awake, aware, sentient, knowing, cognizant, percipient, intelligent. **2.** sensible, sensitive, felt; rational, reasoning. **3.** deliberate, intentional, purposeful. **—Ant.** unconscious. **—Syn. Study.** CONSCIOUS, AWARE, COGNIZANT refer to a realization or recognition of something about oneself or one's surroundings. CONSCIOUS usually implies sensing or feeling certain facts, truths, conditions, etc.: *to be conscious of an extreme weariness; to be conscious of one's own inadequacy.* AWARE implies being mentally awake to something on a sensory level or through observation: *aware of the odor of tobacco; aware of gossip.* COGNIZANT, a more formal term, usually implies having knowledge about some object or fact through reasoning or through outside sources of information: *to be* *cognizant of the drawbacks of a plan.*

consecrate, *v.* **1.** sanctify, hallow, venerate, elevate. **2.** devote, dedicate. —**Ant.** desecrate. —**Syn. Study.** See DEVOTE.

consecutive, *adj.* successive, continuous, regular, uninterrupted. —**Ant.** alternate, random.

consent, *v.* **1.** agree, assent, permit, allow, let, concur, yield, comply, accede, acquiesce. —*n.* **2.** assent, acquiescence, permission, compliance, concurrence, agreement. **3.** accord, concord, agreement, consensus. —**Ant.** refuse, disagree; dissent.

consequence, *n.* **1.** effect, result, outcome, issue, upshot, sequel, event, end. **2.** importance, significance, moment, weight, concern, interest. **3.** distinction, importance, singularity, weight. —**Syn. Study.** See EFFECT. See also IMPORTANCE.

consider, *v.* **1.** contemplate, meditate, reflect, ruminate, ponder, deliberate, weigh, revolve, study, think about. **2.** think, suppose, assume, presume. **3.** regard, respect, honor. —**Ant.** ignore. —**Syn. Study.** See STUDY.

considerate, *adj.* thoughtful, kind, charitable, patient, concerned, well-disposed. —**Ant.** inconsiderate.

consideration, *n.* **1.** considering, meditation, reflection, rumination, deliberation, contemplation, attention, advisement, regard. **2.** regard, account. **3.** recompense, payment, remuneration, fee, compensation, pay. **4.** thoughtfulness, sympathy, kindness, kindliness, patience, concern. **5.** importance, consequence, weight, significance, moment, interest. **6.** estimation, esteem, honor.

consistent, *adj.* **1.** agreeing, concordant, compatible, congruous, consonant, harmonious, suitable, apt, conformable, conforming. **2.** constant, faithful,

assiduous, unwavering.
—Ant. inconsistent.

consolation, *n.* comfort,
solace, relief,
encouragement. **—Ant.**
discomfort,
discouragement.

console, *v.* comfort, solace,
cheer, encourage, soothe,
relieve, calm. **—Ant.**
aggravate, agitate, disturb.
—Syn. Study. See COMFORT.

consonant, *n.* **1.** sonorant,
fricative, stop, continuant.
—adj. **2.** in agreement,
concordant, consistent,
harmonious, compatible,
congruous, conformant,
suitable. **—Ant.** vowel;
discordant, inconsistent.

conspicuous, *adj.* **1.** visible,
manifest, noticeable, clear,
marked, salient,
discernible, perceptible,
plain, open, apparent. **2.**
prominent, outstanding,
obvious, striking,
noteworthy, attractive,
eminent, distinguished,
noted, celebrated,
illustrious. **—Ant.** unclear,
imperceptible;
undistinguished, trifling.

conspiracy, *n.* plot, secret
plan, intrigue, cabal,
scheme, machination,
treason, betrayal. **—Syn.
Study.** CONSPIRACY, PLOT,
INTRIGUE, CABAL refer to
surreptitious or covert
schemes to accomplish
some end, most often an
illegal or evil one. A
CONSPIRACY usually
describes a treacherous or
illicit plan formulated in
secret by a group of
persons: *a conspiracy to
control prices.* A PLOT is a
carefully planned secret
scheme formulated by one
or more persons: *a plot to
seize control of a company.*
An INTRIGUE usually
involves duplicity and
deceit aimed at achieving
personal advantage: *the
petty intrigues of civil
servants.* CABAL usually
refers to a scheme
formulated by a small
group of highly placed
persons to gain control of
a government: *The regime
was overthrown by a cabal
of generals.*

conspire, *v.* **1.** complot,
plot, intrigue, cabal,
contrive, devise. **2.**

combine, concur, cooperate.

constancy, *n.* firmness, fortitude, resolution, determination, inflexibility, decision, tenacity, steadfastness, faithfulness, fidelity, fealty, devotion, loyalty; regularity, stability, immutability, uniformity, permanence, sameness. —**Ant.** randomness, faithlessness, irregularity, instability.

constant, *adj.* **1.** invariable, uniform, stable, unchanging, fixed, immutable, invariable, unvarying, permanent. **2.** perpetual, unremitting, uninterrupted, continual, recurrent, assiduous, unwavering, unfailing, persistent, persevering, determined. **3.** steadfast, faithful, loyal, stanch, true, trusty, devoted, steady, resolute, firm, unshaking, unshakable, unwavering, unswerving, determined. —**Ant.** inconstant, variable, random, unstable, changeable; sporadic; unsteady,

wavering. —**Syn. Study.** See FAITHFUL.

consternation, *n.* amazement, dread, dismay, bewilderment, awe, alarm, terror, fear, panic, fright, horror. —**Ant.** composure, equanimity.

constrain, *v.* **1.** force, compel, oblige, coerce. **2.** confine, check, bind, restrain, curb. —**Ant.** liberate, free.

constrict, *v.* compress, contract, shrink, cramp, squeeze, bind, tighten. —**Ant.** unbind, untie.

construct, *v.* build, frame, form, devise, erect, make, fabricate, raise. —**Ant.** raze.

consult, *v.* confer, deliberate. —**Syn. Study.** CONSULT, CONFER imply talking over a situation or a subject with someone. To CONSULT is to seek advice, opinions, or guidance from a presumably qualified person or source: *to consult with a financial analyst.* To CONFER is to exchange views, ideas, or information in a discussion: *The partners conferred about the decline in sales.*

consume, *v.* **1.** destroy, expend, use up, use, exhaust, spend, waste, dissipate, squander, eat up, devour. **2.** be absorbed *or* engrossed.

consummate, *v.* **1.** complete, perfect, fulfill, accomplish, achieve, finish, effect, execute, do. —*adj.* **2.** complete, perfect, done, finished, effected, fulfilled, excellent, supreme. —**Ant.** imperfect, unfinished, base.

contagious, *adj.* **1.** communicable, infectious, catching. **2.** noxious, pestilential, poisonous, deadly, foul. —**Syn. Study.** CONTAGIOUS, INFECTIOUS are usu. distinguished in technical medical use. CONTAGIOUS, literally "communicable by contact," describes a very easily transmitted disease, as influenza or the common cold. INFECTIOUS refers to a disease involving a microorganism that can be transmitted from one person to another only by a specific kind of contact; venereal diseases are usu. infectious. In nontechnical senses, CONTAGIOUS emphasizes the rapidity with which something spreads: *Contagious laughter ran through the hall.* INFECTIOUS suggests the pleasantly irresistible quality of something: *Her infectious good humor made her a popular guest.*

contain, *v.* hold, accommodate, include, embody, embrace. —**Syn. Study.** CONTAIN, HOLD, ACCOMMODATE express the idea that something is so designed that something else can exist or be placed within it. CONTAIN refers to what is actually within a given container. HOLD emphasizes the idea of keeping within bounds; it refers also to the greatest amount or number that can be kept within a given container. ACCOMMODATE means to contain comfortably or conveniently, or to meet the needs of a certain number. A plane that ACCOMMODATES fifty passengers may be able to HOLD sixty, but at a given time may CONTAIN only thirty.

contaminate, *v.* defile, pollute, sully, stain, soil, tarnish, taint, corrupt, befoul, besmirch, infect, poison, vitiate.

contemplate, *v.* **1.** look at, view, observe, regard, survey. **2.** consider, reflect upon, meditate on, study, ponder, deliberate, think about, revolve. **3.** intend, mean, purpose, design, plan.

contemplative, *adj.* reflective, meditative, thoughtful, studious, musing. —**Ant.** inattentive.

contemporaneous, See Syn. study at CONTEMPORARY.

contemporary, *adj.* coexisting, coeval, contemporaneous, coincident. —**Ant.** antecedent; succeeding. —**Syn. Study.** CONTEMPORARY,

CONTEMPORANEOUS, COEVAL, COINCIDENT mean happening or existing at the same time. CONTEMPORARY often refers to persons or their acts or achievements: *Hemingway and Fitzgerald, though contemporary, shared few values.* CONTEMPORANEOUS is applied chiefly to events: *the rise of industrialism, contemporaneous with the spread of steam power.* COEVAL refers either to very long periods of time, or to remote or distant times: *coeval stars, shining for millennia; coeval with the dawning of civilization.* COINCIDENT means occurring at the same time but without causal relationship: *World War II was coincident with the presidency of Franklin D. Roosevelt.*

contempt, *n.* **1.** scorn, disdain, derision, contumely. **2.** dishonor, disgrace, shame. —**Ant.** respect, reverence; honor. —**Syn. Study.** CONTEMPT, DISDAIN, SCORN imply strong feelings of disapproval and aversion toward what seems base, mean, or worthless. CONTEMPT is disapproval tinged with disgust: *to feel contempt for a weakling.* DISDAIN is a feeling that a person or thing is beneath one's dignity and unworthy of one's notice, respect, or concern: *a disdain for crooked dealing.* SCORN denotes open or undisguised contempt often combined with derision: *He showed only scorn for those who were not as ambitious as himself.*

contemptible, *adj.* despicable, mean, low, miserable, base, vile. —**Ant.** splendid, admirable.

contemptuous, *adj.* disdainful, scornful, sneering, insolent, arrogant, supercilious, haughty. —**Ant.** humble, respectful.

contend, *v.* **1.** struggle, strive, fight, battle, combat, vie, compete, rival. **2.** debate, dispute, argue, wrangle. **3.** assert, maintain, claim. —**Syn. Study.** See COMPETE.

content, *adj.* **1.** satisfied, contented, sanguine. **2.** assenting, acceding, resigned, willing, agreeable. —*v.* **3.** appease, gratify, satisfy. —**Ant.** dissatisfy.

contention, *n.* **1.** struggling, struggle, strife, discord, dissension, quarrel, disagreement, squabble, feud; rupture, break, falling out; opposition, combat, conflict, competition, rivalry, contest. **2.** disagreement, dissension, debate, wrangle, altercation, dispute, argument, controversy. —**Ant.** agreement.

contentment, *n.* happiness, satisfaction, content, ease. —**Ant.** misery.

contest, *n.* **1.** struggle, conflict, battle, combat, fight, encounter. **2.** competition, contention, rivalry, match, tournament, tourney, game. **3.** strife, dispute, controversy, debate, argument, altercation, quarrel, contention. —*v.* **4.** struggle, fight, compete, contend, vie, combat, battle. **5.** argue against, dispute, controvert, litigate, debate, oppose, contend against. **6.** doubt, question, challenge, dispute. **7.** rival, strive, compete, vie, contend for. —**Syn. Study.** See COMPETE.

continual, *adj.* unceasing, incessant, ceaseless, uninterrupted, unremitting, constant, continuous, unbroken, successive, perpetual, unending, habitual, permanent, everlasting, eternal; recurrent, recurring, frequentative, repeated, repetitious, repetitive. —**Ant.** periodic, sporadic.

continue, *v.* **1.** keep on, go onward *or* forward, persist, persevere. **2.** last, endure, remain, persist. **3.** remain, abide, tarry, stay, rest. **4.** persist in, extend, perpetuate, prolong, carry on, maintain, retain; carry over, postpone, adjourn. —**Ant.** cease, interrupt. —**Syn. Study.** CONTINUE,

ENDURE, PERSIST, LAST imply existing uninterruptedly for an appreciable length of time. CONTINUE implies duration or existence without break or interruption: *The rain continued for two days.* ENDURE, used of people or things, implies persistent continuance despite influences that tend to weaken, undermine, or destroy: *The temple has endured for centuries.* PERSIST implies steadfast and longer than expected existence in the face of opposition: *to persist in an unpopular belief.* LAST implies remaining in good condition or adequate supply: *I hope the cake lasts until the end of the party.*

contract, *n.* **1.** agreement, compact, bargain, covenant, arrangement, pact, convention, concordat, treaty, stipulation. —*v.* **2.** draw together, compress, concentrate, condense, reduce, lessen, shorten, narrow, shrivel, shrink. **3.**

elide, abbreviate, apocopate, abridge, epitomize. **—Ant.** disperse, spread. **—Syn. Study.** See AGREEMENT.

contradict, *v.* deny, gainsay, dispute, controvert, impugn, challenge, assail. **—Ant.** corroborate, support.

contradictory, *adj.* contrary, opposed, opposite, opposing, antagonistic, irreconcilable, paradoxical, inconsistent, contrary. **—Ant.** corroborative.

contrary, *adj.* **1.** opposite, opposed, contradictory, conflicting, discordant, counter, opposing. **2.** untoward, unfavorable, adverse, unfriendly, hostile, oppugnant, antagonistic, disagreeable, irreconcilable. **3.** perverse, self-willed, intractable, obstinate, refractory, headstrong, stubborn, pig-headed, contumacious. **—Ant.** obliging, compliant, tractable.

contrast, *v.* **1.** oppose, compare, differentiate, discriminate, distinguish, set off. **—n. 2.** opposition, comparison, differentiation, difference, discrimination, contrariety.

contrive, *v.* plan, devise, invent, design, hatch, brew, concoct, form, make; plot, complot, conspire, scheme; manage, effect.

control, *v.* **1.** dominate, command, manage, govern, rule, direct, reign over. **2.** check, curb, hinder, restrain, bridle, constrain. **3.** test, verify, prove. **—n. 4.** regulation, domination, command, management, direction, government, rule, reign, sovereignty, mastery, superintendence. **—Syn. Study.** See AUTHORITY.

controversy, *n.* dispute, contention, debate, disputation, disagreement, altercation; quarrel, wrangle, argument. **—Ant.** concord, agreement, accord. **—Syn. Study.** See ARGUMENT.

convene, *v.* **1.** assemble, meet, congregate, collect, gather. **2.** convoke, summon. —**Ant.** disperse, adjourn.

convenient, *adj.* **1.** suited, fit, appropriate, suitable, adapted, serviceable, well-suited, favorable, easy, comfortable, agreeable, helpful, advantageous, useful. **2.** at hand, accessible, handy. —**Ant.** inconvenient.

convention, *n.* **1.** assembly, conference, convocation, meeting. **2.** agreement, contract, compact, pact, treaty. **3.** agreement, consent. **4.** custom, precedent. —**Syn. Study.** CONVENTION, ASSEMBLY, CONFERENCE, CONVOCATION refer to meetings for particular purposes. CONVENTION usually suggests a formal meeting of members or delegates of a political, social, or professional group: *an annual medical convention.* ASSEMBLY usually implies a regular meeting for a customary purpose: *an assembly of legislators; a school assembly in the auditorium.* CONFERENCE

suggests a meeting for consultation or discussion: *a sales conference.* CONVOCATION usually refers to an ecclesiastical or academic meeting whose participants were summoned: *a convocation of economic experts.*

conventional, *adj.* **1.** formal, conforming, conformant. **2.** accepted, usual, habitual, customary, regular, common. —**Ant.** unconventional, unusual.

conversant, *adj.* **1.** familiar, versed, learned, skilled, practiced, well-informed, proficient. **2.** acquainted, associating. —**Ant.** unfamiliar, ignorant.

conversational, See Syn. study at COLLOQUIAL.

converse, *v.* **1.** talk, chat, speak, discuss, confabulate. —*n.* **2.** discourse, talk, conversation, discussion, colloquy. **3.** opposite, reverse, transformation.

convert, *v.* **1.** change, transmute, transform, proselyte, proselytize. —*n.* **2.** proselyte, neophyte, disciple. —**Ant.** renegade, recreant. —**Syn. Study.** See TRANSFORM.

convey, *v.* **1.** carry, transport, bear, bring, transmit, lead, conduct. **2.** communicate, impart.

conviction, See Syn. study at BELIEF.

convince, *v.* persuade, satisfy.

convocation, See Syn. study at CONVENTION.

convoy, *v.* **1.** accompany, escort, attend. —*n.* **2.** escort, guard, attendance, protection. —**Ant.** desert. —**Syn. Study.** See ACCOMPANY.

convulsion, *n.* seizure, frenzy, paroxysm, fit, spasm, attack, outburst, outbreak, irruption, upheaval, eruption, storm, tumult, furor.

cool, *adj.* **1.** cold. **2.** calm, unexcited, unmoved, deliberate, composed, collected, self-possessed, unruffled, sedate, undisturbed, placid, quiet, dispassionate, unimpassioned. **3.** frigid, distant, superior, chilling, freezing, apathetic, repellent. **4.** indifferent, lukewarm, unconcerned, cold-blooded. **5.** audacious, impudent, shameless. —*v.* **6.** allay, calm, moderate, quiet, temper, assuage, abate, dampen. —**Ant.** warm, tepid, lukewarm, hot. —**Syn. Study.** See CALM.

copious, *adj.* abundant, large, ample, plentiful, overflowing, profuse, rich, full, plenteous. —**Ant.** scarce, scanty, meager.

copy, *n.* **1.** transcript, reproduction, imitation, carbon, duplicate, facsimile. **2.** original, manuscript, pattern, model, archetype. —*v.* **3.** imitate, duplicate, transcribe. —**Ant.** original.

corporal, *adj.* corporeal, bodily, physical, material. —**Ant.** spiritual. —**Syn. Study.** See PHYSICAL.

corporeal, See Syn. study at PHYSICAL.

corpse, *n.* body, remains, carcass. —**Syn. Study.** See BODY.

correct, *v.* **1.** set right, rectify, amend, emend, reform, remedy, cure. **2.** admonish, warn, rebuke, discipline, chasten, punish, castigate. —*adj.* **3.** factual, truthful, accurate, proper, precise, exact, faultless, perfect, right, true. —**Ant.** ruin, spoil; incorrect, wrong. —**Syn. Study.** CORRECT, ACCURATE, PRECISE imply conformity to fact, standard, or truth. A CORRECT statement is one free from error, mistakes, or faults: *The student gave a correct answer in class.* An ACCURATE statement is one that, as a result of an active effort to comprehend and verify, shows careful conformity to fact, truth, or spirit: *The two witnesses said her account of the accident was accurate.* A PRECISE statement shows scrupulously strict and detailed conformity to fact: *The chemist gave a precise explanation of the experiment.*

correspond, *v.* **1.** conform, agree, harmonize, accord, match, tally, concur, coincide, fit, suit. **2.** communicate. —**Ant.** differ, diverge.

corrode, *v.* **1.** eat, gnaw, consume, erode, wear away. **2.** impair, deteriorate. **3.** canker, rust, crumble.

corrupt, *adj.* **1.** dishonest, venal, false, untrustworthy, bribable. **2.** debased, depraved, base, perverted, wicked, sinful, evil, dissolute, profligate, abandoned, reprobate. **3.** putrid, impure, putrescent, rotten, contaminated, adulterated, tainted, corrupted, spoiled, infected. —*v.* **4.** bribe, lure, entice, demoralize, lead astray. **5.** pervert, deprave, debase, vitiate. **6.** infect, taint, pollute, contaminate, adulterate, spoil, defile, putrefy. —**Ant.** honest; honorable; pure, unspoiled, unadulterated; purify.

corruption, *n.* **1.** perversion, depravity, abandon, dissolution, sinfulness, evil, immorality, wickedness, profligacy. **2.** dishonesty, baseness, bribery. **3.** decay, rot, putrefaction, putrescence, foulness, pollution, defilement, contamination, adulteration. **—Ant.** righteousness; honesty; purity.

cosmetic, *n.* **1.** makeup, greasepaint, cover-up, paint, rouge, foundation, pancake, war paint —*adj.* **2.** beautifying, decorative, enhancing, improving, corrective. **3.** superficial, surface, shallow, cursory, passing, slap-dash, skin-deep.

cost, *n.* **1.** price, charge, expense, expenditure, outlay. **2.** sacrifice, loss, penalty, damage, detriment, suffering, pain.

costly, *adj.* valuable, dear, high-priced, sumptuous, expensive, precious, rich, splendid. **—Ant.** cheap.

coterie, *n.* society, association, set, circle, clique, club, brotherhood, fraternity. **—Syn. Study.** See CIRCLE.

cottage, *n.* cabin, lodge, hut, shack, cot, shanty. **—Ant.** palace, castle.

counsel, *n.* **1.** advice, opinion, instruction, suggestion, recommendation, caution, warning, admonition. **2.** consultation, deliberation, forethought. **3.** purpose, plan, design, scheme. **4.** lawyer, solicitor, barrister, advocate, counselor, adviser. **—Syn. Study.** See ADVICE.

countenance, *n.* **1.** aspect, appearance, look, expression, mien. **2.** face, visage, physiognomy. **3.** favor, encouragement, aid, assistance, support, patronage, sanction, approval, approbation. —*v.* **4.** favor, encourage, support, aid, abet, patronize, sanction, approve. **—Ant.** condemn, prohibit. **—Syn. Study.** See FACE.

counteract, *v.* neutralize, counterbalance, annul, countervail, offset, contravene, thwart, oppose, resist, hinder, check, frustrate, defeat. **—Ant.** cooperate.

counterfeit, *adj.* **1.** spurious, false, fraudulent, forged. **2.** sham, pretended, feigned, simulated, fraudulent, false, mock, fake, unreal, ersatz. —*n.* **3.** imitation, forgery, falsification, sham. —*v.* **4.** imitate, forge, copy, fake, falsify. **5.** resemble. **6.** simulate, feign, sham, pretend. **7.** feign, dissemble. —**Ant.** genuine. —**Syn. Study.** See FALSE.

countryman, *n.* **1.** compatriot, fellow citizen. **2.** native, inhabitant. **3.** rustic, farmer, peasant, husbandman. —**Ant.** alien, foreigner.

couple, *n.* **1.** pair, duo, duet, yoke, brace, two, span. —*v.* **2.** fasten, link, join, unite, associate, pair, conjoin, connect. —**Ant.** separate, disjoin.

courage, *n.* fearlessness, dauntlessness, intrepidity, fortitude, pluck, spirit, heroism, daring, audacity, bravery, mettle, valor, hardihood, bravado, gallantry, chivalry. —**Ant.** cowardice.

courageous, See Syn. study at BRAVE.

course, *n.* **1.** advance, direction, bearing. **2.** path, route, channel, way, road, track, passage. **3.** progress, passage, process. **4.** process, career, race. **5.** conduct, behavior, deportment. **6.** method, mode, procedure. **7.** sequence, succession, order, turn, regularity. **8.** range, row, series, layer, order. —*v.* **9.** chase, pursue, follow, hunt. **10.** run, race.

courteous, *adj.* civil, polite, well-mannered, well-bred, urbane, debonair, affable, gracious, courtly, respectful, obliging. —**Ant.** discourteous, rude, curt, brusque. —**Syn. Study.** See CIVIL.

cover, *v.* **1.** overlay, overspread, envelop, enwrap, clothe, invest. **2.** shelter, protect, shield, guard, defend. **3.** hide, screen, cloak, disguise, secrete, veil, shroud, mask, enshroud. **4.** include, comprise, provide for, take in, embrace, contain, embody, comprehend. **5.** suffice, defray, offset, compensate for, counterbalance. —*n.* **6.** lid, top, case, covering, tegument, integument. **7.** protection, shelter, asylum, refuge, concealment, guard, defense. **8.** woods, underbrush, covert, shrubbery, growth, thicket, copse. **9.** veil, screen, disguise, mask, cloak. —**Ant.** uncover; exposure.

covet, *v.* desire, envy, long for. —**Ant.** relinquish, renounce.

covetous, See Syn. study at AVARICIOUS.

coward, *n.* **1.** poltroon, cad, dastard, milksop. —*adj.* **2.** timid, cowardly.

cowardice, *n.* poltroonery, dastardliness, pusillanimity, timidity. —**Ant.** boldness, bravery, temerity.

cowardly, *adj.* craven, poltroon, dastardly, pusillanimous, recreant, timid, timorous, faint-hearted, white-livered, lily-livered, chicken-hearted, yellow, fearful, afraid, scared. —**Ant.** brave, bold, valiant.

coxcomb, *n.* dandy, fop, dude, exquisite, beau, popinjay, jackanapes.

coy, *adj.* retiring, diffident, shy, self-effacing, bashful, modest, shrinking, timid, demure. —**Ant.** bold, pert, brazen, arch.

cozy, *adj.* comfortable, snug, secure, safe, warm, easeful, comforting, intimate, close, homespun, homelike, homey, soft, comfy. —**Ant.** cold, unwelcoming.

crack, *v.* **1.** snap. **2.** break, snap, split; crackle, craze. —*n.* **3.** snap, report. **4.** break, flaw, split, fissure, cleft, chink, breach, crevice, cranny, interstice.

crackpot, *n* **1.** eccentric, crank, character, oddity, odd duck, oddball, queer fish, crackbrain, screwball, nutcase. **2.** fanatic, zealot, faddist, believer, true believer. —*adj.* **3.** impractical, crazy, lunatic, visionary.

craft, *n.* **1.** skill, ingenuity,

dexterity, talent, ability, aptitude, expertness. **2.** skill, art, artfulness, craftiness, subtlety, artifice, cunning, deceit, guile, shrewdness, deceitfulness, deception. **3.** handicraft, trade, art, vocation, metier, calling. **4.** boat, vessel, ship; aircraft, airplane, plane.

craftsman, *n.* artisan, artificer, mechanic, handicraftsman, workman. —**Ant.** bungler, shoemaker.

crafty, *adj.* skillful, sly, cunning, deceitful, artful, wily, insidious, tricky, designing, scheming, plotting, arch, shrewd. —**Ant.** gullible, naive.

cram, *v.* stuff, crowd, pack, compress, squeeze, overcrowd, gorge, glut, press.

cranky, *adj.* **1.** ill-tempered, cross, crotchety, cantankerous, perverse. **2.** eccentric, queer, odd, strange, peculiar, curious. **3.** shaky, unsteady, loose, disjointed, out of order, broken. **4.** bent, twisted, crooked. —**Ant.** amiable, good-natured; firm; solid.

crash, *v.* **1.** break, shatter, shiver, splinter, dash, smash. —*n.* **2.** falling, collapse, depression, failure, ruin.

crave, *v.* **1.** long for, desire, want, yearn *or* hunger for. **2.** require, need. **3.** beg for, beseech, entreat, implore, solicit, supplicate. —**Ant.** relinquish, renounce.

craven, *adj.* cowardly. —**Ant.** brave, bold, intrepid, fearless.

craving, See Syn. study at DESIRE.

crazy, *adj.* **1.** demented, insane, mad, deranged, crazed, lunatic, cracked. **2.** rickety, shaky, tottering, doddering, loose. **3.** weak, infirm, confused, impaired. —**Ant.** sane, well-balanced; firm; strong.

create, *v.* **1.** produce, originate, invent, cause, occasion. **2.** make, constitute.

credit, *n.* **1.** belief, trust, confidence, faith, reliance, credence. **2.** influence, authority, power. **3.** trustworthiness, credibility. **4.** repute, estimation, character; reputation, name, esteem, regard, standing, position, rank, condition; notoriety. **5.** commendation, honor, merit. **6.** acknowledgment, ascription. —*v.* **7.** believe, trust, confide in, have faith in, rely upon. **—Ant.** discredit.

creditable, *adj.* praiseworthy, meritorious, estimable, reputable, honorable, respectable. **—Ant.** disreputable, dishonorable.

credulous, *adj.* believing, trusting, trustful, unsuspecting, gullible. **—Ant.** incredulous, cautious, wary.

crime, *n.* offense, wrong, sin; infraction, violation, breach, misdemeanor, tort, felony: trespassing, breaking and entering, theft, robbery, assault, battery, statutory rape, rape, embezzlement, slander, libel, treason, manslaughter, murder. **—Syn. Study.** CRIME,

OFFENSE, SIN agree in referring to a breaking of law. CRIME usu. refers to any serious violation of a public law: *the crime of treason.* OFFENSE is used of a less serious violation of a public law, or of a violation of a social or moral rule: *a traffic offense; an offense against propriety.* SIN means a breaking of a moral or divine law: *the sin of envy.*

criminal, *adj.* **1.** felonious, unlawful, illegal, nefarious, flagitious, iniquitous, wicked, sinful, wrong. —*n.* **2.** convict, malefactor, evildoer, transgressor, sinner, culprit, delinquent, offender, felon; crook, hoodlum, gangster. **—Syn. Study.** See ILLEGAL.

cripple, *v.* disable, maim, weaken, impair, break down, ruin, destroy.

crisis, *n.* climax, juncture, exigency, strait, pinch, emergency.

criterion, *n.* standard, rule, principle, measure, parameter, touchstone,

test, proof. **—Syn. Study.**
See STANDARD.

critic, *n.* **1.** reviewer,
censor, judge, connoisseur.
2. censurer, carper,
faultfinder.

critical, *adj.* **1.** captious,
carping, censorious,
faultfinding, caviling,
severe. **2.** discriminating,
tasteful, judicial,
fastidious, nice, exact,
precise. **3.** decisive,
climacteric, crucial,
determining, momentous,
important. **4.** dangerous,
perilous, risky, suspenseful,
hazardous, precarious,
ticklish. **—Ant.**
unimportant, superficial,
trivial.

criticism, *n.* **1.** censure,
faultfinding, stricture,
animadversion, reflection.
2. review, critique,
comment.

crooked, *adj.* **1.** bent,
curved, winding, devious,
sinuous, flexuous,
serpentine. **2.** deformed,
misshapen, disfigured,
twisted, awry, askew,
crippled. **3.** dishonest,
unscrupulous, knavish,
tricky, fraudulent,
dishonorable, unlawful,
illegal, deceitful, insidious,
crafty, treacherous.
—Ant. straight; honest,
upright.

crop, *n.* **1.** harvest,
produce, yield. **2.** craw,
stomach. **—***v.* **3.** cut, cut
short, clip, lop, mow.

cross, *n.* **1.** opposing,
thwarting, opposition,
frustration. **2.** trouble,
misfortune, misery,
burden. **—***v.* **3.** intersect,
traverse. **4.** oppose,
thwart, frustrate, baffle,
contradict, foil. **5.**
interbreed, mongrelize.
—*adj.* **6.** petulant,
fractious, irascible,
waspish, crabbed, cranky,
curmudgeonly, churlish,
sulky, cantankerous,
ill-natured, peevish, sullen,
ill-tempered, intemperate,
impatient, complaining,
snappish, irritable, fretful,
moody, touchy, testy,
unpleasant, unkind, mean,
angry, spiteful, resentful,
gloomy, glowering,
morose, sour. **—Ant.**
supporting; aid, support;

complaisant, amenable, agreeable, sweet.

crowd, *n.* **1.** throng, multitude, swarm, company, host, horde, herd. **2.** masses, proletariat, plebians, rabble, mob, people, populace. —*v.* **3.** assemble, throng, swarm, flock together, herd. **4.** push, shove, cram, pack, press, squeeze, cramp, force. —**Syn. Study.** CROWD, MULTITUDE, SWARM, THRONG refer to large numbers of people. CROWD suggests a jostling, uncomfortable, and possibly disorderly company: *A crowd gathered to listen to the speech.* MULTITUDE emphasizes the great number of persons or things but suggests that there is space enough for all: *a multitude of people at the market.* SWARM as used of people is usu. contemptuous, suggesting a moving, restless, often noisy, crowd: *A swarm of dirty children played in the street.* THRONG suggests a company that presses together or forward, often with some common aim: *The throng pushed forward to see the cause of the excitement.*

crude, *adj.* **1.** unrefined, unfinished, unprepared, coarse, raw. **2.** unripe, immature, undeveloped. **3.** unpolished, unfinished, incomplete, coarse, boorish, uncouth, rough, rude, clumsy, awkward. **4.** undisguised, blunt, bare, rough, direct. —**Ant.** refined; aged, mature, ripe; complete, perfect; indirect, subtle. —**Syn. Study.** See RAW.

cruel, *adj.* **1.** barbarous, bloodthirsty, sanguinary, ferocious, fell, merciless, unmerciful, relentless, implacable, pitiless, distressing, ruthless, truculent, brutal, savage, inhuman, brutish, barbarian, unmoved, unfeeling, unrelenting. **2.** severe, hard, bitter. —**Ant.** kind, benevolent, beneficial.

cruelty, *n.* harshness, brutality, ruthlessness, barbarity, inhumanity, atrocity. —**Ant.** kindness, benevolence.

crush, *v.* **1.** squeeze, press, bruise, crumple, rumple, wrinkle, compress. **2.** break, shatter, pulverize, granulate, powder, mash, smash, crumble, disintegrate. **3.** put down, quell, overpower, subdue, overwhelm, overcome, quash, conquer, oppress.

cry, *v.* **1.** lament, grieve, weep, bawl, sorrow, sob, shed tears, bewail, bemoan, squall, blubber, whimper, mewl, pule, wail. **2.** call, shout, yell, yowl, scream, exclaim, ejaculate, clamor, roar, bellow, vociferate. **3.** yelp, bark, bellow, hoot. —*n.* **4.** shout, scream, wail, shriek, screech, yell, yowl, roar, whoop, bellow. **5.** exclamation, outcry, clamor, ejaculation. **6.** entreaty, appeal. **7.** proclamation, announcement. **8.** weeping, lament, lamentation, tears. —**Ant.** laugh.

crying, *adj.* **1.** weeping, wailing. **2.** flagrant, notorious, demanding, urgent, important, great, enormous. —**Ant.** laughing; nugatory, trifling.

cunning, *n.* **1.** ability, skill, adroitness, expertness. **2.** craftiness, skillfulness, shrewdness, artfulness, wiliness, trickery, finesse, intrigue, artifice, guile, craft, deceit, deceitfulness, slyness, deception. —*adj.* **3.** ingenious, skillful. **4.** artful, wily, tricky, foxy, crafty. —**Ant.** stupidity, inability; dullness; naive, gullible, dull.

curb, *n.* **1.** restraint, check, control, bridle, rein, checkrein. —*v.* **2.** control, restrain, check, bridle, repress. —**Ant.** encourage, further, foster. —**Syn. Study.** See CHECK.

cure, *n.* **1.** remedy, restorative, specific, antidote. —*v.* **2.** remedy, restore, heal, make well *or* whole, mend, repair, correct.

cure-all, *n.* remedy, cure, relief, nostrum, elixir, panacea, sovereign remedy, universal remedy, theriac, catholicon.

curious, *adj.* **1.** inquisitive, inquiring, prying, spying, peeping, meddlesome, interested. **2.** strange, novel, unusual, singular, rare, foreign, exotic, queer, extraordinary, unique. —**Ant.** blasé; common, commonplace, usual, customary.

current, *adj.* **1.** present, prevailing, prevalent, general, common, circulating, widespread, popular, rife. **2.** accepted, stylish, in vogue, *à la mode*, fashionable, du jour. —*n.* **3.** stream, river, tide, course, progress, progression. —**Ant.** outmoded, uncommon, unpopular.

curse, *n.* **1.** imprecation, execration, fulmination, malediction, oath, denunciation, anathema, ban. **2.** evil, misfortune, calamity, trouble, vexation, annoyance, affliction, torment, bane, thorn, plague, scourge. —*v.* **3.** blaspheme, swear, imprecate, execrate,

fulminate, damn, denunciate, accurse, maledict, anathematize, condemn, profane, excommunicate. **4.** doom, destroy, plague, scourge, afflict, trouble, vex, annoy. —**Ant.** blessing, benediction.

cursed, *adj.* **1.** damned, accursed, banned, blighted. **2.** execrable, damnable, hateful, abominable, villainous. —**Ant.** blessed.

curt, *adj.* **1.** short, shortened, brief, abbreviated, concise, laconic, blunt, terse. **2.** rude, snappish, abrupt, dry. —**Ant.** long, drawn-out, lengthy; courteous, courtly. —**Syn. Study.** See BLUNT.

curtail, *v.* lessen, diminish, decrease, dock, shorten, abbreviate, blunt, abridge. —**Ant.** extend, expand. —**Syn. Study.** See SHORTEN.

curtain, *n.* **1.** drape, drapery, hanging, portière, lambrequin, valance, blind, shade, shutter, shutters. **2.** cover, concealment. —**Ant.** window.

cushion, *n.* **1.** pillow, bolster, pad; shock-absorber. —*v.* **2.** absorb, check, slow, alleviate, meliorate.

custody, *n.* **1.** keeping, guardianship, care, custodianship, charge, safekeeping, watch, preserving, protection, preservation; possession, ownership, mastery, holding. **2.** imprisonment, confinement.

custom, *n.* **1.** habit, practice, usage, procedure, rule. **2.** rule, convention, form, observance, formality. **3.** tax, duty, impost, tribute, toll. **4.** patronage, customers, patrons, clientele. —**Syn. Study.** CUSTOM, HABIT, PRACTICE mean an established way of doing things. CUSTOM, applied to a community or to an individual, implies a more or less permanent way of acting reinforced by tradition and social attitudes: *the custom of giving gifts at Christmas.* HABIT, applied particularly to an individual, implies such repetition of the same action as to develop a natural, spontaneous, or rooted tendency or inclination to perform it: *He has an annoying habit of interrupting the speaker.* PRACTICE applies to a regularly followed procedure or pattern in conducting activities: *It is his practice to verify all statements.*

customary, *adj.* usual, habitual, wonted, accustomed, conventional, common, regular. —**Ant.** unusual, rare, uncommon, irregular. —**Syn. Study.** See USUAL.

cut, *v.* **1.** gash, slash, slit, lance, pierce, penetrate, incise, wound. **2.** wound, hurt, move, touch, slight, insult. **3.** divide, sever, carve, cleave, sunder, bisect, chop, hack, hew, fell, saw. **4.** lop off, crop. **5.** reap, mow, harvest. **6.** clip, shear, pare, prune. **7.** cross, intersect, transect. **8.** abridge, edit, shorten, abbreviate, curtail. **9.** lower, lessen, reduce, diminish. **10.** dissolve, dilute, thin, water, water down. **11.** facet, make, fashion. **12.** hollow out, excavate, dig. —*n.* **13.** incision, wound, slash, gash, slit; channel, passage, strait. **14.** style, fashion, mode, kind, sort.

cutting, *n.* **1.** root, shoot, leaf, branch, limb. —*adj.* **2.** sharp, keen, incisive, trenchant, piercing. **3.** mordant, mordacious, caustic, biting, acid, wounding, sarcastic, sardonic, bitter, severe. —**Ant.** dull; kind.

cynical, *adj.* distrustful, pessimistic, sarcastic, satirical, unbelieving, disbelieving, sneering, contemptuous, derisive, cutting, scornful, ridiculing, censorious, captious, waspish, petulant, testy, fretful, touchy, cross, surly, ill-tempered, ill-natured, crusty, cantankerous. —**Ant.** optimistic, hopeful; good-natured, calm, pleasant.

D

dabbler, *adj.* **1.** nonprofessional, amateur, dilettante, putterer, trifler, dallier, sciolist, Sunday painter. **2.** beginner, tyro, starter, novice, neophyte, abecedarian, tenderfoot, greenhorn, raw recruit. —**Ant.** professional, expert, adept.

dainty, *adj.* **1.** delicate, beautiful, charming, exquisite, fine, elegant. **2.** toothsome, delicious, savory, palatable, tender, juicy, delectable, luscious. **3.** particular, fastidious, scrupulous. **4.** squeamish, finical, overnice. —*n.* **5.** delicacy, tidbit, sweetmeat. —**Ant.** clumsy, inelegant; disgusting, distasteful; sloppy. —**Syn. Study.** See DELICATE.

dally, *v.* **1.** sport, play, trifle, fondle, toy, caress.

2. waste time, loiter, delay, dawdle. —**Ant.** hasten, hurry. —**Syn. Study.** See LOITER.

damage, *n.* **1.** injury, harm, hurt, detriment, mischief, impairment, loss. —*v.* **2.** injure, harm, hurt, impair, mar. —**Ant.** improvement; improve, better.

damp, *adj.* **1.** moist, humid, dank, steamy, wet. —*n.* **2.** moisture, humidity, dankness, wet, wetness, dampness, fog, vapor, steam. **3.** dejection, depression, dispiritedness, chill, discouragement, check. —*v.* **4.** dampen, moisten, wet, humidify. **5.** check, retard, slow, inhibit, restrain, moderate, abate, allay, slow, interfere with. **6.** stifle, suffocate, extinguish. —**Ant.** dry, arid.

dandified, *adj.* foppish, dandyish, ultrasmart, fashionable, ulrafashionable, dapper, dressy, stylish, natty, spruce, chic, chichi, showy, flamboyant, peacockish, peacocky, affected, dudish, dandiacal, ostentatious, orchidaceous, bandbox, preening. —**Ant.** plain, dowdy, frumpy.

danger, *n.* hazard, risk, peril, jeopardy, liability, exposure; injury, evil. —**Ant.** security, safety. —**Syn. Study.** DANGER, HAZARD, PERIL imply harm that one may encounter. DANGER is the general word for liability to injury or harm, either near at hand and certain, or remote and doubtful: *to be in danger of being killed.* HAZARD suggests a danger that one can often foresee but cannot avoid: *A mountain climber is exposed to many hazards.* PERIL usually denotes great and imminent danger: *The passengers on the disabled ship were in great peril.*

dappled, *adj.* multicolored, multihued, varicolored, mottled, motley, spotted, polka-dot, flecked, maculate, freckled, freckly, pied, shadowed, shadowy.

dare, *v.* venture, hazard, risk, brave, challenge, defy, endanger.

daredevil, *adj.* daring, rash, adventurous, risk-taking, reckless, heedless, foolhardy, wild, devil-may-care, venturesome, nervy, temerarious, gutsy.

daring, *n.* **1.** courage, adventurousness, boldness, bravery, audacity, intrepidity, heroism. —*adj.* **2.** courageous, venturesome, adventurous, bold, brave, audacious, dauntless, undaunted, intrepid, fearless, valiant, valorous, gallant, chivalrous, doughty, heroic. —**Ant.** cowardice; timid, cowardly, pusillanimous, fearful.

dark, *adj.* **1.** dim, gloomy, murky, umbrageous, shadowy, penumbral, dusky, unilluminated, unlit, sunless, shady, swarthy, black, pitchy, ebon, Cimmerian. **2.** gloomy, cheerless, dismal, sad, morose, morbid, disheartening, discouraging. **3.** sullen, frowning. **4.** unenlightened, ignorant, untaught, untutored, uneducated, unlettered, benighted, in the dark. **5.** obscure, recondite, abstruse, dim, incomprehensible, unintelligible, occult, cabalistic, mysterious, puzzling, enigmatic, enigmatical, mystic, mystical. **6.** hidden, secret, concealed. **7.** silent, reticent. **8.** infernal, wicked, sinful, nefarious, flagitious, foul, infamous, hellish, devilish, evil, bad, satanic. —**Ant.** light, fair; cheerful; pleasant; intelligent, educated; clear, intelligible; open, revealed; voluble; heavenly, godly.

dart, *n.* **1.** arrow, barb. —*v.* **2.** spring, start, dash, bolt, rush, fly, shoot.

dash, *v.* **1.** strike, break; throw, thrust; splash, splatter. **2.** adulterate, mix, deteriorate, mingle. **3.** rush, dart, bolt, fly. —*n.* **4.** pinch, bit, suggestion, soupçon, hint, touch, tinge, smack, sprinkle, sprinkling. **5.** vigor, spirit, élan, flourish, éclat.

daub, **1.** dab, smear,

bedaub, besmear, besmirch, smudge, spot, stain, soil. —*n.* **2.** spot, stain, mark, blot, blotch, smudge, smirch.

daunt, *v.* **1.** intimidate, overawe, subdue, dismay, frighten, appall. **2.** discourage, dispirit, dishearten, thwart, frustrate. —**Ant.** encourage, actuate.

dauntless, *adj.* fearless, bold, undaunted, intrepid, brave, courageous, daring, indomitable, unconquerable, valiant, valorous, heroic, chivalrous, doughty, undismayed. —**Ant.** fearful, cowardly, timid, timorous.

dawdle, *v.* idle, linger, loiter, tarry, lag, poke along, dally, dilly-dally, loll, laze, lallygag, take one's time, procrastinate, temporize, put off. —**Ant.** hasten, hurry. —**Syn. Study.** See LOITER.

dawn, *n.* **1.** daybreak, sunrise, dawning. —*v.* **2.** appear, open, begin, break. —**Ant.** sunset; disappear.

daydream, *v.* **1.** imagine, fantasize, dream, muse, pipe-dream, woolgather, build castles in the air. —*n.* **2.** reverie, dream, fantasy, imagining, woolgathering.

dazzle, *v.* **1.** bedazzle, blind, daze, bedaze. **2.** astonish, amaze, stun, stupefy, overwhelm, astound, confound, flabbergast.

dead, *adj.* **1.** deceased, lifeless, extinct, inanimate, defunct, departed. **2.** insensible, numb, unfeeling, indifferent, cool, cold, callous, obtuse, frigid, unsympathetic, apathetic, lukewarm. **3.** infertile, barren, sterile. **4.** still, motionless, inert, inoperative, useless, dull, inactive, unemployed. **5.** extinguished, out. **6.** complete, absolute, utter, entire, total. **7.** straight, direct, unerring, exact, precise, sure. —**Ant.** alive, live, animate; fervid, eager, warm, animated; fertile;

partial; crooked, indirect, devious.

deadly, *adj.* **1.** fatal, lethal, mortal. **2.** implacable, sanguinary, murderous, bloodthirsty. —**Syn. Study.** See FATAL.

deal, *v.* **1.** act, behave. **2.** trade, do business, traffic. **3.** distribute, dole, mete, dispense, apportion, allot, give, assign. —*n.* **4.** bargain, arrangement, pact, contract. **5.** quantity, amount, extent, degree. **6.** dealing, distribution, share. —**Ant.** gather, collect.

dear, *adj.* **1.** beloved, loved, precious, darling, esteemed. **2.** expensive, high-priced, costly, high; exorbitant. —**Ant.** hateful; cheap.

death, *n.* **1.** decease, demise, passing, departure. **2.** stop, cessation, surcease, estoppage, end, finale. —**Ant.** life.

debar, *v.* **1.** exclude, shut out. **2.** prevent, prohibit, hinder, interdict, outlaw. —**Ant.** include, welcome; encourage, support.

debase, *v.* **1.** adulterate, corrupt, vitiate, contaminate, pollute, defile, foul, befoul. **2.** lower, depress, reduce, impair, deteriorate, degrade, abase, demean. —**Ant.** purify; elevate, raise, exalt.

debate, *n.* **1.** discussion, argument, controversy, disputation, dispute, contention. **2.** deliberation, consideration. —*v.* **3.** discuss, dispute, argue, contend, hold. **4.** deliberate, consider, discuss, argue. —**Ant.** agreement.

debt, *n.* liability, obligation, duty, due, debit.

debut, *n.* **1.** introduction, appearance, arrival, coming out, introduction, inauguration, induction, initiation, unveiling, launching, installation, premiere. —*v.* **2.** come out, appear, arrive, enter, launch, premiere, make a debut.

decadence, *n.* decline, degeneration,

retrogression, decay, fall.
—**Ant.** flourishing,
progress.

decay, *n.* **1.** deteriorate,
decline, retrogress,
degenerate, fall, fall away,
wither, perish. **2.**
decompose, putrefy, rot,
disintegrate. —*n.* **3.**
decline, deterioration,
degeneration, decadence,
impairment, dilapidation.
4. decomposition,
putrefaction, rotting, rot.
—**Ant.** flourish, grow;
progress. —**Syn. Study.**
DECAY, DECOMPOSE,
DISINTEGRATE, ROT imply a
deterioration or falling
away from a sound
condition. DECAY implies
either entire or partial
deterioration by
progressive natural
changes: *Teeth decay.*
DECOMPOSE suggests the
reducing of a substance to
its component elements:
*Moisture makes some
chemical compounds
decompose.* DISINTEGRATE
emphasizes the breaking
up, going to pieces, or
wearing away of anything,
so that its original

wholeness is impaired:
Rocks disintegrate. ROT is
applied esp. to decaying
vegetable matter, which
may or may not emit
offensive odors: *Potatoes
rot.*

deceit, *n.* **1.** deceiving,
concealment, fraud,
deception, cheating, guile,
hypocrisy, craftiness,
slyness, insincerity,
disingenuousness. **2.** trick,
stratagem, artifice, wile,
trickery, chicane,
chicanery, device,
cozenage. **3.** falseness,
duplicity, treachery,
perfidy. —**Ant.** honesty,
forthrightness. —**Syn.
Study.** DECEIT, GUILE,
DUPLICITY, FRAUD refer
either to practices designed
to mislead or to the
qualities in a person that
prompt such behavior.
DECEIT is intentional
concealment or
misrepresentation of the
truth: *Consumers are often
victims of deceit.* GUILE is
crafty or cunning deceit; it
suggests subtle but
treacherous tactics: *The
agent used guile to gain*

access to the documents. DUPLICITY is doing the opposite of what one says or pretends to do; it suggests hypocrisy or pretense: *the duplicity of a friend who does not keep a secret.* FRAUD refers to deceit or trickery by which one may derive benefit at another's expense; it often suggests illegal or dishonest practices: *an advertiser convicted of fraud.*

deceitful, *adj.* **1.** insincere, disingenuous, false, hollow, empty, deceiving, fraudulent, designing, tricky, wily, two-faced. **2.** misleading, fraudulent, deceptive, counterfeit, illusory, fallacious. —**Ant.** sincere, honest, forthright; genuine.

deceive, *v.* mislead, delude, cheat, cozen, dupe, gull, fool, bamboozle, hoodwink, trick, double-cross, defraud, outwit; entrap, ensnare, betray. —**Syn. Study.** See CHEAT.

decent, *adj.* **1.** fitting, appropriate, suited, suitable, apt, proper, fit, becoming. **2.** conformant, tasteful, modest, seemly, proper, decorous. —**Ant.** indecent, indecorous, improper, unfit, unsuitable.

deception, *n.* **1.** deceiving, gulling. **2.** artifice, sham, cheat, imposture, treachery, subterfuge, stratagem, ruse, hoax, fraud, trick, wile.

deceptive, *adj.* deceiving, misleading, delusive, fallacious, specious, false, deceitful. —**Ant.** genuine, authentic.

decide, *v.* determine, settle, resolve, purpose, conclude. —**Ant.** waver, hesitate, vacillate. —**Syn. Study.** DECIDE, RESOLVE, DETERMINE imply settling something in dispute or doubt. To DECIDE is to make up one's mind after consideration: *I decided to go to the party.* To RESOLVE is to settle conclusively with firmness of purpose: *She resolved to ask for a promotion.* To DETERMINE is to settle after investigation or observation: *It is difficult* *to determine the best course of action.*

decided, *adj.* **1.** unambiguous, unquestionable, definite, unmistakable, undeniable, indeniable, indisputable, indubitable, certain, sure, emphatic, pronounced, absolute, unequivocal, categorical, incontrovertible. **2.** resolute, determined, resolved, unwavering, unhesitating. —**Ant.** undecided, ambiguous, indefinite; irresolute, hesitant.

decipher, *v.* decode, decrypt, unravel, break, crack, solve, figure out, translate, unriddle, work out, dope out, puzzle out, explain, elucidate, analyze, interpret, resolve. —**Ant.** encode, encipher, obscure, hide.

decisive, *adj.* incontrovertible, firm, resolute, determined, conclusive, final. —**Ant.** indecisive, irresolute, vacillating, wavering.

deck, *v.* clothe, attire, bedeck, array, garnish, trim, dress, bedizen, adorn, embellish, decorate. —**Ant.** undress.

declaim, *v.* orate, perorate, hold forth, elocute, lecture, preach, sermonize, harangue, speechify, rant, rave, thunder, trumpet, shout, tub-thump, mouth off. —**Ant.** mumble, mutter.

declare, *v.* **1.** announce, proclaim, pronounce. **2.** affirm, assert, aver, protest, make known, state, asseverate, utter. **3.** manifest, reveal, disclose, publish. —**Ant.** deny, controvert; suppress. —**Syn. Study.** DECLARE, AFFIRM, ASSERT imply making something known emphatically, openly, or formally. To DECLARE is to make known, sometimes in the face of actual or potential contradiction: *to declare someone the winner of a contest.* TO AFFIRM is to make a statement based on one's reputation for knowledge or veracity, or so related to a generally recognized truth that denial is not likely: *to affirm the necessity of high standards.* To ASSERT is to state boldly, usu. without other proof than personal authority or conviction: *to assert that the climate is changing.*

decline, *v.* **1.** refuse, avoid, reject, deny. **2.** descend, slope, incline *or* bend downward. **3.** stoop, condescend, lower oneself, abase, debase. **4.** fail, weaken, deteriorate, pale, diminish, degenerate, decay, languish. —*n.* **5.** incline, declivity, slope, hill. **6.** failing, loss, enfeeblement, deterioration, degeneration, enervation, weakening, decay, diminution, lessening, retrogression. —**Ant.** agree; rise; improve, increase; strengthening. —**Syn. Study.** See REFUSE.

decompose, *v.* **1.** separate, distill, fractionate, analyze, disintegrate. **2.** rot, putrefy, decay, mould. —**Syn. Study.** See DECAY.

decorate, *v.* adorn, bedeck, beautify, ornament,

embellish, deck, deck out, bedizen, dress, dress up, trim, spruce up, smarten, appoint, garnish, pretty up, titivate, accouter, furbish, dandify, prettify, doll up, gussy up. —**Ant.** simplify, streamline, strip.

decorous, *adj.* proper, decent, seemly, becoming, sedate, conventional, fitting, fit, suitable. —**Ant.** indecorous, indecent, unseemly, unbecoming, unfit.

decorum, *n.* etiquette, politeness, politesse, manners, manner, behavior, comportment, deportment, decency, propriety, dignity. —**Ant.** indecency, impropriety.

decrease, *v.* **1.** diminish, lessen, abate, fall off, decline, contract, dwindle, shrink, wane, ebb, subside. —*n.* **2.** abatement, diminution, reduction, decline, wane, subsidence, falling-off, contraction, shrinking, dwindling, lessening, ebb, ebbing. —**Ant.** increase. —**Syn. Study.** DECREASE, DIMINISH, DWINDLE, SHRINK imply becoming smaller or less in amount. DECREASE commonly implies a sustained reduction in stages, esp. of bulk, size, volume, or quantity, often from some imperceptible cause or inherent process: *The swelling decreased daily.* DIMINISH usu. implies the action of some external cause that keeps taking away: *Disease caused the number of troops to diminish steadily.* DWINDLE implies an undesirable reduction by degrees, resulting in attenuation: *His followers dwindled to a mere handful.* SHRINK esp. implies contraction through an inherent property under specific conditions: *Many fabrics shrink in hot water.*

decree, *n.* **1.** order, directive, edict, command, commandment, dictum, injunction, mandate, proclamation, declaration, directive, instruction, prescription, prescript, ruling, fiat, ukase, pronunciamento. —*v.* **2.** order, direct, command, dictate, rule, require, prescribe, direct, enjoin, bid, mandate, instruct, pronounce, ordain.

decrepit, *adj.* weak, feeble, enfeebled, infirm, aged, superannuated, effete, broken-down. —**Ant.** sturdy, strong.

decry, *v.* disparage, censure, belittle, discredit, depreciate, condemn. —**Ant.** praise, laud, commend. —**Syn. Study.** DECRY, DENIGRATE, DEPRECATE involve the expression of censure or disapproval. DECRY means to denounce or to express public disapproval of: *to decry all forms of discrimination.* DENIGRATE means to defame or to sully the reputation or character of: *to denigrate the memory of a ruler.* DEPRECATE means to express regretful disapproval of or to plead against: *to deprecate a new policy.*

dedicate, See Syn. study at DEVOTE.

deduce, *v.* conclude, infer,

reason, gather, assume, presume, judge, make out, dope out, conjecture, speculate, guess, glean, reckon, suppose, surmise, think, understand.

deduct, *v.* subtract, remove, detract, withdraw. —**Ant.** add.

deed, *n.* act, performance, exploit, achievement, action, feat.

deem, *v.* judge, regard, think, consider, hold, believe, account, count, suppose.

deep, *adj.* **1.** recondite, abstruse, abstract, difficult, profound, mysterious, obscure, unfathomable. **2.** grave, serious, grievous. **3.** absorbing, absorbed, involved, intense, heartfelt, great, extreme. **4.** penetrating, intelligent, bright, cunning, sagacious, wise, discerning, astute, shrewd, artful. —*n.* **5.** ocean, sea, abyss. —**Ant.** shallow.

deface, *v.* mar, disfigure, deform, spoil, soil, injure, harm; blot out, efface, obliterate, erase, eliminate. —**Ant.** beautify.

defeat, *v.* **1.** overcome, conquer, overwhelm, vanquish, subdue, overthrow, subjugate, suppress, rout, check. **2.** frustrate, thwart, foil, baffle, disconcert, unnerve, balk. —*n.* **3.** overthrow, vanquishment, downfall, rout. **4.** frustration, bafflement. —**Ant.** yield, surrender, submit. —**Syn. Study.** DEFEAT, CONQUER, OVERCOME, SUBDUE imply gaining victory or control over an opponent. DEFEAT usu. means to beat or frustrate in a single contest or conflict: *Confederate forces were defeated at Gettysburg.* CONQUER means to finally gain control over by physical, moral, or mental force, usu. after long effort: *to conquer poverty; to conquer a nation.* OVERCOME emphasizes perseverance and the surmounting of difficulties: *to overcome opposition; to overcome a bad habit.* SUBDUE means to conquer so completely that resistance is broken: *to subdue a rebellious spirit.*

defect, *n.* **1.** blemish, flaw, fault, shortcoming, imperfection, mar, blotch, scar, blot, foible, weakness. **2.** deficiency, want, lack, destitution. —*v.* **3.** desert, abandon, revolt, rebel, betray. —**Ant.** sufficiency, perfection; support. —**Syn. Study.** DEFECT, BLEMISH, FLAW refer to faults, both literal and figurative, that detract from perfection. DEFECT is the general word for any kind of shortcoming, imperfection, or deficiency, whether hidden or visible: *a birth defect; a defect in a plan.* A BLEMISH is usu. a surface defect that mars the appearance; it is also used of a moral fault: *a skin blemish; a blemish on his reputation.* A FLAW is usu. a structural defect or weakness that mars the quality or effectiveness: *a flaw in a diamond; a flaw in Hamlet's character.*

defective, *adj.* imperfect, incomplete, faulty, deficient, insufficient, inadequate, (*euphemism, applied to humans*) challenged. —**Ant.** perfect, complete, adequate.

defend, *v.* **1.** guard, garrison, fortify, shield, shelter, screen, preserve, protect, keep, watch over, safeguard, secure. **2.** uphold, maintain, assert, justify, plead, espouse, vindicate. —**Ant.** attack.

defer, *v.* delay, postpone, put off, prevent, adjourn; procrastinate. —**Ant.** speed, expedite. —**Syn. Study.** DEFER, DELAY, POSTPONE imply keeping something from occurring until a future time. To DEFER is to decide to do something at a more convenient time in the future; it often suggests avoidance: *to defer making a payment.* DELAY is sometimes equivalent to DEFER, but it usu. suggests a hindrance, obstacle, or dilatory tactic: *Completion of the building was delayed by bad weather.* To POSTPONE is to put off to a particular time in the future, often to wait for new information or developments: *to postpone a trial.*

deference, *n.* **1.** homage, honor, veneration, reverence, obeisance, respect, esteem, appreciation, admiration. **2.** submission, subjection, submissiveness, compliance, acquiescence. —**Ant.** disrespect, insolence.

defiant, *adj.* antagonistic, insubordinate, contumacious, refractory, recalcitrant, rebellious, insolent, resistant, in-your-face; daring, courageous, brave, bold. —**Ant.** friendly, amiable; cowardly.

definite, *adj.* **1.** defined, determined, specific, particular, exact, fixed, precise, determinate. **2.** certain, clear, express, sure. —**Ant.** indefinite, undetermined, indeterminate; uncertain, unclear.

deform, *v.* misshape,

deform, disfigure, deface, efface, mar, spoil, ruin; transform.

deformed, *adj.* malformed, misshapen, crippled, disfigured.

deft, See Syn. study at DEXTEROUS.

defy, *v.* challenge, resist, dare, brave, flout, scorn, despise. —**Ant.** encourage, support, help.

degradation, *n.* humiliation, disgrace, debasement, dishonor, degeneration, decline, decadence, degeneracy, perversity. —**Ant.** exaltation.

degrade, *v.* **1.** demote, depose, downgrade, lower, break, cashier. **2.** debase, deprave, lower, abase, vitiate, deteriorate. **3.** humiliate, dishonor, disgrace, discredit. —**Ant.** exalt. —**Syn. Study.** See HUMBLE.

dejected, *adj.* depressed, dispirited, disheartened, low-spirited, discouraged, despondent, downhearted, sad, unhappy, miserable. —**Ant.** happy, cheerful, lighthearted.

delay, *v.* **1.** put off, defer, postpone, procrastinate. **2.** impede, slow, retard, hinder, detain, stop, arrest. **3.** linger, loiter, tarry. —*n.* **4.** delaying, procrastination, loitering, tarrying, dawdling, stay, stop. **5.** deferment, postponement, respite, deferring. —**Ant.** expedite, hasten, speed. —**Syn. Study.** See DEFER.

delegate, *n.* **1.** representative, deputy, envoy, ambassador, legate. —*v.* **2.** depute, entrust, commission.

delete, *v.* cancel, strike *or* take out, dele, erase, expunge, eradicate, remove, efface, blot out.

deleterious, *adj.* injurious, hurtful, harmful, pernicious, destructive, deadly, lethal; noxious, poisonous. —**Ant.** salutary, beneficial, advantageous.

deliberate, *adj.* **1.** weighed, considered, studied, intentional, purposive, purposeful, premeditated, voluntary, willful. **2.** careful, slow, unhurried, leisurely, methodical, thoughtful, circumspect, cautious, wary. —*v.* **3.** weigh, consider, ponder over, reflect, think, ruminate, meditate. **4.** consult, confer. —**Ant.** haphazard, unintentional; careless, unwary, incautious. —**Syn. Study.** DELIBERATE, INTENTIONAL, VOLUNTARY refer to something not happening by chance. DELIBERATE is applied to what is done not hastily but with full realization of what one is doing: *a deliberate attempt to evade justice.* INTENTIONAL is applied to what is definitely intended or done on purpose: *an intentional omission.* VOLUNTARY is applied to what is done by a definite exercise of the will and not because of outside pressures: *a voluntary enlistment.* See also SLOW.

delicacy, *n.* **1.** tenderness, sensitivity, tact, diplomacy, feeling, sensibility, consideration, thoughtfulness, solicitude, solicitousness, refinement, finesse, dexterity, skill, deftness, facility, artistry, artfulness, adroitness, grace. **2.** frailty, unhealthiness, fragility, feebleness, weakness, debility, valetudinarianism. **3.** treat, rare treat, tidbit, morsel, choice morsel, dainty, goody.

delicate, *adj.* **1.** fine, dainty, exquisite, nice, fragile, graceful, elegant, choice. **2.** fine, slight, subtle. **3.** tender, fragile, frail, dainty, slight, weak, slender, sensitive, frangible. **4.** critical, precarious. **5.** scrupulous, careful, painstaking, exact, exacting, precise, accurate. **6.** discriminating, fastidious, careful, demanding. **—Ant.** rude, crude; blunt; rough, insensitive, unbreakable; careless. **—Syn. Study.** DELICATE, DAINTY, EXQUISITE imply beauty or subtle refinement such as might belong in rich surroundings. DELICATE suggests something fragile, soft, light, or fine: *a delicate carving.* DAINTY suggests a smallness, gracefulness, and beauty that forbids rough handling: *a dainty handkerchief;* of persons, it refers to fastidious sensibilities: *a dainty eater.* EXQUISITE suggests an outstanding beauty and elegance that appeals to the most refined taste: *an exquisite tapestry.*

delicious, *adj.* pleasing, luscious, palatable, savory, dainty, delicate. **—Ant.** unpleasant, bitter, acrid, unpalatable.

delight, *n.* **1.** enjoyment, pleasure, transport, delectation, joy, rapture, ecstasy. **—v. 2.** please, satisfy, transport, enrapture, enchant, charm, ravish. **—Ant.** disgust, revulsion, displeasure; displease.

delightful, *adj.* pleasing, pleasant, pleasurable, enjoyable, charming, enchanting, agreeable, delectable, rapturous. **—Ant.** unpleasant, disagreeable, revolting, repellent.

deliver, *v.* **1.** give up, surrender, hand over, transfer, give over, yield, resign, cede, grant, relinquish. **2.** give forth, emit, cast, direct, deal, discharge. **3.** utter, pronounce, announce, proclaim, declare, communicate, publish, impart, promulgate, advance. **4.** set free, liberate, release, free, emancipate. **5.** redeem, rescue, save, release, extricate, disentangle. —**Ant.** limit, confine.

delude, *v.* mislead, deceive, beguile, cozen, cheat, dupe, gull, defraud, trick. —**Ant.** enlighten.

deluge, *n.* inundation, flood, downpour, overflow, cataclysm, catastrophe.

delusion, *n.* illusion, deception, trick, fancy, fallacy, error, mistake, hallucination.

demand, *v.* **1.** claim, require, exact, ask for, call for, challenge. **2.** ask, inquire. —*n.* **3.** claim, requisition, requirement.

4. inquiry, question, asking, interrogation. —**Ant.** waive, relinquish.

demolish, *v.* ruin, destroy, put an end to, lay waste, raze, level. —**Ant.** construct, build, create. —**Syn. Study.** See DESTROY.

demonstrate, *v.* **1.** show, explain, explicate, expound, spell out, illustrate, make clear, make plain, show and tell. **2.** exhibit, manifest, display, evidence, evince, present, disclose, divulge. **3.** protest, object, march, rally, boycott, strike, picket.

demur, *v.* **1.** object, take exception, raise *or* make objection; refuse. —*n.* **2.** objection, hesitation, refusal. —**Ant.** agree, accede, consent.

demure, *adj.* **1.** prudish, prim, overmodest, priggish. **2.** sober, modest, serious, sedate, decorous, coy. —**Ant.** licentious, immodest; indecorous. —**Syn. Study.** See MODEST.

denigrate, See Syn. study at DECRY.

denounce, *v.* **1.** condemn, assail, censure, attack, stigmatize, blame, brand, label. **2.** inform against, accuse, denunciate, give away. —**Ant.** commend, exonerate.

deny, *v.* **1.** dispute, controvert, oppose, gainsay, contradict. **2.** reject, renounce, abjure, disavow. **3.** refuse, repudiate, disown. —**Ant.** concede, agree, concur; accept; receive.

depart, *v.* **1.** go away, start, set out, leave, quit, retire, withdraw, absent, go. **2.** turn aside, diverge, deviate, vary. **3.** die, pass on *or* away. —**Ant.** arrive; converge.

depict, *v.* **1.** represent, portray, paint, limn, delineate, sketch, reproduce, draw. **2.** describe.

deplore, *v.* grieve, regret, lament, bemoan, bewail, mourn. —**Ant.** boast.

deposit, *v.* **1.** place, put, lay down, lay. **2.** throw down, drop, precipitate. **3.** bank, save, store, hoard; secure. —*n.* **4.** sediment, deposition, precipitate; silt, mud, slime, sand, alluvium; snow, rain, sleet, hail. **5.** coating; lode, vein.

depot, *n.* station, terminal; storehouse, warehouse, depository.

depraved, *adj.* corrupt, perverted, corrupted, immoral, wicked, evil, sinful, iniquitous, profligate, debased, dissolute, reprobate, degenerate, licentious, lascivious, lewd. —**Ant.** upright, honest; honorable, decorous, modest.

deprecate, See Syn. study at DECRY.

depress, *v.* **1.** dispirit, deject, oppress, dishearten, discourage, dampen, chill, sadden. **2.** reduce, weaken, dull, lower. **3.** devalue, cheapen. **4.** humble, humiliate, abase, debase, degrade, abash. —**Ant.** inspirit, encourage; elevate; gladden.

depressed, *adj.* dejected, downcast, sad, unhappy, miserable, morose, saddened, blue, despondent, melancholy, gloomy, morbid. —**Ant.** happy, cheerful.

deprive, *v.* dispossess, bereave, strip, divest, disallow, deny. —**Ant.** endow.

dereliction, *n.* neglect, negligence, delinquency, fault, abandonment, desertion, renunciation.

deride, See Syn. study at RIDICULE.

derogatory, *adj.* disparaging, belittling, demeaning, derogative, depreciatory, deprecatory, depreciative, slighting, uncomplimentary, insulting, disdainful, scornful, contemptuous, spiteful, abusive, pejorative, defamatory, malicious, maligning. —**Ant.** flattering, complimentary.

descent, *n.* **1.** falling, fall, sinking, descending. **2.** inclination, declination, slope, declivity, grade, decline. **3.** extraction, lineage, derivation, parentage, genealogy. **4.** incursion, attack, assault, raid, foray. —**Ant.** ascent, rise.

describe, *v.* narrate, account, recount, tell, relate; delineate, portray, characterize, limn, represent, depict.

desert, *n.* **1.** waste, wilderness. —*adj.* **2.** desolate, barren, forsaken, wild, uninhabited. —*v.* **3.** abandon, forsake, leave behind, give up, relinquish, leave, quit, renounce.

design, *v.* **1.** plan, devise, project, contrive. **2.** intend, purpose, mean, propose. **3.** sketch, draw, delineate. —*n.* **4.** plan, scheme, proposal, proposition, project. **5.** sketch, plan, drawings, blueprint, outline, draught. **6.** end, intention, purpose, intent, aim, object. **7.** meaning, purport, drift. —**Ant.** achieve, execute, accomplish; execution; accident, fortuity, chance.

designing, *adj.* contriving, scheming, sly, artful, cunning, tricky, wily, crafty, deceitful, treacherous, arch,

Machiavellian, astute, unscrupulous. **—Ant.** open, candid, frank, honest, guileless, artless, naive.

desire, *v.* **1.** wish *or* long for, crave, want, wish, covet, fancy. **2.** ask, request, solicit. —*n.* **3.** linging, craving, yearning, wish, need, hunger, appetite, thirst. **4.** request, wish, aspiration. **5.** lust. **—Ant.** abominate, loathe, abhor. **—Syn. Study.** DESIRE, CRAVING, LONGING, YEARNING suggest feelings that impel a person to the attainment or possession of something. DESIRE is a strong wish, worthy or unworthy, for something that is or seems to be within reach: *a desire for success.* CRAVING implies a deep and compelling wish for something, arising from a feeling of (literal or figurative) hunger: *a craving for food; a craving for companionship.* LONGING is an intense wish, generally repeated or enduring, for something that is at the moment

beyond reach but may be attainable in the future: *a longing to visit Europe.* YEARNING suggests persistent, uneasy, and sometimes wistful or tender longing: *a yearning for one's native land.*

desolate, *adj.* **1.** barren, laid waste, devastated, ravaged, scorched, destroyed. **2.** deserted, uninhabited, desert, lonely, alone, lone, solitary, forsaken, lonesome. **3.** miserable, wretched, unhappy, sad, woeful, woebegone, disconsolate, inconsolable, forlorn, lost, cheerless. **4.** dreary, dismal, wild. —*v.* **5.** lay waste, devastate, ravage, ruin, sack, destroy, despoil. **6.** depopulate. **7.** sadden, depress. **8.** forsake, abandon, desert. **—Ant.** fertile; populous, crowded; happy, delighted; cultivated; build, create; cheer.

despair, *n.* hopelessness, desperation, despondency, discouragement, gloom, disheartenment. **—Ant.** encouragement, hope,

optimism. —**Syn. Study.**
DESPAIR, DESPERATION,
DESPONDENCY refer to a
state of mind caused by
circumstances that seem
too much to cope with.
DESPAIR suggests total loss
of hope, usu. accompanied
by apathy and low spirits:
*He sank into despair after
the bankruptcy.*
DESPERATION is a state in
which loss of hope drives
a person to struggle
against circumstances, with
utter disregard of
consequences: *In
desperation, they knocked
down the door.*
DESPONDENCY is a state of
deep gloom due to loss of
hope and a sense of
futility and resignation:
*despondency after a serious
illness.*
desperate, *adj.* **1.** reckless,
despairing, rash, headlong,
frantic. **2.** hopeless,
serious, grave, dangerous.
3. wretched, forlorn,
hopeless, desolate. **4.**
extreme, excessive, great,
heroic, prodigious,
foolhardy. —**Ant.** careful;
hopeful.

desperation, See Syn. study
at DESPAIR.
despicable, *adj.* despisable,
contemptible, vile, base,
worthless, mean, abject,
low, pitiful. —**Ant.**
lovable, likable, worth.
despise, *v.* contemn, scorn,
disdain, spurn. —**Ant.**
love, like, admire.
despite, *prep.*
notwithstanding, in spite
of.
despondency, *n.* depression,
dejection, discouragement,
melancholy, gloom,
desperation, despair,
sadness, blues. —**Ant.**
elation, joy, happiness.
—**Syn. Study.** See DESPAIR.
despondent, *adj.*
desponding, depressed,
dejected, discouraged,
disheartened, downhearted,
melancholy, sad, blue,
dispirited, hopeless,
low-spirited. —**Ant.**
elated, joyful, happy.
destiny, *n.* fate, karma,
kismet, lot, fortune, future,
doom, destination. —**Syn.
Study.** See FATE.
destitute, *adj.* needy, poor,
indigent, penniless,

impoverished, poverty-stricken. **—Ant.** affluent, rich, opulent.

destroy, *v.* **1.** smash, dash, demolish, raze, spoil, consume, level, ruin, waste, ravage, devastate, desolate, lay waste. **2.** end, extinguish, extirpate, annihilate, eradicate, slay, kill, uproot. **3.** nullify, invalidate. **—Ant.** create; originate, start. **—Syn. Study.** DESTROY, DEMOLISH, RAZE imply completely ruining or doing away with something. To DESTROY is to reduce something to nothingness or to take away its powers and functions so that restoration is impossible: *Disease destroys tissues.* To DEMOLISH is to destroy something organized or structured by smashing it to bits or tearing it down: *The evidence demolished the attorney's case.* To RAZE is to level a building or other structure to the ground: *to raze a fortress.*

destruction, *n.* **1.** extinction, extermination, desolation, devastation, ruin, eradication. **2.** demolition, annihilation, murder, slaughter, death, massacre, genocide. **3.** plague, shipwreck, holocaust. **—Ant.** birth, origin; creation.

destructive, *adj.* **1.** ruinous, baleful, pernicious, mischievous, deleterious, fatal, deadly, lethal. **2.** extirpative, eradicative. **—Ant.** salutary; creative.

detain, *v.* **1.** delay, arrest, retard, stop, slow, stay, check, keep. **2.** restrain, confine, arrest. **3.** keep back, withhold, retain. **—Ant.** promote, encourage; advance.

detect, *v.* discover, catch, expose, descry, find, find out, ascertain, learn, hear of, hear. **—Syn. Study.** See LEARN.

deter, *v.* discourage, restrain, dissuade, hinder, prevent, stop. **—Ant.** encourage, further, continue.

determine, *v.* **1.** settle, decide, conclude, adjust. **2.** conclude, ascertain, verify, check, certify. **3.**

fix, decide, establish, condition, influence, resolve. **4.** impel, induce, lead, incline. **—Syn. Study.** See DECIDE.

determined, *adj.* staunch, resolute, unflinching, firm, inflexible, rigid, rigorous, unfaltering, unwavering. **—Ant.** irresolute, vacillating, wavering, faltering, flexible.

detest, *v.* abhor, hate, loathe, abominate, execrate, despise. **—Ant.** love, like. **—Syn. Study.** See HATE.

detestable, *adj.* abominable, hateful, execrable, loathsome, vile, odious, abhorred, abhorrent, despicable. **—Ant.** lovable, likable.

detraction, *n.* detracting, disparagement, belittling, defamation, vilification, calumny, abuse, slander, aspersion, depreciation. **—Ant.** praise, commendation.

detriment, *n.* loss, damage, injury, hurt, harm, impairment, disadvantage, prejudice. **—Ant.** advantage, profit.

devastate, *v.* ravage, lay waste, desolate, destroy, strip, pillage, plunder, sack, spoil, despoil. **—Ant.** build, erect, create.

development, *n.* **1.** expansion, growth, elaboration, progress, increase. **2.** opening, disclosure, developing, unfolding, maturing, maturation. **3.** community, project, housing project. **—Ant.** deterioration, decadence, degeneration.

deviate, *v.* **1.** depart, swerve, digress, diverge, part, wander, veer, err, stray. **2.** turn aside, avert. **—Ant.** converge. **—Syn. Study.** DEVIATE, DIGRESS, DIVERGE imply turning or going aside from a path. To DEVIATE is to stray from a usual or established standard, course of action, or route: *Fear caused him to deviate from the truth.* To DIGRESS is to wander from the main theme in speaking or writing: *The speaker digressed to relate an* *amusing anecdote.* To DIVERGE is to differ or to move in different directions from a common point or course: *Their interests gradually diverged.*

device, *n.* **1.** invention, contrivance, gadget. **2.** plan, scheme, project, design, expedient. **3.** wile, ruse, artifice, shift, trick, stratagem, evasion, maneuver. **4.** design, figure, emblem, trademark, badge, logotype, colophon, symbol, crest, seal. **5.** motto, slogan, legend. **6.** (*plural*) will, desire, inclination, bent, abilities, aptitudes.

devilish, *adj.* satanic, diabolic, diabolical, demoniac, infernal, Mephistophelian, fiendish, hellish. —**Ant.** good, fine, upstanding, righteous, godly.

devise, *v.* order, arrange, plan, think out, contrive, invent, prepare, concoct, scheme, project, design. —**Ant.** disorder, disarrange.

devote, *v.* assign, apply, consign, give up, dedicate, consecrate. —**Ant.** resign, relinquish. —**Syn. Study.** DEVOTE, DEDICATE, CONSECRATE share the sense of assigning or committing someone or something to a particular activity, function, or end. DEVOTE is the most general of these terms, although it carries overtones of religious commitment: *He devoted his evenings to mastering the computer.* DEDICATE implies a more solemn or noble purpose and carries an ethical or moral tone: *We are dedicated to the achievement of equality for all.* CONSECRATE, even in nonreligious contexts, implies an intense and sacred commitment: *consecrated to the service of humanity.*

devotee, See Syn. study at FANATIC.

devotion, *n.* **1.** dedication, consecration. **2.** attachment, affection, love. **3.** devotedness, zeal, ardor, eagerness, earnestness. **4.** (*theology*) religion, religiousness, piety, faith, devoutness, sanctity, saintliness, godliness.

devout, *adj.* **1.** pious, devoted, religious, worshipful, holy, saintly. **2.** earnest, sincere, hearty, serious, honest. —**Ant.** atheistic, agnostic; insincere, scornful. —**Syn. Study.** See RELIGIOUS.

dexterous, *adj.* skillful, adroit, deft, handy, nimble, clever, expert, apt, ready, quick, able. —**Ant.** clumsy, awkward, maladroit, unapt. —**Syn. Study.** DEXTEROUS, ADROIT, DEFT imply facility and ease in performance. DEXTEROUS most often refers to physical, esp. manual, ability but can also refer to mental ability: *a dexterous woodcarver; dexterous handling of a delicate situation.* ADROIT usu. implies mental cleverness and ingenuity but can refer to physical ability: *an adroit politician; an adroit juggler.* DEFT suggests a light and assured touch in physical or mental activity: *a deft magician; deft*

handling of the reporters after the tragedy.

dialect, *n.* **1.** provincialism, idiom, localism, jargon, patois, variant. **2.** branch, subfamily, subgroup. **3.** language, tongue, speech. —**Syn. Study.** See LANGUAGE.

diction, *n.* phraseology, wording, style, usage, grammar, language; distinctness, enunciation, pronunciation.

die, *v.* **1.** decease, pass away *or* on, perish, expire, depart. **2.** cease, end, vanish, disappear. **3.** weaken, fail, subside, fade, sink, faint, decline, wither, decay. —*n.* **4.** cube, block. **5.** stamp. —**Syn. Study.** DIE, PERISH mean to relinquish life. To DIE is to cease to live from any cause or circumstance; it is used figuratively of anything that has once displayed activity: *He died of cancer. Her anger died.* PERISH, a more literary term, implies death under harsh circumstances such as hunger or violence; figuratively, it connotes permanent disappearance: *Hardship caused many pioneers to perish. Ancient Egyptian civilization has perished.*

difference, *n.* **1.** discrepancy, disparity, dissimilarity, inconsistency, unlikeness, variation, diversity, imbalance, disagreement, inequality, dissimilitude, divergence, contrast, contrariety. **2.** discrimination, distinction. —**Ant.** similarity; agreement.

different, *adj.* **1.** differing, unlike, diverse, divergent, altered, changed, contrary, contrasted, deviant, deviating, variant. **2.** sundry, divers, miscellaneous, various, manifold. —**Ant.** similar, like; uniform, identical. —**Syn. Study.** See VARIOUS.

differentiate, *v.* **1.** set off, distinguish, alter, change. **2.** distinguish, discriminate, separate, contrast. —**Ant.** group together. —**Syn. Study.** See DISTINGUISH.

difficult, *adj.* **1.** hard,

arduous. **2.** obscure, complex, intricate, perplexing. **3.** austere, rigid, reserved, forbidding, unaccommodating. **4.** fastidious, particular. —**Ant.** easy, simple; clear, plain; accommodating; careless, sloppy.

difficulty, *n.* **1.** dilemma, predicament, quandary, fix, exigency, emergency. **2.** trouble, problem. **3.** reluctance, unwillingness, obstinacy, stubbornness. **4.** demur, objection, obstacle. —**Ant.** ease; willingness.

diffident, *adj.* shy, self-conscious, self-effacing, bashful, abashed, embarrassed, timid, sheepish, modest. —**Ant.** forward, bold, unabashed.

digest, *v.* **1.** understand, assimilate, study, ponder, consider, contemplate, ruminate over, reflect upon. **2.** arrange, systematize, think over, classify, codify. —*n.* **3.** summary, epitome, abstract, synopsis, abridgment, brief, conspectus. **—Ant.** expand. **—Syn. Study.** See SUMMARY.

dignify, *v.* ennoble, exalt, uplift, glorify, honor, elevate, grace, build up, raise, promote, magnify. **—Ant.** demean, humble.

digress, *v.* deviate, diverge, wander. **—Syn. Study.** See DEVIATE.

dilate, *v.* expand, spread out, enlarge, engross, widen, extend, swell, distend. **—Ant.** shrink, constrict.

dilemma, *n.* predicament, problem, question, quandary, difficulty, strait. **—Syn. Study.** See PREDICAMENT.

dilettante, *n.* **1.** amateur, dabble, nonprofessional, tyro, putterer. **2.** connoisseur, aesthete, expert, authority, specialist, collector, maven.

diligence, *n.* persistence, effort, application, industry, assiduity, perseverance, assiduousness. **—Ant.** carelessness, laziness.

diligent, *adj.* **1.** industrious, assiduous, sedulous, occupied, busy, constant, attentive, persistent. **2.** painstaking, persevering, indefatigable, untiring, tireless, unremitting, industrious. **—Ant.** lazy, careless; remiss.

dim, *adj.* **1.** obscure, dark, shadowy, dusky, nebulous, hazy, cloud, faint, indistinct. **2.** indistinct, unclear, ill-defined, blurred, vague, confused, indefinite. **3.** dull, tarnished, blurred, slow, stupid, dense, foggy. **4.** disparaging, adverse, uncomplimentary. **—v. 5.** darken, cloud, obscure, dull. **6.** blur, dull, fade. **—Ant.** clear, bright, distinct; definite.

diminish, *v.* lessen, reduce, decrease, subside, ebb, dwindle, shrink, abate, contract, shrivel up. **—Ant.** increase. **—Syn. Study.** See DECREASE.

diminutive, *adj.* little, small, tiny, dwarf, dwarflike, dwarfish, minute, microscopic, submicroscopic. **—Ant.** large, immense.

din, See Syn. study at
NOISE.

dip, *v.* **1.** plunge, immerse,
dive, duck. **2.** sink, drop,
incline, decline, slope
downward. —**Ant.** rise.
—**Syn. Study.** DIP, IMMERSE,
PLUNGE refer to putting
something into liquid. To
DIP is to put down into a
liquid quickly or partially
and lift out again: *to dip a
finger into water to test the
temperature.* IMMERSE
denotes a lowering into a
liquid until covered by it:
*to immerse meat in salt
water.* PLUNGE adds a
suggestion of force or
suddenness to the action
of dipping: *to plunge a
lobster into boiling water.*

diplomatic, *adj.* politic,
tactful, artful. —**Ant.**
tactless, rude, naive.
—**Syn. Study.** DIPLOMATIC,
POLITIC, TACTFUL imply
ability to avoid offending
others, esp. in situations
where this is important.
DIPLOMATIC suggests a
smoothness and skill in
handling others, usually in
such a way as to attain
one's own ends and yet

avoid any unpleasantness
or opposition: *diplomatic
inquiries about the
stockbroker's finances.*
POLITIC emphasizes
expediency or prudence in
looking out for one's own
interests, thus knowing
how to treat people of
different types in delicate
situations: *a truth which it
is not politic to insist on.*
TACTFUL suggests a nice
touch in the handling of
delicate matters or
situations; it often involves
a sincere desire not to hurt
the feelings of others: *a
tactful way of correcting
someone.*

direct, *v.* **1.** guide, advise,
regulate, conduct, manage,
control, dispose, lead,
govern, rule. **2.** order,
command, instruct. **3.**
point, aim. —*adj.* **4.**
straight, undeviating. **5.**
immediate, personal,
unbroken, simple, evident.
6. straightforward,
downright, plain,
categorical, unequivocal,
unambiguous, express,
open, sincere, outspoken,
frank, earnest, ingenuous,

obvious, naive. **—Ant.** divert, mislead; crooked; devious; ambiguous, sly. **—Syn. Study.** DIRECT, ORDER, COMMAND mean to issue instructions. DIRECT suggests also giving explanations or advice; the emphasis is on steps necessary to accomplish a purpose: *He directed me to organize the files.* ORDER connotes a more personal relationship and instructions that leave no room for refusal: *She ordered him out of the class.* COMMAND suggests greater formality and a more fixed authority: *The officer commanded the troops to advance.*

directly, See Syn. study at IMMEDIATELY.

dirty, *adj.* **1.** soiled, foul, unclean, filthy, squalid, defiled, grimy. **2.** dirtying, soiling, befouling, besmirching. **3.** vile, mean, base, vulgar, low, groveling, scurvy, shabby, contemptible, despicable. **4.** indecent, obscene, nasty, lascivious, lewd, lecherous, licentious, immoral, amoral. **5.** contaminated, radioactive. **6.** stormy, squally, rainy, foul, sloppy, disagreeable, nasty. **7.** dark-colored, dingy, dull, dark, sullied, clouded. **—Ant.** clean; elevated, exalted; decent, moral; fair; clear.

disability, *n.* incapacity, disqualification, inability, incompetence, impotence, incapability. **—Ant.** ability, capacity, capability.

disable, *v.* **1.** weaken, destroy, cripple, incapacitate, enfeeble, paralyze. **2.** disqualify, incapacitate, eliminate. **—Ant.** strengthen; qualify; include.

disadvantage, *n.* **1.** drawback, inconvenience, hindrance, deprivation. **2.** detriment, hurt, harm, damage, injury, loss, disservice. **—Ant.** advantage.

disaffect, See Syn. study at ESTRANGE.

disappear, *v.* vanish, fade, cease, pass away, end. **—Ant.** appear. **—Syn.**

Study. DISAPPEAR, FADE, VANISH mean that something or someone passes from sight or existence. DISAPPEAR is used of whatever suddenly or gradually goes away: *We watched them turn down a side street and disappear.* FADE suggests a complete or partial disappearance that proceeds gradually and often by means of a blending into something else: *Dusk faded into darkness.* VANISH suggests complete, generally rapid disappearance: *The sun vanished behind clouds.*

disappointment, *n.* **1.** failure, defeat, frustration, unfulfillment. **2.** mortification, frustration, chagrin. **—Ant.** fulfillment, victory; consummation.

disaster, *n.* misfortune, calamity, mischance, mishap, accident, misadventure, blow, reverse, catastrophe, adversity, affliction. **—Ant.** luck, fortune. **—Syn. Study.** DISASTER, CALAMITY, CATASTROPHE, CATACLYSM refer to adverse happenings usu. occurring suddenly and unexpectedly. DISASTER may be caused by negligence, bad judgment, or the like, or by natural forces, as a hurricane or flood: *a railroad disaster that claimed many lives.* CALAMITY suggests great affliction, either personal or general; the emphasis is on the grief or sorrow caused: *the calamity of losing a child.* CATASTROPHE refers esp. to the tragic outcome of a personal or public situation; the emphasis is on the destruction or irreplaceable loss: *the catastrophe of a defeat in battle.* CATACLYSM, physically a sudden and violent change in the earth's surface, also refers to a personal or public upheaval of unparalleled violence: *a cataclysm that turned our lives in a new direction.*

disband, *v.* break up, disorganize, demobilize, dissolve, disperse, dismiss, scatter, separate. **—Ant.** organize, unite.

disburse, *v.* spend, pay, expend, lay out. **—Ant.** bank, save.

discern, *v.* **1.** perceive, see, recognize, notice, apprehend, discover, descry, espy, come upon, behold. **2.** discriminate, distinguish, differentiate, judge. **—Syn. Study.** See NOTICE.

discharge, *v.* **1.** unload, disburden, relieve, unburden. **2.** remove, send forth, get rid of, expel, eject, emit. **3.** fire, shoot, set off, detonate. **4.** relieve, release, absolve, exonerate, clear, acquit, liberate, set free, free. **5.** fulfill, perform, execute, observe. **6.** dismiss, cashier, fire, remove, expel, send down, break. **7.** pay, honor, disburse, make good on, liquidate, dissolve, settle. **—***n.* **8.** emission, ejection, expulsion, removal, evacuation, voiding. **9.** detonation, firing, shooting. **10.** fulfillment, execution, performance,

observance. **—Ant.** load, burden. **—Syn. Study.** See RELEASE.

disciple, *n.* follower, adherent, supporter; pupil, student, scholar. **—Ant.** leader; rebel.

discipline, *n.* **1.** training, drill, exercise, instruction, practice. **2.** punishment, chastisement, castigation, correction. **3.** subjection, order, control, regulation, subjugation, government. **4.** rules, regulations. **—***v.* **5.** train, exercise, drill, practice, instruct, teach, educate. **6.** punish, correct, chastise, castigate.

disclose, *v.* **1.** reveal, make known, divulge, show, tell, unveil, communicate. **2.** uncover, lay open, expose, bring to light; muckrake. **—Ant.** conceal, hide; cover.

disconcert, *v.* disturb, confuse, perturb, ruffle, discompose, perplex, bewilder, frustrate, embarrass, abash; disarrange, disorder. **—Ant.** calm; order, arrange.

disconsolate, *adj.*
inconsolable, unhappy,
desolate, forlorn,
heart-broken, sad,
melancholy, dejected,
gloomy, miserable,
cheerless, sorrowful.
—**Ant.** happy, cheerful,
delighted.

discontent, *adj.* **1.**
discontented, dissatisfied.
—*n.* **2.** discontentment,
dissatisfaction, uneasiness,
inquietude, restlessness,
displeasure. —**Ant.**
contentment; satisfaction,
pleasure, ease, restfulness.

discontinue, *v.* put an end
to, interrupt, stop, cease,
quit; desist. —**Ant.**
continue, further.

discourage, *v.* **1.**
dishearten, dispirit, daunt,
depress, deject, overawe,
cow, awe, subdue, abash,
embarrass, dismay,
intimidate, frighten. **2.**
dissuade, deter, hinder,
prevent, obstruct. —**Ant.**
encourage, hearten,
embolden. —**Syn. Study.**
DISCOURAGE, DISMAY,
INTIMIDATE mean to
dishearten or frighten a
person so as to prevent

some action. To
DISCOURAGE is to dishearten
by expressing disapproval
or by suggesting that a
contemplated action will
probably fail: *He was
discouraged from going into
business.* To DISMAY is to
dishearten, shock, or
bewilder by sudden
difficulties or danger: *a
prosecutor dismayed by
disclosures of new evidence.*
To INTIMIDATE is to deter
by making timid: *The
prospect of making a
speech intimidates me.*

discouragement, *n.* **1.**
depression, dejection,
hopelessness, despair. **2.**
deterrent, damper, wet
blanket, cold water,
chilling effect, impediment,
obstacle, obstruction.
—**Ant.** encouragement.

discover, *v.* **1.** learn of,
ascertain, unearth,
determine, ferret out, dig
up; find out, detect, espy,
descry, discern, see, notice.
2. originate, bring to light,
invent. —**Ant.** conceal.
—**Syn. Study.** See LEARN.

discreet, *adj.* wise,
judicious, prudent,

circumspect, cautious, careful, heedful, considerate, wary. —**Ant.** indiscreet, careless, imprudent; incautious, inconsiderate. —**Syn. Study.** See CAREFUL.

discrepancy, *n.* difference, inconsistency, incongruity, disagreement, discordance, contrariety, variance, variation. —**Ant.** similarity, congruity, consistency, concord, accord, agreement.

discriminate, *v.* **1.** distinguish, set apart, differentiate. —*adj.* **2.** critical, distinguishing, discriminative, discriminatory. —**Ant.** group, unite; indiscriminate, undistinguished. —**Syn. Study.** See DISTINGUISH.

discuss, *v.* examine, reason, deliberate, argue, debate, talk over, sift, consider.

disdain, *v.* **1.** contemn, despise, scorn, spurn. —*n.* **2.** contempt, scorn, contumely, contemptuousness, haughtiness, arrogance, superciliousness, hauteur. —**Ant.** accept, like, love; love, admiration, regard. —**Syn. Study.** See CONTEMPT.

disdainful, *adj.* contemptuous, scornful, haughty, arrogant, supercilious, contumelious. —**Ant.** friendly, amiable, considerate, attentive.

disease, *n.* morbidity, illness, sickness, ailment, complaint, affection, disorder, malady, abnormality, derangement, distemper, indisposition, infirmity. —**Ant.** health, salubriety.

disfigure, *v.* mar, deface, injure, deform, spoil, ruin, blemish. —**Ant.** beautify.

disgrace, *n.* **1.** ignominy, shame, dishonor, infamy, disfavor, disapproval, disapprobation, disparagement, stain, taint, notoriety, baseness. **2.** odium, obloquy, degradation, opprobrium, scandal. —*v.* **3.** shame, dishonor, defame, disfavor, humiliate, disapprove, discredit, degrade, debase, stain, sully, taint, tarnish, reproach. —**Syn. Study.** DISGRACE, DISHONOR, IGNOMINY, INFAMY imply a very low position in the opinion of others. DISGRACE implies being excluded and held in strong disfavor by others: *to bring disgrace to one's family by not paying debts.* DISHONOR suggests a loss of honor or honorable reputation; it usu. relates to one's own conduct: *He preferred death to dishonor.* IGNOMINY is disgrace that invites public contempt: *the ignominy of being caught cheating.* INFAMY is shameful notoriety, or baseness of action or character that is widely known and recognized: *The children never outlived their father's infamy.*

disgust, *v.* **1.** sicken, nauseate, turn one's stomach. **2.** offend, displease, repel, repulse, revolt, abhor, detest. —*n.* **3.** distaste, nausea, loathing, hatred, abhorrence, disrelish. **4.**
dislike, detestation, repugnance, aversion, dissatisfaction, antipathy. —**Ant.** please, delight, attract; relish, liking, love; satisfaction.

disgusting, *adj.* offensive, offending, loathsome, sickening, nauseous, nauseating, repulsive, revolting, odious, hateful, repugnant, foul, abominable, abhorrent, distasteful, detestable. —**Ant.** delightful, delectable, attractive, beautiful.

dishonest, *adj.* unscrupulous, conniving, corrupt, knavish, thievish, deceitful, treacherous, perfidious; false, fraudulent, counterfeit. —**Ant.** honest.

dishonor, See Syn. study at DISGRACE.

dishonorable, *adj.* **1.** ignoble, base, disgraceful, shameful, shameless, false, fraudulent. **2.** infamous, notorious, unscrupulous, unprincipled, disreputable, disgraceful, scandalous,

ignominious, discreditable.
—**Ant.** honorable.

disintegrate, *v.* reduce to particles *or* fragments, break up, decay, rot, fall apart, separate. —**Ant.** integrate. —**Syn. Study.** See DECAY.

disinterested, *adj.* unbiased, unprejudiced, unselfish, impartial, fair, generous, liberal. —**Ant.** biased, prejudiced, illiberal, bigoted, selfish, partial. —**Syn. Study.** See FAIR.

dislike, *v.* **1.** have an aversion *or* be averse to, be disinclined *or* reluctant. —*n.* **2.** disrelish, disgust, distaste, repugnance, antipathy, loathing, aversion, antagonism. —**Ant.** like; relish, delight, delectation.

disloyal, *adj.* unfaithful, false, perfidious, treacherous, traitorous, treasonable, subversive, disaffected, untrue, unpatriotic. —**Ant.** loyal, faithful, true, honest.

disloyalty, *n.* unfaithfulness, perfidy, treachery, treason, betrayal, disaffection, faithlessness, subversion. —**Ant.** loyalty, fealty, allegiance.

dismay, *v.* **1.** discourage, dishearten, daunt, appall, terrify, horrify, frighten, scare, intimidate, disconcert, put out, alarm, paralyze. —*n.* **2.** consternation, terror, horror, panic, fear, alarm. —**Ant.** encourage, hearten, embolden; security, confidence. —**Syn. Study.** See DISCOURAGE.

dismiss, *v.* release, let go, discharge, discard, reject, set *or* put aside; fire. —**Ant.** hire, employ. —**Syn. Study.** See RELEASE.

disobedient, *adj.* insubordinate, contumacious, defiant, refractory, unruly, rebellious, obstinate, stubborn, unsubmissive, uncompliant. —**Ant.** obedient.

disobey, *v.* transgress, violate, disregard, defy, infringe. —**Ant.** obey.

disorder, *n.* **1.**

disorderliness, disarray, jumble, mess, litter, clutter, disarrangement, confusion, irregularity, disorganization, derangement. **2.** disturbance, tumult, brawl, uproar, fight, unrest, quarrel, bustle, clamor, riot, turbulence. **3.** ailment, malady, derangement, illness, complaint, sickness, disease, indisposition. —*v.* **4.** disarrange, disarray, mess up, disorganize, unsettle, disturb, derange, discompose, upset, confuse, confound. —**Ant.** order.

disparity, *n.* dissimilarity, inequality, difference, distinction, dissimilitude. —**Ant.** similarity, equality, similitude.

dispel, See Syn. study at SCATTER.

dispense, *v.* deal, distribute, apportion, allot, dole.

disperse, *v.* **1.** scatter, dissipate, separate. **2.** spread, diffuse, disseminate, broadcast, sow, scatter. **3.** dispel. **4.** vanish, disappear, evanesce. —**Ant.** unite, combine; appear. —**Syn. Study.** See SCATTER.

displace, *v.* **1.** misplace, move, dislocate. **2.** replace, remove, depose, oust, dismiss, cashier.

display, *v.* **1.** show, exhibit, demonstrate, make visible, evince, manifest. **2.** reveal, uncover, betray. **3.** unfold, open out, spread out. **4.** show, flourish, flaunt, parade, show off. —*n.* **5.** show, exhibition, manifestation. **6.** parade, ostentation, flourish, flaunting. —**Ant.** conceal, hide; cover. —**Syn. Study.** DISPLAY, EXHIBIT, MANIFEST mean to show or bring to the attention of another or others. To DISPLAY is literally to spread something out so that it may be most completely and favorably seen: *to display goods for sale.* To EXHIBIT is to display something to the public for inspection or appraisal: *to exhibit African violets at a flower show.* They may both refer to showing or revealing one's qualities or feelings: *to display wit; to exhibit surprise.* MANIFEST means to show feelings or qualities plainly or clearly: *He manifested his anger with a scowl.*

displeasure, *n.* dissatisfaction, annoyance, disapprobation, disapproval, distaste, dislike; anger, ire, wrath, indignation, vexation; offense. —**Ant.** pleasure, satisfaction, approval, delight; calm, peace.

disposition, *n.* **1.** temper, temperament, nature, character, humor. **2.** inclination, willingness, bent, tendency, proneness, bias, predisposition, proclivity. **3.** arrangement, order, grouping, location, placement. **4.** settlement, outcome, finale, result, dispensation. **5.** regulation, appointment, management, control, direction. **6.** bestowal, endowment. —**Ant.** indisposition, unwillingness.

dispute, *v.* **1.** argue, discuss, debate, agitate. **2.** wrangle, contest, quarrel, bicker, spat, squabble, spar, brawl. **3.** oppose, controvert, contradict, deny, impugn. —*n.* **4.** argumentation, argument, contention, debate, controversy, disputation, altercation, quarrel, wrangle, bickering, spat, squabble, tiff. —**Ant.** agree, concur; agreement, concurrence. —**Syn. Study.** See ARGUMENT.

disregard, *v.* **1.** ignore, neglect, overlook, disobey, pay no attention *or* heed *or* regard to, take no notice of. **2.** slight, insult. —*n.* **3.** neglect, inattention, inattentiveness, oversight. **4.** disrespect, slight, indifference. —**Ant.** regard, view, notice, note; attention; respect. —**Syn. Study.** See SLIGHT.

disrespectful, *adj.* discourteous, impolite, rude, crude, uncivil, impudent, impertinent, irreverent. —**Ant.** respectful, courteous, polite, civil, reverent.

dissatisfaction, *n.*

discontent, displeasure, dislike, disappointment, disapproval, disapprobation, uneasiness. **—Ant.** satisfaction, approval, approbation.

dissension, See Syn. study at QUARREL.

dissent, *v.* **1.** differ, disagree. —*n.* **2.** difference, dissidence, disagreement, dissatisfaction, opposition, nonconformity, separation. **—Ant.** agree, concur; agreement, concurrence, satisfaction, unity.

dissipate, *v.* **1.** scatter, disperse, dispel, disintegrate. **2.** waste, squander. **3.** scatter, disappear, vanish, disintegrate. **4.** debauch. **—Ant.** integrate, unite; appear; join. **—Syn. Study.** See SCATTER.

dissolve, *v.* **1.** melt, liquefy. **2.** sever, loose, loosen, free, disunite, break up; dismiss, disperse, adjourn. **3.** destroy, dispel, ruin, disintegrate, break down, terminate, end; perish, crumble, die, expire.

—Ant. solidify; unite; meet; integrate; originate.

distaste, *n.* dislike, disinclination, aversion, repugnance, disgust, displeasure, dissatisfaction; disrelish. **—Ant.** taste, delectation, liking, love, satisfaction; relish.

distasteful, *adj.* **1.** disagreeable, displeasing, offensive, repugnant, repulsive, unpleasant. **2.** unpalatable, unsavory, nauseating, loathsome, disgusting, sickening. **—Ant.** tasteful, agreeable, pleasant, inoffensive; attractive, delightful.

distend, *v.* expand, swell, stretch, dilate, bloat, enlarge. **—Ant.** contract, shrink, reduce.

distinct, *adj.* **1.** distinguished, distinguishable, different, individual, separate, dividual, various, varied; dissimilar. **2.** definite, well-defined, clear, plain, unmistakable, unconfused. **—Ant.** indistinct, blurred, same; similar; indefinite, unclear, confused. **—Syn. Study.** See VARIOUS.

distinction, *n.* **1.** difference, differentiation, discrimination. **2.** honor, repute, name, fame, celebrity, renown, importance, note, account, eminence, superiority. **—Ant.** indifference; similarity; disrepute, dishonor.

distinguish, *v.* **1.** mark, characterize. **2.** discriminate, differentiate, separate, divide, classify, categorize. **3.** discern, recognize, perceive, know, tell. **4.** make prominent *or* conspicuous *or* eminent. **—Syn. Study.** DISTINGUISH, DIFFERENTIATE, DISCRIMINATE mean to note the difference between two or more similar things. To DISTINGUISH is to recognize differences based on characteristic features or qualities: *to distinguish a light cruiser from a heavy cruiser.* To DIFFERENTIATE is to find and point out the exact differences in detail: *The symptoms of both diseases are so similar that it is hard to differentiate one from the other.* To DISCRIMINATE is to note fine or subtle distinctions and to judge their significance: *to discriminate prejudiced from unprejudiced testimony.*

distinguished, *adj.* **1.** conspicuous, marked, extraordinary. **2.** noted, eminent, famed, famous, celebrated, renowned, illustrious. **3.** distingué, refined. **—Ant.** undistinguished, common; infamous; unknown; unrefined, coarse.

distress, *n.* **1.** pain, anxiety, sorrow, grief, agony, anguish, misery, adversity, hardship, trial, tribulation, suffering, trouble, affliction. **2.** need, necessity, want, privation, deprivation, destitution, poverty, indigence. *—v.* **3.** trouble, worry, afflict, bother, grieve, pain, make miserable *or* unhappy. **—Ant.** comfort; fulfillment, opulence; console, mitigate, delight.

distribute, *v.* **1.** deal out, deal, allot, apportion, assign, mete, dole, dispense, give. **2.** disperse, spread, scatter. **3.** divide, separate, classify, categorize, dispose, sort, arrange. —**Ant.** collect, keep; unite.

distrust, *v.* **1.** doubt, suspect, mistrust. —*n.* **2.** doubt, suspicion, mistrust, misgiving. —**Ant.** trust, depend. —**Syn. Study.** See SUSPICION.

disturbance, *n.* **1.** perturbation, agitation, commotion, disorder, confusion, derangement. **2.** disorder, tumult, riot, uproar. —**Ant.** order, organization; calm, serenity.

diverge, *v.* **1.** branch off, separate, fork, bifurcate, divide. **2.** differ, deviate, disagree, vary. —**Ant.** converge, unite; agree, concur. —**Syn. Study.** See DEVIATE.

diverse, *adj.* **1.** unlike, dissimilar, separate, different, disagreeing. **2.** various, varied, multiform, manifold, variant, divergent. —**Ant.** similar, like. —**Syn. Study.** See VARIOUS.

divert, *v.* **1.** turn aside, deflect. **2.** draw aside *or* away, turn aside, distract. **3.** distract, entertain, amuse, delight, gratify, exhilarate. —**Ant.** fix; weary, bore, tire. —**Syn. Study.** See AMUSE.

divest, *v.* **1.** strip, unclothe, denude, disrobe, undress. **2.** strip, dispossess, deprive. —**Ant.** invest.

divide, *v.* **1.** separate, sunder, cut off, sever, shear, cleave, part. **2.** apportion, share, deal out, partition, distribute, portion. **3.** alienate, disunite, cause to disagree, estrange. **4.** distinguish, classify, sort, arrange, distribute. —**Ant.** unite; keep, retain; disarrange.

division, *n.* **1.** partition, dividing, separation, apportionment, allotment, distribution, sharing. **2.** mark, boundary, partition, demarcation. **3.** section, part, compartment, partition, segment. **4.** disagreement, dissension, difference, variance, rupture, disunion, discord, breach, rift, estrangement, alienation, feud. **—Ant.** agreement, union, accord.

divulge, *v.* disclose, reveal, make known, impart, tell, broadcast. **—Ant.** conceal.

do, *v.* **1.** perform, act. **2.** execute, finish, carry out, conclude, end, terminate, complete. **3.** accomplish, finish, achieve, attain, effect, bring about, execute, carry out. **4.** exert, put forth. **5.** cover, traverse. **6.** serve, suffice for. **7.** behave, proceed, act, fare, manage.

doctrine, *n.* tenet, dogma, theory, precept, belief, principle; teachings.

dodge, *v.* equivocate, quibble, evade, be evasive, elude.

dogged, See Syn. study at STUBBORN.

dominant, *adj.* **1.** ruling, governing, controlling, most influential, prevailing, prevalent, common, principal, predominant, paramount, preeminent, outstanding, important, first, ascendant. **2.** commanding, advantageous. **—Ant.** secondary, disadvantageous. **—Syn. Study.** DOMINANT, PREDOMINANT, PARAMOUNT describe something outstanding or supreme. DOMINANT applies to something that exerts control or influence: *the dominant powers at an international conference.* PREDOMINANT applies to something that is foremost at a specific time: *English is one of the world's predominant languages.* PARAMOUNT refers to something that is first in rank or order: *Safety is of paramount importance.*

donation, *n.* gift, contribution, offering, grant, benefaction, boon, largess, present, gratuity.

doom, *n.* **1.** fate, destiny, lot, fortune. **2.** ruin, death. **3.** judgment, decision, sentence, condemnation. **—v. 4.** destine, predestine, foreordain, decree. **5.** condemn, sentence, ordain.

dormant, *adj.* **1.** asleep, inactive, torpid, quiescent. **2.** quiescent, inoperative, in abeyance, latent, potential, inert, suspended. **—Ant.** awake, active; operative; kinetic. **—Syn. Study.** See INACTIVE.

doubt, *v.* **1.** distrust, mistrust, suspect, question. **2.** hesitate, waver. **—***n.* **3.** undecidedness, indecision, uncertainty, faltering, irresolution, hesitation, hesitancy, vacillation, misgiving, suspense; mistrust, distrust, suspicion. **—Ant.** trust; decision, certainty, conviction.

doubtful, *adj.* **1.** uncertain, unsure, ambiguous, equivocal, indeterminate, undecided, fifty-fifty. **2.** undetermined, unsettled, indecisive, dubious, enigmatic, problematic, puzzled. **3.** hesitating, hesitant, wavering, irresolute, vacillating, dubious, skeptical, incredulous. **—Ant.** certain, sure, unambiguous, decided; settled; unhesitating,

resolute. **—Syn. Study.** DOUBTFUL, DUBIOUS, INCREDULOUS, SKEPTICAL all involve a reluctance to be convinced. DOUBTFUL implies a strong feeling of uncertainty or indecision about something or someone: *to be doubtful about the outcome of a contest.* DUBIOUS usu. implies vacillation or hesitation caused by mistrust or suspicion: *dubious about the statements of a witness.* INCREDULOUS suggests an unwillingness or reluctance to believe: *incredulous at the good news.* SKEPTICAL implies a general disposition to doubt or question: *skeptical of human progress.*

dowdy, *adj.* ill-dressed, frumpy, shabby, old-maidish, old-fashioned. **—Ant.** fashionable, chic, modish, à la mode.

downhearted, *adj.* dejected, discouraged, depressed, downcast, despondent, disheartened, sad, sorrowful, unhappy,

dispirited, crestfallen.
—**Ant.** happy.

downright, *adj.* utter, absolute, complete, outright, positive, perfect, arrant, out-and-out, thoroughgoing, flat-out, unqualified, unmitigated.

drag, *v.* **1.** draw, pull, haul, trail, tug. **2.** trail, linger, loiter, slow. —**Ant.** drive, push; speed, expedite.

draw, *v.* **1.** drag, haul, pull, tug, tow, lead. **2.** attract, magnetize. **3.** delineate, sketch, draught, depict, trace. **4.** frame, formulate, compose, write, draw up, prepare, form. **5.** suck, inhale, drain. **6.** get, derive, deduce, infer, understand. **7.** produce, bring in, bear. **8.** draw *or* pull out, attenuate; extend, stretch, lengthen. **9.** extract. —**Ant.** drive, push.

dread, *v.* **1.** fear. —*n.* **2.** terror, fear, apprehension. **3.** awe, reverence, veneration. —*adj.* **4.** frightful, dire, terrible, dreadful, horrible. —**Ant.**

intrepidity, bravery; pleasant, delightful.

dreary, *adj.* **1.** gloomy, dismal, drear, cheerless, chilling, chill, depressing, comfortless. **2.** monotonous, tedious, wearisome, dull, boring, uninteresting, tiresome. —**Ant.** cheerful, comforting; interesting, engaging.

drench, *v.* steep, wet, soak, ret, saturate. —**Ant.** dry.

dress, *n.* **1.** costume, frock, gown. **2.** clothing, raiment, garb, attire, apparel, vesture, garments, vestments, clothes, suit, habit, habiliment. **3.** regalia, array, panoply. —*v.* **4.** attire, robe, garb, clothe, array, accouter, apparel, rig, deck out. **5.** trim, ornament, adorn, decorate. **6.** straighten, align. **7.** prepare, fit. —**Ant.** undress.

drink, *v.* **1.** imbibe, sip, quaff, swallow. **2.** tipple, tope. —*n.* **3.** beverage, potion, liquid refreshment, draft. —**Syn. Study.** DRINK, IMBIBE, SIP refer to taking liquids into the mouth. They are also used figuratively in the sense of taking in something through the mind or the senses. DRINK is the general word: *to drink coffee; to drink in the music.* IMBIBE is a more formal word, used most often in a figurative sense but also in reference to liquids, esp. alcohol: *to imbibe culture; to imbibe with discretion.* SIP implies drinking or absorbing little by little: *to sip a soda; to sip the words of Shakespeare.*

drive, *v.* **1.** push, force, impel, propel, send. **2.** overwork, overtask, overburden, overtax. **3.** urge, constrain, impel, compel, force. **4.** go, travel, ride. —*n.* **5.** vigor, pressure, effort, energy. —**Ant.** curb, restrain.

droll, *adj.* **1.** queer, odd, diverting, amusing, comical, waggish, witty, funny. —*n.* **2.** wag, buffoon, jester, comedian, clown, zany, punch, merry-andrew. **3.** joke, jest, clown. —**Ant.**

common; serious. —**Syn. Study.** See AMUSING.

droop, *v.* sink, bend, hang down, flag, languish, fail, weaken, decline, faint, wilt, wither, fade. —**Ant.** rise.

drove, *n.* herd, flock, company, crowd, host, collection.

drudgery, *n.* work, labor. —**Syn. Study.** See WORK.

drunkard, *n.* toper, sot, tippler, drinker, inebriate, dipsomaniac, alcoholic. —**Ant.** teetotaler, dry.

drunken, *adj.* drunk, sotted, besotted, tipsy, inebriated, intoxicated, befuddled. —**Ant.** sober.

dry, *adj.* **1.** arid, parched. **2.** wiped *or* drained away, evaporated. **3.** thirsty. **4.** plain, bald, unadorned, unembellished. **5.** dull, uninteresting, dreary, tiresome, boring, tedious, jejune, barren, vapid. **6.** humorous, sarcastic, biting, sardonic, keen, sharp, pointed, sly. —**Ant.** wet, drenched; interesting, fascinating; dull. —**Syn. Study.** DRY, ARID both mean without moisture. DRY is the general word indicating absence of water or freedom from moisture, which may be favorable or unfavorable: *a dry well; a dry bath towel.* ARID suggests intense dryness in a region or climate, resulting in bareness or in barrenness: *arid tracts of desert.*

dubious, *adj.* **1.** doubtful, undecided, indeterminate, uncertain, dubitable, fluctuating, wavering. **2.** questionable, equivocal, ambiguous, obscure, unclear. **—Ant.** definite, incisive, certain; unquestionable, unequivocal, clear. **—Syn. Study.** See DOUBTFUL.

dull, *adj.* **1.** slow, obtuse, stupid, blunted, unimaginative, sluggish, unintelligent, stolid. **2.** insensible, unfeeling, insensate, apathetic, unimpassioned, lifeless, callous, dead. **3.** listless, spiritless, torpid, inactive, lifeless, inert, inanimate. **4.** boring, depressing, ennuyant, tedious, uninteresting, tiresome, drear, dreary, vapid, wearisome, dry, jejune. **5.** blunt, dulled. **—v. 6.** blunt, deaden, stupefy, paralyze, obtund, benumb. **7.** depress, dishearten, discourage, dispirit, sadden, deject. **—Ant.** bright, imaginative, quick; sensitive; spirited, active, animated; interesting; sharp, clever; encourage, inspirit, hearten.

dumb, *adj.* **1.** mute, speechless, silent, voiceless. **2.** stupid. **—Ant.** voluble, talkative, loquacious.

duplicate, *adj.* **1.** double, twofold. **—n. 2.** facsimile copy, replica, reproduction, transcript. **—v. 3.** copy, replicate, reproduce, repeat, double, imitate. **—Ant.** original.

duplicity, *n.* deceitfulness, deceit, double-dealing, deception, guile, hypocrisy, dissimulation, chicanery, artifice, fraud, dishonesty, perfidy, treachery. **—Ant.** naiveté, honesty, openness, simplicity. **—Syn. Study.** See DECEIT.

durable, *adj.* lasting, enduring, stable, constant, permanent. —**Ant.** unstable, temporary, temporal.

dusky, *adj.* **1.** swarthy, dark. **2.** dim, shadowy, murky, cloudy, shady, obscure, clouded, penumbral. —**Ant.** fair, blond, light; clear, unclouded.

dutiful, *adj.* respectful, docile, submissive, deferential, reverential, obedient. —**Ant.** disrespectful, disobedient, irreverent.

duty, *n.* **1.** obligation. **2.** office, function, responsibility, service, business. **3.** homage, respect, deference, reverence. **4.** levy, tax, impost, custom, toll, excise. —**Syn. Study.** DUTY, OBLIGATION refer to something a person feels bound to do. A DUTY often applies to what a person performs in fulfillment of the permanent dictates of conscience, piety, right, or law: *one's duty to tell the truth; a parent's duty to raise children properly. An* OBLIGATION is what is expected at a particular time in fulfillment of a specific and often personal promise, contract, or agreement: *social or financial obligations.*

dwarf, *n.* **1.** homunculus, manikin, pygmy, midget, Lilliputian. **2.** runt. —*adj.* **3.** diminutive, tiny, small, little, Lilliputian, stunted, dwarfed, undersized. —*v.* **4.** stunt. —**Ant.** giant, colossus; huge, gigantic, immense, colossal. —**Syn. Study.** DWARF, MIDGET, PYGMY are terms for a very small person. A DWARF is someone checked in growth or stunted, or in some way not normally formed. A MIDGET (not in technical use) is someone normally proportioned, but diminutive. A PYGMY is properly a member of one of certain small-sized peoples of Africa and Asia, but the word is often used imprecisely to mean dwarf or midget. DWARF is a term often used to describe very small plants.

PYGMY is used to describe very small animals.

dwell, *v.* **1.** abide, reside, stay, live, inhabit. **2.** continue, perpetuate. **3.** linger, emphasize. **—Ant.** leave, depart; cease, end, terminate, stop.

dwelling, See Syn. study at HOUSE.

dwindle, *v.* diminish, lessen, decline, decrease, wane, shrink, waste away, degenerate, sink, decay. **—Ant.** increase, grow, wax. **—Syn. Study.** See DECREASE.

E

eager, *adj.* avid, ardent, enthusiastic, zealous, breathless, impatient, anxious, atingle, champing at the bit, raring to go. **—Ant.** reluctant, disinclined, hesitant.

earn, *v.* **1.** gain, acquire, win, get, obtain, secure, procure. **2.** merit, deserve. **—Syn. Study.** See GAIN.

earnest, *adj.* **1.** sincere, zealous, ardent, eager, fervent, resolute, serious, fervid, determined, purposeful. **2.** deep, firm, stable, intent, steady, faithful, true. **—Ant.** insincere, apathetic; faithless, unfaithful,

wavering. **—Syn. Study.** EARNEST, RESOLUTE, SERIOUS, SINCERE imply having qualities of steady purposefulness. EARNEST implies having a purpose and being steadily and soberly eager in pursuing it: *an earnest student.* RESOLUTE adds a quality of determination: *resolute in defending the rights of others.* SERIOUS implies having depth and a soberness of attitude that contrasts with gaiety and frivolity; it may include the qualities of both earnestness and resolution: *serious and thoughtful.* SINCERE suggests genuineness, trustworthiness, and absence of superficiality: *a sincere interest in a person's welfare.*

earth, *n.* **1.** globe, world. **2.** ground, soil, turf, sod, dirt, terra firma. —**Ant.** heaven; sky.

earthly, *adj.* **1.** terrestrial, worldly, mundane, earthy. **2.** possible, conceivable, imaginable. —**Ant.** spiritual; impossible, inconceivable. —**Syn. Study.** EARTHLY, TERRESTRIAL, WORLDLY, MUNDANE refer to that which is concerned with the earth literally or figuratively. EARTHLY now almost always implies a contrast to that which is heavenly: *earthly pleasures; our earthly home.* TERRESTRIAL applies to the earth as a planet or to land as opposed to water: *the terrestrial globe; terrestrial areas.* WORLDLY is commonly used in the sense of being devoted to the vanities, cares, advantages, or gains of physical existence to the exclusion of spiritual interests or the afterlife: *worldly success; worldly standards.* MUNDANE is a formal equivalent of WORLDLY and suggests that which is bound to the earth, is not exalted, and therefore is commonplace: *mundane pursuits.*

earthy, *adj.* **1.** plain, simple, unadorned, down-to-earth, unpretentious, matter-of-fact, unsophisticated, uncomplicated, direct, practical, pragmatic, clear-eyed. **2.** unrefined, impolite, rude, crude, vulgar, scatological, obscene, blue, gross. —**Ant.** refined, elevated, delicate.

ease, *n.* **1.** comfort, relaxation, rest, repose, well-being, effortlessness, contentment, happiness. **2.** tranquillity, serenity, calmness, quiet, quietude, peace. **3.** informality, unaffectedness, naturalness, lightness, flexibility, freedom. —*v.* **4.** comfort, relieve, disburden. **5.** tranquilize, soothe, allay, alleviate, mitigate, abate, assuage, lighten, lessen, reduce. **6.** facilitate. **—Ant.** discomfort, effort; disturbance, perturbation; affectation; burden; increase.

easy, *adj.* **1.** facile, light, gentle, moderate. **2.** tranquil, untroubled, comfortable, contented, satisfied, quiet, at rest. **3.** easygoing, compliant, submissive, complying, accommodating, agreeable, yelding. **4.** lenient. **5.** informal, unrestrained, unconstrained, brash, unembarrassed, smooth. **—Ant.** difficult, hard, immoderate; troubled, disturbed, uncomfortable, disagreeable, unyielding; restrained, embarrassed.

easygoing, *adj.* relaxed, placid, calm, serene, tranquil, even-tempered, composed, collected, easy, unruffled, posed, self-possessed, imperturbable, nonchalant, insouciant, laid-back, cool. **—Ant.** tense, rigid, demanding.

ebb, *n.* **1.** reflux, regression, regress, retrogression. **2.** decline, decay, deterioration, degeneration, wane. **—v. 3.** subside, abate, recede, retire. **4.** decline, sink, wane, decrease, decay, waste *or* fade away. **—Ant.** flow, neap; wax; increase, swell, well; rise.

eccentric, *adj.* **1.** off-center, uncentered, off-balance, unbalanced. **2.** odd, unusual, peculiar, unconventional, strange, curious, bizarre, aberrant, weird, freakish, offbeat, off-the-wall, oddball, bizzarro. **—n. 3.** character, oddity, original, strange one, crank, freak, oddball, odd duck.

eccentricity, *n.* idiosyncrasy, quirk, peculiarity, foible, odd characteristic, uncommon behavior, quirkiness. **—Syn. Study.** ECCENTRICITY, PECULIARITY, QUIRK, IDIOSYNCRASY all refer to some noticeable deviation in behavior, style, or manner from what is normal or expected. ECCENTRICITY usu. suggests a mildly amusing but harmless characteristic or style: *a whimsical eccentricity of dress.* PECULIARITY is the most general of these words, referring to almost any perceptible oddity or departure from any norm: *a peculiarity of the language.* QUIRK often refers to a minor, unimportant kind of oddity: *Her one quirk was a habit of writing long, rambling letters.* Sometimes QUIRK has overtones of strangeness: *sexual quirks.* IDIOSYNCRASY refers to a variation in behavior or manner exclusive to or characteristic of a single individual: *idiosyncrasies of style that irritated editors but often delighted readers.*

economical, *adj.* saving, provident, sparing, thrifty, frugal; stingy, tight, penurious. **—Ant.** lavish, spendthrift. **—Syn. Study.** ECONOMICAL, THRIFTY, FRUGAL imply careful and efficient use of resources. ECONOMICAL implies prudent planning in the disposition of resources so as to avoid unnecessary waste or expense: *It is economical to buy in large quantities.* THRIFTY adds the idea of industry and successful management: *a thrifty shopper looking for bargains.* FRUGAL suggests saving by denying oneself luxuries: *so frugal that he never takes taxis.*

economy, *n.* **1.** frugality, thriftiness, thrift, saving. **2.** management, system, method. **—Ant.** lavishness.

ecstasy, *n.* rapture, transport, exultation, apotheosis, jubilation, happiness, elation, delight, happiness, joy, bliss. **—Syn. Study.** ECSTASY, RAPTURE, TRANSPORT, EXULTATION share a sense of being taken out of oneself or one's normal state and entering a state of heightened feeling. ECSTASY suggests an emotion so overpowering and engrossing as to produce a trancelike state: *religious ecstasy; an ecstasy of grief.* RAPTURE most often refers to an elevated sensation of bliss or delight, either carnal or spiritual: *the rapture of first love.* TRANSPORT suggests a strength of feeling that often results in expression of some kind: *They jumped up and down in a transport of delight.* EXULTATION refers to a heady sense of personal well-being so powerful that one is lifted above normal emotional levels: *wild exultation at having finally broken the record.*

ecstatic, *adj.* overjoyed, joyful, elated, bursting, rapturous, delirious, exultant, jubilant, transported, on cloud nine, in seventh heaven, beside oneself, happy as a lark. —**Ant.** glum, dispirited, downhearted.

edge, *n.* **1.** border, rim, lip, margin, boundary, verge, brink. —*v.* **2.** inch, sidle. —**Ant.** center.

edifice, *n.* structure, building, construction, erection, pile.

edify, *v.* enlighten, educate, illuminate, improve, better, transform, uplift, raise, boost, lift, elevate.

educate, *v.* teach, instruct, school, drill, indoctrinate, train, discipline. —**Syn. Study.** See TEACH.

education, *n.* **1.** instruction, schooling, tuition, training. **2.** learning, knowledge, enlightenment, culture. —**Ant.** illiteracy.

eerie, *adj.* fearful, awesome, weird, uncanny, strange. —**Ant.** common, ordinary. —**Syn. Study.** See WEIRD.

effect, *n.* **1.** result, consequence, end, outcome, issue. **2.** power, efficacy, force, validity, weight. **3.** operation, execution; accomplishment, fulfillment. **4.** purport, intent, tenor, significance, signification, meaning, import. —*v.* **5.** bring about, accomplish, make happen, achieve, do, perform, complete, consummate, bring about, realize. —**Ant.** cause. —**Syn. Study.** EFFECT, CONSEQUENCE, RESULT refer to something produced by an action or a cause. An EFFECT is that which is produced, usu. more or less immediately and directly: *The drug had the effect of producing sleep.* A CONSEQUENCE, something that follows naturally or logically, as in a train of events or sequence of time, is less intimately connected with its cause than is an effect: *One consequence of a recession is a rise in unemployment.* A RESULT may be near or remote, and often is the sum of effects or consequences as making an end or final outcome: *The English language is the result of the fusion of many different elements.*

effective, *adj.* **1.** capable, competent, efficient, efficacious, effectual. **2.** operative, in force, active. —**Ant.** ineffective, incompetent, inefficient, ineffectual; inactive, inoperative. —**Syn. Study.** EFFECTIVE, EFFECTUAL, EFFICACIOUS, EFFICIENT refer to that which produces or is able to produce an effect. EFFECTIVE is applied to something that produces a desired or expected effect, often a lasting one: *an effective speech.* EFFECTUAL usually refers to something that produces a decisive outcome or result: *an effectual settlement.* EFFICACIOUS refers to something capable of achieving a certain end or purpose: *an efficacious remedy.* EFFICIENT, usually used of a person, implies skillful accomplishment of a purpose with little waste of effort: *an efficient manager.*

effects, See Syn. study at PROPERTY.

effectual, *adj.* effective. —**Ant.** ineffectual. —**Syn. Study.** See EFFECTIVE.

effeminate, See Syn. study at FEMALE.

efficacious, *adj.* effective.

—**Ant.** ineffective. —**Syn. Study.** See EFFECTIVE.

efficient, *adj.* effective.
—**Ant.** inefficient, ineffective. —**Syn. Study.** See EFFECTIVE.

effort, *n.* application, endeavor, exertion, nisus, attempt, struggle, striving.
—**Ant.** ease. —**Syn. Study.** EFFORT, APPLICATION, ENDEAVOR, EXERTION imply energetic activity and expenditure of energy. EFFORT is an expenditure of physical or mental energy to accomplish some objective: *He made an effort to control himself.* APPLICATION is continuous effort plus careful attention and diligence: *application to one's studies.* ENDEAVOR means a continued and sustained series of efforts to achieve some end, often worthy and difficult: *an endeavor to rescue survivors.* EXERTION is vigorous action or effort, frequently without an end in view: *out of breath from exertion.*

effusive, *adj.* demonstrative, extravagant, gushing, profuse, unrestrained, unrepressed, expansive, unreticent, talkative.
—**Ant.** taciturn, laconic.

egocentric, *adj.* self-centered, self-referencing, conceited, egotistic, egotistical, egomaniacal, selfish, spoiled, narcissistic, self-loving, self-absorbed, vain, vainglorious, stuck-up, stuck on oneself.
—**Ant.** modest, self-effacing, humble.

egoism, *n.* self-love, egotism, selfishness, self-conceit. —**Ant.** altruism. —**Syn. Study.** See EGOTISM.

egotism, *n.* self-centeredness, egoism, boastfulness, conceit.
—**Ant.** altruism, modesty. —**Syn. Study.** EGOTISM, EGOISM refer to preoccupation with one's ego or self. EGOTISM is the common word for a tendency to speak or write about oneself too much; it suggests selfishness and an inordinate sense of one's

own importance: *His egotism alienated most of his colleagues.* EGOISM, a less common word, emphasizes the moral justification of a concern for one's own welfare and interests, but carries less of an implication of boastful self-importance: *a healthy egoism that stood him well in times of trial.*

elaborate, *adj.* **1.** perfected, painstaking, labored, studied; detailed, ornate, intricate, complicated, complex. —*v.* **2.** produce, develop, work out, refine, improve. —**Ant.** simple; simplify.

elate, *v.* cheer, cheer up, excite, exhilarate, inspirit, exalt, lift, uplift. —**Ant.** depress, discourage.

elect, *v.* **1.** select, choose, prefer, pick out. —*adj.* **2.** select, chosen, choice. —**Ant.** refuse, reject; spurned.

elegant, *adj.* tasteful, fine, luxurious; refined, polished, cultivated, genteel, courtly, graceful; choice, nice, superior; excellent. —**Ant.** inelegant, distasteful; unrefined, disgraceful; inferior.

element, *n.* **1.** component, constituent, ingredient, unit, part, essential. **2.** rudiments, principle, basis, basics. **3.** habitat, environment, medium, milieu. —**Ant.** whole, nonessential; compound. —**Syn. Study.** ELEMENT, COMPONENT, CONSTITUENT, INGREDIENT refer to units that are parts of whole or complete substances, systems, compounds, or mixtures. ELEMENT denotes a fundamental, ultimate part: *the elements of matter; the elements of a problem.* COMPONENT refers to one of a number of separate parts: *Iron and carbon are components of steel.* CONSTITUENT refers to an active and necessary part: *The constituents of a molecule of water are two atoms of hydrogen and one of oxygen.* INGREDIENT is most frequently used in nonscientific contexts to denote any part that is combined into a mixture: *the ingredients of a cake; the ingredients of a successful marriage.*

elementary, *adj.* primary, rudimentary, basic, fundamental, rudimental; uncompounded, simple, uncomplicated. **—Ant.** advanced, secondary; complex, complicated.

elevate, *v.* raise, lift up, exalt, heighten, increase, intensify, promote, advance, improve, enhance, dignify, refine; animate, cheer. **—Ant.** lower, debase, decrease; depress. **—Syn. Study.** ELEVATE, ENHANCE, EXALT, HEIGHTEN mean to raise or make higher in some respect. To ELEVATE is to raise up to a higher level, position, or state: *to elevate the living standards of a group.* To ENHANCE is to add to the attractions or desirability of something: *Landscaping enhances the beauty of the grounds.* To EXALT is to raise very high in rank, character, estimation, mood, etc.: *A king is*

exalted above his subjects. To HEIGHTEN is to increase the strength or intensity: *to heighten one's powers of concentration.*

elevation, *n.* **1.** eminence, height, hill; altitude. **2.** loftiness, grandeur, dignity, nobility, nobleness, refinement, exaltation. **—Ant.** valley; depths. **—Syn. Study.** See HEIGHT.

elf, See Syn. study at FAIRY.

eligible, *adj.* suitable, qualified, acceptable, fitted, fit, worthy, admissible, desirable. **—Ant.** unsuitable, ineligible.

eliminate, *v.* get rid of, expel, remove, exclude, reject, omit, ignore. **—Ant.** include, accept.

elocution, *n.* oratory, declamation, rhetoric.

eloquent, *adj.* articulate, communicative, fluent, facile, persuasive, powerful, silver-tongued, stirring. **—Syn. Study.** ELOQUENT, ARTICULATE both refer to effective language or an effective user of language. ELOQUENT implies vivid, moving, and convincing expression: *an eloquent plea for disarmament*. ARTICULATE suggests fluent, clear, and coherent expression: *an articulate speaker.*

elucidate, *v.* explain, explicate, clarify, make plain *or* clear. —**Ant.** becloud, bedim, confuse. —**Syn. Study.** See EXPLAIN.

elude, *v.* **1.** avoid, escape, evade, slip away from, shun, dodge. **2.** baffle, confound, foil, thwart, confuse, frustrate, disconcert. —**Ant.** pursue, follow. —**Syn. Study.** See ESCAPE.

emanate, *v.* emerge, issue, proceed, come forth, originate, arise, spring, flow. —**Syn. Study.** See EMERGE.

embarrass, *v.* **1.** disconcert, abash, make uncomfortable, confuse, discomfit, discompose, chagrin. **2.** complicate, make difficult, perplex, mystify. **3.** impede, hamper, hinder, annoy, vex, trouble, harass, distress. —**Ant.** comfort, console; simplify.

embarrassment, *n.* **1.** disconcertment, abashment, perplexity, confusion, discomposure, discomfort, mortification, chagrin. **2.** trouble, annoyance, vexation, distress, harassment, hindrance, deterrent. —**Ant.** comfort, composure; encouragement. —**Syn. Study.** See SHAME.

embellish, *v.* **1.** beautify, ornament, adorn, decorate, garnish, bedeck, embroider. **2.** enhance, embroider, exaggerate about. —**Ant.** mar, disfigure, deface.

emblem, *n.* token, sign, symbol, figure, image, badge, device, mark.

embrace, *v.* **1.** clasp, hug. **2.** accept, adopt, espouse, welcome, seize. **3.** encircle, surround, enclose, contain. **4.** include, contain, comprise, comprehend, cover, embody. —**Ant.** exclude.

emend, See Syn. study at AMEND.

emerge, *v.* come forth, emanate, issue, spread, stream. —**Ant.** enter. —**Syn. Study.** EMERGE, EMANATE, ISSUE mean to come forth from a place or source. EMERGE is used of coming forth from concealment, obscurity, or something that envelops: *The sun emerged from behind the clouds.* EMANATE is used of intangible or immaterial things, as light or ideas, spreading from a source: *Rumors often emanate from irresponsible persons.* ISSUE is most often used of a number of persons, a mass of matter, or a volume of smoke, sound, or the like, coming forth through any outlet or outlets: *The crowd issued from the building.*

emergency, *n.* crisis, straits, urgency, turning-point, exigency, necessity, extremity, pinch, dilemma, quandary.

emigrate, See Syn. study at MIGRATE.

eminence, *n.* **1.** repute, distinction, prominence, celebrity, renown, conspicuousness, note, fame, rank, position. **2.** elevation, hill, prominence. —**Ant.** disrepute.

eminent, *adj.* **1.** distinguished, signal, notable, noteworthy, noted, reputable, prominent, celebrated, renowned, outstanding, illustrious, conspicuous, exalted. **2.** lofty, high, prominent, projecting, protruding, protuberant. —**Ant.** disreputable, commonplace, ordinary; low, debased; inconspicuous.

emit, *v.* **1.** send *or* give forth, discharge, eject, vent, exhale, exude, expel. **2.** issue, circulate, publish. —**Ant.** inspire, inhale, accept; hide.

emotion, *n.* feeling; sympathy, empathy. —**Ant.** apathy. —**Syn. Study.** See FEELING.

empathy, *n.* compassion, understanding, responsiveness, concern, caring, sensitivity, identification, involvement, sharing, fellow feeling, perceptiveness, perceptivity, sympathy. —**Ant.** callousness, indifference. —**Syn. Study.** See SYMPATHY.

emphasize, *v.* stress, accent, accentuate, italicize, bring out, underline, underscore, play up, highlight, feature, mark, spotlight, single out, punctuate. —**Ant.** de-emphasize, play down, underplay.

emphatic, *adj.* significant, marked, striking, positive, energetic, forcible, forceful, pronounced, strong, decided, unequivocal, definite. —**Ant.** insignificant, uncertain, unsure.

empire, *n.* **1.** power, sovereignty, dominion, rule, supremacy, authority. **2.** command, sway, rule, government, control.

employ, *v.* **1.** use, engage, hire, retain, occupy. **2.** use, apply, make use of. —*n.* **3.** service, employment.

employee, *n.* worker, servant, agent, clerk, wage earner. —**Ant.** employer, boss.

empower, *v.* **1.** enable, enfranchise, inspire, actualize, self-actualize. **2.** authorize, sanction, entitle, warrant, license. —**Ant.** disenfranchise, marginalize.

empty, *adj.* **1.** void, vacant, blank, unoccupied, uninhabited. **2.** unsatisfactory, meaningless, superficial, hollow, delusive, vain, ineffectual, ineffective, unsatisfying. **3.** frivolous, foolish. —*v.* **4.** unload, unburden, pour out, evacuate, drain, discharge. —**Ant.** full, replete, occupied, inhabited; satisfactory, effectual; serious.

emulation, *n.* competition, rivalry, contention, strife, envy.

enamor, *v.* inflame, captivate, bewitch, charm, fascinate, enchant.

enchant, *v.* fascinate, captivate, charm,

enrapture, transport, bewitch, delight. **—Ant.** bore.

encircle, *v.* surround, encompass, environ, gird, enfold, enclose.

enclose, *v.* surround, encircle, encompass, circumscribe. **—Ant.** exclude.

encounter, *v.* **1.** meet, confront, face. **2.** contend against, engage with, attack, cope with, compete with. **—***n.* **3.** meeting. **4.** battle, combat, conflict.

encourage, *v.* **1.** inspirit, embolden, hearten, stimulate, incite; reassure, assure, console, comfort. **2.** urge, abet, second, support, favor, countenance, advance, foster, promote, aid, help, foment. **—Ant.** discourage, dispirit.

encroach, *v.* trespass, intrude, invade, infringe. **—Syn. Study.** See TRESPASS.

encumber, *v.* **1.** impede, hamper, retard, embarrass, obstruct, complicate, involve, entangle. **2.** load, oppress, overload, burden.

—Ant. disencumber; unload, unburden.

end, *n.* **1.** extremity, extreme. **2.** limit, bound, boundary, termination, tip, terminus. **3.** close, termination, conclusion, finish, outcome, issue, consequence, result, completion, attainment. **4.** finale, conclusion, peroration. **5.** purpose, aim, object, objective, intention, design, intent, drift. **—***v.* **6.** terminate, conclude, wind up, finish, complete, close. **7.** stop, cease, discontinue, conclude. **—Ant.** beginning, start; begin, commence, open; continue. **—Syn. Study.** See AIM.

endeavor, *v.* **1.** attempt, essay, try, make an effort, strive, struggle, labor; seek, aim. **—***n.* **2.** exertion, struggle, essay, attempt, trial. **—Syn. Study.** See TRY. See also EFFORT.

endless, *adj.* limitless, unlimited, vast, illimitable, immeasurable, unending, boundless, infinite, interminable, incessant, unceasing, eternal, continuous, perpetual, everlasting. —**Ant.** limited, finite. —**Syn. Study.** See ETERNAL.

endow, *v.* equip, invest, clothe, endue, enrich; confer, bestow, give. —**Ant.** divest.

endowment, *n.* gift, grant, bequest, largess, bounty, present; capacity, talent, faculties, quality, power, ability, aptitude, capability, genius. —**Ant.** incapacity.

endure, *v.* **1.** sustain, hold out against, undergo, bear, support, suffer, experience. **2.** experience, stand, tolerate, bear, brook, allow, permit, submit. **3.** continue, last, persist, remain. —**Ant.** fail, subside; refuse; die, perish, fail. —**Syn. Study.** See BEAR. See also CONTINUE.

enemy, *n.* foe, adversary, opponent, antagonist. —**Ant.** friend, ally.

energetic, *adj.* **1.** forcible, vigorous, active. **2.** powerful, effective, effectual, strong, efficacious, potent. —**Ant.** lazy, inactive; ineffective, impotent, weak.

energy, *n.* **1.** activity, exertion, power, force, operation, dynamism, vigor, potency, zeal, push, spirit, animation, life. **2.** force, power, might, efficacy, strength, intensity. —**Ant.** inertia, inactivity; weakness.

engender, *v.* **1.** produce, cause, give rise to, beget, create, occasion, excite, stir up, incite, generate, breed. **2.** procreate, beget, create, generate, breed. —**Ant.** terminate; kill.

enhance, See Syn. study at ELEVATE.

enigma, *n.* puzzle, riddle, problem, question.

enjoin, *v.* **1.** charge, order, direct, prescribe, bid, command, require. **2.** prohibit, proscribe, interdict, ban, preclude. —**Ant.** encourage, allow.

enjoyment, *n.* delight, delectation, pleasure, gratification, happiness. —**Ant.** detestation, abhorrence, displeasure.

enlarge, *v.* extend,

augment, amplify, dilate, increase, aggrandize, magnify, expand, greaten. —**Ant.** limit, decrease, lessen, abate.

enlighten, *v.* illumine, edify, teach, inform, instruct, educate. —**Ant.** confuse.

enliven, *v.* **1.** invigorate, animate, inspirit, vivify, stimulate, quicken. **2.** exhilarate, gladden, cheer, brighten, inspire, delight. —**Ant.** dispirit, slow; depress.

enormous, *adj.* **1.** huge, immense, vast, colossal, mammoth, gigantic, prodigious, elephantine, monstrous. **2.** outrageous, atrocious, flagitious, depraved, wicked, flagrant, scandalous, egregious. —**Ant.** small, diminutive, tiny; honorable. —**Syn. Study.** See HUGE.

enrage, *v.* infuriate, anger, incense, inflame, provoke, madden, exasperate, aggravate. —**Ant.** tranquilize, calm, assuage. —**Syn. Study.** ENRAGE, INCENSE, INFURIATE imply

stirring to violent anger. To ENRAGE or to INFURIATE is to provoke wrath: *They enrage (infuriate) her by their deliberate and continual harassment.* To INCENSE is to inflame with indignation or anger: *to incense a person by making insulting remarks.*

ensue, *v.* follow, succeed; issue, arise, result, flow. —**Ant.** lead; precede. —**Syn. Study.** See FOLLOW.

entangle, *v.* **1.** complicate, ensnare, enmesh, tangle, knot, mat. **2.** embarrass, confuse, perplex, bewilder, involve, ensnare. —**Ant.** simplify.

enterprise, *n.* **1.** project, plan, undertaking, venture. **2.** boldness, readiness, spirit, energy.

enterprising, *adj.* ambitious, ready, resourceful, adventurous, venturesome, dashing, bold, energetic, spirited, eager, zealous. —**Ant.** smug, phlegmatic. —**Syn. Study.** See AMBITIOUS.

entertain, *v.* **1.** divert, amuse, please. **2.** receive, consider, admit. **3.** harbor, cherish, hold. —**Ant.** bore; refuse, reject; expel. —**Syn. Study.** See AMUSE.

enthusiasm, *n.* eagerness, earnestness, sincerity, interest, warmth, fervor, zeal, ardor, passion, devotion. —**Ant.** coolness.

enthusiast, *n.* **1.** zealot, devotee, fan. **2.** zealot, bigot, fanatic.

enthusiastic, *adj.* ardent, zealous, eager, fervent, passionate, vehement, fervid, burning, impassioned. —**Ant.** blasé, dispassionate, cool, unenthusiastic.

entice, *v.* allure, inveigle, excite, lure, attract, decoy, tempt, seduce, coax, cajole, wheedle, persuade. —**Ant.** discourage, deter, dissuade.

entire, *adj.* **1.** whole, complete, unbroken, perfect, unimpaired, intact, undiminished, undivided, continuous. **2.** full, complete, thorough, unqualified, unrestricted, unmitigated. —*n.* **3.** entirety. —**Ant.** partial,

imperfect, divided; restricted, incomplete. —**Syn. Study.** See COMPLETE.

entitle, *v.* **1.** empower, qualify. **2.** name, designate, call, title, dub. —**Ant.** disqualify.

entrance, *n.* **1.** entry, ingress, access, entree. **2.** entry, door, portal, gate, doorway, stoa, passage, inlet. **3.** admission, entry, admittance. —*v.* **4.** enrapture, enchant, charm, delight, transport. —**Ant.** exit; disenchant.

entreat, *v.* appeal, implore, beg, beseech, obsecrate, obtest, supplicate, crave, solicit, pray, importune, petition, sue.

entreaty, *n.* supplication, appeal, suit, plea, solicitation, petition.

enumerate, *v.* count, name, recount, recapitulate, rehearse, cite.

envelop, *v.* **1.** wrap, cover, enfold, hide, conceal. **2.** surround, enclose, encompass, cover, enfold.

environment, *n.* surroundings, atmosphere,

environs, setting, milieu, ambience, medium, situation, position, site. —**Syn. Study.** ENVIRONMENT, MILIEU, AMBIANCE, SETTING refer to the objects, conditions, or circumstances that influence the life of an individual or community. ENVIRONMENT may refer to physical or to social and cultural surroundings: *an environment of grinding poverty.* MILIEU, encountered most often in literary writing, refers to intangible surroundings: *a milieu of artistic innovation.* AMBIANCE applies to the mood or tone of the surroundings: *an ambiance of ease and elegance.* SETTING tends to highlight the person or thing surrounded by or set against a background: *a lovely setting for a wedding.*

envy, *n.* **1.** jealousy, enviousness, grudge, covetousness. —*v.* **2.** covet, begrudge, resent. —**Ant.** generosity. —**Syn. Study.** ENVY and JEALOUSY are very close in meaning. ENVY denotes a longing to possess something awarded to or achieved by another: *to feel envy when a friend inherits a fortune.* JEALOUSY, on the other hand, denotes a feeling of resentment that another has gained something that one more rightfully deserves: *to feel jealousy when a coworker receives a promotion.* JEALOUSY also refers to anguish caused by fear of losing someone or something to a rival: *a husband's jealousy of other men.*

ephemeral, *adj.* **1.** short-lived, transitory, temporary, fleeting, momentary, brief, evanescent. —*n.* **2.** will o' the wisp, St. Elmo's fire, corposant, ephemeron. —**Ant.** concrete, permanent.

epicure, *n.* gastronome, gourmet, epicurean, voluptuary, sensualist, glutton, gourmand.

episode, *n.* occurrence, event, incident, happening. —**Syn. Study.** See EVENT.

epoch, *n.* age, era, period, date. —**Syn. Study.** See AGE.

equable, *adj.* even, uniform, tranquil, steady, regular, even-tempered, temperate. —**Ant.** uneven, irregular, turbulent, intemperate.

equal, *adj.* **1.** proportionate, commensurate, balanced, coordinate, correspondent, equivalent, tantamount, like, alike. **2.** uniform, even, regular, unvarying, invariant. **3.** adequate, sufficient, competent, suitable, fit. —*n.* **4.** peer, compeer, match, mate, fellow. —*v.* **5.** match, be commensurate with. —**Ant.** unequal, disproportionate, incommensurate, dissimilar; uneven, irregular, variable; inadequate, insufficient, unsuitable.

equip, *v.* furnish, provide, fit out, outfit, rig, array, accouter. —**Syn. Study.** See FURNISH.

equipment, *n.* apparatus, paraphernalia, gear, accouterment.

equivocal, *adj.* **1.** ambiguous, uncertain. **2.** doubtful, uncertain, questionable, dubious, indeterminate. —**Ant.** unequivocal, certain; definite, unquestionable. —**Syn. Study.** See AMBIGUOUS.

era, See Syn. study at AGE.

eradicate, *v.* remove, destroy, extirpate, abolish, obliterate, uproot, exterminate, annihilate. —**Ant.** insert, add; originate, create.

erase, *v.* efface, expunge, cancel, obliterate. —**Ant.** create.

erect, *adj.* **1.** upright, standing, vertical. —*v.* **2.** build, raise, construct, upraise. **3.** set up, found, establish, institute. —**Ant.** horizontal; raze, destroy; dissolve, liquidate.

erroneous, *adj.* mistaken, incorrect, inaccurate, false, wrong, untrue. —**Ant.** correct, accurate, true.

error, *n.* **1.** mistake, blunder, slip, oversight. **2.**

offense, wrongdoing, fault, sin, transgression, trespass, misdeed, iniquity. —**Syn. Study.** See MISTAKE.

erudition, See Syn. study at LEARNING.

escape, *v.* **1.** flee, abscond, decamp, fly, steal away, run away. **2.** shun, fly, elude, evade, avoid. —*n.* **3.** flight; release. —**Syn. Study.** ESCAPE, ELUDE, EVADE mean to keep free of something. To ESCAPE is to succeed in keeping away from danger, pursuit, observation, etc.: *to escape punishment.* To ELUDE is to slip through an apparently tight net, thus avoiding, often by a narrow margin, whatever threatens; it implies using adroitness or slyness to baffle or foil: *The fox eluded the hounds.* To EVADE is to turn aside from or go out of reach of a person or thing, usually by directing attention elsewhere: *to evade the police.*

escort, *n.* **1.** convoy, guard, guide, protection, safeguard, guidance. —*v.* **2.** conduct, usher, guard, guide, convoy, accompany, attend. —**Syn. Study.** See ACCOMPANY.

especially, *adv.* particularly, chiefly, principally, unusually, significantly, prominently, signally, specially, markedly.

espouse, *v.* adopt, embrace, take up, ratify, endorse, accept. —**Ant.** renounce, apostatize, abjure.

espy, *v.* catch sight of, descry, discover, perceive, make out.

essential, *adj.* **1.** indispensable, necessary, vital, fundamental, rudimentary, elementary, basic, inherent, intrinsic, important. —*n.* **2.** necessity, basic, element. —**Ant.** dispensable, unnecessary, unimportant. —**Syn. Study.** ESSENTIAL, INHERENT, INTRINSIC refer to that which is in the natural composition of a thing. ESSENTIAL suggests that which is in the very essence or constitution of a thing: *Quiet is essential*

in a public library.
INHERENT means inborn or fixed from the beginning as a permanent quality or constituent of a thing: *properties inherent in iron.* INTRINSIC implies belonging to the nature of a thing itself and comprised within it, without regard to external considerations or accidentally added properties: *the intrinsic value of diamonds.* See also NECESSARY.

establish, *v.* **1.** set up, found, institute, form, organize, fix, settle, install. **2.** verify, substantiate, prove. **3.** appoint, ordain, fix, enact, decree. —**Ant.** liquidate, dissolve; disprove.

estate, See Syn. study at PROPERTY.

esteem, *v.* **1.** prize, value, honor, revere, respect, appreciate, estimate, regard. —*n.* **2.** respect, regard, favor, admiration, honor, reverence, veneration. **3.** estimation, valuation, estimate, appreciation. —**Ant.** disregard; disrespect,

disfavor; depreciation. —**Syn. Study.** See APPRECIATE. See also RESPECT.

estimable, *adj.* respectable, reputable, worthy, deserving, meritorious, good, excellent. —**Ant.** disreputable, unworthy, bad, inferior.

estimate, *v.* **1.** judge, compute, reckon, gauge, count, assess, value, evaluate, appraise. —*n.* **2.** judgment, calculation, valuation, estimation, opinion, computation.

estimation, *n.* judgment, opinion, appreciation, regard, honor, veneration, esteem, respect, reverence.

estrange, *v.* alienate, disaffect, antagonize, drive apart, make hostile, make unfriendly. —**Syn. Study.** ESTRANGE, ALIENATE, DISAFFECT share the sense of turning away from a state of affection, comradeship, or allegiance. ESTRANGE refers to the replacement of affection by apathy or hostility; it often involves physical separation: *lovers estranged by a misunderstanding.* ALIENATE often emphasizes the cause of antagonism: *His inconsiderate behavior alienated his friends.* DISAFFECT usu. refers to relationships involving allegiance or loyalty rather than love or affection: *disaffected workers ready to strike.*

eternal, *adj.* **1.** endless, everlasting, infinite, unending, never-ending, interminable, unceasing, perpetual, ceaseless, permanent. **2.** timeless, immortal, deathless, undying, imperishable, indestructible. **—Ant.** transitory, ephemeral; perishable, mortal. **—Syn. Study.** ETERNAL, ENDLESS, EVERLASTING, PERPETUAL imply lasting or going on without ceasing. That which is ETERNAL is, by its nature, without beginning or end: *God, the eternal Father.* That which is ENDLESS never stops but goes on continuously as if in a circle: *an endless succession of years.* That

which is EVERLASTING will endure through all future time: *a promise of everlasting life.* PERPETUAL implies continuous renewal far into the future: *perpetual strife between nations.*

ethical, *adj.* moral, virtuous, principled, high-principled, honest, upright, decent, honorable, conscientious, righteous, right-minded, right-thinking, upstanding, just, scrupulous. **—Ant.** unethical, immoral.

etiquette, *n.* decorum, propriety, code of behavior, convention, dignity. **—Ant.** impropriety, indignity.

eulogize, *v.* praise, extol, laud, commend, panegyrize, applaud. **—Ant.** criticize, condemn.

evade, *v.* **1.** escape, elude, escape from, avoid, shun, sidestep, dodge. **2.** baffle, foil, elude. **3.** prevaricate, equivocate, quibble, fence. **—Ant.** face, confront. **—Syn. Study.** See ESCAPE.

evaporate, *v.* **1.** vaporize,

dehydrate, dry. **2.** disappear, fade, vanish, evanesce. **—Ant.** condense, sublimate.

evasion, *n.* **1.** avoidance, dodging, escape. **2.** prevarication, equivocation, quibbling, subterfuge, sophistry.

even, *adj.* **1.** level, flat, smooth, plane. **2.** parallel, level. **3.** regular, equable, uniform, steady, well-balanced, in equilibrium, conforming, standard. **4.** commensurate, equal; square, balanced. **5.** calm, placid, tranquil, even-tempered, temperate, composed, peaceful. **6.** fair, just, equitable, impartial. **—adv. 7.** still, yet; just; fully, quite, completely; indeed. **—v. 8.** level, smooth; balance, equilibrate, counterpoise. **—Ant.** uneven, irregular; unsteady; unequal; agitated, intemperate; unfair, unjust, prejudiced, biased.

evening, *n.* eventide, dusk, twilight, gloaming, nightfall, eve, even, sundown. **—Ant.** dawn, sunrise.

event, *n.* **1.** occurrence, happening, affair, case, circumstance, episode, incident. **2.** result, issue, consequence, outcome. **—Syn. Study.** EVENT, EPISODE, INCIDENT refer to a happening. An EVENT is usu. an important happening, esp. one that comes out of and is connected with previous happenings: *historical events.* An EPISODE is one of a series of happenings, frequently distinct from the main course of events but arising from them and having an interest of its own: *an episode in her life.* An INCIDENT is usu. a minor happening that is connected with an event or series of events of greater importance: *an amusing incident in a play.*

ever, *adv.* **1.** continuously, eternally, perpetually, constantly, always. **2.** by any chance, at all, at any time. **—Ant.** never.

everlasting, *adj.* eternal. **—Ant.** ephemeral,

transitory. —**Syn. Study.**
See ETERNAL.

evidence, *n.* **1.** ground,
grounds, proof, testimony.
2. indication, sign, signal.
3. information, deposition,
affidavit, exhibit,
testimony, proof. —*v.* **4.**
make clear, show,
manifest, demonstrate.

evident, *adj.* plain, clear,
obvious, manifest,
palpable, patent,
unmistakable, apparent.
—**Ant.** concealed, hidden.
—**Syn. Study.** See
APPARENT.

evil, *adj.* **1.** wicked, bad,
immoral, amoral, sinful,
iniquitous, flagitious,
depraved, vicious, corrupt,
perverse, wrong, base, vile,
nefarious, malicious,
malignant, malevolent. **2.**
harmful, injurious, wrong,
bad, pernicious,
destructive, mischievous.
3. unfortunate, disastrous,
miserable. —*n.* **4.**
wickedness, depravity,
iniquity, unrighteousness,
sin, corruption, baseness,
badness. **5.** harm,
mischief, misfortune,
disaster, calamity, misery,

pain, woe, suffering,
sorrow. —**Ant.** good.

exact, *adj.* **1.** accurate,
correct, precise, literal,
faithful, close. **2.** strict,
rigorous, rigid, unbending,
exacting, demanding,
severe, scrupulous. **3.**
methodical, careful,
punctilious, accurate,
critical, nice, regular,
precise, orderly. —*v.* **4.**
call for, demand, require,
force, compel. **5.** extort,
wrest, wring, extract.
—**Ant.** inexact, inaccurate,
imprecise, unfaithful, free.

exalt, *v.* **1.** elevate,
promote, dignify, raise,
ennoble. **2.** praise, extol,
glorify, bless. **3.** elate,
make proud, please. **4.**
stimulate. **5.** intensify.
—**Ant.** lower, debase;
damn, condemn; displease.
—**Syn. Study.** See ELEVATE.

examination, *n.* **1.**
inspection, inquiry,
observation, investigation,
scrutiny, scanning,
inquisition. **2.** test, trial.
—**Syn. Study.** EXAMINATION,
INSPECTION, SCRUTINY refer
to a looking at something.
An EXAMINATION is an

orderly attempt to test or to obtain information about something, often something presented for observation: *an examination of merchandise for sale.* An INSPECTION is usu. a formal and official examination: *An inspection of the plumbing revealed a defective pipe.* SCRUTINY implies a critical and minutely detailed examination: *His testimony was given close scrutiny.*

examine, *v.* **1.** inspect, scrutinize, search, probe, explore, study, investigate, test. **2.** catechize.

example, *n.* sample, specimen, representative, illustration, case, pattern, model.

exasperate, *v.* irritate, annoy, vex, infuriate, exacerbate, anger, incense, provoke, nettle, needle, enrage, inflame. **—Ant.** calm, assuage, tranquilize.

exceed, *v.* overstep, transcend, surpass, cap, top, outdo, excel, outstrip, beat.

excel, *v.* surpass, outdo, exceed, transcend, outstrip, eclipse, beat, win over, cap, top.

excellence, *n.* superiority, eminence, preeminence, transcendence, distinction; merit, virtue, purity, goodness, uprightness. **—Ant.** baseness; inferiority.

excellent, *adj.* good, choice, worthy, fine, first-rate, estimable, superior, better, admirable, prime, (*slang*) def. **—Ant.** bad, inferior, base.

except, *prep.* **1.** but, save, excepting, excluding. **—***v.* **2.** exclude, leave out, omit, bar, reject. **—Ant.** including; include, admit.

exceptional, *adj.* unusual, extraordinary, irregular, peculiar, rare, strange, unnatural, anomalous, abnormal, aberrant. **—Ant.** customary, common, usual, normal, regular, natural.

excess, *n.* **1.** superfluity, superabundance, nimiety, redundancy. **2.** surplus, remainder. **3.** immoderation, intemperance, over-indulgence, dissipation. **—Ant.** lack, need, want.

excessive, *adj.* immoderate, extravagant, extreme, exorbitant, inordinate, outrageous, unreasonable, disproportionate. **—Ant.** reasonable, proportionate.

exchange, *v.* **1.** barter, trade, interchange, commute, swap, reciprocate. *—n.* **2.** interchange, trade, traffic, business, commerce, reciprocity, barter. **3.** market, bourse. **—Ant.** embargo.

exchangeable, *adj.* interchangeable, replaceable, returnable.

excitable, *adj.* emotional, passionate, fiery, quick-tempered, hot-tempered, hasty, irascible, irritable, choleric. **—Ant.** unemotional, cool, calm, serene, tranquil.

excite, *v.* **1.** stir, arouse, rouse, awaken, stimulate, animate, kindle, inflame, incite. **2.** stir up, provoke, disturb, agitate, irritate,

discompose. **—Ant.** pacify, calm, soothe.

excited, *adj.* ruffled, discomposed, stormy, perturbed, impassioned, stimulated, brisk, agitated, stirred up, agog, eager, enthusiastic. **—Ant.** calm, unruffled, composed.

excitement, *n.* agitation, commotion, ado, to do, perturbation, disturbance. **—Ant.** serenity, peace.

exclamation, *n.* outcry, ejaculation, interjection, cry, complaint, protest, vociferation, shout, clamor.

exclude, *v.* **1.** bar, restrain, keep out, shut out. **2.** debar, eliminate, expel, eject, reject, prohibit, withhold, except, omit, preclude; proscribe, prevent. **—Ant.** include; accept.

exclusive, *adj.* **1.** incompatible, excluding, barring. **2.** restrictive, cliquish, snobbish, fastidious. **3.** single, sole, only, special. **4.** select, narrow, clannish, snobbish, selfish, illiberal, narrow, narrow-minded, uncharitable. **5.** fashionable, chic, aristocratic, choice. —**Ant.** inclusive, including; general; liberal; poor.

excursion, *n.* **1.** journey, tour, trip, jaunt, junket, outing, cruise. **2.** deviation, digression, episode.

excuse, *v.* **1.** forgive, pardon, overlook, acquit, absolve, exonerate, exculpate. **2.** apologize for, exonerate, exculpate, clear, vindicate. **3.** extenuate, palliate, justify. **4.** release, disoblige, free, liberate, disencumber. —*n.* **5.** plea, apology, absolution, justification. **6.** pretext, pretense, subterfuge, evasion, makeshift. —**Ant.** condemn; oblige, shackle. —**Syn. Study.** EXCUSE, FORGIVE, PARDON imply being lenient or giving up the wish to punish. EXCUSE means to overlook some (usu.) slight offense, because of circumstance, realization that it was unintentional, or the like:

to excuse rudeness. FORGIVE is applied to excusing more serious offenses; the person wronged not only overlooks the offense but harbors no ill feeling against the offender: *to forgive and forget.* PARDON often applies to an act of leniency or mercy by an official or superior; it usu. involves a serious offense or crime: *The governor was asked to pardon the condemned criminal.*

execute, *v.* **1.** carry out, accomplish, do, perform, achieve, effect, consummate, finish, complete. **2.** kill, put to death, hang. **3.** enforce, effectuate, administer; sign, seal, and deliver.

exemption, *n.* immunity, impunity, privilege, freedom, exception. —**Ant.** culpability. —**Syn. Study.** EXEMPTION, IMMUNITY, IMPUNITY imply special privilege or freedom from requirements imposed on others. EXEMPTION implies release or privileged freedom from sharing with others some duty or legal requirement: *exemption from military service.* IMMUNITY implies freedom from a penalty or from some natural or common liability, esp. one that is disagreeable or threatening: *immunity from prosecution; immunity from disease.* IMPUNITY (limited mainly to the expression *with impunity*) suggests freedom from punishment: *The police force was so inadequate that crimes could be committed with impunity.*

exercise, *n.* **1.** exertion, labor, toil, work, action, activity. **2.** drill, practice, training, schooling, discipline. **3.** practice, use, application, employment, performance, operation. **4.** ceremony, ritual, procedure, observance, service. —*v.* **5.** discipline, drill, train, school. **6.** practice, use, apply, employ, effect, exert. **7.** discharge, perform. **8.** worry, annoy, make uneasy, try, burden,

trouble, pain, afflict. —**Ant.** laziness.

exertion, *n.* effort, action, activity, endeavor, struggle, attempt, strain, trial. —**Syn. Study.** See EFFORT.

exhaust, *v.* **1.** empty, drain, void. **2.** use up, expend, consume, waste, squander, dissipate, spend, fritter away. **3.** enervate, tire, prostrate, wear out, fatigue, weaken, cripple, debilitate. —*n.* **4.** fumes, smoke, vapor, effluvium. —**Ant.** fill; use; innervate, invigorate, strengthen.

exhaustion, *n.* weariness, lassitude, weakness, fatigue. —**Ant.** energy, exhilaration, strength.

exhibit, *v.* **1.** expose, present, display, show, demonstrate, offer. **2.** manifest, display, show, betray, reveal, express, disclose, indicate, evince. —*n.* **3.** exhibition, showing, show, display, demonstration, offering, exposition, manifestation. **4.** evidence, testimony.

—**Ant.** conceal, hide.
—**Syn. Study.** See DISPLAY.

exhilarate, *v.* make cheerful *or* merry, cheer, gladden, enliven, inspirit, animate, inspire, elate. —**Ant.** depress, sadden, deject.

exonerate, *v.* **1.** absolve, exculpate, clear, acquit, vindicate, justify. **2.** relieve, release, discharge, except, exempt, free. —**Ant.** blame, condemn; imprison. —**Syn. Study.** See ABSOLVE.

exorbitant, *adj.* exceeding, excessive, inordinate, extravagant, unreasonable, unconscionable, enormous. —**Ant.** reasonable, inexpensive.

expand, *v.* increase, extend, swell, enlarge, dilate, distend, inflate, bloat, aggrandize, spread *or* stretch out, unfold, develop. —**Ant.** contract, shrink. —**Syn. Study.** See INCREASE.

expect, *v.* look forward to, anticipate, await, hope for, wait for, count on, rely on.

expectation, *n.* expectancy, anticipation, hope, trust, prospect.

expedient, *adj.* **1.** advantageous, fit, suitable, profitable, advisable, proper, appropriate, desirable. —*n.* **2.** device, contrivance, means, resource, shift, resort. —**Ant.** unsuitable, inapt, undesirable.

expedite, *v.* speed up, hasten, quicken, speed, push, accelerate, hurry, precipitate; dispatch. —**Ant.** slow.

expedition, *n.* **1.** excursion, journey, voyage, trip, junket, safari. **2.** promptness, speed, haste, quickness, dispatch, alacrity. —**Ant.** sloth. —**Syn. Study.** See TRIP.

expel, *v.* drive *or* force away, drive *or* force out, discharge, eject; dismiss, oust, banish, exile, expatriate, (*British*) send down. —**Ant.** accept, invite.

expend, *v.* **1.** use, employ, consume, spend, exhaust, use up. **2.** pay, disburse, spend, lay out. **—Ant.** save, husband, conserve.

expense, *n.* **1.** cost, charge, price, outlay, expenditure. **2.** loss, injury, harm, debit, detriment.

expensive, *adj.* costly, dear, high-priced. **—Ant.** inexpensive, cheap, tawdry.

experience, *n.* **1.** undergoing, feeling, encountering. **2.** knowledge, wisdom, sagacity. —*v.* **3.** meet with, undergo, feel, encounter, live through, know, observe; endure; suffer. **—Ant.** inexperience, naiveté.

experienced, *adj.* skilled, expert, veteran, practiced, accomplished, versed, qualified, adroit, adept. **—Ant.** inexperienced, inexpert, naive, artless, unqualified.

experiment, *n.* **1.** test, trial, examination, proof, assay, procedure. **2.** experimentation, research, investigation. —*v.* **3.** try, test, examine, prove, assay.

expert, *n.* **1.** specialist, authority, connoisseur, master. —*adj.* **2.** trained, skilled, skillful, experienced, proficient, dexterous, adroit, clever, apt, quick. **—Ant.** butcher, shoemaker, dolt; untrained, inexperienced, maladroit. **—Syn. Study.** See SKILLFUL.

explain, *v.* **1.** elucidate, expound, explicate, interpret, clarify, throw light on, make plain *or* manifest. **2.** account for, justify. **—Ant.** confuse. **—Syn. Study.** EXPLAIN, ELUCIDATE, EXPOUND, INTERPRET imply making the meaning of something clear or understandable. To EXPLAIN is to make plain, clear, or intelligible something that is not known or understood: *to explain a theory.* To ELUCIDATE is to throw light on what before was dark and obscure, usu. by illustration and commentary and sometimes by elaborate explanation: *They asked her to elucidate her statement.* To EXPOUND is to give a methodical, detailed, scholarly explanation of something, usu. Scriptures, doctrines, or philosophy: *to expound the doctrine of free will.* To INTERPRET is to give the meaning of something by paraphrase, by translation, or by an explanation based on personal opinion: *to interpret a poem.*

explanation, *n.* **1.** explaining, elucidation, explication, exposition, definition, interpretation, description. **2.** meaning, interpretation, solution, key, answer, definition, account, justification.

explicit, *adj.* **1.** clear, unequivocal, express, unambiguous, precise, definite, exact, categorical, determinate. **2.** open, outspoken, definite, unashamed, unabashed. —**Ant.** unclear, equivocal, ambiguous, indefinite; clandestine, concealed.

exploit, *n.* **1.** deed, feat, accomplishment, achievement. —*v.* **2.** use, utilize, take advantage of.

expose, *v.* **1.** lay open, subject, endanger, imperil, jeopardize. **2.** bare, uncover; exhibit, display. **3.** make known, betray, uncover, unveil, disclose, reveal, unmask, bring to light; muckrake. —**Ant.** conceal, hide.

exposition, *n.* **1.** exhibit, exhibition, show, demonstration, display. **2.** explanation, elucidation, commentary, treatise, critique, interpretation, exegesis, explication.

exposure, *n.* **1.** exposing; disclosure, unmasking, presentation, display, divulgement, revelation, exposé. **2.** aspect, orientation. —**Ant.** hiding, concealment.

expound, See Syn. study at EXPLAIN.

express, *v.* **1.** utter, declare, state, word, speak, assert, asseverate. **2.** show, manifest, reveal, expose, indicate, exhibit, represent. **3.** indicate, signify, designate, denote. **4.** press *or* squeeze out. —*adj.* **5.** clear, distinct, definite, explicit, plain, obvious, positive, unambiguous, categorical; unsubtle. **6.** special, particular, singular, signal. **7.** faithful, exact, accurate, precise, true, close. **8.** swift, direct, fast, rapid, nonstop. —*n.* **9.** courier, special messenger. **—Ant.** conceal.

expression, *n.* **1.** utterance, declaration, assertion, statement. **2.** phrase, term, idiom. **3.** language, diction, phraseology, wording, phrasing, presentation. **4.** manifestation, sign. **5.** look, countenance, aspect, air, mien, intonation, tone. **—Ant.** silence.

expressive, *adj.* **1.** meaning, significant, suggestive, meaningful, indicative. **2.** lively, vivid, strong, emphatic. **—Ant.** expressionless, meaningless.

exquisite, *adj.* **1.** dainty, beautiful, elegant, rare, delicate, appealing, charming. **2.** fine, admirable, consummate, perfect, matchless, complete, valuable, precious. **3.** intense, acute, keen, poignant. **4.** sensitive, responsive. **5.** rare, select, choice, excellent, precious, valuable, priceless; vintage. **6.** refined, elegant, delicate, discriminating, polished, debonair. **—Ant.** ugly, hideous; imperfect, valueless, worthless; dull; vacuous, vapid; common, ordinary; poor, inferior; boorish. **—Syn. Study.** See DELICATE.

extemporaneous, *adj.* extemporary, extempore, impromptu, improvised, unpremeditated, offhand, off the cuff. **—Ant.** prepared, premeditated. **—Syn. Study.** EXTEMPORANEOUS, IMPROMPTU are used of expression that is not planned. EXTEMPORANEOUS may refer to a speech given without any advance preparation: *extemporaneous remarks.* IMPROMPTU is also used of a speech, but often refers to a poem, song, etc., delivered without preparation and at a moment's notice: *She entertained the guests with some impromptu rhymes.*

extend, *v.* **1.** stretch *or* draw out, attenuate. **2.** lengthen, prolong, protract, continue. **3.** expand, spread out, dilate, enlarge, widen, diffuse, fill out. **4.** hold forth, offer, bestow, grant, give, impart, yield. **—Ant.** shorten, abbreviate; discontinue; shrink, curtail. **—Syn. Study.** See LENGTHEN.

extension, *n.* **1.** stretching, expansion, enlargement, dilation, dilatation, increase. **2.** prolongation, lengthening, protraction, continuation; delay. **3.** extent, limit. **—Ant.** shrinking, decrease; curtailment.

extensive, *adj.* **1.** wide, broad, large, extended, spacious, ample, vast. **2.** far-reaching, comprehensive, thorough; inclusive.

extent, *n.* space, degree, magnitude, measure, amount, scope, compass, range, expanse, stretch, reach, size; length, area, volume.

exterior, *adj.* **1.** outer, outside, outward, external, outer, superficial. **2.** outlying, extraneous, foreign, extrinsic. **—n. 3.** outside, face. **4.** appearance, mien, aspect, face. **—Ant.** interior, inner; important; interior, inside.

exterminate, *v.* extirpate, annihilate, destroy, eradicate, abolish, eliminate. **—Ant.** create, generate, originate.

extinct, *adj.* **1.** extinguished, quenched, out, put out. **2.** obsolete, archaic. **3.** ended, terminated, over, dead, gone, vanished. **—Ant.** extant; modern; begun, initiated.

extol, *v.* praise, laud, eulogize, commend, glorify, exalt, celebrate, applaud, panegyrize. **—Ant.** condemn, damn.

extort, *v.* extract, exact, wrest, wring, blackmail, bleed.

extract, *v.* **1.** draw forth *or* out, get, pull *or* pry out. **2.** deduce, divine, understand. **3.** extort, exact, evoke, educe, draw out, elicit, wrest, wring, bleed. **4.** derive, withdraw, distill. —*n.* **5.** excerpt, quotation, citation, selection. **6.** decoction, distillate, solution.

extraneous, *adj.* external, extrinsic, foreign, alien, adventitious; inappropriate, not germane, not pertinent, nonessential, superfluous. —**Ant.** internal, intrinsic; appropriate, pertinent, essential, vital.

extraordinary, *adj.* exceptional, special, inordinate, uncommon, singular, signal, rare, phenomenal, remarkable, unusual, egregious, unheard-of, drop-dead. —**Ant.** ordinary, common, usual, customary.

extravagant, *adj.* **1.** imprudent, wasteful, lavish, spendthrift, prodigal, immoderate, excessive, inordinate, exorbitant. **2.** unreasonable, fantastic, wild, foolish, absurd. —**Ant.** prudent, thrifty, moderate; reasonable, thoughtful, sensible.

extreme, *adj.* **1.** utmost, greatest, rarest, highest; superlative. **2.** outermost, endmost, ultimate, last, uttermost, remotest. **3.** extravagant, immoderate, excessive, fanatical, uncompromising, radical, outré, unreasonable. **4.** last, final, ultimate. —*n.* **5.** farthest, furthest, remotest. **6.** acme, limit, end; extremity. —**Ant.** reasonable.

extremity, *n.* **1.** terminal, limit, end, termination, extreme, verge, border, boundary, bounds. **2.** utmost, extreme.

exuberance, *n.* exuberancy, superabundance, excess, copiousness, profusion, luxuriance, lavishness, superfluity, redundancy, overflow. —**Ant.** paucity, lack, need, want.

exultation, See Syn. study at ECSTASY.

F

fable, *n.* **1.** legend, tale, apologue, parable, allegory, myth, story. **2.** lie, untruth, falsehood, fib, fiction, invention, fabrication, forgery. —*v.* **3.** lie, fib, fabricate, invent. —**Ant.** truth, gospel. —**Syn. Study.** See LEGEND.

fabricate, *v.* **1.** construct, build, frame, erect, make, manufacture. **2.** assemble, put together, erect. **3.** devise, invent, coin, feign; forge, fake. —**Ant.** destroy, raze.

fabulous, *adj.* **1.** unbelievable, incredible, amazing, astonishing, astounding. **2.** untrue, unreal, unrealistic, invented, fabled, fictional, fictitious, fabricated, coined, made up, imaginary. —**Ant.** commonplace; real, natural.

face, *n.* **1.** countenance, visage, front, features, look, expression, appearance, aspect, mien; sight, presence. **2.** show, pretense, pretext, exterior. **3.** name, prestige, reputation. —*v.* **4.** meet face to face, confront, encounter, meet, meet with. **5.** oppose. **6.** cover, veneer. —**Ant.** back; absence; interior. —**Syn. Study.** FACE, COUNTENANCE, VISAGE refer to the front of the (usu. human) head. FACE is used when referring to physical features: *a pretty face with high cheekbones.* COUNTENANCE, a more formal word, denotes the face as it is affected by or reveals a person's state of mind; hence, it often signifies the look or expression on the face: *a thoughtful countenance.* VISAGE, still more formal, refers to the face as seen in a certain aspect, esp. as revealing a person's character: *a stern visage.*

facet, *n.* aspect, side, angle, position, posture, phase, view, viewpoint, feature, light, slant, particular, detail.

facetious, *adj.* amusing, humorous, comical, funny, witty, droll, jocular. —**Ant.** sad.

facile, *adj.* **1.** effortless, easy, adroit, deft, dexterous, fluent, flowing, smooth, graceful, elegant. **2.** superficial, glib, slick, surface, shallow, slight. —**Ant.** labored, laborious, profound.

faction, *n.* side, bloc, camp. group, party, sect, interest, division, wing, denomination, order, school, society, body.

factory, *n.* manufactory, mill, workshop, plant.

factual, *adj.* actual, real, true, demonstrable, provable, evidential, evidentiary, verifiable, de facto, genuine, certain, undoubted, unquestioned, valid. —**Ant.** imaginary, groundless, illusory.

faculty, *n.* ability, capacity, aptitude, capability, knack, turn, talent. —**Ant.** inability, incapacity. —**Syn. Study.** See ABILITY.

fade, *v.* **1.** wither, droop, languish, decline, decay. **2.** blanch, bleach, pale. **3.** disappear, vanish, die out, pass away, evanesce. —**Ant.** flourish; flush; appear. —**Syn. Study.** See DISAPPEAR.

fail, *v.* **1.** come short, fall short, disappoint. **2.** fall off, dwindle, pass *or* die away, decline, fade, weaken, sink, wane, give out, cease, disappear. **3.** desert, forsake, disappoint. —**Ant.** succeed.

failing, *n.* shortcoming, weakness, foible, deficiency, defect, frailty, imperfection, fault, flaw. —**Ant.** success, sufficiency; strength. —**Syn. Study.** See FAULT.

failure, *n.* **1.** unsuccessfulness, miscarriage, abortion, failing. **2.** neglect, omission, dereliction, nonperformance. **3.**

deficiency, insufficiency, defectiveness. **4.** decline, decay, deterioration, loss. **5.** bankruptcy, insolvency, failing, bust; dud. **—Ant.** success; adequacy, sufficiency, effectiveness.

faint, *adj.* **1.** indistinct, ill-defined, dim, faded, dull. **2.** feeble, half-hearted, faltering, irresolute, weak, languid, drooping. **3.** feeble, languid, swooning. **4.** cowardly, timorous, pusillanimous, fearful, timid, dastardly, faint-hearted. —*v.* **5.** swoon, pass out, black out. —*n.* **6.** swoon, unconsciousness. **—Ant.** strong; distinct; brave, bold.

fair, *adj.* **1.** unbiased, equitable, just, honest, impartial, disinterested, unprejudiced. **2.** reasonable, passable, tolerable, average, middling. **3.** likely, favorable, promising, hopeful. **4.** bright, sunny, cloudless; fine. **5.** unobstructed, open, clear, distinct, unencumbered,

plain. **6.** clean, spotless, pure, untarnished, unsullied, unspotted, unblemished, unstained. **7.** clear, legible, distinct. **8.** light, blond, white, pale. **9.** beautiful, lovely, comely, pretty, attractive, pleasing, handsome. **10.** courteous, civil, polite, gracious. —*adv.* **11.** straight, directly. **12.** favorably, auspiciously. —*n.* **13.** exhibit, exhibition, festival, kermis. **—Ant.** unfair. **—Syn. Study.** FAIR, IMPARTIAL, DISINTERESTED refer to lack of bias in opinions, judgments, etc. FAIR implies the treating of all sides alike, justly and equitably: *a fair compromise.* IMPARTIAL also implies showing no more favor to one side than another, but suggests particularly a judicial consideration of a case: *an impartial judge.* DISINTERESTED implies a fairness arising from lack of desire to obtain a selfish advantage: *a disinterested concern that the best person win.*

fairy, *n.* fay, pixy, leprechaun, nix, nixie, brownie, elf, sprite.

faith, *n.* **1.** confidence, trust, reliance, credit, credence, assurance. **2.** belief, doctrine, tenet, creed, dogma, religion, persuasion. —**Ant.** discredit, distrust.

faithful, *adj.* **1.** strict, thorough, true, devoted. **2.** true, reliable, trustworthy, trusty. **3.** stable, dependable, steadfast, stanch, loyal, constant. **4.** credible, creditable, believable, trustworthy, reliable. **5.** strict, rigid, accurate, precise, exact, conscientious, close. —*n.* **6.** believers. —**Ant.** unfaithful, faithless. —**Syn. Study.** FAITHFUL, CONSTANT, LOYAL imply qualities of stability, dependability, and devotion. FAITHFUL implies enduring fidelity to what one is bound to by a pledge, duty, or obligation: *a faithful friend.* CONSTANT suggests lack of change in affections or loyalties: *a constant companion through thick and thin.* LOYAL implies firm support and defense of a person, cause, institution, or idea considered to be worthy: *a loyal citizen.*

faithless, *adj.* **1.** disloyal, false, inconstant, fickle, perfidious, treacherous. **2.** unreliable, untrustworthy, untrue. **3.** untrusting; unbelieving, doubting. **4.** atheistic, agnostic, heathen, infidel. —**Ant.** faithful.

fake, *adj.* **1.** fraudulent, false, unreal, forged, fabricated, counterfeit, bogus, phony, sham, spurious, pretend, pinchbeck. —*n.* **2.** fraud, hoax, imposture, deception, counterfeit, sham, phony. —*v.* **3.** pretend, feign, affect, counterfeit, sham, simulate, act.

false, *adj.* **1.** erroneous, incorrect, mistaken, wrong, untrue, improper. **2.** untruthful, lying, mendacious, untrue. **3.** deceitful, treacherous, faithless, insincere, hypocritical, disingenuous, disloyal, unfaithful, two-faced, inconstant, recreant, perfidious, traitorous. **4.** deceptive, deceiving, misleading, fallacious. **5.** spurious, artificial, bogus, phony, forged, sham, counterfeit. **6.** substitute, ersatz, supplementary, stand-in. —**Ant.** true; genuine. —**Syn. Study.** FALSE, SHAM, COUNTERFEIT agree in referring to something that is not genuine. FALSE is used mainly of imitations of concrete objects; it sometimes implies an intent to deceive: *false teeth; false hair.* SHAM is rarely used of concrete objects and usu. has the suggestion of intent to deceive: *sham title; sham tears.* COUNTERFEIT always has the implication of cheating; it is used particularly of spurious imitation of coins and paper money.

falsehood, *n.* lie, fib, untruth, distortion, fabrication, fiction. —**Ant.** truth.

falsify, *v.* See Syn. study at MISREPRESENT.

falter, *v.* **1.** hesitate, vacillate, waver, tremble. **2.** stammer, stutter.

fame, *n.* reputation, estimation, opinion, consensus, repute, renown, eminence, celebrity, honor, glory; notoriety. —**Ant.** infamy, disrepute.

familiar, *adj.* **1.** common, well-known, frequent. **2.** well-acquainted, conversant, well-versed. **3.** easy, informal, unceremonious, unconstrained, free. **4.** intimate, close, friendly, amicable. **5.** presuming, presumptive, unreserved, disrespectful. **6.** tame, domesticated. —*n.* **7.** friend, associate, companion. —**Ant.** unfamiliar, unknown. —**Syn. Study.** FAMILIAR, CONFIDENTIAL, INTIMATE suggest a friendly relationship between persons, based on frequent association, common interests, etc. FAMILIAR suggests an easygoing and unconstrained relationship between persons who are well-acquainted: *on familiar terms with one's neighbors.* CONFIDENTIAL implies a sense of mutual trust that extends to the sharing of confidences and secrets: *a confidential adviser.* INTIMATE connotes a very close and warm relationship characterized by empathy and sharing of private thoughts: *intimate letters to a friend.*

familiarity, *n.* **1.** acquaintance, knowledge, understanding. **2.** intimacy, liberty, freedom, license, disrespect. **3.** informality, unconstraint, freedom. —**Ant.** unfamiliarity.

famous, *adj.* celebrated, renowned, well-known, famed, notable, eminent, distinguished, illustrious, honored. —**Ant.** unknown, undistinguished. —**Syn. Study.** FAMOUS, CELEBRATED, RENOWNED, NOTORIOUS refer to someone or something widely known. FAMOUS is the general word for a person or thing that receives wide public notice, usu. favorable: *a famous lighthouse.* CELEBRATED refers to a famous person or thing that enjoys wide public praise or honor for merit, services, etc.: *a celebrated poet.* RENOWNED usu. implies wider, greater, and more enduring fame and glory: *a renowned hospital.* NOTORIOUS means widely known and discussed because of some bad or evil quality or action: *a notorious criminal.*

fanatic, *n.* zealot, devotee, extremist, maniac, hothead, *(slang)* freak, nut. —**Syn. Study.** FANATIC, ZEALOT, DEVOTEE refer to persons showing more than ordinary enthusiasm or support for a cause, belief, or activity. FANATIC and ZEALOT both suggest extreme or excessive devotion. FANATIC further implies unbalanced or obsessive behavior: *a wild-eyed fanatic.* ZEALOT, slightly less unfavorable in implication, implies single-minded partisanship:

a tireless zealot for tax reform. DEVOTEE is a milder term, suggesting enthusiasm but not to the exclusion of other interests or possible points of view: *a devotee of baseball.*

fanatical, *adj.* zealous, enthusiastic, visionary, frenzied, rabid. —**Ant.** apathetic.

fancy, *n.* **1.** imagination, fantasy. **2.** image, conception, idea, thought, notion, impression; hallucination. **3.** caprice, whim, vagary, quirk, humor, crotchet. **4.** preference, liking, inclination, fondness. **5.** judgment, taste, sensitivity, sensitiveness. —*adj.* **6.** fine, elegant, choice. **7.** ornamental, decorated, ornate. **8.** fanciful, capricious, whimsical, irregular, extravagant. —*v.* **9.** picture, envision, conceive, imagine. **10.** like, be pleased with, take a fancy to. —**Ant.** plain; regular, ordinary; dislike, abhor.

fantastic, *adj.* bizarre, grotesque, eccentric, outlandish, outre, odd, queer, absurd, unbelievable, strange, outlandish, singular, unnatural, weird. —**Syn. Study.** FANTASTIC, BIZARRE, GROTESQUE share a sense of deviation from what is normal or expected. FANTASTIC suggests a wild lack of restraint and a fancifulness so extreme as to lose touch with reality: *a fantastic new space vehicle.* BIZARRE implies striking or odd elements that surprise and captivate the observer: *bizarre costumes for Mardi Gras.* GROTESQUE implies shocking distortion or incongruity, sometimes ludicrous, but more often pitiful or tragic: *the grotesque gestures of a mime.*

fascinate, *v.* bewitch, charm, enchant, entrance, enrapture, captivate, allure, infatuate, enamor. —**Ant.** repel, disgust.

fashion, *n.* **1.** custom, style, vogue, mode, fad, rage, craze. **2.** custom, style, conventionality, conformity. **3.** haut monde, beau monde, four hundred, society. **4.** manner, way, mode, method, approach. **5.** make, form, figure, shape, stamp, mold, pattern, model, cast. **6.** kind, sort. —*v.* **7.** make, shape, frame, construct, mold, form. **8.** accommodate, adapt, suit, fit, adjust.

fashionable, *adj.* stylish, chic, in vogue, in fashion, in style, smart, trendy, du jour, voguish, exclusive, inside, swank, tony, au courant, à la mode, soigné, soignée, all the rage, hip, with-it. —**Ant.** unfashionable, dowdy.

fast, *adj.* **1.** quick, swift, rapid, fleet. **2.** energetic, active, alert, quick. **3.** dissolute, dissipated, profligate, unmoral, wild, reckless, extravagant, prodigal. **4.** strong, resistant, impregnable. **5.** immovable, fixed, secure, steadfast, stanch, firm. **6.** inescapable, inextricable. **7.** tied, knotted, fastened, fixed, tight, close. **8.** permanent, lasting, enduring, eternal. **9.** loyal, faithful, steadfast. **10.** deep, sound, profound. **11.** deceptive, insincere, inconstant, unreliable. —*adv.* **12.** tightly, fixedly, firmly, securely, tenaciously. **13.** quickly, swiftly, rapidly, speedily. **14.** energetically, recklessly, extravagantly, wildly, prodigally. —**Ant.** slow, lethargic; upright, moral; weak, defenseless; feeble; temporary; disloyal, faithless; shallow; sincere, constant, reliable. —**Syn. Study.** See QUICK.

fasten, *v.* make fast, fix, secure, attach, pin, rivet, bind, tie, connect, link, hook, clasp, clinch, clamp, tether. —**Ant.** loosen, loose, untie.

fat, *adj.* **1.** fleshy, plump, corpulent, obese, adipose, stout, portly, chubby, pudgy. **2.** oily, fatty, unctuous, greasy, pinguid. **3.** rich, profitable, remunerative, lucrative. **4.** fertile, rich, fruitful, productive. **5.** thick, broad, extended, wide. **6.** plentiful, copious, abundant. **7.** dull, stupid, sluggish, coarse. —**Ant.** thin, skinny, cadaverous; poor; scarce, scanty; barren; clever.

fatal, *adj.* **1.** deadly, mortal, lethal; destructive, ruinous, pernicious, calamitous, catastrophic. **2.** fateful, inevitable, doomed, predestined, foreordained, damned. —**Ant.** lifegiving, constructive; indeterminate. —**Syn. Study.** FATAL, DEADLY, LETHAL, MORTAL apply to something that has caused or is capable of causing death or dire misfortune. FATAL may refer to the future or the past; in either case, it emphasizes inevitability or inescapable consequences: *a fatal illness; fatal errors.* DEADLY refers to the future, and suggests something that causes death by its very nature, or has death as its purpose: *a deadly disease; a deadly poison.* LETHAL is usu. used in technical contexts: *Carbon monoxide is a lethal gas.* MORTAL usu. refers to death that has

actually occurred: *He received a mortal blow.*

fate, *n.* **1.** fortune, luck, lot, chance, destiny, karma, kismet, doom. **2.** death, destruction, ruin. —*v.* **3.** predetermine, destine, predestine, foreordain, preordain. —**Syn. Study.** FATE, DESTINY refer to a predetermined and usu. inescapable course or outcome of events. The two words are frequently interchangeable. FATE stresses the irrationality and impersonal character of events: *It was Napoleon's fate to be exiled.* The word is often used lightly: *It was my fate to meet her that very afternoon.* DESTINY is often used of a favorable or exalted lot in life: *It was her destiny to save her people.*

fateful, See Syn. study at OMINOUS.

fatherly, *adj.* paternal, protecting, protective; kind, tender, benign.

fatuous, *adj.* stupid, dense, dull, dimwitted, foolish, silly, idiotic. —**Ant.** clever, bright, intelligent. —**Syn. Study.** See FOOLISH.

fault, *n.* **1.** defect, imperfection, blemish, flaw, failing, frailty, foible, weakness, shortcoming, vice. **2.** error, mistake, slip. **3.** misdeed, sin, transgression, trespass, misdemeanor, offense, wrong, delinquency, indiscretion, culpability. —**Ant.** strength. —**Syn. Study.** FAULT, FOIBLE, WEAKNESS, FAILING, VICE refer to human shortcomings or imperfections. FAULT refers to any ordinary shortcoming; condemnation is not necessarily implied: *Of his many faults the greatest is vanity.* FOIBLE suggests a weak point that is slight and often amusing, manifesting itself in eccentricity rather than in wrongdoing: *the foibles of an artist.* WEAKNESS suggests that a person is unable to control a particular impulse or response, and gives way to it: *a weakness for ice cream.* FAILING is particularly applied to humanity at large, suggesting common, often venial, shortcomings: *Procrastination is a common failing.* VICE is the strongest term and designates a habit that is detrimental, immoral, or evil: *to succumb to the vice of compulsive gambling.*

faulty, *adj.* **1.** defective, imperfect, incomplete, bad. **2.** blameworthy, culpable, reprehensible, censurable. —**Ant.** perfect, complete, consummate; exonerated, blameless.

favor, *n.* **1.** kindness, good will, benefit, good deed. **2.** partiality, bias, patronage, prejudice. **3.** gift, present. —*v.* **4.** prefer, encourage, patronize, approve, countenance, allow. **5.** facilitate, ease; propitiate, conciliate, appease. **6.** aid, help, support, assist. —**Ant.** cruelty; disfavor; disapprove, disallow, discourage.

favorite, *adj.* **1.** preferred, chosen, pet, best-liked, best-loved, fair-haired, popular, beloved, loved, prized, treasured, dearest, precious, adored, esteemed, dearly beloved. —*n.* **2.** preference, pet, darling, chosen one, apple of one's eye, fair-haired one.

fear, *n.* **1.** apprehension, consternation, dismay, alarm, trepidation, dread, terror, fright, horror, panic. **2.** anxiety, solicitude, concern. **3.** awe, reverence, veneration. —*v.* **4.** be afraid of, apprehend, dread. **5.** revere, venerate, reverence. —**Ant.** boldness, bravery, intrepidity; security, confidence.

fearless, *adj.* brave, intrepid, bold, courageous, heroic. —**Ant.** cowardly. —**Syn. Study.** See BRAVE.

feasible, *adj.* **1.** practicable, workable, possible. **2.** suitable, suited, usable, practical, practicable. **3.** likely, probable. —**Ant.** unfeasible, impractical, impossible; unsuitable, unsuited; unlikely,

improbable. —**Syn. Study.** See POSSIBLE.

feast, *n.* **1.** celebration, anniversary, commemoration, ceremony, banquet, fête, entertainment, carousal. **2.** repast, sumptuous repast. —*v.* **3.** eat, gourmandize, glut *or* stuff *or* gorge oneself. **4.** gratify, delight.

feat, *n.* achievement, accomplishment, deed, action, act, exploit.

feature, *n.* characteristic, peculiarity, trait, property, mark. —**Syn. Study.** FEATURE, CHARACTERISTIC, PECULIARITY refer to a distinctive trait of an individual or of a class. FEATURE suggests an outstanding or marked property that attracts attention: *A large art exhibit was a feature of the convention.* CHARACTERISTIC means a distinguishing mark or quality always associated in one's mind with a particular person or thing: *A fine sense of humor is one of his characteristics.* PECULIARITY means a distinctive and often unusual property exclusive to one individual, group, or thing: *A blue-black tongue is a peculiarity of the chow chow.*

feeble, *adj.* **1.** weak, feckless, ineffective, ineffectual. **2.** infirm, sickly, debilitated, enervated, declining, frail. **3.** faint, dim, weak. —**Ant.** strong, effective, effectual; healthy; clear.

feed, *v.* **1.** nourish, sustain, purvey. **2.** satisfy, minister to, gratify, please. **3.** eat. **4.** subsist. —*n.* **5.** fodder, forage, provender, food. —**Ant.** starve. —**Syn. Study.** FEED, FODDER, FORAGE, PROVENDER mean food for animals. FEED is the general word; however, it most often applies to grain: *chicken feed.* FODDER is applied to coarse feed that is fed to livestock: *Cornstalks are good fodder.* FORAGE is feed that an animal obtains (usu. grass, leaves, etc.) by grazing or searching about for it: *Lost cattle can usually live on forage.* PROVENDER

denotes dry feed for livestock, such as hay, oats, or corn: *a supply of provender in the haymow.*

feeling, *n.* **1.** consciousness, impression; emotion, passion, sentiment, sensibility; sympathy, empathy. **2.** tenderness, sensitivity, sentiment, sentimentality, susceptibility, pity. **3.** sentiment, opinion, tenor. —*adj.* **4.** sentient, emotional, sensitive, tender; sympathetic. **5.** emotional, impassioned, passionate. —**Ant.** apathy, coolness; unemotional, insensitive, unsympathetic; cool. —**Syn. Study.** FEELING, EMOTION, PASSION, SENTIMENT refer to pleasurable or painful sensations experienced when one is stirred to sympathy, anger, fear, love, grief, etc. FEELING is a general term for a subjective point of view as well as for specific sensations: *to be guided by feeling rather than by facts; a feeling of pride, of dismay.* EMOTION is applied to an intensified feeling: *agitated by emotion.* PASSION is strong or violent emotion, often so overpowering that it masters the mind or judgment: *stirred to a passion of anger.* SENTIMENT is a mixture of thought and feeling, esp. refined or tender feeling: *Recollections are often colored by sentiment.*

feign, *v.* **1.** invent, concoct, devise, fabricate, forge, counterfeit. **2.** simulate, pretend, counterfeit, affect; emulate, imitate, mimic. **3.** make believe, pretend, imagine. **—Syn. Study.** See PRETEND.

felicitous, *adj.* **1.** apt, suitable, appropriate, cogent, germane, relevant, fitting, fit, applicable, proper, meet, just, happy. **2.** enjoyable, pleasant, delightful, pleasing, pleasurable, happy, felicific.

female, *n.* **1.** woman, girl. *—adj.* **2.** feminine, delicate, womanly, soft, gentle, maternal, nurturing. **—Ant.** male; masculine,

manly. **—Syn. Study.** FEMALE, FEMININE, EFFEMINATE describe women and girls or whatever is culturally attributed to them. FEMALE classifies individuals on the basis of their genetic makeup or their ability to produce offspring in sexual reproduction. It contrasts with MALE in all uses: *her oldest female relative; the female parts of the flower.* FEMININE refers to qualities and behavior deemed especially appropriate to or ideally associated with women and girls. In American and Western European culture, these have traditionally included such features as charm, gentleness, and patience: *to dance with feminine grace; a feminine sensitivity to moods.* FEMININE is sometimes used of physical features too: *small, feminine hands.* EFFEMINATE is most often applied derogatorily to men or boys, suggesting that they have traits culturally regarded as appropriate to women and girls rather than to men: *an effeminate speaking style.* See also WOMAN, WOMANLY.

feminine, See Syn. study at FEMALE.

ferocious, *adj.* fierce, savage, wild, cruel, violent, ravenous, rapacious. —**Ant.** mild, tame, calm. —**Syn. Study.** See FIERCE.

fertile, *adj.* productive, prolific, fecund, fruitful, rich, teeming. —**Ant.** sterile, barren. —**Syn. Study.** See PRODUCTIVE.

fervent, *adj.* fervid, ardent, earnest, warm, heated, hot, burning, glowing, fiery, inflamed, eager, zealous, vehement, impassioned, passionate, enthusiastic. —**Ant.** cool, apathetic.

fervor, *n.* ardor, intensity, earnestness, eagerness, enthusiasm, passion, fire, heat, vehemence. —**Ant.** coolness, apathy.

feud, *n.* hostility, quarrel, argument, difference, falling-out.

fickle, *adj.* inconstant, disloyal, faithless, changeable,

shifting, unstable, capricious, unpredictable, irresolute, inconsistent, volatile. —**Syn. Study.** FICKLE, INCONSTANT, CAPRICIOUS describe persons or things that are not firm or steady in affection, behavior, opinion, or loyalty. FICKLE implies an underlying perversity as a cause for the lack of stability: *once lionized, now rejected by a fickle public.* INCONSTANT suggests an innate disposition to change: *an inconstant lover, flitting from affair to affair.* CAPRICIOUS implies unpredictable changeability arising from sudden whim: *a capricious reversal of policy.*

fiction, *n.* **1.** novel, fantasy. **2.** fabrication, figment, unreality, falsity. —**Ant.** nonfiction, fact; reality.

fictitious, *adj.* **1.** imaginary, illusory, fanciful, fancied, invented, created, concocted, made-up, dreamed-up, unreal, visionary, chimerical, mythical. **2.** artificial, bogus, fake, mock, ungenuine, deceptive, counterfeit, factitious, synthetic. —**Ant.** real, genuine.

fidelity, *n.* **1.** loyalty, faithfulness, devotion, fealty. **2.** accuracy, precision, faithfulness, exactness, closeness. —**Ant.** disloyalty, unfaithfulness; inaccuracy.

fierce, *adj.* **1.** ferocious, wild, vehement, violent, savage, cruel, fell, brutal, bloodthirsty, murderous, homicidal. **2.** truculent, barbarous, untamed, furious, passionate, turbulent, impetuous. —**Ant.** tame, domesticated; calm; civilized; cool, temperate. —**Syn. Study.** FIERCE, FEROCIOUS, TRUCULENT suggest vehement hostility and unrestrained violence. FIERCE implies an aggressive, savage, or wild temperament and appearance: *the fiercest of foes; a fierce tribe.* FEROCIOUS implies merciless cruelty or brutality, esp. of a bloodthirsty kind: *a ferocious tiger.* TRUCULENT

implies an intimidating or menacing fierceness: *a truculent bully.*

fiery, *adj.* **1.** hot, flaming, heated, fervent, fervid, burning, afire, glowing. **2.** fervent, fervid, vehement, inflamed, impassioned, spirited, ardent, impetuous, passionate, fierce. —**Ant.** cool, cold; dispassionate.

fight, *n.* **1.** battle, war, combat, encounter, conflict, contest, scrimmage, engagement, fray, affray, action, skirmish, affair, struggle. **2.** melee, struggle, scuffle, tussle, riot, row, fray. —*v.* **3.** contend, strive, battle, combat, conflict, contest, engage, struggle.

figment, *n.* invention, fiction, fabrication, fable. —**Ant.** fact, reality.

filthy, *adj.* **1.** dirty, foul, unclean, defiled, squalid. **2.** obscene, vile, dirty, pornographic, licentious, lascivious. —**Ant.** clean, spotless, immaculate.

final, *adj.* **1.** last, latest, ultimate, drop-dead. **2.**

conclusive, decisive.
—**Ant.** prime, primary.

financial, *adj.* monetary, fiscal, pecuniary. —**Syn. Study.** FINANCIAL, FISCAL, MONETARY, PECUNIARY refer to matters concerned with money. FINANCIAL usu. refers to money matters or transactions of some size or importance: *a lucrative financial deal.* FISCAL is used esp. in connection with government funds, or funds of any organization: *the end of the fiscal year.* MONETARY relates esp. to money as such: *The dollar is a monetary unit.* PECUNIARY refers to money as used in making ordinary payments: *a pecuniary obligation; pecuniary rewards.*

fine, *adj.* **1.** superior, high-grade, choice, excellent, admirable, elegant, exquisite, finished, consummate, perfect, refined, select, delicate. **2.** powdered, pulverized, minute, small, little. **3.** keen, sharp, acute. **4.** skilled, accomplished, brilliant. **5.** affected,

ornate, ornamented, fancy.
—**Ant.** inferior, poor, bad, unfinished; dull; unskilled, maladroit; plain.

finery, *n.* regalia, dress-up, frills, frillery, frippery, trappings, toggery, fancy dress, Sunday best.
—**Ant.** rags, tatters.

finish, *v.* **1.** bring to an end, end, terminate, conclude, close. **2.** use up, complete, consume. **3.** complete, perfect, consummate, polish. **4.** accomplish, achieve, execute, complete, perform, do. —*n.* **5.** end, conclusion, termination, close. **6.** polish, elegance, refinement. —**Ant.** begin, start, commence; originate, create; beginning.

finished, *adj.* **1.** ended, completed, consummated, over, done, done with; complete, consummate, perfect. **2.** polished, refined, elegant, perfected; trained, experienced, practiced, qualified, accomplished, proficient, skilled, gifted, talented.
—**Ant.** begun; incomplete, imperfect; unrefined,

inelegant; inexperienced, unqualified, unskilled, maladroit.

firm, *adj.* **1.** hard, solid, stiff, rigid, inelastic, compact, condensed, compressed, dense. **2.** steady, unshakable, rooted, fast, fixed, stable, secure, immovable. **3.** fixed, settled, unalterable, established, confirmed. **4.** steadfast, unwavering, determined, immovable, resolute, stanch, constant, steady, reliable. —*n.* **5.** company, partnership, association, business, concern, house, corporation. —**Ant.** flabby, flaccid, elastic, soft; unsteady, unstable; wavering, irresolute, inconstant, unreliable.

fiscal, See Syn. study at FINANCIAL.

fitness, *n.* **1.** condition, physical condition, conditioning, tone, shape, fettle, health, healthfulness, trim, repair, order, salubrity, salubriousness. **2.** appropriateness, suitability, applicability, aptness, cogency, propriety.

fix, *v.* **1.** make, fast, fasten, pin, attach, tie, secure, stabilize, establish, set, plant, implant. **2.** settle, determine, establish, define, limit. **3.** assign, refer. **4.** repair, mend, correct, emend. —*n.* **5.** predicament, dilemma, plight, spot. —**Ant.** loosen, loose, detach; unsettle; break.

flagrant, *adj.* glaring, overdone, excessive, gross, shameless, bodacious, brazen, blatant, scandalous, shocking, disgraceful, outrageous, heinous, monstrous. —**Syn. Study.** FLAGRANT, GLARING, GROSS suggest something offensive that cannot be overlooked. FLAGRANT implies a conspicuous offense so far beyond the limits of decency as to be insupportable: *a flagrant violation of the law.* GLARING emphasizes conspicuousness but lacks the imputation of evil or immorality: *a glaring error* *by a bank teller.* GROSS suggests a mistake or impropriety of major proportions: *a gross miscarriage of justice.*

flame, *n.* **1.** blaze, conflagration, holocaust, inferno, fire. **2.** heat, ardor, zeal, passion, fervor, warmth, enthusiasm. —*v.* **3.** burn, blaze. **4.** glow, burn, warm; shine, flash. **5.** inflame, fire.

flash, *n.* **1.** flame, outburst, flare, gleam, glare. **2.** instant, split second, moment, twinkling, wink. **3.** ostentation, display. —*v.* **4.** glance, glint, glitter, scintillate, gleam. —*adj.* **5.** showy, ostentatious, flashy, gaudy, tawdry, flaunting, pretentious, superficial. **6.** counterfeit, sham, fake, false, fraudulent.

flat, *adj.* **1.** horizontal, level, even, equal, plane, smooth. **2.** low, supine, prone, prostrate. **3.** collapsed, deflated. **4.** unqualified, downright, positive, outright, peremptory, absolute. **5.** uninteresting, dull, tedious, lifeless, boring, spiritless, prosaic, unanimated. **6.** insipid, vapid, tasteless, stale, dead, unsavory. **7.** pointless. —*adv.* **8.** horizontally, levelly. **9.** positively, absolutely, definitely. —*n.* **10.** apartment, suite. —**Ant.** vertical, upright, perpendicular; doubtful, dubious; spirited, animated; tasteful, savory; pointed.

flatter, *v.* apple-polish, fawn, toady, kowtow, truckle, blandish, cajole, wheedle, coax, beguile, entice, inveigle, flatter, soft-soap, honey, sweet-talk, butter up, bootlick, suck up to. —**Ant.** insult, affront, offend.

flavor, *n.* **1.** taste, savor. **2.** seasoning, extract, flavoring. **3.** characteristic, essence, quality, spirit, soul. **4.** smell, odor, aroma, perfume, fragrance.

flaw, *n.* defect, imperfection, blot, blemish, spot, fault, crack, crevice, breach, break,

cleft, fissure, rift, fracture.
—**Syn. Study.** See DEFECT.

fleet, *adj.* swift, fast, quick, rapid, speedy, expeditious, fleet-footed, nimble-footed, hasty, express, snappy.
—**Ant.** slow, sluggish.

flexible, *adj.* **1.** pliable, pliant, flexile, limber, plastic, elastic, supple. **2.** adaptable, tractable, compliant, yielding, gentle.
—**Ant.** inflexible, rigid, solid, firm; intractable, unyielding.

flit, *v.* fly, dart, skim along; flutter.

flock, *n.* bevy, covey, flight, gaggle; brood, hatch, litter; shoal, school; swarm; pride; drove, herd, pack; group, company, crowd.

flood, *n.* **1.** deluge, inundation, overflow, flash flood, freshet. —*v.* **2.** overflow, inundate, deluge, flow.

flourish, *v.* **1.** thrive, prosper, be successful, grow, increase, succeed. **2.** luxuriate. **3.** brandish, wave. **4.** parade, flaunt, display, show off, be

ostentatious, boast, brag, vaunt. **5.** embellish, adorn, ornament, decorate. —*n.* **6.** parade, ostentation, show, display, dash. **7.** decoration, ornament, adornment, embellishment.
—**Ant.** decline, die, fail; disfigure, mar. —**Syn. Study.** See SUCCEED.

flow, *v.* **1.** gush, spout, stream, spurt, jet, discharge. **2.** proceed, run, pour, roll on. **3.** overflow, abound, teem, pour. —*n.* **4.** current, flood, stream. **5.** stream, river, rivulet, rill, streamlet. **6.** outpouring, discharge, overflowing.

flowery, See Syn. study at BOMBASTIC.

fluctuate, *v.* waver, vacillate, change, vary; wave, undulate, oscillate.

fluent, *adj.* flowing, glib, voluble, copious, smooth.
—**Ant.** terse, curt, silent.
—**Syn. Study.** FLUENT, GLIB, VOLUBLE may refer to an easy flow of words or to a person able to communicate with ease. FLUENT suggests the easy

and ready flow of an accomplished speaker or writer; it is usually a term of commendation: *a fluent orator.* GLIB implies an excessive fluency and lack of sincerity or profundity; it suggests talking smoothly and hurriedly to cover up or deceive: *a glib salesperson.* VOLUBLE implies the copious and often rapid flow of words characteristic of a person who loves to talk and will spare the audience no details: *a voluble gossip.*

fluid, *n.* **1.** liquid; gas, vapor. —*adj.* **2.** liquid, gaseous. —**Ant.** solid. —**Syn. Study.** See LIQUID.

fly, *v.* **1.** take wing, soar, hover, flutter, flit, wing, flap. **2.** elapse, pass, glide, slip.

fodder, See Syn. study at FEED.

foe, *n.* enemy, opponent, adversary, antagonist. —**Ant.** friend, ally, associate.

fog, *n.* **1.** cloud, mist, haze; smog. **2.** cloud, confusion, obfuscation, dimming, blurring, darkening. —*v.* **3.** befog, becloud, obfuscate, dim, blur, darken. **4.** daze, bewilder, befuddle, muddle. —**Ant.** clarity; clear, brighten; clarify.

foible, *n.* weakness, fault, failing, frailty, defect, imperfection, infirmity. —**Ant.** strength, perfection. —**Syn. Study.** See FAULT.

folderol, *n.* **1.** ornament, decoration, trifle, bauble, frippery, gewgaw. **2.** nonsense, humbug, trumpery, balderdash, flummery, fiddle-faddle.

follow, *v.* **1.** succeed, ensue. **2.** conform, obey, heed, comply, observe. **3.** accompany, attend. **4.** pursue, chase, trail, track, trace. **5.** ensue, succeed, result, come next, arise, proceed. —**Ant.** lead; order. —**Syn. Study.** FOLLOW, ENSUE, RESULT, SUCCEED imply coming after something else, in a natural sequence. FOLLOW is the general word: *We must wait to see what follows. A detailed account* *follows.* ENSUE implies a logical sequence, what might be expected normally to come after a given act, cause, etc.: *When the power lines were cut, a paralysis of transportation ensued.* RESULT emphasizes the connection between a cause or event and its effect, consequence, or outcome: *The accident resulted in injuries to those involved.* SUCCEED implies coming after in time, particularly coming into a title, office, etc.: *Formerly the oldest son succeeded to his father's title.*

follower, *n.* **1.** adherent, partisan, disciple, pupil. **2.** attendant, servant; supporter, retainer, companion, associate. **—Ant.** leader, teacher; enemy, foe. **—Syn. Study.** FOLLOWER, ADHERENT, PARTISAN refer to someone who demonstrates allegiance to a person, doctrine, cause, or the like. FOLLOWER often has an implication of personal relationship or of deep devotion to authority or to a leader: *a follower of Gandhi.* ADHERENT, a more formal word, suggests active championship of a person or point of view: *an adherent of monetarism.* PARTISAN suggests firm loyalty, as to a party, cause, or person, that is based on emotions rather than on reasoning: *a partisan of the conservatives.*

food, *n.* provisions, rations, nutrition, nutriment, aliment, bread, sustenance, victuals; meat, viands; diet, regimen, fare, menu.

fool, *n.* **1.** simpleton, dolt, dunce, blockhead, nincompoop, ninny, numskull, ignoramus, booby, sap, dunderhead, dunderpate, idiot. **2.** jester, buffoon, drool, harlequin, zany, clown, merry-andrew. **3.** imbecile, moron, idiot. —*v.* **4.** impose on, trick, deceive, delude, hoodwink, cozen, cheat, gull, gudgeon, hoax, dupe. **5.** joke, jest, play, toy, trifle, dally, idle,

dawdle, loiter, tarry.
—**Ant.** genius.

foolish, *adj.* **1.** silly,
senseless, fatuous, stupid,
inane, dull, vacant, vapid,
slow, asinine, simple,
witless. **2.** ill-considered,
unwise, thoughtless,
irrational, imprudent,
unreasonable, absurd,
ridiculous, nonsensical,
preposterous, foolhardy.
—**Ant.** bright, brilliant,
clever, intelligent; wise,
sage, sagacious. —**Syn.**
Study. FOOLISH, FATUOUS,
INANE imply weakness of
intellect and lack of
judgment. FOOLISH implies
lack of common sense or
good judgment or,
sometimes, weakness of
mind: *a foolish decision; a
foolish child.* FATUOUS
implies being not only
foolish, dull, and vacant in
mind, but complacent and
highly self-satisfied as well:
a fatuous grin. INANE
suggests a lack of content,
meaning, or purpose: *inane
conversation about the
weather.*

forage, See Syn. study at
FEED.

forbid, *v.* inhibit, prohibit,
taboo, interdict, prevent,
preclude, stop, obviate,
deter, discourage. —**Ant.**
allow, permit, encourage.

forbidding, *adj.*
unappealing, dismaying,
grim, disagreeable,
rebarbative, off-putting,
menacing, threatening,
minatory. —**Ant.**
attractive, appealing.

force, *n.* **1.** strength,
power, impetus, intensity,
might, vigor, energy. **2.**
coercion, violence,
compulsion, constraint,
enforcement. **3.** efficacy,
effectiveness, effect,
efficiency, validity,
potency, potential. **4.**
effect, operation. —*v.* **5.**
compel, constrain, oblige,
coerce, necessitate. **6.**
drive, propel, impel. **7.**
overcome, overpower,
violate, ravish, rape.
—**Ant.** weakness, frailty;
ineffectiveness, inefficiency.

forecast, *v.* **1.** predict,
augur, foretell, foresee,
anticipate. **2.** prearrange,
plan, contrive, project. **3.**
conjecture, guess, estimate.
—*n.* **4.** prediction, augury,

conjecture, guess, estimate, foresight, prevision, anticipation, forethought, prescience. **—Syn. Study.** See PREDICT.

foreigner, *n.* alien, stranger, non-native, outsider, outlander. **—Ant.** native. **—Syn. Study.** See STRANGER.

foresee, See Syn. study at PREDICT.

foresight, *n.* **1.** prudence, forethought, prevision, anticipation, precaution; forecast. **2.** prescience, prevision, foreknowledge, prospect.

forest, *n.* grove, wood, woods, woodland. **—Ant.** plain.

foreword, See Syn. study at INTRODUCTION.

forgive, *v.* pardon, excuse; absolve, acquit. **—Ant.** blame, condemn, censure. **—Syn. Study.** See EXCUSE.

forlorn, *adj.* **1.** abandoned, deserted, forsaken, desolate, alone, lost, solitary. **2.** desolate, dreary, unhappy, miserable, wretched, pitiable, pitiful, helpless, woebegone, disconsolate, comfortless, destitute. **—Ant.** accompanied; happy, cheerful.

form, *n.* **1.** shape, figure, outline, mold, appearance, cast, cut, configuration. **2.** mold, model, pattern. **3.** manner, style, arrangement, sort, kind, order, type. **4.** assemblage, group. **5.** ceremony, ritual, formula, formality, conformity, rule, convention. **6.** document, paper, application, business form, blank. **7.** method, procedure, system, mode, practice, formula, approach. **—v. 8.** construct, frame, shape, model, mold, fashion, outline, cast. **9.** make, produce, create, originate. **10.** compose, make up, serve for, constitute. **11.** order, arrange, organize, systematize, dispose, combine. **12.** instruct, teach, educate, discipline, train. **13.** frame, invent, contrive, devise.

formal, *adj.* **1.** academic, conventional, conformal, conforming, conformist. **2.**

ceremonial, ceremonious, ritual, conventional. **3.** ceremonious, stiff, prim, precise, punctilious, starched. **4.** perfunctory, external. **5.** official, express, explicit, strict, rigid, rigorous, stodgy. **6.** rigorous, methodical, regular, set, fixed, rigid, stiff.

formidable, *adj.* dread, dreadful, appalling, threatening, menacing, fearful, terrible, frightful, horrible. **—Ant.** pleasant, friendly, amiable.

forsake, *v.* **1.** quit, leave, desert, abandon. **2.** give up, renounce, forswear, relinquish, recant, drop, forgo.

fortification, *n.* **1.** fortifying, strengthening, bolstering, arming. **2.** fort, castle, fortress, citadel, stronghold, bulwark, fastness.

fortuitous, *adj.* accidental, chance, casual, incidental. **—Ant.** purposeful, intentional.

fortunate, *adj.* lucky, happy, propitious, favorable, advantageous, auspicious; successful, prosperous. **—Ant.** unlucky, unfortunate. **—Syn. Study.** FORTUNATE, HAPPY, LUCKY refer to persons who enjoy, or events that produce, good fortune. FORTUNATE implies that the success is obtained by the operation of favorable circumstances more than by direct effort: *fortunate in one's choice of a wife; a fortunate investment.* HAPPY emphasizes a pleasant ending or something that happens at just the right moment: *By a happy accident I received the package on time.* LUCKY, a more colloquial word, is applied to situations that turn out well by chance: *lucky at cards; my lucky day.*

forward, *adv.* **1.** onward, ahead, up ahead, in advance, frontward. **2.** out, forth. **—***adj.* **3.** well-advanced, up front, ahead. **4.** ready, prompt, eager, willing, sincere, earnest, zealous. **5.** pert, bold, presumptuous, assuming, confident, impertinent, impudent, brazen, flippant. **6.** radical, extreme, unconventional, progressive. **7.** early, premature, future, preliminary. **—Ant.** backward.

foster, *v.* **1.** promote, encourage, further, favor, patronize, forward, advance. **2.** bring up, rear, breed, nurse, nourish, sustain, support. **3.** care for, cherish. **—Ant.** discourage. **—Syn. Study.** See CHERISH.

foul, *adj.* **1.** offensive, gross, disgusting, loathsome, repulsive, repellent, noisome, fetid, putrid, stinking. **2.** filthy, dirty, unclean, squalid, polluted, sullied, soiled, tarnished, stained, tainted, impure. **3.** stormy, unfavorable, rainy, tempestuous. **4.** abominable, wicked, vile, base, shameful, infamous, sinful, scandalous. **5.** scurrilous, obscene, smutty, profane, vulgar, low, coarse. **6.** unfair, dishonorable, underhanded, cheating. **7.** entangled, caught, jammed, tangled. *—adv.* **8.** unfairly, foully. *—v.* **9.** soil, defile, sully, stain, dirty, besmirch, smut, taint, pollute, poison. **10.** entangle, clog, tangle, catch. **11.** defile, dishonor, disgrace, shame. **—Ant.** delightful, attractive, pleasant; pure; saintly, angelic; fair, honorable; clean, purify; clear; honor.

foundation, *n.* **1.** base, basis, ground, footing. **2.** establishment, settlement; endowment. **—Ant.** superstructure. **—Syn. Study.** See BASE.

fractious, *adj.* cross, fretful, peevish, testy, captious, petulant, touchy, splenetic, pettish, waspish, snappish, irritable; unruly, refractory, stubborn. **—Ant.** temperate, kind, even-tempered; amenable, tractable, obedient.

fragile, See Syn. study at FRAIL.

fragrance, See Syn. study at PERFUME.

fragrant, *adj.* perfumed, odorous, redolent, sweet-smelling, sweet-scented, aromatic, odoriferous. **—Ant.** noxious.

frail, *adj.* brittle, fragile, breakable, frangible, delicate, weak, feeble. **—Ant.** strong, pliant, elastic, unbreakable. **—Syn. Study.** FRAIL, BRITTLE, FRAGILE imply a delicacy or weakness of substance or construction. FRAIL applies particularly to health and immaterial things: *a frail constitution; frail hopes.* BRITTLE implies a hard material that snaps or breaks to pieces easily: *brittle as glass.* FRAGILE implies that the object must be handled carefully to avoid breakage or damage: *fragile bric-a-brac.*

frank, *adj.* **1.** open, unreserved, unrestrained, unrestricted, nonrestrictive, outspoken, candid, sincere, free, bold, truthful, uninhibited. **2.** artless, ingenuous, undisguised, avowed, downright, outright, direct. *—n.* **3.** signature, mark, sign, seal; franchise. **—Ant.** secretive, restrained, restricted; sly, artful, dissembling. **—Syn. Study.** FRANK, CANDID, OPEN, OUTSPOKEN imply a freedom and boldness in speaking. FRANK implies a straightforward, almost tactless expression of one's real opinions or sentiments: *He was frank in his rejection of the proposal.* CANDID suggests sincerity, truthfulness, and impartiality: *a candid appraisal of her work.* OPEN implies a lack of reserve or of concealment: *open antagonism.* OUTSPOKEN suggests free and bold expression, even when inappropriate: *an outspoken and unnecessary show of disapproval.*

fraud, *n.* deceit, trickery, duplicity, treachery, sharp practice, breach of confidence, trick, deception, guile, artifice, ruse, stratagem, wile, hoax, humbug. **—Ant.**

honesty. —**Syn. Study.**
See DECEIT.

free, *adj.* **1.** unfettered,
independent, at liberty,
unrestrained, unrestricted.
2. unregulated,
unrestricted, unimpeded,
open, unobstructed. **3.**
clear, immune, exempt,
uncontrolled, decontrolled.
4. easy, firm, swift,
unimpeded,
unencumbered. **5.** loose,
unattached, lax. **6.** frank,
open, unconstrained,
unceremonious, familiar,
informal, easy. **7.** loose,
licentious, ribald, lewd,
immoral, libertine. **8.**
liberal, lavish, generous,
bountiful, unstinted,
munificent, charitable,
open-handed. —*v.* **9.**
liberate, set free, release,
unfetter, emancipate,
manumit, deliver,
disenthrall. **10.** exempt,
deliver. **11.** rid, relieve,
disengage, clear. —**Ant.**
dependent, restrained,
restricted; close,
obstructed; difficult;
unfamiliar; moral, upright;
stingy, niggardly; confine,

enthrall. —**Syn. Study.**
See RELEASE.

freedom, *n.* **1.** liberty,
independence. **2.**
immunity, franchise,
privilege. **3.** ease, facility.
4. frankness, openness,
ingenuousness. **5.**
familiarity, license,
looseness, laxity. —**Ant.**
dependence; restriction;
difficulty; secrecy;
unfamiliarity, restraint.

freight, *n.* **1.** cargo,
shipment, load. **2.**
freightage, transportation,
expressage. —*v.* **3.** load,
lade, burden, charge.

frenzy, *n.* agitation,
excitement, paroxysm,
enthusiasm; rage, fury,
raving, mania, insanity,
delirium, derangement,
aberration, lunacy,
madness. —**Ant.** calm,
coolness; sanity, judgment.

frequently, *adv.* often,
many times, repeatedly.
—**Ant.** seldom. —**Syn.**
Study. See OFTEN.

fresh, *adj.* **1.** new, recent,
novel. **2.** youthful,
healthy, robust, vigorous,
well, hearty, hardy, strong.

3. refreshing, pure, cool, unadulterated, sweet, invigorating. **4.** inexperienced, artless, untrained, raw, green, uncultivated, unskilled. —**Ant.** stale, old; impure, contaminated; experienced, skilled. —**Syn. Study.** See NEW.

fret, *v.* **1.** worry, fume, rage. **2.** torment, worry, harass, annoy, irritate, vex, taunt, goad, tease, nettle, needle. **3.** wear away, erode, gnaw, corrode, rust. —*n.* **4.** annoyance, vexation, harassment, agitation, worry, irritation. **5.** erosion, corrosion, eating away, gnawing. **6.** fretwork, ornament.

fretful, *adj.* irritable, peevish, petulant, querulous, touchy, testy, waspish, pettish, splenetic, captious, snappish, short-tempered, ill-tempered. —**Ant.** calm, even-tempered, temperate, easy-going.

friction, *n.* discord, disaccord, disharmony, conflict, dissension, antagonism, strain, incompatibility, contentiousness, enmity. —**Ant.** friendliness, amity, cooperation.

friend, *n.* **1.** companion, crony, chum, acquaintance, intimate, confidant. **2.** well-wisher, patron, supporter, backer, encourager, advocate, defender. **3.** ally, associate, confrère. —**Ant.** enemy, foe, adversary. —**Syn. Study.** See ACQUAINTANCE.

friendly, *adj.* **1.** kind, kindly, amicable, fraternal, amiable, cordial, genial, well-disposed, benevolent, affectionate, kind-hearted. **2.** helpful, favorable, advantageous, propitious. —**Ant.** unfriendly, inimical; unfavorable.

fright, *n.* dismay, consternation, terror, fear, alarm, panic. —**Ant.** bravery, boldness.

frighten, *v.* scare, terrify, alarm, appall, shock, dismay, intimidate.

frightful, *adj.* dreadful, terrible, alarming, terrific, fearful, awful, shocking, dread, dire, horrid, horrible, hideous, ghastly, gruesome. —**Ant.** delightful, attractive, beautiful.

frivolous, *adj.* **1.** unimportant, trifling, petty, paltry, trivial, flimsy. **2.** idle, silly, foolish, childish, puerile. —**Ant.** important, vital; mature, adult, sensible.

frontier, See Syn. study at BOUNDARY.

froward, *adj.* perverse, contrary, refractory, obstinate, willful, disobedient, uncooperative, fractious, contumacious, wayward, unmanageable, difficult, defiant, fresh, impudent. —**Ant.** tractable, lenient, cooperative, easy.

frugal, *adj.* economical, thrifty, chary, provident, saving, sparing, careful; parsimonious, stingy, penurious. —**Ant.** lavish, wasteful. —**Syn. Study.** See ECONOMICAL.

fruitful, *adj.* prolific, fertile, fecund, productive, profitable; plentiful, abudant, rich, copious.

—**Ant.** barren, scarce, scanty, unprofitable, fruitless. —**Syn. Study.** See PRODUCTIVE.

fruitless, *adj.* **1.** useless, inutile, unavailing, profitless, ineffectual, unprofitable, vain, idle, futile, abortive. **2.** barren, sterile, unfruitful, unproductive, infecund, unprolific. —**Ant.** fruitful, useful, profitable, effectual; abundant, fertile.

frustrate, *v.* defeat, nullify, baffle, disconcert, foil, disappoint, balk, check, thwart. —**Ant.** encourage, foster.

fulfill, *v.* **1.** carry out, consummate, execute, discharge, accomplish, achieve, complete, effect, realize, perfect. **2.** perform, do, obey, observe, discharge. **3.** satisfy, meet, anwer, fill, comply with. **4.** complete, end, terminate, bring to an end, finish, conclude. —**Ant.** fail; dissatisfy; create, originate.

fume, *n.* **1.** smoke, vapor, exhalation, steam. **2.** rage, fury, agitation, storm. —*v.* **3.** smoke, vaporize. **4.** chafe, fret, rage, rave, flare up, bluster, storm.

fun, *n.* merriment, enjoyment, pleasure, amusement, divertissement, sport, diversion, joking, jesting, playfulness, gaiety, frolic. —**Ant.** misery, melancholy.

fundamental, *adj.* **1.** basic, underlying, principal, main, central, chief, essential, primary, elementary, necessary, indispensable. **2.** original, first. —*n.* **3.** principle, rule, basic law, essence, essential. —**Ant.** superficial, superfluous, dispensable; last, common; nonessential.

funny, *adj.* amusing, diverting, comical, farcical, absurd, ridiculous, droll, witty, facetious, humorous, laughable, ludicrous, incongruous, foolish. —**Ant.** sad, melancholy, humorless.

furnish, *v.* **1.** provide, supply; purvey, cater. **2.** appoint, equip, fit up, rig, deck out, decorate, outfit, fit out. —**Syn. Study.** FURNISH, APPOINT, EQUIP refer to providing something necessary or useful. FURNISH often refers to providing necessary or customary objects or services that increase living comfort: *to furnish a bedroom with a bed, desk, and chair.* APPOINT, a more formal word, now usu. used in the past participle, means to supply completely with all requisites or accessories, often in an elegant style: *a well-appointed hotel; a fully appointed suite.* EQUIP means to supply with necessary materials or apparatus for a particular action, service, or undertaking; it emphasizes preparation: *to equip a vessel; to equip a soldier.*

fury, *n.* **1.** passion, furor, frenzy, rage, ire, anger, wrath. **2.** violence, turbulence, fierceness, impetuousness, impetuosity, vehemence. **3.** shrew, virago, termagant, vixen, nag, hag, maenad, bacchante. —**Ant.** calm, serenity. —**Syn. Study.** See ANGER.

fuse, *v.* **1.** melt, liquefy, dissolve, smelt; combine, blend, intermingle, coalesce, intermix, commingle, amalgamate, homogenize, merge. —*n.* **2.** match, fusee, fuze. —**Ant.** solidify, separate.

fuss, *n.* **1.** activity, ado, bustle, pother, to-do, stir, commotion. —*v.* **2.** bother, annoy, pester. —**Ant.** inactivity.

futile, *adj.* **1.** ineffectual, useless, unsuccessful, vain, unavailing, idle, profitless, unprofitable, bootless, worthless, valueless, fruitless, unproductive. **2.** trivial, frivolous, minor, nugatory, unimportant, trifling. —**Ant.** effective, effectual, successful; profitable, worthy; basic, important, principal, major. —**Syn. Study.** See USELESS.

G

gadget, *n.* device, tool, appliance, implement, instrument, utensil, mechanism, contrivance, contraption, invention, creation, doohickey, dingus, thingamabob, gizmo, thingamajig, doodad, widget, whatchamacallit.

gaiety, *n.* **1.** merriment, mirth, glee, jollity, joyousness, liveliness, sportiveness, hilarity, vivacity, life, cheerfulness, joviality, animation, spirit. **2.** showiness, finery, gaudiness, brilliance, glitter, flashiness, flash. —**Ant.** sadness, melancholy, misery.

gain, *v.* **1.** obtain, secure, procure, get, acquire, attain, earn, win. **2.** reach, get to, arrive at, attain. **3.** improve, better, progress, advance, forward; near, approach. —*n.* **4.** profit, increase, advantage, advance; profits, winnings. —**Ant.** lose; worsen; retreat; losses. —**Syn. Study.** GAIN, ATTAIN, EARN, WIN imply obtaining a reward or something advantageous. GAIN suggests the expenditure of effort to get or reach something desired: *After battling the blizzard, we finally gained our destination.* ATTAIN suggests a sense of personal satisfaction in having reached a lofty goal: *to attain stardom.* EARN emphasizes a deserved reward for labor or services: *to earn a promotion.* WIN stresses attainment in spite of competition or opposition: *to win support in a campaign.*

gall, *v.* **1.** irritate, annoy, irk, vex, nettle, peeve, provoke, aggravate, exasperate, get one's goat. *n.* **2.** effrontery, brazenness, brashness, impudence, insolence, nerve, cheek, gall, face, crust, brass.

gallant, *adj.* **1.** brave, high-spirited, valorous, valiant, chivalrous, courageous, bold, intrepid, fearless, daring. **2.** gay, showy, magnificent, splendid, fine. **3.** polite, courtly, chivalrous, noble, courteous. —*n.* **4.** suitor, wooer, lover, paramour. —**Ant.** cowardly, fearful; tawdry; impolite, discourteous.

gambol, *v.*, *n.* frolic, spring, caper, romp, dance.

game, *n.* **1.** amusement, pastime, diversion, divertissement, play, sport, contest, competition. **2.** scheme, artifice, strategy, stratagem, plan, plot, undertaking, venture, adventure. **3.** fun, sport, joke, diversion. **4.** prey, quarry. —*adj.* **5.** plucky, brave, bold, resolute, intrepid, dauntless, valorous, fearless, heroic, gallant.

gang, *n.* **1.** band, group, crew, crowd, company, party, set, clique, coterie; horde. **2.** squad, shift, team.

gape, *v.* **1.** yawn. **2.** stare, wonder, gaze. **3.** split, open, dehisce, separate.

garb, *n.* **1.** fashion, mode, style, cut. **2.** clothes, clothing, dress, costume, attire, apparel, habiliments, habit, garments, raiment, vesture. —*v.* **3.** dress, clothe, attire, array, apparel.

garish, *adj.* **1.** glaring, loud, showy, tawdry, gaudy, flashy. **2.** ornate, ornamented, decorated. —**Ant.** elegant; plain, simple.

garnish, *v.* **1.** adorn, decorate, ornament, embellish, grace, enhance, beautify, trim, bedeck, bedizen, set off. —*n.* **2.** decoration, ornamentation, ornament, adornment, garniture, garnishment. —**Ant.** strip.

garrulous, *adj.* talkative, loquacious, prating, prattling, wordy, diffuse, babbling, verbose, prolix. —**Ant.** taciturn, silent, reticent. —**Syn. Study.** See TALKATIVE.

gasp, *v.* pant, puff, blow.

gather, *v.* **1.** get together, collect, aggregate, assemble, muster, marshal, bring *or* draw together. **2.** learn, infer, understand, deduce, assume, conclude. **3.** accumulate, amass, garner, hoard. **4.** pluck, garner, reap, harvest, glean, cull, crop. **5.** select, cull, sort, sort out. **6.** grow, increase, accrete, collect, thicken, condense. —*n.* **7.** contraction, drawing together, tuck, pucker, fold, pleat, plait. —**Ant.** separate, disperse; decrease. —**Syn. Study.** GATHER, ASSEMBLE, COLLECT, MUSTER, MARSHAL imply bringing or drawing together. GATHER expresses the general idea usu. with no implication of arrangement: *to gather seashells.* ASSEMBLE is used of persons, objects, or facts brought together in a specific place or for a specific purpose: *to assemble data for a report.* COLLECT implies purposeful accumulation to form an ordered whole: *to collect evidence.* MUSTER, primarily a military term, suggests thoroughness in the process of collection: *to muster all one's resources.* MARSHAL, another chiefly military term, suggests rigorously ordered, purposeful arrangement: *to marshal facts for effective presentation.*

gathering, *n.* **1.** assembly, meeting, assemblage, crowd, convocation, congregation, concourse, company, throng, muster. **2.** swelling, boil, abscess, carbuncle, pimple, sore, pustule, tumor.

gaudy, *adj.* showy, tawdry, garish, brilliant, loud, flashy, conspicuous, obvious, vulgar, unsubtle. —**Ant.** elegant, refined, subtle.

gaunt, *adj.* **1.** thin, emaciated, haggard, lean, spare, skinny, scrawny, lank, angular, raw-boned, meager, attenuated, slender. **2.** bleak, desolate, grim, dreary. —**Ant.** obese, fat; populous.

gay, *adj.* **1.** joyous, gleeful, jovial, glad, happy, lighthearted, lively, convivial, vivacious, animated, frolicsome, sportive, hilarious, jolly, joyful, merry, good-humored, expansive, cheerful, sprightly, blithe, airy. **2.** bright, showy, fine, brilliant. **3.** homosexual; lesbian. —**Ant.** unhappy, miserable; dull; straight.

gaze, *v., n.* stare, gape, wonder.

genealogy, See Syn. study at PEDIGREE.

general, *adj.* **1.** impartial, unparticular, catholic, universal. **2.** common, usual, prevalent, customary, regular, ordinary, popular, nonexclusive, widespread, prevailing. **3.** miscellaneous, unrestricted, unspecialized, nonspecific. **4.** vague, lax, indefinite, ill-defined, inexact, imprecise. —**Ant.** special, partial; uncommon, unusual, extraordinary; specific; definite, exact, precise. —**Syn. Study.** GENERAL, COMMON, POPULAR, UNIVERSAL agree in the idea of being nonexclusive and widespread. GENERAL means pertaining to or true of all or most of a particular class or body, irrespective of individuals: *a general belief.* COMMON means shared or experienced frequently or by a majority of group members: *a common problem.* POPULAR means belonging to or favored by the people or the public generally, rather than a particular class: *a popular misconception.* UNIVERSAL means found everywhere with no exception: *a universal need.*

generally, *adv.* usually, commonly, ordinarily, often, in general. —**Ant.** especially, particularly, unusually. —**Syn. Study.** See OFTEN.

generosity, *n.* **1.** readiness, liberality, munificence, charity, bounteousness. **2.** nobleness, disinterestedness, magnanimity. —**Ant.** stinginess, niggardliness, parsimony.

generous, *adj.* **1.**

munificent, bountiful, unselfish, unstinting, liberal, charitable, open-handed, beneficent. **2.** noble, high-minded, magnanimous; large, big. **3.** ample, plentiful, abudant, flowing, overflowing, copious. —**Ant.** stingy, tightfisted, selfish, niggardly; small, parsimonious; scarce, scanty, barren. —**Syn. Study.** GENEROUS, CHARITABLE, LIBERAL, MUNIFICENT all describe giving or sharing something of value. GENEROUS stresses the warm and sympathetic nature of the giver: *a retired executive, generous with her time.* CHARITABLE stresses the goodness and kindness of the giver and the indigence or need of the receiver: *a charitable contribution to a nursing home.* LIBERAL emphasizes the large size of the gift and the openhandedness of the giver: *a liberal bequest to the university.* MUNIFICENT refers to a gift or award so strikingly large as to evoke amazement or admiration: *a lifetime income, a truly munificent reward for his loyalty.*

genial, *adj.* **1.** cheerful, sympathetic, cordial, friendly, pleasant, agreeable, kindly, well-disposed, hearty, encouraging. **2.** enlivening, lively, warm, mild. **—Ant.** unsympathetic, unpleasant, discouraging; cool.

genius, *n.* **1.** capacity, ability, talent, gift, aptitude, faculty, bent. **2.** spirit, guardian angel, genie, jinn. **—Ant.** inability, incapacity.

gentle, *adj.* **1.** soft, bland, peaceful, clement, moderate, pacific, soothing, kind, tender, humane, lenient, merciful, meek, mild, kindly, amiable, submissive, gentle-hearted, kind-hearted. **2.** gradual, moderate, temperate, tempered, light, mild. **3.** wellborn, noble, highborn. **4.** honorable, respectable, refined, cultivated, polished, well-bred, polite, elegant, courteous, courtly. **5.** manageable, tractable, tame, docile, trained, peaceable, quiet. **—Ant.** immoderate, turbulent, unkind, cruel, heartless; sudden, abrupt; unrefined, unpolished, impolite; intractable, wild, noisy.

gentleman, See Syn. study at MAN.

genuine, *adj.* authentic, real, true, bona fide, verifiable, factual, provable, honest-to-God, the real McCoy. **—Ant.** false, counterfeit.

get, *v.* **1.** obtain, acquire, procure, secure, gain. **2.** earn, win, gain. **3.** learn, apprehend, grasp. **4.** capture, seize upon. **5.** prepare, get ready. **6.** prevail on *or* upon, persuade, induce, influence, dispose. **7.** beget, engender, generate, breed, procreate. **8.** come to, reach, arrive. **9.** become, grow. **—Ant.** lose. **—Syn. Study.** GET, OBTAIN, ACQUIRE, PROCURE, SECURE imply gaining possession of something. GET suggests gaining possession in any manner, either voluntarily or without effort: *to get a copy of a book.* OBTAIN suggests putting forth effort to gain possession of something wanted: *to obtain information.* ACQUIRE often suggests possessing something after a prolonged effort: *to acquire a fortune in the oil business.* PROCURE stresses the use of special means or measures to get something: *to procure a rare etching from an art dealer.* SECURE suggests obtaining something and making possession safe and sure: *to secure benefits for striking workers.*

ghastly, *adj.* **1.** dreadful, horrible, frightful, hideous, grisly, dismal, terrible, shocking. **2.** pale, deathly, white, wan, cadaverous. —**Ant.** lovely, attractive, beautiful; ruddy, robust, healthy.

ghost, *n.* **1.** apparition, phantom, spirit, phantasm, wraith, revenant, shade, spook, specter,

supernatural being. **2.** shadow, hint, suggestion.

giant, *adj.* **1.** oversize, outsize, huge, enormous, great, grand, king-size, gigantic, mammoth, jumbo, colossal, gargantuan, immense, massive, monstrous, monster, vast, Brobdingnagian. **2.** colossus, titan, Atlas, Goliath, amazon, behemoth, monster. —**Ant.** Lilliputian, tiny.

giddy, *adj.* **1.** light-headed, light, dizzy, vertiginous, swimmy, reeling, spacey, seeing double, groggy, confused. **2.** silly, frivolous, lighthearted, merry, playful, whimsical, pixilated, foolish, goofy, wacky. **3.** empty-headed, flighty, featherbrained, witless. **4.** high, tipsy, tiddly, pixilated. —**Ant.** sober.

gift, *n.* **1.** donation, present, contribution, offering, boon, alms, gratuity, tip, benefaction, grant, largess, subsidy, allowance, endowment, bequest, legacy, dowry, inheritance, bounty. **2.** talent, endowment, power, faculty, ability, capacity, forte, capability, genius, bent.

gigantic, *adj.* huge, enormous, tremendous, colossal, mammoth, monstrous, elephantine, immense, prodigious, herculean, titanic, cyclopean, vast, extensive, infinite. —**Ant.** small, tiny, infinitesimal, microscopic. —**Syn. Study.** GIGANTIC, COLOSSAL, MAMMOTH are used of whatever is physically or metaphorically of great magnitude. GIGANTIC refers to the size of a giant, or to anything that is of unusually large size: *a gigantic country.* COLOSSAL refers to the awesome effect and extraordinary size or power of a colossus or of something of similar size, scope, or effect: *a colossal mistake.* MAMMOTH refers to the size of the animal of that name and is used esp. of anything large and heavy: *a mammoth battleship.*

gingerly, *adj.* **1.** cautious, careful, circumspect, mindful, heedful, prudent, discreet, guarded, politic. —*adv.* **2.** cautiously, carefully, heedfully.

give, *v.* **1.** deliver, bestow, hand over, offer, vouchsafe, impart, accord, furnish, provide, supply, donate, contribute, afford, spare, accommodate with, confer, grant, cede, relinquish, yield, turn over, assign, present. **2.** enable, assign, award. **3.** set forth, issue, show, present, offer. **4.** assume, suppose, assign. **5.** afford, yield, produce. **6.** perform, make do. **7.** issue, put forth, emit, publish, utter, give out (with), pronounce, render. **8.** communicate, impart, divulge. **9.** draw back, recede, retire, relax, cede, yield, give over, give away, sink, give up. **10.** break down, fail. —**Ant.** receive. —**Syn. Study.** GIVE, CONFER, GRANT, PRESENT mean that something concrete or abstract is bestowed on one person by another. GIVE is the general word:

to give someone a book. CONFER usu. means to give as an honor or as a favor; it implies courteous and gracious giving: *to confer a medal.* GRANT is usu. limited to the idea of acceding to a request or fulfilling an expressed wish; it often involves a formal act or legal procedure: *to grant a prayer; to grant immunity.* PRESENT, a more formal word than GIVE, usu. implies a certain ceremony in the giving: *to present an award.*

glad, *adj.* **1.** delighted, pleased, elated, happy, gratified, contented. **2.** cheerful, joyous, joyful, happy, merry, cheery, animated, light. —**Ant.** miserable, unhappy, sad.

glamour, *n.* allure, allurement, attraction, seductiveness, appeal, charm, charisma, fascination, magnetism, exoticism, star quality. —**Ant.** ordinariness.

glance, *v.* **1.** glitter, flash, glimpse, gleam, glisten, scintillate, shine. **2.** cast, reflect. —*n.* **3.** glitter, gleam; glimpse, look.

glare, *n.* **1.** dazzle, flare, glitter, luster, brilliance, sparkle, flash. **2.** showiness. **3.** scowl, glower. —*v.* **4.** shine, dazzle, gleam. **5.** glower, gloat, scowl.

glaring, See Syn. study at FLAGRANT.

gleam, *n.* **1.** ray, flash, beam, glimmer, glimmering. —*v.* **2.** shine, glimmer, flash, glitter, sparkle, beam.

glee, *n.* joy, exultation, merriment, jollity, hilarity, mirth, joviality, gaiety, liveliness, verve, life. —**Ant.** misery, sadness, melancholy.

glib, *adj.* **1.** fluent, voluble, talkative, ready. **2.** slippery, smooth, facile, artful. —**Ant.** taciturn, silent, quiet; artless, guileless. —**Syn. Study.** See FLUENT.

glide, *v., n.* slide, slip, flow. —**Ant.** stick.

glisten, *v.* glimmer, shimmer, sparkle, shine, gleam, glitter.

gloom, *n.* **1.** darkness, dimness, shadow, shade, obscurity, gloominess. **2.** melancholy, sadness, depression, dejection, despondency. **—Ant.** brightness, effulgence; joy, glee, happiness.

gloomy, *adj.* **1.** dark, shaded, obscure, shadowy, dim, dusky; dismal, lowering. **2.** depressed, dejected, sad, melancholy, despondent, downcast, crestfallen, downhearted, glum, dispirited, disheartened. **—Ant.** bright, effulgent, dazzling; happy, delighted, gleeful.

glorious, *adj.* **1.** admirable, delightful. **2.** famous, renowned, noted, celebrated, famed, eminent, distinguished, illustrious. **—Ant.** horrible; unknown; notorious.

glory, *n.* **1.** praise, honor, distinction, renown, fame, eminence, celebrity. **2.** resplendence, splendor, magnificence, grandeur, pomp, brilliance, effulgence. **—v. 3.** exult, rejoice, triumph. **—Ant.** infamy, dishonor; gloom.

gloss, *n.* **1.** luster, sheen, polish, glaze, shine. **2.** front, mien, appearance, pretext, pretence. **3.** explanation, exegesis, critique, comment, note, interpretation, analysis, annotation, commentary. **—v. 4.** polish, shine, glaze, varnish. **5.** annotate, explain, interpret, analyze. **—Syn. Study.** See POLISH.

glossy, *adj.* **1.** lustrous, shiny, shining, glazed, smooth, sleek. **2.** specious, plausible.

glum, *adj.* morose, depressed, gloomy, sad, dejected; moody, sullen, sulky, sour, dour **—Syn. Study.** GLUM, MOROSE, SULLEN describe a gloomy, unsociable attitude. GLUM suggests a depressed, spiritless disposition or manner, usu. temporary: *The runner had a glum expression after losing the race.* MOROSE, which adds a sense of bitterness and peevishness, implies a habitual and pervasive gloominess: *His chronic* *illness put him in a morose mood.* SULLEN usu. implies a reluctance or refusal to speak, accompanied by a glowering look expressing anger or a sense of injury: *The child had a sullen look after being scolded.*

gluttonous, *adj.* greedy, devouring, voracious, ravenous, grasping, insatiable, ravening, hoggish, piggish, piggy, avid, rapacious, edacious. —**Ant.** abstinent, abstemious, restrained.

gnome, *n.* goblin, troll, sylph, gremlin. —**Syn. Study.** See GOBLIN.

gobble, *v.* gulp, bolt, devour, swallow.

goblin, *n.* gnome, gremlin, troll, elf, bogeyman, ogre, demon —**Syn. Study.** GOBLIN, GNOME, GREMLIN refer to supernatural beings thought to be malevolent to people. GOBLINS are demons of any size, usu. in human or animal form, that are supposed to assail, afflict, and even torture human beings. GNOMES are small ugly creatures that live in the earth, guarding mines, treasures, etc. They are mysteriously malevolent and terrify human beings by causing dreadful mishaps to occur. GREMLINS are thought to disrupt machinery and are active in modern folklore.

godly, *adj.* pious, saintly, devout, religious, holy, righteous, good. —**Ant.** ungodly.

good, *adj.* **1.** moral, righteous, religious, pious, pure, virtuous, conscientious, meritorious, worthy, exemplary, upright. **2.** commendable, adroit, efficient, proficient, able, skillful, expert, ready, dexterous, clever, capable, qualified, fit, suited, suitable, convenient. **3.** satisfactory, excellent, exceptional, valuable, precious, capital, admirable, commendable. **4.** well-behaved, obedient, heedful. **5.** kind, beneficent, friendly, kindly, benevolent, humane, favorable, well-disposed, gracious, obliging. **6.**

honorable, worthy, deserving, fair, unsullied, immaculate, unblemished, unimpeached. **7.** reliable, safe, trustworthy, honest, competent. **8.** genuine, sound, valid. **9.** agreeable, pleasant, genial, cheering. **10.** satisfactory, advantageous, favorable, auspicious, propitious, fortunate, profitable, useful, serviceable, beneficial. **11.** ample, sufficient. **12.** full, adequate, all of. **13.** great, considerable, large. —*n.* **14.** profit, worth, advantage, benefit, usefulness, utility, gain. **15.** excellence, merit, righteousness, kindness, virtue. **16.** (*plural*) property, belongings, effects, chattel, furniture. **17.** (*plural*) wares, merchandise, stock, commodities. —**Ant.** bad. —**Syn. Study.** See PROPERTY.

goodness, *n.* **1.** virtue, morality, integrity, honesty, uprightness, probity, righteousness, good. **2.** kindness, benevolence, generosity, kindliness, benignity, humanity. **3.** excellence, worth, value, quality. **4.** essence, strength. —**Ant.** evil. —**Syn. Study.** GOODNESS, MORALITY, VIRTUE refer to qualities of character or conduct that entitle the possessor to approval and esteem. GOODNESS is the simple word for a general quality recognized as an inherent part of one's character: *Many could tell of her goodness and honesty.* MORALITY implies conformity to the recognized standards of right conduct: *a citizen of the highest morality.* VIRTUE is a rather formal word, and usually suggests GOODNESS that is consciously or steadily maintained, often in spite of temptations or evil influences: *a man of unassailable virtue.*

good will, **1.** friendliness, benevolence, favor, kindness. **2.** acquiescence, heartiness, ardor, zeal, earnestness.

gorge, *n.* **1.** defile, pass, cleft, fissure, ravine, notch. **2.** disgust, repulsion, revulsion. —*v.* **3.** stuff, glut, cram, fill. **4.** bolt, gulp, gobble, devour, gormandize.

gorgeous, *adj.* sumptuous, magnificent, splendid, rich, grand, resplendent, brilliant, glittering, dazzling, superb, to die for. —**Ant.** poor; ugly.

gossip, *n.* **1.** scandal, small talk, hearsay, palaver, idle talk, newsmongering. **2.** chatterer, babbler, gabber, nosy Parker. —*v.* **3.** chatter, prattle, prate, palaver, tattle.

govern, *v.* **1.** rule, reign, hold sway, control, command, sway, influence, have control. **2.** direct, guide, restrain, check, conduct, manage, supervise, superintend. —**Ant.** obey; follow.

gown, *n.* dress, robe, frock, evening gown *or* dress.

grace, *n.* **1.** attractiveness, charm, gracefulness, comeliness, ease, elegance, symmetry, beauty; polish, refinement. **2.** favor, kindness, kindliness, love, good will, benignity, condescension. **3.** mercy, clemency, pardon, leniency, lenity, forgiveness. **4.** love, sanctity, holiness, devoutness, devotion, piety. —*v.* **5.** adorn, embellish, beautify, enhance, deck, decorate, ornament; honor, dignify. —**Ant.** ugliness; disfavor; condemnation; hate, abhorrence; dishonor, disgrace.

gracious, *adj.* **1.** kind, kindly, benevolent, benign, courteous, polite, courtly, friendly, well-disposed, favorable. **2.** compassionate, tender, merciful, lenient, clement, mild, gentle. **3.** indulgent, beneficent, condescending, patronizing. —**Ant.** ungracious, unkind, impolite, unfavorable; dispassionate, cool, cruel, inclement.

gradual, *adj.* slow, by degrees, little by little, step by step, moderate, gentle. —**Ant.** sudden, precipitous, abrupt, immoderate. **—Syn. Study.** See SLOW.

grand, *adj.* **1.** imposing, stately, august, majestic, dignified, exalted, elevated, eminent, princely, regal, kingly, royal, great, illustrious. **2.** lofty, magnificent, great, large, palatial, splendid, brilliant, superb, glorious, sublime, noble, fine. **3.** main, principal, chief. **4.** important, distinctive, pretentious. **5.** complete, comprehensive, inclusive, all-inclusive. **—Ant.** base, undignified; ignoble; secondary; unimportant; incomplete.

grandeur, *n.* magnificence, splendor, grandness, resplendence, magnitude, sweep, amplitude, scope, loftiness, nobility, stateliness, majesty. **—Ant.** insignificance, nullity.

grandiloquent, *adj.* lofty, pompous, bombastic, turgid, inflated, declamatory, rhetorical, oratorical, high-flown, pretentious, haughty, highfalutin. **—Ant.** base, servile, lowly.

grandiose, *adj.* ostentatious, pretentious, pompous, overblown, inflated, highfalutin, in poor taste, brassy; awesome, dramatic, formidable. **—Syn. Study.** GRANDIOSE, OSTENTATIOUS, PRETENTIOUS, POMPOUS refer to a conspicuous outward display designed to attract attention. GRANDIOSE may suggest impressiveness that is not objectionable; however, it most often implies exaggeration or affectation to the point of absurdity: *the grandiose sweep of an arch; a grandiose idea to take a limousine to work.* OSTENTATIOUS has the negative connotation of trying to impress or outdo others: *ostentatious furnishings.* PRETENTIOUS is always derogatory, suggesting falseness or exaggeration in claims made or implied: *pretentious language that masked the absence of real content.* POMPOUS implies a display of exaggerated dignity or importance: *a pompous bureaucrat.*

grant, *v.* **1.** bestow, confer, award, bequeath, give. **2.** agree *or* accede to, admit, allow, concede, accept, cede, yield. **3.** transmit, convey, transfer. —*n.* **4.** cession, concession, bequest, conveyance. —**Ant.** receive. —**Syn. Study.** See GIVE.

graphic, *adj.* **1.** lifelike, vivid, picturesque, striking, telling. **2.** diagrammatic, well-delineated, detailed.

grasp, *v.* **1.** seize, hold, clasp, grip, clutch, grab, catch. **2.** lay hold of, seize upon, fasten on; concentrate on, comprehend, understand. —*n.* **3.** grip, hold, clutches. **4.** hold, possession, mastery. **5.** reach, comprehension, compass, scope. —**Ant.** loose, loosen; misunderstand.

grateful, *adj.* **1.** appreciative, thankful, obliged, indebted. **2.** pleasing, agreeable, welcome, refreshing,

pleasant, gratifying, satisfying, satisfactory. —**Ant.** ungrateful; unpleasant, disagreeable, unsatisfactory.

gratify, *v.* please, indulge, humor, satisfy. —**Ant.** displease, dissatisfy.

grave, *n.* **1.** place of interment, tomb, sepulchre, pit, excavation. —*adj.* **2.** sober, solemn, serious, dignified, sedate, earnest, staid, thoughtful. **3.** weighty, momentous, important, serious, consequential, critical. —**Ant.** undignified, thoughtless; unimportant, trivial, trifling. —**Syn. Study.** GRAVE, SOBER, SOLEMN refer to the condition of being serious in demeanor or appearance. GRAVE indicates a dignified seriousness due to heavy responsibilities or cares: *The jury looked grave while pondering the evidence.* SOBER implies a determined but sedate and restrained manner: *a wise and sober judge.* SOLEMN suggests an impressive and earnest seriousness marked by the absence of gaiety or mirth: *The minister's voice was solemn as he announced the text.*

great, *adj.* **1.** immense, enormous, huge, gigantic, vast, ample, grand, large, big. **2.** numerous, countless. **3.** unusual, considerable, important, momentous, serious, weighty. **4.** notable, remarkable, noteworthy. **5.** distinguished, famous, famed, eminent, noted, prominent, celebrated, illustrious, grand, renowned. **6.** consequential, important, vital, critical. **7.** chief, principal, main, grand, leading. **8.** noble, lofty, grand, exalted, elevated, dignified, majestic, august. **9.** admirable, notable. —**Ant.** small; insignificant; paltry; infamous, notorious; trivial; secondary.

greed, *n.* desire, avidity, avarice, cupidity, covetousness, greediness, voracity, ravenousness, rapacity. —**Ant.** generosity.

greedy, *adj.* **1.** grasping, rapacious, selfish, avaricious. **2.** gluttonous, voracious, ravenous, starved, insatiable. **3.** desirous, covetous, eager, anxious. —**Ant.** generous, unselfish. —**Syn. Study.** See AVARICIOUS.

greet, *v.* address, welcome, hail, accost, salute.

gremlin, See Syn. study at GOBLIN.

grief, *n.* suffering, distress, sorrow, regret, anguish, heartache, woe, misery, sadness, melancholy, moroseness. —**Ant.** joy, happiness, glee, delight.

grieve, *v.* **1.** lament, weep, mourn, sorrow, suffer, bewail, bemoan. **2.** distress, sadden, depress, agonize, break one's heart, pain. —**Ant.** delight in.

grievous, *adj.* **1.** distressing, sad, sorrowful, painful, lamentable, regrettable. **2.** deplorable, lamentable, calamitous, heinous, outrageous, flagrant, atrocious, flagitious, dreadful, gross, shameful, iniquitous. —**Ant.**

delighted, happy, joyful; delightful, pleasant, favorable.

grim, *adj.* **1.** stern, unrelenting, merciless, uncompromising, harsh, unyielding. **2.** sinister, ghastly, repellent, frightful, horrible, dire, appalling, horrid, grisly, gruesome, hideous, dreadful. **3.** severe, stern, harsh, hard, fierce, forbidding, ferocious, cruel, savage, ruthless. —**Ant.** merciful, lenient, sympathetic; wonderful, delightful, pleasant; amenable, genial, congenial, amiable.

grind, *v.* **1.** smooth, sharpen. **2.** bray, triturate, pulverize, powder, crush, comminute, pound. **3.** oppress, torment, harass, persecute, plague, afflict, trouble. **4.** grate, rub, abrade.

grit, *n.* **1.** sand, gravel. **2.** spirit, pluck, fortitude, courage, resolution.

groggy, *adj.* confused, muddled, dazed, muzzy, dopey, woozy, punchy, slap-happy. —**Ant.** clear-headed, alert.

gross, *adj.* **1.** whole, entire, total, aggregate. **2.** glaring, flagrant, outrageous, shameful, heinous, grievous. **3.** coarse, indelicate, indecent, low, animal, sensual, vulgar, broad, lewd. **4.** large, big, bulky, massive, great. **5.** thick, dense, heavy. —*n.* **6.** body, bulk, mass. —**Ant.** partial, incomplete; delicate, decent; small, dainty. —**Syn. Study.** See FLAGRANT.

grotesque, See Syn. study at FANTASTIC.

grouchy, *adj.* cantankerous, irritable, irascible, fractious, cross, crotchety, choleric, foul-tempered, mean-tempered, grumpy, ornery, testy, touchy, peevish, surly, vinegary. —**Ant.** even-tempered, gracious.

ground, *n.* **1.** land, earth, soil, mold, loam, dirt. **2.** (*often plural*) foundation, basis, base, premise, motive, reason, cause, consideration, factor, account. **3.** (*plural*) lees, dregs, sediment, silt, deposit. —*v.* **4.** found, fix, settle, establish, base, set. **5.** instruct, train. —**Ant.** sky, heaven; embellishment.

grow, *v.* **1.** increase, swell, enlarge, dilate, greaten, expand, extend. **2.** sprout, germinate; arise, originate. **3.** swell, wax, extend, advance, improve. **4.** raise, cultivate, produce. —**Ant.** decrease, shrink; wane, deteriorate.

growl, *v.* **1.** snarl. **2.** grumble, complain, mumble.

growth, *n.* **1.** development, increase, augmentation, expansion. **2.** product, outgrowth, result; produce. **3.** (*pathology*) tumor, excrescence. **4.** source, production. —**Ant.** failure, stagnation.

grudge, *n.* **1.** malice, ill will, spite, resentment, bitterness, rancor, malevolence, enmity, hatred. —*v.* **2.** suffer, yield, submit to. **3.**

begrudge, envy. —**Ant.** good will, amiability.

grudging, *adj.* reluctant, unenthusiastic, unwilling, begrudging, apathetic, indifferent, perfunctory, lukewarm, tepid, ungenerous, mean-spirited. —**Ant.** enthusiastic, generous.

grumble, See Syn. study at COMPLAIN.

guarantee, *n.* **1.** guaranty, warrant, pledge, assurance, promise, surety, security. —*v.* **2.** guaranty, secure, ensure, insure, warrant.

guard, *v.* **1.** protect, keep safe, preserve, save, watch over, shield, defend, shelter. **2.** hold, check, watch, be careful. —*n.* **3.** protector, guardian, sentry, watchman, defender, sentinel. **4.** convoy, escort. **5.** defense, protection, shield, bulwark, security, aegis, safety. —**Ant.** attack, assault; ignore; danger.

guardian, *n.* **1.** guard, protector, defender. **2.** trustee, warden, keeper. —**Ant.** assailant.

guess, *v.* **1.** conjecture, hazard, suppose, fancy, believe, imagine, think. **2.** estimate, solve, answer, penetrate. —*n.* **3.** notion, judgment, conclusion, conjecture, surmise, supposition. —**Ant.** know. —**Syn. Study.** GUESS, CONJECTURE, SURMISE imply attempting to form an opinion as to the probable. To GUESS is to risk an opinion regarding something one does not know about, or, wholly or partly by chance, to arrive at the correct answer to a question: *to guess the outcome of a game.* To CONJECTURE is to make inferences in the absence of sufficient evidence to establish certainty: *to conjecture the circumstances of the crime.* SURMISE implies making an intuitive conjecture that may or may not be correct: *to surmise the motives that led to the crime.*

guest, *n.* visitor, company. —**Ant.** host.

guide, *v.* **1.** lead, pilot, steer, conduct, direct, show *or* point the way, escort, instruct, induce, influence, regulate, manage, govern, rule. —*n.* **2.** pilot, steersman, helmsman, director, conductor. **3.** mark, sign, signal, indication, key, clue. —**Ant.** follow.

guile, *n.* cunning, treachery, deceit, artifice, duplicity, deception, trickery, fraud, craft, artfulness. —**Ant.** ingenuousness. —**Syn. Study.** See DECEIT.

guileless, *adj.* artless, honest, sincere, open, candid, frank, truthful, ingenuous, naive, unsophisticated, simple-minded. —**Ant.** cunning, sly, deceitful, artful, treacherous.

guilt, *n.* guiltiness, culpability, criminality. —**Ant.** exoneration.

guiltless, *adj.* innocent, spotless, blameless, immaculate, pure, unsullied, unpolluted, untarnished. —**Ant.**

culpable, guilty, sullied, tarnished.

guise, *n.* appearance, aspect, semblance, form, shape, fashion, mode, manner. **—Syn. Study.** See APPEARANCE.

guru, *n.* teacher, guide, instructor, tutor, coach, trainer, handler, preceptor, master, docent, expert. **—Ant.** student, acolyte, follower.

gush, *v.* pour, stream, spurt, flow, spout, flood.

gust, See Syn. study at WIND.

H

habit, *n.* **1.** disposition, tendency, bent, wont. **2.** custom, practice, way, usage, wont, manner. **3.** garb, dress, rig, habiliment. **—v. 4.** dress, clothe, garb, array, attire, deck out, rig, equip. **—Syn. Study.** See CUSTOM.

habitat, *n.* home, locality, haunt, environment, turf, locale, site, neighborhood, precincts, range, territory, surroundings, environs, vicinity, stamping ground, home ground, milieu.

habitual, *adj.* confirmed, inveterate, accustomed, customary, usual, common, regular, familiar, ordinary. **—Ant.** rare, unaccustomed, unusual, uncommon, irregular. **—Syn. Study.** See USUAL.

habituate, *v.* accustom, familiarize, acclimate, acclimatize, train, inure, harden, make used (to).

hack, *v.* **1.** cut, notch, chop, hew, mangle. **2.** let, hire, lease, rent. **3.** hackney. **—n. 4.** cut, notch, gash. **5.** jade, nag. **—adj. 6.** hired, hackney, mercenary. **7.** hackneyed, trite, clichéd, overdone, old, used, worn out, commonplace, stale, stereotyped; old hat. **—Ant.** novel, new.

hackneyed, *adj.* trite, clichéd, stale, timeworn, overused, tired, well-worn, unoriginal, bromidic, platitudinous, commonplace, pedestrian, worn-out, banal, cornball, bathetic, stock, set, old-hat, warmed-over, moth-eaten, threadbare, corny. —**Ant.** original, inventive. —**Syn. Study.** See COMMONPLACE.

haggard, *adj.* wild-looking, careworn, gaunt, emaciated, drawn, hollow-eyed, meager, spare, worn, wasted. —**Ant.** hale, hearty, robust.

haggle, *v.* **1.** bargain, chaffer, higgle, palter, negotiate. **2.** wrangle, dispute, cavil, argue. **3.** harass, annoy, vex, tease, worry, badger, bait, fret. **4.** hack, mangle, chop, cut. —*n.* **5.** haggling, wrangle, dispute, argument, disagreement.

hale, *adj.* **1.** robust, healthy, vigorous, sound, strong, hearty. —*v.* **2.** drag, haul, pull, tug, draw.

—**Ant.** haggard, weak, feeble.

half-hearted, *adj.* unenthusiastic, indifferent, uninterested, cold, cool, perfunctory, curt, abrupt, discouraging. —**Ant.** enthusiastic, eager, encouraging.

hallowed, *adj.* sacred, consecrated, holy, blessed; honored, revered. —**Ant.** execrative, blasphemous. —**Syn. Study.** See HOLY.

hallucination, *n.* illusion, delusion, aberration, phantasm, vision. —**Ant.** reality.

halt, *v.* **1.** hold, stop, cease, desist. **2.** waver, hesitate. —**Ant.** continue, persist. —**Syn. Study.** See STOP.

hamlet, *n.* village, community, town, dorp.

hamper, *v.* **1.** impede, hinder, hold back, encumber, prevent, obstruct, restrain, clog. —*n.* **2.** basket; crate. —**Ant.** further, encourage. —**Syn. Study.** See PREVENT.

handsome, *adj.* **1.** comely, fine, admirable, good-looking. **2.** liberal, considerable, ample, large, generous, magnanimous. **3.** gracious, generous. —**Ant.** ugly, unattractive; stingy, penurious, parsimonious. —**Syn. Study.** See BEAUTIFUL.

handy, *adj.* **1.** convenient, useful, practical, functional, serviceable. **2.** near, nearby, at hand, close, adjacent, convenient, close-by, near-at-hand, close-at-hand. **3.** adept, dexterous, skilled, skillful, artful, adroit, deft, clever, proficient.

hang, *v.* **1.** suspend, dangle. **2.** execute, lynch. **3.** drape, decorate, adorn, furnish. **4.** depend, rely, rest; hold fast, cling, adhere. **5.** be doubtful *or* undecided, waver, hesitate, demur, halt. **6.** loiter, linger, hover, flot. **7.** impend, be imminent.

hanker, See Syn. study at YEARN.

happen, *v.* come to pass, take place, occur, chance; befall, betide.

happiness, *n.* good fortune, pleasure, contentment, gladness, bliss, content, contentedness, beatitude, blessedness, delight, joy, enjoyment, gratification, satisfaction. —**Ant.** misery, dissatisfaction.

happy, *adj.* **1.** joyous, joyful, glad, blithe, merry, cheerful, contented, gay, blissful, delighted, satisfied, pleased, gladdened. **2.** favored, lucky, fortunate, propitious, advantageous, successful, prosperous. **3.** appropriate, fitting, apt, felicitous, opportune, befitting, pertinent. —**Ant.** unhappy, sad, cheerless, melancholy; unlucky, luckless, unfortunate; inappropriate, inapt.

harangue, *n.* **1.** address, speech, bombast. —*v.* **2.** declaim, address. —**Syn. Study.** See SPEECH.

harass, *v.* trouble, harry, raid, molest, disturb, distress; plague, vex, worry, badger, pester, annoy, torment, torture.

harbinger, *n.* **1.** forerunner, herald, precursor,

announcer, messenger,
outrider, evangel,
evangelist, stormy petrel.
—*v.* **2.** announce, herald,
presage, forerun, foreshow,
preindicate, augur, foretell.
harbor, *n.* **1.** haven, port.
2. shelter, refuge, asylum,
protection, cover,
sanctuary, retreat. —*v.* **3.**
shelter, protect, lodge. **4.**
conceal, hide, secrete. **5.**
entertain, indulge, foster,
cherish. —**Syn. Study.**
HARBOR, PORT, HAVEN refer
to a shelter for ships. A
HARBOR is a natural or an
artificially constructed
shelter and anchorage for
ships: *a fine harbor on the
eastern coast.* A PORT is a
harbor viewed esp. with
reference to its commercial
activities and facilities: *a
thriving port.* HAVEN is a
literary word meaning
refuge, although
occasionally referring to a
natural harbor that can be
utilized by ships as a place
of safety: *to seek a haven
in a storm.* See also
CHERISH.
hard, *adj.* **1.** solid, firm,
inflexible, rigid, unyielding,

resistant, resisting,
adamantine, flinty,
impenetrable, compact. **2.**
difficult, toilsome,
burdensome, wearisome,
exhausting, laborious,
arduous, onerous,
fatiguing, wearying. **3.**
difficult, complex,
intricate, complicated,
perplexing, tough,
puzzling. **4.** vigorous,
severe, violent, stormy,
tempestuous; inclement. **5.**
oppressive, harsh, rough,
cruel, severe, unmerciful,
grinding, unsparing,
unrelenting. **6.** severe,
harsh, stern, austere, strict,
exacting, callous,
unfeeling, unsympathetic,
impassionate, insensible,
unimpressible, insensitive,
indifferent, unpitying,
inflexible, relentless,
unyielding, cruel,
obdurate, adamant,
hard-hearted. **7.**
undeniable, irrefutable,
incontrovertible. **8.**
unfriendly, unkind; harsh,
unpleasant. **9.**
unsympathetic,
unsentimental, shrewd,
hard-headed, callous. **10.**

strong, spirituous, intoxicating. —*adv.* **11.** energetically, vigorously, violently. **12.** earnestly, intently, incessantly. **13.** harshly, severely, gallingly, with difficulty. **14.** solidly, firmly. —**Ant.** soft; easy; fair; merciful; sympathetic; kind.

harden, *v.* **1.** solidify, indurate, ossify, petrify. **2.** strengthen, confirm, fortify, steel, brace, nerve, toughen, inure; habituate, accustom, season, train, discipline.

hardly, *adv.* **1.** barely, scarcely, nearly. **2.** harshly, severely, roughly, cruelly, unkindly, rigorously. —**Syn. Study.** HARDLY, BARELY, SCARCELY imply a narrow margin of sufficiency. HARDLY usu. emphasizes the difficulty or sacrifice involved: *We could hardly endure the winter.* BARELY implies no more than the minimum, as in performance or quantity: *We barely succeeded.* SCARCELY implies an even narrower margin, usu. below a satisfactory level: *He can scarcely read.*

hardship, *n.* trial, oppression, privation, need, austerity, trouble, affliction, burden, suffering, misfortune, grievance.

hardy, *adj.* **1.** vigorous, hearty, sturdy, hale, robust, stout, strong, sound, healthy. **2.** bold, daring, courageous, brave. —**Ant.** weak, feeble, unsound, unhealthy; cowardly, pusillanimous.

harm, *n.* **1.** injury, damage, hurt, mischief, detriment. **2.** wrong, evil, wickedness, sinfulness. —*n.* **3.** injure, hurt, damage; maltreat, molest, abuse. —**Ant.** good.

harmful, *adj.* injurious, detrimental, hurtful, deleterious, pernicious, mischievous. —**Ant.** beneficial.

harmonious, *adj.* **1.** amicable, congenial, sympathetic. **2.** consonant, congruous, concordant, consistent, correspondent, symmetrical. **3.** melodious, tuneful, agreeable, concordant. **—Ant.** unsympathetic; discordant, incongruous, asymmetrical; cacophonous, noisy.

harmony, *n.* **1.** agreement, concord, unity, peace, amity, friendship, accord, unison. **2.** congruity, consonance, conformity, correspondence, consistency, congruence, fitness, suitability. **3.** melody, melodiousness, concord, euphony. **—Ant.** discord, disagreement; nonconformity, unfitness; cacophony, noise. **—Syn. Study.** See SYMMETRY.

harrowing, *adj.* trying, stressful, distressing, painful, agonizing, torturous, frightening, excruciating, harsh, hairy. **—Ant.** pleasant, relaxing.

harry, *v.* **1.** harass, torment, worry, molest, plague, trouble, vex, gall, fret, disturb, harrow, chafe, annoy, pester. **2.** ravage, devastate, plunder, strip, rob, pillage. **—Ant.** please, delight, enrapture.

harsh, *adj.* **1.** rough;

ungentle, unpleasant, severe, austere, brusque, rough, hard, unfeeling, unkind, brutal, cruel, stern, acrimonious, bad-tempered, ill-natured, crabbed, morose. **2.** jarring, unaesthetic, inartistic, discordant, dissonant, unharmonious. **—Ant.** gentle, pleasant, kind, good-natured; artistic, aesthetic, harmonious. **—Syn. Study.** See STERN.

haste, *n.* **1.** swiftness, celerity, alacrity, quickness, rapidity, dispatch, speed, expedition, promptitude. **2.** need, hurry, flurry, bustle, ado, precipitancy, precipitation. **—Ant.** sloth.

hasten, *v.* hurry, accelerate, urge, press, expedite, quicken, speed, precipitate, dispatch.

hasty, *adj.* **1.** speedy, quick, hurried, swift, rapid, fast, fleet, brisk. **2.** precipitate, rash, foolhardy, reckless, indiscreet, thoughtless, headlong, unthinking. **3.**

quick-tempered, testy, touchy, irascible, petulant, waspish, fretful, fiery, pettish, excitable, irritable, peevish. **—Ant.** slow, deliberate; discreet, thoughtful; even-tempered, amiable.

hatch, *v.* **1.** incubate, breed, brood. **2.** contrive, devise, plan, plot, concoct, design, scheme, project. **3.** shade, line. —*n.* **4.** brood. **5.** door, cover, deck, hatchway.

hate, *v.* **1.** dislike; detest, abhor, loathe, despise, execrate, abominate. —*n.* **2.** hatred. **—Ant.** like, love. **—Syn. Study.** HATE, ABHOR, DETEST imply feeling intense dislike or aversion toward something. HATE, the simple and general word, suggests passionate dislike and a feeling of enmity: *to hate autocracy.* ABHOR expresses a deep-rooted horror and a sense of repugnance or complete rejection: *to abhor cruelty.* DETEST implies intense, even vehement, dislike and antipathy, besides a sense of disdain: *to detest a combination of ignorance and arrogance.*

hateful, *adj.* detestable, odious, abominable, execrable, loathsome, abhorrent, repugnant, invidious, obnoxious, offensive, disgusting, nauseating, revolting, vile, repulsive. **—Ant.** lovable, appealing, attractive, likable. **—Syn. Study.** HATEFUL, ODIOUS, OFFENSIVE, OBNOXIOUS refer to something that provokes strong dislike or aversion. HATEFUL implies causing dislike along with hostility and ill will: *a hateful task.* ODIOUS emphasizes a disgusting or repugnant quality: *odious crimes.* OFFENSIVE is a general term that stresses the resentment or displeasure aroused by something that is insulting or unpleasant: *an offensive remark; an offensive odor.* OBNOXIOUS implies causing annoyance or discomfort by objectionable qualities: *His constant bragging is obnoxious.*

hatred, *n.* aversion, animosity, hate, detestation, loathing, abomination, odium, horror, repugnance. —**Ant.** attraction, love, favor.

haughty, *adj.* disdainful, proud, arrogant, supercilious, snobbish, lordly, contemptuous. —**Ant.** humble, shy, self-effacing.

have, *v.* **1.** hold, occupy, possess, own, contain. **2.** get, receive, take, obtain, acquire, gain, secure, procure. **3.** experience, enjoy, suffer, undergo. **4.** permit, allow. **5.** assert, maintain, hold, aver, state, asseverate, testify.

haven, See Syn. study at HARBOR.

havoc, *n.* devastation, ruin, destruction, desolation, waste, damage.

hazard, *n.* **1.** danger, peril, jeopardy, risk. **2.** chance, hap, accident, luck, fortuity, fortuitousness. **3.** uncertainty, doubt. —*v.* **4.** venture, offer. **5.** imperil, risk, endanger. —**Ant.**
safety, security; certainty, surety. —**Syn. Study.** See DANGER.

haze, *n.* **1.** vapor, dust, mist, cloud, fog, smog. **2.** obscurity, dimness, cloud, vagueness. —*v.* **3.** torment, torture, abuse, trick. —**Ant.** clearness, clarity.

head, *n.* **1.** command, authority. **2.** commander, director, chief, chieftain, leader, principal, commander in chief, master. **3.** top, summit, acme. **4.** culmination, crisis, conclusion. **5.** cape, headland, promontory, ness. **6.** source, origin, rise, beginning, headwaters. **7.** froth, foam. —*adj.* **8.** front, leading, topmost, chief, principal, main, cardinal, foremost, first. —*v.* **9.** lead, precede, direct, command, rule, govern. **10.** outdo, excel, surpass, beat.

headlong, *adj.* rushed, precipitate, precipitous, hasty, abrupt, hurried, impetuous, sudden, impulsive, reckless.

headstrong, *adj.* willful, stubborn, obstinate, intractable, self-willed, dogged, pigheaded, froward. —**Ant.** amenable, tractable, genial, agreeable. —**Syn. Study.** See WILLFUL.

heal, *v.* **1.** cure, remedy, restore. **2.** amend, settle, harmonize, compose, soothe. **3.** cleanse, purify, purge, disinfect. —**Ant.** discompose; soil, pollute, infect.

healthful, See Syn. study at HEALTHY.

healthy, *adj.* **1.** healthful, hale, sound, hearty, well, robust, vigorous, strong. **2.** nutritious, nourishing, salubrious, salutary, hygienic, invigorating, bracing, wholesome. —**Ant.** unhealthy, ill, sick, weak; unwholesome, enervating. —**Syn. Study.** HEALTHY, HEALTHFUL, WHOLESOME refer to physical, mental, or moral health and well-being. HEALTHY most often applies to what possesses health, but may apply to what promotes health: *a healthy child; a healthy climate.* HEALTHFUL is usu. applied to something conducive to physical health: *a healthful diet.* WHOLESOME, connoting freshness and purity, applies to something that is physically or morally beneficial: *wholesome food; wholesome entertainment.*

heap, *n.* **1.** mass, stack, pile, accumulation, collection. —*v.* **2.** pile *or* heap up, amass, accumulate. **3.** bestow, confer, cast.

hear, *v.* **1.** listen, perceive, attend. **2.** regard, heed, attend.

heat, *n.* **1.** warmth, caloricity, caloric, hotness. **2.** warmth, intensity, ardor, fervor, zeal. **3.** ardor, flush, fever, excitement, impetuosity, vehemence, violence. —*v.* **4.** stimulate, warm, stir, animate, arouse, excite, rouse. —**Ant.** coolness; phlegm; cool, discourage.

heathen, *n.* **1.** gentile, pagan. —*adj.* **2.** gentile, pagan, heathenish, irreligious, unenlightened, barbarous. —**Ant.** Christian. —**Syn. Study.** HEATHEN, PAGAN are both applied to peoples who are not Christian, Jewish, or Muslim; these terms may also refer to irreligious peoples. HEATHEN is often used of those whose religion is unfamiliar and therefore regarded as primitive, unenlightened, or uncivilized: *heathen idols; heathen rites.* PAGAN is most frequently used of the ancient Greeks and Romans who worshiped many deities: *a pagan civilization.*

heave, *v.* **1.** raise, lift, hoist, elevate. **2.** pant, exhale, breathe. **3.** vomit, retch. **4.** rise, swell, dilate, bulge, expand.

heavenly, *adj.* **1.** blissful, beautiful, divine, seraphic, cherubic, angelic, saintly, sainted, holy, beatific, blessed, beatified, glorified. **2.** celestial. —**Ant.** hellish, satanic, diabolical, devilish.

heavy, *adj.* **1.** weighty, ponderous, massive. **2.** burdensome, harsh, oppressive, depressing, onerous, distressing, severe, grievous, cumbersome. **3.** broad, thick, coarse, blunt. **4.** serious, intense, momentous, weighty, important, pithy, concentrated. **5.** trying, difficult. **6.** depressed, serious, grave, sorrowful, gloomy, mournful, melancholy, morose, morbid, dejected, sad, disconsolate, crushed, despondent, heavy-hearted, downcast, crestfallen, downhearted. **7.** overcast, cloudy, lowering, oppressive, gloomy. **8.** clumsy, slow. **9.** ponderous, dull, tedious, tiresome, wearisome, burdensome, boring, lifeless. **10.** thick, unleavened, dense, concentrated. —**Ant.** light.

hectic, *adj.* **1.** frantic, rushed, overactive, bustling, furious, frenzied, frenetic, perfervid, hysterical, hyper. **2.** feverish, fevered, febrile, hot, heated, burning, flushed. —**Ant.** calm. cool.

heed, *v.* **1.** pay *or* give attention to, consider, regard, notice, mark, observe, obey. —*n.* **2.** attention, notice, observation, consideration, care, caution, heedfulness, watchfulness, vigilance. —**Ant.** disregard, ignore.

height, *n.* **1.** altitude, stature, elevation, tallness. **2.** hill, prominence, mountain. **3.** top, peak, pinnacle, apex, eminence, acme, summit, zenith, culmination. —**Ant.** depth, abyss. —**Syn. Study.** HEIGHT, ALTITUDE, ELEVATION refer to distance above a level. HEIGHT denotes extent upward (as from foot to head) as well as any measurable distance above a given level: *The tree grew to a height of ten feet. They looked down from a great height.* ALTITUDE usually refers to the distance, determined by instruments, above a given level, commonly mean sea level: *The airplane flew at an altitude of 30,000 feet.* ELEVATION implies a distance to which something has been raised or uplifted above a level: *a hill's elevation above the surrounding country.*

heighten, See Syn. study at ELEVATE.

heinous, *adj.* hateful, odious, reprehensible, grave, wicked, infamous, flagrant, flagitious, atrocious, villainous, nefarious. —**Ant.** good, beneficial.

hell, *n.* Gehenna, Tartarus, inferno, Abaddon, Avernus, Hades, Erebus, pandemonium, abyss, limbo. —**Ant.** heaven.

help, *v.* **1.** cooperate, aid, assist, encourage, befriend, support, second, uphold, back, abet, succor, save. **2.** further, facilitate, promote, ease, foster. **3.** relieve, ameliorate, alleviate, remedy, cure, heal, restore, improve, better. **4.** refrain from, avoid, forbear. —*n.* **5.** support, backing, aid, assistance, relief, succor. **6.** helper, handyman, assistant. **—Ant.** discourage, attack. **—Syn. Study.** HELP, AID, ASSIST, SUCCOR agree in the idea of furnishing someone with something that is needed. HELP implies furnishing anything that furthers one's efforts or satisfies one's needs: *I helped her plan the party.* AID and ASSIST, somewhat more formal, imply a furthering or seconding of another's efforts. AID suggests an active helping; ASSIST suggests less need and less help: *to aid the poor; to assist a teacher in the classroom.* To SUCCOR, still more formal and literary, is to give timely help and relief to someone in difficulty or distress: *Succor him in his hour of need.*

helper, *n.* aid, assistant, supporter, auxiliary, ally, colleague, partner.

helpful, *adj.* useful, convenient, beneficial, advantageous, profitable. **—Ant.** useless, inconvenient, disadvantageous, uncooperative.

herd, *n.* **1.** drove, flock, clutch, crowd. **—v. 2.** flock, assemble, associate, keep company.

hereditary, See Syn. study at INNATE.

heritage, *n.* inheritance, estate, patrimony.

heroic, *adj.* intrepid, dauntless, gallant, valorous, brave, courageous, bold, daring, fearless; epic. **—Ant.** cowardly, fearful.

heroism, *n.* intrepidity, valor, prowess, gallantry, bravery, courage, daring, fortitude, boldness. **—Ant.** cowardice.

hesitate, *v.* **1.** waver, vacillate, falter. **2.** demur, delay, pause, wait. **—Ant.** resolve, decide.

hesitation, *n.* **1.** hesitancy, indecision, vacillation, irresolution, delay, uncertainty, doubt. **2.** halting, stammering, faltering. **—Ant.** resolution, certainty.

heterogeneous, *adj.* mixed,

assorted, miscellaneous, motley, varied, multifarious, jumbled, scrambled. **—Ant.** uniform, homogeneous.

hew, *v.* **1.** cut, chop, hack. **2.** make, shape, fashion, form. **3.** sever, cut down, fell.

hide, *v.* **1.** conceal, secrete, screen, mask, cloak, veil, shroud, cover, disguise, withhold, suppress. *—n.* **2.** skin, pelt, rawhide. **—Ant.** open, reveal. **—Syn. Study.** HIDE, CONCEAL, SECRETE mean to keep something from being seen or discovered. HIDE is the general word: *A rock hid them from view.* CONCEAL, somewhat more formal, usually means to intentionally cover up something: *He concealed the evidence of the crime.* SECRETE means to put away carefully, in order to keep secret: *The spy secreted the important papers.*

hideous, *adj.* horrible, frightful, ugly, grisly, grim, revolting, repellent, repulsive, detestable, odious, monstrous, dreadful, appalling, terrifying, terrible, ghastly, macabre, shocking. **—Ant.** beautiful, lovely, attractive.

high, *adj.* **1.** lofty, tall, elevated, towering, skyscraping. **2.** intensified, energetic, intense, strong. **3.** expensive, costly, dear, high-priced. **4.** exalted, elevated, eminent, prominent, preeminent, distinguished. **5.** shrill, sharp, acute, high-pitched, strident. **6.** chief, main, principal, head. **7.** consequential, important, grave, serious, capital, extreme. **8.** lofty, haughty, arrogant, snobbish, proud, lordly, supercilious. **9.** elated, merry, hilarious, happy. **10.** remote, primeval, early, antediluvian, prehistoric; northerly, arctic, southerly, polar. **—Ant.** low.

highminded, See Syn. study at NOBLE.

hilarity, *n.* glee, mirth, merriment, levity, jollity, hilariousness, hysterics, joy, jocularity.

hill, *n.* elevation, prominence, eminence, mound, monticule, knoll, hillock, foothill. **—Ant.** valley, dale, glen, hollow, depth.

hind, See Syn. study at BACK.

hinder, *v.* **1.** interrupt, check, retard, impede, encumber, delay, hamper, obstruct, trammel. **2.** block, thwart, prevent, obstruct. **—Ant.** encourage, disencumber. **—Syn. Study.** See PREVENT.

hindrance, *n.* **1.** impeding, stopping, stoppage, estoppage, preventing. **2.** impediment, deterrent, hitch, encumbrance, obstruction, check, restraint, hobble, obstacle. **—Ant.** help, aid, support. **—Syn. Study.** See OBSTACLE.

hint, *n.* **1.** suggestion, implication, intimation, allusion, insinuation, innuendo, memorandum, reminder, inkling. **—v. 2.** imply, intimate, insinuate, suggest, mention. **—Syn. Study.** HINT, INTIMATE, INSINUATE, SUGGEST denote the conveying of an idea to the mind indirectly or without full or explicit statement. To HINT is to convey an idea covertly or indirectly, but in a way that can be understood: *She hinted that she would like a bicycle for her birthday.* To INTIMATE is to give a barely perceptible hint, often with the purpose of influencing action: *He intimated that a conciliation was possible.* To INSINUATE is to hint artfully, often at what one would not dare to say directly: *Someone insinuated that the defendant was guilty.* SUGGEST denotes recalling something to the mind or starting a new train of thought by means of association of ideas: *Her restlessness suggested that she wanted to leave.*

hire, *v.* **1.** engage, employ; let, lease, rent, charter. **2.** bribe, reward. **—n. 3.** rent, rental; pay, stipend, salary, wages, remuneration. **—Syn. Study.** HIRE,

CHARTER, RENT refer to paying money for the use of something. HIRE is most commonly applied to paying money for a person's services, but is also used in reference to paying for the temporary use of something: *to hire a gardener; to hire a convention hall.* CHARTER is applied to hiring a vehicle for the exclusive use of a group or individual: *to charter a boat.* RENT, although used in the above senses, is most often applied to paying a set sum at regular intervals for the use of a dwelling or other property: *to rent an apartment.*

history, *n.* record, chronicle, account, annals, story, relation, narrative.

hit, *v.* **1.** strike. **2.** reach, attain, gain, win, accomplish, achieve. **3.** touch, suit, fit, befit, affect. **4.** find, come upon, meet with, discover, happen upon. **5.** collide, strike, clash. **6.** assail. —*n.* **7.** blow, stroke; success. —**Syn. Study.** See BEAT.

hitch, *v.* **1.** make fast, fasten, connect, hook, tether, attach, tie, unite, harness, yoke. —*n.* **2.** halt, obstruction, hindrance, catch, impediment. —**Ant.** loose, loosen, untie.

hoarse, *adj.* husky, throaty, guttural, gruff, harsh, grating, raucous, rough.

hobble, *v.* **1.** restrain, hamper, hinder, shackle, fetter, encumber, entrammel, trammel, handicap. **2.** limp, halt, totter, stagger. —**Ant.** enable, empower.

hoist, *v.* **1.** raise, elevate, lift, heave. —*n.* **2.** derrick, crane, elevator, lift. —**Ant.** lower.

hold, *v.* **1.** have, keep, retain, possess, occupy. **2.** bear, sustain, hold up, support, maintain, keep (up), continue, carry on. **3.** engage in, observe, celebrate, preside over, carry on, pursue. **4.** hinder, restrain, keep back, deactivate, confine, detain. **5.** occupy, possess, own. **6.** contain, admit. **7.** think, believe, embrace, espouse, entertain, have, regard, consider, esteem, judge, deem. **8.** continue, persist, last, endure, remain. **9.** adhere, cling, remain, stick. —*n.* **10.** grasp, grip. **11.** control, influence. **12.** prison, keep, tower, cell, dungeon, deep. —**Syn. Study.** See CONTAIN.

hole, *n.* **1.** aperture, opening, cavity, excavation, pit, hollow, concavity. **2.** burrow, lair, den, retreat, cave. **3.** hovel, den, cot.

holy, *adj.* **1.** blessed, sacred, consecrated, hallowed, dedicated. **2.** saintly, godly, divine, pious, devout, spiritual, pure. —**Ant.** unholy, desecrated, impious, piacular, sinful, impure, corrupt. —**Syn. Study.** HOLY, SACRED, HALLOWED refer to something that is the object of worship or veneration. HOLY refers to the divine, that which has its sanctity directly from God or is connected with Him: *Remember the Sabbath day to keep it holy.* Something that is SACRED is usually dedicated to a religious purpose by human authority: *a sacred shrine.* Something that is HALLOWED has been made holy by being worshiped or venerated: *The church graveyard is hallowed ground.*

homage, *n.* **1.** respect, reverence, deference, obeisance, honor, tribute. **2.** fealty, allegiance, faithfulness, fidelity, loyalty, devotion. **3.** devotion, worship, adoration. —**Ant.** disrespect, irreverence, dishonor; faithlessness, disloyalty.

home, *n.* **1.** house, apartment, residence, household, abode, dwelling, domicile, habitation. **2.** refuge, retreat, institution, asylum. **3.** hearth, fireside, family; rightful place. —**Syn. Study.** See HOUSE.

homely, *adj.* plain, simple, unpretentious, unattractive, coarse, inelegant, uncomely, ugly. —**Ant.** beautiful.

homograph, See Syn. study at HOMONYM.

homonym, *n.* homophone, homograph —**Syn. Study.** HOMONYM, HOMOPHONE, and HOMOGRAPH designate words that are identical to other words in spelling or pronunciation, or both, while differing from them in meaning and usu. in origin. HOMOPHONES are words that sound alike, whether or not they are spelled differently. The words *pear* "fruit," *pare* "cut off," and *pair* "two of a kind" are HOMOPHONES that are different in spelling; *bear* "carry; support" and *bear* "animal" are HOMOPHONES that are spelled alike. HOMOGRAPHS are words that are spelled identically but may or may not share a pronunciation. *Spruce* "tree" and *spruce* "neat" are HOMOGRAPHS, but so are *row* (rō) "line" and *row* (rou) "fight" as well as *sewer* (soo′ər) "conduit for waste" and *sewer* (sō′ər) "person who sews." HOMONYMS are, in the strictest sense, both HOMOPHONES and HOMOGRAPHS, alike in spelling *and* pronunciation, as the two forms *bear.* HOMONYM, however, is used more frequently than HOMOPHONE, a technical term, when referring to words with the same pronunciation without regard to spelling. HOMONYM is also used as a synonym of HOMOGRAPH. Thus, it has taken on a broader scope than either of the other two terms and is often the term of choice in a nontechnical context.

homophone, See Syn. study at HOMONYM.

honest, *adj.* **1.** honorable, upright, fair, just, incorruptible, trusty, trustworthy, truthful, virtuous, moral. **2.** open, sincere, candid, straightforward, frank, unreserved, ingenuous. **3.** genuine, pure, unadulterated. **4.** chaste, virtuous, pure, virginal, decent. —**Ant.** dishonest; corrupt, disingenuous, untrustworthy, secretive;

false, counterfeit; impure, venal, indecent.

honesty, *n.* **1.** uprightness, probity, integrity, justice, fairness, rectitude, equity, honor. **2.** truthfulness, sincerity, candor, frankness, truth, veracity. —**Ant.** dishonesty, inequity; deceit, insincerity. —**Syn. Study.** See HONOR.

honor, *n.* **1.** esteem, fame, glory, repute, reputation, credit. **2.** credit, distinction, dignity. **3.** respect, deference, homage, reverence, veneration, consideration, distinction. **4.** privilege, favor. **5.** character, principle, probity, uprightness, honesty, integrity, nobleness. **6.** purity, chastity, virginity. —*v.* **7.** revere, esteem, venerate, respect, reverence; adore, worship, hallow. —**Ant.** dishonor, disrepute, discredit; indignity; disfavor; indecency; execrate, abominate. —**Syn. Study.** HONOR, HONESTY, INTEGRITY, SINCERITY refer to the highest moral principles.

HONOR denotes a fine sense of, and a strict conformity to, what is considered morally right or due: *The soldier conducted himself with honor.* HONESTY denotes moral virtue and particularly the absence of deceit or fraud: *known for her honesty in business dealings.* INTEGRITY indicates a soundness of moral principle that no power or influence can impair: *a judge of unquestioned integrity.* SINCERITY particularly implies the absence of dissimulation or deceit and a strong adherence to the truth: *Your sincerity was evident in every word.*

honorable, *adj.* **1.** upright, honest, noble, highminded, just, fair, trusty, trustworthy, true, virtuous. **2.** dignified, distinguished, noble, illustrious, great. **3.** creditable, reputable, estimable, right, proper, equitable. —**Ant.** ignoble, untrustworthy, corrupt; undignified; disreputable.

hope, *n.* **1.** expectation, expectancy, longing,

desire. **2.** confidence, trust, reliance, faith. —*v.* **3.** trust, expect. —**Ant.** hopelessness.

hopeful, *adj.* expectant, sanguine, optimistic, confident. —**Ant.** hopeless.

hopeless, *adj.* **1.** desperate, despairing, despondent, forlorn, disconsolate. **2.** irremediable, remediless, incurable. —**Ant.** hopeful.

horrendous, *adj.* terrible, overwhelming, frightful, fearful, horrific, dreadful, ghastly, terrifying, stupefying, dire, atrocious.

horrible, *adj.* **1.** horrendous, terrible, horrid, dreadful, awful, appalling, frightful, hideous, grim, ghastly, shocking, revolting, repulsive, repellent, dire, formidable, horrifying, harrowing. **2.** unpleasant, deplorable, shocking, abominable, odious. —**Ant.** attractive, delightful, beautiful; pleasant.

horror, *n.* **1.** fear, abhorrence, terror, dread, dismay, consternation, panic, alarm. **2.** aversion, repugnance, loathing, antipathy, detestation, hatred, abomination. —**Ant.** calm, serenity; attraction, delight, love.

hospital, *n.* retreat, sanatorium, asylum, sanitarium, clinic.

hostile, *adj.* opposed, adverse, averse, unfriendly, inimical, antagonistic, contrary, warlike, oppugnant, repugnant. —**Ant.** friendly, amiable, amicable.

hostility, *n.* **1.** enmity, antagonism, animosity, animus, ill will, unfriendliness, opposition, hatred. **2.** (*plural*) war, warfare, fighting, conflict. —**Ant.** friendliness, good will, love; peace, truce.

hot, *adj.* **1.** heated, torrid, sultry, burning, fiery. **2.** pungent, piquant, sharp, acrid, spicy, peppery, biting, blistering. **3.** ardent, fervent, fervid, angry, furious, vehement, intense, excited, excitable, irascible, animated, violent, passionate, impetuous. **—Ant.** cold.

hotel, *n.* hostelry, hostel, inn, house, guest house, motel, tavern.

hotheaded, *adj.* reckless, rash, incautious, headstrong, impetuous, emotional, hot-tempered, passionate, fiery. **—Ant.** cool, serene, phlegmatic.

house, *n.* **1.** domicile, dwelling, residence, home, household. **2.** firm, company, partnership, business, establishment. **—v. 3.** lodge, harbor, shelter, reside, dwell. **—Syn. Study.** HOUSE, HOME, RESIDENCE, DWELLING are terms applied to a place in which people live. HOUSE is generally applied to a structure built for one or two families or social units: *a ranch house in the suburbs.* HOME may be used of an apartment or a private house; it retains connotations of domestic comfort and family ties: *Their home is full of charm and character.* RESIDENCE is characteristic of formal usage and often implies spaciousness and elegance: *the private residence of the prime minister.* DWELLING is a general and neutral word (*a houseboat is a floating dwelling*) and therefore commonly used in legal, scientific, and other technical contexts, as in a lease or in the phrases *multiple dwelling, single-family dwelling.*

household, *n.* **1.** family, ménage, people, brood, folks, occupants, dwellers, home, homestead, hearth, fireside, hearth and home. **—adj. 2.** domestic, family, home, domiciliary, residential. **3.** simple, ordinary, common, commonplace, plain, prosaic, everyday, garden-variety, homespun, plain-Jane. **4.** familiar, well-known, public, famous, unmistakable, notorious.

hubbub, *n.* noise, tumult, uproar, clamor, din, racket, disorder, confusion, disturbance, riot. **—Ant.** serenity, calm. **—Syn. Study.** See NOISE.

huge, *adj.* large, extensive, mammoth, vast, gigantic, colossal, stupendous, bulky, enormous, immense, tremendous, Cyclopean. **—Ant.** tiny, small, infinitesimal, microscopic. **—Syn. Study.** HUGE, ENORMOUS, TREMENDOUS, IMMENSE imply great magnitude. HUGE, when used of concrete objects, usually adds the idea of massiveness, bulkiness, or even lack of shape: *a huge mass of rock.* ENORMOUS applies to what exceeds a norm or standard in extent, magnitude, or degree: *an enormous iceberg.* TREMENDOUS suggests something so large as to be astonishing or to inspire awe: *a tremendous amount of equipment.* IMMENSE, literally not measurable, is particularly applicable to what is exceedingly great, without reference to a standard: *immense buildings.* All of these terms are used figuratively: *a huge success; enormous curiosity; tremendous effort; immense joy.*

humane, *adj.* **1.** merciful, kind, kindly, kindhearted, tender, human, benevolent, sympathetic, compassionate, gentle, accommodating, benignant, charitable. **2.** refining, polite, cultivating, elevating, humanizing, spiritual. **—Ant.** inhumane, cruel, ruthless, merciless; boorish, degrading.

humble, *adj.* **1.** low, lowly, unassuming, plain, common, poor, meek, modest, submissive, unpretending, unpretentious. **2.** respectful, polite, courteous, courtly. **—v. 3.** lower, abase, debase, degrade, humiliate, reduce, mortify, shame, subdue, abash, crush, break. **—Ant.** haughty, immodest, snobbish, conceited, pretentious; impolite, discourteous; raise, elevate. **—Syn. Study.** HUMBLE, DEGRADE, HUMILIATE suggest a lowering in self-respect or in the estimation of others. HUMBLE most often refers to a lowering of pride or arrogance, but may refer to a lessening of power or importance: *humbled by failure; to humble an enemy.* DEGRADE literally means to demote in rank or standing, but commonly refers to a bringing into dishonor or contempt: *You degrade yourself by cheating.* To HUMILIATE is to make another feel inadequate or unworthy, esp. in a public setting: *humiliated by criticism.*

humbug, *n.* **1.** trick, hoax, fraud, imposture, deception, imposition. **2.** falseness, deception, sham, pretense, hypocrisy, charlatanism. **3.** cheat, impostor, swindler, charlatan, pretender, confidence man, deceiver, quack. —*v.* **4.** impose upon, delude, deceive, cheat, swindle, trick, fool, dupe.

humid, *adj.* damp, dank, wet, moist. —**Ant.** dry.

humiliate, *v.* mortify, degrade, debase, dishonor, disgrace, abash, shame, humble. —**Ant.** honor, elevate, exalt. —**Syn. Study.** See HUMBLE.

humiliation, *n.* mortification, shame, abasement, degradation, humbling, dishonoring. —**Ant.** honor, elevation. —**Syn. Study.** See SHAME.

humility, *n.* lowliness, meekness, humbleness, submissiveness. —**Ant.** haughtiness.

humongous, *adj.* **1.** huge, bulky, giant, jumbo, king-size. **2.** remarkable, amazing, outstanding, awesome.

humor, *n.* **1.** wit, fun, facetiousness, pleasantry. **2.** disposition, tendency, temperament, mood; whim, caprice, fancy, vagary. —*v.* **3.** indulge, gratify. —**Syn. Study.** HUMOR, WIT refer to an ability to perceive and express a sense of the clever or amusing. HUMOR consists principally in the recognition and expression of incongruities or peculiarities present in a situation or character. It is frequently used to illustrate some fundamental absurdity in human nature or conduct, and is generally thought of as a kindly trait: *a genial and mellow type of humor.* WIT is a purely intellectual, often spontaneous, manifestation of cleverness and quickness in discovering analogies between things really unlike, and expressing them in brief, diverting, and often sharp observations or remarks: *biting wit.* See also SPOIL.

humorous, *adj.* amusing, funny, jocose, jocular, droll, comic, comical, witty, facetious, waggish, sportive, ludicrous, laughable. —**Ant.** serious, sad, melancholy.

hunch, *n.* feeling, impression, presentiment, suspicion, premonition, intimation, gut sense, instinct, foreboding, funny feeling.

hungry, *adj.* ravenous, famishing, famished, starved, starving. —**Ant.** sated.

hunt, *v.* **1.** chase, pursue, track. **2.** search for, seek, scour. —*n.* **3.** chase, pursuit, hunting; search.

hurly-burly, *n.* commotion, activity, busyness, excitement, whirl, hurry, hurry-scurry, ferment, tumult, turmoil, uproar, agitation, frenzy. —**Ant.** calm, torpor.

hurry, *v.* **1.** rush, haste, hasten, be quick, move swiftly *or* quickly. **2.** hasten, urge, forward, accelerate, quicken, expedite, hustle, dispatch. —*n.* **3.** bustle, haste, dispatch, celerity, speed, quickness, alacrity, promptitude, expedition. **4.** bustle, ado, precipitation, flurry, flutter, confusion, perturbation. —**Ant.** delay, slow.

hurt, *v.* **1.** injure, harm, damage, mar, impair. **2.** pain, ache, grieve, afflict, wound. —*n.* **3.** injury, harm, damage, detriment, disadvantage; bruise, wound.

hut, *n.* cottage, cot, cabin, shed, hovel.

hybrid, *n.* half-breed, mongrel, mutt.

hypocrite, *n.* deceiver, pretender, dissembler, pharisee.

hypocritical, *adj.* sanctimonious, pharisaical, Pecksniffian; insincere, deceiving, dissembling, pretending, false, hollow, empty, deceptive, misleading, deceitful. —**Ant.** honest, direct, forthright, sincere.

hypothesis, See Syn. study at THEORY.

I

icon, *n.* picture, image, symbol, idol, representation, sign.

iconoclast, *n.* unbeliever, disbeliever, doubter, questioner, challenger, heretic, nonconformist. —**Ant.** believer, supporter.

idea, *n.* **1.** thought, conception, notion; impression, apprehension, fancy. **2.** opinion, view, belief, sentiment, judgment, supposition. **3.** intention, plan, object, objective, aim. —**Syn. Study.** IDEA, THOUGHT, CONCEPTION, NOTION refer to a product of mental activity. IDEA refers to a mental representation that is the product of understanding or creative imagination: *She had an excellent idea for the party.* THOUGHT emphasizes the intellectual processes of reasoning, contemplating, reflecting, or recollecting: *I welcomed his thoughts on the subject.* CONCEPTION suggests imaginative, creative, and somewhat intricate mental activity: *The architect's conception of the building was a glass skyscraper.* NOTION suggests a fleeting, vague, or imperfect thought: *I had only a bare notion of how to proceed.*

ideal, *n.* **1.** example, model, conception, epitome, standard. **2.** aim, object, intention, objective. —*adj.* **3.** perfect, consummate, complete. **4.** unreal, unpractical, impractical, imaginary, visionary, fanciful, fantastic, illusory, chimerical.

identical, *adj.* same, alike, twin, indistinguishable, exact, equal, selfsame, undifferentiated, duplicated, reduplicated, clonal, cloned, one and the same, same-old same-old. —**Ant.** unique, nonpareil.

ideology, *n.* philosophy, belief, belief system, credo, creed, ethos, ethic, view, outlook, faith, religion, school, cult, *Weltanschauung.* —**Ant.** nihilism.

idiosyncrasy, *n.* mannerism, quirk, tic, trait, habit, trick, peculiarity, characteristic, attribute, property, mark, hallmark, token, singularity, trademark, affectation. —**Syn. Study.** See ECCENTRICITY.

idiotic, *adj.* foolish, senseless, half-witted, stupid, fatuous, imbecilic. —**Ant.** intelligent, sensible.

idle, *adj.* **1.** unemployed, unoccupied, inactive. **2.** indolent, slothful, lazy, sluggish. **3.** worthless, unimportant, trivial, trifling, insignificant, useless, fruitless, vain, ineffective, unavailing, ineffectual, abortive, baseless, groundless. **4.** frivolous, vain, wasteful. —*v.* **5.** waste, fritter away, idle away, loiter. —**Ant.** employed, occupied; active, energetic; worthy, important; thrifty. —**Syn. Study.** IDLE, INDOLENT, LAZY, SLOTHFUL apply to a person who is not active. IDLE means to be inactive or not working at a job; it is not necessarily derogatory: *pleasantly idle on a vacation.* INDOLENT means naturally disposed to avoid exertion: *an indolent and contented fisherman.* LAZY means averse to exertion or work, and esp. to continued application; the word is usually derogatory: *too lazy to earn a living.* SLOTHFUL denotes a reprehensible unwillingness to do one's share; it describes a person who is slow-moving and lacking in energy: *The heat made the workers slothful.* See also LOITER.

idol, *n.* **1.** image, icon, symbol, statue, false god, pagan deity. **2.** favorite, fair-haired boy, darling, pet. **3.** figment, delusion, illusion.

if, *conj.* **1.** in case, provided, providing, granting, supposing, even though, though; whether, whether or not. —*n.* **2.** condition, supposition.

iffy, *adj.* uncertain, unsure, doubtful, problematic, chancy, unsettled, ambiguous, conjectural, speculative, unpredictable, incalculable, unforeseeable, dicey. —**Ant.** certain, sure.

ignite, *v.* kindle, fire, set fire to, set on fire. —**Ant.**

quench. —**Syn. Study.** See KINDLE.

ignoble, *adj.* **1.** mean, base, ignominious, degraded, dishonorable, contemptible, vulgar, low, peasant. **2.** inferior, base, mean, insignificant. **3.** lowly, humble, obscure, plebeian, contemptible. —**Ant.** noble, honorable; superior, significant; haughty.

ignominious, *adj.* discreditable, humiliating, degrading, disgraceful, dishonorable, shameful, infamous, disreputable, opprobrious, despicable, scandalous, contemptible. —**Ant.** creditable, honorable, reputable.

ignominy, *n.* disgrace, dishonor, disrepute, contempt, discredit, shame, infamy, obloquy, opprobrium, scandal, odium, abasement. —**Ant.** credit, honor, repute, fame, distinction. —**Syn. Study.** See DISGRACE.

ignorant, *adj.* illiterate, unlettered, uneducated, unlearned, uninstructed,

untutored, untaught,
unenlightened, nescient.
—**Ant.** literate, lettered,
educated. —**Syn. Study.**
IGNORANT, ILLITERATE,
UNEDUCATED mean lacking
in knowledge or training.
IGNORANT may mean
knowing little or nothing,
or it may mean
uninformed about a
particular subject: *An
ignorant person can be
dangerous. I confess I'm
ignorant of higher
mathematics.* ILLITERATE
most often means unable
to read or write; however,
it sometimes means not
well-read or not well
versed in literature: *classes
for illiterate soldiers; an
illiterate mathematician.*
UNEDUCATED particularly
refers to lack of schooling:
*an intelligent but
uneducated clerk.*

ignore, *v.* overlook, slight,
disregard, neglect. —**Ant.**
notice, note, regard, mark.

ill, *adj.* **1.** unwell, sick,
indiposed, unhealthy,
ailing, diseased, afflicted.
2. evil, wicked, bad,
wrong, iniquitous,

naughty. **3.** objectionable,
unsatisfactory, poor,
faulty. **4.** hostile,
unkindly, unkind,
unfavorable, adverse. —*n.*
5. evil, wickedness,
depravity, badness. **6.**
harm, injury, hurt, pain,
affliction, misery, trouble,
misfortune, calamity. **7.**
disease, ailment, illness,
affliction. —*adv.* **8.** illy,
wickedly, badly. **9.** poorly,
unsatisfactorily. **10.**
unfavorably,
unfortunately. **11.** faultily,
improperly. —**Ant.** well,
hale, healthy; good;
satisfactory; favorably,
properly. —**Syn. Study.**
ILL, SICK mean being in bad
health, not being well. ILL
is the more formal word.
In the U.S. the two words
are used practically
interchangeably except
that SICK is always used
when the word modifies
the following noun: *He
looks sick (ill); a sick
person.* In England, SICK is
not interchangeable with
ILL, but usu. has the
connotation of nauseous:
She got sick and threw up.

SICK, however, is used before nouns just as in the U.S.: *a sick man.*

illegal, *adj.* unauthorized, unlawful, illegitimate, illicit, unlicensed. **—Ant.** legal, licit, authorized. **—Syn. Study.** ILLEGAL, UNLAWFUL, ILLICIT, CRIMINAL describe actions not in accord with law. ILLEGAL refers to violation of statutes or, in games, codified rules: *an illegal seizure of property; an illegal block in football.* UNLAWFUL is a broader term that may refer to lack of conformity with any set of laws or precepts, whether natural, moral, or traditional: *an unlawful transaction.* ILLICIT most often applies to matters regulated by law, with emphasis on the way things are carried out: *the illicit sale of narcotics.* CRIMINAL refers to violation of a public law that is punishable by a fine or imprisonment: *Robbery is a criminal act.*

illicit, See Syn. study at ILLEGAL.

illiterate, See Syn. study at IGNORANT.

ill-mannered, *adj.* impolite, uncivil, discourteous, uncourtly, rude, coarse, uncouth, unpolished, crude, rough, ill-bred.

ill-natured, *adj.* cross, cranky, petulant, testy, snappish, unkindly, unpleasant, sulky, ill-tempered, crabbed, morose, sullen, dour, gloomy, sour, crusty, perverse, acerb, bitter. **—Ant.** good-natured, kindly, pleasant, amiable, friendly.

illusion, *n.* delusion, hallucination, deception, fantasy, chimera. **—Ant.** fact, reality.

illusory, *adj.* deceptive, misleading, unreal, fancied, fanciful, visionary, imaginary, misleading, delusional, chimerical. **—Ant.** real, concrete.

illustration, *n.* comparison, example, case, elucidation, explanation, explication.

image, *n.* **1.** icon, idol, representation, statue. **2.** reflection, likeness, effigy, figure, representation. **3.** idea, conception, notion, mental picture. **4.** form, appearance, semblance. **5.** counterpart, facsimile, copy. —*v.* **6.** imagine, conceive. —**Ant.** original.

imagery, *n.* picture, pictures, pictorialization, illustration, visualization, iconography, representation, portrayal, depiction, rendering, rendition.

imaginary, *adj.* fanciful, unreal, visionary, baseless, chimerical, shadowy, fancied, illusory, imagined. —**Ant.** real.

imagine, *v.* conceive, image, picture, conceive of, realize, think, believe, fancy, assume, suppose, guess, conjecture, hypothesize.

imbibe, *v.* drink, absorb, swallow, take in, receive. —**Syn. Study.** See DRINK.

imbue, *v.* fill, infuse, steep, suffuse, permeate, pervade, inform, perfuse.

imitate, *v.* follow, mimic, ape, mock, impersonate, copy, duplicate, reproduce, simulate, counterfeit.

immediate, *adj.* **1.** instant, without delay, present, instantaneous. **2.** present, next, near, close, proximate. **3.** direct, unmediated. —**Ant.** later.

immediately, *adv.* **1.** instantly, at once, without delay, presently, directly, instanter, instantaneously, forthwith; *esp. in business contexts* ASAP. **2.** directly, closely, without intervention. —**Ant.** later, anon. —**Syn. Study.** IMMEDIATELY, INSTANTLY, DIRECTLY, PRESENTLY were once close synonyms, all denoting complete absence of delay or any lapse of time. IMMEDIATELY and INSTANTLY still almost always have that sense and usu. mean at once: *He got up immediately.* She responded instantly to the request. DIRECTLY is usu. equivalent to soon, in a little while rather than at once: *You go ahead, we'll join you directly.* PRESENTLY changes sense according to the tense of the verb with which it is used. With a present tense verb it usu. means now, at the present time: *The author presently lives in San Francisco. She is presently working on a new novel.* In some contexts, esp. those involving a contrast between the present and the near future, PRESENTLY can mean soon or in a little while: *She is at the office now but will be home presently.*

immense, *adj.* huge, great, vast, extensive. —**Ant.** small, tiny, submicroscopic. —**Syn. Study.** See HUGE.

immerse, *v.* **1.** plunge, dip, sink, immerge, duck, douse. **2.** embed, bury; involve, absorb, engage. —**Ant.** withdraw; disinter. —**Syn. Study.** See DIP.

immigrate, See Syn. study at MIGRATE.

imminent, *adj.* **1.** impending, threatening, near, at hand. **2.** overhanging, leaning forward. —**Ant.** delayed, far off.

immoderate, *adj.* excessive, extreme, exorbitant, unreasonable, inordinate, extravagant, intemperate. —**Ant.** moderate, reasonable, temperate.

immoral, *adj.* abandoned, depraved, self-indulgent, dissipated, licentious, dissolute, profligate, unprincipled, vicious, sinful, corrupt, amoral, wicked, bad, wrong, evil. —**Ant.** moral, pious, good.

immortal, *adj.* undying, eternal, everlasting, deathless, enduring, imperishable, indestructible, endless, unending, perpetual, perdurable, permanent, never-ending. —**Ant.** passing, ephemeral.

immunity, *n.* **1.** insusceptibility. **2.** exemption, franchise, privilege, license, charter, right, liberty, prerogative. —**Ant.** susceptibility; proneness. —**Syn. Study.** See EXEMPTION.

impair, *v.* injure; worsen, diminish, deteriorate,

lessen. —**Ant.** repair. —**Syn. Study.** See INJURE.

impart, *v.* **1.** communicate, disclose, divulge, reveal, make known, tell, relate. **2.** give, bestow, grant, cede, confer. —**Ant.** conceal, hide.

impartial, *adj.* unbiased, just, fair, unprejudiced, disinterested, equitable. —**Ant.** partial. —**Syn. Study.** See FAIR.

impatient, *adj.* **1.** uneasy, restless, unquiet. **2.** hasty, impetuous, vehement, precipitate, sudden, curt, brusque, abrupt. **3.** irritable, testy, fretful, violent, hot. —**Ant.** patient, restful, quiet; gradual, slow; calm, unperturbed.

impeach, *v.* censure, accuse, blame, reproach, charge, indict, arraign.

impecunious, *adj.* penniless, poor, destitute, poverty-stricken. —**Ant.** wealthy, rich. —**Syn. Study.** See POOR.

impede, *v.* retard, slow, delay, hinder, hamper, prevent, obstruct, check, stop, block, thwart, interrupt, restrain. —**Ant.** aid, encourage. —**Syn. Study.** See PREVENT.

impediment, *n.* bar, hindrance, obstacle, obstruction, encumbrance, check. —**Ant.** help, support, encouragement. —**Syn. Study.** See OBSTACLE.

impel, *v.* compel, drive, urge, press on, incite, constrain, force, actuate. —**Ant.** restrain. —**Syn. Study.** See COMPEL.

imperfect, *adj.* **1.** defective, faulty, incomplete. **2.** rudimentary, undeveloped, underdeveloped, incomplete; immature.

imperious, *adj.* **1.** domineering, overbearing, dictatorial, tyrannical, despotic, arrogant. **2.** urgent, imperative, necessary. —**Ant.** submissive; unnecessary.

impersonate, *v.* act, personate, mimic, ape, mime, parrot, enact, act out, personify, represent, portray, illustrate.

impertinent, *adj.* **1.**

intrusive, presumptuous, impudent, insolent, rude, fresh, bold, arrogant, insulting, officious, saucy, pert, brazen. **2.** irrelevant, inappropriate, incongruous, inapplicable. **3.** trivial, silly, absurd, ridiculous, inane. —**Ant.** polite, courteous; appropriate; important, serious. —**Syn. Study.** IMPERTINENT, IMPUDENT, INSOLENT refer to bold and rude persons or behavior. IMPERTINENT, from its primary meaning of not pertinent and hence inappropriate or out of place, has come to imply an unseemly intrusion into the affairs of others; it may also refer to a presumptuous rudeness toward persons entitled to respect: *impertinent questions; an impertinent interruption.* IMPUDENT suggests a bold and shameless rudeness: *an impudent young rascal.* INSOLENT suggests the insulting or contemptuous behavior of an arrogant

person: *The boss fired the insolent employee.*

impetuous, *adj.* impulsive, rash, precipitate, spontaneous, violent, hasty, furious, hot. —**Ant.** planned, careful. —**Syn. Study.** IMPETUOUS, IMPULSIVE both refer to persons who are hasty and precipitate in action, or to actions not preceded by thought. IMPETUOUS suggests great energy, overeagerness, and impatience: *an impetuous lover; impetuous words.* IMPULSIVE emphasizes spontaneity and lack of reflection: *an impulsive act of generosity.*

implacable, *adj.* unappeased, unpacified, inexorable, inflexible, unbending, relentless, unappeasable, rancorous, merciless. —**Ant.** flexible, merciful.

implement, See Syn. study at TOOL.

implicate, *v.* involve, concern, entangle. —**Ant.** disentangle.

implore, *v.* call upon,

supplicate, beseech,
entreat, crave, beg, solicit.

impolite, *adj.* uncivil, rude,
discourteous, disrespectful,
insolent, unpolished,
unrefined, boorish,
ill-mannered, rough,
savage. **—Ant.** polite.

importance, *n.*
consequence, weight,
moment, significance,
import, momentousness,
weightiness. **—Ant.**
unimportance,
insignificance. **—Syn.
Study.** IMPORTANCE,
CONSEQUENCE, SIGNIFICANCE,
MOMENT refer to something
valuable, influential, or
worthy of note.
IMPORTANCE is the most
general of these terms,
assigning exceptional value
or influence to a person or
thing: *the importance of
Einstein's discoveries.*
CONSEQUENCE may suggest
personal distinction, or
may suggest importance
based on results to be
produced: *a woman of
consequence in world
affairs; an event of great
consequence for our future.*
SIGNIFICANCE carries the

implication of importance
not readily or immediately
recognized: *The
significance of the
discovery became clear
many years later.* MOMENT,
on the other hand, usu.
refers to immediately
apparent, self-evident
importance: *an
international treaty of great
moment.*

impostor, *n.* pretender,
deceiver, cheat, confidence
man, con man, intruder,
trickster, knave, hypocrite,
charlatan, mountebank.

impotent, *adj.* powerless,
helpless, enfeebled,
forceless, weak, ineffectual,
ineffective, uninfluential,
lightweight, wimpish,
wimpy, nebbishy. **—Ant.**
powerful, strong.

impoverished, See Syn.
study at POOR.

impregnable, *adj.*
unassailable, invincible,
invulnerable. **—Ant.**
pregnable, vulnerable.
—Syn. Study. See
INVINCIBLE.

impromptu, See Syn. study
at EXTEMPORANEOUS.

improper, *adj.* **1.** inapplicable, unsuited, unfit, inappropriate, unsuitable. **2.** indecent, unbecoming, unseemly, indecorous, unfitting. **3.** abnormal, irregular. —**Ant.** proper. —**Syn. Study.** IMPROPER, INDECENT, UNBECOMING, UNSEEMLY are applied to that which is inappropriate or not in accordance with propriety. IMPROPER has a wide range, being applied to whatever is not suitable or fitting, and often specifically to what does not conform to the standards of conventional morality: *an improper diet; improper clothes; improper behavior in church.* INDECENT, a strong word, is applied to what is offensively contrary to standards of propriety and esp. of modesty: *indecent photographs.* UNBECOMING is applied to what is especially unfitting in the person concerned: *conduct unbecoming a minister.* UNSEEMLY is applied to whatever is unfitting or improper under the circumstances: *unseemly mirth.*

impropriety, *n.* **1.** misbehavior, misconduct, indecorousness, indecorum, unseemliness, naughtiness, vulgarity, disorderliness. **2.** error, indiscretion, faux pas, solecism, gaffe, vulgarism, indecency.

improve, *v.* **1.** ameliorate, better, amend, emend, correct, right, rectify. **2.** mend, gain, get better. —**Ant.** worsen, impair; fail, sink. —**Syn. Study.** IMPROVE, AMELIORATE, BETTER imply bringing to a more desirable state. IMPROVE usu. implies remedying a lack or a felt need: *to improve a process.* AMELIORATE, a formal word, implies improving oppressive, unjust, or difficult conditions: *to ameliorate working conditions.* BETTER implies improving conditions that are adequate but could be more satisfactory: *to better a previous attempt; to better oneself by study.*

improvident, *adj.* **1.** incautious, unwary, thoughtless, careless, imprudent, heedless, without *or* lacking foresight. **2.** thriftless, shiftless, neglectful, wasteful, prodigal. —**Ant.** provident, cautious; thrifty.

improvised, *adj.* extemporaneous, impromptu, unpremeditated, unrehearsed, spontaneous. —**Ant.** premeditated.

impudence, *n.* impertinence, effrontery, insolence, rudeness, brass, brazenness, face, lip, boldness, presumption, presumptiveness, sauciness, pertness, flippancy; (*colloquial*) nerve. —**Ant.** politeness, courtesy.

impudent, *adj.* bold, brazen, brassy, presumptuous, insolent, impertinent, insulting, rude, presumptive, saucy, pert, flippant, fresh. —**Ant.** polite, courteous, well-behaved. —**Syn. Study.** See IMPERTINENT.

impulsive, *adj.* emotional, impetuous, rash, quick, hasty, unpremeditated. —**Ant.** cool, cold, unemotional, premeditated. —**Syn. Study.** See IMPETUOUS.

impunity, *n.* exemption, license, permission. —**Ant.** responsibility, blame, culpability. —**Syn. Study.** See EXEMPTION.

impute, *v.* attribute, charge, ascribe, refer. —**Syn. Study.** See ATTRIBUTE.

inability, *n.* incapability, incapacity, disqualification, impotence, incompetence. —**Ant.** ability.

inaccuracy, *n.* **1.** incorrectness, erroneousness, inexactness, inexactitude. **2.** error, blunder, mistake, slip. —**Ant.** accuracy.

inaccurate, *adj.* inexact, loose, general, unspecific; incorrect, wrong, erroneous, faulty, improper. —**Ant.** accurate.

inactive, *adj.* inert, dormant, unmoving, immobile, inoperative;

indolent, lazy, sluggish, torpid, passive, idle, slothful, dilatory. —**Ant.** active. —**Syn. Study.** INACTIVE, DORMANT, INERT, TORPID suggest lack of activity. INACTIVE describes a person or thing that is not acting, moving, functioning, or operating: *an inactive board member; inactive laws.* DORMANT suggests the quiescence or inactivity of that which sleeps or seems to sleep, but may be roused to action: *a dormant geyser.* INERT suggests something with no inherent power of motion or action; it may also refer to a person disinclined to move or act: *the inert body of an accident victim.* TORPID suggests a state of suspended activity, esp. of animals that hibernate: *Snakes are torpid in cold weather.*

inadequate, *adj.* inapt, incompetent, insufficient, incommensurate, defective, imperfect, incomplete. —**Ant.** adequate.

inadvertent, *adj.* heedless, inattentive, unintentional, thoughtless, careless, negligent. —**Ant.** intentional, purposive, purposeful.

inane, See Syn. study at FOOLISH.

inanimate, *adj.* **1.** lifeless, inorganic, vegetable, mineral, mechanical. **2.** spiritless, lifeless, sluggish, inert, spiritless; dead, defunct. —**Ant.** animate, alive; spirited.

inapt, *adj.* **1.** unsuited, unsuitable, inappropriate, not pertinent. **2.** incapable, clumsy, awkward, slow, dull. —**Ant.** apt, suitable, appropriate, fit; capable, efficient.

inborn, *adj.* innate, inbred, native, natural, congenital, inherent, instinctive, inherited. —**Ant.** acquired, learned, conditioned, environmental. —**Syn. Study.** See INNATE.

incapable, *adj.* unable, incompetent, inefficient, impotent, unqualified; incapacious. —**Ant.**

capable, competent,
efficient, potent, qualified.
—**Syn. Study.** INCAPABLE,
INCOMPETENT are applied to
a person or thing lacking
in ability, preparation, or
power for whatever is to
be done. INCAPABLE usu.
means inherently lacking
in ability or power to meet
and fill ordinary
requirements: *a bridge
incapable of carrying heavy
loads; a worker described
as clumsy and incapable.*
INCOMPETENT, generally
used only of persons,
means unfit or unqualified
for a particular task:
*incompetent as an
administrator.*

incarcerate, *v.* imprison,
commit, confine, jail;
constrict, enclose, restrict.
—**Ant.** liberate, free.

incense, *n.* **1.** perfume,
aroma, scent, fragrance.
—*v.* **2.** inflame, enrage,
exasperate, provoke,
irritate, goad, vex, excite.
—**Syn. Study.** See ENRAGE.

incentive, *n.* motive,
inducement, incitement,
enticement, stimulus, spur,
impulse, goad,
encouragement, prod.
—**Ant.** discouragement.
—**Syn. Study.** See MOTIVE.

incessant, *adj.*
uninterrupted, unceasing,
ceaseless, continual,
continuous, constant,
unending, never-ending,
relentless, unrelenting,
unremitting, perpetual,
eternal, everlasting.
—**Ant.** interrupted,
spasmodic, sporadic;
temporary.

incident, *n.* event,
occurrence, happening,
circumstance. —**Syn.
Study.** See EVENT.

incidental, *adj.* fortuitous,
chance, accidental, casual,
contingent. —**Ant.**
fundamental.

incisive, *adj.* **1.**
penetrating, trenchant,
biting, acute, sarcastic,
sardonic, satirical, acid,
severe, cruel. **2.** sharp,
keen, acute. —**Ant.**
superficial; dull.

incite, *v.* urge on,
stimulate, encourage, back,
prod, push, spur, goad,
instigate, provoke, arouse,
fire; induce. —**Ant.**

discourage. —**Syn. Study.**
INCITE, ROUSE, PROVOKE
mean to goad or inspire
an individual or group to
take some action or
express some feeling.
INCITE means to induce
activity of any kind,
although it often refers to
violent or uncontrolled
behavior: *incited to greater
effort; incited to rebellion.*
ROUSE is used in a similar
way, but has an
underlying sense of
awakening from sleep or
inactivity: *to rouse an
apathetic team.* PROVOKE
means to stir to sudden,
strong feeling or vigorous
action: *Kicking the animal
provoked it to attack.*

inclination, *n.* **1.** bent,
leaning, tendency, set,
propensity, liking,
preference, predilection,
predisposition, proclivity,
bias, proneness, prejudice,
penchant. **2.** slope, slant,
leaning, inclining; verging,
tending, tendency. —**Ant.**
dislike, antipathy.

include, *v.* contain,
embrace, comprise,
comprehend, embody.

—**Ant.** exclude, preclude.
—**Syn. Study.** INCLUDE,
COMPREHEND, COMPRISE,
EMBRACE imply containing
parts of a whole. INCLUDE
means to contain as a part
or member of a larger
whole; it may indicate one,
several, or all parts: *This
anthology includes works
by Sartre and Camus. The
price includes appetizer,
main course, and dessert.*
COMPREHEND means to have
within the limits or scope
of a larger whole: *The plan
comprehends several
projects.* COMPRISE means to
consist of; it usu. indicates
all of the various parts
serving to make up the
whole: *This genus
comprises 50 species.*
EMBRACE emphasizes the
extent or assortment of
that which is included: *The
report embraces a great
variety of subjects.*

income, *n.* return, returns,
receipts, revenue, profits,
salary, wages, pay,
stipend, interest, annuity,
gain, earnings. —**Ant.**
expense, expenditure.

incommode, *v.* **1.**

inconvenience, discomfort, disturb, annoy, vex, trouble, discommode. **2.** impede, hinder, interfere, delay. **—Ant.** comfort; encourage, aid, abet, support, expedite.

incompatible, *adj.* **1.** inconsistent, incongruous, unsuitable, unsuited, contradictory, irreconcilable. **2.** discordant, contrary, opposed, difficult, contradictory, inharmonious. **—Ant.** compatible, consistent, appropriate; harmonious.

incompetent, *adj.* unqualified, unable, incapable, inadequate, unfit, insufficient. **—Ant.** competent, efficient, able, capable. adequate, fit. **—Syn. Study.** See INCAPABLE.

incongruous, *adj.* **1.** unbecoming, inappropriate, incompatible, out of keeping, discrepant, absurd. **2.** inconsonant, inharmonious, discordant. **3.** inconsistent, incoherent, illogical, unfitting,

contrary, contradictory. **—Ant.** congruous, becoming, appropriate, proper; harmonious; logical, consistent, coherent, sensible.

inconsistent, *adj.* incompatible, inharmonious, incongruous, unsuitable, irreconcilable, incoherent, discrepant, out of keeping, inappropriate. **—Ant.** consistent, coherent, harmonious, suitable.

inconstant, *adj.* changeable, fickle, inconsistent, variable, moody, capricious, vacillating, wavering, mercurial, volatile, unsettled, unstable, mutable, uncertain. **—Ant.** constant, steady, invariant, settled, staid. **—Syn. Study.** See FICKLE.

incontrovertible, *adj.* undeniable, indisputable, incontestable, unquestionable. **—Ant.** deniable, controvertible, disputable, questionable.

inconvenient, *adj.* awkward, inopportune,

disadvantageous, troublesome, annoying, vexatious, untimely, incommodious, discommodious. **—Ant.** convenient, opportune, advantageous.

incorrect, *adj.* **1.** wrong, not valid, untrue, false, erroneous, inexact, inaccurate. **2.** improper, faulty; indecent. **—Ant.** correct.

increase, *v.* **1.** augment, add to, enlarge, greaten; extend, prolong. **2.** grow, dilate, expand, enlarge, multiply. **—***n.* **3.** growth, augmentation, enlargement, expansion, addition, extension. **—Ant.** decrease.

incredulous, *adj.* unbelieving, skeptical, doubtful, dubious. **—Ant.** credulous. **—Syn. Study.** See DOUBTFUL.

inculpate, *v.* charge, blame, accuse, incriminate, censure, impeach. **—Ant.** exonerate.

indecent, *adj.* offensive, distasteful, improper, unbecoming, unseemly,

outrageous, vulgar, indelicate, coarse, rude, gross, immodest, unrefined, indecorous, obscene, filthy, lewd, licentious, lascivious, pornographic. **—Ant.** decent. **—Syn. Study.** See IMPROPER.

indefinite, *adj.* **1.** unlimited, unconfined, unrestrained, undefined, undetermined, indistinct, confused. **2.** vague, obscure, confusing, equivocal, dim, unspecific, doubtful, unsettled, uncertain. **—Ant.** definite.

independence, *n.* freedom, liberty. **—Ant.** dependence, reliance.

indifference, *n.* **1.** unconcern, listlessness, apathy, insensibility, coolness, insensitiveness, inattention. **2.** unimportance, triviality, insignificance. **3.** mediocrity, inferiority. **—Ant.** concern, warmth, sensibility; importance, significance, superiority.

indignation, *n.* consternation, resentment,

exasperation, wrath, anger, ire, fury, rage, choler. —**Ant.** calm, serenity, composure. —**Syn. Study.** See ANGER.

indignity, *n.* injury, slight, contempt, humiliation, affront, insult, outrage, scorn, obloquy, contumely, reproach, abuse, opprobrium, dishonor, disrespect. —**Ant.** dignity; honor, respect. —**Syn. Study.** See INSULT.

indiscriminate, *adj.* **1.** miscellaneous, undiscriminating, undistinguishing. **2.** confused, undistinguishable, mixed, promiscuous. —**Ant.** discriminating; distinguishing.

indispensable, *adj.* necessary, requisite, essential, needed. —**Ant.** dispensable, disposable, unnecessary, nonessential. —**Syn. Study.** See NECESSARY.

indisposed, *adj.* **1.** sick, ill, unwell, ailing. **2.** disinclined, unwilling, reluctant, averse, loath. —**Ant.** well, healthy, hardy, hale; eager, willing.

indisputable, *adj.* incontrovertible, incontestable, unquestionable, undeniable, indubitable; evident, apparent, obvious, certain, sure. —**Ant.** questionable, dubitable, dubious; uncertain.

indolent, *adj.* idle, lazy, slothful, slow, inactive, sluggish, torpid, listless, inert. —**Ant.** energetic, active, industrious. —**Syn. Study.** See IDLE.

indomitable, *adj.* invincible, unconquerable, unyielding. —**Ant.** yielding, weak, feeble. —**Syn. Study.** See INVINCIBLE.

induce, *v.* **1.** persuade, influence, move, actuate, prompt, instigate, incite, urge, impel, spur, prevail upon. **2.** bring about, produce, cause, effect, bring on. —**Ant.** dissuade. —**Syn. Study.** See PERSUADE.

inducement, *n.* incentive, motive, cause, stimulus, spur, incitement. —**Ant.**

discouragement. **—Syn. Study.** See MOTIVE.

indulge, *v.* yield to, satisfy, gratify, humor, pamper, give way to, favor; suffer, foster, permit, allow. **—Ant.** dissatisfy; disallow, forbid. **—Syn. Study.** See SPOIL.

industrious, *adj.* busy, hard-working, diligent, assiduous, operose, sedulous, persistent, persevering. **—Ant.** lazy, indolent.

inebriate, *v.* **1.** intoxicate, make drunk; exhilarate. **—***n.* **2.** drunkard.

ineffectual, *adj.* **1.** useless, unavailing, futile, nugatory, ineffective, fruitless, pointless, abortive, purposeless. **2.** powerless, impotent, feeble, weak. **—Ant.** effectual, efficacious, efficient.

inefficient, *adj.* incapable, ineffective, feeble, weak. **—Ant.** efficient, effectual, efficacious.

inept, *adj.* **1.** inapt, unfitted, unfitting, unsuitable, unsuited,

inappropriate, out of place, anomalous. **2.** absurd, foolish, stupid, pointless, inane, ridiculous. **—Ant.** fit, suitable, apt, appropriate.

inert, *adj.* inactive, immobile, unmoving, lifeless, passive, motionless. **—Ant.** active, kinetic. **—Syn. Study.** See INACTIVE.

inexorable, *adj.* unyielding, unalterable, inflexible, unbending, firm, solid, steadfast, severe; relentless, unrelenting, implacable, merciless, cruel, pitiless. **—Ant.** flexible, yielding; merciful, relenting.

inexpensive, *adj.* cheap, low-priced. **—Ant.** expensive. **—Syn. Study.** See CHEAP.

inexperienced, *adj.* untrained, unskilled, raw, green, unknowledgeable, unpracticed, unschooled, untutored, uninformed, naive, uninitiated. **—Ant.** experienced, skilled, practiced.

infallible, *adj.* trustworthy, sure, certain, reliable, unfailing. **—Ant.** fallible, unreliable, uncertain.

infamous, *adj.* **1.** disreputable, ill-famed, notorious. **2.** disgraceful, scandalous, detestable, dishonorable, shameful, bad, nefarious, odious, wicked, outrageous, shocking, vile, base, ignominious, dark, heinous, villainous. **—Ant.** reputable, famed; honorable, good.

infamy, *n.* notoriety, disgrace, dishonor, discredit, shame, disrepute, obloquy, odium, opprobrium, scandal, debasement, abasement, ignominy. **—Ant.** honor, credit, repute. **—Syn. Study.** See DISGRACE.

infantile, *adj.* babyish, childish, puerile, immature, weak. **—Ant.** mature, adult. **—Syn. Study.** See CHILDISH.

infectious, *adj.* contagious, catching, communicable. **—Syn. Study.** See CONTAGIOUS.

infidel, See Syn. study at ATHEIST.

inflame, *v.* kindle, excite, rouse, arouse, incite, fire, stimulate. **—Ant.** discourage. **—Syn. Study.** See KINDLE.

inflate, *v.* distend, swell, swell out, dilate, expand, puff up *or* out, bloat, blow up. **—Ant.** deflate.

inflexible, *adj.* rigid, unbending, undeviating, unyielding, rigorous, implacable, stern, relentless, unrelenting, inexorable, unremitting, immovable, resolute, steadfast, firm, stony, solid, persevering, stubborn, dogged, pigheaded, obstinate, refractory, willful, headstrong, intractable, obdurate, adamant. **—Ant.** flexible.

influence, *n.* **1.** sway, rule, authority, power, control, predominance, direction. **—***v.* **2.** modify, affect, sway, impress, bias, direct, control. **3.** move, impel, actuate, activate, incite, rouse, arouse, instigate, induce, persuade. **—Syn. Study.** See AUTHORITY.

inform, *v.* **1.** apprise, make known, advise, notify, tell, acquaint. **2.** animate, inspire, quicken, enliven, inspirit. —**Ant.** conceal, hide.

informal, *adj.* **1.** irregular, unusual, anomalous, unconventional, natural, easy, unceremonious. **2.** colloquial, flexible. —**Ant.** formal, regular, customary, conventional; inflexible. —**Syn. Study.** See COLLOQUIAL.

information, *n.* knowledge, news, data, facts, circumstances, situation, intelligence, advice. —**Ant.** secret.

infraction, See Syn. study at BREACH.

infringe, *v.* **1.** violate, transgress, breach, break, disobey. **2.** trespass, encroach; poach. —**Ant.** obey. —**Syn. Study.** See TRESPASS.

infuriate, *v.* enrage, anger, incense. —**Ant.** calm, pacify. —**Syn. Study.** See ENRAGE.

ingenious, *adj.* clever, skillful, adroit, bright, gifted, able, resourceful, inventive. —**Ant.** unskillful, maladroit.

ingenuous, *adj.* unreserved, unrestrained, frank, candid, free, open, guileless, artless, innocent, naive, straightforward, sincere, open-hearted. —**Ant.** reserved, restrained, secretive, sly, insincere.

ingredient, *n.* constituent, element, component. —**Ant.** whole.

inherent, *adj.* innate, inherited, native, natural, inborn, inbred, essential. —**Ant.** acquired. —**Syn. Study.** See ESSENTIAL.

inheritance, *n.* heritage, patrimony.

inhibit, *v.* **1.** restrain, hinder, arrest, check, repress, obstruct, stop; discourage. **2.** prohibit, forbid, interdict, prevent. —**Ant.** encourage, support, abet.

inimical, *adj.* **1.** adverse, unfavorable, harmful, noxious. **2.** unfriendly, hostile, antagonistic, contrary. **—Ant.** friendly, favorable.

initiate, *v.* **1.** begin, originate, set going, start, commence, introduce, inaugurate, open. **2.** teach, instruct, indoctrinate, train. —*adj.* **3.** initiated, begun, started. —*n.* **4.** new member, pledge, tyro, beginner, learner, amateur, freshman. **—Ant.** terminate, conclude, finish. **—Syn. Study.** See BEGIN.

injure, *v.* **1.** damage, impair, harm, hurt, spoil, ruin, break, mar. **2.** wrong, maltreat, mistreat, abuse. **—Syn. Study.** INJURE, IMPAIR mean to harm or damage something. INJURE is a general term referring to any kind or degree of damage: *to injure one's spine; to injure one's reputation.* To IMPAIR is to make imperfect in any way, often with a suggestion of progressive deterioration: *One's health can be impaired by overwork.*

injurious, *adj.* **1.** harmful, hurtful, damaging, ruinous, detrimental, pernicious, deleterious, baneful, destructive, mischievous. **2.** unjust, wrongful, prejudicial, biased, inequitable, iniquitous. **3.** offensive, insulting, abusive, derogatory, defamatory, slanderous, libelous, contumelious, scornful, deprecatory. **—Ant.** beneficial; just, right; complimentary.

injury, *n.* **1.** harm, damage, ruin, detriment, wound, impairment, mischief. **2.** wrong, injustice.

inn, *n.* hotel, hostelry, hostel, tavern.

innate, *n.* inborn, congenital, hereditary, inbred, native, genetic, familial **—Syn. Study.** INNATE, INBORN, CONGENITAL, HEREDITARY describe qualities, characteristics, or possessions acquired before or at the time of birth. INNATE, of Latin origin, and INBORN, a native English word, share the literal basic sense "existing at the time of birth," and they are interchangeable in most contexts: *innate* (or *inborn*) *stodginess, strength, abilities.* CONGENITAL refers most often to characteristics acquired during fetal development, esp. defects or undesirable conditions: *a congenital deformity; congenital blindness.* HEREDITARY describes qualities or things passed on from ancestors, either through the genes or by social or legal means: *Hemophilia is a hereditary condition; a hereditary title.*

innocent, *adj.* **1.** pure, untainted, sinless, virtuous, virginal, blameless, faultless, impeccable, spotless, immaculate. **2.** guiltless, blameless. **3.** upright, honest, forthright. **4.** naive, simple, unsophisticated, artless, guileless, ingenuous. —**Ant.** impure, tainted, sinful, piacular; guilty, culpable; dishonest; disingenuous, sophisticated, artful.

innocuous, *adj.* **1.** harmless, inoffensive, innocent, unhurtful, benign. **2.** well-meaning, unthreatening, insipid, neutral, dull.

innumerable, *adj.* countless, numberless, many, numerous; infinite. —**Syn. Study.** See MANY.

inquire, *v.* ask, question, query, investigate, examine. —**Ant.** answer, reply.

inquiry, *n.* **1.** investigation, examination, study, scrutiny, exploration, research. **2.** inquiring, questioning, interrogation; query, question. —**Ant.** anwer, reply.

inquisitive, *adj.* inquiring, prying, curious, scrutinizing, questioning.

insane, *adj.* deranged, demented, lunatic, crazed, crazy, maniacal, *non compos mentis,* of unsound mind, mad; paranoiac, schizophrenic, delirious; foolish, senseless, stupid, thoughtless. —**Ant.** sane.

insanity, *n.* derangement, dementia, lunacy, madness, craziness, mania, aberration; dementia praecox, schizophrenia, paranoia. —**Ant.** sanity, probity.

inscrutable, *adj.* impenetrable, unpenetrable, mysterious, hidden, incomprehensible, undiscoverable, inexplicable, unexplainable, unfathomable. —**Ant.** penetrable, comprehensible, understandable. —**Syn. Study.** See MYSTERIOUS.

insecure, *adj.* **1.** unsafe, exposed, unprotected. **2.** uncertain, unsure, risky. —**Ant.** secure, safe; certain, sure.

insensibility, *n.* **1.** unconsciousness. **2.** indifference, apathy, insusceptibility. —**Ant.** consciousness; concern, sensibility.

inside, *prep.* **1.** within, inside of, in. —*n.* **2.** interior. **3.** (*plural*) innards, organs. —**Ant.** outside.

insidious, *adj.* **1.** corrupting, entrapping, beguiling, guileful. **2.**

treacherous, stealthy, deceitful, artful, cunning, sly, wily, intriguing, subtle, crafty, tricky, arch, crooked, foxy. —**Ant.** upright, forthright; artless, ingenuous.

insinuate, *v.* **1.** hint, suggest, intimate. **2.** instill, infuse, introduce, inject, inculcate. —**Syn. Study.** See HINT.

insolent, *adj.* bold, rude, disrespectful, impertinent, brazen, brassy, abusive, overbearing, contemptuous, insulting. —**Ant.** polite, courteous, retiring; complimentary. —**Syn. Study.** See IMPERTINENT.

inspection, *n.* examination, investigation, scrutiny. —**Syn. Study.** See EXAMINATION.

instance, *n.* case, example, illustration, exemplification.

instant, *n.* moment, minute, second, twinkling, flash, jiffy, trice. —**Syn. Study.** See MINUTE.

instantly, *adv.* immediately, at once, instanter,

instantaneously, forthwith, in a flash *or* trice *or* jiffy. —**Ant.** later. —**Syn. Study.** See IMMEDIATELY.

instruct, *v.* **1.** direct, command, order, prescribe. **2.** teach, train, educate, tutor, coach, drill, discipline, indoctrinate, school, inform, enlighten, apprise. —**Ant.** learn, study. —**Syn. Study.** See TEACH.

instruction, *n.* **1.** education, tutoring, coaching, training, drill, exercise, indoctrination, schooling, teaching. **2.** order, direction, mandate, command.

instructor, *n.* teacher, tutor, pedagogue, schoolmaster, preceptor. —**Ant.** student, pupil.

instrument, *n.* tool, implement, utensil. —**Syn. Study.** See TOOL.

insult, *v.* **1.** affront, offend, scorn, injure, slander, abuse. —*n.* **2.** affront, indignity, offense, contumely, scorn, outrage. —**Ant.** compliment, dignify; dignity. —**Syn.**

Study. INSULT, INDIGNITY, AFFRONT, SLIGHT refer to acts or words that offend or demean. INSULT refers to a deliberately discourteous or rude remark or act that humiliates, wounds the feelings, and arouses anger: *an insult about her foreign accent.* INDIGNITY refers to an injury to one's dignity or self-respect: *The prisoners suffered many indignities.* AFFRONT implies open offense or disrespect, esp. to one's face: *Criticism of my book was a personal affront.* SLIGHT implies inadvertent indifference or disregard, but may also indicate ill-concealed contempt: *Not inviting me was an unforgivable slight.*

insurrection, *n.* revolt, uprising, rebellion, mutiny, insurgency.

intact, *adj.* uninjured, unaltered, sound, whole, unimpaired, complete, undiminished, unbroken, entire. —**Ant.** impaired, unsound, incomplete. —**Syn. Study.** See COMPLETE.

integrity, *n.* **1.** uprightness, honesty, honor, rectitude, right, righteousness, probity, principle, virtue, goodness. **2.** wholeness, entirety, completeness. —**Ant.** dishonesty, disrepute; part. —**Syn. Study.** See HONOR.

intellect, *n.* mind, understanding, reason, sense, common sense, brains. —**Ant.** inanity. —**Syn. Study.** See MIND.

intellectual, *adj.* **1.** mental; intelligent; high-brow. —*n.* **2.** (*colloquial*) high-brow, egghead, professor, brain, mental giant, longhair. —**Ant.** sensual, low-brow; dunderpate, fool.

intelligence, *n.* **1.** mind, understanding, discernment, reason, acumen, aptitude, penetration. **2.** knowledge, news, information, tidings. —**Ant.** stupidity.

intelligent, *adj.* **1.** understanding, intellectual, quick, bright. **2.** astute, clever, quick, alert, bright, apt, discerning, shrewd, smart. —**Ant.** stupid, unintelligent, slow; dull. —**Syn. Study.** See SHARP.

intend, *v.* have in mind, mean, design, propose, contemplate, expect, meditate, project, aim for *or* at, purpose.

intensify, *v.* aggravate, deepen, quicken, strengthen; concentrate. —**Ant.** alleviate, lessen, weaken, dilute.

intent, *n.* **1.** intention, design, purpose, meaning, plan, plot, aim, end, object, mark. —*adj.* **2.** fixed, steadfast, bent, resolute, set, concentrated, unshakable, eager. —**Ant.** phlegmatic, undetermined, irresolute, apathetic.

intention, *n.* intent.

intentional, *adj.* deliberate, purposeful, premeditated, designed, planned, intended. —**Ant.** unintentional, purposeless, unpremeditated; involuntary. —**Syn. Study.** See DELIBERATE.

interesting, *adj.* pleasing, attractive, gratifying, engaging, absorbing, exciting, fulfilling, entertaining. —**Ant.** uninteresting, dull, prosaic.

interpret, *v.* **1.** explain, explicate, elucidate, shed *or* cast light on, define, translate, decipher, decode. **2.** explain, construe, understand. —**Syn. Study.** See EXPLAIN.

interrupt, *v.* **1.** discontinue, suspend, intermit. **2.** stop, cease, break off, disturb, hinder, interfere with. —**Ant.** continue.

intimate, *adj.* **1.** close, closely associated, familiar, dear, confidential. **2.** private, personal, privy, secret. **3.** detailed, deep, cogent, exacting, exact, precise. **4.** inmost, deep within; intrinsic, inner, deep-rooted, deep-seated. —*n.* **5.** friend, associate, confidant, crony, familiar. —*v.* **6.** hint, suggest, insinuate, allude to. —**Ant.** open, public, known, blatant; enemy, foe; announce, proclaim. —**Syn. Study.** See FAMILIAR.

intimidate, *v.* overawe, cow, subdue, dismay, frighten, alarm;

discourage, dissuade. —**Ant.** encourage, calm. —**Syn. Study.** See DISCOURAGE.

intolerable, *adj.* unbearable, unendurable, insufferable, insupportable. —**Ant.** tolerable, bearable, endurable.

intolerant, *adj.* bigoted, illiberal, narrow, proscriptive, prejudiced, biased, dictatorial, fascistic, totalitarian, fanatical. —**Ant.** tolerant, liberal, unprejudiced.

intractable, *adj.* stubborn, obstinate, unmanageable, perverse, fractious, refractory, headstrong, pigheaded, dogged, unbending, inflexible, obdurate, adamant, stony, willful, unyielding, contumacious, froward. —**Ant.** tractable, amiable, amenable, easygoing, flexible. —**Syn. Study.** See UNRULY.

intrigue, See Syn. study at CONSPIRACY.

intrinsic, *adj.* essential, native, innate, inborn, inbred, natural, true, real,

genuine. —**Ant.** extrinsic.
—**Syn. Study.** See
ESSENTIAL.

introduce, *v.* present,
acquaint; lead, bring,
conduct. —**Syn. Study.**
INTRODUCE, PRESENT mean
to bring persons into
personal acquaintance with
each other, as by
announcement of names.
INTRODUCE is the ordinary
term, referring to making
persons acquainted who
are ostensibly equals: *to
introduce a friend to one's
sister.* PRESENT, a more
formal term, suggests a
degree of ceremony in the
process, and implies (if
only as a matter of
compliment) superior
dignity, rank, or
importance in the person
to whom another is
presented: *to present a
visitor to the president.*

introduction, *n.* foreword,
preface, front matter;
preamble. —**Syn. Study.**
INTRODUCTION, FOREWORD,
PREFACE refer to material in
the front of a book that
introduces and explains it
to the reader. An
INTRODUCTION is a formal
preliminary statement,
often extensive, that serves
as a guide to the book. It
is written by the author
and usu. printed as part of
the text: *The introduction
outlined the subjects
covered in the book.* A
FOREWORD is a short
introductory statement
that precedes the text
proper. It is usu. written
by someone other than the
author, often an authority
on the subject of the book:
*The writer of the foreword
praised the book and its
author.* A PREFACE, also
separate from the text
proper, is the author's
informal statement about
the purpose, preparation,
etc., of the book; it usu.
includes acknowledgments:
*The author thanked her
family in the preface.* A
PREFACE usu. follows a
FOREWORD, if there is one.

introductory, See Syn. study
at PRELIMINARY.

intrude, *v.* trespass,
obtrude, encroach, violate,
infringe. —**Syn. Study.**
See TRESPASS.

inundate, *v.* flood, deluge, overflow, overspread, overwhelm, glut.

invaluable, *adj.* priceless, precious, valuable, inestimable. —**Ant.** worthless.

invariable, *adj.* unalterable, unchanging, uniform, constant, invariant, changeless, unvarying; unchangeable, immutable. —**Ant.** variable, changing, varying, mutable.

invective, *n.* **1.** denunciation, censure, reproach, abuse, contumely, scorn. **2.** accusation, vituperation, railing. —*adj.* **3.** abusive, censorious, denunciatory, vituperative, captious. —**Ant.** praise, honor; commendatory. —**Syn. Study.** See ABUSE.

invent, *v.* **1.** devise, contrive, originate, discover. **2.** produce, create, imagine, fancy, conceive, fabricate, concoct.

inventory, *n.* roll, list, roster, listing, record, account, catalogue, register. —**Syn. Study.** See LIST.

invert, *v.* reverse, turn around *or* upside down.

investigation, *n.* examination, inspection, inquiry, scrutiny, research, exploration.

invigorate, *v.* animate, innerve, enliven, strengthen, fortify, energize, quicken, vitalize. —**Ant.** enervate, enfeeble, weaken, devitalize.

invincible, *adj.* unconquerable, unvanquishable, insuperable, insurmountable, impregnable, impenetrable, indomitable, persistent, unyielding, irrepressible. —**Ant.** conquerable, pregnable, penetrable. —**Syn. Study.** INVINCIBLE, IMPREGNABLE, INDOMITABLE suggest that which cannot be overcome or mastered. INVINCIBLE is applied to that which cannot be conquered in combat or war, or overcome or subdued in any manner: *an invincible army;*

invincible courage.
IMPREGNABLE is applied to a place or position that cannot be taken by assault or siege, and hence to whatever is proof against attack: *an impregnable fortress; impregnable virtue.* INDOMITABLE implies having an unyielding spirit, or stubborn persistence in the face of opposition or difficulty: *indomitable will.*

invite, *v.* **1.** call, request, ask, bid, summon, solicit. **2.** attract, allure, lure, tempt, entice, draw.

involuntary, *adj.* **1.** unintentional, reluctant, accidental. **2.** automatic, reflex, unwilled, instinctive, uncontrolled. —**Ant.** voluntary, intentional.

involve, *v.* **1.** include, embrace, contain, comprehend, comprise, entail, imply. **2.** entangle, implicate, connect, tie, bind. —**Ant.** exclude, preclude.

iota, *n.* tittle, jot, bit, whit, particle, atom, grain, mite, scrap, scintilla, trace, glimmer, shadow, spark.

irascible, *adj.* testy, short-tempered, hot-tempered, quick-tempered, touchy, temperamental, irritable, waspish, snappish, petulant, peppery, choleric. —**Ant.** calm, even-tempered, temperate. —**Syn. Study.** See IRRITABLE.

irate, *adj.* angry, enraged, furious, piqued, provoked, irritated. —**Ant.** pleased, calm.

irony, *n.* sarcasm, satire, mockery, derision. —**Syn. Study.** IRONY, SATIRE, SARCASM indicate mockery of a person or thing. IRONY is exhibited in the organization or structure of either language or literary material. It indirectly presents a contradiction between an action or expression and the context in which it occurs. One thing is said and its opposite implied, as in "Beautiful weather, isn't it?" said when it is raining. Ironic literature

exploits the contrast
between an ideal and an
actual condition, as when
events turn out contrary to
expectations. SATIRE, also a
literary and rhetorical
form, is the use of ridicule
in exposing human vice
and folly. Jonathan Swift
wrote social and political
satires. SARCASM is a harsh
and cutting type of humor.
Its distinctive quality is
present in the spoken
word; it is manifested
chiefly by vocal inflection.
Sarcastic language may
have the form of irony, as
in "What a fine musician
you turned out to be!", or
it may be a direct
statement, as in "You
couldn't play one piece
correctly if you had two
assistants!"

irregular, *adj.* **1.**
unsymmetrical, uneven. **2.**
unmethodical,
unsystematic, disorderly,
capricious, erratic,
eccentric, lawless, aberrant,
devious, unconforming,
nonconformist, unusual,
abnormal, anomalous.
—**Ant.** regular.

irrepressible, *adj.*
unrestrained,
unconstrained,
enthusiastic, effervescent,
vivacious, uninhibited,
exuberant, high-spirited.
—**Ant.** gloomy, depressive.

irritable, *adj.* testy,
irascible, touchy, cranky,
snappish, petulant,
argumentative,
cantankerous, fractious
—**Syn. Study.** IRRITABLE,
TESTY, IRASCIBLE, TOUCHY
mean easily excited,
provoked, or disturbed.
IRRITABLE means easily
annoyed or bothered; it
implies cross and snappish
behavior, often of short
duration: *The irritable
clerk had no patience for
my questions.* TESTY
describes the same kind of
response, particularly to
minor annoyances: *Too
little sleep put her in a
testy mood.* IRASCIBLE is a
stronger term that means
habitually angry or easily
angered: *an irascible boss,
roaring at employees for
the slightest error.* TOUCHY
stresses oversensitivity and
readiness to take offense,

even though none is intended: *touchy about any reference to shyness.*

irritate, *v.* vex, annoy, chafe, fret, gall, nettle, ruffle, pique, incense, anger, ire, enrage, infuriate, exasperate, provoke. —**Ant.** please, delight.

isolation, *n.* solitude, loneliness; separation, disconnection, segregation, detachment.

issue, *n.* **1.** delivery, emission, sending, promulgation. **2.** copy, number, edition, printing. **3.** point, crux; problem, question. **4.** product, effect, result, consequence, event, outcome, upshot, denouement, conclusion, end, consummation. **5.** egress, outlet, vent. **6.** offspring, progeny, children. —*v.* **7.** put out, deliver, circulate, publish, distribute. **8.** send out, discharge, emit. **9.** come forth, emerge, flow out. **10.** come, proceed, emanate, flow, arise, spring, originate, ensue. —**Syn. Study.** See EMERGE.

itinerant, *adj.* wandering, nomadic, unsettled, roving, roaming, traveling, journeying, itinerating. —**Ant.** stationary, fixed, settled.

J

jabber, *v.* prattle, chatter, babble, prate, run on, natter, palaver, gabble, blather, tittle-tattle. —**Ant.** discourse, orate.

jaded, *adj.* **1.** world-weary, bored, blasé, spoiled, sated, satiated, glutted, burned-out. **2.** tired, weary, spent, exhausted, worn-out, fatigued. —**Ant.** fresh, bright-eyed, eager.

jam, *v.* **1.** wedge, pack, crowd, ram, force, squeeze, bruise, crush. —*n.* **2.** preserve, conserve, marmalade.

jargon, *n.* **1.** idiom, vocabulary, phraseology, language, vernacular, argot, patois, patter, lingo, cant, slang. **2.** mumbo-jumbo, nonsense, double-talk, gibberish. —**Syn. Study.** See LANGUAGE.

jaunty, *adj.* **1.** sprightly, cheerful, lighthearted, upbeat, buoyant, perky, carefree, debonair, breezy. **2.** dashing, smart, natty, spruce, dapper. —**Ant.** dull, drab, subfusc.

jealous, *adj.* **1.** envious, resentful; suspicious. **2.** solicitous, watchful, vigilant. —**Ant.** generous, open, trusting.

jealousy, See Syn. study at ENVY.

jeer, *v.* **1.** deride, scoff, gibe, mock, taunt, sneer at, ridicule, flout. —*n.* **2.** sneer, scoff, gibe, derision, ridicule, flout. —**Syn. Study.** See SCOFF.

jeopardy, *n.* hazard, risk, danger, peril. —**Ant.** security.

jest, *n.* **1.** witticism, joke, pleasantry, mot, quip. **2.** raillery, banter; sport, fun, jape, gibe. —*v.* **3.** joke, trifle (with). **4.** deride, jeer, scoff, gibe.

job, *n.* position, situation, post, employment. —**Ant.** unemployment. —**Syn. Study.** See TASK.

jocose, *adj.* joking, jesting, jovial, humorous, playful, facetious, waggish, witty, funny, comical, droll, sportive, jocular, merry. —**Ant.** serious, morose, melancholy.

jocular, *adj.* jocose. —**Syn. Study.** See JOVIAL.

jocund, *adj.* cheerful, merry, gay, blithe, happy, glad, joyous, joyful, frolicsome, frolicking, blithesome, jolly, playful, lively, debonair. —**Ant.** sad, cheerless, unhappy, miserable.

join, *v.* **1.** link, couple, fasten, attach, conjoin, combine, confederate, associate, consolidate, amalgamate, connect, unite, bring together. **2.** adjoin, abut, touch, be adjacent to. —**Ant.** separate, divide. —**Syn.**

Study. JOIN, CONNECT, UNITE imply bringing two or more things together more or less closely. JOIN may refer to a connection or association of any degree of closeness, but often implies direct contact: *to join pieces of wood to form a corner.* CONNECT implies a joining as by a tie, link, or wire: *to connect two batteries.* UNITE implies a close joining of two or more things, so as to form one: *to unite layers of veneer sheets to form plywood.*

joke, *n.* witticism, jape, quip, jest, sally, trick, raillery, prank.

jolly, *adj.* gay, glad, happy, spirited, jovial, merry, sportive, playful, cheerful, convivial, festive, joyous, mirthful, jocund, frolicsome. **—Ant.** serious, morose, mirthless. **—Syn. Study.** See JOVIAL.

journey, *n.* **1.** excursion, trip, jaunt, tour, expedition, pilgrimage, travel. **—***v.* **2.** travel, tour, peregrinate, roam, rove;

go, proceed, fare. **—Syn. Study.** See TRIP.

jovial, *adj.* merry, jolly, convivial, gay, jocose, jocular, jocund, joyous, joyful, blithe, happy, glad, mirthful. **—Ant.** serious, mirthless, cheerless, unhappy. **—Syn. Study.** JOVIAL, JOCULAR, JOLLY refer to someone who is in good spirits. JOVIAL suggests a sociable and friendly person, full of hearty good humor: *The jovial professor enlivened the party.* JOCULAR refers to an amusing person, given to joking or jesting in a playful way: *His jocular sister teased him about his haircut.* JOLLY suggests a cheerful person, full of fun and laughter: *a jolly Santa Claus.*

joy, *n.* **1.** satisfaction, exultation, gladness, delight, rapture. **2.** happiness, felicity, bliss, pleasure, ecstasy, transport. **—Ant.** dissatisfaction, misery; unhappiness.

joyful, *adj.* glad, delighted, joyous, happy, blithe,

buoyant, elated, jubilant, gay, merry, jocund, blithesome, jolly, jovial. —**Ant.** sad, unhappy, melancholy, depressed.

joyless, *adj.* sad, cheerless, unhappy, gloomy, dismal, miserable. —**Ant.** joyous.

judge, *n.* **1.** justice, magistrate; arbiter, arbitrator, umpire, referee. —*v.* **2.** try, pass sentence upon. **3.** estimate, consider, regard, esteem, appreciate, reckon, deem. **4.** decide, determine, conclude, form an opinion, pass judgment. —**Syn. Study.** JUDGE, REFEREE, UMPIRE indicate a person who is entrusted with decisions affecting others. JUDGE, in its legal and other uses, implies that the person has qualifications and authority for rendering decisions in matters at issue: *a judge appointed to the Supreme Court; a judge in a baking contest.* REFEREE refers to an officer who examines and reports on the merits of a case as an aid to a court; it is also used of a

person who settles disputes, esp. in a game or sport: *a referee in bankruptcy; a basketball referee.* UMPIRE refers to a person who gives the final ruling when arbitrators of a case disagree; it is also used of a person who enforces the rules in a game: *an umpire to settle the labor dispute; a baseball umpire.*

judgment, *n.* **1.** verdict, decree, decision, determination, conclusion, opinion, estimate. **2.** understanding, discrimination, discernment, perspicacity, sagacity, wisdom, intelligence, prudence, brains, taste, penetration, discretion, common sense.

judicial, *adj.* critical, discriminating, judicious, juridical, forensic.

judicious, *adj.* **1.** practical, expedient, discreet, prudent, politic. **2.** wise, sensible, well-advised, rational, reasonable, sober, sound, enlightened, sagacious, considered, common-sense. —**Ant.**

impractical, indiscreet, imprudent; silly, nonsensical, unsound, unreasonable. —**Syn. Study.** See PRACTICAL.

jumble, *v.* **1.** mix, confuse, mix up. —*n.* **2.** medley, mixture, hodgepodge, hotchpotch, muddle, mess, farrago, chaos, disorder, confusion, gallimaufry, potpourri. —**Ant.** separate, isolate; order.

jump, *v.* **1.** spring, bound, skip, hop, leap, vault. —*n.* **2.** leap, bound, spring, caper, vault, hop, skip.

junction, *n.* combination, union, joining, connection, linking, coupling; juncture; seam, welt, joint. —**Syn. Study.** JUNCTION, JUNCTURE refer to a place, line, or point at which two or more things join. A JUNCTION is also a place where things come together: *the junction of two rivers.* A JUNCTURE is a line or point at which two bodies are joined, or a point of exigency or crisis in time: *the juncture of the head and neck; a critical juncture in a struggle.*

juncture, See Syn. study at JUNCTION.

junket, *n.* excursion.

just, *adj.* **1.** upright, equitable, fair, impartial, evenhanded, right, lawful. **2.** true, correct, accurate, exact, proper, regular, normal. **3.** rightful, legitimate, lawful, legal; deserved, merited, appropriate, condign, suited, suitable, apt, due. **4.** righteous, blameless, honest, upright, pure, conscientious, good, uncorrupt, virtuous, honorable, straightforward. —**Ant.** unjust.

justify, *v.* vindicate, exonerate, exculpate, absolve, acquit, defend, warrant, excuse. —**Ant.** inculpate, convict, indict, accuse, condemn.

K

keen, *adj.* **1.** sharp, acute, honed, razor-sharp. **2.** sharp, cutting, biting, severe, bitter, poignant, caustic, acrimonious. **3.** piercing, penetrating, discerning, astute, sagacious, sharp-witted, quick, shrewd, clever, keen-eyed, keen-sighted, clear-sighted, clear-headed. **4.** ardent, eager, zealous, earnest, fervid. —**Ant.** dull. —**Syn. Study.** See SHARP.

keep, *v.* **1.** maintain, reserve, preserve, retain, hold, withhold, have, continue. —*n.* **2.** subsistence, board and room. **3.** tower, dungeon, stronghold. —**Ant.** lose. —**Syn. Study.** KEEP, RETAIN, RESERVE, WITHHOLD refer to having or holding in one's possession, care, or control. KEEP means to continue to have or hold, as opposed to losing, parting with, or giving up: to keep a book for a week. RETAIN, a more formal word, often stresses keeping something in spite of resistance or opposition: *The dictator managed to retain power.* To RESERVE is to keep for some future use, occasion, or recipient, or to hold back for a time: *to reserve a seat; to reserve judgment.* To WITHHOLD is generally to hold back altogether: *to withhold evidence.*

keeper, *n.* guard, warden, custodian, jailer, guardian.

keeping, *n.* **1.** congruity, harmony, conformity, consistency, agreement. **2.** custody, protection, care, charge, guardianship, trust. —**Ant.** incongruity, nonconformity, inconsistency.

kibitz, *v.* **1.** meddle, interfere, second-guess, Monday-morning quarterback, pry, snoop.

2. advise, counsel, coach, direct.

kill, *v.* **1.** slaughter, slay, assassinate, massacre, butcher, execute; murder; hang, electrocute, behead, guillotine, strangle, garrote. **2.** extinguish, destroy, do away with. —**Ant.** create, originate.

killjoy, *n.* doomsayer, Cassandra, pessimist, damper, crepehanger, worrywart, spoilsport, wet blanket, grouch, sourpuss, grinch, drag, party pooper, gloomy Gus, dog in the manger. —**Ant.** optimist, positivist, enthusiast.

kind, *adj.* **1.** gracious, kindhearted, kindly, good, mild, benign, bland; benevolent, benignant, beneficent, friendly, humane, generous, bounteous, accommodating; gentle, affectionate, living, tender, compassionate, sympathetic, tender-hearted, soft-hearted, good-natured. —*n.* **2.** sort, nature, character, race, genus, species, breed, set, class. —**Ant.** unkind.

kindhearted, *adj.* kind. —**Ant.** hardhearted, cruel.

kindle, *v.* **1.** set fire to, ignite, inflame, fire, light. **2.** rouse, arouse, awaken, bestir, inflame, provoke, incite, stimulate, animate, foment. —**Ant.** extinguish, quench. —**Syn. Study.** KINDLE, IGNITE, INFLAME literally mean to set something on fire. To KINDLE is to cause something gradually to begin burning; it is often used figuratively: *to kindle logs; to kindle someone's interest.* To IGNITE is to set something on fire with a sudden burst of flame; it also has figurative senses: *to ignite straw; to ignite dangerous hatreds.* INFLAME is most often used figuratively, meaning to intensify, excite, or rouse: *to inflame passions.*

kindly, *adj.* **1.** benevolent, kind, good-natured, sympathetic, compassionate. **2.** gentle, mild, benign. **3.** pleasant, genial, benign. —*adv.* **4.**

cordially, politely, heartily; favorably. —**Ant.** unkindly, malevolent, unsympathetic; cruel, harsh; unpleasant; unfavorable.

kindness, *n.* **1.** service, favor, good turn. **2.** benevolence, beneficence, humanity, benignity, generosity, philanthropy, charity, sympathy, compassion, tenderness, amiability. —**Ant.** unkindness, malevolence.

kingdom, *n.* monarchy, realm, sovereignty, dominion, empire, domain.

kingly, *adj.* kinglike, princely, regal, royal, imperial, sovereign, majestic, august, magnificent, grand, grandiose. —**Ant.** serflike, slavish, low, lowly.

kinship, *n.* relationship, affinity, connection, bearing.

knack, *n.* **1.** aptitude, aptness, facility, dexterity, skill, adroitness, dexterousness, skillfulness, expertness. **2.** habit, practice.

knave, *n.* rascal, rogue, scoundrel, blackguard, villain, scamp, scapegrace, swindler. —**Ant.** hero. —**Syn. Study.** KNAVE, RASCAL, ROGUE, SCOUNDREL are disparaging terms applied to persons considered base, dishonest, or unprincipled. KNAVE, which formerly meant a male servant, in modern use emphasizes baseness of nature and intention: *a swindling knave.* RASCAL suggests a certain shrewdness and trickery: *The rascal ran off with my money.* ROGUE often refers to a worthless person who preys on the community: *pictures of criminals in a rogues' gallery.* SCOUNDREL, a stronger term, suggests a base, immoral, even wicked person: *Those scoundrels finally went to jail.* RASCAL and ROGUE are often used affectionately or humorously to describe a mischievous person: *I'll bet that rascal hid my slippers. The little rogues ate all the cookies.*

knot, *n.* **1.** group,

company, cluster, clique, hand, crew, gang, squad, crowd. **2.** lump, knob. **3.** difficulty, perplexity, puzzle, conundrum, rebus.

knotty, *adj.* complicated, complex, involved, intricate, difficult, hard, tough, thorny, perplexing. **—Ant.** easy, straightforward, uncomplicated.

know, *v.* **1.** perceive, understand, apprehend, comprehend, discern. **2.** recognize. **3.** distinguish, discriminate. **—Syn. Study.** KNOW, COMPREHEND, UNDERSTAND refer to perceiving or grasping facts and ideas. To KNOW is to be aware of, sure of, or familiar with something through observation, study, or experience: *She knows the basic facts of the subject. I know that he agrees with me.* To COMPREHEND is to grasp something mentally and to perceive its relationships to certain other facts or ideas: *to comprehend a difficult text.* To UNDERSTAND is to be fully aware not only of the meaning or nature of something but also of its implications: *I could comprehend everything you said, but did not understand that you were joking.*

knowledge, *n.* **1.** enlightenment, erudition, wisdom, science, information, learning, scholarship, lore. **2.** understanding, discernment, perception, apprehension, comprehension, judgment.

kvetch, *v.* **1.** complain, whine, find fault, grouse, gripe, bellyache. **—***n.* **2.** complainer, whiner, faultfinder, nitpicker, smellfungus.

L

labor, *n.* **1.** toil, work, exertion, drudgery. **2.** travail, childbirth, parturition, delivery. **3.** workingmen, working class; bourgeoisie. —*v.* **4.** work, toil, strive, drudge. **5.** be burdened *or* troubled *or* distressed, suffer. **6.** overdo, elaborate. —**Ant.** idleness, indolence, sloth. —**Syn. Study.** See WORK.

labored, *adj.* overdone, overworked, overwrought, ornate, unnatural.

laborious, *adj.* **1.** toilsome, arduous, onerous, burdensome, difficult, tiresome, wearisome, fatiguing. **2.** diligent, hard-working, assiduous, industrious, sedulous, painstaking. —**Ant.** easy, simple.

lacerate, *v.* **1.** tear, mangle, maim, rend, claw. **2.** hurt, injure, harm, wound, damage.

lachrymose, *adj.* **1.** tearful, weeping, teary, weepy, crying, sobbing, blubbering, blubbery. **2.** mournful, disconsolate, sorrowful, grief-stricken, woeful, anguished. —**Ant.** cheerful, happy, sunny.

lack, *n.* **1.** deficiency, need, want, dearth, scarcity, paucity, shortcoming, deficit, scantiness, insufficiency, defectiveness. —*v.* **2.** want, need. —**Ant.** sufficiency, copiousness, abundance. —**Syn. Study.** LACK, WANT, NEED, REQUIRE indicate the absence of something desirable, important, or necessary. LACK means to be without or to have less than a desirable quantity of something: *to lack courage; to lack sufficient money.* WANT stresses the urgency of fulfilling a desire or providing what is lacking: *The room wants some final touch to make it homey.* NEED suggests even more urgency, stressing the necessity of supplying something essential: *to need an operation.* REQUIRE has a similar sense, although it is used in formal or serious contexts: *The report requires some editing.*

lackadaisical, *adj.* listless, indolent, enervated, blasé, indifferent, languid, languorous, lazy, unconcerned, uninvolved, apathetic, nonchalant, lethargic, sluggish, limp, bovine, numb. —**Ant.** effervescent, peppy, alert.

lackluster, *adj.* dull, ordinary, plain, pedestrian, routine, unexceptional, banal, colorless, prosaic, commonplace, everyday, mediocre, so-so, wishy-washy, drab, lifeless, flat, leaden. —**Ant.** brilliant.

laconic, *adj.* brief, concise, succinct, sententious, pithy, concentrated, terse, compact. —**Ant.** voluble.

lady, See Syn. study at WOMAN.

lag, *v.* **1.** fall behind *or* back, loiter, linger. —*n.* **2.** retardation, slowing, slowdown. —**Ant.** speed, quicken, expedite; expedition.

laggard, *n.* **1.** lingerer, dawdler, slowpoke, plodder, foot-dragger, procrastinator, delayer, dillydallier. —*adj.* **2.** slow, lingering, poky, delaying, dilatory, foot-dragging, procrastinating, lagging, indolent, slothful. —**Ant.** go-getting, industrious.

laid-back, *adj.* relaxed, easygoing, at ease, casual, off-hand, free-and-easy, dégagé, undemanding, loose, lax, nonchalant, blasé, flexible. —**Ant.** rigid, strict, severe.

lament, *v.* **1.** bewail, bemoan, deplore, grieve, weep, mourn *or* sorrow over *or* for. —*n.* **2.** lamentation, moan, wail, wailing, moaning. **3.** dirge, elegy, monody, threnody. —**Ant.** rejoice.

lane, *n.* path, way, passage, track, channel, course, alley.

language, *n.* **1.** speech,

communication, tongue. **2.** dialect, jargon, terminology, vernacular; lingo, lingua franca. **3.** speech, phraseology, jargon, style, expression, diction. —**Syn. Study.** LANGUAGE, DIALECT, JARGON, VERNACULAR refer to patterns of vocabulary, syntax, and usage characteristic of communities of various sizes and types. LANGUAGE is applied to the general pattern of a people or nation: *the English language.* DIALECT is applied to regionally or socially distinct forms or varieties of a language, often forms used by provincial communities that differ from the standard variety: *the Scottish dialect.* JARGON is applied to the specialized language, esp. the vocabulary, used by a particular (usu. occupational) group within a community or to language considered unintelligible or obscure: *technical jargon.* The

VERNACULAR is the natural, everyday pattern of speech, usu. on an informal level, used by people indigenous to a community.

languid, *adj.* **1.** faint, weak, feeble, weary, exhausted, debilitated. **2.** indifferent, spiritless, listless, inactive, inert, sluggish, torpid, dull. —**Ant.** strong, distinct, sharp, tireless; active, energetic.

large, *adj.* **1.** big, huge, enormous, immense, gigantic, colossal, massive, vast, great, extensive, broad, sizeable, grand, spacious; pompous. **2.** multitudinous; abundant, copious, ample, liberal, plentiful. —**Ant.** small, tiny; scanty, sparse, scarce, rare.

lascivious, *adj.* lustful, lecherous, salacious, lewd, libidinous, lubricious, lickerish, goatish, horny, randy, obscene, prurient. —**Ant.** chaste.

last, *adj.* **1.** final, ultimate, latest, concluding, conclusive, utmost,

extreme, terminal,
hindmost. —*v.* **2.** go on,
continue, endure,
perpetuate, remain.
—**Ant.** first; fail, die.
—**Syn. Study.** See
CONTINUE.

late, *adj.* **1.** tardy, slow,
dilatory, delayed, belated.
2. continued, lasting,
protracted. **3.** recent,
modern, advanced. **4.**
former, recently deceased.
—**Ant.** early, fast.

latent, *adj.* hidden,
concealed, veiled;
potential. —**Ant.** kinetic,
open.

latitude, *n.* range, scope,
extent, liberty, freedom,
indulgence. —**Syn. Study.**
See RANGE.

laud, *v.* praise, extol,
applaud, celebrate, esteem,
honor. —**Ant.** censure,
condemn, criticize.

laugh, *v.* **1.** chortle, cackle,
cachinnate, hawhaw,
guffaw, roar; giggle,
snicker, snigger, titter.
—*n.* **2.** chuckle, grin, smile;
laughter, cachinnation.
—**Ant.** cry, mourn, wail.

laughable, *adj.* funny,

amusing, humorous, droll,
comical, ludicrous,
farcical, ridiculous, risible.
—**Ant.** sad, melancholy.

lavish, *adj.* **1.** unstinted,
extravagant, excessive,
prodigal, profuse,
generous, openhanded;
wasteful, improvident. —*v.*
2. expend, bestow, endow;
waste, dissipate, squander.
—**Ant.** stingy, niggardly;
provident; save. —**Syn.
Study.** LAVISH, PRODIGAL,
PROFUSE refer to that which
exists in abundance and is
poured out in great
amounts. LAVISH suggests
an unlimited, sometimes
excessive generosity and
openhandedness: *lavish
hospitality.* PRODIGAL
suggests wastefulness,
improvidence, and reckless
impatience: *He has lost his
inheritance because of his
prodigal ways.* PROFUSE
emphasizes abundance, but
may suggest exaggeration,
emotionalism, or the like:
*profuse thanks; profuse
apologies.*

lawful, *adj.* **1.** legal,
legitimate, valid. **2.** licit,
sanctioned, allowed.

—**Ant.** illegal, illicit, illegitimate; forbidden.

lax, *adj.* **1.** loose, relaxed, slack, drooping, droopy. **2.** negligent, careless, remiss, neglectful, unrigorous, heedless, slipshod, slovenly. —**Ant.** rigorous, responsible.

lay, *v.* **1.** place, put, deposit, set, locate. **2.** allay, appease, calm, still, quiet, suppress. **3.** wager, bet, stake, risk. **4.** impute, ascribe, attribute, charge. **5.** burden, penalize, assess, impose. —*n.* **6.** position, lie, site. **7.** song, lyric, musical poem, poem, ode. —*adj.* **8.** unclerical, laic, laical. **9.** unprofessional, amateur.

lazy, *adj.* idle, indolent, slothful, slow-moving, sluggish, inert, inactive, torpid. —**Ant.** industrious, quick. —**Syn. Study.** See IDLE.

lead, *v.* **1.** conduct, go before, precede, guide, direct, escort. **2.** guide, influence, induce, persuade, convince, draw, entice, lure, allure, seduce, lead on. **3.** excel, outstrip, surpass. —*n.* **4.** precedence, advance, vanguard, head. **5.** weight, plumb. —**Ant.** follow.

leading, *n.* **1.** guidance, direction, lead. **2.** lead, spacing, space. —*adj.* **3.** chief, principal, most important, foremost, capital, ruling, governing. —**Ant.** deputy; secondary, following.

league, *n.* **1.** covenant, compact, alliance, confederation, combination, coalition, confederacy, union. —*v.* **2.** unite, combine, confederate. —**Syn. Study.** See ALLIANCE.

lean, *v.* **1.** incline, tend toward, bend, slope. **2.** repose, rest, rely, depend, trust, confide. —*adj.* **3.** skinny, thin, gaunt, emaciated, lank, meager. **4.** sparse, barren, unfruitful, inadequate, deficient, jejune. —*n.* **5.** meat, essence. —**Ant.** fat, obese; fertile, fruitful, adequate; superfluity, excess.

leap, *v., n.* jump, bound, spring, vault, hop.

learn, *v.* ascertain, detect, discover, memorize, acquire, hear. **—Syn. Study.** LEARN, DISCOVER, ASCERTAIN, DETECT imply adding to one's store of knowledge or information. To LEARN is to come to know by chance, or by study or other application: *to learn of a friend's death; to learn to ski.* To DISCOVER is to find out something previously unseen or unknown; it suggests that the new information is surprising to the learner: *I discovered that they were selling their house.* To ASCERTAIN is to find out and verify information through inquiry or analysis: *to ascertain the truth about the incident.* To DETECT is to become aware of something obscure, secret, or concealed: *to detect a flaw in reasoning.*

learning, *n.* erudition, lore, knowledge, scholarship, store of information. **—Syn. Study.** LEARNING, ERUDITION, SCHOLARSHIP refer to facts or ideas acquired through systematic study. LEARNING usu. refers to knowledge gained from extensive reading and formal instruction: *Her vast learning is reflected in her many books.* ERUDITION suggests a thorough and profound knowledge of a difficult subject: *His erudition in languages is legendary.* SCHOLARSHIP suggests a high degree of mastery in a specialized field, along with an analytical or innovative ability suited to the academic world: *The author is renowned for several works of classical scholarship.*

leave, *v.* **1.** quit, vacate, abandon, forsake, desert, depart from, retire from, withdraw *or* escape from, relinquish, renounce. **2.** desist from, stop, forbear, cease, abandon, let alone. **3.** omit, forget, exclude. **4.** bequeath, will, devise, transmit. **—n. 5.** permission, allowance,

freedom, liberty, license.
—**Ant.** arrive, gain.

legend, *n.* fable, myth, story, fiction. —**Ant.** fact, history. —**Syn. Study.** LEGEND, MYTH, FABLE refer to stories handed down from earlier times, often by word of mouth. A LEGEND is a story associated with a people or a nation; it is usu. concerned with a real person, place, or event and is popularly believed to have some basis in fact: *the legend of King Arthur.* A MYTH is one of a class of purportedly historical stories that attempt to explain some belief, practice, or natural phenomenon; the characters are usu. gods or heroes: *the Greek myth about Demeter.* A FABLE is a fictitious story intended to teach a moral lesson; the characters are usu. animals: *the fable about the fox and the grapes.*

legitimate, *adj.* **1.** legal, lawful, licit, sanctioned. **2.** normal, regular. **3.** reasonable, logical, sensible, common-sense, valid, warranted, called-for, correct, proper. —*v.* **4.** authorize, justify, legalize. —**Ant.** illegitimate; unreasonable, incorrect, improper.

leisurely, *adj.* deliberate, slow, premeditated, unhurried, easily. —**Ant.** unpremeditated, quick, hurried, hasty. —**Syn. Study.** See SLOW.

lengthen, *v.* extend, stretch, prolong, protract, attenuate, elongate, draw out, continue, increase. —**Ant.** shorten, abbreviate. —**Syn. Study.** LENGTHEN, EXTEND, PROLONG, PROTRACT agree in the idea of making longer. To LENGTHEN is to make longer, either in a material or immaterial sense: *to lengthen a dress; to lengthen human life.* To EXTEND is to lengthen beyond some original point or so as to reach a certain point: *to extend a railway line another fifty miles.* Both PROLONG and PROTRACT mean esp. to lengthen in time. To

PROLONG is to continue beyond the desired, estimated, or allotted time: *to prolong an interview.* To PROTRACT is to draw out to undue length or to be slow in coming to a conclusion: *to protract a discussion.*

lenient, *adj.* mild, clement, merciful, easy, gentle, soothing, tender, forbearing, long-suffering. **—Ant.** harsh, cruel, brutal, merciless.

lessen, *v.* **1.** diminish, decrease, abate, dwindle, fade, shrink. **2.** diminish, decrease, depreciate, disparage, reduce, micrify, lower, degrade. **3.** decrease, diminish, abate, abridge, reduce. **—Ant.** increase; raise; lengthen, enlarge.

let, *v.* **1.** allow, permit, suffer, grant. **2.** disappoint, fail. **3.** lease, rent, sublet, hire. **—Ant.** prevent, disallow. **—Syn. Study.** See ALLOW.

lethal, See Syn. study at FATAL.

level, *adj.* **1.** even, flat, smooth, uniform, plain, flush. **2.** horizontal. **3.** equal, on a par, equivalent. **4.** even, equable, uniform. **—***v.* **5.** even, equalize, smooth, flatten. **6.** raze, demolish, destroy. **7.** aim, direct, point. **—Ant.** uneven; vertical; unequal.

liable, *adj.* **1.** subject, exposed, likely, open. **2.** obliged, responsible, answerable, accountable. **—Ant.** protected, secure.

liberal, *adj.* **1.** progressive, reform. **2.** tolerant, unbigoted, broad-minded, unprejudiced, magnanimous, generous, honorable. **3.** generous, bountiful, beneficent, free, charitable, openhanded, munificent; abundant, ample, bounteous, unstinting, lavish, plentiful. **—Ant.** illiberal; intolerant, prejudiced; stingy, parsimonious, niggardly.

liberate, *v.* set free, release, emancipate, free, disengage, unfetter, disenthrall, deliver, set loose, loose, let out, discharge. —**Ant.** imprison, incarcerate; enthrall, enslave. —**Syn. Study.** See RELEASE.

libertine, *n.* **1.** rake, roué, debauchee, lecher, sensualist, profligate. —*adj.* **2.** amoral, licentious, lascivious, lewd, dissolute, depraved, corrupt, perverted, immoral, sensual. —**Ant.** prude.

liberty, *n.* freedom, liberation, independence; franchise, permission, leave, license, privilege, immunity.

licentious, *adj.* sensual, libertine, lewd, lascivious, libidinous, lustful, lecherous, lawless, immoral, wanton, concupiscent, loose, amoral, unchaste, impure. —**Ant.** prudish, moral; chaste, pure.

lie, *n.* **1.** falsehood, prevarication, mendacity, untruth, falsification, fib. **2.** place, position, location, lay, site. —*v.* **3.** falsify, prevaricate, fib. **4.** recline. —**Ant.** truth.

life, *n.* **1.** animation, vigor, vivacity, vitality, sprightliness, verve, effervescence, sparkle, spirit, activity, energy. **2.** biography, memoir. **3.** existence, being.

lifeless, *adj.* **1.** inanimate, inorganic, mineral. **2.** dead, defunct, extinct. **3.** dull, inactive, inert, passive, sluggish, torpid, spiritless. —**Ant.** alive, animate, live, organic; alive, extant; active, animated, spirited.

lift, *v.* raise, elevate, hold up, exalt, uplift. —**Ant.** lower.

light, *n.* **1.** illumination, radiance, daylight; dawn, sunrise, daybreak. **2.** aspect, viewpoint, point of view, angle, approach. —*adj.* **3.** pale, whitish, blanched. **4.** buoyant, lightsome, easy. **5.** shallow, humorous, slight, trivial, trifling, inconsiderable, unsubstantial, flimsy, insubstantial, gossamer, airy, flighty. **6.** airy, nimble, agile, alert. **7.** carefree, gay, cheery,

cheerful, happy,
light-hearted. **8.** frivolous,
lightsome, light-headed,
volatile. **9.** wanton. **10.**
dizzy, delirious,
light-headed, giddy. —*v.*
11. alight, get *or* come
down, descend, land,
disembark. **12.** kindle, set
fire to, ignite, set afire,
fire. —**Ant.** darkness,
sunset; swarthy; difficult;
deep, considerable,
substantial; cheerless, sad;
serious; board, embark,
mount; quench.

lighten, *v.* **1.** illuminate,
brighten, shine, gleam,
illume. **2.** mitigate,
disburden, unburden, ease.
3. cheer, gladden. —**Ant.**
darken, adumbrate;
intensify, aggravate;
sadden.

light-hearted, *adj.* carefree,
cheerful, lightsome, gay,
cheery, joyous, joyful,
blithe, glad, happy, merry,
jovial, jocund. —**Ant.**
heavy-hearted, cheerless,
morose, sad, gloomy,
melancholy.

likely, *adj.* apt, liable,
probable, possible,

suitable, appropriate.
—**Ant.** unlikely.

liking, *n.* preference,
inclination, favor,
disposition, bent, bias,
leaning, propensity,
capacity, proclivity,
proneness, predilection,
predisposition, tendency;
partiality, fondness,
affection. —**Ant.** dislike,
disfavor, disinclination.

limb, *n.* **1.** part, member,
extremity; leg, arm, wing.
2. branch, bough,
offshoot.

limber, *adj.* pliant, flexible,
supple, pliable, lithe.
—**Ant.** rigid, unbending,
unyielding.

limelight, *n.* public eye,
public notice, cynosure,
publicness, fame,
notoriety, exposure,
publicity, réclame. —**Ant.**
reclusiveness, seclusion.

limit, *n.* **1.** bound, extent,
boundary, confine,
frontier, termination. **2.**
restraint, restriction,
constraint, check,
hindrance. —*v.* **3.** restrain,
restrict, confine, check,

hinder, bound,
circumscribe, define.

limpid, *adj.* clear,
transparent, pellucid, lucid,
crystal-clear. —**Ant.**
cloudy, dim, dull.

linger, *v.* remain, stay on,
tarry, delay, dawdle, loiter.

link, *n.* **1.** bond, tie,
connection, connective,
copula, vinculum. —*v.* **2.**
bond, join, unite, connect,
league, conjoin, fasten,
pin, bind, tie. —**Ant.**
separation; separate, split,
rive.

liquid, *n., adj.* fluid, liquor.
—**Ant.** solid, gas. —**Syn.**
Study. LIQUID, FLUID agree
in referring to matter that
is not solid. LIQUID
commonly refers to
substances, as water, oil,
alcohol, and the like, that
are neither solids nor
gases: *Water ceases to be a
liquid when it is frozen or
turned to steam.* FLUID is
applied to anything that
flows, whether liquid or
gaseous: *Pipes can carry
fluids from place to place.*

lissome, *adj.* lithesome,
lithe, limber, supple, agile,

active, energetic. —**Ant.**
inflexible, rigid, clumsy,
awkward.

list, *n.* **1.** catalogue,
inventory, roll, schedule,
series, register. **2.** border,
strip, selvage, band, edge.
3. leaning, tilt, tilting,
careening. —*v.* **4.** register,
catalogue, enlist, enroll. **5.**
border, edge. **6.** careen,
incline, lean. —**Syn.**
Study. LIST, CATALOG,
INVENTORY, ROLL imply a
meaningful arrangement of
items. LIST denotes a series
of names, figures, or other
items arranged in a row or
rows: *a grocery list.*
CATALOG adds the idea of
an alphabetical or other
orderly arranged list of
goods or services, usu.
with descriptive details: *a
mail-order catalog.*
INVENTORY refers to a
detailed, descriptive list of
goods or property, made
for legal or business
purposes: *The company's
inventory consists of 2,000
items.* A ROLL is a list of
names of members of a
group, often used to check

attendance: *The teacher called the roll.*

listen, *v.* hearken, hear, hark, attend, give ear, lend an ear.

listlessness, *n.* indifference, inattention, inattentiveness, heedlessness; thoughtlessness, carelessness. **—Ant.** concern, care, attention, attentiveness.

literature, *n.* belles-lettres, letters, humanities, writings.

litter, *n.* **1.** rubbish, shreds, fragments. **2.** untidiness, disorder, confusion. **3.** brood. **4.** stretcher. **5.** straw *or* hay bedding. —*v.* **6.** strew, scatter, derange, mess up, disarrange, disorder.

little, *adj.* **1.** small, diminutive, minute, tiny, infinitesimal, wee. **2.** short, brief. **3.** weak, feeble, slight, inconsiderable, trivial, paltry, insignificant, unimportant, petty, scanty. **4.** mean, narrow, illiberal, paltry, stingy, selfish, small, niggardly. —*adv.* **5.**

slightly, barely, just. **—Ant.** large, immense, huge; important; liberal, generous.

livelihood, *n.* maintenance, living, sustenance, support, subsistence.

lively, *adj.* **1.** energetic, active, vigorous, brisk, peart, vivacious, alert, spry, nimble, agile, quick. **2.** animated, spirited, vivacious, sprightly, gay, blithe, blithesome, buoyant, gleeful. **3.** eventful, stirring, moving. **4.** strong, keen, distinct, vigorous, forceful, clear, piquant. **5.** striking, telling, effective. **6.** vivid, bright, brilliant, fresh, clear, glowing. **7.** sparkling, fresh. **—Ant.** inactive, torpid; leaden; uneventful; weak, dull, unclear; ineffective; dim; stale.

living, *adj.* **1.** alive, live, quick, existing; extant, surviving. **2.** active, lively, strong, vigorous, quickening. —*n.* **3.** livelihood, maintenance, sustenance, subsistence, support. **—Ant.** dead.

load, *n.* **1.** burden, onus, weight, encumbrance, incubus, pressure. —*v.* **2.** lade, weight, weigh down, burden, encumber, freight, oppress. —**Ant.** disburden, unload, lighten.

loath, *adj.* reluctant, averse, unwilling, disinclined, backward. —**Ant.** eager, anxious, willing. —**Syn. Study.** See RELUCTANT.

loathe, *v.* abominate, detest, hate, abhor. —**Ant.** adore, love.

loathing, *n.* disgust, dislike, aversion, abhorrence, hatred, hate, antipathy; animus, animosity, hostility. —**Ant.** liking, love; friendship, regard.

loathsome, *adj.* disgusting, nauseating, sickening, repulsive, offensive, repellent, revolting, detestable, abhorrent, hateful, odious, abominable, execrable. —**Ant.** attractive, delightful, lovable.

locale, *n.* place, location, site, spot, locality.

lodge, *n.* **1.** shelter, habitation, cabin, hut, cottage, cot. **2.** club, association, society. —*v.* **3.** shelter, harbor, house, quarter. **4.** place, put, set, plant, infix, deposit, lay, settle.

lofty, *adj.* **1.** high, elevated, towering, tall. **2.** exalted, elevated, sublime. **3.** haughty, proud, arrogant, prideful. —**Ant.** lowly; debased; humble.

loiter, *v.* linger, dally, dawdle, idle, loaf, delay, tarry, lag. —**Syn. Study.** LOITER, DALLY, DAWDLE, IDLE imply moving or acting slowly, stopping for unimportant reasons, and in general wasting time. To LOITER is to linger aimlessly: *to loiter outside a building.* To DALLY is to loiter indecisively or to delay as if free from care or responsibility: *to dally on the way home.* To DAWDLE is to saunter, stopping often, and taking a great deal of time, or to fritter away time working in a halfhearted way: *to dawdle over a task.* To IDLE is to move slowly and aimlessly, or to spend a great deal of time doing nothing: *to idle away the hours.*

lone, *adj.* **1.** alone, unaccompanied, solitary, lonely, secluded, apart, separate, separated; deserted, uninhabited, unoccupied, unpopulated, empty. **2.** isolated, solitary, sole, unique, lonely. **—Ant.** accompanied, together; inhabited, occupied.

lonely, *adj.* lone, solitary, lonesome, sequestered, remote, dreary. **—Ant.** crowded, populous.

lonesome, *adj.* lonely, alone, secluded; desolate, isolated.

long, *adj.* **1.** lengthy, extensive, drawn out, attenuated, protracted, stretched, prolonged, extended. **2.** overlong, long-winded, tedious, boring, wordy, prolix. **—v. 3.** crave, desire, yearn for, pine for, hanker for *or* after. **—Ant.** short, abbreviated; interesting; forgo. **—Syn. Study.** See YEARN.

longing, *n.* craving, desire, hankering, yearning, aspiration. **—Ant.** disinterest, antipathy, apathy.

look, *v.* **1.** gaze, glance, watch. **2.** appear, seem. **3.** await, wait for, expect, anticipate. **4.** face, front. **5.** seek, search for. **—n. 6.** gaze, glance. **7.** search, examination. **8.** appearance, aspect, mien, manner, air. **—Syn. Study.** See SEEM.

loose, *adj.* **1.** free, unfettered, unbound, untied, unrestrained, unrestricted, released, unattached, unfastened, unconfined. **2.** uncombined. **3.** lax, slack, careless, negligent, heedless. **4.** wanton, libertine, unchaste, immoral, dissolute, licentious. **5.** general, vague, indefinite, inexact, imprecise, ill-defined, indeterminate, indistinct. **—v. 6.** loosen, free, set free, unfasten, undo, unlock, unbind, untie, unloose, release, liberate. **7.** relax, slacken, ease, loosen. —**Ant.** bound, fettered; combined; tight, taut; moral, chaste; definite, specific; bind, commit; tighten.

loot, *n.* **1.** spoils, plunder, booty. —*v.* **2.** plunder, rob, sack, rifle, despoil, ransack, pillage, rape.

loquacious, *adj.* talkative, garrulous, wordy, verbose, voluble. —**Ant.** taciturn, close-mouthed. —**Syn. Study.** See TALKATIVE.

lordly, *adj.* **1.** grand, magnificent, majestic, royal, regal, kingly, aristocratic, dignified, noble, lofty. **2.** haughty, arrogant, lofty, imperious, domineering, insolent, overbearing, despotic, dictatorial, tyrannical. —**Ant.** menial, servile; humble, obedient.

lore, *n.* **1.** learning, kowledge, erudition. **2.** wisdom, counsel, advice, teaching, doctrine, lesson.

loss, *n.* **1.** detriment, disadvantage, damage, injury, destruction. **2.** privation, deprivation. —**Ant.** gain.

lost, *adj.* **1.** forfeited, gone, missing, missed. **2.** bewildered, confused, perplexed, puzzled. **3.** wasted, misspent, squandered, dissipated. **4.** defeated, vanquished. **5.** destroyed, ruined. **6.** depraved, abandoned, dissolute, corrupt, reprobate, profligate, licentious, shameless, hardened, irredeemable, irreclaimable. —**Ant.** found; pure, honorable, chaste.

loud, *adj.* **1.** noisy, clamorous, resounding, deafening, stentorian, boisterous, tumultuous. **2.** gaudy, flashy, showy, obtrusive, vulgar, obvious, blatant, coarse, rude, crude, cheap. —**Ant.** soft, quiet; sedate, tasteful, artistic.

loutish, *adj.* boorish, unrefined, uncouth, ill-bred, rough, cloddish, clumsy, crass, churlish, coarse, crude, brutish, beastly. —**Ant.** refined, gracious, graceful.

love, *n.* **1.** affection, predilection, liking,

inclination, regard, friendliness, kindness, tenderness, fondness, devotion, warmth, attachment, passion, adoration. —*v.* **2.** like, be fond of, have affection for, be enamored of, be in love with, adore, adulate, worship. —**Ant.** hatred, dislike; detest, abhor, abominate, hate.

lovely, *adj.* beautiful, charming, exquisite, enchanting, winning. —**Ant.** ugly, unattractive, homely. —**Syn. Study.** See BEAUTIFUL.

low, *adj.* **1.** prostrate, dead, prone, supine. **2.** profound, deep. **3.** feeble, weak, exhausted, sinking, dying, expiring. **4.** depressed, dejected, dispirited, unhappy, sad, miserable. **5.** undignified, infra dig, lowly, dishonorable, disreputable, unbecoming, disgraceful. **6.** groveling, abject, sordid, mean, base, lowly, degraded, menial, servile, ignoble, vile. **7.** humble, lowly, meek, lowborn, poor, plain, plebeian,

vulgar, base. **8.** coarse, vulgar, rude, crude. **9.** soft, subdued, gentle, quiet. —*adv.* **10.** cheaply, inexpensively. —*v., n.* **11.** moo, bellow. —**Ant.** high, upright. —**Syn. Study.** See MEAN.

lowbred, *adj.* unrefined, vulgar, coarse, rude, lowborn. —**Ant.** refined, noble, highborn.

lower, *v.* **1.** reduce, decrease, diminish, lessen. **2.** soften, turn down, quiet down. **3.** degrade, humble, abase, humiliate, disgrace, debase. **4.** let down, drop, depress, take down, sink. **5.** darken, threaten, glower; frown, scowl. —**Ant.** raise, increase; elevate, honor; brighten.

loyal, *adj.* faithful, true, patriotic, devoted, constant. —**Ant.** faithless, disloyal, treacherous. —**Syn. Study.** See FAITHFUL.

loyalty, *n.* faithfulness, allegiance, fealty, devotion, constancy, patriotism, fidelity. —**Ant.** faithlessness, disloyalty.

lubricous, *adj.* **1.** slippery,

oily, smooth. **2.** unsteady, unstable, uncertain, shifty, wavering, undependable. **3.** lewd, lascivious, licentious, salacious, wanton, unchaste, incontinent, lecherous, perverse, perverted, immoral, vulgar, lustful, carnal, libidinous, dissolute, libertine, profligate, depraved, corrupt, loose, sensual, concupiscent, impure, pornographic, obscene, dirty, filthy. **—Ant.** dependable, sure, certain, reliable; prudish, chaste, moral.

lucid, *adj.* **1.** shining, bright, lucent, radiant, brilliant, resplendent, luminous. **2.** clear, transparent, pellucid, limpid, crystalline; luculent, intelligible, plain, unmistakable, obvious, distinct, evident, understandable; rational, sane, sober, sound, reasonable. **—Ant.** dull; unclear, dull; unreasonable.

lucky, *adj.* fortunate, fortuitous, happy, favored, blessed; auspicious, propitious, favorable, prosperous. **—Ant.** unfortunate, unlucky.

ludicrous, *adj.* laughable, ridiculous, amusing, comical, funny, droll, absurd, farcical. **—Ant.** miserable, serious, tragic.

lugubrious, *adj.* doleful, mournful, dismal, sorrowful, melancholy, gloomy, depressing. **—Ant.** cheerful, happy.

lukewarm, *adj.* **1.** tepid, warmish, moderately warm, room-temperature. **2.** halfhearted, unenthusiastic, so-so, unimpassioned, unmoved, indifferent, unsympathetic, Laodicean. **—Ant.** dedicated, enthusiastic.

luminous, *adj.* **1.** bright, shining, lucid, lucent, radiant, brilliant, resplendent. **2.** lighted, lit, illuminated. **3.** brilliant, bright, intelligent, smart, clever, enlightening. **4.** clear, intelligible, understandable, perspicacious, perspicuous, plain, lucid. **—Ant.** dull;

dark; stupid; unclear, unintelligible.

lunacy, *n.* **1.** madness, craziness, insanity, psychosis, daftness, mania, dementia, dementedness. **2.** folly, foolishness, foolhardiness, absurdity, fatuity, silliness. —**Ant.** sanity, normalcy, sobriety.

lure, *n.* **1.** enticement, decoy, attraction, allurement, temptation, bait; fly, minnow. —*v.* **2.** allure, decoy, entice, draw, attract, tempt, seduce.

lurid, *adj.* **1.** vivid, glaring, sensational; shining, fiery, red, intense, fierce, terrible, unrestrained, passionate. **2.** wan, pale, pallid, ghastly, gloomy, murky, dismal, lowering. —**Ant.** mild, controlled; cheery.

lurk, *v.* skulk, sneak, prowl, slink, steal; lie in wait, lie in ambush, lie hidden *or* concealed. —**Syn. Study.** LURK, SKULK, SNEAK, PROWL suggest avoiding observation, often because of a sinister purpose. To LURK is to lie in wait for someone or to move stealthily: *The thief lurked in the shadows.* SKULK has a similar sense, but usu. suggests cowardice or fear: *The dog skulked about the house.* SNEAK emphasizes the attempt to avoid being seen or discovered; it suggests a sinister intent or the desire to avoid punishment: *The children sneaked out the back way.* PROWL usu. implies seeking prey or loot; it suggests quiet and watchful roaming: *The cat prowled around in search of mice.*

luscious, *adj.* **1.** delicious, juicy, delectable, palatable, savory. **2.** sweet, cloying, saccharine, honeyed. —**Ant.** unpalatable, disgusting, nauseating; bitter, acrid, acid.

lush, *adj.* **1.** tender, juicy, succulent, luxuriant, fresh. —*n.* **2.** *(slang)* drunk, toper, tippler, dipsomaniac, alcoholic, heavy drinker. —**Ant.** stale, moldy.

lust, *n.* **1.** desire, passion, appetite, craving, eagerness, cupidity. **2.**

lechery, concupiscence, carnality, lubricity, salaciousness, licentiousness, wantonness, lasciviousness, libertinism, license. —*v.* **3.** crave, desire, need, want, demand, hunger for.

luster, *n.* **1.** glitter, glisten, sheen, gloss. **2.** brillance, brightness, radiance, luminosity, resplendence. **3.** excellence, merit, distinction, glory, honor, repute, renown, eminence, celebrity, dash, élan, éclat. **4.** chandelier, sconce, candelabrum. —**Ant.**

dullness, tarnish; disrepute, dishonor.

lusty, *adj.* hearty, vigorous, strong, healthy, robust, sturdy, stout. —**Ant.** weak, frail, unhealthy.

luxurious, *adj.* **1.** splendid, rich, sumptuous, ornate, delicate, opulent, well-appointed. **2.** voluptuous, sensual, self-indulgent, epicurean. —**Ant.** poor, squalid.

lyrical, *adj.* lilting, airy, songful, graceful, lighthearted, lightsome, buoyant, sunny, exuberant, rhapsodic. —**Ant.** sorrowful, elegiac.

M

macabre, *adj.* gruesome, horrible, grim, ghastly, morbid, weird. —**Ant.** beautiful, lovely, attractive, delightful.

Machiavellian, *adj.* crafty, deceitful, cunning, wily. astute, unscrupulous, clever, artful, designing, insidious, sly, shrewd,

subtle, arch, crooked, tricky, intriguing, double-dealing, equivocal. —**Ant.** naive, ingenuous, honest.

machination, *n.* manipulation, maneuver, stratagem, ploy, artifice, tactic, wile, device, trick, plot, cabal, intrigue, scheme, conspiracy,

machismo, *n.* manliness, supermanliness, virility, potency, boldness, courageousness, dominance, prepotency, primacy, arrogance.

mad, *adj.* **1.** insane, lunatic, deranged, raving, distracted, crazed, maniacal, crazy. **2.** furious, exasperated, angry, enraged, raging, incensed, provoked, wrathful, irate. **3.** violent, furious, stormy. **4.** excited, frantic, frenzied, wild, rabid. **5.** senseless, foolish, imprudent, impractical, ill-advised, excessive, reckless, unsound, unsafe, harmful, dangerous, perilous. **6.** infatuated, wild about, desirous. —**Ant.** sane; calm; serene; sensible, wise.

madden, *v.* infuriate, irritate, provoke, vex, annoy, enrage, anger, inflame, exasperate. —**Ant.** calm, mollify.

maelstrom, *n.* **1.** whirlpool, vortex, eddy, whirl,

Charybdis, sea puss. **2.** turmoil, agitation, bustle, turbulence, ferment, hubbub, commotion, confusion, storm. —**Ant.** tranquillity, smoothness.

magic, *n.* enchantment, sorcery, necromancy, witchcraft, legerdemain, conjuring, sleight of hand.

magician, *n.* sorcerer, necromancer, witch doctor, enchanter, conjuror.

magisterial, *adj.* **1.** dictatorial, dominating, dogmatic, doctrinaire, imperious, authoritarian, lordly. **2.** masterful, masterly, authoritative, commanding, expert.

magnanimous, *adj.* **1.** big, large, generous, forgiving, unselfish, liberal, disinterested. **2.** noble, lofty, honorable, elevated, high-minded, exalted. —**Ant.** small, niggardly; base, vile. —**Syn. Study.** See NOBLE.

magnificence, *n.* splendor, grandeur, impressiveness, sumptuousness, pomp, state, majesty, luxury,

luxuriousness, éclat.
—**Ant.** squalor, poverty.

magnificent, *adj.* **1.**
splendid, fine, superb,
august, stately, majestic,
imposing, sumptuous, rich,
lavish, luxurious, grand,
gorgeous, beautiful,
princely, impressive,
dazzling, brilliant, radiant,
excellent, exquisite,
elegant, superior,
extraordinary; showy,
ostentatious. **2.** noble,
sublime, dignified, great.
—**Ant.** squalid, poor; base.

magnify, *v.* **1.** enlarge,
augment, increase, add to,
amplify. **2.** exaggerate,
overstate. —**Ant.**
decrease, micrify;
understate.

maid, *n.* **1.** girl, maiden,
demoiselle, lass, lassie,
virgin. **2.** maidservant.

maim, *v.* mutilate, cripple,
lacerate, mangle, injure,
disable, wound, deface,
mar, impair.

main, *adj.* **1.** chief,
cardinal, prime,
paramount, primary,
principal, leading, capital.
2. pure, sheer, utmost,

direct. —*n.* **3.** pipe, duct,
conduit, channel. **4.** force,
power, strength, might,
effort. **5.** point, idea, crux.
6. ocean, sea, high seas.
—**Ant.** secondary,
unimportant; least;
weakness.

mainstay, *n.* support,
backbone, spine, sine qua
non, supporter, upholder,
sustainer, pillar, brace,
standby, prop, crutch.

maintain, *v.* **1.** keep,
continue, preserve, retain,
keep up, uphold, support.
2. affirm, assert, aver,
asseverate, state, hold,
allege, declare. **3.** contend,
hold, claim, defend,
vindicate, justify. **4.**
provide for, support,
sustain, keep up. —**Ant.**
discontinue.

maintenance, *n.*
subsistence, support,
livelihood, living, bread,
victuals, food, provisions.
—**Ant.** desuetude.

majestic, *adj.* regal, royal,
princely, kingly, imperial,
noble, lofty, stately, grand,
august, dignified,
imposing, pompous,

splendid, magnificent, sublime. —**Ant.** base, squalid.

major, *adj.* greater, larger, capital. —**Ant.** minor. —**Syn. Study.** See CAPITAL.

make, *v.* **1.** form, build, produce, fabricate, create, construct, manufacture, fashion, mold, shape. **2.** cause, render, constitute. **3.** transform, convert, change, turn, compose. **4.** give rise to, prompt, occasion. **5.** get, gain, acquire, obtain, secure, procure, earn, win. **6.** do, effect, bring about, perform, execute, accomplish, practice, act. **7.** estimate, reckon, judge, gauge. **8.** cause, induce, compel, force. —*n.* **9.** style, form, build, shape, brand, trade name, construction, structure, constitution. **10.** disposition, character, nature. **11.** quantity made, output, produce, production, product. —**Ant.** destroy.

makeshift, *adj.* **1.** improvised, stopgap, provisional, expedient, temporary, substitute, reserve, spare, make-do, jerry-built. —*n.* **2.** improvisation, expedient, substitute, reserve, stopgap, resort, make-do.

maladroit, *adj.* **1.** unskillful, awkward, clumsy, bungling, inept. **2.** tactless, gauche. —**Ant.** adroit; tactful, subtle.

malady, *n.* disease, illness, sickness, affliction, disorder, complaint, ailment, indisposition.

malcontent, *adj.* dissatisfied, discontented, unsatisfied, unfulfilled. —**Ant.** satisfied, contented, content.

male, *adj.* masculine, manly, virile, paternal. —**Ant.** female. —**Syn. Study.** MALE, MASCULINE, VIRILE describe men and boys or whatever is culturally attributed to them. MALE classifies individuals on the basis of their genetic makeup or their ability to fertilize an ovum in bisexual reproduction. It contrasts with FEMALE in all uses: *his* oldest male relative; the male parts of the flower. MASCULINE refers to qualities or behavior deemed especially appropriate to or ideally associated with men and boys. In American and W European culture, this has traditionally included such traits as strength, aggressiveness, and courage: a firm, masculine handshake; masculine impatience at indecision. VIRILE implies the muscularity, vigor, and sexual potency of mature manhood: a swaggering, virile walk. See also MANLY, MAN.

malediction, *n.* curse, imprecation, denunciation, cursing, damning, damnation, execration; slander. —**Ant.** benediction, blessing.

malefactor, *n.* evildoer, culprit, criminal, felon, outlaw, offender. —**Ant.** benefactor.

malevolence, *n.* ill will, rancor, malignity, resentment, malice, maliciousness, spite, spitefulness, grudge, hate, hatred, venom. —**Ant.** benevolence, good will.

malevolent, *adj.* malicious, malignant, resentful, spiteful, begrudging, hateful, venomous, vicious, hostile, ill-natured, evil-minded, rancorous, mischievous, envious. —**Ant.** benevolent, friendly, amiable.

malfeasance, *n.* misbehavior, misconduct, misdemeanor, misdeed, badness, wrongdoing, malpractice, delinquency, criminality, illegality, wickedness. —**Ant.** lawfulness, honesty.

malice, *n.* ill will, spite, spitefulness, animosity, animus, enmity, malevolence, grudge, venom, hate, hatred, bitterness, rancor. —**Ant.** good will, benevolence.

malicious, *adj.* malevolent. —**Ant.** benevolent.

malign, *v.* **1.** slander, libel, revile, abuse, calumniate, defame, disparage, vilify. —*adj.* **2.** evil, pernicious, baleful, injurious, unfavorable, baneful. **3.** malevolent. —**Ant.** compliment, praise; good, favorable; benevolent.

malignant, *adj.* **1.** malicious, spiteful, malevolent, rancorous, bitter. **2.** dangerous, perilous, harmful, hurtful, virulent, pernicious, lethal, deadly. —**Ant.** benevolent; benign.

malignity, *n.* malevolence. —**Ant.** benignity.

malinger, *v.* shirk, slack, slack off, dodge, duck duty, get out of, goldbrick.

malleable, *adj.* adaptable, plastic, shapable, bendable, ductile, moldable, pliant, pliable, supple, flexile, elastic, compliant. —**Ant.** rigid, refractory.

maltreat, *v.* mistreat, abuse, injure, ill-treat. —**Ant.** amuse, entertain.

mammoth, *adj.* huge, gigantic, immense, colossal. —**Ant.** tiny, microscopic. —**Syn. Study.** See GIGANTIC.

man, *n.* **1.** male, gentleman, adult male **2.** humanity, humankind, mankind; human being, human —**Syn. Study.** MAN, MALE, GENTLEMAN refer to adult humans of the sex that produces sperm for procreation. MAN, the most commonly used of the three, can be neutral: *a man of deep faith.* It can also signify possession of typical or desirable masculine qualities: *to take one's punishment like a man.* MALE emphasizes physical or sexual characteristics and can also apply to an animal or a plant: *two males and three females in the pack.* GENTLEMAN, once used only of men of high social rank, now also specifies a man of courtesy and consideration: *to behave like a gentleman.* It is used too as a polite term of reference (*This gentleman is next*) or, only in the plural, of address (*Are we ready, gentlemen?*). See also MANLY, MALE.

manage, *v.* **1.** bring about, succeed, accomplish, arrange, contrive. **2.**

conduct, handle, direct, govern, control, guide, regulate, engineer, rule, administer, supervise, superintend. **3.** handle, wield, manipulate, control. **4.** dominate, influence; train, educate, handle. —**Ant.** mismanage, bungle.

management, *n.* handling, direction, control, regulation, conduct, charge, administration, superintendence, care, guidance, disposal, treatment, oversight, surveillance. —**Ant.** mismanagement.

manager, *n.* administrator, executive, superintendent, supervisor, boss, director, overseer, governor. —**Ant.** employee.

mandate, *n.* command, order, fiat, decree, ukase, injunction, edict, ruling, commission, requirement, precept, requisite, prerequisite.

maneuver, *n.* **1.** procedure, move; scheme, plot, plan, design, stratagem, ruse, artifice, trick. —*v.* **2.** manipulate, handle,

intrigue, trick, scheme, plot, plan, design, finesse.

manful, *adj.* manly. —**Ant.** feminine, cowardly. —**Syn. Study.** See MANLY.

mangle, *v.* cut, lacerate, crush, slash, disfigure, maim, ruin, spoil, mar, deface, mutilate, destroy.

mania, *n.* **1.** excitement, enthusiasm, craze, fad. **2.** insanity, madness, aberration, derangement, dementia, frenzy, lunacy. —**Ant.** phobia; rationality.

manifest, *adj.* **1.** evident, obvious, apparent, plain, clear, distinct, patent, open, palpable, visible, unmistakable, conspicuous. —*v.* **2.** show, display, reveal, disclose, open, exhibit, evince, evidence, demonstrate, declare, express, make known. —**Ant.** latent, hidden, inconspicuous; conceal. —**Syn. Study.** See DISPLAY.

manifold, *adj.* **1.** various, many, numerous, multitudinous. **2.** varied, various, divers, multifarious, multifaceted.

—**Ant.** simple, singular.
—**Syn. Study.** See MANY.

manly, *adj.* **1.** manful, mannish, masculine, male, virile. **2.** strong, brave, honorable, courageous, bold, valiant, intrepid, undaunted. —**Ant.** feminine; weak, cowardly. —**Syn. Study.** MANLY, MANFUL, MANNISH mean having traits or qualities considered typical of or appropriate to adult males. MANLY, a term of approval, suggests such admirable traits as maturity and steadiness: *a manly acceptance of responsibility.* MANFUL, also an approving term, stresses such qualities as courage and strength: *a manful effort to overcome great odds.* MANNISH is most often used, esp. derogatorily, in referring to the qualities or accouterments of a woman considered more appropriate to a man: *the mannish abruptness of her speech; She wore a severely mannish suit.* See also MALE.

manner, *n.* **1.** mode,

fashion, style, way, habit, custom, method, form. **2.** demeanor, department, air, bearing, behavior, carriage, mien, aspect, look, appearance. **3.** kind, sort. **4.** nature, guise, character.

mannish, *adj.* manly. —**Ant.** feminine; cowardly, pusillanimous. —**Syn. Study.** See MANLY.

manufacture, *v.* assemble, fabricate, make, construct, build, compose. —**Ant.** destroy.

many, *adj.* numerous, multifarious, abundant, myriad, innumerable, manifold, divers, sundry, various, varied. —**Ant.** few. —**Syn. Study.** MANY, NUMEROUS, INNUMERABLE, MANIFOLD imply the presence of a large number of units. MANY is a general word that refers to a large but indefinite number of units or individuals: *many years ago; many friends and supporters.* NUMEROUS, a more formal word, stresses the individual and separate quality of the units: *to receive numerous* *letters.* INNUMERABLE denotes a number that is too large to be counted or, more loosely, that is very difficult to count: *the innumerable stars.* MANIFOLD implies that the number is large, but also varied or complex: *manifold responsibilities.*

map, *n.* chart, graph, plan, outline, diagram.

mar, *v.* damage, impair, ruin, spoil, injure, blot, deface, disfigure, deform, distort, maim.

maraud, *v.* raid, plunder, pillage, ravage, ransack.

margin, *n.* border, edge, rim, limit, confine, bound, marge, verge, brink. —**Ant.** center.

mariner, *n.* sailor, seaman, tar, seafarer, seafaring man. —**Ant.** landlubber. —**Syn. Study.** See SAILOR.

mark, *n.* **1.** trace, impression, line, cut, dent, stain, bruise. **2.** badge, brand, sign. **3.** symbol, sign, token, inscription, indication. **4.** note, importance, distinction, eminence, consequence. **5.**
trait, characteristic, stamp, print. **6.** aim, target, end, purpose, object, objective. —*v.* **7.** label, tag, mark up, mark down. **8.** indicate, designate, point out, brand, identify, imprint, impress, characterize. **9.** destine, single out. **10.** note, pay attention to, heed, notice, observe, regard, eye, spot.

marriage, *n.* **1.** wedding, nuptials; wedlock, matrimony. **2.** union, alliance, association, confederation. —**Ant.** divorce; separation.

marshal, *v.* arrange, array, order, rank, dispose; gather, convoke. —**Ant.** disorder; scatter. —**Syn. Study.** See GATHER.

marvelous, *adj.* **1.** wonderful, wondrous, extraordinary, amazing, astonishing, astounding, miraculous. **2.** improbable, incredible, unbelievable, surprising. —**Ant.** terrible, ordinary, commonplace; believable.

masculine, See Syn. study at MALE.

mask, *n.* **1.** face-covering, veil, false face. **2.** disguise, concealment, pretense, pretext, ruse, trick, subterfuge, evasion. **3.** masquerade, revel, *bal masqué*, *ballo in maschera*, mummery. —*v.* **4.** disguise, conceal, hide, veil, screen, cloak, shroud, cover.

mass, *n.* **1.** aggregate, aggregation, assemblage, heap, congeries, combination. **2.** collection, accumulation, conglomeration, pile, assemblage, quantity. **3.** main body, bulk, majority. **4.** size, bulk, massiveness, magnitude, dimension. **5.** *(plural)* proletariat, working class, common people, plebeians. —*v.* **6.** assemble; collect, gather, marshal, amass, convoke; heap *or* pile up, aggregate.

massacre, *n.* **1.** killing, slaughter, carnage, extermination, annihilation, butchery, murder, genocide. —*v.* **2.** kill, butcher, slaughter, murder, slay. —**Syn. Study.** See SLAUGHTER.

massive, *adj.* **1.** bulky, heavy, large, immense, huge, tremendous. **2.** solid, substantial, great, imposing, massy, ponderous. —**Ant.** diminutive; flimsy.

master, *n.* **1.** adept, expert. **2.** employer, boss. **3.** commander, chief, head, commander in chief, captain. —*adj.* **4.** chief, principal, head, leading, cardinal, primary, prime, main. **5.** dominating, predominant. **6.** skilled, adept, expert, skillful. —*v.* **7.** conquer, subdue, subject, subjugate, overcome, overpower. **8.** rule, direct, govern, manage, superintend, oversee.

matchless, *adj.* peerless, unrivaled, unequaled, inimitable, unparalleled, incomparable, unmatched, consummate, exquisite. —**Ant.** unimportant, unimpressive.

material, *n.* **1.** substance, matter, stuff. **2.** element, constituent. —*adj.* **3.** physical, corporeal. **4.** important, essential, vital, consequent, momentous.

—**Ant.** spiritual;
immaterial. —**Syn. Study.**
See MATTER.

matter, *n.* **1.** substance,
material, stuff. **2.** thing,
affair, business, question,
subject, topic. **3.**
consequence, importance,
essence, import,
significance, moment. **4.**
trouble, difficulty. **5.**
ground, reason, cause.
—*v.* **6.** signify, be of
importance, count. —**Ant.**
insignificance; ease.

mature, *adj.* **1.** ripe, aged,
complete, grown, adult,
full-grown,
fully-developed, maturated.
2. completed, perfected,
elaborated, ready,
prepared. —*v.* **3.** ripen,
age, develop. **4.** perfect,
complete. —**Ant.**
immature, childish,
adolescent.

maxim, *n.* proverb,
aphorism, saying, adage,
apothegm. —**Syn. Study.**
See PROVERB.

meager, *adj.* scanty,
deficient, sparse, mean,
insignificant; thin, lean,
emaciated, spare, gaunt,

skinny, lank. —**Ant.**
abundant. —**Syn. Study.**
See SCANTY.

mealymouthed, *adj.*
devious, hypocritical, false,
duplicitous, two-faced,
insincere, smarmy. —**Ant.**
straightforward, candid.

mean, *v.* **1.** intend,
purpose, contemplate,
destine, foreordain,
predestinate, design. **2.**
signify, indicate, denote,
imply, express. —*adj.* **3.**
inferior. **4.** common,
humble, low, undignified,
ignoble, plebeian, coarse,
rude, vulgar. **5.**
unimportant, unessential,
nonessential, inconsequent,
dispensable, insignificant,
petty, paltry, little, poor,
wretched, despicable,
contemptible, low, base,
vile, foul, disgusting,
repulsive, repellent,
depraved, immoral;
small-minded. **6.**
unimposing, shabby,
sordid, unclean,
unscrupulous, squalid,
poor. **7.** penurious,
parsimonious, illiberal,
stingy, miserly, tight,
niggardly, scotch, selfish,

narrow, mercenary. **8.** intermediate, middle, medium, average, moderate. —*n. (plural)* **9.** agency, instrumentality, method, approach, mode, way. **10.** resources, backing, support. **11.** revenue, income, substance, wherewithal, property, wealth. **12.** (*sing.*) average, median, middle, midpoint, center. —**Ant.** exalted, dignified; important, essential; imposing, splendid, rich, generous; superior. —**Syn. Study.** MEAN, LOW, BASE refer to characteristics worthy of dislike, contempt, or disgust. MEAN suggests a petty selfishness or lack of generosity, and may describe spiteful, unkind, or even vicious behavior: *mean rumors; a mean bully.* LOW means dishonorable in purpose or character; it describes that which is morally reprehensible or vulgar: *low deeds; low company.* BASE suggests moral depravity, greed, and cowardice; it describes

dishonorable or exploitative behavior: *base motives.*

meander, *v.* **1.** wander, stroll; wind, turn. —*n.* **2.** labyrinth, maze, intricacy.

meaning, *n.* **1.** tenor, gist, trend, idea, purport, significance, signification, sense, import, denotation, connotation, interpretation. **2.** intent, intention, aim, object, purpose, design. —*adj.* **3.** expressive, significant, poignant, pointed, knowing, meaningful. —**Ant.** insignificant, meaningless. —**Syn. Study.** MEANING, SENSE, SIGNIFICANCE, PURPORT denote that which is expressed or indicated by language or action. MEANING is a general word describing that which is intended to be, or actually is, expressed: *the meaning of a statement.* SENSE often refers to a particular meaning of a word or phrase: *The word "run" has many senses.* SENSE may also be used of meaning that is intelligible or reasonable: *There's no sense in what you say.* SIGNIFICANCE refers to a meaning that is implied rather than expressed: *the significance of a glance.* It may also refer to a meaning the importance of which is not immediately perceived: *We did not grasp the significance of the event until years later.* PURPORT usu. refers to the gist or essential meaning of something fairly complicated: *the purport of a theory.*

measureless, *adj.* limitless, boundless, immeasurable, immense, vast, endless, infinite, unending. —**Ant.** limited, finite.

mechanic, *n.* repairman, workman, machinist; craftsman, artificer, artisan.

meddlesome, *adj.* prying, curious, interfering, intrusive, officious.

mediate, *v.* intercede, interpose, arbitrate, reconcile, settle.

medicine, *n.* medication,

medicament, remedy, drug, physic.

mediocre, *adj.* indifferent, ordinary, common, commonplace, medium, average, middling, passable, mean. —**Ant.** superior.

meditate, *v.* **1.** contemplate, plan, reflect on, devise, scheme, plot, concoct, contrive, think over, dwell on. **2.** reflect, ruminate, contemplate, ponder, muse, cogitate, think, study.

meditative, *adj.* pensive, thoughtful, reflecting, contemplative; studious. —**Ant.** impetuous. —**Syn. Study.** See PENSIVE.

medium, *n.* **1.** mean, average, mean proportion, mean average. **2.** means, agency, instrumentality, instrument. **3.** environment, atmosphere, ether, air, temper, conditions, influences. —*adj.* **4.** average, mean, middling; mediocre.

meek, *adj.* humble, patient, submissive, spiritless, tame, yielding, forbearing, docile, unassuming, mild, peaceful, pacific, calm, soft, gentle, modest. —**Ant.** forward, unyielding, immodest.

meet, *v.* **1.** join, connect, intersect, cross, converge, come together, unite. **2.** encounter, come upon, confront, face. **3.** encounter, oppose, conflict. **4.** settle, discharge, fulfill, satisfy, gratify, answer, comply with. **5.** gather, assemble, congregate, convene, collect, muster. **6.** concur, agree, see eye to eye, unite, conjoin. —*n.* **7.** meeting, contest, competition, match. —*adj.* **8.** suited, suitable, apt, fitting, proper, appropriate, fit, befitting, adapted. —**Ant.** diverge; dissatisfy; scatter; disagree, diverge; unsuited, unapt.

melancholy, *n.* **1.** gloom, depression, sadness, dejection, despondency, gloominess, blues, hypochondria. **2.** pensiveness, thoughtfulness, sobriety, seriousness. —*adj.* **3.** sad,

depressed, dejected, gloomy, despondent, blue, dispirited, sorrowful, unhappy, disconsolate, inconsolable, miserable, dismal, doleful, lugubrious, moody, glum, down-in-the-mouth, downhearted, downcast, low-spirited. **4.** sober, serious, thoughtful, pensive. —**Ant.** cheer, happiness; cheerful, happy.

mellifluous, *adj.* flowing, smooth, honeyed, melodious, musical, euphonious, pleasant-sounding, lyrical, dulcet, sweet, sweet-sounding, sonorous, silvery, golden-tongued. —**Ant.** harsh, discordant.

mellow, *adj.* **1.** ripe, full-flavored, soft, mature, well-matured. **2.** softened, toned down, improved. **3.** soft, rich, delicate, mellifluous, dulcet, melodious, tuneful, sweet, smooth. **4.** genial, jovial, good-humored, good-natured. —*v.* **5.** soften, ripen, develop, mature, improve, perfect. —**Ant.** immature.

melody, *n.* tune, song, air, descant, theme.

melt, *v.* **1.** liquefy, fuse, dissolve, thaw. **2.** pass, dwindle, fade, fade out, blend. **3.** soften, gentle, mollify, relax. —**Ant.** freeze.

member, *n.* **1.** limb, leg, arm, wing, head, branch. **2.** constituent, element, part, portion.

memento, *n.* keepsake, remembrance, souvenir, token, reminder, relic, memorial, trophy, monument, favor, commemoration, testimonial, memento mori.

memorable, *adj.* notable, noteworthy, newsworthy, impressive, significant, remarkable, marked, signal, unforgettable, outstanding, standout, extraordinary, exceptional, indelible, haunting. —**Ant.** forgettable, unimpressive, fleeting.

menace, *n.* **1.** threat, minaciousness, minacity, threatening. —*v.* **2.** threaten, intimidate.

mend, *v.* **1.** darn, patch, repair, renew, fix, restore, retouch. **2.** correct, rectify, make better, amend, emend, ameliorate, meliorate, improve, set right. **3.** heal, recover, amend, improve, become better. —*n.* **4.** repair, improvement, amelioration, emendation, correction, restoration, rectification, amendment, renewal. —**Ant.** ruin, destroy; die, languish.

mendacious, *adj.* lying, untrue, false, untruthful, deceitful. —**Ant.** truthful, honest.

menial, *adj.* **1.** servile, mean, base, low. —*n.* **2.** servant, domestic, attendant, footman, butler, valet, maid, maidservant, waiter; flunky, slave, underling, hireling, serf, minion, lackey. —**Ant.** noble, dignified; master.

mental, *adj.* **1.** intellectual, cerebral, intellective, rational, reasoning, cognitive, psychological, psychic. **2.** neurotic, delusional, irrational, crazy, insane, psychotic, daft, batty.

mention, *v.* **1.** refer to, allude to, name, specify, speak of, make known, impart, disclose, divulge, communicate, declare, state, tell, aver. —*n.* **2.** reference, indirect reference, allusion.

mercenary, *adj.* venal, grasping, sordid, acquisitive, avaricious, covetous, penurious, parsimonious, stingy, tight, miserly, mean, niggardly, selfish. —**Ant.** generous, unselfish.

merciful, *adj.* compassionate, kind, clement, lenient, forgiving, gracious, benignant, beneficent, generous, big, large; tender, humane, kindhearted, tender-hearted, soft-hearted, sympathetic. —**Ant.** merciless.

merciless, *adj.* pitiless, cruel, hard, hard-hearted, severe, relentless, unrelenting, fell, unsympathetic, uncompassionate, unfeeling, inexorable. —**Ant.** merciful.

mercurial, *adj.* **1.** sprightly, volatile, active, spirited, lively, nimble, energetic. **2.** flighty, fickle, changeable, volatile, inconstant, undecided. —**Ant.** inactive, dispirited, phlegmatic; constant, steady.

mercy, *n.* **1.** compassion, pity, benevolence, consideration, forgiveness, indulgence, clemency, leniency, forbearance, lenity, kindness, tenderness, mildness, gentleness. **2.** disposal, discretion, disposition. —**Ant.** cruelty, pitilessness, harshness.

mere, *adj.* bare, scant, simple, pure, sheer, unmixed, entire. —**Ant.** considerable.

meretricious, *adj.* tawdry, showy, gaudy, ornate, spurious, sham, false. —**Ant.** genuine, sincere.

merit, *n.* **1.** worth, excellence, value, desert, entitlement, due, credit.

—*v.* **2.** deserve, be worthy of, earn, be entitled to.

merriment, *n.* gaiety, mirth, hilarity, laughter, jollity, joviality, jocularity. —**Ant.** misery, melancholy.

merry, *adj.* jolly, gay, happy, jovial, joyful, joyous, mirthful, hilarious, gleeful, blithe, blithesome, frolicsome, cheery, cheerful, glad. —**Ant.** sad, unhappy.

mess, *n.* **1.** dirtiness, untidiness. **2.** confusion, muddle, medley, farrago, hodgepodge, hotchpotch, jumble, litter, mixture, miscellany, mélange, salmagundi. **3.** unpleasantness, difficulty, predicament, plight, muddle, pickle. —*v.* **4.** muddle, confuse, mix, mix up. —**Ant.** tidiness; order, system; arrange.

metamorphosis, *n.* change, transformation, transmutation, mutation. —**Ant.** stasis.

mete, *v.* **1.** distribute, apportion, parcel out, dole, allot, deal, measure.

—*n.* **2.** limit, bound, boundary, term.

method, *n.* **1.** mode, procedure, way, means, manner, fashion, technique, process, course. **2.** order, system, arrangement, disposition, rule. —**Syn. Study.** METHOD, MODE, WAY refer to the manner in which something is done. METHOD implies a fixed procedure, usu. following a logical and systematic plan: *the open-hearth method of making steel.* MODE, a more formal word, implies a customary or characteristic manner: *Kangaroos have an unusual mode of carrying their young.* WAY is a general word that may often be substituted for more specific words: *the best way to solve a problem; an attractive way of wearing the hair.*

methodical, See Syn. study at ORDERLY.

meticulous, *adj.* careful, finical, finicky, solicitous, exact, precise, demanding. —**Ant.** careless, inexact,

imprecise. —**Syn. Study.**
See PAINSTAKING.

mettle, *n.* **1.** disposition, temper, character, spirit. **2.** spirit, courage, valor, pluck, vigor, ardor, fire, nerve, fiber. —**Ant.** cowardice, pusillanimity.

middle, *adj.* **1.** central, equidistant, halfway, medial. **2.** intermediate, intervening. —*n.* **3.** center, midpoint, midst. —**Ant.** end, final, initial.

midget, See Syn. study at DWARF.

midst, *n.* middle, center stage, arena, center, thick, heart, core. —**Ant.** rim, edge.

miffed, *adj.* offended, insulted, resentful, angry, annoyed, irritated, peeved, nettled, vexed, aggravated, put-out, teed off, bugged. —**Ant.** pleased.

might, *n.* power, ability, force, main, puissance, strength, efficacy. —**Ant.** weakness, inability.

mighty, *adj.* **1.** powerful, strong, vigorous, robust, sturdy, puissant, potent. **2.** sizable, huge, immense, enormous, vast, tremendous. —**Ant.** feeble, weak, impotent; small, negligible.

migrate, *v.* immigrate, emigrate, move, resettle. —**Ant.** remain, stay.

mild, *adj.* **1.** amiable, gentle, temperate, kind, compassionate, indulgent, clement, soft, pleasant. **2.** placid, peaceful, tranquil, pacific, calm. **3.** bland, emollient, mollifying, assuasive, soothing. —**Ant.** intemperate, unkind, unpleasant; stormy, turbulent; piquant, biting, bitter.

milieu, *n.* environment, medium, background, class, sphere, surroundings, element. —**Syn. Study.** See ENVIRONMENT.

mind, *n.* **1.** intellect, intelligence, understanding, reason, sense. **2.** brain, brains. **3.** sanity, reason, mental balance. **4.** disposition, temper, inclination, bent, intention, leaning, proclivity, bias. **5.** opinion, sentiments, belief, contemplation, judgment, consideration. **6.** purpose, intention, intent, will, wish, liking, desire, wont. **7.** remembrance, recollection, recall, memory. —*v.* **8.** pay attention, heed, obey, attend, attend to, mark, regard, notice, note. **9.** tend, take care of, watch, look after. **10.** be careful *or* cautious *or* wary. **11.** care, object. —**Syn. Study.** MIND, INTELLECT, BRAIN refer to that part of a conscious being that thinks, feels, wills, perceives, or judges. MIND is a philosophical, psychological, and general term for the center of all mental activity, as contrasted with the body and the spirit: *His mind grasped the complex issue.* INTELLECT refers to reasoning power, as distinguished from the faculties of feeling: *a book that appeals to the intellect, rather than the emotions.* BRAIN is a physiological term for the organic structure that makes mental activity possible, but is often applied to mental ability or capacity: *a fertile brain.* These words may also refer to a person of great mental ability or capacity: *a great mind of our age; a fine scholar and intellect; the brain in the family.*

mindless, *adj.* **1.** inane, simple, unthinking, undemanding, silly, purposeless, unpurposeful, aimless, pointless, uninvolved, uninvolving, stupid, no-brain. **2.** heedless, careless, unmindful, thoughtless. —**Ant.** aware, dutiful.

mingle, *v.* **1.** mix, blend, unite, commingle, intermix, join, conjoin, combine, intermingle, concoct, compound. **2.** participate, associate. —**Syn. Study.** See MIX.

minor, *adj.* **1.** lesser, smaller, inferior, secondary, subordinate, petty, inconsiderable, unimportant, small. —*n.* **2.** child, adolescent. —**Ant.** major.

minute, *n.* **1.** moment,

instant; jiffy, second. **2.** *(plural)* note, memorandum, record, proceedings. —*adj.* **3.** small, tiny, little, infinitesimal, minuscule, diminutive. **4.** detailed, exact, precise, critical. —**Ant.** tremendous, huge, large; general, inexact, rough.

miraculous, *adj.* **1.** marvelous, wonderful, wondrous, extraordinary, incredible. **2.** supernatural, preternatural. —**Ant.** prosaic, commonplace; natural. —**Syn. Study.** MIRACULOUS, PRETERNATURAL, SUPERNATURAL refer to that which seems to transcend the laws of nature. MIRACULOUS refers to something that apparently contravenes known laws governing the universe: *a miraculous recovery.* PRETERNATURAL suggests the possession of supernormal qualities: *Dogs have a preternatural sense of smell.* It may also mean *supernatural: Elves are preternatural beings.* SUPERNATURAL suggests divine or superhuman properties: *supernatural aid in battle.*

mirth, *n.* rejoicing, joy, joyousness, gaiety, jollity, glee, merriment, joviality, laughter, hilarity. —**Ant.** sadness, misery.

misadventure, *n.* mischance, mishap, ill fortune, ill luck, misfortune; accident, disaster, calamity, catastrophe. —**Ant.** luck, fortune.

miscellaneous, *adj.* indiscriminate, promiscuous, mixed, heterogeneous, divers, diversified, varied, various, mingled, confused. —**Ant.** specific, special, discerning.

mischief, *n.* **1.** harm, trouble, injury, damage, hurt, detriment, disadvantage. **2.** evil, malice, malicious mischief, vandalism; misfortune, trouble. —**Ant.** good, advantage.

misconstrue, *v.* misinterpret, misread, misunderstand, misapprehend, misjudge, mistake. **—Ant.** construe, understand.

misdemeanor, *n.* misbehavior, misdeed, transgression, fault, misconduct; offense, trespass.

miser, *n.* niggard, skinflint, tightwad, pinchpenny. **—Ant.** Maecenas.

miserable, *adj.* **1.** wretched, unhappy, uneasy, uncomfortable, distressed, disconsolate, doleful, forlorn, broken-hearted, heartbroken. **2.** poverty-stricken, poor, needy, destitute, penniless. **3.** contemptible, bad, wretched, mean, despicable, low, abject, worthless. **4.** deplorable, pitiable, lamentable, unfortunate, unlucky, ill-starred, star-crossed, luckless; calamitous, catastrophic. **—Ant.** happy; wealthy; good; fortunate, lucky.

miserly, *adj.* penurious, niggardly, cheap, stingy, parsimonious, tightfisted, penny-pinching, close, mean. **—Ant.** generous, unselfish. **—Syn. Study.** See STINGY.

misery, *n.* **1.** wretchedness, distress, tribulation, woe, trial, suffering, agony, anguish, torture. **2.** grief, anguish, woe, unhappiness, sorrow, torment, desolation. **—Ant.** happiness, joy; delight.

misfortune, *n.* **1.** ill luck, bad luck, ill fortune. **2.** accident, disaster, calamity, catastrophe, reverse, affliction, mishap, mischance, adversity, distress, hardship, trouble, blow. **—Ant.** luck, fortune.

misgiving, *n.* apprehension, doubt, distrust, suspicion, mistrust, hesitation. **—Ant.** trust.

mislead, *v.* misguide, lead astray, misconduct, delude, deceive, misdirect. **—Ant.** lead, conduct.

misplace, *v.* **1.** displace, mislay, lose. **2.** misapply, misbestow. **—Ant.** find; apply, place.

misprint, *n.* typographical error, erratum, typo.

misshapen, *adj.* distorted,

deformed, malformed, contorted, warped, misproportioned, disproportionate, ill-formed, crooked, twisted, unshapely, irregular. —**Ant.** shapely, well-formed.

mist, *n.* **1.** cloud, fog, fogbank, haze, smog; soup. **2.** bewilderment, haze, perplexity, obscurity. —*v.* **3.** fog, cloud over, drizzle, foggle. —**Ant.** clarity.

mistake, *n.* **1.** error, blunder, slip, inaccuracy, erratum, typo, misprint, fault, oversight. **2.** misapprehension, misconception, misunderstanding. —*v.* **3.** misapprehend, misconceive, misunderstand, misjudge, err. —**Ant.** accuracy; understanding.

mistaken, *adj.* erroneous, wrong, incorrect, misconceived, inaccurate. —**Ant.** correct, accurate.

misunderstanding, *n.* **1.** mistake, misapprehension, error, misconception. **2.**

disagreement, dissension, discord, difference, difficulty, quarrel. —**Ant.** understanding; agreement, concord.

mix, *v.* **1.** blend, combine, mingle, commingle, confuse, jumble, unite, compound, amalgamate, homogenize. **2.** consort, mingle, associate, join. —*n.* **3.** mixture, concoction. —**Ant.** separate; dissociate. —**Syn. Study.** MIX, BLEND, COMBINE, MINGLE concern the bringing of two or more things into more or less intimate association. MIX means to join elements or ingredients into one mass, generally with a loss of distinction between them: *to mix fruit juices.* BLEND suggests a smooth and harmonious joining, often a joining of different varieties to obtain a product of a desired quality: *to blend whiskeys.* COMBINE means to bring similar or related things into close union, usu. for a particular purpose: *to combine forces.* MINGLE usu.

suggests a joining in which the identity of the separate elements is retained: *voices mingling at a party.*

mixed, *adj.* mingled, commingled, joined; coeducational, coed. —**Ant.** separated.

mixture, *n.* **1.** blend, combination, compound. **2.** hodgepodge, hotchpotch, gallimaufry, conglomeration, jumble, medley, melange, olio, potpourri, miscellany, farrago, salmagundi; variety, diversity. —**Ant.** element, constituent.

moan, *n.* **1.** groan, wail, lament, lamentation; dirge, elegy, threnody, monody. —*v.* **2.** bemoan, bewail, grieve, lament, mourn, deplore.

mock, *v.* **1.** ridicule, deride, taunt, flout, gibe, tantalize, tease, jeer, chaff, scoff, banter, make sport of; mimic, ape, satirize, imitate. **2.** defy. **3.** deceive, delude, disappoint, cheat, dupe, fool, defeat, mislead. —*n.* **4.** mockery, derision, ridicule, banter, sport, sneer. —*adj.* **5.** feigned, pretended, counterfeit, sham, false, spurious, fake. —**Ant.** praise, honor. —**Syn. Study.** See RIDICULE.

mockery, *n.* **1.** ridicule, derision, scorn, contumely. **2.** imitation, show, mimicry. **3.** travesty, pretense, pretext, sham, satire.

mode, *n.* **1.** method, way, manner, style, fashion. **2.** form, variety, degree, modification, graduation. —**Syn. Study.** See METHOD.

model, *n.* **1.** standard, paragon, prototype, ideal, pattern, example, archetype, mold, original. **2.** representation, facsimile, copy, image, imitation. —*v.* **3.** form, plan, pattern, mold, shape, fashion, design. —**Syn. Study.** See IDEAL.

moderate, *adj.* **1.** reasonable, temperate, judicious, just, fair, deliberate, mild, cool, steady, calm, peaceful. **2.** medium, average, usual. **3.** mediocre, fair. **4.**

middle-of-the-road, conservative, temperate. —*n.* **5.** mugwump, middle-of-the-roader, conservative. —*v.* **6.** allay, meliorate, pacify, calm, assuage, sober, mitigate, soften, mollify, temper, qualify, appease, abate, lessen, diminish, reduce. **7.** preside, chair, arbitrate, referee, regulate, umpire. —**Ant.** immoderate; unusual; radical; disturb, increase, intensify.

modern, *adj.* recent, up-to-date, late, present, new, novel, fresh, neoteric. —**Ant.** old, archaic, ancient, obsolete. —**Syn. Study.** MODERN, RECENT, LATE apply to that which is near to or characteristic of the present as contrasted with any other time. MODERN, which is applied to those things that exist in the present age, sometimes has the connotation of up-to-date and, thus, good: *modern ideas.* That which is RECENT is separated from the present or the time of action by only a short interval; it is new, fresh, and novel: *recent developments.* LATE may mean nearest to the present moment: *the late reports on the battle.*

modest, *adj.* **1.** moderate, humble, unpretentious, decent, becoming, proper. **2.** inextravagant, unostentatious, retiring, unassuming, unobtrusive. **3.** decent, demure, prudish, chaste, pure, virtuous. —**Ant.** immodest, immoderate, improper; extravagant.

modesty, *n.* **1.** unobtrusiveness. **2.** moderation, decency, propriety, simplicity, purity, chastity, prudery, prudishness. —**Ant.** indecency, licentiousness.

modify, *v.* **1.** change, alter, vary, qualify, temper, adjust, restrict, limit, shape, reform. **2.** reduce, qualify, moderate.

moil, *v.* **1.** work hard, toil, drudge, labor. —*n.* **2.** toil, drudgery, labor. **3.** confusion, turmoil, trouble. **—Ant.** indolence, laziness.

moist, *adj.* damp, humid, dank, wet. **—Ant.** dry, arid.

molest, *v.* attack, assail; harass, harry, disturb, trouble, annoy, vex, plague, tease, pester, torment, torture, irritate, fret, hector, inconvenience, discommode, worry, bother.

moment, *n.* **1.** minute, instant, second, jiffy, trice, flash, twinkling. **2.** importance, consequence, significance, weight, gravity, import, consideration. **3.** momentum, force, power, impetus, drive. **—Ant.** insignificance, inertia. **—Syn. Study.** See IMPORTANCE.

momentous, *adj.* important, consequent, vital, weighty, serious. **—Ant.** unimportant, trivial, trifling.

monarchy, *n.* kingdom, realm, empire.

monetary, *adj.* pecuniary, financial; nummary,

nummular. **—Syn. Study.** See FINANCIAL.

money, *n.* **1.** coin, cash, currency, specie, change; coin of the realm. **2.** funds, capital, assets, property, wealth, riches. **3.** (*slang*) mazuma, long green, lettuce, dough, (*small amt.*) chump change.

mongrel, *n.* **1.** cross, hybrid, mutt, half-breed. **—***adj.* **2.** hybrid. **—Ant.** purebred, thoroughbred.

monk, *n.* friar, brother; cenobite, eremite.

monopolize, *v.* consume, possess, corner, control, appropriate, co-opt, engross, usurp, arrogate, preempt, take over, gobble up, grab, hog. **—Ant.** share.

monotonous, *adj.* tedious, humdrum, tiresome, uniform, boring, dull, unvaried, unvarying. **—Ant.** interesting, amusing, diverting.

monster, *n.* **1.** brute, griffin, gargoyle, sphinx, centaur, hippogriff. **2.** mooncalf, monstrosity. **3.**

fiend, brute, miscreant, wretch, villain, demon, devil. —*adj.* **4.** huge, enormous, monstrous.

monstrous, *adj.* **1.** huge, great, large, tremendous, gigantic, monster, prodigious, enormous, immense, vast, stupendous, colossal. **2.** frightful, hideous, revolting, shocking, repulsive, horrible, atrocious, terrible, dreadful, horrendous. **—Ant.** small, tiny; delightful, attractive.

mooch, *v.* beg, scrounge, cadge, panhandle, hit up, bum.

mood, *n.* **1.** disposition, frame of mind, humor, temper, vein. **2.** mode.

moody, *adj.* gloomy, sullen, ill-humored, perverse, sulky, waspish, snappish, pettish, testy, short-tempered, irritable, irascible, captious, peevish, fretful, spleeny, spenetic, spiteful, morose, intractable, stubborn. **—Ant.** amiable, temperate, tractable.

moonstruck, *adj.* **1.**

romantic, starry-eyed, moony, sentimental, mushy. **2.** unbalanced, mental, touched, daft. **—Ant.** down-to-earth.

moot, *adj.* **1.** doubtful, debatable, disputable, disputed, unsettled. —*v.* **2.** argue, debate, dispute, discuss. **—Ant.** indubitable, indisputable; agree, concur.

moral, *adj.* **1.** ethical, upright, honest, straightforward, righteous, open, just, good, virtuous, honorable. —*n.* **2.** (*plural*) ethics, integrity, standards, morality. **—Ant.** immoral, amoral.

morality, See Syn. study at GOODNESS.

morbid, *adj.* **1.** gloomy, sensitive, extreme. **2.** unwholesome, diseased, unhealthy, sick, sickly, tainted, corrupted, vitiated. **—Ant.** cheerful; wholesome, salubrious.

moreover, *adv.* besides, further, furthermore, and, also, too, likewise.

morning, *n.* morn,

daybreak, sunrise, dawn.
—**Ant.** evening.

morose, *adj.* sullen, gloomy, moody, sour, sulky, churlish, splenetic, surly, ill-humored, ill-natured, perverse. —**Ant.** cheerful, happy, good-natured. —**Syn. Study.** See GLUM.

mortal, *adj.* **1.** human. **2.** fatal, final, lethal, deadly. —*n.* **3.** human being, man. —**Ant.** immortal. —**Syn. Study.** See FATAL.

mortify, *v.* **1.** shame, humiliate, humble, abash, abase, subdue, restrain. **2.** gangrene, necrose. —**Ant.** honor.

mostly, *adv.* in the main, generally, chiefly, especially, particularly, for the most part, customarily. —**Ant.** seldom.

motion, *n.* **1.** movement, move, action. **2.** gait, deportment, bearing, air. **3.** gesture, movement, move. —*v.* **4.** move, gesture. —**Ant.** stasis.

motionless, *adj.* stable, fixed, unmoving, still, transfixed, quiescent, stationary. —**Ant.** mobile.

motive, *n.* motivation, inducement, incentive, incitement, stimulus, spur, influence, occasion, reason, ground, cause, purpose. —**Syn. Study.** MOTIVE, INDUCEMENT, INCENTIVE apply to something that moves or prompts a person to action. MOTIVE is usu. applied to an inner urge that moves a person; it may also apply to a contemplated goal, the desire for which moves the person: *Her motive was a wish to be helpful. Money was the motive for the crime.* INDUCEMENT is used mainly of opportunities offered by another person or by situational factors: *The salary they offered me was a great inducement.* INCENTIVE is usu. applied to something offered as a reward or to stimulate competitive activity: *Profit sharing is a good incentive for employees.*

mount, *v.* **1.** go up, ascend, climb, scale, get up on. **2.** raise, put into position, fix on. **3.** prepare, produce, make ready, ready. —*n.* **4.** horse, steed, charger, palfrey. **5.** mountain, hill. —**Ant.** descend.

mountebank, *n.* quack, pitchman, charlatan, pretender, phony.

mourn, *v.* **1.** grieve, lament, bewail, bemoan, sorrow for. **2.** deplore. —**Ant.** laugh, rejoice.

move, *v.* **1.** stir, advance, budge, progress, make progress, proceed, move on, remove. **2.** turn, revolve, spin, gyrate, rotate, operate. **3.** act, bestir oneself, take action. **4.** stir, shake, agitate, excite, arouse, rouse; shift, transfer, propel. **5.** prompt, actuate, induce, influence, impel, activate, incite, rouse, instigate. **6.** affect, touch. **7.** propose, recommend, suggest, bring up *or* forward. —*n.* **8.** motion, movement, action.

movement, *n.* **1.** move, motion, change. **2.** motion, progress, activity, eventfulness. **3.** (*music*) part, section, division;

motion, rhythm, time, tempo. —**Ant.** inertia, stasis.

multifarious, *adj.* numerous, various, many, abundant, multitudinous, manifold, diverse, sundry, multifold, multivarious, legion, myriad, various and sundry. —**Ant.** singular, unique.

multitude, *n.* host, crowd, throng, mass, army, swarm, collection. —**Syn. Study.** See CROWD.

mumble, *v.* murmur, mutter, muffle. —**Ant.** articulate, enunciate, pronounce.

mundane, *adj.* worldly, earthly, terrestrial, terraqueous, secular, temporal. —**Ant.** unearthly, clerical. —**Syn. Study.** See EARTHLY.

munificent, *adj.* liberal, generous, bountiful, beneficent, bounteous. —**Ant.** stingy, penurious, mean, niggardly. —**Syn. Study.** See GENEROUS.

murder, *n.* **1.** killing, assassination, homicide, manslaughter. —*v.* **2.** kill, slay, assassinate, destroy, put an end to. **3.** spoil, mar, ruin, abuse.

murky, *adj.* dark, gloomy, cheerless, obscure, dim, cloudy, dusky, lowering, overcast, misty, hazy. —**Ant.** bright, light, clear.

murmur, *n.* **1.** grumble, susurration, susurrus, mumble, complaint, plaint, whimper, mutter. —*v.* **2.** mumble, mutter, whisper. **3.** complain, grumble, grouse.

muscular, *adj.* brawny, sinewy, well-muscled, well-built, well-knit, beefy, sturdy, burly, husky, strong, powerful, mighty, Bunyanesque, (*slang*) hunky, buff. —**Ant.** weak, feeble, underdeveloped.

muse, *v.* reflect, meditate, ponder, contemplate, think of *or* about, cogitate, deliberate, ruminate, think, brood; dream.

muster, *v.* **1.** assemble, gather, summon, convoke, collect, marshal, convene, congregate. —*n.* **2.** gathering, assembly, assemblage, collection, convention, congregation. —**Ant.** scatter, separate.

mutable, *adj.* **1.** changeable, alterable, variable. **2.** fickle, changing, inconstant, unstable, vacillating, unsettled, wavering, unsteady, flickering, varying, variable. —**Ant.** immutable, invariable; stable, settled, motionless.

mute, *adj.* silent, dumb, speechless, still. —**Ant.** loquacious, voluble, talkative.

mutilate, *v.* injure, disfigure, maim, damage, mar, cripple, mangle.

mutinous, *adj.* **1.** seditious, insurrectionary, revolutionary, insurgent. **2.** rebellious, refractory, insubordinate, unruly, contumacious, turbulent, riotous. —**Ant.** patriotic; obedient.

mutiny, *n.* **1.** revolt, rebellion, insurrection, revolution, uprising, sedition. —*v.* **2.** revolt, rebel, rise up. —**Ant.** obedience.

mutter, *v.* murmur.

mutual, *adj.* reciprocal, balanced, correlative, common, interchangeable. —**Ant.** single, singular.

mysterious, *adj.* secret, esoteric, occult, cryptic, inscrutable, mystical, obscure, puzzling, inexplicable, unexplainable, unintelligible, incomprehensible, enigmatic, impenetrable, recondite, hidden, concealed, dark, abstruse, cabalistic, unfathomable. —**Ant.** open. —**Syn. Study.** MYSTERIOUS, INSCRUTABLE, MYSTICAL, OBSCURE refer to that which is not easily comprehended or explained. That which is MYSTERIOUS, by being unknown or puzzling, excites curiosity, amazement, or awe: *a mysterious disease.* INSCRUTABLE applies to that which is impenetrable, so enigmatic that one cannot interpret its significance: *an inscrutable smile.* That which is MYSTICAL has a secret significance, such as that attaching to certain rites or signs: *mystical symbols.* That which is OBSCURE is discovered or comprehended dimly or with difficulty: *obscure motives.*

mystical, See Syn. study at MYSTERIOUS.

myth, *n.* legend, story, fiction, fable, tradition, epic. —**Syn. Study.** See LEGEND.

N

nag, *v.* **1.** torment, pester, harass, harry, hector, importune, irritate, annoy, vex. —*n.* **2.** shrew, virago, pest, termagant, maenad. **3.** horse, pony.

naive, *adj.* unsophisticated, ingenuous, simple, unaffected, natural, unsuspecting, artless, guileless, candid, open, plain. —**Ant.**

sophisticated, disingenuous, artful, sly.

naked, *adj.* **1.** nude, bare, uncovered, undressed, unclothed. **2.** bare, stripped, destitute, desert, denuded. **3.** unsheathed, exposed, bare. **4.** unfurnished, bare. **5.** defenseless, unprotected, unguarded, exposed, unarmed, open. **6.** simple, plain, manifest, evident, undisguised, unadorned, mere, bare, sheer. **7.** plainspoken, blunt, direct, outspoken, unvarnished, uncolored, unexaggerated, plain. **—Ant.** covered, dressed; protected; ornate; exaggerated, embellished.

namby-pamby, *adj.* **1.** insipid, bland, wishy-washy, insubstantial, overrefined, overnice, unnourishing, precious, jejune, goody-goody. **2.** weak, spineless, indecisive, wavering, wimpish, wimpy. **—Ant.** strong, forthright, decisive.

name, *n.* **1.** appellation, title, label, tag, designation, epithet. **2.** reputation, repute, character, credit. **3.** fame, repute, note, distinction, renown, eminence, honor, praise. **—v. 4.** call, title, entitle, dub, denominate. **5.** specify, mention, indicate, designate, identify, nominate.

nameless, *adj.* **1.** anonymous, unknown, obscure, undistinguished, unremarked, unnamed, untitled, unspecified, incognito. **2.** ineffable, unnamable, indescribable, inexpressible, unutterable, unspeakable.

narrate, *v.* recount, relate, tell, retail, describe, detail, recite.

narrative, *n.* story, account, recital, history, chronicle, tale, description.

narrow-minded, *adj.* prejudiced, biased, bigoted, intolerant, illiberal, partial. **—Ant.** liberal, broad-minded, tolerant, unprejudiced.

nasty, *adj.* **1.** filthy, dirty, disgusting, unclean, foul, impure, loathsome, polluted, defiled. **2.** nauseous, nauseating, disgusting, sickening, offensive, repulsive, repellent, objectionable. **3.** obscene, smutty, pornographic, lewd, licentious, lascivious, indecent, ribald, gross, indelicate. **4.** vicious, spiteful, ugly, bad-tempered, disagreeable. **5.** unpleasant, inclement, stormy. —**Ant.** clean, pure, unpolluted; delightful; decent, honorable; amiable, agreeable; pleasant, fair.

nation, *n.* **1.** race, stock, ethnic group, population, people, tribe. **2.** state, country, commonwealth, kingdom, realm.

native, *adj.* **1.** inborn, inherent, inherited, natural, innate, inbred, congenital. **2.** indigenous, autochthonous, aboriginal, natural. **3.** unadorned, natural, real, genuine, original. —*n.* **4.** inhabitant, aborigine. —**Ant.** acquired; imported; decorated; foreigner, alien.

nature, *n.* **1.** character, quality, attributes, qualification. **2.** kind, sort, character, type, species, quality. **3.** universe, world, earth. **4.** reality, matter.

naughty, *adj.* **1.** ill-behaved, misbehaved, bad, disobedient. **2.** risqué, improper, off-color, ribald, profane, dirty.

nauseate, *v.* **1.** sicken, revolt, disgust. **2.** loathe, abhor, abominate, detest, reject. —**Ant.** delight, enchant, attract; like, love, adore.

nauseous, *adj.* **1.** sickening, revolting, nasty, repellent, disgusting, loathsome, abhorrent, detestable, despicable, nauseating, offensive. **2.** ill, sick to one's stomach. —**Ant.** attractive, lovable; well.

near, *adj.* **1.** close, nigh, at, within, at hand, nearby, adjacent, contiguous, touching, adjoining, bordering, abutting. **2.** imminent, impending, approaching, forthcoming, at hand. **3.** related, connected, intimate, familiar, allied, attached. **4.** faithful, close, accurate, literal. **5.** narrow, close, niggardly, parsimonious, stingy, miserly, tight, tightfisted. **—Ant.** far; generous.

nearly, *adv.* **1.** almost, approximately, well-nigh. **2.** intimately, closely. **3.** parsimoniously, penuriously.

neat, *adj.* **1.** orderly, ordered, trim, tidy, spruce, smart, nice. **2.** clever, effective, adroit, finished, well-planned, dexterous, apt. **3.** unadulterated, undiluted, straight, unmixed, pure. **—Ant.** disorderly, sloppy; maladroit, ineffective; adulterated; impure.

nebulous, *adj.* **1.** hazy, vague, confused, indistinct. **2.** cloudy, cloudlike, nebular. **—Ant.** clear, fair, distinct.

necessary, *adj.* **1.** essential, indispensable, required, requisite, needed, needful, vital, unavoidable. **2.** involuntary. **—***n.* **3.** requisite, prerequisite, requirement, necessity, *sine qua non,* essential. **—Ant.**

unnecessary, dispensable; voluntary; nonessential.

—Syn. Study. NECESSARY, REQUISITE, INDISPENSABLE, ESSENTIAL indicate something that cannot be done without. NECESSARY refers to something needed for existence, for proper functioning, or for a particular purpose: *Food is necessary for life. Sugar is a necessary ingredient in this recipe.* REQUISITE refers to something required for a particular purpose or by particular circumstances: *She has the requisite qualifications for the job.* INDISPENSABLE means absolutely necessary to achieve a particular purpose or to complete or perfect a unit: *He made himself indispensable in the laboratory.* ESSENTIAL refers to something that is part of the basic nature or character of a thing and is vital to its existence or functioning: *Water is essential to life.*

necessity, *n.* **1.** needfulness, indispensability, need, indispensableness. **2.** requirement, requisite, demand, necessary, *sine qua non,* essential, prerequisite. **3.** compulsion, fate, destiny, kismet, karma, inevitability, inevitableness, unavoidability, unavoidableness, irresistibility. **4.** poverty, neediness, indigence, necessitousness, need, want. **—Ant.** dispensability; wealth.

necromancy, *n.* magic, enchantment, conjuration, sorcery, divination.

need, *n.* **1.** requirement, want, necessity, exigency, emergency, urgency. **2.** want, necessity, lack, demand. **3.** destitution, poverty, neediness, want, deprivation, necessity, indigence, penury, distress, privation. **—**v*.* **4.** require, want, lack. **—Ant.** wealth, opulence. **—Syn. Study.** See LACK.

nefarious, *adj.* wicked, depraved, iniquitous, evil, abominable, detestable, atrocious, execrable, flagitious, heinous, vile,

horrible, dreadful, horrendous, infamous, villainous, base. **—Ant.** good, honest, honorable, exalted.

neglect, *v.* **1.** disregard, ignore, slight, overlook, omit, be remiss. **—**n*.* **2.** disregard, dereliction, negligence, remissness, carelessness, failure, omission, default, inattention, heedlessness. **—Ant.** regard, attend; regard, attention, care.

neglectful, *adj.* disregardful, remiss, careless, negligent, inattentive, indifferent, heedless, thoughtless. **—Ant.** regardful, careful, thoughtful.

negligence, *n.* neglect. **—Ant.** regard.

negligent, *adj.* neglectful. **—Ant.** regardful.

negligible, *adj.* remote, insignificant, slight, marginal, small, slender, slim, minuscule, outside, off. **—Ant.** significant, important.

negotiate, *v.* **1.** arrange, arrange for, settle. **2.**

circulate; sell, transfer, deliver, assign.

neophyte, *n.* **1.** convert, proselyte. **2.** beginner, tyro, amateur, greenhorn, novice, novitiate, pupil, student. —**Ant.** old hand, expert.

nerve, *n.* **1.** strength, vigor, energy, power, force, might. **2.** courage, firmness, steadfastness, intrepidity, fortitude, resolution, resoluteness, endurance. —*v.* **3.** strengthen, fortify, innervate, invigorate, steel, brace. —**Ant.** weakness, frailty, cowardice; weaken, enervate.

nerveless, *adj.* feeble, weak, enervated, flaccid, spiritless, flabby, cowardly, pusillanimous. —**Ant.** strong, brave, bold, fearless.

nervous, *adj.* excitable, uneasy, apprehensive, fearful, timid, timorous. —**Ant.** confident, bold, intrepid.

new, *adj.* **1.** recent, modern, up to date, late, neoteric, novel, fresh. **2.**
further, additional, fresh. **3.** unaccustomed, unused, fresh. —*adv.* **4.** recently, lately; freshly, anew, newly, afresh. —**Ant.** old, stale. —**Syn.** NEW, FRESH, NOVEL describe things that have not existed or have not been known or seen before. NEW refers to something recently made, grown, or built, or recently found, invented, or discovered: *a new car; new techniques.* FRESH refers to something that has retained its original properties, or has not been affected by use or the passage of time: *fresh strawberries; fresh ideas.* NOVEL refers to something new that has an unexpected, strange, or striking quality, generally pleasing: *a novel experience.*

nice, *adj.* **1.** pleasing, pleasant, agreeable, delightful, good. **2.** kind, amiable, pleasant, friendly. **3.** accurate, precise, skilled, delicate, fastidious, exact, exacting, critical, rigorous, strict, demanding, scrupulous. **4.** tactful, careful, delicate, discriminating, discerning, particular. **5.** minute, fine, subtle, refined. **6.** refined, well-mannered, well-spoken. **7.** suitable, proper, polite. **8.** neat, trim, fastidious, finical, finicky, dainty, squeamish, fussy. **—Ant.** unpleasant; unkind; inaccurate; tactless, careless; unrefined; improper, impolite; sloppy.

nickname, *n.* sobriquet.

niggardly, *adj.* stingy, parsimonious, penurious, miserly, mean, tightfisted, close-fisted, small, avaricious, mercenary; illiberal, niggard, close, tight; scanty, poor, saving, chary, sparing. **—Ant.** generous, liberal.

nimble, *adj.* agile, quick, lively, active, brisk, spry, ready, alert, swift, light, awake, on the qui vive. **—Ant.** slow, clumsy, awkward.

noble, *adj.* **1.** high-born, aristocratic. **2.** high-minded, magnanimous, superior, elevated, exalted, worthy, lofty, honorable, great, large, generous. **3.** admirable, dignified, imposing, stately, magnificent, impressive, grand, lordly, splendid. —*n.* **4.** nobleman, peer, aristocrat, lord, lady. **—Ant.** lowborn; base; undignified; serf, slave. **—Syn. Study.** NOBLE, HIGH-MINDED, MAGNANIMOUS suggest moral excellence and high ideals. NOBLE implies superior moral qualities and an exalted mind, character, or spirit that scorns the petty, base, or dishonorable: *a noble sacrifice.* HIGH-MINDED suggests exalted moral principles, thoughts, or sentiments: *a high-minded speech on social reform.* MAGNANIMOUS adds the idea of generosity, shown by a willingness to forgive injuries or overlook insults: *The magnanimous ruler granted amnesty to the rebels.*

noise, *n.* **1.** clamor, din, hubbub, racket, clatter, rattle, blare, uproar, outcry, tumult, ado. —*v.* **2.** spread, rumor, bruit about. —**Ant.** quiet, peace. —**Syn. Study.** NOISE, CLAMOR, HUBBUB, DIN, RACKET refer to nonmusical or confused sounds. NOISE is a general word that usu. refers to loud, harsh, or discordant sounds: *noise from the street.* CLAMOR refers to loud noise, as from shouting or cries, that expresses feelings, desires, or complaints: *the clamor of an angry crowd.* HUBBUB refers to a confused mingling of sounds, usu. voices; it may also mean tumult or confused activity: *the hubbub on the floor of the stock exchange.* DIN is a very loud, continuous noise that greatly disturbs or distresses: *the din of a factory.* RACKET refers to a rattling sound or clatter: *to make a racket when doing the dishes.*

noiseless, *adj.* silent, quiet, still, inaudible, soundless. —**Ant.** noisy, clamorous, tumultuous.

noisome, *adj.* **1.** offensive, disgusting, fetid, putrid, foul, rotten. **2.** harmful, injurious, poisonous, noxious, nocuous, lethal, deadly, mephitic, miasmatic, miasmal, miasmic, pestilential, hurtful, pernicious, unhealthy, detrimental, deleterious, unwholesome, baneful, destructive. —**Ant.** delightful; pleasant, wholesome, healthful.

noisy, *adj.* loud, stentorian, clamorous, boisterous, tumultuous, riotous, vociferous, obstreperous, blustering, blatant, uproarious. —**Ant.** quiet, silent, peaceful.

nominal, *adj.* titular, so-called, formal.

nonchalant, *adj.* unconcerned, indifferent, cool, apathetic, unexcited, calm, casual. —**Ant.** concerned, excitable.

nondescript, *adj.* odd, peculiar, strange, unclassifiable, amorphous, indescribable. —**Ant.** regular, natural, ordinary.

nonesuch, *n.* paragon,

ideal, model, pattern, nonpareil.

nonpareil, *adj.* **1.** peerless, unequaled, unparalleled. —*n.* **2.** nonesuch. —**Ant.** average, common, ordinary.

nonplus, *v.* puzzle, confound, confuse, perplex, disconcert.

nonsense, *n.* twaddle, balderdash, senselessness, moonshine, absurdity, folly, trash.

notable, *adj.* **1.** noteworthy, noted, noticeable, remarkable, signal, distinguished, unusual, uncommon, extraordinary, great, conspicuous, memorable. **2.** prominent, important, eminent, distinguished, famed, famous, well-known, conspicuous, notorious. **3.** capable, thrifty, industrious, diligent, sedulous, assiduous, careful, clever, smart, alert, watchful. —*n.* **4.** celebrity. —**Ant.** common, ordinary; unimportant, undistinguished; careless.

note, *n.* **1.** memorandum, record, minute. **2.** comment, remark, commentary, criticism, critique, assessment, annotation, footnote. **3.** IOU. **4.** eminence, distinction, repute, celebrity, fame, renown, reputation, name. **5.** notice, heed, observation; consideration, regard. —*v.* **6.** mark down, jot down, record, make a note of, register. **7.** mention, designate, refer to, indicate, denote. **8.** notice, see, perceive, spot, remark, observe, regard, look at.

noted, *adj.* famous, celebrated, distinguished, famed, notable, renowned, eminent, illustrious, well-known. —**Ant.** unknown, undistinguished; notorious, infamous.

noteworthy, *adj.* notable, significant, remarkable, newsworthy, impressive, signal, outstanding, standout, extraordinary, exceptional, great, major. —**Ant.** insignificant.

notice, *n.* **1.** information, intelligence, advice, news, notification, mention, announcement. **2.** intimation, warning, premonition. **3.** sign, placard, poster, billboard, advertisement. **4.** observation, perception, attention, heed, note, cognizance. **5.** comment, mention, account, criticism, critique, review. —*v.* **6.** discern, perceive, see, become aware of, pay attention to, distinguish, discriminate, recognize, understand, regard, heed, note, observe, mark, remark. **—Syn. Study.** NOTICE, PERCEIVE, DISCERN imply becoming aware of something through the senses or the intellect. NOTICE means to pay attention to something one sees, hears, or senses: *to notice a newspaper ad; to notice someone's absence; to notice one's lack of enthusiasm.* PERCEIVE is a more formal word meaning to detect by means of the senses; with reference to the mind, it implies realization, understanding, and insight: *to perceive the sound of*

hoofbeats; to perceive the significance of an event. DISCERN means to detect something that is obscure or concealed; it implies keen senses or insight: *to discern the outlines of a distant ship; to discern the truth.*

notify, *v.* give notice to, inform, apprise, acquaint, make known to.

notion, *n.* **1.** conception, idea, concept. **2.** opinion, view, belief, sentiment, impression, judgment. **3.** whim, caprice, fancy, crotchet. **—Syn. Study.** See IDEA.

notorious, See Syn. study at FAMOUS.

notwithstanding, *prep.* **1.** despite, in spite of. —*adv.* **2.** nevertheless, yet, however. —*conj.* **3.** although, though, however, yet, nevertheless. **—Ant.** on account of, because of.

nourish, *v.* **1.** nurture, nurse, sustain, support, tend, attend. **2.** foster, promote, promulgate, foment, succor, aid, help, encourage. **—Ant.** discourage; neglect.

novel, *n.* **1.** romance, fiction, tale, story. *—adj.* **2.** new, different. **—Syn. Study.** See NEW.

novelty, *n.* **1.** originality, newness, innovation, uniqueness, freshness, inventiveness. **2.** fad, rage, wrinkle, craze. **3.** knickknack, curio, trinket, trifle, bibelot, whatnot, gewgaw, gimcrack, tchotchke.

noxious, *adj.* **1.** harmful, hurtful, unhealthy, unwholesome, injurious, mephitic, miasmatic, nocuous, noisome, detrimental, baneful, deleterious, pestilential, poisonous, destructive, deadly. **2.** corrupting, immoral, pernicious. **—Ant.** harmless, wholesome, beneficial; moral.

nucleus, *n.* center, kernel, core, heart.

nude, *adj.* uncovered, undressed, unclothed, undraped, naked, bare, exposed, denuded, stark

naked, *au naturel,* in the altogether. **—Ant.** covered, dressed.

nugatory, *adj.* **1.** trifling, worthless, futile, vain, trivial. **2.** useless, ineffectual, inoperative. **—Ant.** important, vital; useful, effectual.

nullify, *v.* invalidate, negate, annul, abrogate, quash, undo, cancel out, vitiate. **—Ant.** confirm, establish.

number, *n.* **1.** sum, total, count, aggregate, collection. **2.** numeral, digit, figure. **3.** issue, copy, edition. **4.** quantity, collection, company, multitude, horde, many. **5.** beat, rhythm. *—v.* **6.** count, enumerate, calculate, compute, reckon, numerate, tell; account; include, consist of.

numberless, *adj.* myriad, innumerable, numerous, countless, uncounted, untold, infinite. **—Ant.** finite.

numerous, *adj.* many, numberless. **—Ant.** few. **—Syn. Study.** See MANY.

nurse, *v.* **1.** tend, take care of, attend. **2.** foster, cherish, succor, promote, foment, encourage, aid, abet, help. **3.** nourish, nurture, feed, rear, raise. **4.** suckle, feed, give suck to. —**Ant.** neglect.

nurture, *v.* nurse.

nutrition, *n.* food, nutriment, aliment, nourishment, sustenance, subsistence.

nymph, *n.* sylph, naiad, nereid, oceanid, oread, dryad, hamadryad.

O

oaf, *n.* **1.** simpleton, blockhead, dunce, dolt, fool, nincompoop, ninny. **2.** idiot, imbecile, moron. **3.** changeling. —**Ant.** genius.

oath, *n.* **1.** promise, vow, pledge, affirmation. **2.** profanity, curse, blasphemy, malediction, imprecation.

obdurate, *adj.* **1.** hard-hearted, hardened, hard, firm, obstinate, callous, stubborn, pigheaded, unyielding, unbending, inflexible, inexorable. **2.** penitent, lost, unregenerate, reprobate, irreclaimable, shameless, graceless.

—**Ant.** soft-hearted, soft, malleable; abashed, humble.

obedient, *adj.* submissive, compliant, docile, tractable, yielding, deferential, respectful, dutiful, subservient. —**Ant.** disobedient, recalcitrant, refractory.

obeisance, *n.* **1.** deference, honor, homage, reverence, fealty, allegiance, respect, submission. **2.** bow, curtsy, salaam, genuflection, kowtow, bob, prostration. —**Ant.** disrespect, impertinence.

obese, *adj.* fat, stout, plump, pudgy, corpulent,

portly, gross. —**Ant.** thin, skinny, slender, slim.

obfuscate, *v.* **1.** confuse, stupefy, muddle, bewilder, perplex. **2.** darken, obscure, adumbrate, cloud. —**Ant.** clarify; brighten.

object, *n.* **1.** thing, reality, fact, manifestation, phenomenon. **2.** target, objective, goal, end, destination, aim. **3.** purpose, reason, basis, base, target, goal, end, motive, intent, intention. —*v.* **4.** protest, disapprove, be averse, refuse. —**Ant.** approve. —**Syn. Study.** See AIM.

objective, *n.* **1.** end, termination, object, destination, aim, target, butt. —*adj.* **2.** unprejudiced, unbiased, impartial, fair, impersonal. —**Ant.** subjective, biased, personal.

obligation, *n.* **1.** requirement, duty, responsibility, accountableness. **2.** agreement, contract, covenant, bond, stipulation. —**Syn. Study.** See DUTY.

oblige, *v.* **1.** require, constrain, compel, force, necessitate, bind, coerce. **2.** obligate, bind. **3.** favor, accommodate, serve, please, benefit. —**Ant.** disoblige, liberate, free; unfetter. —**Syn. Study.** OBLIGE, ACCOMMODATE imply making a gracious and welcome gesture of some kind. OBLIGE emphasizes the idea of doing a favor (and often of taking some trouble to do it): *to oblige someone with a loan.* ACCOMMODATE emphasizes providing a service or convenience: *to accommodate someone with lodgings and meals.*

obliging, *adj.* helpful, accommodating, amiable, friendly, outgoing, considerate, courteous, thoughtful, solicitous. —**Ant.** unhelpful, selfish.

obliterate, *v.* destroy, erase, efface, do away with, expunge, rub out, cancel, dele, delete, blot out. —**Ant.** construct, create, originate; restore.

oblivious, *adj.* heedless, disregardful, neglectful, careless, negligent. —**Ant.** heedful, regardful, careful.

obloquy, *n.* **1.** discredit, disgrace. **2.** censure, blame, reproach, odium, calumny, contumely, scorn, defamation, aspersion, revilement. —**Ant.** credit; exoneration, favor.

obnoxious, *adj.* **1.** objectionable, offensive, odious, hateful. **2.** exposed, liable, subject, answerable. —**Ant.** delightful, favorable; franchised, licensed, irresponsible. —**Syn. Study.** See HATEFUL.

obscene, *adj.* immodest, indecent, lewd, pornographic, coarse, ribald, smutty, offensive, filthy, immoral, indelicate, impure, unchaste, gross, disgusting, lubricious. —**Ant.** modest, decent, moral, pure, chaste.

obscure, *adj.* **1.** unclear, uncertain, doubtful, dubious, ambiguous, mysterious. **2.** inconspicuous, unnoticeable, unnoticed, unknown, undistinguished, undistinguishable, unnoted. **3.** remote, retired, secluded. **4.** indistinct, blurred, blurry, imperfect, dim, veiled. **5.** dark, murky, dim, clouded, cloudy, gloomy, dusky, somber, shadowy, lurid, unilluminated. —**Ant.** clear, certain, unambiguous, conspicuous, noted; distinct; bright. —**Syn. Study.** See MYSTERIOUS.

obsequious, *adj.* **1.** servile, compliant, deferential, cringing, slavish, mean, submissive. **2.** deferential, fawning, sycophantic, flattering. —**Ant.** haughty, overbearing, domineering. —**Syn. Study.** See SERVILE.

observant, *adj.* **1.** attentive, watchful, heedful, mindful, aware. **2.** perceptive, quick, alert. **3.** careful, obedient. —**Ant.** inattentive, careless; dull; disobedient.

observation, *n.* **1.** noticing, perceiving, watching, regarding, attending. **2.**

notice, observance, attention. **3.** information, record, memorandum. **4.** remark, comment, aside, utterance.

observe, *v.* **1.** perceive, notice, see, discover, detect. **2.** regard, witness, mark, watch, note, view. **3.** remark, comment, mention; utter, say. **4.** obey, comply, conform, follow, fulfill. **5.** solemnize, celebrate, keep. —**Ant.** ignore.

obsession, *n.* preoccupation, domination.

obsolete, *adj.* antiquated, old-fashioned, ancient, old, archaic. —**Ant.** modern, new, up-to-date.

obstacle, *n.* obstruction, hindrance, impediment, interference, check, block, barrier. —**Ant.** aid, support; license, franchise, permission. —**Syn. Study.** OBSTACLE, OBSTRUCTION, HINDRANCE, IMPEDIMENT refer to something that interferes with or prevents action or progress and must be removed, overcome, or bypassed. An OBSTACLE is something, material or nonmaterial, that stands in the way of progress: *an obstacle in a steeplechase; an obstacle to success.* An OBSTRUCTION is something that more or less completely blocks passage: *an obstruction in a drainpipe.* A HINDRANCE interferes and causes delay or difficulty: *Interruptions are a hindrance to my work.* An IMPEDIMENT slows down proper functioning or interferes with free movement: *Heavy rain was an impediment to our departure.*

obstinate, *adj.* **1.** mulish, obdurate, unyielding, recusant, stubborn, perverse, unbending, contumacious, inflexible, willful, headstrong, refractory, firm, intractable, resolute, pertinacious, persistent, dogged. **2.** uncontrollable, wild. —**Ant.** submissive, flexible, tractable, irresolute; controlled, tame. —**Syn. Study.** See STUBBORN.

obstreperous, *adj.* unruly, uncontrolled, boisterous, noisy, clamorous, tumultuous, riotous, uproarious. —**Ant.** obedient, calm.

obstruct, *v.* block, stop, close, occlude, oppilate, choke, clog, bar, hinder, barricade, dam up, impede, prevent; retard, slow, check, arrest, interrupt. —**Ant.** encourage, help, support, further.

obstruction, *n.* **1.** obstacle, hindrance, barrier, occlusion, impediment, bar. **2.** stopping, estoppage. —**Ant.** encouragement, furtherance; continuation. —**Syn. Study.** See OBSTACLE.

obtain, *v.* get, acquire, procure, secure, gain, achieve, earn, win, attain. —**Ant.** lose, forgo. —**Syn. Study.** See GET.

obtrusive, *adj.* **1.** meddlesome, intrusive, interfering, impertinent, invasive, interruptive, disruptive, presumptuous, officious, busybody, forward, prying, pushy, nosy. **2.** protruding, prominent, pronounced, noticeable, conspicuous. —**Ant.** reticent, circumspect.

obviate, *v.* preclude, prevent, avert, anticipate. —**Ant.** include, foster.

obvious, *adj.* plain, manifest, evident, clear, open, apparent, patent, palpable, perceptible, distinct, unmistakable. —**Ant.** concealed, hidden, indistinct, imperceptible. —**Syn. Study.** See APPARENT.

occasion, *n.* **1.** occurrence, event, time, incident. **2.** opportunity, chance, convenience, opening. **3.** ground, reason, cause, motive, inducement, influence. —*v.* **4.** bring about, cause, motivate, originate, create, move, give rise to, produce. —**Ant.** cease, stop.

occult, *adj.* **1.** mysterious, hidden, concealed, secret, undisclosed, unrevealed, unknown, mystical recondite, cabalistic, veiled, shrouded. **2.** supernatural, metaphysical. **—Ant.** open, manifest, obvious; natural.

occupation, *n.* **1.** calling, trade, business, profession, metier, vocation, employment, pursuit, craft. **2.** possession, tenure, use, occupancy. **3.** seizure, invasion, capture.

occupy, *v.* **1.** take up, use, engage, employ, busy. **2.** possess, capture, seize, keep, take hold of.

occur, *v.* **1.** come to pass, take place, happen, befall. **2.** appear, be met with, be found, arise, offer, meet the eye.

occurrence, *n.* event, incident, circumstance, affair, proceeding, transaction.

odd, *adj.* **1.** different, extraordinary, unusual, strange, weird, peculiar, singular, unique, queer, quaint, eccentric, uncommon, rare, fantastic, bizarre, whimsical. **2.** out-of-the-way, secluded, retired. **3.** occasional,

casual. **—n. 4.** (*plural*) bits, scraps, remnants, oddments. **—Ant.** ordinary, common, unexceptional, usual.

odious, *adj.* **1.** hateful, despicable, detestable, execrable, abominable, invidious. **2.** obnoxious, offensive, disgusting, loathsome, repellent, repulsive, forbidding. **—Ant.** attractive, lovable; inviting. **—Syn. Study.** See HATEFUL.

odium, *n.* **1.** hatred, detestation, abhorrence, dislike, antipathy. **2.** reproach, discredit, opprobrium, obloquy. **—Ant.** love.

odor, *n.* smell, aroma, fragrance, redolence, scent, perfume. **—Syn. Study.** ODOR, SMELL, SCENT, STENCH all refer to a sensation perceived by means of the olfactory nerves. ODOR refers to a relatively strong sensation that may be agreeable or disagreeable, actually or figuratively: *the odor of freshly roasted coffee; the odor of duplicity.* SMELL is used in similar contexts, although it is a more general word: *cooking smells; the sweet smell of success.* SCENT may refer to a distinctive smell, usu. delicate and pleasing, or to a smell left in passing: *the scent of lilacs; the scent of an antelope.* STENCH refers to a foul, sickening, or repulsive smell: *the stench of rotting flesh.*

odoriferous, *adj.* odorous, fragrant, aromatic, perfumed, redolent. —**Ant.** noisome, noxious.

offbeat, *adj.* unusual, unconventional, uncommon, unexpected, out-of-the-ordinary, out-of-the-way, rare, special, eccentric, unique, way-out, far-out. —**Ant.** commonplace, conventional.

offend, *v.* **1.** irritate, annoy, vex, chafe, provoke, nettle, mortify, gall, fret, displease, affront, insult. **2.** sin, transgress, err, stumble. —**Ant.** please, delight, compliment.

offense, *n.* **1.** transgression, wrong, sin, trespass, misdemeanor, crime, fault, felony. **2.** displeasure, unpleasantness, umbrage, resentment, wrath, indignation, anger, ire. **3.** attack, assault, onset, aggression. **4.** besiegers, enemy, foe, attackers. —**Ant.** delight, pleasure; defense; allies, friends. —**Syn. Study.** See CRIME.

offensive, *adj.* **1.** displeasing, irritating, annoying, vexing, vexatious, unpleasant, impertinent, rude, insolent, hateful, detestable, opprobrious, insulting, abusive. **2.** disagreeable, distasteful, disgusting, repulsive, obnoxious, unpalatable, unpleasant, revolting, repellent, nauseating, nauseous, sickening, loathsome. **3.** repugnant, insulting, execrable, abominable, shocking, revolting. **4.** aggressive, assailant, invading, attacking. —**Ant.** pleasing, pleasant, polite, courteous; agreeable, tasteful, attractive; delightful;

defensive. —**Syn. Study.** See HATEFUL.

offer, *v.* **1.** present, proffer, tender. **2.** propose, give, move, put forward, tender. **3.** volunteer, sacrifice, immolate, present. —*n.* **4.** proposal, proposition, overture; bid. —**Ant.** refuse; refusal, denial. —**Syn. Study.** OFFER, PROFFER, TENDER mean to put something forward for acceptance or rejection. OFFER is the general word for presenting anything for acceptance, sale, consideration, or the like: *to offer help; to offer a cold drink.* PROFFER, chiefly a literary word, implies presenting something freely and unselfishly: *to proffer one's services.* TENDER is used in formal, legal, business, and polite social contexts: *to tender one's resignation; to tender payment.*

offhand, *adj.* **1.** casual, nonchalant, informal, unceremonious, relaxed, easygoing, unstudied, laid-back. **2.** unpremeditated,

spontaneous, impromptu, improvisatory, extemporaneous, impulsive, ad-lib, spur-of-the-moment, off-the-cuff. —**Ant.** studied, formal.

office, *n.* **1.** staff, organization. **2.** position, post, station, berth, situation. **3.** duty, function, responsibility, charge, appointment, trust. **4.** service, task, work, duty.

officious, *adj.* forward, obtrusive, forceful, direct, interfering, meddlesome. —**Ant.** retiring, shy, backward.

often, *adv.* frequently, generally, usually, repeatedly, customarily. —**Ant.** seldom. —**Syn. Study.** OFTEN, FREQUENTLY, GENERALLY, USUALLY refer to experiences that are habitual or customary. OFTEN and FREQUENTLY are used interchangeably in most cases, but OFTEN implies numerous repetitions: *We often go there;* whereas FREQUENTLY suggests repetition at comparatively short intervals: *It happens frequently.* GENERALLY emphasizes a broad or nearly universal quality: *It is generally understood. He is generally liked.* USUALLY emphasizes time, and means in numerous instances: *We usually have hot summers.*

ointment, *n.* unguent, nard, salve, balm.

old, *adj.* **1.** aged, elderly. **2.** familiar, known. **3.** former, past, ancient, primeval, olden, primitive, antediluvian, antiquated, passé, antique, old-fashioned. **4.** deteriorated, dilapidated, worn, decayed. **5.** experienced, practiced, skilled, adroit. **6.** sedate, sensible, wise, intelligent, thoughtful. **—Ant.** new, modern; inexperienced, green; wild, senseless.

old-fashioned, *adj.* outmoded, obsolete, antique, passé, antiquated, old, ancient, archaic. **—Ant.** modern.

omen, *n.* sign, augury, foreboding, portent. **—Syn. Study.** See SIGN.

ominous, *adj.* **1.** portentous, inauspicious, threatening, unpropitious. **2.** significant, foreboding. **—Ant.** favorable, propitious; insignificant, meaningless. **—Syn. Study.** OMINOUS, PORTENTOUS, FATEFUL, THREATENING describe something that foretells a serious and significant outcome or consequence. OMINOUS suggests an evil or harmful consequence: *ominous storm clouds.* PORTENTOUS, although it may point to evil or disaster, more often describes something momentous or important: *a portentous change in foreign policy.* FATEFUL also stresses the great or decisive importance of what it describes: *a fateful encounter between two influential leaders.* THREATENING may point to calamity or mere unpleasantness, but usu. suggests that the outcome is imminent: *a threatening rumble from a volcano.*

omnipresent, *adj.* ubiquitous, present. **—Ant.** nowhere.

only, *adv.* **1.** alone, solely, exclusively. **2.** merely, but, just, no more than. **3.** singly, uniquely. *—adj.* **4.** sole, single, unique, solitary, lone. **5.** distinct, exclusive, alone. *—conj.* **6.** but, excepting *or* except that, however.

onus, *n.* burden, responsibility, load. **—Ant.** relief.

onward, *adv.* **1.** forward, ahead. *—adj.* **2.** forward, advanced, improved; advancing. **—Ant.** backward; retreating, retrograde.

ooze, *v.* **1.** percolate, exude, seep, drip, drop. *—n.* **2.** mire, slime, mud. **—Ant.** pour, flood.

opalescent, *adj.* iridescent, nacreous, polychromatic.

open, *adj.* **1.** unclosed, uncovered, unenclosed. **2.** accessible, available, public, unrestricted, free. **3.** unfilled, unoccupied. **4.** undecided, unsettled, undetermined, debatable, disputable. **5.** liable, subject to, unprotected, bare, undefended, exposed. **6.** mild, moderate. **7.** unreserved, candid, frank, ingenuous, artless, guileless, unconcealed, undisguised; sincere, honest, fair, aboveboard. **8.** perforated, porous, reticulated. **9.** expanded, patulous, extended, spread out, unclosed. **10.** generous, liberal, free, bounteous, bountiful, munificent, magnanimous, open-handed. **11.** obvious, evident, clear, apparent, plain. *—v.* **12.** unclose. **13.** recall, revoke. **14.** uncover, lay bare, bare, expose, reveal, divulge, disclose. **15.** expand, extend, spread out. **16.** begin, start, commence, initiate. **—Ant.** closed; close. **—Syn. Study.** See FRANK.

opening, *n.* **1.** gap, hole, aperture, orifice, perforation; slit, slot, breach, rift, chasm, cleft, fissure, rent. **2.** beginning, start, commencement, initiation, dawn. **3.** vacancy, chance, opportunity. **—Ant.** closing.

operate, *v.* **1.** work, run, use, act. **2.** manage, carry on, perform. **3.** bring about, effect, produce, occasion, cause. **—Ant.** fail.

operation, *n.* **1.** action, process, procedure, manipulation, performance, proceeding. **2.** efficacy, influence, virtue, effect, force, action. **3.** course, transaction, business, affair, maneuver. **—Ant.** failure.

operative, *n.* **1.** worker, workman, artisan, hand, laborer. **2.** detective, investigator, private eye, agent. **—***adj.* **3.** operating, exerting, influencing, influential. **4.** effective, efficacious, efficient, effectual, serviceable. **—Ant.** inoperative; ineffectual, inefficient.

opiate, *n.* narcotic, drug, anodyne, sedative,

sedation, soporific. **—Ant.** stimulant.

opinion, *n.* sentiment, view, conclusion, persuasion, belief, judgment, notion, conception, idea, impression, estimation. **—Syn. Study.** OPINION, SENTIMENT, VIEW are terms for one's conclusion about something. An OPINION is a belief or judgment that falls short of absolute conviction, certainty, or positive knowledge: *an opinion about modern art.* SENTIMENT refers to a rather fixed opinion, usu. based on feeling or emotion rather than reasoning: *sentiments on the subject of divorce.* A VIEW is an intellectual or critical judgment based on one's particular circumstances or standpoint; it often concerns a public issue: *views on government spending.*

opinionated, *adj.* obstinate, stubborn, conceited, dogmatic, prejudiced, biased, bigoted. **—Ant.**

liberal, open-minded, unprejudiced.

opponent, *n.* adversary, antagonist, competitor, rival, contestant; enemy, foe. **—Ant.** ally, friend, associate.

opportune, *adj.* **1.** appropriate, favorable, suitable, apt, suited, fit, fitting, fitted, fortunate, propitious. **2.** convenient, timely, well-timed, lucky, felicitous, seasonable, timely. **—Ant.** inopportune, inappropriate; inconvenient.

opportunity, *n.* chance, occasion, time, opportune moment.

oppose, *v.* **1.** resist, combat, withstand, thwart, confront, contravene, interfere, oppugn. **2.** hinder, obstruct, prevent, check. **3.** offset, contrast. **4.** contradict, gainsay, deny, refuse. **—Ant.** support, aid, help. **—Syn. Study.** OPPOSE, RESIST, WITHSTAND imply holding out or acting against something. OPPOSE implies offensive action against the opposite side in a conflict or contest; it may also refer to attempts to thwart displeasing ideas, methods, or the like: *to oppose an enemy; to oppose the passage of a bill.* RESIST suggests defensive action against a threatening force or possibility; it may also refer to an inner struggle in which the will is divided: *to resist an enemy onslaught; hard to resist chocolate.* WITHSTAND generally implies successful resistance; it stresses the determination and endurance necessary to emerge unharmed: *to withstand public criticism; to withstand a siege.*

opposite, *adj.* **1.** facing, fronting. **2.** contrary, reverse, incompatible, irreconcilable, inconsistent, unlike, differing, different. **3.** opposed, adverse, refractory, hostile, antagonistic, inimical. **—Ant.** compatible, consistent, like, same; friendly, amiable.

opposition, *n.* **1.** opposing, resisting, combating. **2.** antagonism, hostility, resistance, counteraction. **3.** competition, enemy, foe, adversary, antagonist. **4.** offset, antithesis, contrast. **5.** contrariety, inconsistency, incompatibility, difference. —**Ant.** help, support, furtherance; consistency, compatibility.

oppress, *v.* **1.** depress, weigh down, burden, load. **2.** maltreat, persecute, wrong. **3.** overwhelm, crush, overpower, subdue, suppress. —**Ant.** unburden, liberate, disencumber.

oppression, *n.* **1.** cruelty, injustice, tyranny, despotism, persecution, severity. **2.** hardship, misery, suffering, calamity. **3.** depression, sadness, misery. —**Ant.** kindness, justice; happiness, joy.

opprobrious, *adj.* **1.** reproachful, infamous, abusive, scurrilous, vituperative, contemptuous, insolent, offensive, insulting, scandalous. **2.** disgraceful, shameful, infamous, dishonorable, disreputable, ignominious, hateful. —**Ant.** complimentary, praising, laudatory; honorable, reputable.

oppugn, *v.* criticize, argue *or* act against, dispute, doubt, question, oppose. —**Ant.** favor.

optimistic, *adj.* hopeful, upbeat, sanguine, full of hope, expectant, confident, sunny, rosy, cheerful, Pollyanna, Pollyannaish, Panglossian. —**Ant.** pessimistic, discouraged, doubtful.

option, *n.* choice, election, selection, preference. —**Syn. Study.** See CHOICE.

opulent, *adj.* **1.** wealthy, rich, affluent, moneyed, sumptuous, luxurious. **2.** abundant, copious, plentiful. —**Ant.** poor, squalid; scarce.

oracular, *adj.* **1.** prophetic, portentous, auspicious. **2.** authoritative, inspired, inspirational, dogmatic, sententious. **3.** ambiguous, obscure, equivocal, two-faced.

oral, *adj.* verbal, spoken, mouthed, uttered, said, vocal. **—Ant.** tacit, silent, taciturn.

oration, *n.* speech, address, lecture, discourse, declamation, harangue. **—Syn. Study.** See SPEECH.

orb, *n.* sphere, globe, ball.

orbit, *n.* **1.** path, course. **—v. 2.** circle, circumvent.

ordain, *v.* **1.** appoint, call, nominate, elect, select, destine. **2.** decree, order, enact, prescribe, determine. **3.** predetermine, predestine, destine, fate.

ordeal, *n.* trial, test, proof, assay.

order, *n.* **1.** direction, injunction, mandate, law, ukase, command, instruction, rule, canon, prescription. **2.** succession, sequence. **3.** method, arrangement, harmony, regularity, symmetry. **4.** disposition, array, arrangement. **5.** class, kind, sort, genus, subclass; tribe, family. **6.** rank, status, grade, class, degree.

7. fraternity, society, brotherhood, community. **8.** peace, calm, serenity. **9.** custom, usage. **10.** direction, commission. **—v. 11.** direct, command, instruct, bid, require; ordain. **12.** regulate, conduct, manage, run, operate, adjust, arrange, systematize. **—Syn. Study.** See DIRECT.

orderly, *adj.* **1.** regular, systematic, methodical. **2.** well-regulated, neat, trim, organized, well-organized. **3.** well-disciplined, well-trained, well-behaved. **—Ant.** irregular, unsystematic; sloppy, unregulated; undisciplined. **—Syn. Study.** ORDERLY, SYSTEMATIC, METHODICAL characterize that which is efficient, thorough, and carefully planned. ORDERLY emphasizes neatness, harmony, and logical sequence or arrangement: *an orderly library.* SYSTEMATIC emphasizes an extensive, detailed plan and a relatively complex procedure designed to achieve some purpose: *a*

systematic search.
METHODICAL is similar in meaning, but stresses a carefully developed plan and rigid adherence to a fixed procedure: *methodical examination of the evidence.*

ordinary, *adj.* **1.** common, usual, customary, regular, normal, accustomed, habitual, frequent. **2.** inferior, second-rate, mean, mediocre, indifferent. **3.** plain, homely, common-looking, commonplace. —**Ant.** uncommon, extraordinary, unusual; superior; beautiful. —**Syn. Study.** See COMMON.

organic, *adj.* **1.** systematic, systematized, organized. **2.** constitutional, structural, inherent, fundamental, essential, vital, radical. —**Ant.** inorganic.

organize, *v.* **1.** coordinate, harmonize, unite, construct, form, dispose, constitute, make, shape, frame. **2.** systematize, order. **3.** combine, unionize. —**Ant.** destroy, ruin; disorder.

origin, *n.* **1.** source, rise, fountainhead, derivation, beginning, root, cradle, foundation, birthplace. **2.** parentage, birth, extraction, lineage, heritage, descent. —**Ant.** end; posterity.

original, *adj.* **1.** primary, primordial, primeval, primitive, aboriginal. **2.** new, fresh, novel, inventive, creative. —*n.* **3.** archetype, pattern, prototype, model. —**Ant.** secondary; old, old-fashioned.

originate, *v.* **1.** arise, spring, rise, begin, emanate, flow, proceed. **2.** initiate, invent, discover, create, author. —**Ant.** terminate; follow.

ornament, *n.* **1.** accessory, detail, embellishment, adornment, decoration, ornamentation, design. —*v.* **2.** decorate, adorn, embellish, beautify, trim, garnish, grace, bedeck. —**Ant.** essential, necessity.

ornate, *adj.* elaborate, adorned, embellished, showy, splendid, sumptuous, elegant, decorated, florid; flowery. —**Ant.** simple, plain.

orthodox, *adj.* conventional, regular, customary, expected, accepted, recognized, approved, sanctioned, canonical, received, traditional, standard, conformable, conformist, conforming, correct, regular, kosher, conservative, reactionary, die-hard, hidebound, pedantic. —**Ant.** free-thinking, unconventional, rebellious.

oscillate, *v.* vibrate, vacillate, swing, fluctuate, vary.

ostensible, *adj.* apparent, professed, pretended, ostensive, specious, plausible. —**Ant.** concealed, hidden, implausible.

ostentation, *n.* pretension, pretentiousness, semblance, show, showiness, pretense, pretext, display, pageantry, pomp, pompousness, flourish.

ostentatious, See Syn. study at GRANDIOSE.

ostracize, *v.* banish, exile, expatriate, disenfranchise, excommunicate. —**Ant.** accept.

outcome, *n.* end, result, consequence, issue.

outdo, *v.* surpass, excel, exceed, beat, outstrip, outdistance.

outgoing, *adj.* friendly, sociable, approachable, open, gregarious, communicative, talkative, extroverted, demonstrative, expansive, effusive. —**Ant.** restrained, shy.

outgrowth, *n.* **1.** development, product, result. **2.** offshoot, excrescence.

outlaw, *n.* **1.** criminal, highwayman, holdup man, robber, thief, bandit, brigand. —*v.* **2.** proscribe, prohibit.

outline, *n.* **1.** contour, silhouette. **2.** plan, draft, drawing, rough, sketch, cartoon. —*v.* **3.** delineate, draft, draw.

outlive, *v.* survive, outlast. —**Syn. Study.** See SURVIVE.

outrage, *n.* **1.** violence,

violation. **2.** affront, insult, offense, abuse, indignity. —*v.* **3.** shock, abuse, maltreat, injure, offend. **4.** ravish, rape.

outspoken, *adj.* frank, open, unreserved, candid, free. —**Ant.** reserved, taciturn. —**Syn. Study.** See FRANK.

outstanding, *adj.* **1.** prominent, eminent, conspicuous, striking. **2.** unsettled, unpaid, owing, due. —**Ant.** inconspicuous; paid, settled.

overbearing, *adj.* domineering, dictatorial, haughty, arrogant, imperious, supercilious. —**Ant.** humble, servile.

overcome, *v.* **1.** conquer, defeat, subdue, vanquish, rout, crush. **2.** surmount. **3.** overpower, overwhelm, discomfit. —**Syn. Study.** See DEFEAT.

overlook, *v.* **1.** slight, disregard, miss, neglect, ignore. **2.** excuse, forgive, pardon. **3.** oversee, superintend, supervise. **4.** bewitch. —**Ant.** regard,

attend. —**Syn. Study.** See SLIGHT.

overpower, *v.* overcome, overwhelm, vanquish, subjugate, subdue, conquer, overmaster, rout, crush, defeat, beat.

overrule, *v.* disallow, rescind, revoke, repeal, recall, repudiate, set aside, nullify, cancel, annul; prevail over, influence. —**Ant.** allow, permit, approve.

oversee, *v.* supervise, direct, manage, superintend, survey, watch, overlook.

oversight, *n.* **1.** mistake, blunder, slip, error, erratum, omission, lapse, neglect, fault, inattention. **2.** management, direction, control, superintendence, supervision, charge, surveillance, care. —**Ant.** attention.

overt, *adj.* open, plain, manifest, showing, apparent, public. —**Ant.** private, concealed, clandestine, secret.

overthrow, *v.* **1.** cast down, overcome, defeat,

vanquish, overwhelm, conquer, master, overpower, subjugate, crush. **2.** upset, overturn. **3.** knock down, demolish, destroy, raze, level. **4.** subvert, ruin, destroy. —*n.* **5.** deposition, fall, displacement. **6.** defeat, destruction, ruin, rout, dispersion, demolition. **—Ant.** support.

overture, *n.* **1.** opening, proposal, proposition, offer. **2.** prelude, introduction; prologue.

—Ant. finale, termination, close, end, epilogue.

overturn, *v.* **1.** overthrow, destroy, vanquish, conquer, upset. **2.** upset, capsize, founder.

overwhelm, *v.* **1.** overpower, crush, overcome, subdue, defeat, vanquish. **2.** overload, overburden, cover, bury, sink, drown, inundate.

own, *v.* **1.** have, hold, possess. **2.** acknowledge, admit, allow, confess, concede, avow; recognize.

P

pace, *n.* **1.** step, rate; gait. **2.** step, walk, trot, jog, singlefoot, amble, rack, canter, gallop, run. **3.** dais, platform. —*v.* **4.** step, plod, trudge, walk, move, go. **—Syn. Study.** PACE, PLOD, TRUDGE refer to a steady and monotonous kind of walking. PACE suggests steady, measured steps, as of someone lost in thought or impelled by

some distraction: *to pace up and down the hall.* PLOD implies a slow, heavy, laborious walk: *The mail carriers plod their weary way.* TRUDGE implies a spiritless but usu. steady and doggedly persistent walk: *The farmer trudged to the village to buy supplies.*

pacific, *adj.* **1.** conciliatory, appeasing. **2.** peaceable, peaceful, calm, tranquil, at peace, quiet, unruffled, gentle. —**Ant.** hostile; agitated, perturbed.

pacify, *v.* **1.** quiet, calm, tranquilize, assuage, still, smooth, moderate, soften, ameliorate, mollify, meliorate, better, soothe. **2.** appease, conciliate. —**Ant.** agitate, perturb, aggravate, worsen; estrange.

pack, *n.* **1.** package, bundle, parcel, packet; knapsack. **2.** set, gang, group, band, company, crew, squad. —*v.* **3.** stow, compress, cram. **4.** load, burden, lade.

package, *n.* **1.** bundle, parcel, packet, pack, bale. **2.** case, crate, carton, box.

pact, *n.* agreement, compact, contract, deal, arrangement, treaty, bond, covenant, league, union, concordat, alliance, bargain.

paean, *n.* hymn, anthem, hosanna, hallelujah, laudation, laud, praise, encomium, tribute, homage, accolade.

pagan, *n.* **1.** heathen, idolater, gentile. —*adj.* **2.** heathen, heathenish, gentile, irreligious, idolatrous. —**Ant.** Christian, believer; pious, religious. —**Syn. Study.** See HEATHEN.

pageant, *n.* **1.** spectacle, extravaganza, show, masque. **2.** display, show, procession, parade.

pain, *n.* **1.** suffering, distress, torture, misery, anguish, agony, torment, throe, pang, ache, twinge, stitch. **2.** (*plural*) care, efforts, labor. —*v.* **3.** afflict, torture, torment, distress, hurt, harm, injure, trouble, grieve, aggrieve, disquiet, discommode, incommode, inconvenience, displease, worry, tease, irritate, vex, annoy. —**Ant.** joy, delight, pleasure; ease; please.

painful, *adj.* **1.** distressing, torturous, agonizing, tormenting, excruciating. **2.** laborious, difficult, arduous, severe. —**Ant.** pleasant, soothing; easy, simple.

painstaking, *adj.* careful, assiduous, diligent, sedulous, strenuous.
—**Ant.** careless, frivolous.
—**Syn. Study.** PAINSTAKING, METICULOUS, CONSCIENTIOUS mean extremely careful or precise about details. PAINSTAKING stresses laborious effort and diligent attention to detail in achieving a desired objective: *the painstaking editing of a manuscript.* METICULOUS suggests a more extreme attention to minute details: *to be meticulous about matching shoes and clothing.* CONSCIENTIOUS stresses scrupulous effort to obey one's sense of moral obligation to perform tasks well: *a conscientious description of the facts.*

pair, *n.* **1.** brace, couple, span, yoke, two, team.
—*v.* **2.** match, mate, couple, marry, join.

palatable, *adj.* agreeable, savory, sapid, tasty, gustatory, luscious, delicious, delectable, flavorsome. —**Ant.** unpalatable, distasteful, tasteless, flavorless.
—**Syn. Study.** PALATABLE, APPETIZING, TASTY, SAVORY refer to tastes or aromas pleasing to the palate, and sometimes to the senses of sight and smell. PALATABLE usu. refers to food that is merely acceptable: *a barely palatable plate of vegetables.* APPETIZING suggests stimulation of the appetite by the smell, taste, or sight of food: *an appetizing display of meats and cheeses.* TASTY refers to food that has an appealing taste: *a tasty sausage.* SAVORY refers most often to well or highly seasoned food that is pleasing to the taste or smell: *a savory stew.*

palatial, *adj.* magnificent, grand, grandiose, imposing, noble, stately, majestic, splendid, splendiferous, sumptuous, luxurious, extravagant, swank, posh, ritzy. —**Ant.** humble, simple.

pale, *adj.* **1.** pallid, wan, white, ashy, ashen, colorless. **2.** dim, faint, feeble, obscure. —*v.* **3.**

blanch, etiolate, whiten.
—*n.* **4.** picket, stake. **5.**
enclosure, fence, barrier,
paling, limits, bounds,
confines. —**Ant.** ruddy,
hale, hearty; robust;
blacken, soil. —**Syn.**
Study. PALE, PALLID, WAN
imply an absence of color,
esp. from the human
countenance. PALE implies
a faintness or absence of
color, which may be
natural when applied to
things (*the pale blue of a
violet*), but when used to
refer to the human face
usu. means an unnatural
and often temporary
absence of color, as arising
from sickness or sudden
emotion: *pale cheeks.*
PALLID, limited mainly to
the human countenance,
implies an excessive
paleness induced by
intense emotion, disease,
or death: *the pallid lips of
the dying man.* WAN implies
a sickly paleness, as after a
long illness: *wan and thin;*
or it may suggest
weakness: *a wan smile.*

pall, *n.* **1.** shroud, blanket,
cover, covering, veil. —*v.*

2. glut, satiate, fill, cloy,
sate, surfeit, overstuff,
gorge. **3.** weary, tire,
fatigue, wear on, jade.

palliate, *v.* **1.** moderate,
abate, relieve, alleviate,
ease, modify, reduce,
diminish, lessen, mitigate,
soften, cushion. **2.** qualify,
hedge, temper, season,
excuse, sugarcoat, gloss
over, prettify, whitewash,
varnish, camouflage.
—**Ant.** intensify, worsen.

pallid, *adj.* **1.** pale, faded,
washed-out, colorless,
white, whitish, ashen,
sallow, wan, pasty,
ghastly, whey-faced. **2.**
dull, colorless, insipid,
anemic, unexciting, flat,
lifeless. —**Ant.** robust.
—**Syn. Study.** See PALE.

palpable, *adj.* **1.** obvious,
evident, manifest, plain,
unmistakable. **2.** tangible,
material, real, corporeal.
—**Ant.** obscure, unclear;
intangible, spiritual.

palpitate, *v.* pulsate, throb,
flutter, beat.

paltry, *adj.* trifling, petty,
minor, trashy, mean,
worthless, contemptible,

insignificant, unimportant, trivial, inconsiderable, slight. **—Ant.** important, major, significant, considerable, essential. **—Syn. Study.** See PETTY.

pamper, *v.* indulge, gratify, humor, coddle, baby, cater to, spoil. **—Ant.** discipline.

pan, *v.* criticize, faultfind, deprecate, dispraise, censure, put down, fault, disparage, denigrate, disdain, despise, excoriate, reject, ridicule, knock, rap, flame. **—Ant.** praise, extol.

panacea, *n.* cure, cure-all, remedy, relief, nostrum, catholicon, theriac.

panache, *n.* showiness, dash, flair, style, flamboyance, dazzle, showmanship, élan, verve, bravura, brilliance, virtuosity.

pandemic, *adj.* general, prevalent, universal, epidemic. **—Ant.** isolated, unique, singular.

panegyric, *n.* eulogy, encomium, tribute; commendation, praise.

—Ant. condemnation, invective.

pang, *n.* **1.** pain, stab, stitch, twinge, prick, throe. **2.** qualm, scruple, compunction, scrupulousness.

panic, *n.* **1.** terror, fright, alarm. —*v.* **2.** terrorize, frighten. **—Ant.** security; soothe, calm.

pant, *v.* **1.** gasp, breathe heavily, puff, blow. **2.** long, yearn, thirst, hunger, desire. **3.** throb, pulsate, palpitate. —*n.* **4.** puff, gasp, heave; throb.

paradigm, *n.* model, ideal, guide, archetype, example, exemplar, standard, pattern, blueprint, criterion, classic example, locus classicus.

paragon, *n.* model, ideal, pattern, nonesuch, masterpiece.

parallel, *adj.* **1.** corresponding, similar, analogous, like, resembling, correspondent. **2.** tonic, harmonic. —*n.* **3.** match, counterpart. **4.** correspondence, analogy, similarity, resemblance, likeness. —*v.* **5.** match, resemble. **6.** equal, be equivalent to. —**Ant.** unique, unlike, singular, unusual; dissimilarity; differ.

paralyze, *v.* stun, shock, benumb, unnerve, deaden.

paramount, *adj.* superior, preeminent, chief, principal. —**Ant.** base, inferior, unimportant. —**Syn. Study.** See DOMINANT.

paraphernalia, *n.* belongings, effects; equipment, apparatus, appointments, appurtenances, accouterments, trappings, rig, equipage.

paraphrase, *n.* **1.** rendering, version, translation. —*v.* **2.** restate, render, translate; explain, explicate, interpret.

parasite, *n.* yes-man, sycophant, leech, hanger-on, bloodsucker, toady, flatterer, flunky.

parcel, *n.* **1.** package, bundle, pack, packet. **2.** quantity, lot, group, batch, collection. **3.** lot, plot, tract, acreage, portion, land. —*v.* **4.** divide, distribute, mete out, apportion, deal out, allot.

pardon, *n.* **1.** indulgence, allowance, excuse, forgiveness; remission, amnesty, absolution. —*v.* **2.** forgive, absolve, remit, condone, excuse, overlook; acquit, clear, release. —**Ant.** censure, blame. —**Syn. Study.** PARDON, AMNESTY, REPRIEVE refer to the remission or delay of a penalty or punishment for an offense; these terms do not imply absolution from guilt. A PARDON is often granted by a government official; it releases the individual from any punishment due: *The governor granted a pardon to the prisoner.* AMNESTY is usu. a general pardon granted to a group of persons for offenses against a government; it often includes an assurance of no further prosecution: *to grant amnesty to the rebels.* A REPRIEVE is a delay of impending punishment, usu. for a specific period of time or until a decision can be made as to the possibility of pardon or reduction of sentence: *a last-minute reprieve, allowing the prisoner to file an appeal.* See also EXCUSE.

pare, *v.* **1.** peel; clip, cut, shave. **2.** diminish, lessen, clip, reduce. **—Ant.** increase.

parentage, *n.* birth, descent, lineage, ancestry, origin, extraction, pedigree, family, stock.

pariah, *n.* outcast, undesirable, untouchable, castaway, castoff, Ishmael, persona non grata.

parity, *n.* equality; equivalence, correspondence, similarity, analogy, parallelism, likeness; sameness. **—Ant.** inequality, dissimilarity, difference.

parlance, *n.* phraseology, language, idiom, diction, wording, words, phrasing, usage, grammar, wordage, locution, expression, formulation, tongue, lingo.

parley, *n.* **1.** conference, discussion, talk, conversation, discourse. **—***v.* **2.** confer, discuss, speak, converse, talk, discourse.

parody, *n.* travesty, burlesque, imitation, caricature. **—Syn. Study.** See BURLESQUE.

paroxysm, *n.* fit, spasm, attack, access, seizure, throe, convulsion, outburst, eruption, irruption, explosion, storm.

parry, *v.* **1.** ward off, avert, avoid, evade, elude; prevent, obviate, preclude. **—***n.* **2.** prevention; avoidance, evasion. **—Ant.** encourage, further.

parsimonious, *adj.* sparing, frugal, stingy, tight, tight-fisted, close, niggardly, miserly, illiberal, mean, close-fisted, grasping, avaricious, penurious, covetous. **—Ant.** generous, open-handed, unsparing. **—Syn. Study.** See STINGY.

parsimony, *n.* economy, frugality, niggardliness, stinginess, miserliness, sparingness, closeness, illiberality, close-fistedness, tight-fistedness, cupidity, meanness. —**Ant.** generosity, liberality.

part, *n.* **1.** portion, division, piece, fragment, fraction, section, constituent, component, ingredient, element, member, organ. **2.** allotment, share, apportionment, portion, lot, dividend, concern, participation, interest, stock. **3.** (*usually plural*) region, quarter, district, section. **4.** duty, function, role, office, responsibility, charge. —*v.* **5.** divide, break, cleave, separate, sever, sunder, disunite, dissociate, dissever, disconnect, disjoin, detach. **6.** share, allot, portion, parcel out, apportion, distribute, deal out, mete out. **7.** depart, leave, go, quit; pass on *or* away, die. —**Ant.** all, none, nothing, everything.

partake, *v.* participate, share.

partial, *adj.* **1.** incomplete, unfinished, imperfect, limited. **2.** constituent,

component. **3.** biased, prejudiced, one-sided, unfair, unjust, influenced. —**Ant.** complete, perfect; unbiased, unprejudiced, liberal, just, fair.

partiality, *n.* **1.** bias, favor, prejudice, one-sidedness, injustice, unfairness, favoritism. **2.** fondness, liking, preference, bent, leaning, tendency, predilection, inclination. —**Ant.** justice, fairness; dislike, disfavor.

participate, *v.* share, partake.

particle, *n.* **1.** mite, whit, jot, iota, tittle, bit, mote, grain, ace, scrap, speck. **2.** molecule, atom, meson, deuteron, electron, positron, neutron, neutrino.

particular, *adj.* **1.** special, specific, especial. **2.** one, individual, single, separate, distinct, discrete. **3.** noteworthy, marked, unusual, notable, extraordinary; peculiar, singular, strange, odd, uncommon. **4.** exceptional, especial,

characteristic, distinctive.
5. certain, personal,
special. **6.** detailed,
descriptive, minute,
circumstantial, critical,
scrupulous, strict, careful,
exact, precise. **7.** critical,
finical, finicky,
discriminating, dainty,
nice, fastidious,
scrupulous. —*n.* **8.** point,
detail, circumstance, item,
feature, particularity.
—**Ant.** general, overall;
common, ordinary;
inexact, imprecise;
undiscriminating,
indiscriminate.

particularly, *adv.* **1.**
exceptionally, especially,
specially. **2.** specially,
especially, individually,
characteristically, uniquely,
separately, discretely,
unusually, specifically,
singly. **3.** in detail,
minutely, exactly,
precisely, strictly. —**Ant.**
generally; commonly,
usually, customarily.

partisan, *n.* **1.** adherent,
supporter, follower,
disciple. —*adj.* **2.** biased,
partial. —**Ant.** leader;
unbiased, impartial.

—**Syn. Study.** See
FOLLOWER.

partition, *n.* **1.** division,
distribution, portion,
share, allotment,
apportionment. **2.**
separation, division. **3.**
part, section, division,
segment, piece. **4.** barrier,
wall, dividing wall, screen.
—*v.* **5.** divide, separate,
apportion, portion, parcel
out, deal out, mete out,
share. —**Ant.** unity; unite,
blend.

partner, *n.* **1.** sharer,
partaker, associate,
accessory, accomplice,
participant, colleague. **2.**
husband, wife, spouse.

party, *n.* **1.** group,
gathering, assembly,
assemblage, company. **2.**
body, faction, circle,
coterie, clique, set,
combination, ring, league,
alliance. **3.** attachment,
devotion, partisanship.

parvenu, *n.* upstart, snob,
Johnny-come-lately,
climber.

pass, *v.* **1.** go, move,
proceed. **2.** disregard, pass
over, skim over, skim,

ignore. **3.** transcend, exceed, surpass, excel. **4.** spend; circulate. **5.** convey, transfer, transmit, send, deliver. **6.** sanction, approve, okay, enact. **7.** express, pronounce, utter, deliver. **8.** leave, go away, depart. **9.** end, terminate, expire, cease. **10.** go on, happen, take place, occur. **11.** vanish, fade, die, disappear. —*n.* **12.** notch, defile, ravine, gorge, gulch, canyon, channel. **13.** permission, license, ticket, passport, visa. **14.** thrust, lunge. **15.** stage, state, juncture, situation, condition. **—Ant.** attend, regard, note, notice; disapprove; arrive, come; initiate, begin, start; appear.

passage, *n.* **1.** paragraph, verse, line, section, clause, text, passus. **2.** way, route, avenue, channel, road, path, byway, lane, street, thoroughfare. **3.** movement, transit, transition, passing. **4.** voyage, trip, tour, excursion, journey. **5.** progress, course. **6.** passing, enactment. **7.** exchange, altercation, dispute, encounter, combat, skirmish, conflict, affair. **8.** transference, transmission. —*v.* **9.** cross, pass, voyage.

passion, *n.* **1.** feeling, emotion, zeal, ardor, fervor, transport, rapture, excitement, impulse; hope, fear, joy, grief, anger, love, desire. **2.** love, desire, attachment, affection, fondness, warmth. **3.** anger, ire, resentment, fury, wrath, rage, vehemence, indignation. **—Ant.** coolness, apathy. **—Syn. Study.** See FEELING.

passionate, *adj.* **1.** impassioned, emotional, ardent, vehement, excited, excitable, impulsive, fervent, fervid, zealous, warm, enthusiastic, earnest, glowing, burning, fiery; animated, impetuous, violent. **2.** quick-tempered, irascible, short-tempered, testy, touchy, choleric, hasty, hotheaded, fiery. **—Ant.** dispassionate, cool, cold; calm, collected.

passive, *adj.* **1.** inactive, quiescent, inert, receptive, prone. **2.** suffering, receiving, submitting, submissive, patient, unresisting. —**Ant.** active, energetic; hostile, resisting.

password, *n.* watchword, shibboleth, countersign.

pastime, *n.* diversion, amusement, sport, entertainment, recreation.

patch, *v.* mend, repair, restore, fix, correct, emend; settle, smooth. —**Ant.** break, crack, ruin, spoil.

patent, *n.* **1.** invention. —*adj.* **2.** patented, trademarked, copyrighted. **3.** open, manifest, evident, plain, clear, apparent, obvious, palpable, unmistakable, conspicuous, unconcealed. —**Ant.** concealed, hidden, unclear, dim.

path, *n.* way, walk, lane, trail, footpath, pathway, route, course, track, passage, road, avenue.

pathetic, *adj.* **1.** pitiable, touching, moving, affecting, tender, plaintive. **2.** emotional, pathetical. —**Ant.** cruel, ruthless; unemotional, apathetical.

patience, *n.* **1.** calmness, composure, endurance, fortitude, stoicism, stability, courage, self-possession, inner strength, submissiveness, submission, sufferance, resignation. **2.** perseverance, diligence, assiduity, sedulousness, indefatigability, indefatigableness, persistence. —**Ant.** hostility; weakness, frailty; fatigue.

patient, *n.* **1.** invalid. —*adj.* **2.** persevering, diligent, persistent, sedulous, assiduous, indefatigable, untiring. **3.** long-suffering, submissive, resigned, passive, unrepining, calm. **4.** quiet, calm, serene, unruffled, unexcited, self-possessed, stoical, composed. **5.** susceptible. —**Ant.** hostile, agitated; excited, perturbed; unsusceptible, impervious.

patron, *n.* **1.** customer, client. **2.** protector,

supporter, advocate, defender. —**Ant.** critic.

pattern, *n.* **1.** decoration, design, figure. **2.** style, type, kind, sort. **3.** original, model, paragon, example, exemplar, guide, archetype, prototype. **4.** sample, example, specimen; illustration. —*v.* **5.** model, imitate, copy, follow.

paucity, *n.* smallness, fewness, sparseness, scarcity, poverty. —**Ant.** abundance.

pause, *n.* **1.** rest, wait, hesitation, suspension, lacuna, hiatus, interruption, delay, intermission, break; stop, halt, cessation, stoppage. —*v.* **2.** hesitate, waver, deliberate, wait, rest, interrupt, tarry, delay. **3.** cease, stop, arrest, halt, desist, forbear. —**Ant.** continuity, continuousness.

pay, *v.* **1.** settle, liquidate, discharge. **2.** satisfy, compensate, reimburse, remunerate, recompense; reward; indemnify. **3.** yield, be profitable to, repay, requite. **4.** punish, repay, retaliate, requite, revenge. **5.** make amends, suffer, be punished, make compensation. —*n.* **6.** payment, wages, salary, income, stipend, remuneration, emolument, fee, allowance. **7.** requital, reward, punishment, just deserts. —*adj.* **8.** profitable, interest-bearing, gold-bearing, precious, valuable. —**Ant.** dissatisfy; unprofitable.

payment, *n.* pay.

peace, *n.* **1.** agreement, treaty, armistice, truce, pact, accord, entente, entente cordiale, amity, harmony, concord. **2.** order, security. **3.** calm, quiet, tranquillity, peacefulness, calmness. —**Ant.** insecurity; agitation, disturbance.

peaceable, *adj.* pacific, peaceful, amicable, friendly, amiable, mild, gentle; calm, tranquil, serene, quiet. —**Ant.** hostile, unfriendly; noisy.

peaceful, *adj.* tranquil, placid, serene, unruffled,

calm, complacent;
composed, dignified,
gracious, mellow;
unexcited, unagitated,
pacific. —**Ant.** perturbed,
disturbed. —**Syn. Study.**
PEACEFUL, PLACID, SERENE,
TRANQUIL refer to what is
characterized by lack of
strife or agitation.
PEACEFUL is rarely applied
to persons; it refers to
situations, scenes, and
activities free of
disturbances or,
occasionally, of warfare: *a
peaceful afternoon; a
peaceful protest.* PLACID,
SERENE, TRANQUIL are used
mainly of persons; when
used of things (usu.
elements of nature) there
is a touch of
personification. PLACID
suggests an unruffled calm
that verges on
complacency: *a placid
disposition; a placid
stream.* SERENE is a
somewhat nobler word;
when used of persons it
suggests dignity,
composure, and
graciousness; when applied
to nature there is a
suggestion of mellowness:
a serene summer landscape.
TRANQUIL implies a
command of emotions that
keeps one unagitated even
in the midst of excitement
or danger: *She remained
tranquil despite the chaos
around her.*

peak, *n.* point, top, crest,
summit, arete, acme,
pinnacle. —**Ant.** base,
bottom, abyss.

peaked, *adj.* pale, sickly,
wan, drawn, haggard,
pinched, emaciated,
unhealthy, infirm, wasted,
hollow-eyed. —**Ant.** hale,
hearty, robust.

pearly, *adj.* opalescent,
opaline, nacreous,
iridescent, mother-of-pearl,
pale, whitish, light, snowy,
dove-gray, pearl-gray.

peccadillo, *n.* petty sin *or*
offense, slight crime,
trifling fault; shortcoming,
weakness.

peculiar, *adj.* **1.** strange,
odd, queer, eccentric,
bizarre, uncommon,
unusual, extraordinary,
singular, exceptional. **2.**
distinguished, distinctive.

3. characteristic, appropriate, proper, individual, particular, select, especial, special, specific, unique, exclusive. —**Ant.** usual, common, ordinary; general, unspecific.

peculiarity, *n.* **1.** idiosyncrasy, characteristic, odd trait. **2.** singularity, oddity, rarity, eccentricity. **3.** distinction, feature, characteristic. —**Syn. Study.** See ECCENTRICITY. See also FEATURE.

pecuniary, *adj.* monetary, financial, nummular. —**Syn. Study.** See FINANCIAL.

pedestrian, *n.* **1.** walker, stroller. —*adj.* **2.** on foot, walking, afoot. **3.** commonplace, prosaic, dull. —**Ant.** interesting, fascinating, engaging.

pedigree, *n.* genealogy, descent, family tree, family, heritage, ancestry, lineage, line, race, derivation; patrimony. —**Syn. Study.** PEDIGREE, GENEALOGY refer to an account of ancestry. A PEDIGREE is a table or chart recording a line of ancestors, either of persons or (more commonly) of animals, as horses, cattle, and dogs; in the case of animals, such a table is used as proof of superior qualities: *a detailed pedigree.* A GENEALOGY is an account of the descent of a person or family traced through a series of generations, usu. from the first known ancestor: *a genealogy that includes a king.*

peek, *v.* peep, peer, pry.

peel, *v.* **1.** strip, skin, decorticate, pare, flay. —*n.* **2.** skin, rind, bark. —**Ant.** cover, plate.

peer, *n.* **1.** equal, compeer, match. **2.** nobleman, lord; duke, count, marquis, earl, viscount, baron.

peerless, *adj.* matchless, unequaled, unsurpassed, unique, superlative, unmatched.

peevish, *adj.* cross, querulous, fretful, vexatious, vexed, captious, discontented, petulant,

testy, irritable, crusty,
snappish, waspish,
acrimonious, splenetic,
short-tempered,
ill-tempered, ill-natured,
unpleasant, disagreeable,
nasty. **—Ant.**
good-natured, friendly,
pleasant, amiable,
agreeable.

pejorative, *adj.*
depreciative, deprecatory,
disparaging, opprobrious.
—Ant. favorable,
complimentary.

pell-mell, *adv.* headlong,
hurriedly, recklessly,
agitatedly, frantically,
frenziedly, wildly,
higgledy-piggledy.

pellucid, *adj.* translucent;
limpid, clear, crystalline,
crystal-clear, transparent.
—Ant. dull, opaque.

pelt, *v.* **1.** strike (*with
missiles*), beat, belabor,
batter. **—***n.* **2.** blow,
stroke. **3.** skin, hide,
peltry.

penchant, *n.* liking, leaning,
inclination, taste, fondness,
bent, propensity,
proclivity, affinity,
preference, predilection,

disposition, predisposition,
prejudice, bias, partiality,
soft spot.

pendulous, *adj.* **1.** hanging,
suspended, overhanging,
pendent, dangling,
swinging. **2.** hesitant,
vacillating, wavering,
tentative, uncertain,
indecisive, irresolute,
waffling. **—Ant.** resolute,
certain.

penetrate, *v.* **1.** pierce,
bore, probe, enter;
permeate, sink in. **2.** affect
or impress deeply, touch.
3. understand, discern,
comprehend, fathom.
—Syn. Study. See PIERCE.

penetrating, *adj.* **1.**
piercing, sharp, acute,
subtle. **2.** acute,
discerning, critical, keen,
shrewd, sharp,
sharp-witted, intelligent,
wise, sagacious. **—Ant.**
blunt; uncritical, silly,
stupid, undiscriminating.

penitent, *adj.* sorry,
contrite, repentant,
atoning, amending,
remorseful.

penniless, *adj.* poor,
indigent, poverty-stricken,

destitute, needy,
necessitous, inpecunious.
—**Ant.** rich, wealthy.
—**Syn. Study.** See POOR.
pensive, *adj.* serious, sober,
thoughtful, meditative,
reflective, dreamy, wistful;
contemplative, thinking.
—**Ant.** frivolous, silly,
unthinking, thoughtless,
vapid. —**Syn. Study.**
PENSIVE, MEDITATIVE,
REFLECTIVE suggest quiet
modes of apparent or real
thought. PENSIVE suggests
dreaminess or wistfulness,
and may involve little or
no thought to any
purpose: *a pensive,
faraway look.* MEDITATIVE
involves thinking of
certain facts or
phenomena, perhaps in the
religious sense of
"contemplation," without
necessarily having a goal
of complete understanding
or of action: *a slow,
meditative reply.* REFLECTIVE
has a strong implication of
orderly, perhaps analytic,
processes of thought, usu.
with a definite goal of
understanding: *a reflective
critic.*

pent-up, *adj.* confined,
restrained; frustrated.
penurious, *adj.* mean,
parsimonious, stingy, tight,
tightfisted, close-fisted,
close, miserly, niggardly,
mercenary. —**Ant.**
generous.
penury, *n.* poverty,
destitution, indigence,
need, want. —**Ant.**
wealth, opulence,
abundance.
people, *n.* **1.** community,
tribe, race, nation, clan,
family. **2.** persons, human
beings, humans, men,
man; folks. **3.** populace,
commonalty, public. —*v.*
4. populate; stock.
peppery, *adj.* **1.** pungent,
hot, spicy. **2.** sharp,
stinging, biting. **3.**
irascible, irritable,
hottempered,
short-tempered, hotheaded,
touchy, testy, petulant,
snarling, snappish,
waspish, churlish, choleric.
—**Ant.** mild, tasteless;
insipid; calm, amiable,
friendly, good-natured.
perceive, *v.* **1.** see, discern,
notice, note, discover,

observe, descry, espy, distinguish. **2.** apprehend, understand, see, discern, appreciate. —**Ant.** ignore. —**Syn. Study.** See NOTICE.

perceptible, *adj.* cognizable, appreciable, understandable, discernible, apparent, perceivable. —**Ant.** undiscernible, concealed.

perception, *n.* **1.** cognition, recognition, perceiving, apprehension, understanding, discernment. **2.** percept. —**Ant.** misapprehension, misunderstanding.

perceptive, *adj.* astute, discerning, sensitive, responsive, keen, sharp, insightful, perspicacious, understanding, appreciative, sagacious, judicious. —**Ant.** obtuse, insensitive.

perdition, *n.* ruin, damnation, destruction, downfall, hell. —**Ant.** blessedness, sanctity.

peremptory, *adj.* **1.** imperative, undeniable, irrefutable; categorical, positive, absolute. **2.**
dictatorial, imperious, dogmatic, arbitrary, authoritative. —**Ant.** refutable, indefinite, uncertain, unsure; obedient; lenient.

perennial, *adj.* lasting, enduring, perpetual, perdurable, everlasting, permanent, imperishable, undying, deathless, eternal, immortal; constant, incessant, continual, uninterrupted, unceasing. —**Ant.** evanescent, temporary, flimsy, mortal; inconstant; sporadic.

perfect, *adj.* **1.** complete, finished, completed, full, consummate. **2.** faultless, spotless, unblemished, excellent, exquisite. **3.** skilled, adept, adroit, expert, accomplished. **4.** typical, exact; thorough, sound, unqualified, pure, unmixed, unadulterated. —*v.* **5.** complete, finish, bring to perfection, consummate, accomplish. —**Ant.** incomplete, unfinished; imperfect; maladroit; mixed, impure.

perfidious, *adj.* faithless, treacherous, false, disloyal, dishonest; unfaithful, traitorous, deceitful, venal, untrustworthy. **—Ant.** faithful, honest, loyal, trustworthy.

perfidy, *n.* treachery, faithlessness, traitorousness, treason, disloyalty. **—Ant.** allegiance, faithfulness, faith, loyalty.

perform, *v.* **1.** carry out, execute, do, discharge, transact. **2.** fulfill, accomplish, achieve, effect. **—Ant.** fail.

perfume, *n.* **1.** essence, attar, scent, toilet water; incense. **2.** redolence, scent, odor, smell, aroma, fragrance. **—Ant.** stench, stink, noxiousness. **—Syn. Study.** PERFUME, FRAGRANCE, AROMA all refer to agreeable odors. PERFUME often indicates a strong, rich smell: *the perfume of flowers.* FRAGRANCE is usu. applied to a sweet, delicate, and fresh smell, esp. from growing things: *the fragrance of new-mown hay.* AROMA is usu. restricted to a distinctive,

pervasive, somewhat spicy smell: *the aroma of coffee.*

perfunctory, *adj.* mechanical, indifferent, careless, superficial, negligent, slovenly, heedless, reckless, uninterested, thoughtless. **—Ant.** careful, diligent, thoughtful.

peril, *n.* **1.** risk, jeopardy, danger, hazard. **—v. 2.** imperil, endanger, risk. **—Ant.** safety, security. **—Syn. Study.** See DANGER.

period, *n.* **1.** interval, age, era, epoch, term, time. **2.** course, cycle. **—Syn. Study.** See AGE.

periphery, *n.* **1.** boundary, circumference, perimeter. **2.** surface, outside. **—Ant.** center; meat.

perish, *v.* **1.** die, pass away, pass on, expire, decease. **2.** decay, wither, shrivel, rot, molder, disappear, vanish. **—Ant.** appear. **—Syn. Study.** See DIE.

perky, *adj.* jaunty, pert, brisk. **—Ant.** flaccid, retiring.

permanent, *adj.* lasting, unchanging, unchanged,

unaltered, stable, immutable, invariant, invariable, constant; enduring, durable, abiding, perpetual, everlasting, remaining, perdurable. **—Ant.** unstable, temporary, variable, inconstant; temporal.

permeate, *v.* pass through, penetrate, pervade, diffuse through, osmose, saturate, sink in.

permission, *n.* liberty, license, enfranchisement, franchise, leave, permit, liberty, freedom, allowance, consent. **—Ant.** refusal.

permit, *v.* **1.** allow, let, tolerate, agree to, endure, suffer. **—n. 2.** license, franchise, permission. **—Ant.** refuse, disallow. **—Syn. Study.** See ALLOW.

permutation, *n.* change, variation, modification, transformation, mutation, transmutation, transmogrification, metamorphosis, vicissitude, rearrangement, interchange, transposition, replacement, commutation.

—Ant. sameness, regularity.

pernicious, *adj.* **1.** ruinous, harmful, hurtful, detrimental, deleterious, injurious, destructive, damaging, baneful, noxious. **2.** deadly, fatal, lethal. **3.** evil, wicked, malevolent, malicious, bad. **—Ant.** beneficial, salubrious, healthful; good.

perorate, *v.* orate, declaim, elocute, lecture, sermonize, harangue, rant, rave, spout, run off at the mouth.

perpendicular, *adj.* vertical, upright, standing. **—Ant.** horizontal, parallel.

perpetrate, *v.* do, cause, effect, effectuate, commit, bring about, bring off, perform, carry out, pull off, accomplish, execute.

perpetual, *adj.* everlasting, permanent, continuing, continuous, enduring, constant, eternal, ceaseless, unceasing, incessant, unending, endless, uninterrupted, interminable, infinite.

—**Ant.** temporary, finite, impermanent; discontinuous. —**Syn. Study.** See ETERNAL.

perplex, *v.* **1.** confuse, puzzle, bewilder, mystify, confound. **2.** complicate, confuse, tangle, snarl, entangle, involve, encumber. **3.** hamper, discourage, vex, annoy, bother, trouble, harass, disturb. —**Ant.** clarify; disencumber; encourage, calm.

persecute, *v.* **1.** oppress, harass, badger, molest, vex, afflict. **2.** punish, discriminate against; torture, torment. **3.** importune, annoy, tease, bother, pester, harass, harry.

perseverance, *n.* persistence, tenacity, pertinacity, resolution, doggedness, determination, steadfastness, indefatigability. —**Ant.** irresolution. —**Syn. Study.** PERSEVERANCE, PERSISTENCE, TENACITY imply determined continuance in a state or in a course of action. PERSEVERANCE suggests effort maintained in spite of difficulties or long-continued application; it is used in a favorable sense: *The scientist's perseverance finally paid off in a coveted prize.* PERSISTENCE, which may be used in a favorable or unfavorable sense, implies steadfast, unremitting continuance in spite of opposition or protest: *an annoying persistence in a belief.* TENACITY is a dogged and determined holding on: *the stubborn tenacity of a salesman.*

persevere, *v.* persist, continue, keep on, last, stick it out, hold on. —**Ant.** fail, cease, desist.

persist, *v.* **1.** persevere, continue, last, endure, remain. **2.** insist. —**Ant.** stop, discontinue. —**Syn. Study.** See CONTINUE.

persistence, See Syn. study at PERSEVERANCE.

persistent, *adj.* **1.** persisting, persevering, enduring, indefatigable, pertinacious, tenacious, stubborn, pigheaded, immovable, steadfast. **2.** continued, continual, continuous, repeated, constant, steady. **—Ant.** amenable, obedient; inconstant, sporadic. **—Syn. Study.** See STUBBORN.

person, *n.* **1.** human being, human, man, somebody, individual, personage, one. **2.** character, part, role.

personality, *n.* character; personal identity. **—Syn. Study.** See CHARACTER.

perspicacious, *adj.* keen, perceptive, discerning, acute, penetrating, sharp-witted, clear-sighted. **—Ant.** dull, stupid, dim-witted.

perspicacity, *n.* perception, discernment, penetration, shrewdness, acuity, astuteness, insight, sharpness, acumen. **—Ant.** dullness, stupidity.

perspicuity, *n.* clearness, clarity, lucidity, transparency, plainness, distinctness, explicitness, intelligibility. **—Ant.** dimness, opacity.

perspicuous, *adj.* clear, lucid, intelligible, plain, distinct, explicit, transparent, unequivocal. **—Ant.** opaque, unintelligible, indistinct, unclear, confused, clouded.

perspiration, *n.* sweat, diaphoresis, water **—Syn. Study.** PERSPIRATION, SWEAT refer to moisture exuded by animals and people from the pores of the skin. PERSPIRATION is the more polite word, and is often used overfastidiously by those who consider SWEAT coarse: *a deodorant that retards perspiration.* However, SWEAT is a strong word and in some cases is more appropriate: *the sweat of one's brow.* SWEAT is always used when referring to animals: *Sweat dripped from the horse's flanks.* It may also be used metaphorically of objects: *Sweat forms on apples after they are gathered.*

persuade, *v.* **1.** prevail on, induce, urge, influence, actuate, move, entice, impel. **2.** win over, convince, satisfy. **—Ant.** dissuade, discourage.

—**Syn. Study.** PERSUADE, INDUCE imply influencing someone's thoughts or actions. They are used mainly in the sense of winning over a person to a certain course of action: *I persuaded her to call a doctor. I induced her to join the club.* They differ in that PERSUADE suggests appealing more to the reason and understanding: *I persuaded him to go back to work;* INDUCE emphasizes only the idea of successful influence, whether achieved by argument or promise of reward: *What can I say that will induce you to stay at your job?* Owing to this idea of compensation, INDUCE may be used in reference to the influence of factors as well as of persons: *The prospect of a raise in salary induced me to stay.*

pert, *adj.* bold, forward, impertinent, saucy, presumptuous, impudent, flippant. —**Ant.** retiring, shy, bashful; polite, courteous.

pertinacious, *adj.* tenacious, persevering, persistent, dogged. —**Ant.** relenting, flexible.

pertinacity, *n.* perseverance, persistence, tenacity, tenaciousness, inflexibility, firmness, steadfastness, determination, resolution. —**Ant.** flexibility.

pertinent, *adj.* pertaining, relating, relevant, apt, appropriate, apposite, fit, fitting, fitted, suited, suitable, applicable, proper. —**Ant.** irrelevant, inappropriate, unsuited, unsuitable, improper. —**Syn. Study.** See APT.

perturb, *v.* **1.** disturb, disquiet, agitate, stir up, trouble. **2.** disturb, derange, disorder, confuse, addle, muddle. —**Ant.** pacify, calm, tranquilize; clarify.

peruse, *v.* study, read, scrutinize, examine, survey, pore over, inspect, review, vet. —**Ant.** skim.

pervade, *v.* permeate, diffuse, fill; penetrate, pass through.

perverse, *adj.* **1.** contrary,

contumacious, disobedient, wayward, cantankerous. **2.** willful, persistent, obstinate, stubborn, headstrong, pigheaded, dogged, intractable, unyielding. **3.** wicked, evil, bad, sinful, piacular, perverted, distorted. —**Ant.** amiable, obedient; amenable, tractable; good. —**Syn. Study.** See WILLFUL.

perverted, *adj.* wicked, misguided, misapplied, distorted. —**Ant.** straight, good, sensible.

pessimistic, *adj.* cynical, gloomy, dark, foreboding. —**Ant.** optimistic, rosy, bright.

pest, *n.* **1.** nuisance, annoyance. **2.** pestilence, plague, scourge, bane; epidemic, pandemic.

pester, *v.* harass, annoy, vex, torment, torture, molest, harry, hector, tease, trouble, plague, nettle, disturb, provoke, bother, worry, gall, badger, irritate, chafe. —**Ant.** please, delight, entertain, divert.

pet, *n.* **1.** favorite, darling; lap-dog. **2.** peevishness, cantankerousness, moodiness. —*v.* **3.** fondle, indulge, baby, caress. **4.** sulk, be peevish.

petition, *n.* **1.** request, supplication, suit, prayer, entreaty, solicitation, appeal, application. —*v.* **2.** entreat, supplicate, beg, pray, appeal, solicit, sue.

petty, *adj.* **1.** unimportant, trifling, paltry, nugatory, trivial, lesser, little, small, insignificant, negligible, inconsiderable, slight, diminutive. **2.** narrow, narrow-minded, small. **3.** mean, ungenerous, stingy, miserly. —**Ant.** important, considerable, significant; broad-minded; generous. —**Syn. Study.** PETTY, PALTRY, TRIVIAL, TRIFLING apply to something that is so insignificant as to be almost unworthy of notice. PETTY implies lack of significance or worth: *petty quarrels.* PALTRY applies to something that is contemptibly small or worthless: *I was paid a paltry sum.* TRIVIAL applies to something that is slight or insignificant, often being in contrast to something that is important: *a trivial task.* TRIFLING is often interchangeable with TRIVIAL; however, TRIFLING implies an even lesser, almost negligible, importance or worth: *to ignore a trifling error.*

petulance, *n.* petulancy, irritability, peevishness, fretfulness, pettishness, testiness, waspishness. —**Ant.** calm, tranquillity.

petulant, *adj.* irritable, peevish, fretful, vexatious, waspish, snappish, testy, short-tempered, hotheaded, hot-tempered, peppery, pettish, touchy, irascible, cross, snarling, captious, acrimonious. —**Ant.** even-tempered, temperate, pleasant.

phantasm, *n.* apparition, specter, phantom, vision, illusion, ghost. —**Ant.** reality.

phantom, *n.* **1.** phantasm. —*adj.* **2.** unreal, illusive, spectral, illusory, phantasmal; imaginary, hallucinatory. —**Ant.** real, flesh-and-blood, material.

phenomenon, *n.* **1.** fact, occurrence, event, incident, circumstance. **2.** prodigy, marvel, wonder, miracle.

philander, *v.* flirt, coquet, trifle, dally.

phlegm, *n.* **1.** mucus. **2.** sluggishness, stoicism, apathy, indifference. **3.** coolness, calm, self-possession, coldness, impassivity, impassiveness. —**Ant.** concern; interest, warmth.

phobia, *n.* dread, fear; aversion, hatred. —**Ant.** like, attraction, love.

phony, *adj.* **1.** false, sham, counterfeit, inauthentic, bastard, mock, phony, spurious, brummagem, pinchbeck, pseudo. —*n.* **2.** impostor, faker, mountebank, charlatan, pretender, fraud, humbug, bluffer, four-flusher. **3.** imposture, counterfeit, sham, pretense. —**Ant.** genuine, authentic.

phraseology, *n.* diction, expression, style, language.

physical, *adj.* **1.** bodily,

corporeal, corporal, mortal; tangible, sensible. **2.** material, real, natural. —**Ant.** mental, spiritual; unnatural, unreal. —**Syn. Study.** PHYSICAL, BODILY, CORPOREAL, CORPORAL agree in pertaining to the body. PHYSICAL means connected with or pertaining to the animal or human body as a material organism: *physical strength.* BODILY means belonging to or concerned with the human body as distinct from the mind or spirit: *bodily sensations.* CORPOREAL, a more poetic and philosophical word, refers esp. to the mortal substance of which the body is composed, as opposed to spirit: *our corporeal existence.* CORPORAL is usu. reserved for reference to suffering inflicted on the human body: *corporal punishment.*

pick, *v.* **1.** choose, select, cull. **2.** criticize, find fault with. **3.** steal, rob, pilfer. **4.** pierce, indent, dig into, break up, peck. **5.** pluck, gather, reap, collect, get,

acquire. —*n.* **6.** pickax. **7.** choice, selection, choicest part, best. **8.** plectrum.

picture, *n.* **1.** painting, drawing, photograph, representation. **2.** image, representation, similitude, semblance, likeness. **3.** description, account, representation. **4.** motion picture, movie, screen play, photoplay, film. —*v.* **5.** imagine; depict, describe, delineate, paint, draw, represent.

picturesque, *adj.* **1.** striking, interesting, colorful, scenic, beautiful. **2.** graphic, vivid, impressive; intense, lively. —**Ant.** uninteresting, dull.

piece, *n.* **1.** portion, quantity, segment, section, scrap, shred, fragment, part. **2.** thing, example, instance, specimen. **3.** short story, story, article, essay, composition, paper, theme, novella; poem, ode, sonnet; play. —*v.* **4.** mend, patch. **5.** complete, enlarge, extend, augment, add to. —**Ant.** all, everything; none, nothing.

piecemeal, *adv.* **1.** gradually, bit by bit, inchmeal, inchwise, by degrees. **2.** separately, fractionally, disjointedly, spasmodically.

pierce, *v.* **1.** penetrate, enter, run through *or* into, perforate, stab, puncture, bore, drill. **2.** affect, touch, move, rouse, strike, thrill, excite. —**Syn. Study.** PIERCE, PENETRATE suggest the action of one object passing through another or making a way through and into another. These terms are used both concretely and figuratively. To PIERCE is to perforate quickly, as by stabbing; it suggests the use of a sharp, pointed instrument impelled by force: *to pierce the flesh with a knife; a scream that pierced my ears.* PENETRATE suggests a slow or difficult movement: *No ordinary bullet can penetrate an elephant's hide; to penetrate the depths of one's ignorance.*

piety, *n.* **1.** reverence, regard, respect. **2.** godliness, devoutness, devotion, sanctity, grace, holiness. —**Ant.** irreverence, disrespect.

pile, *n.* **1.** assemblage, collection, mass, heap, accumulation. **2.** pyre, burning ghat. **3.** building, edifice, structure. **4.** pier, post. **5.** hair, down; wool, fur, pelage; nap. —*v.* **6.** heap up, accumulate, assemble, amass, collect.

pilfer, *v.* steal, rob, thieve, appropriate, take, purloin, pinch, filch, lift, nick, pocket, swipe, rifle, shoplift, rip off.

pilgrim, *n.* **1.** palmer, crusader. **2.** wayfarer, sojourner, traveler, wanderer.

pilgrimage, *n.* journey, trip, excursion, tour, expedition. —**Syn. Study.** See TRIP.

pillage, *v.* **1.** rob, plunder, rape, despoil, sack, spoil. —*n.* **2.** booty, plunder, spoils. **3.** rapine, depredation, devastation, spoliation.

pillar, *n.* shaft, column,

stele, Lally column, support, pier, prop.

pillory, *v.* mock, ridicule, deride, scorn, revile, sneer at, vilify, slur, stigmatize, brand, besmirch, smear, tarnish, blacken, skewer, crucify. —**Ant.** praise, esteem.

pillow, *n.* cushion, pad, bolster.

pin, *n.* **1.** peg, fastening, bolt. **2.** brooch. —*v.* **3.** fasten, fix.

pine, *v.* **1.** yearn, long, ache, hunger, thirst, crave, itch, sigh. **2.** languish, fade, dwindle, wilt, droop, pine away. —**Syn. Study.** See YEARN.

pinnacle, *n.* peak, eminence, culmination, tower, summit, apex, acme, zenith. —**Ant.** base.

pioneer, *v.* **1.** lead, precede, blaze a trail, guide, forerun. **2.** initiate, introduce, invent, create, dream up. —*n.* **3.** forerunner, precursor, pathfinder, trailblazer, vanguard, bellwether, point man, point woman, point person. —*adj.* **4.**

first, earliest, advance, original, maiden, initial, avant-garde, trail-blazing, cutting-edge.

pious, *adj.* **1.** devout, reverent, godly, religious, holy. **2.** sacred. —**Ant.** impious, irreligious, unholy; unsacred, defiled. —**Syn. Study.** See RELIGIOUS.

piquant, *adj.* **1.** pungent, sharp, flavorsome, tart, spicy. **2.** stimulating, interesting, attractive, sparkling. **3.** smart, racy, sharp, clever. —**Ant.** insipid; uninteresting, unattractive; dull.

pique, *v.* **1.** offend, nettle, sting, irritate, chafe, vex; affront, wound, displease. **2.** interest, stimulate, excite, incite, stir, spur, prick, goad. —**Ant.** please, delight; compliment.

pirate, *n.* plunderer, filibuster, freebooter, picaroon, buccaneer, corsair.

pit, *n.* **1.** hole, cavity, burrow, hollow. **2.** excavation, well, pitfall, trap. **3.** hollow, depression, dent, indentation. **4.** stone, pip, seed, core.

piteous, *adj.* pathetic, pitiable, deplorable, wretched, miserable; affecting, distressing, moving, pitiful, lamentable, woeful, sorrowful, sad, mournful, morose, doleful. —**Ant.** good, fine, pleasant, delightful. —**Syn. Study.** See PITIFUL.

pithy, *adj.* terse, concise, brief, short, compact, epigrammatic, succint, compendious, laconic, summary, to the point, short and sweet. —**Ant.** expansive, prolix, verbose.

pitiable, See Syn. study at PITIFUL.

pitiful, *adj.* **1.** pitiable, pathetic, piteous. **2.** contemptible, deplorable, mean, low, base, vile, despicable. —**Ant.** superior, delightful, lovable. —**Syn. Study.** PITIFUL, PITIABLE, PITEOUS apply to that which arouses pity (with

compassion or with contempt). That which is PITIFUL is touching and excites pity or is mean and contemptible: *a pitiful leper; a pitiful exhibition of cowardice.* PITIABLE may mean lamentable, or wretched and paltry: *a pitiable hovel.* PITEOUS refers only to that which exhibits suffering and misery, and is therefore heartrending: *piteous poverty.*

pitiless, *adj.* merciless, cruel, mean, unmerciful, ruthless, implacable, relentless, inexorable, hard-hearted. —**Ant.** merciful, soft-hearted, kind, kindly.

pity, *n.* **1.** sympathy, compassion, commiseration, condolence, mercy. —*v.* **2.** commiserate, be *or* feel sorry for, sympathize with, feel for. —**Ant.** apathy, cruelty, ruthlessness. —**Syn. Study.** See SYMPATHY.

placate, *v.* appease, satisfy, conciliate. —**Ant.** dissatisfy, displease.

place, *n.* **1.** space, plot, spot, location, locale, locality, site. **2.** position, situation, circumstances. **3.** job, post, office, function, duty, charge, responsibility, employment, rank. **4.** region, area, section, sector. **5.** residence, dwelling, house, home, domicile, abode. **6.** stead, lien. **7.** opportunity, occasion, reason, ground, cause. —*v.* **8.** position, range, order, dispose, arrange, situate, put, set, locate, station, deposit, lay, seat, fix, establish. **9.** appoint, hire, induct. **10.** identify, connect. —**Ant.** misplace, displace; forget.

placid, *adj.* calm, peaceful, unruffled, tranquil, serene, quiet, undisturbed. —**Ant.** turbulent, tumultuous, perturbed. —**Syn. Study.** See PEACEFUL.

plague, *n.* **1.** epidemic, pestilence, disease, Black Death, Great Plague, Oriental Plague. **2.** affliction, calamity, evil, curse. **3.** trouble, vexation, annoyance, nuisance,

torment. —*v.* **4.** trouble, torment, torture, molest, bother, incommode. discommode. **5.** vex, harry, hector, harass, fret, worry, pester, badger, annoy, tease, irritate, disturb. —**Syn. Study.** See BOTHER.

plain, *adj.* **1.** clear, distinct, lucid, unambiguous, unequivocal, intelligible, understandable, perspicuous, evident, manifest, obvious, unmistakable, patent, apparent. **2.** downright, sheer, direct, transparent. **3.** unambiguous, candid, outspoken, blunt, direct, frank, guileless, artless, ingenuous, open, unreserved, honest, sincere, open-hearted. **4.** homely, unpretentious, homey, simple, unadorned, frugal. **5.** ugly, homely, unattractive. **6.** ordinary, common, commonplace, unostentatious. **7.** flat, level, plane, smooth, even. —*n.* **8.** mesa, plateau, savanna, prairie, pampas. —**Ant.** unclear, ambiguous, unintelligible;

artful, sly, cunning, deceptive, insincere; beautiful, attractive; uncommon, extraordinary.

plaint, *n.* **1.** protest, complaint, accusation, reproach. **2.** lament, cry, grieving, lamentation, wail, keening.

plaintive, *adj.* sorrowful, melancholy, mournful, sad, wistful; discontented. —**Ant.** happy, pleasant.

plan, *n.* **1.** scheme, plot, complot, procedure, project, formula, method, system, design, contrivance. **2.** drawing, sketch, floorplan, draft, map, chart, diagram, representation. —*v.* **3.** arrange, scheme, plot, design, devise, contrive, invent, concoct, hatch.

platform, *n.* **1.** stage, dais, rostrum, pulpit; landing. **2.** principles, beliefs, tenets.

platitude, *n.* cliché, commonplace, banality, bromide, truism, generalization, prosaicism, old saw, chestnut. —**Ant.** witticism, mot.

plausible, *adj.* **1.** specious, deceptive, deceiving, deceitful, hypocritical. **2.** fair-spoken, glib, convincing. —**Ant.** implausible.

play, *n.* **1.** drama, piece, show; comedy, tragedy, melodrama, farce. **2.** amusement, recreation, game, sport, diversion, pastime. **3.** fun, jest, trifling, frolic. **4.** action, activity, movement, exercise, operation, motion. **5.** freedom, liberty, scope, elbow-room. —*v.* **6.** act, perform, enact, characterize, impersonate, personate. **7.** compete, contend with *or* against, engage. **8.** use, employ. **9.** stake, bet, wager. **10.** represent, imitate, emulate, mimic. **11.** do, perform, bring about, execute. **12.** toy, trifle, sport, dally, caper, romp, disport, frolic, gambol, skip, revel, frisk. —**Ant.** work.

playful, *adj.* frisky, coltish, antic, frolicsome, sportive, sprightly, prankish, puckish, impish, puppyish, kittenish, whimsical, larky. —**Ant.** somber, sober.

plead, *v.* **1.** entreat, appeal, beg, supplicate. **2.** argue, persuade, reason. **3.** allege, cite, make a plea, apologize, answer, make excuse.

pleasant, *adj.* **1.** pleasing, agreeable, enjoyable, pleasurable, acceptable, welcome, gratifying. **2.** delightful, congenial, polite, courteous, friendly, personable, amiable. **3.** fair, sunny. **4.** gay, sprightly, merry, cheery, cheerful, lively, sportive, vivacious. **5.** jocular, facetious, playful, humorous, witty, amusing, clever, jocose. —**Ant.** unpleasant, displeasing.

pleasing, *adj.* agreeable, pleasant, acceptable, pleasurable, charming, delightful, interesting, engaging. —**Ant.** disagreeable, unpleasant, unacceptable.

pleasure, *n.* **1.** happiness, gladness, delectation, enjoyment, delight, joy, well-being, satisfaction, gratification. **2.** luxury, sensuality, voluptuousness. **3.** will, desire, choice, preference, purpose, wish, mind, inclination, predilection. —**Ant.** displeasure, unhappiness; disinclination.

plentiful, *adj.* bountiful, ample, plenteous, copious, abundant, full, rich, fertile, fruitful, bounteous, productive, exuberant, luxuriant. —**Ant.** sparse, scanty, barren, fruitless. —**Syn. Study.** PLENTIFUL, AMPLE, ABUNDANT, BOUNTIFUL describe a more than adequate supply of something. PLENTIFUL suggests a large or full quantity: *a plentiful supply of fuel.* AMPLE suggests a quantity that is sufficient for a particular need or purpose: *an auditorium with ample seating for students.* ABUNDANT and BOUNTIFUL both imply a greater degree of plenty: *an abundant rainfall; a bountiful harvest.*

plenty, *n.* fullness, abundance, copiousness, plenteousness, plentifulness, profusion, luxuriance, exuberance, affluence, overflow, extravagance, prodigality; superabundance, overfullness, plethora. —**Ant.** paucity, scarcity.

pliant, *adj.* pliable, supple, flexible, flexile, lithe, limber; compliant, easily influenced, yielding, adaptable, manageable, tractable, ductile, facile, docile. —**Ant.** inflexible; unyielding, rigid, intractable.

plight, *n.* **1.** condition, state, situation, predicament, category, case, dilemma. —*v.* **2.** propose, pledge, hypothecate. —**Syn. Study.** See PREDICAMENT.

plod, *v.* **1.** walk heavily, pace, trudge. **2.** toil, moil, labor, drudge, sweat. —**Syn. Study.** See PACE.

plot, *n.* **1.** plan, scheme, complot, intrigue, conspiracy, cabal, stratagem, machination. **2.** story, theme, thread, story line. —*v.* **3.** devise, contrive, concoct, brew,

hatch, frame. **4.** conspire, scheme, contrive.

ploy, *n.* stratagem, strategy, tactic, trick, maneuver, artifice, tactic, scheme, gimmick, dodge, wile, device, feint, gambit, ruse.

pluck, *v.* **1.** pull, jerk, yank, snatch, tug, tear, rip. —*n.* **2.** courage, resolution, spirit, bravery, boldness, determination, mettle, nerve.

plump, *adj.* **1.** fleshy, fat, chubby, stout, portly, corpulent, obese, round. **2.** direct, downright, blunt, unqualified, unreserved, complete, full. —*v.* **3.** gain weight; fatten. **4.** drop, sink, fall. —*n.* **5.** fall, drop. —*adv.* **6.** directly, bluntly, suddenly, abruptly. —**Ant.** thin, slender, skinny; subtle.

plunder, *v.* **1.** rob, despoil, fleece, pillage, ravage, rape, sack, devastate, strip, lay waste. —*n.* **2.** pillage, rapine, spoliation, robbery, theft, plundering. **3.** loot, booty, spoils.

plunge, *v.* **1.** immerse, submerge, dip. **2.** dive;

rush, hasten; descend, drop, hurtle over. —*n.* **3.** leap, dive, rush, dash, dip. —**Syn. Study.** See DIP.

poetry, *n.* verse, meter, rhythm, poesy, numbers.

poignant, *adj.* **1.** distressing, heartfelt, serious, intense, severe, bitter, sincere. **2.** keen, strong, biting, mordant, caustic, acid, pointed. **3.** pungent, piquant, sharp, biting, acrid, stinging. —**Ant.** superfluous, trivial; mild.

pointed, *adj.* **1.** sharp, piercing, penetrating, epigrammatic, stinging, piquant, biting, mordant, sarcastic, caustic, severe, keen. **2.** directed, aimed, explicit, marked, personal. **3.** marked, emphasized, accented, accentuated. —**Ant.** blunt, dull, mild.

poise, *n.* **1.** balance, equilibrium, equipoise, counterpoise. **2.** composure, self-possession, steadiness, stability, self-control, control. **3.** suspense, indecision. **4.** carriage, mien, demeanor,

savoir-faire, breeding, behavior. —*v.* **5.** balance, equilibrate. —**Ant.** instability, unsteadiness; decision.

poison, *n.* **1.** toxin, venom, virus. —*v.* **2.** envenom, infect. **3.** corrupt, ruin, vitiate, contaminate, pollute, taint, canker. —**Syn. Study.** POISON, TOXIN, VENOM are terms for any substance that injures the health or destroys life when absorbed into the system. POISON is the general word: *a poison for insects.* A TOXIN is a poison produced by an organism; it is esp. used in medicine in reference to disease-causing bacterial secretions: *A toxin produces diphtheria.* VENOM is esp. used of the poisons injected by bite, sting, etc.: *snake venom; bee venom.*

policy, *n.* **1.** course (*of action*), expediency, tactic, approach, procedure, rule, management, administration, handling. **2.** prudence, widsom, sagacity, shrewdness, acumen, astuteness, discretion, skill, art, cunning, stratagem. —**Ant.** ingenuousness, naiveté.

polish, *v.* **1.** brighten, smooth, burnish, shine. **2.** finish, refine, civilize, make elegant. —*n.* **3.** smoothness, gloss, shine, sheen, luster, brightness, brilliance. **4.** refinement, elegance, poise, grace. —**Ant.** dull. —**Syn. Study.** POLISH, GLOSS, LUSTER, SHEEN refer to a smooth, shining, or bright surface from which light is reflected. POLISH suggests the smooth, bright reflection often produced by friction: *a lamp rubbed to a high polish.* GLOSS suggests a superficial, hard smoothness characteristic of lacquered, varnished, or enameled surfaces: *a gloss on oilcloth.* LUSTER denotes the characteristic quality of the light reflected from the surfaces of certain materials, as pearls or freshly cut metals: *a pearly luster.* SHEEN sometimes suggests a glistening brightness such as that reflected from the surface of silk: *the sheen of a satin gown.*

polished, *adj.* **1.** smooth, glossy, burnished, shining, shiny, shined, lustrous, brilliant. **2.** refined, cultured, finished, elegant, polite, poised. **3.** flawless, excellent, perfect. —**Ant.** dull, dim; unrefined, impolite; inelegant; imperfect.

polite, *adj.* well-mannered, courteous, civil, well-bred, gracious, genteel, urbane, polished, poised, courtly, cultivated, refined, finished, elegant. —**Ant.** impolite, rude, discourteous, uncivil. —**Syn. Study.** See CIVIL.

politic, *adj.* **1.** sagacious, prudent, wise, tactful, diplomatic, discreet, judicious, provident, astute, wary, prudential. **2.** shrewd, artful, sly, cunning, underhanded, tricky, foxy, clever, subtle, Machiavellian, wily, intriguing, scheming, crafty, unscrupulous, strategic. **3.** expedient, judicious, political. —**Ant.**

imprudent, indiscreet, improvident; artless, ingenuous, direct, open, honest. —**Syn. Study.** See DIPLOMATIC.

politician, *n.* statesman, political leader, national leader; politico, *Slang* pol —**Syn. Study.** POLITICIAN, STATESMAN refer to one skilled in politics. POLITICIAN is more often derogatory, and STATESMAN laudatory. POLITICIAN suggests the schemes of a person who engages in politics for party ends or personal advantage: *a dishonest politician.* STATESMAN suggests the eminent ability, foresight, and patriotic devotion of a person dealing with important affairs of state: *a distinguished statesman.*

pollute, *v.* **1.** befoul, dirty, defile, soil, taint, tarnish, stain, contaminate, vitiate, corrupt, debase, deprave. **2.** desecrate, profane, blaspheme, violate, dishonor, defile. —**Ant.** purify; honor, revere, respect.

pompous, See Syn. study at GRANDIOSE.

ponder, *v.* consider, meditate, reflect, cogitate, deliberate, ruminate, muse, think, study; weigh, contemplate, examine. —**Ant.** forget, ignore.

ponderous, *adj.* **1.** heavy, massive, weighty, bulky. **2.** important, momentous, weighty. —**Ant.** light, weightless; unimportant.

poor, *adj.* **1.** needy, indigent, necessitous, straitened, destitute, penniless, poverty-stricken, impecunious, impoverished, reduced, hard up, distressed. **2.** deficient, insufficient, meager, lacking, incomplete. **3.** faulty, inferior, unsatisfactory, substandard, shabby, jerry-built, seedy, worthless, valueless. **4.** sterile, barren, unfertile, fruitless, unproductive. **5.** lean, emaciated, thin, skinny, meager, hungry, underfed, lank, gaunt, shrunk. **6.** cowardly, abject, mean, base. **7.** scanty, paltry, meager, insufficient, inadequate. **8.** humble, unpretentious. **9.** unfortunate, hapless, unlucky, star-crossed, doomed, luckless, miserable, unhappy, pitiable, piteous. —**Ant.** rich, wealthy; sufficient, adequate, complete; superior; fertile; well-fed; bold, brave; bold, pretentious; fortunate, lucky. —**Syn. Study.** POOR, IMPECUNIOUS, IMPOVERISHED, PENNILESS refer to those lacking money. POOR is the simple word for the condition of lacking the means to obtain the comforts of life: *a very poor family.* IMPECUNIOUS often suggests that the poverty is a consequence of unwise habits: *an impecunious actor.* IMPOVERISHED often implies a former state of greater plenty: *the impoverished aristocracy.* PENNILESS refers to extreme poverty; it means entirely without money: *The widow was left penniless.*

popular, *adj.* **1.** favorite, approved, accepted, received, liked. **2.** common, prevailing, current, general, prevalent, in vogue, faddish. —**Ant.** unpopular; uncommon, rare, unusual. —**Syn. Study.** See GENERAL.

populous, *adj.* crowded, filled, overcrowded, packed, jam-packed, crammed, teeming, swarming, bristling, crawling, alive.

port, *n.* harbor, haven, refuge, anchorage. —**Syn. Study.** See HARBOR.

portent, *n.* indication, omen, augury, sign, warning, presage. —**Syn. Study.** See SIGN.

portentous, See Syn. study at OMINOUS.

portion, *n.* **1.** part, section, segment, piece, bit, scrap, morsel, fragment. **2.** share, allotment, quota, dole, dividend, division, apportionment, lot. **3.** serving. **4.** dowry, dot. —*v.* **5.** divide, distribute, allot, apportion, deal *or* parcel out. **6.** endow. —**Ant.** all, everything; none, nothing.

portray, *v.* picture, delineate, limn, depict, paint, represent, sketch.

pose, *v.* **1.** sit, model; attitudinize. **2.** state, assert, propound. —*n.* **3.** attitude, posture, position; affectation.

position, *n.* **1.** station, place, locality, spot, location, site, locale, situation, post. **2.** situation, condition, state, circumstances. **3.** status, standing, rank, place. **4.** post, job, situation, place, employment. **5.** placement, disposition, array, arrangement. **6.** posture, attitude, pose. **7.** proposition, thesis, contention, principle, dictum, predication, assertion, doctrine. —*v.* **8.** put, place, situate. **9.** locate, fix, discover. —**Syn. Study.** POSITION, POSTURE, ATTITUDE, POSE refer to an arrangement or disposal of the body or its parts. POSITION is the general word for the arrangement of the body: *in a reclining position.* POSTURE is usu. an assumed arrangement of the body, esp. when standing: *a relaxed posture.* ATTITUDE is often a posture assumed for imitative effect or the like, but may be one adopted for a purpose (as that of a fencer or a tightrope walker): *an attitude of prayer.* A POSE is an attitude assumed, in most cases, for artistic effect: *an attractive pose.*

positive, *adj.* **1.** explicit, express, sure, certain, definite, precise, clear, unequivocal, categorical, unmistakable, direct. **2.** arbitrary, enacted, decided, determined, decisive, unconditional. **3.** incontrovertible, substantial, indisputable, indubitable. **4.** stated, expressed, emphatic. **5.** confident, self-confident, self-assured, assured, convinced, unquestioning, over-confident, stubborn, peremptory, obstinate, dogmatic, overbearing. **6.** absolute. **7.** practical. —**Ant.** unsure, indefinite, unclear, equivocal; conditional; doubtful;

tacit; tractable, self-effacing; relative; impractical, unpractical.

possess, *v.* **1.** have, hold, own. **2.** occupy, hold, have, control. **3.** impart, inform, familiarize, acquaint, make known. —**Ant.** lose.

possession, *n.* **1.** custody, occupation, tenure. **2.** ownership. —**Ant.** loss.

possible, *adj.* feasible, practicable, likely, potential. —**Ant.** impossible, impractical, unlikely. —**Syn. Study.** POSSIBLE, FEASIBLE, PRACTICABLE refer to that which may come about or take place without prevention by serious obstacles. That which is POSSIBLE is naturally able or even likely to happen, other circumstances being equal: *He offered a possible compromise.* FEASIBLE refers to the ease with which something can be done and implies a high degree of desirability for doing it: *Which plan is the most feasible?* PRACTICABLE applies to that which can be done with the means at hand and with conditions as they are: *We ascended the slope as far as was practicable.*

post, *n.* **1.** column, pillar, pole, support, upright. **2.** position, office, assignment, appointment. **3.** station, round, beat, position. —*v.* **4.** announce, advertise, publicize. **5.** station, place, set.

posterior, See Syn. study at BACK.

postpone, *v.* **1.** put off, defer, delay, procrastinate, adjourn. **2.** subordinate. —**Syn. Study.** See DEFER.

posture, *n.* **1.** position, pose, attitude. **2.** position, condition, state. —**Syn. Study.** See POSITION.

potent, *adj.* **1.** powerful, mighty, strong, puissant. **2.** cogent, influential, efficacious. —**Ant.** weak, impotent, powerless, feeble, frail; ineffectual.

potential, *adj.* **1.** possible. **2.** capable, able, latent. —*n.* **3.** possibility, potentiality. —**Ant.** kinetic, impossible;

incapable, unable; impossibility.

pound, *v.* **1.** strike, beat, thrash. **2.** crush, bray, pulverize, powder, triturate, comminute. **3.** impound, imprison, pen, jail, shut up, confine, coop up. —*n.* **4.** pound avoirdupois, pound troy, pound sterling, pound Scots. **5.** enclosure, pen, confine, trap. —**Syn. Study.** See BEAT.

poverty, *n.* **1.** destitution, need, lack, want, privation, necessitousness, necessity, neediness, indigence, penury, distress. **2.** deficiency, sterility, barrenness, unfruitfulness. **3.** scantiness, jejuneness, sparingness, meagerness. —**Ant.** wealth; abundance, fertility, fruitfulness.

power, *n.* **1.** ability, capability, capacity, faculty, competence, competency, might, strength, puissance. **2.** strength, might, force, energy. **3.** control, command, dominion, authority, sway, rule, ascendancy, influence, sovereignty, suzerainty, prerogative. —**Ant.** inability, incapacity, incompetence.

powerful, *adj.* **1.** mighty, potent, forceful, strong. **2.** cogent, influential, forcible, convincing, effective, efficacious, effectual. —**Ant.** weak, frail, feeble; ineffective, ineffectual.

practicable, *adj.* possible, feasible, workable, performable, doable, achievable, attainable. —**Ant.** impracticable, impossible, unattainable. —**Syn. Study.** See POSSIBLE.

practical, *adj.* **1.** sensible, businesslike, pragmatic, efficient. **2.** judicious, discreet, sensible, discriminating, balanced, reasoned, sound, shrewd. —**Ant.** impractical, inefficient; indiscreet, unsound. —**Syn. Study.** PRACTICAL, JUDICIOUS, SENSIBLE refer to good judgment in action, conduct, and the handling of everyday matters. PRACTICAL suggests the ability to adopt means to an end or to turn what is at hand to account: *to adopt practical measures for settling problems.* JUDICIOUS implies the possession and use of discreet judgment, discrimination, and balance: *a judicious use of one's time.* SENSIBLE implies the possession and use of reason and shrewd common sense: *a sensible suggestion.*

practice, *n.* **1.** custom, habit, wont. **2.** exercise, drill, experience, application, study. **3.** performance, operation, action, process. **4.** plotting, intriguing, trickery, chicanery; plot, intrigue, stratagem, ruse, maneuver. —*v.* **5.** carry out, perform, do, drill, exercise. **6.** follow, observe. —**Ant.** inexperience. —**Syn. Study.** See CUSTOM.

praise, *n.* **1.** praising, commendation, acclamation, plaudit, compliment, laudation, approval, approbation, applause, kudos. **2.**

enconium, eulogy, panegyric. —*v.* **3.** laud, approve, commend, admire, extol, celebrate, eulogize, panegyrize. **4.** glorify, magnify, exalt, worship, bless, adore, honor. —**Ant.** condemnation, disapprobation, disapproval, criticism.

pray, *v.* importune, entreat, supplicate, beg, beseech, implore, sue, petition, invoke.

precarious, *adj.* **1.** uncertain, unstable, unsure, insecure, dependent, unsteady. **2.** doubtful, dubious, unreliable, undependable, risky, perilous, hazardous, dangerous. **3.** groundless, unfounded, baseless. —**Ant.** certain, stable, sure, secure, independent, reliable, dependable; well-founded.

precaution, *n.* foresight, prudence, providence, wariness, forethought.

precious, *adj.* **1.** valuable, costly, dear, invaluable, priceless. **2.** dear, beloved, darling, cherished. **3.** choice, fine, delicate, select, pretty. **4.** arrant, gross, egregious. —**Ant.** inexpensive, cheap; worthless; ugly, unattractive.

precipitate, *v.* **1.** hasten, accelerate, hurry, speed up, expedite, speed, rush, quicken, advance, dispatch. **2.** cast down, hurl *or* fling down, plunge. —*adj.* **3.** headlong, hasty, rash, reckless, indiscreet. **4.** sudden, abrupt, violent. —**Ant.** slow, retard; considered.

precipitous, *adj.* steep, abrupt, sheer, perpendicular. —**Ant.** gradual, sloping.

precise, *adj.* **1.** definite, exact, defined, fixed, correct, strict, explicit, accurate. **2.** rigid, particular, puritanical, demanding, crucial. —**Ant.** indefinite, incorrect, inexact, lenient; flexible, tractable. —**Syn. Study.** See CORRECT.

predatory, *adj.* predacious, plundering, ravaging, pillaging, rapacious, voracious.

predicament, *n.* dilemma, plight, quandary; situation, state, condition, position, case. —**Syn. Study.** PREDICAMENT, PLIGHT, DILEMMA, QUANDARY refer to unpleasant or puzzling situations. PREDICAMENT and PLIGHT stress more the unpleasant nature, DILEMMA and QUANDARY the puzzling nature, of a situation. PREDICAMENT, though often used lightly, may also refer to a crucial situation: *Stranded in a strange city without money, he was in a predicament.* PLIGHT, however, though originally meaning peril or danger, is most often used lightly: *When her suit wasn't ready at the cleaners, she was in a terrible plight.* DILEMMA means a position of doubt or perplexity in which a person is faced by two equally undesirable alternatives: *the dilemma of a person who must support one of two friends in an election.* QUANDARY is the state of mental perplexity of one faced with a difficult situation: *There seemed to be no way out of the quandary.*

predict, *v.* foretell, prophesy, foresee, forecast, presage, augur, prognosticate, foretoken, portend, divine. —**Syn. Study.** PREDICT, PROPHESY, FORESEE, FORECAST mean to know or tell beforehand what will happen. To PREDICT is usu. to foretell with precision of calculation, knowledge, or shrewd inference from facts or experience: *Astronomers can predict an eclipse;* it may, however, be used without the implication of knowledge or expertise: *I predict it will be a successful party.* To PROPHESY is usu. to predict future events by the aid of divine or supernatural inspiration: *Merlin prophesied that two knights would meet in conflict;* this verb, too, may be used in a less specific sense: *I prophesy she'll be back in the old job.* FORESEE refers specifically not to the uttering of predictions but to the mental act of seeing ahead; there is often a practical implication of preparing for what will happen: *He was able to foresee their objections.* FORECAST means to predict by observation or study; however, it is most often used of phenomena that cannot be accurately predicted: *Rain is forecast for tonight.*

prediction, *n.* prophecy, forecast, augury, prognostication, foretoken, portent, divination, soothsaying, presage.

predilection, *n.* prepossession, favoring, partiality, predisposition, disposition, inclination, bent, preference, leaning, bias, prejudice. —**Ant.** disfavor, disinclination, dislike.

predominant, *adj.* ascendant, prevailing, prevalent, dominant, in sway, sovereign. —**Ant.** rare, retrograde. —**Syn. Study.** See DOMINANT.

predominate, *v.*
preponderate, prevail,
outweigh, overrule,
surpass, dominate.

preeminent, *adj.* eminent,
surpassing, dominant,
superior, over, above,
distinguished, excellent,
peerless, unequalled,
paramount, consummate,
predominant, supreme.
—**Ant.** undistinguished,
inferior.

preface, *n.* introduction,
foreword, preamble,
prologue, proem, prelude,
preliminary, prolegomena.
—**Ant.** appendix, epilogue.
—**Syn. Study.** See
INTRODUCTION.

prefer, *v.* **1.** like better,
favor, choose, elect, select,
pick out, pick, single out,
fix upon, fancy. **2.** put
forward, advance, present,
offer, proffer, tender,
promote. —**Ant.** exclude,
dislike; retract, withdraw.

preference, *n.* choice,
selection, pick,
predilection. —**Ant.**
exclusion.

prejudice, *n.* **1.**
preconception, bias,

partiality, prejudgment,
predilection,
predisposition, disposition.
—*v.* **2.** bias, influence,
warp, twist. —**Ant.**
judgment, decision.
—**Syn. Study.** See BIAS.

preliminary, *adj.* **1.**
preceding, introductory,
preparatory, prefatory,
precursive, prior. —*n.* **2.**
introduction, prelude,
preface, prolegomena,
preparation. —**Ant.**
resulting, concluding;
conclusion, end, appendix,
epilogue. —**Syn. Study.**
PRELIMINARY, INTRODUCTORY
both refer to that which
comes before the principal
subject of consideration.
That which is PRELIMINARY
is in the nature of
preparation or of clearing
away details that would
encumber the main subject
or problem; it often deals
with arrangements and the
like that have to do only
incidentally with the
principal subject:
preliminary negotiations.
That which is
INTRODUCTORY leads with
natural, logical, or close

connection directly into the main subject of consideration: *introductory steps.*

premeditate, *v.* consider, plan, deliberate, precontrive, predetermine, prearrange, predesign.

premium, *n.* **1.** prize, door prize, bounty. **2.** bonus, gift, reward, recompense. —**Ant.** punishment. —**Syn. Study.** See BONUS.

preoccupied, *adj.* absorbed, engrossed, meditating, meditative, pondering, musing, concentrating, inattentive, in a brown study. —**Ant.** unthinking, thoughtless, frivolous.

prepare, *v.* **1.** contrive, devise, plan, plan for, anticipate, get *or* make ready, provide, arrange, order. **2.** manufacture, make, compound, fix, compose. —**Ant.** destroy, ruin.

preposterous, *adj.* absurd, senseless, foolish, inane, asinine, unreasonable, ridiculous, excessive, extravagant, irrational. —**Ant.** rational,

reasonable, sensible. —**Syn. Study.** See ABSURD.

prerogative, *n.* right, privilege, precedence, license, franchise, immunity, freedom, liberty. —**Syn. Study.** See PRIVILEGE.

presage, *n.* **1.** presentiment, foreboding, foreshadowing, indication, premonition, foreknowledge. **2.** portent, omen, sign, token, augury, warning, signal, prognostic. **3.** forecast, prediction. —*v.* **4.** portend, foreshadow, forecast, predict.

prescribe, *v.* lay down, predetermine, appoint, ordain, enjoin, direct, dictate, decree, establish, hand down, institute.

presence, *n.* **1.** attendance, company. **2.** nearness, vicinity, neighborhood, proximity, vicinage, closeness. **3.** personality; bearing, carriage, mien, aspect, impression, appearance. —**Ant.** absence.

present, *adj.* **1.** current,

existing, extant; here, at hand, near, nearby. —*n.* **2.** now. **3.** gift, donation, bonus, benefaction, largess, grant, gratuity, boon, tip. —*v.* **4.** give, endow, bestow, grant, confer, donate. **5.** afford, furnish, yield, offer, proffer. **6.** show, exhibit; introduce. **7.** represent, personate, act, enact, imitate, impersonate. **8.** point, level, aim, direct. —**Ant.** absent; then; receive. —**Syn. Study.** See GIVE. See also INTRODUCE.

presently, *adv.* anon, at once, immediately, directly, right away, without delay, shortly, forthwith, soon. —**Ant.** later. —**Syn. Study.** See IMMEDIATELY.

preserve, *v.* **1.** keep, conserve. **2.** guard, safeguard, shelter, shield, protect, defend, save. **3.** keep up, maintain, continue, uphold, sustain. **4.** retain, keep. —**Ant.** forgo; lose.

prestige, *n.* reputation, influence, weight, importance, distinction.

—**Ant.** disrepute, notoriety.

presume, *v.* **1.** assume, presuppose, suppose, take for granted, believe. **2.** venture, undertake.

presumptuous, *adj.* bold, impertinent, forward, arrogant, insolent, audacious, rude, fresh. —**Ant.** modest, polite. —**Syn. Study.** See BOLD.

pretend, *v.* **1.** feign, affect, put on, assume, falsify, simulate, fake, sham, counterfeit. **2.** allege, profess; lie. **3.** make believe. —**Syn. Study.** PRETEND, AFFECT, ASSUME, FEIGN imply an attempt to create a false appearance. To PRETEND is to create an imaginary characteristic or to play a part: *to pretend sorrow.* To AFFECT is to make a consciously artificial show of having qualities that one thinks would look well and impress others: *to affect shyness.* To ASSUME is to take on or put on a specific outward appearance, often with intent to deceive: *to* *assume an air of indifference.* To FEIGN implies using ingenuity in pretense, and some degree of imitation of appearance or characteristics: *to feign surprise.*

pretense, *n.* **1.** pretending, feigning, shamming, make-believe; subterfuge, fabrication, pretext, excuse. **2.** show, cover, cover-up, semblance, dissembling, mask, cloak, veil; pretension.

pretentious, *adj.* vain, vainglorious, affected, ostentatious, showy, la-di-da, posy, highfalutin, mannered, precious. —**Ant.** earthy, plain. —**Syn. Study.** See BOMBASTIC. See also GRANDIOSE.

preternatural, *adj.* abnormal, unusual, peculiar, odd, strange, extraordinary, irregular, unnatural, anomalous; supernatural. —**Ant.** usual, common, regular, natural. —**Syn. Study.** See MIRACULOUS.

pretty, *adj.* **1.** fair, attractive, comely, pleasing, beautiful. **2.** fine, pleasant, excellent, splendid. —*adv.* **3.** moderately, fairly, somewhat, to some extent. **4.** very, quite. —**Ant.** ugly; unpleasant; completely. —**Syn. Study.** See BEAUTIFUL.

prevail, *v.* **1.** predominate, preponderate. **2.** win, succeed. —**Ant.** lose.

prevailing, *adj.* **1.** prevalent, predominant, preponderating, dominant, preponderant. **2.** current, general, common. **3.** superior, influential, effectual, effective, efficacious, successful. —**Ant.** rare, uncommon; inferior, ineffectual, ineffective, unsuccessful.

prevalent, *adj.* widespread, current, common, prevailing, extensive, predominant, predominating, accepted, used, general. —**Ant.** rare, unusual, uncommon.

prevaricate, *v.* equivocate, quibble, cavil, shift; fib, lie.

prevent to pride

prevent, v. hinder, stop, obstruct, hamper, impede, forestall, thwart, intercept, preclude, obviate, interrupt. —**Ant.** encourage, aid, help, abet, support, continue. —**Syn. Study.** PREVENT, HAMPER, HINDER, IMPEDE refer to different degrees of stoppage of action or progress. To PREVENT is to stop something effectually by forestalling action and rendering it impossible: *to prevent the sending of a message.* To HAMPER is to clog or entangle or put an embarrassing restraint upon: *to hamper preparations for a trip.* To HINDER is to keep back by delaying or stopping progress or action: *to hinder the progress of an expedition.* To IMPEDE is to make difficult the movement or progress of anything by interfering with its proper functioning: *to impede a discussion by demanding repeated explanations.*

previous, adj. prior, earlier, former, preceding, foregoing. —**Ant.** later, following.

price, n. charge, cost, expense, outlay, expenditure.

pride, n. **1.** conceit, self-esteem, vanity, arrogance, vainglory, self-importance. **2.** insolence, haughtiness, snobbishness, superciliousness, hauteur, presumption. —**Ant.** modesty; humility. —**Syn. Study.** PRIDE, CONCEIT, EGOTISM, VANITY imply a favorable view of one's own appearance, advantages, achievements, etc., and often apply to offensive characteristics. PRIDE is a lofty and often arrogant assumption of superiority in some respect: *Pride must have a fall.* CONCEIT implies an exaggerated estimate of one's own abilities or attainments, together with pride: *blinded by conceit.* EGOTISM implies an excessive preoccupation with oneself or with one's own concerns, usu. but not always accompanied by pride or conceit: *Her egotism blinded her to others' difficulties.* VANITY implies self-admiration and an excessive desire to be admired by others: *His vanity was easily flattered.*

prim, *adj.* stiff, starched, formal, straitlaced, precise, proper, puritanical, rigid, blue, priggish; prunes and prisms. —**Ant.** flexible, informal; lewd, licentious, profligate.

primary, *adj.* **1.** first, highest, chief, principal, main. **2.** first, earliest, primitive, original, primeval, aboriginal. **3.** elementary, beginning, opening, fundamental, basic, ordinate. **4.** direct, immediate. —**Ant.** last, final, ultimate; secondary; indirect.

prime, *adj.* primary. —**Ant.** last.

primeval, *adj.* prime, primary, primordial, primitive, original, primigenial, pristine.

primitive, *adj.* **1.** prehistoric, primal, primeval, prime, primary, primordial, original, aboriginal, pristine, prehistoric, first, antediluvian. **2.** uncivilized, uncultured, simple, unsophisticated, quaint. —**Ant.** secondary; civilized, sophisticated, cultured.

principal, *adj.* **1.** first, highest, prime, paramount, capital, chief, foremost, main, leading, cardinal, preeminent. —*n.* **2.** chief, head, leader, chieftain. **3.** headmaster, dean, master. —**Ant.** ancillary, secondary. —**Syn. Study.** See CAPITAL.

principally, *adv.* especially, chiefly, mainly, primarily, firstly, particularly. —**Ant.** lastly.

principle, *n.* **1.** canon, rule, standard, test, parameter. **2.** theorem, axiom, postulate, maxim, law, proposition. **3.** doctrine, tenet, belief, opinion. **4.** integrity, honesty, probity, righteousness, uprightness, rectitude, virtue, incorruptibility, goodness, trustworthiness, honor.

private, *adj.* **1.** individual, personal, singular, especial, special, particular, peculiar. **2.** confidential, secret, top secret, "eyes only." **3.** alone, secluded, cloistered, sequestered, solitary, retired. —**Ant.** public, general; known; open.

privation, *n.* hardship, deprivation, loss; destitution, want, need, necessity, distress, lack. —**Ant.** ease, wealth.

privilege, *n.* right, immunity, leave, prerogative, advantage, license, freedom, liberty, permission, franchise. —**Syn. Study.** PRIVILEGE, PREROGATIVE refer to a special advantage or right possessed by an individual or group. A PRIVILEGE is a right or advantage gained by birth, social position, effort, or concession. It can have either legal or personal sanction: *the privilege of paying half fare; the privilege of calling whenever one wishes.* PREROGATIVE refers to an exclusive right claimed and granted, often officially or legally, on the basis of social status, heritage, sex, etc.: *the prerogatives of a king; the prerogatives of management.*

prize, *n.* **1.** reward, premium. —*v.* **2.** value, esteem, appraise. —**Syn. Study.** See APPRECIATE.

probe, *v.* examine, explore, question, investigate, scrutinize, search, sift, prove, test. —**Ant.** overlook, ignore.

probity, *n.* honesty, uprightness, rectitude, integrity. —**Ant.** dishonesty.

problem, *n.* question, doubt, uncertainty, puzzle, riddle, enigma. —**Ant.** certainty, certitude, surety.

procedure, *n.* **1.** proceeding, conduct, management, operation, course, process. **2.** act, deed, transaction, maneuver, goings-on.

proceed, *v.* **1.** advance, go on, progress, move on, continue, pass on. **2.** go *or* come forth, issue, emanate, spring, arise,

result, ensue, originate.
—**Ant.** retreat.

process, *n.* course, procedure, operation, proceeding.

proclaim, *v.* announce, declare, advertise, promulgate, publish.
—**Syn. Study.** See ANNOUNCE.

proclivity, *n.* inclination, tendency, bent, leaning, propensity, predisposition, disposition, proneness, favor, bias, prejudice.
—**Ant.** dislike, aversion.

procrastinate, *v.* delay, postpone, put off, defer, adjourn, prolong. —**Ant.** speed, expedite.

procure, *v.* **1.** acquire, gain, get, secure, win, obtain. **2.** bring about, effect, cause, contrive. **3.** pander, bawd, pimp. —**Ant.** lose.
—**Syn. Study.** See GET.

prod, *v.* poke, jab; goad, rouse, incite.

prodigal, *adj.* **1.** reckless, profligate, extravagant, lavish, wasteful, profuse. **2.** abundant, profuse, plenteous, copious, plentiful, bounteous,

bountiful. —*n.* **3.** spendthrift, waster, wastrel, squanderer, carouser, playboy. —**Ant.** cautious, provident, thrifty; scarce, scanty.
—**Syn. Study.** See LAVISH.

prodigious, *adj.* **1.** enormous, immense, huge, gigantic, tremendous, monstrous. **2.** wonderful, marvelous, amazing, stupendous, astonishing, astounding, extraordinary, miraculous, wondrous, uncommon, unusual, strange. **3.** abnormal, monstrous, anomalous.
—**Ant.** small, tiny, infinitesimal; negligible, common; normal, usual.

produce, *v.* **1.** give rise to, cause, generate, occasion, originate, create, effect, make, manufacture, bring about. **2.** bear, bring forth, yield, furnish, supply, afford, give. **3.** exhibit, show, demonstrate, bring forward. —*n.* **4.** yield, product, crops, fruits, production. —**Ant.** destroy, ruin; subdue, squelch; hide, conceal.

productive, *adj.* generative, creative; prolific, fertile, fruitful. —**Ant.** barren, sterile, unproductive. —**Syn. Study.** PRODUCTIVE, FERTILE, FRUITFUL, PROLIFIC apply to the generative aspect of something. PRODUCTIVE refers to a generative source of continuing activity: *productive soil; a productive influence.* FERTILE applies to that in which seeds, literal or figurative, take root: *fertile soil; a fertile imagination.* FRUITFUL refers to that which has already produced and is capable of further production: *fruitful species; fruitful discussions.* PROLIFIC means highly productive: *a prolific farm; a prolific writer.*

profane, *adj.* **1.** irreverent, irreligious, blasphemous, sacrilegious, piacular, wicked, impious, ungodly, godless, unredeemed, unredeemable. **2.** unconsecrated, secular, temporal. **3.** unholy, heathen, pagan, unhallowed, impure,
polluted. **4.** common, low, mean, base, vulgar. —*v.* **5.** debase, misuse, defile, desecrate, violate, pollute. —**Ant.** sacred, repentant; spiritual; pure, hallowed, holy; elevated, exalted.

profession, *n.* **1.** vocation, calling, occupation, business, employment. **2.** professing, avowal, declaration, asseveration, assertion.

proffer, *v.* offer, tender, volunteer, propose, suggest, hint. —**Ant.** refuse. —**Syn. Study.** See OFFER.

proficient, *adj.* skilled, adept, skillful, competent, practiced, experienced, qualified, trained, conversant, accomplished, finished, able, apt. —**Ant.** unskilled, maladroit, awkward, clumsy, untrained, unable, inept.

profit, *n.* **1.** gain, return. **2.** returns, proceeds, revenue, dividend. **3.** advantage, benefit, gain, good, welfare, improvement, advancement. —*v.* **4.** gain, improve, advance, better.

—**Ant.** loss; lose. —**Syn. Study.** See ADVANTAGE.

profound, *adj.* deep, intense, extreme, penetrating, sagacious; abstruse. —**Ant.** shallow, superficial.

profuse, *adj.* extravagant, abundant, lavish, prodigal, wasteful, profligate, improvident. —**Ant.** scarce, scanty, thrifty. —**Syn. Study.** See LAVISH.

profusion, *n.* abundance, plenty, copiousness, bounty, prodigality, profligacy, excess, waste. —**Ant.** scarcity, need, want; penury, niggardliness.

progress, *n.* **1.** proceeding, advancement, advance, progression. **2.** growth, development, improvement, increase, betterment. —*v.* **3.** advance, proceed; develop, improve, grow, increase. —**Ant.** retrogression; recession; recede, decrease, diminish.

prohibit, *v.* **1.** forbid, interdict, disallow. **2.** prevent, hinder, preclude, obstruct. —**Ant.** allow, permit; encourage, foster, further.

prohibition, *n.* interdiction, prevention, embargo, ban, restriction. —**Ant.** permission.

project, *n.* **1.** plan, scheme, design, proposal. **2.** activity, lesson, homework. —*v.* **3.** propose, contemplate, plan, contrive, scheme, plot, devise, concoct, brew, frame. **4.** throw, cast, toss. **5.** extend, protrude, obtrude, bulge, jut out, stick out.

prolific, *adj.* **1.** fruitful, fertile, productive, teeming. **2.** abundant. —**Ant.** fruitless, unfruitful, barren, sterile; scarce. —**Syn. Study.** See PRODUCTIVE.

prolix, See Syn. study at WORDY.

prolong, *v.* lengthen, extend, protract. —**Ant.** abbreviate, shorten, curtail. —**Syn. Study.** See LENGTHEN.

prominent, *adj.* **1.** conspicuous, noticeable,

outstanding, manifest, principal, chief, important, main. **2.** projecting, jutting out, protuberant, embossed. **3.** important, leading, well-known, eminent, celebrated, famed, famous, distinguished. **—Ant.** inconspicuous, unimportant; recessed; negligible, unknown.

promiscuous, *adj.* **1.** miscellaneous, hodgepodge, hotchpotch, indiscriminate, confused, mixed, intermixed, intermingled, mingled, jumbled, garbled. **2.** nonselective, indiscriminate, careless. **—Ant.** special, discriminate, pure, unmixed; selective, careful, select.

promise, *n.* **1.** word, pledge, assurance. **—v. 2.** pledge, covenant, agree, engage.

promote, *v.* **1.** further, advance, encourage, forward, assist, aid, help, support. **2.** elevate, raise, exalt. **—Ant.** discourage, obstruct; lower, debase.

prone, *adj.* **1.** inclined, disposed, liable, tending, bent. **2.** prostrate, recumbent. **—Ant.** averse; upright.

proof, *n.* **1.** evidence, testimony, certification, confirmation, demonstration. **2.** test, trial, examination, essay. **3.** impression. *—adj.* **4.** impenetrable, impervious, invulnerable, steadfast, firm.

propensity, *n.* inclination, bent, leaning, tendency, disposition, bias. **—Ant.** disinclination, aversion, distaste.

proper, *adj.* **1.** appropriate, fit, suitable, suited, adapted, convenient, fitting, befitting, correct, right, becoming, meet. **2.** correct, decorous, decent, respectable, polite, well-mannered. **3.** special, specific, individual, peculiar. **4.** strict, accurate, precise, exact, just, formal, correct. **—Ant.** improper.

property, *n.* **1.** possession, possessions, goods, effects, chattels, estate, belongings. **2.** land, real estate, acreage. **3.** ownership, right. **4.** attribute, quality, characteristic, feature. —**Syn. Study.** PROPERTY, CHATTELS, EFFECTS, ESTATE, GOODS refer to what is owned. PROPERTY is the general word: *She owns a great deal of property. He said that the umbrella was his property.* CHATTELS is a term for pieces of personal property or movable possessions; it may be applied to livestock, automobiles, etc.: *a mortgage on chattels.* EFFECTS is a term for any form of personal property, including even things of the least value: *All my effects were insured against fire.* ESTATE refers to property of any kind that has been, or is capable of being, handed down to descendants or otherwise disposed of in a will: *He left most of his estate to his niece.* It may consist of personal estate (money, valuables, securities, chattels, etc.) or real estate (land and buildings). GOODS refers to household possessions or other movable property, esp. the stock in trade of a business: *The store arranged its goods on shelves.* See also QUALITY.

prophesy, *v.* foretell, predict, augur, prognosticate, divine. —**Syn. Study.** See PREDICT.

propitiate, *v.* appease, conciliate, pacify. —**Ant.** anger, arouse. —**Syn. Study.** See APPEASE.

proportion, *n.* **1.** relation, arrangement; comparison, analogy. **2.** size, extent, dimensions. **3.** portion, part, piece, share. **4.** symmetry, harmony, agreement, balance, distribution, arrangement. —*v.* **5.** adjust, regulate, redistribute, arrange, balance, harmonize. —**Ant.** disproportion. —**Syn. Study.** See SYMMETRY.

proposal, *n.* plan, scheme, offer, recommendation, suggestion, design, overture, approach, proposition.

propose, *v.* **1.** offer, proffer, tender, suggest, recommend, present. **2.** nominate, name. **3.** plan, intend, design, mean, purpose. **4.** state, present, propound, pose, posit. —**Ant.** refuse.

proposition, *n.* proposal.

propriety, *n.* **1.** decorum, etiquette, protocol, good behavior, decency, modesty. **2.** suitability, appropriateness, aptness, fitness, suitableness, seemliness. **3.** rightness, justness, correctness, accuracy. —**Ant.** impropriety, immodesty, indecency; unseemliness, ineptitude; inaccuracy.

prosaic, *adj.* prosy, commonplace, dull, matter-of-fact, unimaginative, vapid, humdrum, tedious, tiresome, wearisome, uninteresting. —**Ant.** interesting, fascinating, beguiling.

prospect, *n.* **1.** anticipation, expectation, expectance, contemplation. **2.** view, scene, outlook, survey, vista, perspective. —*v.* **3.** search, explore. —**Syn. Study.** See VIEW.

prosper, *v.* succeed, thrive, flourish. —**Ant.** fail, die. —**Syn. Study.** See SUCCEED.

prosperous, *adj.* **1.** fortunate, successful, flourishing, thriving. **2.** wealthy, rich, well-to-do, well-off. **3.** favorable, propitious, fortunate, lucky, auspicious, golden, bright. —**Ant.** unfortunate, unsuccessful; poor, impoverished; unfavorable.

prostitute, *n.* **1.** harlot, whore, strumpet, call girl, trollop, quean, street walker, courtesan. —*v.* **2.** misapply, misuse, abuse.

protect, *v.* defend, guard, shield, cover, screen, shelter, save, harbor, house, secure. —**Ant.** attack, assail.

protection, *n.* **1.** preservation, guard, defense, shelter, screen, cover, security, refuge, safety. **2.** shield, aegis, bulwark. **3.** treaty, safe-conduct, passport, visa, pass, permit. **4.** aegis, patronage, sponsorship. **—Ant.** attack.

protest, *n.* **1.** objection, disapproval, protestation. **—v. 2.** remonstrate, complain, object. **3.** declare, affirm, assert, asseverate, avow, aver, testify, attest. **—Ant.** approval; approve.

prototype, *n.* model, pattern, example, exemplar, original, archetype.

protract, *v.* draw out, lengthen, extend, prolong, continue. **—Ant.** curtail, abbreviate, discontinue. **—Syn. Study.** See LENGTHEN.

proud, *adj.* **1.** contented, self-satisfied, egotistical, vain, conceited. **2.** arrogant, overweening, haughty, overbearing, self-important, overconfident, disdainful, supercilious, snooty, imperious, presumptuous. **3.** honorable, creditable. **4.** stately, majestic, magnificent, noble, imposing, splendid. **—Ant.** discontented, dissatisfied; humble, self-effacing; dishonorable; ignoble, base.

prove, *v.* **1.** demonstrate, show, confirm, manifest, establish, evince, evidence, substantiate, verify, justify, ascertain, determine. **2.** try, test, examine, assay. **—Ant.** disprove.

provender, See Syn. study at FEED.

proverb, *n.* maxim, saying, adage, epigram, precept, truth, saw, aphorism, by-word, apothegm. **—Syn. Study.** PROVERB, MAXIM are terms for short, pithy sayings. A PROVERB is such a saying popularly known and repeated, usu. expressing simply and concretely, though often metaphorically, a truth based on common sense or practical human experience: *"A stitch in time saves nine."* A MAXIM is a brief statement of a general and practical truth, esp. one that serves as a rule of conduct: *"It is* *wise to risk no more than one can afford to lose."*

provide, *v.* **1.** furnish, supply, afford, yield, produce, contribute, give. **2.** prepare, get ready, procure, provide for, make provision for. —**Ant.** deprive.

provided, *conj.* on the condition *or* supposition that, if, in case, granted. —**Ant.** lest.

provision, *n.* **1.** stipulation, condition, if, proviso. **2.** catering, purveying, supplying. **3.** (*plural*) food, supplies, stores, provender, stock.

provoke, *v.* **1.** anger, enrage, exasperate, irk, vex, irritate, incense, annoy, chafe, aggravate, exacerbate, infuriate, ire, nettle, affront. **2.** stir up, arouse, call forth, incite, stimulate, excite, fire, rouse, inflame, animate, inspirit, instigate. **3.** give rise to, induce, bring about. —**Ant.** assuage, calm, propitiate. —**Syn. Study.** See INCITE.

prowl, *v.* lurk, rove, roam, wander; prey, plunder, pillage, steal. —**Syn. Study.** See LURK.

prudence, *n.* **1.** calculation, foresight, forethought, judgment, discretion, common sense, circumspection, caution, wisdom. **2.** providence, care, economy, frugality, carefulness. —**Ant.** carelessness, imprudence, incaution.

prudent, *adj.* **1.** wise, judicious, cautious, discreet, tactful, sensible, sagacious, circumspect, careful, wary, provident. **2.** provident, frugal, sparing, economical, thrifty, saving, careful. —**Ant.** imprudent, indiscreet, tactless, careless; improvident, prodigal.

prudish, *adj.* modest, proper, demure, pure, coy, reserved. —**Ant.** immodest, indecent. —**Syn. Study.** See MODEST.

prying, *adj.* curious, inquisitive, peeping, peering, peeking; nosy.

—**Ant.** blasé, unconcerned, uninterested.

pseudo, *adj.* sham, counterfeit, false, spurious, pretended, fake. —**Ant.** genuine, real.

publish, *v.* **1.** issue, distribute. **2.** announce, proclaim, promulgate, declare, disclose, divulge, reveal, impart, advertise, publicize. —**Ant.** conceal, hide. —**Syn. Study.** See ANNOUNCE.

puerile, *adj.* **1.** boyish, juvenile, childish, youthful. **2.** childish, immature, foolish, irrational, trivial, nugatory, silly, ridiculous, idle. —**Ant.** manly; mature, rational.

pulsate, *v.* beat, palpitate, pulse, throb; vibrate, quiver.

punctilious, *adj.* strict, exact, precise, demanding, scrupulous, nice, careful, conscientious. —**Ant.** inexact, careless. —**Syn. Study.** See SCRUPULOUS.

pungent, *adj.* **1.** biting, acrid, hot, peppery, piquant, sharp. **2.** poignant, distressing, painful. **3.** caustic, biting, sarcastic, sardonic, mordant, penetrating, piercing, trenchant, cutting, severe, acrimonious, bitter, waspish. **4.** stimulating, acute, keen, sharp. —**Ant.** mild, bland; painless; dull.

punish, *v.* **1.** correct, discipline, penalize, reprove. **2.** castigate, scold, berate, chastise, chasten, flog, whip, lash, scourge. —**Ant.** praise, laud; forgive.

pupil, *v.* disciple, scholar, student, learner, tyro, greenhorn, neophyte, novice, beginner. —**Ant.** teacher, expert.

purblind, *adj.* blind, sightless, dim-sighted, myopic, short-sighted, nearsighted. —**Ant.** sighted, clear-sighted, presbyopic.

purchase, *v.* **1.** buy, acquire, get, obtain, procure. **2.** haul, draw, raise. —*n.* **3.** buying, acquisition. **4.** bargain. **5.** tackle, lever, winch, capstan. —**Ant.** sell, lose; lower; sale.

pure, *adj.* **1.** unmixed, unadulterated, uncontaminated, unalloyed, clean, unsullied, untainted, unstained, undefiled, spotless, untarnished, immaculate, unpolluted, uncorrupted. **2.** unmodified, simple, homogeneous, genuine, faultless, perfect. **3.** thoroughbred, purebred, pedigreed. **4.** utter, sheer, unqualified, absolute. **5.** innocent, chaste, undefiled, unsullied, modest, virtuous. **6.** guiltless, innocent, true, guileless, honest, upright. —**Ant.** impure.

purge, *v.* purify, cleanse, clear, clean, clarify. —**Ant.** pollute.

purport, *v.* **1.** profess, claim, mean, intend, signify. **2.** express, imply. —*n.* **3.** tenor, import, meaning, intention, claim, design, significance, signification, implication, drift, suggestion, gist,

spirit. —**Ant.** understand, see; infer; insignificance, meaninglessness. —**Syn. Study.** See MEANING.

purpose, *n.* **1.** object, intent, intention, determination, aim, end, design, view. **2.** result, effect, advantage, consequence. —*v.* **3.** propose, design, intend, mean, contemplate, plan. —**Ant.** purposelessness.

push, *v.* **1.** shove, shoulder, thrust, drive, move, slide. **2.** press, urge, persuade, drive, impel. —*n.* **3.** attack, effort, onset.

put, *v.* **1.** place, lay, set, deposit. **2.** set, levy, impose, inflict. **3.** render, translate. **4.** express, state, utter.

puzzle, *n.* **1.** riddle, enigma, problem, poser, maze, question. —*v.* **2.** bewilder, perplex, confound, mystify, confuse.

pygmy, *n.* dwarf, midget, Lilliputian, runt. —**Ant.** giant, colossus. —**Syn. Study.** See DWARF.

Q

quagmire, *n.* **1.** swamp, marsh, fen, bog, mire, morass, slough. **2.** predicament, difficulty, dilemma, pickle, tight spot, fix, jam, corner, box.

quail, See Syn. study at WINCE.

quaint, *adj.* **1.** strange, odd, curious, unusual, extraordinary, unique, uncommon. **2.** picturesque, charming, old-fashioned, antiquated, antique, archaic. **—Ant.** common, usual, ordinary; modern, new-fangled.

quake, *v.* **1.** shake, shudder, tremble, shiver, quaver, quiver. *—n.* **2.** temblor, earthquake.

qualify, *v.* **1.** fit, suit, adapt, prepare, equip. **2.** characterize, call, name, designate, label, signify. **3.** modify, limit, mitigate, restrain, narrow, restrict. **4.** moderate, mitigate, meliorate, soften, mollify, soothe, ease, assuage, temper, reduce, diminish.

quality, *n.* **1.** characteristic, attribute, property, character, feature, trait. **2.** nature, grade, kind, sort, description, status, rank, condition. **3.** excellence, superiority, standing. **4.** accomplishment, deed, feat, attainment. **5.** distinction, class. **—Ant.** inferiority, baseness; failure. **—Syn. Study.** QUALITY, ATTRIBUTE, PROPERTY refer to a distinguishing feature or characteristic of a person, thing, or group. A QUALITY is an innate or acquired characteristic that, in some particular, determines the nature and behavior of a person or thing: *the qualities of patience and perseverance.* An ATTRIBUTE is a quality that we assign or ascribe to a person or to something personified; it may also mean a fundamental or innate characteristic: *an attribute of God; attributes of a logical mind.* PROPERTY is applied only to a thing; it refers to a principal characteristic that is part of the constitution of a thing and serves to define or describe it: *the physical properties of limestone.*

qualm, *n.* uneasiness, compunction, scruple, twinge, remorse, misgiving. —**Ant.** ease, confort, security.

quandary, *n.* dilemma, predicament, strait, uncertainty, doubt. —**Ant.** certainty, assurance. —**Syn. Study.** See PREDICAMENT.

quarrel, *n.* **1.** dispute, altercation, disagreement, argument, contention, controversy, dissension, feud, breach, break, rupture, difference, spat, tiff, fight, misunderstanding, wrangle, brawl, tumult. —*v.* **2.** squabble, fall out, disagree with, differ, disagree, bicker, dispute, argue, wrangle, spar, brawl,

clash, jar, fight. —**Syn. Study.** QUARREL, DISSENSION refer to disagreement and conflict. QUARREL applies chiefly to a verbal disagreement between individuals or groups and is used with reference to a large variety of situations, from a slight and petty difference of opinion to a violent altercation: *It was little more than a domestic quarrel. Their quarrel led to an actual fight.* DISSENSION usu. implies a profound disagreement and bitter conflict. It also applies chiefly to conflict within a group or between members of the same group: *dissension within the union; dissension among the Democrats.*

quarrelsome, *adj.* argumentative, disputatious, cantankerous, combative, belligerent, bellicose, truculent, pugnacious, antagonistic. —**Ant.** peaceable, amicable.

queasy, *adj.* **1.** squeamish, fastidious, overfastidious, delicate, finicky, finical, picky, particular. **2.** nauseated, nauseous, qualmish, sickish, seasick, airsick, carsick, queer, queerish, puky, barfy.

queer, *adj.* strange, unconventional, odd, singular, curious, fantastic, uncommon, weird, peculiar, extraordinary, eccentric, freakish. **—Ant.** conventional, ordinary, common.

quell, *v.* **1.** suppress, stifle, extinguish, put an end to, crush, quash, subdue, overpower, overcome. **2.** vanquish, put down, defeat, conquer. **3.** quiet, allay, calm, pacify, compose, lull, hush. **—Ant.** encourage, foster; defend, lose; agitate, disturb, perturb.

querulous, *adj.* complaining, petulant, peevish, snappish, abrupt, waspish, testy; caviling, carping, discontented, fault-finding. **—Ant.** calm, equable; pleased, contented.

question, *n.* **1.** inquiry, query, interrogation. **2.** dispute, controversy. **—***v.* **3.** interrogate; ask, inquire, query, examine. **4.** doubt. **5.** dispute, challenge. **—Ant.** answer, reply; agree, concur.

questionable, *adj.* doubtful, uncertain, dubitable, dubious, debatable, disputable, controvertible. **—Ant.** certain, sure, positive.

quibble, *n.* **1.** evasion, prevarication, equivocation, sophism, shift, subterfuge, cavil. **—***v.* **2.** evade, prevaricate, equivocate, cavil, shuffle, trifle.

quick, *adj.* **1.** prompt, immediate, rapid, fast, swift, speedy, instantaneous, fleet, hasty, hurried, expeditious. **2.** impatient, hasty, abrupt, curt, short, precipitate, sharp, unceremonious; testy, waspish, snappish, irritable, peppery, irascible, petulant, touchy. **3.** lively, keen, acute, sensitive, alert, sharp, shrewd, intelligent, discerning. **4.** vigorous, energetic, active, nimble, animated, agile, lively, alert, brisk. **—Ant.** slow; patient, deliberate; calm; dull, stupid; lethargic, lazy. **—Syn. Study.** QUICK, FAST, SWIFT, RAPID describe a speedy rate of motion or progress. QUICK applies particularly to an action or reaction that is almost instantaneous, or of brief duration: *to take a quick look around.* FAST refers to a person or thing that acts or moves speedily; when used of communication or transportation, it suggests a definite goal and continuous movement: *a fast swimmer; a fast train.* SWIFT, a more formal word, suggests great speed as well as graceful movement: *The panther is a swift animal.* RAPID applies to one or a series of actions or movements; it stresses the rate of speed: *to perform rapid calculations.* See also SHARP.

quiet, *n.* **1.** tranquillity, rest, repose, calm, stillness, quietude, serenity, peace, calmness, silence. **2.** peace.

—adj. **3.** peaceable, peaceful, pacific, calm, tranquil, serene, silent. **4.** motionless, still, unmoving, unmoved. **5.** inconspicuous, subdued; repressed, unstrained, unobtrusive. *—v.* **6.** still, hush, silence. **7.** tranquilize, pacify, calm, compose, lull, soothe. **—Ant.** disturbance, perturbation; war; warlike, noisy, clamorous; conspicuous, obvious, blatant; disturb, perturb.

quip, *v.* **1.** joke, banter, jest, gibe, wisecrack, josh, crack wise. *—n.* **2.** witticism, joke, jape, gibe, wisecrack, gag, bon mot, sally.

quirk, See Syn. study at ECCENTRICITY.

quit, *v.* **1.** stop, cease, discontinue, desist. **2.** depart from, leave, go, withdraw *or* retire from. **3.** give up, let go, relinquish, release, resign, surrender. *—adj.* **4.** released, free, clear, liberated, rid, absolved, acquitted, discharged. **—Ant.** start; initiate, originate; continue; arrive, enter; chained, confined.

quiver, *v.* **1.** shake, tremble, vibrate, quake, shudder, shiver. —*n.* **2.** tremble, tremor, shudder, shiver, trembling, shake. **3.** arrow-case.

quixotic, *adj.* visionary, impracticable, romantic, imaginary, wild. —**Ant.** realistic, practicable, practical.

quizzical, *adj.* **1.** questioning, curious, inquisitive, inquiring, interrogatory. **2.** skeptical, suspicious, dubious, doubting, wary, distrustful, incredulous, unbelieving.

R

rabid, *adj.* **1.** overwrought, frantic, frenzied, frenetic, furious, raging, wild, mad, maniacal. **2.** extreme, extremist, radical, fanatic, fanatical, fervent, perfervid, overzealous, irrational, wild-eyed, over-the-top. —**Ant.** calm, composed, reasonable.

race, *n.* **1.** competition, contest. **2.** course, stream. **3.** nation, people, clan, family, tribe, generation, stock, line, lineage, breed, kin, kindred, progeny, descendants, offspring, children. **4.** man, mankind. —*v.* **5.** run, speed, hurry, hasten, hie.

rack, *n.* **1.** frame, framework, crib. **2.** torment, anguish, torture, pain, agony. —*v.* **3.** torture, distress, torment, agonize, excruciate. **4.** strain, force, wrest, stretch.

racket, *n.* **1.** din, uproar, noise, clamor, fuss, tumult, hubbub, outcry, disturbance. **2.** excitement, gaiety, dissipation. —**Ant.** quiet, tranquillity, peace. —**Syn. Study.** See NOISE.

racy, *adj.* **1.** vigorous, lively, animated, spirited. **2.** sprightly, piquant,

pungent, strong, flavorful.
3. suggestive, risqué.
—**Ant.** dispirited, dejected;
mild, bland.

radiant, *adj.* shining,
bright, brilliant, beaming,
effulgent, resplendent,
sparkling, splendid,
glittering. —**Ant.** dull.

radiate, *v.* **1.** shine, beam,
glow, gleam, burn,
luminesce, incandesce,
twinkle, glimmer, sparkle,
flash, glare, dazzle. **2.**
diffuse, disperse, emit,
spread, propagate, scatter,
emanate, throw off, give
off.

radical, *adj.* **1.**
fundamental, basic,
original, constitutional,
essential, innate, ingrained.
2. thoroughgoing, extreme,
complete, unqualified,
thorough, fanatical,
excessive, immoderate,
extravagant, violent. —*n.*
3. extremist. —**Ant.**
superfluous; incomplete,
moderate.

radioactive, *adj.* hot, dirty.
—**Ant.** clean.

rage, *n.* **1.** anger, ire, fury,
frenzy, passion,
vehemence, wrath,
madness, raving. **2.** fury,
violence, turbulence,
tumultuousness, storm. **3.**
ardor, fervor, enthusiasm,
eagerness, desire,
vehemence. **4.** mode,
fashion, fad, craze, vogue.
—*v.* **5.** rave, fume, storm,
chafe, fret. —**Ant.** calm,
equanimity. —**Syn. Study.**
See ANGER.

ragged, *adj.* **1.** tattered,
torn, shredded, rent. **2.**
shabby, poor, mean.
—**Ant.** neat, whole.

raid, *n.* **1.** onset, attack,
seizure. **2.** invasion,
inroad, incursion. —**Ant.**
defense.

raillery, *n.* banter, kidding,
kidding around, teasing,
joshing, ribbing, ragging,
twitting, fooling around,
badinage, persiflage,
give-and-take,
back-and-forth.

raiment, *n.* clothes,
clothing, garments,
apparel, attire, dress,
habiliment, things,
costume, habit, togs,
toggery, gear, duds, getup,
threads.

raise, *v.* **1.** lift, lift up, elevate, heave, hoist, loft. **2.** rouse, arouse, awake, awaken, call forth, evoke, stir up, excite. **3.** build, erect, construct, rear, set up. **4.** cause, promote, cultivate, grow, propagate. **5.** originate, engender, give rise to, bring up *or* about, produce, effect, cause. **6.** invigorate, animate, inspirit, heighten, intensify. **7.** advance, elevate, promote, exalt. **8.** gather, collect, assemble, bring together. **9.** increase, intensify, heighten, aggravate, amplify, augment, enhance, enlarge. —*n.* **10.** increase, rise. —**Ant.** lower; pacify; destroy, raze; kill; weaken, dispirit; debase, dishonor; scatter, disperse, broadcast; decrease.

ramble, *v.* **1.** stroll, amble, walk, wander, saunter, stray, roam, rove, range, straggle. —*n.* **2.** walk, stroll, amble, excursion, tour.

rambling, *adj.* wandering, aimless, irregular, straggling, straying,

discursive. —**Ant.** direct, pointed.

rambunctious, *adj.* boisterous, high-spirited, exuberant, roisterous, rollicking, unrestrained, uninhibited, irrepressible, untamed, knockabout, uproarious, wild, rowdy. —**Ant.** docile.

rampage, *n.* **1.** spree, tear, binge, outburst, orgy, riot, furor, furore, convulsion. —*v.* **2.** rage, storm, rave, rant, tear, tear around, riot.

rampart, *n.* fortification, breastwork, bulwark, barricade, stronghold, security, guard, defense.

ramshackle, *adj.* shaky, rickety, flimsy, dilapidated. —**Ant.** luxurious, sumptuous.

rancor, *n.* resentment, bitterness, ill will, hatred, malice, spite, venom, malevolence, animosity, enmity. —**Ant.** amiability, good will, benevolence.

random, *adj.* haphazard, chance, fortuitous, casual, stray, aimless. —**Ant.** specific, particular.

range, *n.* **1.** extent, limits, scope, sweep, latitude, reach, compass. **2.** rank, class, order, kind, sort. **3.** row, line, series, tier, file. **4.** area, trace, region. —*v.* **5.** align, rank, classify, class, order, arrange, array, dispose. **6.** vary, course. **7.** extend, stretch out, run, go, lie. **8.** roam, rove, wander, stroll, straggle. **9.** extend, be found, occupy, lie, run. —**Syn. Study.** RANGE, COMPASS, LATITUDE, SCOPE refer to extent or breadth. RANGE emphasizes extent and diversity: *the range of one's interests.* COMPASS suggests definite limits: *within the compass of one's mind.* LATITUDE emphasizes the idea of freedom from narrow confines, thus breadth or extent: *granted latitude of action.* SCOPE suggests great freedom but a proper limit: *the scope of one's obligations.*

rank, *n.* **1.** position, standing, station, order, class, level, division. **2.** row, line, tier, series, range. **3.** distinction, eminence, dignity. **4.** membership, body, rank and file. **5.** order, arrangement, array, alignment. —*v.* **6.** arrange, line up, align, array, range. **7.** classify, dispose, sort, class, arrange. —*adj.* **8.** tall, vigorous, luxuriant, abundant, over-abundant, exuberant. **9.** strong, gamy, pungent, offensive, noxious, fetid, rancid, putrid. **10.** utter, absolute, complete, entire, sheer, gross, extravagant, excessive. **11.** offensive, disgusting, repulsive, repellent, miasmatic, mephitic. **12.** coarse, indecent, foul, gross.

rankle, *v.* irritate, annoy, vex, distress, plague, nettle, fester, gall, inflame, incense, embitter, rile, aggravate. —**Ant.** placate, please.

ransom, *n.* **1.** redemption, deliverance, liberation, release. —*v.* **2.** redeem, release, restore, deliver, deliver up.

rapacious, *adj.* greedy, predatory, extortionate, ravenous, voracious,

avaricious, grasping;
predacious, raptorial,
preying. —**Ant.** generous,
yielding; parasitic.

rapid, *adj.* speedy, fast,
quick, swift, fleet. —**Ant.**
slow. —**Syn. Study.** See
QUICK.

rapidity, *n.* swiftness, speed,
fleetness, quickness, haste,
velocity, alacrity, celerity.
—**Ant.** sloth, lethargy.

rapport, *n.* relationship,
interrelationship, affinity,
attraction, sympathy,
empathy, closeness,
understanding,
like-mindedness, accord,
concord, harmony,
compatibility, goodwill,
fellow feeling, fellowship,
kinship, oneness, unity.
—**Ant.** enmity,
discordance.

rapt, *adj.* **1.** engrossed,
preoccupied, occupied,
absorbed, abstracted,
thoughtful, bemused,
faraway, single-minded,
concentrated, fixed,
fixated. **2.** enraptured,
rapturous, transported,
ecstatic, transfigured,
enthralled, fascinated,

enchanted, gripped, held,
riveted. —**Ant.** distracted,
distrait.

rapture, *n.* ecstasy, joy,
delight, transport, bliss,
beatitude, exultation.
—**Ant.** misery, disgust,
revulsion. —**Syn. Study.**
See ECSTASY.

rare, *adj.* **1.** scarce,
uncommon, exceptional,
unusual, sparse,
infrequent, extraordinary,
singular. **2.** excellent,
admirable, fine, choice,
exquisite, incomparable,
inimitable. **3.** underdone.
—**Ant.** common, usual,
frequent, ordinary; base,
inferior; medium, well
done.

rarefied, *adj.* **1.** thin,
attenuated, tenuous,
ethereal, vaporous,
insubstantial, airy,
gaseous, diffuse, diluted,
dilute, adulterated, weak,
watered-down, porous. **2.**
refined, esoteric, special,
secret, recondite, inside,
privileged.

rascal, *n.* **1.** rapscallion,
knave, rogue, scamp,
villain, scoundrel,

miscreant, scapegrace.
—*adj.* **2.** knavish, roguish,
miscreant, dishonest, base,
paltry, mean, low, rascally.
—**Syn. Study.** See KNAVE.

rash, *adj.* **1.** hasty,
impetuous, reckless,
headlong, precipitate,
impulsive, thoughtless,
heedless, indiscreet,
incautious, unwary,
foolhardy, audacious. —*n.*
2. eruption, efflorescence,
eczema, dermatitis,
breaking out, exanthema.
—**Ant.** thoughtful,
considered, discreet,
cautious.

ratify, *v.* confirm,
corroborate, consent to,
agree to, approve,
sanction, substantiate,
validate, establish. —**Ant.**
refute, veto, disapprove.

ration, *n.* **1.** allowance,
portion, food. —*v.* **2.**
apportion, distribute,
mete, dole, deal, parcel
out. **3.** put on rations,
restrict to rations.

rational, *adj.* **1.** reasonable,
sensible. **2.** intelligent,
wise; judicious, discreet,
sagacious, enlightened. **3.**

sane, lucid, sound, sober.
—**Ant.** irrational,
unreasonable;
unintelligent, stupid,
unwise, indiscreet;
unsound, dim.

rationalize, *v.* **1.** explain,
clarify, elucidate, explicate,
illuminate. **2.** justify,
excuse, alibi, exculpate,
palter, extenuate, explain
away, whitewash, gloss
over.

raucous, *adj.* **1.** noisy,
discordant, strident, harsh,
dissonant, rackety,
cacophonous, stridulant,
shrill, grating, piercing,
jarring, screechy, shrieky,
squawky. **2.** obstreperous,
riotous, disorderly,
boisterous, unruly, rowdy.
—**Ant.** melodious,
sweet-sounding.

ravage, *n.* **1.** devastation,
destruction, ruin, waste,
desolation, damage, havoc,
despoilment, plunder,
pillage. —*v.* **2.** damage,
mar, ruin, devastate,
destroy, lay waste, despoil,
plunder, pillage, sack.
—**Ant.** construction,
creation; build; repair.

ravening, *adj.* ravenous.

ravenous, *adj.* ravening, voracious, greedy, starved, hungry, famished, insatiable, gluttonous, devouring; rapacious, raptorial, predacious, predatory. **—Ant.** sated, satisfied.

raw, *adj.* **1.** unprepared, unfinished, unrefined, unmade, crude, rude, rough, makeshift. **2.** uncooked. **3.** ignorant, inexperienced, untrained, undisciplined, green, unskilled, untried, unpracticed. **4.** frank, candid, bold, exposed. **5.** damp, chilly, cold, wet, windy. **—Ant.** prepared, finished, refined, done, polished; cooked, done; intelligent, disciplined, skilled, secretive, dry, warm, arid. **—Syn. Study.** RAW, CRUDE, RUDE refer to something not in a finished or highly refined state. RAW applies particularly to material not yet changed by a process, by manufacture, or by preparation for consumption: *raw leather.*

CRUDE refers to that which still needs refining: *crude petroleum.* RUDE refers to what is still in a condition of rough simplicity or in a roughly made form: *rude agricultural implements.*

raze, See Syn. study at DESTROY.

reach, *v.* **1.** get to, attain, arrive at, come to. **2.** touch, seize. **3.** stretch, extend. **—***n.* **4.** extent, distance, range, compass, area, sphere, influence, stretch, scope, grasp. **—Ant.** fail.

reactionary, *n., adj.* conservative. **—Ant.** radical.

readily, *adv.* promptly, quickly, easily; willingly, cheerfully. **—Ant.** slowly, lethargically; reluctantly.

ready, *adj.* **1.** prepared, set, fitted, fit. **2.** equipped, geared, completed, adjusted, arranged. **3.** willing, agreeable, cheerful, disposed, inclined. **4.** prompt, quick, alert, acute, sharp, keen, adroit, facile, clever, skillful, nimble. **—***v.* **5.** make ready, prepare. **—Ant.** unprepared, unfit; unwilling, indisposed, disinclined; slow, deliberate, unskillful.

real, *adj.* true, actual, faithful, factual, authentic, genuine; sincere, unfeigned. **—Ant.** false, fake, counterfeit, fraudulent; insincere.

realistic, *adj.* practical, hardheaded, clear-eyed, clear-sighted, clear-headed, sober, blunt, factual, pragmatic, tough-minded, undeceived, ungullible, unsentimental, unromantic. **—Ant.** impractical, flighty.

realize, *v.* **1.** grasp, understand, comprehend, conceive. **2.** imagine. **3.** accomplish, effect, effectuate, perform. **—Ant.** misunderstand; begin.

realm, *n.* **1.** kingdom. **2.** sovereignty, sphere, domain, province, department.

rear, *n.* **1.** back, background. **—v. 2.** bring up, nurture, raise, nurse. **3.** raise, elevate, lift, loft,

lift up, hold up. **4.** build, put up, erect, construct. **5.** rise; buck. **—Ant.** front; face. **—Syn. Study.** See BACK.

reason, *n.* **1.** ground, cause, motive, purpose, end, design, *raison d'être*, objective, aim, object. **2.** justification, explanation, excuse, rationale, ratiocination, rationalization. **3.** judgment, common sense, understanding, intellect, intelligence, mind. **4.** sanity. **—v. 5.** argue, ratiocinate, justify; rationalize. **6.** conclude, infer. **7.** bring, persuade, convince, influence. **—Syn. Study.** REASON, CAUSE, MOTIVE are terms for a circumstance (or circumstances) that brings about or explains certain results. A REASON is an explanation of a situation or circumstance that made certain results seem possible or appropriate: *The reason for the robbery was the victim's careless display of money.* The CAUSE is the way in which the circumstances produce the effect; that is, make a specific action seem necessary or desirable: *The cause was the robber's immediate need of money.* A MOTIVE is the hope, desire, or other force that starts the action (or an action) in an attempt to produce specific results: *The motive was to use the stolen money to gamble.*

reasonable, *adj.* **1.** rational, logical, sensible, intelligent, wise, judicious, right, fair, equitable. **2.** moderate, tolerable. **3.** sane, rational, sober, sound. —**Ant.** unreasonable, illogical, irrational; immoderate, intolerable; unsound, insane.

reassure, *v.* encourage, hearten, embolden, bolster, comfort, inspirit. —**Ant.** disconcert, unnerve, dishearten, discourage.

rebel, *n.* **1.** insurgent, insurrectionist, mutineer, traitor. —*adj.* **2.** insurgent, mutinous, rebellious, insubordinate. —*v.* **3.** revolt. —**Ant.** patriot; loyal, obedient.

rebellion, *n.* resistance, defiance, insurrection, mutiny, sedition, revolution, revolt; insubordination, disobedience, contumacy.

rebellious, *adj.* defiant, insubordinate, mutinous, rebel, seditious, insurgent, refractory, disobedient, contumacious. —**Ant.** subordinate, obedient, patriotic.

rebuff, *v.* **1.** reject, snub, slight, spurn, cut, dismiss, drop, repulse, repel, brush off, high-hat, kiss off. —*n.* **2.** rejection, snub, dismissal, repulsion, brush-off, kiss-off. —**Ant.** welcome, embrace.

rebuke, *v.* **1.** reprove, reprimand, censure, upbraid, chide, reproach, reprehend, admonish, scold, remonstrate with. —*n.* **2.** reproof, reprimand, censure, reproach, reprehension, chiding, scolding, remonstration, expostulation. —**Ant.** praise.

recalcitrant, *adj.* resistant, resistive, disobedient,

uncompliant, refractory, rebellious, contumacious, opposing. —**Ant.** obedient, compliant. —**Syn. Study.** See UNRULY.

recall, *v.* **1.** recollect, remember. **2.** call back, revoke, rescind, retract, withdraw, recant, repeal, annul, countermand, nullify. —*n.* **3.** memory, recollection. **4.** revocation, retraction, repeal, withdrawal, recantation, nullification; impeachment. —**Ant.** forget; enforce; ratify; sanction.

recapitulate, *v.* review, summarize, repeat, reiterate. —**Syn. Study.** See REPEAT.

recent, *adj.* late, modern, up-to-date, fresh, new, novel. —**Ant.** early, old, ancient.

receptive, *adj.* responsive, open, open-minded, hospitable, welcoming, sympathetic, impressionable, susceptible, amenable, reachable, teachable, educable, influenceable, swayable, persuadable,

suggestible. —**Ant.** resistant, recalcitrant.

recherché, *adj.* **1.** unusual, exotic, rare, novel, uncommon, unfamiliar, strange, foreign, unheard-of, mysterious. **2.** quaint, choice, exquisite, precious, special, superior, select, peerless, superlative. **3.** affected, over-refined, unnatural, artificial, put-on, stagy, theatrical. —**Ant.** down-to-earth, everyday.

reciprocal, *adj.* **1.** mutual, correlative, interchangeable. —*n.* **2.** equivalent, counterpart, complement. —**Ant.** unequal.

recital, *n.* account, narrative, description, relation, history, story.

recite, *v.* **1.** repeat, relate, narrate, recount, describe. **2.** enumerate, count, number, detail, recapitulate. —**Syn. Study.** See RELATE.

reckless, *adj.* careless, rash, heedless, incautious, negligent, thoughtless, imprudent, improvident,

remiss, inattentive,
indifferent, regardless,
unconcerned. —**Ant.**
careful, heedful, cautious,
thoughtful, provident.

reckon, *v.* **1.** count,
compute, calculate,
enumerate. **2.** esteem,
consider, regard, account,
deem, estimate, judge,
evaluate.

reclaim, *v.* recover, bring
or get back, regain,
restore.

recoil, *v.* **1.** draw *or* shrink
back, falter, flinch, quail.
2. rebound, spring *or* fly
back, react, reverberate.
—**Ant.** advance. —**Syn.**
Study. See WINCE.

recollect, *v.* recall,
remember. —**Ant.** forget.

recommend, *v.* **1.**
commend, approve,
condone. **2.** advise,
counsel. —**Ant.** condemn,
disapprove.

recompense, *v.* **1.** repay,
remunerate, reward,
requite, compensate for.
—*n.* **2.** compensation,
payment, reward, requital,
remuneration, repayment,

amends, indemnification,
satisfaction, retribution.

reconcile, *v.* **1.** content,
win over, convince,
persuade. **2.** pacify,
conciliate, placate,
propitiate, appease. **3.**
compose, settle, adjust,
make up, harmonize, make
compatible *or* consistent.
—**Ant.** dissuade; anger,
arouse, disturb.

recondite, *adj.* **1.** abstruse,
profound, deep. **2.**
obscure, dim, mysterious,
hidden, occult, dark,
secret, concealed. —**Ant.**
clear, obvious, patent.

record, *v.* **1.** set down,
enter, register, enroll. —*n.*
2. account, chronicle,
history, note, register,
memorandum.

recount, *v.* relate, narrate,
tell, recite, describe,
enumerate. —**Syn. Study.**
See RELATE.

recourse, *n.* resource,
resort, refuge, hope,
expedient, means, device,
help, strength, last resort,
pis aller.

recover, *v.* **1.** regain, get
again, reclaim, retrieve,

restore. **2.** heal, mend, recuperate, rally.

recreant, *adj.* **1.** cowardly, craven, dastardly, base, pusillanimous, faint-hearted, yellow. **2.** unfaithful, disloyal, false, faithless, untrue, treacherous, apostate. —*n.* **3.** coward, craven, dastard. **4.** apostate, traitor, renegade. —**Ant.** bold, brave; faithful, loyal, true; hero; patriot.

rectify, *v.* **1.** set right, correct, remedy, mend, emend, amend, improve, better, ameliorate. **2.** adjust, regulate, put right, straighten. —**Ant.** worsen, ruin.

redeem, *v.* **1.** buy *or* pay off, ransom, recover, buy back, repurchase. **2.** ransom, free, liberate, rescue, save. **3.** discharge, fulfill, perform.

redress, *n.* **1.** reparation, restitution, amends, indemnification, compensation, satisfaction, indemnity, restoration, remedy, relief, atonement, *Wiedergutmachung.* —*v.* **2.**

remedy, repair, correct, amend, mend, emend, right, rectify, adjust, relieve, ease. —**Ant.** blame, punishment; damage. —**Syn. Study.** REDRESS, REPARATION, RESTITUTION suggest making amends or giving compensation for a wrong. REDRESS may refer either to the act of setting right an unjust situation or to satisfaction sought or gained for a wrong suffered: *the redress of grievances.* REPARATION refers to compensation or satisfaction for a wrong or loss inflicted. The word may have the moral idea of amends, but more frequently it refers to financial compensation: *to make reparation for one's neglect; the reparations demanded of the aggressor nations.* RESTITUTION means literally the giving back of what has been taken from the lawful owner, but may refer to restoring the equivalent of what has been taken: *The servant* *convicted of robbery made restitution to his employer.*

reduce, *v.* **1.** diminish, decrease, shorten, abridge, curtail, retrench, abate, lessen, attenuate, contract. **2.** subdue, suppress, subject, subjugate, conquer, vanquish, overcome, overpower, overthrow, depose. **3.** debase, depress, lower, degrade. **4.** control, adjust, correct. —**Ant.** increase; defend; honor, exalt, elevate.

redundant, See Syn. study at WORDY.

reel, See Syn. study at STAGGER.

refer, *v.* **1.** direct, commit, deliver, consign. **2.** assign, attribute, ascribe, impute. **3.** relate, apply, obtain, pertain, belong, respect. **4.** advert, allude, hint at.

referee, *n.* **1.** arbitrator, umpire, judge, arbiter. —*v.* **2.** judge, arbitrate, umpire. —**Syn. Study.** See JUDGE.

reference, *n.* **1.** direction, allusion, referral, mention, citation. **2.** witness. **3.** testimonial, endorsement.

4. relation, regard, respect, conern.

refined, *adj.* **1.** cultivated, polished, genteel, elegant, polite, courteous, courtly, civilized, well-bred. **2.** purified, clarified, distilled, strained. **3.** subtle. **4.** minute, precise, exact, exquisite. —**Ant.** unrefined, inelegant, impolite, discourteous; polluted, contaminated; obvious, direct, candid; general, inexact.

reflect, *v.* **1.** mirror, cast *or* throw back, rebound. **2.** reproduce, show, manifest, espouse. **3.** meditate, think, ponder, ruminate, cogitate, muse, deliberate, study, comtemplate, consider. —**Syn. Study.** See STUDY.

reflection, *n.* **1.** image, representation, counterpart. **2.** consideration, deliberation, cogitation, rumination, meditation, study, comtemplation, thinking, musing. **3.** imputation, aspersion, reproach, censure. —**Ant.** original; thoughtlessness; praise.

reflective, *adj.* pensive, meditative, contemplative, thoughtful, pondering, deliberating, reflecting, reasoning, cogitating. —**Ant.** thoughtless, inconsiderate, unthinking. —**Syn. Study.** See PENSIVE.

reform, *n.* **1.** improvement, amendment, correction, reformation, betterment, amelioration. —*v.* **2.** better, rectify, correct, amend, emend, ameliorate, mend, improve, repair, restore. —**Ant.** deterioration; worsen, deteriorate.

reformation, *n.* improvement, betterment, correction, reform, amendment.

refractory, *adj.* stubborn, unmanageable, obstinate, perverse, mulish, headstrong, pigheaded, contumacious, intractable, disobedient, recalcitrant, cantankerous, ungovernable, unruly. —**Ant.** obedient, tractable. —**Syn. Study.** See UNRULY.

refrain, *v.* **1.** restrain, cease, abstain, desist, curb oneself, hold oneself back, withhold. —*n.* **2.** chorus, verse, theme, burden. —**Ant.** continue, persist.

refresh, *v.* **1.** reinvigorate, revive, stimulate, freshen, cheer, enliven, reanimate. **2.** restore, repair, renovate, renew, retouch. —**Ant.** dispirit, discourage.

refuge, *n.* **1.** shelter, protection, security, safety. **2.** asylum, retreat, sanctuary, hiding place, haven, harbor, stronghold, cloister.

refurbish, *v.* renovate, refurnish, redecorate, brighten.

refuse, *v.* **1.** decline, reject, spurn, turn down, deny, rebuff, repudiate. —*n.* **2.** rubbish, trash, waste, garbage; slag, lees, dregs, scum, sediment, marc, scoria, dross. —**Ant.** allow, permit, sanction, approve. —**Syn. Study.** REFUSE, REJECT, SPURN, DECLINE imply nonacceptance of something. REFUSE is direct and emphatic in expressing a determination not to accept what is offered or proposed: *to refuse an offer of help*. REJECT is even more forceful and definite: *to reject an author's manuscript*. To SPURN is to reject with scorn: *to spurn a bribe*. DECLINE is a milder and more courteous term: *to decline an invitation*.

refute, *v.* disprove, rebut, confute. —**Ant.** agree, concur.

regain, *v.* recover, recapture, repossess, retrieve, get back. —**Ant.** lose, miss.

regal, *adj.* royal, kingly; stately, princely, splendid. —**Ant.** servile.

regale, *v.* amuse, divert, entertain, beguile, refresh, please, delight, gladden, titillate, tickle.

regard, *v.* **1.** look upon, think of, consider, esteem, account, judge, deem, hold, suppose, estimate. **2.** respect, esteem, honor, revere, reverence, value. **3.** look at, observe, notice, note, see, remark, mark. **4.** relate to, concern, refer to, respect. —*n.* **5.** reference, relation. **6.** point, particular, detail, matter, consideration. **7.** thought, concern, attention. **8.** look, gaze, view. **9.** respect, deference, concern, esteem, estimation, consideration, reverence. **10.** liking, affection, interest, love. —**Ant.** disregard; disrespect, dishonor; inattention; dislike.

regardless, *adj.* inattentive, negligent, neglectful, indifferent, heedless, disregarding, ignoring, unmindful, unconcerned. —**Ant.** attentive, mindful.

region, *n.* part, area, division, district, section, portion, quarter, territory, locale, site, sphere, vicinity, vicinage, space, tract.

register, *n.* **1.** record, catalogue, account book, ledger, archive. **2.** roll, roster, catalogue, list, record, chronicle, schedule, annals. **3.** registry, entry, registration, enrollment. —*v.* **4.** enroll, list, record, catalogue, chronicle, enter.

5. demonstrate, show, evince.

regret, *v.* **1.** deplore, lament, feel sorry about, grieve at, bemoan, bewail, rue, mourn for, repent. —*n.* **2.** sorrow, lamentation, grief. **3.** remorse, penitence, contrition, repentance, compunction. **—Ant.** rejoice; joy; unregeneracy. **—Syn. Study.** REGRET, REMORSE imply a sense of sorrow about events in the past, usu. wrongs committed or errors made. REGRET is a feeling of sorrow or disappointment for what has been done or not been done: *I remembered our bitter quarrel with regret.* REMORSE is a deep sense of guilt and mental anguish for having done wrong: *The killer seemed to have no remorse.*

regular, *adj.* **1.** usual, normal, customary. **2.** conforming, symmetrical, uniform, even, systematic, formal, fixed, orderly, invariant, unvarying, methodical, constant. **3.**

recurrent, periodic, habitual, established, fixed. **4.** (*colloquial*) out-and-out, thorough, complete, unregenerate, perfect. **—Ant.** irregular.

regulate, *v.* control, direct, manage, rule, order, adjust, arrange, set, systematize, dispose, conduct, guide.

regulation, *n.* **1.** rule, order, direction, law, precept. **2.** direction, control, management, arrangement, ordering, disposition, disposal, adjustment. **—Ant.** misdirection, mismanagement.

rehearse, *v.* **1.** recite, act, practice, drill, train, repeat. **2.** relate, enumerate, recount, delineate, describe, portray, narrate, recapitulate. **—Ant.** extemporize.

reign, *n.* **1.** rule, sway, dominion, sovereignty, suzerainty, power, influence. —*v.* **2.** rule, govern, prevail, predominate, hold sway, influence. —**Ant.** obey.

reiterate, *v.* repeat. —**Syn. Study.** See REPEAT.

reject, *v.* **1.** refuse, repudiate, decline, deny, rebuff, repel, renounce. **2.** discard, throw away, exclude, eliminate; jettison. —*n.* **3.** second. —**Ant.** accept. —**Syn. Study.** See REFUSE.

rejoinder, *n.* answer, reply, riposte, response, replication, surrejoinder. —**Syn. Study.** See ANSWER.

relate, *v.* **1.** tell, recite, narrate, recount, rehearse, report, describe, delineate, detail, repeat. **2.** associate, connect, ally. —**Ant.** dissociate, disconnect, separate, alienate. —**Syn. Study.** RELATE, RECITE, RECOUNT mean to tell, report, or describe in some detail an occurrence or circumstance. To RELATE is to give an account of happenings, events, circumstances, etc.: *to relate one's adventures.* To RECITE may mean to give details consecutively, but more often applies to the repetition from memory of something learned with verbal exactness: *to recite a poem.* To RECOUNT is usu. to set forth consecutively the details of an occurrence, argument, experience, etc., to give an account in detail: *to recount an unpleasant experience.*

relation, *n.* **1.** connection, relationship, association, alliance, dependence. **2.** reference, regard, respect. **3.** narration, recitation, recital, description, rehearsal, relating, telling. **4.** narrative, account, recital, report, story, chronicle, tale, history. —**Ant.** independence.

relationship, *n.* **1.** relation, connection, association. **2.** kinship, affinity, family tie, consanguinity. —**Ant.** dissociation.

relax, *v.* **1.** loosen, slacken. **2.** diminish, mitigate, weaken, lessen, reduce, remit, abate, debilitate, enfeeble, enervate. **3.** ease, unbend, relent, soften.

—**Ant.** tighten; intensify, increase; harden.

release, *v.* **1.** free, liberate, set free, loose, unloose, unfasten, set at liberty, discharge, deliver, dismiss. **2.** disengage, loose, extricate. **3.** proclaim, publish, announce. —*n.* **4.** liberation, deliverance, emancipation, discharge, freedom. —**Ant.** fasten, fetter, imprison; engage, involve; hide, conceal; incarceration, imprisonment. —**Syn. Study.** RELEASE, FREE, DISMISS, DISCHARGE, LIBERATE all mean to let loose or let go. RELEASE and FREE both suggest a helpful action; they may be used of delivering a person from confinement or obligation: *to release prisoners; to free a student from certain course requirements.* DISMISS usually means to force to go unwillingly; however, it may also refer to giving permission to go: *to dismiss an employee; to dismiss a class.* DISCHARGE usually means to relieve of an obligation, office, etc.;

it may also mean to permit to go: *The soldier was discharged.* The hospital discharged the patient. LIBERATE suggests particularly the deliverance from unjust punishment, oppression, or the like, and often means to set free through forcible or military action: *to liberate occupied territories.*

relentless, *adj.* unrelenting, inflexible, rigid, stern, severe, unbending, unforgiving, unappeasable, implacable, merciless, ruthless, unmerciful, pitiless, unpitying, hard, obdurate, adamant, unyielding, remorseless, inexorable. —**Ant.** relenting, flexible, soft, pliant, merciful, remorseful.

relevant, *adj.* pertinent, applicable, germane, apposite, appropriate, suitable, fitting, apt, proper, suited. —**Ant.** irrelevant. —**Syn. Study.** See APT.

reliable, *adj.* trustworthy, trusty, dependable, infallible, unfailing.

—**Ant.** unreliable, untrustworthy, undependable.

relief, *n.* **1.** deliverance, alleviation, ease, assuagement, mitigation, comfort. **2.** help, assistance, aid, succor, redress, remedy. **3.** release, replacement. —**Ant.** intensity, intensification.

relieve, *v.* **1.** ease, alleviate, assuage, mitigate, allay, lighten, comfort, soothe, lessen, abate, diminish. **2.** unburden, disburden, ease. **3.** aid, help, assist, succor, remedy, support, sustain. —**Ant.** intensify, increase; burden.

religious, *adj.* **1.** pious, holy, devout, faithful, reverent, godly. **2.** conscientious, scrupulous, exacting, punctilious, strict, rigid, demanding. —*n.* **3.** monk, friar, nun. —**Ant.** irreligious, impious, unfaithful, irreverent; flexible, lenient. —**Syn. Study.** RELIGIOUS, DEVOUT, PIOUS indicate a spirit of reverence toward God. RELIGIOUS is a general word, indicating adherence to a particular set of beliefs and practices: *a religious family.* DEVOUT indicates a fervent spirit, usu. genuine and often independent of outward observance: *a deeply devout though unorthodox church member.* PIOUS implies constant attention to, and extreme conformity with, outward observances; it can also suggest sham or hypocrisy: *a pious hypocrite.*

relinquish, *v.* renounce, surrender, give up, resign, yield, cede, waive, forswear, forgo, abdicate, leave, forsake, desert, renounce, quit, abandon, let go, resign. —**Ant.** demand, require.

relish, *n.* **1.** liking, taste, enjoyment, appreciation, gusto, zest, inclination, bent, partiality, predilection, preference. **2.** condiment, appetizer. **3.** taste, flavor, savor. —*v.* **4.** like, enjoy, appreciate, prefer. —**Ant.** distaste, disfavor.

reluctant, *adj.* unwilling, disinclined, hesitant, loath, averse, indisposed. **—Ant.** willing, agreeable, amenable, unhesitating. **—Syn. Study.** RELUCTANT, LOATH, AVERSE describe disinclination toward something. RELUCTANT implies some sort of mental struggle, as between disinclination and sense of duty: *reluctant to expel students.* LOATH describes extreme disinclination: *loath to part from a friend.* AVERSE describes a long-held dislike or unwillingness, though not a particularly strong feeling: *averse to an idea; averse to getting up early.*

remain, *v.* **1.** continue, stay, last, abide, endure. **2.** wait, tarry, delay, stay, rest. —*n.* **3.** remnant, scrap, remainder, refuse, leavings, crumbs, orts, residue, relics. **4.** corpse, dead body, cadaver. **—Ant.** leave, depart.

remainder, *n.* residuum, remnant, excess, residue, rest, balance, surplus. **—Ant.** insufficiency, inadequacy.

remark, *v.* **1.** say, observe, note, perceive, heed, regard, notice. **2.** comment, say, state. —*n.* **3.** notice, regard, observation, heed, attention, consideration. **4.** comment, utterance, note, observation, declaration, assertion, asseveration, statement. **—Ant.** disregard, ignore; inattention.

remarkable, *adj.* notable, conspicuous, unusual, extraordinary, noteworthy, striking, wonderful, uncommon, strange, rare, distinguished, prominent, singular. **—Ant.** common, usual, ordinary.

remedy, *n.* **1.** cure, relief, medicine, treatment, restorative, specific, medicament, medication, ointment, nard, balm. **2.** antidote, corrective, antitoxin, counteraction. —*v.* **3.** cure, heal, put *or* set right, restore, recondition, repair, redress. **4.** counteract, remove, correct, right. **—Ant.** sicken, worsen.

remember, *v.* **1.** recall,

recollect. **2.** retain, memorize, keep *or* bear in mind. **—Ant.** forget.

remembrance, *n.* **1.** recollection, reminiscence; memory. **2.** keepsake, memento, souvenir, remembrancer, trophy, token, memorial.

remiss, *adj.* **1.** negligent, careless, thoughtless, lax, neglectful; inattentive, heedless. **2.** languid, sluggish, dilatory, slothful, slow, tardy, lax. **—Ant.** careful, thoughtful, attentive; energetic, quick.

remission, *n.* **1.** pardon, forgiveness, absolution, indulgence, exoneration, discharge. **2.** abatement, diminution, lessening, relaxation, moderation, mitigation. **3.** release, relinquishment. **4.** decrease, subsidence, respite, stoppage, pause, interruption, relief, hiatus, suspense, suspension, abatement. **—Ant.** blame, censure, conviction; increase, intensification; increase.

remissness, *n.* slackness,

neglect, dilatoriness, languor, languidness. **—Ant.** responsibility.

remit, *v.* **1.** transmit, send, forward. **2.** pardon, release, forgive, excuse, overlook, absolve. **3.** slacken, abate, diminish, relax. **4.** return, give back, restore, replace. **5.** put off, postpone. **—Ant.** retain, keep, hold; condemn; increase.

remnant, *n.* **1.** remainder, remains, residue, residuum, rest. **2.** trace, vestige.

remorse, *n.* regret, compunction, penitence, contrition. **—Ant.** conviction, assertion, assertiveness. **—Syn. Study.** See REGRET.

remorseful, *adj.* regretful, penitent, contrite, repentant. **—Ant.** impenitent.

remorseless, *adj.* relentless, pitiless, uncompassionate, unrelenting, merciless, unmerciful, ruthless, cruel, savage, implacable, inexorable. **—Ant.** merciful, relenting.

remote, *adj.* **1.** distant, far

apart, far off, removed, alien, foreign, unrelated, unconnected. **2.** slight, faint, inconsiderable. **3.** separated, abstracted. —**Ant.** close, near, connected, related; considerable, substantial.

remove, *v.* **1.** replace, displace, dislodge, transfer, transport, carry. **2.** take, withdraw, separate, extract, eliminate. **3.** kill, assassinate, do away with, destroy, murder.

rend, *v.* tear apart, split, divide, rip, rive, sunder, sever, cleave, chop, fracture, tear, dissever, crack, snap, lacerate, rupture.

render, *v.* **1.** make, cause to be, cause to become. **2.** do, perform. **3.** furnish, supply, give, contribute, afford. **4.** exhibit, show, demonstrate. **5.** present, give, assign. **6.** deliver. **7.** translate, interpret. **8.** give back, restore, return. **9.** give up, surrender, cede, yield.

renew, *v.* **1.** restore, replenish, restock. **2.**

re-create, rejuvenate, regenerate, restore, reinstate, renovate, repair, mend. **3.** revive, reestablish. —**Syn. Study.** RENEW, RENOVATE, REPAIR, RESTORE suggest making something the way it formerly was. RENEW means to bring back to an original condition of freshness and vigor: *to renew one's faith.* RENOVATE means to bring back to a good condition, or to make as good as new: *to renovate an old house.* To REPAIR is to put into good or sound condition after damage, wear and tear, etc.: *to repair the roof of a house.* To RESTORE is to bring back to a former, original, or normal condition or position: *to restore a painting.*

renounce, *v.* **1.** give up, put aside, forsake, forgo, relinquish, abandon, forswear, leave, quit, resign, abdicate. **2.** repudiate, disown, disclaim, reject, disavow, deny, recant. —**Ant.** claim, accept, desire.

renovate, *v.* renew. —**Syn. Study.** See RENEW.

renown, *n.* repute, fame, celebrity, glory, distinction, note, eminence, reputation, name, honor. —**Ant.** disrepute, infamy.

renowned, See Syn. study at FAMOUS.

rent, *n.* **1.** rental, return, payment. **2.** tear, split, fissure, slit, crack, crevice, cleft, rift, gap, opening, rip, rupture, breach, break, fracture, laceration. **3.** schism, separation, disunion, breach. —*v.* **4.** lease, let, hire. —**Syn. Study.** See HIRE.

repair, *v.* **1.** restore, mend, remodel, renew, renovate, patch, amend, fix. **2.** make good, make up for, remedy, retrieve. **3.** make amends for, atone for, redress. —**Ant.** break, destroy, ruin. —**Syn. Study.** See RENEW.

reparation, *n.* **1.** (*usually plural*) amends, indemnification, atonement, restitution, satisfaction, compensation, *Wiedergutmachung.* **2.**
restoration, repair, renewal, renovation. —**Ant.** destruction. —**Syn. Study.** See REDRESS.

repay, *v.* payback, return, reimburse, indemnify, refund.

repeat, *v.* **1.** reiterate, recapitulate, iterate, recite, rehearse, relate. **2.** reproduce, echo, reecho, redo. —*n.* **3.** repetition, iteration. —**Syn. Study.** REPEAT, RECAPITULATE, REITERATE refer to saying or doing a thing more than once. To REPEAT is to say or do something over again: *to repeat an order.* To RECAPITULATE is to restate in brief form often by repeating the principal points in a discourse: *to recapitulate a news broadcast.* To REITERATE is to say (or, sometimes, to do) something over and over again, often for emphasis: *to reiterate a refusal.*

repel, *v.* **1.** repulse, parry, ward off. **2.** resist, withstand, rebuff, oppose, confront. **3.** reject, decline, refuse, discourage. —**Ant.** attract; approve, accept.

repent, *v.* regret, atone.

repentance, *n.* compunction, contrition; contriteness, penitence, remorse, sorrow, regret. —**Ant.** impenitence.

replace, *v.* **1.** supersede, supplant, substitute, succeed. **2.** restore, return, make good, refund, repay; replenish. —**Syn. Study.** REPLACE, SUPERSEDE, SUPPLANT refer to putting one thing or person in place of another. To REPLACE is to take the place of, to succeed: *Ms. Jones will replace Mr. Smith as president.* SUPERSEDE implies that that which is replacing another is an improvement: *The typewriter has superseded the pen.* SUPPLANT implies that that which takes the other's place has ousted the former holder and usurped the position or function, esp. by art or fraud: *to supplant a former favorite.*

reply, *v.* **1.** answer,

respond, echo, rejoin. —*n.* **2.** answer, rejoinder, riposte, replication, surrejoinder, response. —**Syn. Study.** See ANSWER.

represent, *v.* **1.** designate, stand for, denote, symbolize, exemplify, image, depict, express, portray, personate, delineate, figure, present. **2.** set forth, describe, state.

repress, *v.* **1.** check, suppress, subdue, put down, quell, quash, reduce, crush. **2.** check, restrain, curb, bridle, control. —**Ant.** foster, support, help, aid.

reprieve, See Syn. study at PARDON.

reprimand, *v.* upbraid, admonish, censure, berate, rebuke, chide, scold, dress down; *Informal* bawl out, chew out —**Syn. Study.** REPRIMAND, UPBRAID, ADMONISH, CENSURE mean to criticize or find fault with someone for behavior deemed reprehensible. REPRIMAND implies a formal criticism, as by an official or person in authority:

The lawyer was reprimanded by the judge. UPBRAID suggests relatively severe criticism, but of a less formal kind: *The minister upbraided the parishioners for their poor church attendance.* ADMONISH refers to a more gentle warning or expression of disapproval, often including suggestions for improvement: *I admonished the children to make less noise.* CENSURE suggests harsh, vehement criticism, often from an authoritative source: *The legislators voted to censure their fellow senator.*

reprisal, *n.* **1.** retaliation, revenge, vengeance, redress. **2.** vendetta. —**Syn. Study.** See REVENGE.

reproach, *v.* **1.** chide, abuse, reprimand, condemn, criticize, rebuke, scold, reprove, call to account, censure, blame, find fault with, shame, abash, discredit, reprehend, upbraid. —*n.* **2.** blame, censure, upbraiding, reproof, abuse, vilification, discredit,

reprehension, rebuke, criticism, remonstrance, condemnation, expostulation, disapproval, disapprobation. **3.** disgrace, dishonor, shame, disrepute, odium, scandal, obloquy, opprobrium, ignominy, indignity, infamy, insult, scorn, offense. —**Ant.** praise, honor.

reproduce, *v.* **1.** copy, duplicate, repeat, imitate, represent. **2.** generate, propagate, beget. —**Ant.** initiate, originate.

reprove, *v.* rebuke, blame, censure, reproach, reprimand, upbraid, chide, lecture, reprehend, admonish, remonstrate *or* expostulate with. —**Ant.** praise; exonerate.

repudiate, *v.* **1.** reject, disclaim, disavow, disown, discard, renounce. **2.** condemn, disapprove. —**Ant.** accept; approve, commend.

repugnance, *n.* **1.** objection, distaste, aversion, dislike, reluctance, hatred, hostility, antipathy. **2.** contradictoriness, inconsistency, contrariety, unsuitableness, irreconcilableness, incompatibility. **—Ant.** attractiveness, attraction, liking, sympathy; consistency, compatibility.

repugnant, *adj.* **1.** distasteful, objectionable, offensive. **2.** opposing, objecting, protesting, averse, unfavorable, antagonistic, inimical, adverse, contrary, hostile, opposed. **—Ant.** attractive, tasteful; favorable, amiable.

reputation, *n.* **1.** estimation, regard, repute, standing, position, name, character. **2.** credit, esteem, honor, fame, celebrity, distinction, renown. **—Ant.** disrepute; dishonor, infamy. **—Syn. Study.** REPUTATION and CHARACTER are often confused. REPUTATION, however, is the word which refers to the position one occupies or the standing that one has in the opinion of others, in respect to attainments, integrity, and the like: *a fine reputation; a reputation for honesty.* CHARACTER is the combination of moral and other traits which make one the kind of person one actually is (as contrasted with what others think of one): *Honesty is an outstanding trait of her character.*

repute, *n.* **1.** estimation, reputation. **2.** name, distinction, credit, honor. **—v. 3.** consider, esteem, account, regard, hold, deem, reckon. **—Ant.** disrepute; dishonor; condemn, scorn.

request, *n.* **1.** solicitation, petition, suit, entreaty, supplication, prayer. **2.** demand. **—v. 3.** ask for, sue, petition, entreat, beg, supplicate, solicit, beseech, require.

require, *v.* **1.** need, demand, request, order, enjoin, direct, ask. **2.** obligate, necessitate, want, need, call for. **—Ant.** forgo. **—Syn. Study.** See LACK.

requirement, *n.* **1.** requisite, need, claim, requisition, prerequisite, demand. **2.** mandate, order, command, directive, injunction, ukase, charge, claim, precept. —**Syn. Study.** REQUIREMENT, REQUISITE refer to that which is necessary. A REQUIREMENT is some quality or performance demanded of a person in accordance with certain fixed regulations: *requirements for admission to college.* A REQUISITE is not imposed from outside; it is a factor that is judged necessary according to the nature of things, or to the circumstances of the case: *Efficiency is a requisite for success in business.* REQUISITE may also refer to a concrete object judged necessary: *the requisites for perfect grooming.*

requisite, *adj.* **1.** required, necessary, essential, indispensable, needed, needful. —*n.* **2.** necessity, requirement. —**Ant.** dispensable, unnecessary; luxury, superfluity. —**Syn.**

Study. See NECESSARY. See also REQUIREMENT.

requite, *v.* **1.** repay, remunerate, reimburse, recompense, pay, satisfy, compensate. **2.** retaliate, avenge, revenge, punish. —**Ant.** dissatisfy; forgive.

rescue, *v.* **1.** save, deliver, liberate, set free, release, redeem, ransom, extricate; recover, preserve. —*n.* **2.** liberation, release, redemption, ransom, recovery, deliverance. —**Ant.** incarceration, imprisonment.

research, *n.* **1.** inquiry, investigation, examination, scrutiny, study. —*v.* **2.** investigate, study, inquire, examine, scrutinize.

resemblance, *n.* **1.** similarity, likeness, analogy, semblance, similitude. **2.** appearance, representation, semblance, image. —**Ant.** dissimilarity; misrepresentation.

reserve, *v.* **1.** keep back, save, retain, husband, keep, hold, store up. **2.** set apart, set aside, bank. —*n.*

3. reservation, qualification, exception. **4.** store, stock, supply. **5.** self-restraint, restraint, reticence, silence, taciturnity, constraint, coldness, coolness, retention. —**Ant.** splurge, squander, waste; prodigality; warmth, enthusiasm. —**Syn. Study.** See KEEP.

reside, *v.* **1.** dwell, abide, live, sojourn, stay, lodge, inhabit, remain. **2.** abide, lie, be present, habituate, inhere, exist.

residence, *n.* **1.** dwelling, house, home, habitation, domicile, mansion, manse. **2.** habitancy, stay, abode, sojourn, inhabitancy. —**Syn. Study.** See HOUSE.

residue, *n.* remainder, rest, remains, residuum; surplus.

resign, *v.* **1.** give up, submit, yield, cede, surrender, abdicate, relinquish, forgo, abandon, forsake, quit, leave. **2.** renounce, withdraw.

resignation, *n.* **1.** abdication, abandonment, surrender, relinquishment. **2.** submission, meekness, patience, acquiescence, endurance, compliance, forbearance, sufferance. —**Ant.** application; boldness, recalcitrance.

resilient, *adj.* rebounding, elastic, recoiling; buoyant, cheerful. —**Ant.** rigid, inflexible, inelastic.

resist, *v.* **1.** withstand, strive against, oppose, impugn, confront, assail, attack, counteract, rebuff. **2.** refrain *or* abstain from. —**Ant.** defend; continue. —**Syn. Study.** See OPPOSE.

resolute, *adj.* resolved, firm, steadfast, determined, set, opinionated, purposeful, earnest, sincere, fixed, unflinching, unwavering, inflexible, hardy, unshaken, bold, undaunted, pertinacious. —**Ant.** weak, feeble, frail, flexible, lenient. —**Syn. Study.** See EARNEST.

resolve, *v.* **1.** fix *or* settle on, determine, decide, confirm, establish. **2.** break up, disintegrate, separate, analyze, reduce. **3.** convert, transform, reduce, change. **4.** explain, explicate, solve. **5.** clear, dispel, scatter, disperse. —*n.* **6.** resolution, determination, decision, purpose, intention. **—Ant.** unite, amalgamate; consolidate; indecision. **—Syn. Study.** See DECIDE.

respect, *n.* **1.** particular, detail, point, regard, feature, matter. **2.** relation, reference, connection, regard. **3.** esteem, deference, regard, estimation, veneration, reverence, homage, honor, admiration, approbation, approval, affection, feeling. **4.** discrimination, bias, partiality, prejudice, preference, inclination. —*v.* **5.** honor, revere, reverence, esteem, venerate, regard, consider, defer to, admire, adulate, adore, love. **6.** regard, heed, attend, notice, consider. **7.** regard, relate to, refer to. **—Ant.** disregard. **—Syn. Study.** RESPECT, ESTEEM, VENERATION imply recognition of a person's worth, or of a personal quality, trait, or ability. RESPECT is commonly the result of admiration and approbation, together with deference: *to feel respect for a great scholar.* ESTEEM is deference combined with admiration and often with affection: *to hold a friend in great esteem.* VENERATION is an almost religious attitude of reverence and love, such as one feels for persons or things of outstanding superiority, endeared by long association: *veneration for noble traditions.*

respectable, *adj.* **1.** estimable, worthy, honorable. **2.** proper, decent, honest, respected, reputable. **3.** fair, fairly good, moderate, middling, passable, tolerable. **4.** considerable, large, moderate. **—Ant.** unworthy, dishonorable; improper; poor, intolerable; small, insignificant.

respectful, *adj.* courteous, polite, well-mannered,

well-bred, courtly,
decorous, civil, deferential.
—Ant. disrespectful,
discourteous, impolite.

respite, *n.* **1.** relief, delay,
hiatus, cessation,
postponement, interval,
rest, recess. **2.** stay,
reprieve, suspension. **—v.**
3. relieve, delay, alleviate,
postpone, put off, suspend.
—Ant. intensity,
perseverance.

response, *n.* answer, reply,
rejoinder, replication.
—Syn. Study. See ANSWER.

responsible, *adj.* **1.**
accountable, answerable,
liable. **2.** chargeable,
blamable, censurable. **3.**
capable, able, reliable,
solvent, trustworthy,
trusty, dutiful, honest.
—Ant. irresponsible;
innocent; incapable,
unable, unreliable.

restful, *adj.* calm, tranquil,
peaceful, undisturbed,
serene, pacific. **—Ant.**
perturbed, disturbed,
agitated.

restitution, *n.* reparation,
redress, indemnification,
restoration, recompense,

amends, compensation,
remuneration, requital,
satisfaction, repayment,
Wiedergutmachung.
—Syn. Study. See REDRESS.

restive, *adj.* **1.** uneasy,
restless, nervous,
impatient, ill at ease,
recalcitrant, unquiet. **2.**
refractory, disobedient,
obstinate, mulish,
stubborn, pigheaded.
—Ant. restful, patient,
quiet, serene; obedient.

restore, *v.* **1.** reestablish,
replace, reinstate, renew.
2. renew, renovate, repair,
mend. **3.** return, give
back. **4.** reproduce,
reconstruct, rebuild.
—Ant. disestablish,
destroy; break, ruin;
accept, receive; raze.
—Syn. Study. See RENEW.

restrain, *v.* **1.** check, keep
down, repress, curb,
bridle, suppress, hold,
keep, constrain. **2.** restrict,
circumscribe, confine,
hinder, abridge, narrow.
—Ant. unbridle; broaden,
widen. **—Syn. Study.** See
CHECK.

restrict, *v.* confine, limit,

restrain, abridge, curb, circumscribe, bound. **—Ant.** free, broaden, disencumber.

result, *n.* **1.** outcome, consequence, effect, conclusion, issue, event, end, termination, product, fruit. **—***v.* **2.** spring, arise, proceed, follow, flow, come, issue, ensue, rise, originate. **3.** terminate, end, resolve, eventuate. **—Ant.** cause. **—Syn. Study.** See FOLLOW. See also EFFECT.

retain, *v.* **1.** keep, hold, withhold, preserve, detain, reserve. **2.** remember, recall. **3.** hire, engage, employ. **—Ant.** loose, lose; forget; disengage, fire. **—Syn. Study.** See KEEP.

retaliate, *v.* avenge, requite, return, repay, revenge. **—Ant.** forgive, pardon.

retard, *v.* slow, delay, hinder, impede, decelerate, clog, obstruct, check. **—Ant.** speed, expedite, accelerate.

reticent, *adj.* taciturn, silent, reserved, quiet, uncommunicative. **—Ant.** voluble, communicative.

retire, *v.* withdraw, leave, depart, go away, retreat, retrograde, retrocede, fall back, recede; retract. **—Ant.** advance, attack.

retired, *adj.* withdrawn, secluded, sequestered, cloistered, isolated, enisled, removed, apart, solitary, abstracted. **—Ant.** advanced.

retort, *v.* **1.** reply, respond, return, answer, retaliate, rejoin. **—***n.* **2.** reply, response, answer, riposte, rejoinder, surrejoinder, replication; repartee. **—Syn. Study.** See ANSWER.

retreat, *n.* **1.** departure, withdrawal, retirement, seclusion, privacy, solitude. **2.** shelter, refuge, asylum. **—***v.* **3.** retire, retrocede, retrograde, withdraw, leave, depart, draw back. **4.** recede, slope backward. **—Ant.** advance.

retribution, *n.* requital, revenge, vengeance, retaliation, repayment, reward, recompense, compensation. —**Ant.** forgiveness, pardon. —**Syn. Study.** See REVENGE.

retrieve, *v.* **1.** recover, regain, restore. **2.** make good, repair, make amends for. **3.** rescue, save.

reveal, *v.* make known, communicate, disclose, divulge, unveil, uncover, discover, publish, impart, tell, announce, proclaim. —**Ant.** conceal, hide, veil, cover.

revenge, *n.* **1.** vengeance, retaliation, requital, reprisal, retribution. **2.** vindictiveness, revengefulness, vengefulness. —*v.* **3.** avenge, retaliate, requite, vindicate. —**Ant.** forgiveness, pardon. —**Syn. Study.** REVENGE, REPRISAL, RETRIBUTION, VENGEANCE suggest a punishment or injury inflicted in return for one received. REVENGE is the carrying out of a bitter desire to injure another for a wrong done to oneself or to those who are close to oneself: *to plot revenge for a friend's betrayal.*

REPRISAL is used specifically in the context of warfare; it means retaliation against an enemy: *The guerrillas expected reprisals for the raid.* RETRIBUTION usu. suggests deserved punishment for some evil done: *a just retribution for wickedness.* VENGEANCE is usu. vindictive, furious revenge: *He swore vengeance against his enemies.*

revengeful, *adj.* vindictive, spiteful, malevolent, resentful, malicious, malignant, implacable. —**Ant.** forgiving, benevolent.

reverence, *n.* **1.** worship, veneration, respect, homage, awe. **2.** bow, curtsy, obeisance. —*v.* **3.** venerate, revere, honor, adore, adulate. —**Ant.** disrespect; despise.

reverse, *adj.* **1.** opposite, contrary, converse. —*n.* **2.** opposite, contrary, converse, counterpart. **3.** back, rear, hind. **4.** check, misfortune, defeat, mishap, misadventure, affliction. —*v.* **5.** transpose, invert. **6.**

alter, change. **7.** revoke, annul, repeal, veto, rescind, overthrow, countermand. **—Ant.** same.

review, *n.* **1.** critique, criticism, judgment, survey. **2.** rereading, study, reconsideration, reexamination. **3.** inspection, examination, investigation. —*v.* **4.** survey, inspect, criticize.

revive, *v.* **1.** reactivate, revitalize, reanimate, resuscitate, revivify, reinvigorate, reinspirit. **2.** bring back, quicken, renew, refresh, rouse. **3.** recover, recall, reawake. **—Ant.** kill; languish, die.

revoke, *v.* take back, withdraw, annul, cancel, reverse, rescind, repeal, retract.

revolt, *v.* **1.** rebel, mutiny, rise. **2.** disgust, repel, shock, nauseate, sicken. —*n.* **3.** insurrection, rebellion, mutiny, revolution, uprising, overthrow, sedition. **4.** aversion, disgust, loathing. **—Ant.** attract, delight.

revolution, *n.* **1.** overthrow, change, revolt, rebellion, mutiny. **2.** cycle, rotation, circuit, turn, round.

revolve, *v.* **1.** rotate, spin, circulate, turn, roll. **2.** orbit, circle. **3.** consider, think about, ruminate upon, ponder, reflect upon, brood over, study. **—Syn. Study.** See TURN.

reward, *n.* **1.** recompense, prize, desert, compensation, pay, remuneration, requital, merit. **2.** bounty, premium, bonus. —*v.* **3.** recompense, requite, compensate, pay, remunerate.

ribald, *adj.* scurrilous, offensive, coarse, mocking, abusive, wanton, irreverent, loose, indecent, low, base, mean, vile, obscene, gross, filthy, dirty, vulgar. **—Ant.** pure, inoffensive, refined, polished, elegant.

rich, *adj.* **1.** well-to-do, wealthy, moneyed, opulent, affluent. **2.** abounding, abundant, bounteous, bountiful, fertile, plenteous, plentiful, copious, ample, luxuriant, productive, fruitful, prolific. **3.** valuable, valued, precious, costly, estimable, sumptuous. **4.** dear, expensive, high-priced, elegant. **5.** deep, strong, vivid, bright, gay. **6.** full, mellow, pear-shaped, harmonious, sweet. **7.** fragrant, aromatic. —**Ant.** poor, impoverished; scarce, barren, sterile; cheap; weak; dull; flat; noisome.

riddle, *n.* **1.** conundrum, puzzle, enigma, poser, question, problem. **2.** sieve, colander, strainer. —*v.* **3.** perforate, pierce, puncture.

ridicule, *n.* **1.** derision, mockery, gibes, jeers, taunts, raillery, satire, burlesque, sarcasm, sneer, banter, wit, irony. —*v.* **2.** deride, banter, rally, chaff, twit, mock, taunt, make fun of, sneer at, burlesque, satirize, rail at, lampoon, jeer *or* scoff at. —**Ant.** praise, honor; respect. —**Syn. Study.** RIDICULE, DERIDE, MOCK, TAUNT mean to make fun of a person. To RIDICULE is to make fun of, either playfully or with the intention of humiliating: *to ridicule a pretentious person.* To DERIDE is to laugh at scornfully: *a student derided for acting silly.* To MOCK is to make fun of by imitating the appearance or actions of another: *She mocked the seriousness of his expression.* To TAUNT is to call attention to something annoying or humiliating, usu. maliciously and in the presence of others: *The bully taunted the smaller boy.*

ridiculous, *adj.* absurd, preposterous, laughable, nonsensical, funny, ludicrous, droll, comical, farcical. —**Ant.** sensible. —**Syn. Study.** See ABSURD.

rife, *adj.* **1.** common, prevalent, widespread, prevailing. **2.** current. **3.** abundant, plentiful, numerous, plenteous, abounding, multitudinous. —**Ant.** rare, unusual; scarce, scanty.

right, *adj.* **1.** just, good, equitable, fair, upright, honest, lawful. **2.** correct, proper, suitable, fit, appropriate, convenient, becoming, *de rigueur*, befitting, seemly, *comme il faut*. **3.** correct, true, accurate. **4.** sound, sane, normal. **5.** healthy. **6.** principal, front, upper, obverse. **7.** genuine, legitimate, rightful. **8.** straight, true, direct. —*n.* **9.** claim, title, due, ownership. **10.** virtue, justice, fairness, integrity, equity, equitableness, uprightness, recitude, goodness, lawfulness. —*adv.* **11.** straight, directly. **12.** quite, completely. **13.** immediately. **14.** precisely, exactly, just, truly, actually. **15.** uprightly, righteously, rightfully, lawfully, rightly, justly, fairly, equitably. **16.** properly, fittingly, appropriately, fitly, suitably. **17.** advantageously, favorably, well. —**Ant.** wrong.

righteous, *adj.* moral, upright, justifiable, virtuous, good, honest, fair, right, equitable. —**Ant.** immoral, bad, dishonest, unfair.

rigid, *adj.* **1.** stiff, unyielding, unbending, firm, hard, inflexible. **2.** unmoving, immovable, static, stationary. **3.** inflexible, strict, severe, stern, rigorous, austere, unbending, harsh, stringent, inelastic. —**Ant.** flexible, soft; compliant, elastic, lenient. —**Syn. Study.** See STRICT.

rigorous, *adj.* **1.** rigid, severe, harsh, stern, austere, strict, hard, inflexible, stiff, unyielding, stringent. **2.** exact, demanding, finical, accurate. **3.** inclement, bitter, severe, sharp. —**Ant.** flexible, soft; inaccurate; fair, mild, bland. —**Syn. Study.** See STRICT.

rim, *n.* **1.** edge, border, lip, margin, brim, boundary, verge, skirt, confine. —*v.* **2.** edge, border, bound, margin, confine. —**Ant.** center, inside. —**Syn.**

Study. RIM, BRIM refer to the boundary of a circular or curved area. A RIM is a line or surface bounding such an area; an edge or border: *the rim of a glass.* BRIM usu. means the inside of the rim, at the top of a hollow object (except of a hat), and is used particularly when the object contains something: *The cup was filled to the brim.*

ring, *n.* **1.** circlet, loop, hoop; annulus. **2.** arena, rink, circle. **3.** competition, contest. **4.** clique, coterie, set, combination, confederacy, league; gang, mob, syndicate. —*v.* **5.** surround, encircle, circle. **6.** peal, resonate, vibrate, reverberate, resound, reecho; tinkle, jingle, jangle. **7.** announce, proclaim, usher in *or* out, summon, call, signal.

riot, *n.* **1.** outbreak, disorder, brawl, uproar, tumult, disturbance, commotion, fray, melee, altercation. **2.** disorder, confusion. **3.** revelry,

festivity. —*v.* **4.** create disorder, disturb the peace, create a disturbance, brawl, fight. **5.** carouse, revel.

rip, *v.* **1.** cut, tear, tear apart, slash, slit, rend. —*n.* **2.** rent, tear, laceration, cut.

ripe, *adj.* **1.** mature, mellow, grown, aged. **2.** ruddy, full, complete, consummate, perfect, finished. **3.** developed, ready, prepared, set. —**Ant.** immature; imperfect, unfinished; undeveloped, unprepared.

ripen, *v.* mature, age, grow, develop, mellow, grow up, maturate, evolve, blossom, flower, come into season.

ripple, *v.* **1.** wave, undulate, ruffle, purl. **2.** agitate, curl, dimple. —*n.* **3.** wavelet, wave, ruffling, undulation.

rise, *v.* **1.** get up, arise, stand, stand up. **2.** revolt, rebel, oppose, resist. **3.** spring up, grow. **4.** come into existence, appear, come forth. **5.** occur, happen. **6.** originate, issue, arise, come up, be derived, proceed. **7.** move upward, ascend, mount, arise. **8.** succeed, be promoted, advance. **9.** swell, puff up, enlarge, increase. **10.** adjourn, close. —*n.* **11.** rising, ascent, mounting. **12.** advance, elevation, promotion. **13.** increase, augmentation, enlargement, swelling. **14.** source, origin, beginning. —**Ant.** sink; support; die; fail; decrease, deflate; open; end.

risible, *adj.* funny, amusing, comic, comical, laugh-provoking, laughable, droll, humorous, hilarious, rich, ludicrous, absurd, ridiculous, farcical, priceless, hysterical. —**Ant.** sober, solemn.

risk, *n.* **1.** hazard, chance, dangerous chance, venture, peril, jeopardy, exposure. —*v.* **2.** hazard, take a chance, endanger, imperil; jeopardize. **3.** venture upon, dare.

rite, *n.* ceremony, procedure, practice, observance, form, usage.

ritual, *n.* **1.** ceremony, rite. —*adj.* **2.** ceremonial, formal, sacramental. —**Ant.** unceremonious, informal.

rival, *n.* **1.** competitor, contestant, emulator, antagonist, opponent. —*adj.* **2.** competing, competitive, opposed, emulating, opposing. —*v.* **3.** compete *or* contend with, oppose. **4.** match, equal, emulate. —**Ant.** ally, friend; associate with.

roam, *v.* walk, go, travel, ramble, wander, peregrinate, rove, stray, stroll, range; prowl.

roar, *v.* **1.** cry, bellow, bawl, shout, yell, vociferate. **2.** laugh. **3.** resound, boom, thunder, peal.

rob, *v.* **1.** rifle, sack, steal, deprive, plunder, pillage, pilfer, pinch, shoplift. **2.** defraud, cheat, deprive, rook.

robber, *n.* thief, highwayman, footpad, second-story man, kleptomaniac, shoplifter, pilferer, brigand, bandit, marauder, freebooter, pirate, picaroon. —**Syn. Study.** See THIEF.

robust, *adj.* **1.** sturdy, healthy, strong, hardy, vigorous, stalwart, hale, dusty, powerful, firm, sound, athletic, brawny, muscular, sinewy. **2.** rough, rude, coarse, boisterous, rambunctious, wild. —**Ant.** weak, feeble, unhealthy; refined, cultivated.

rogue, *n.* rascal, scamp, rapscallion, knave, mischief-maker, villain, scoundrel, scapegrace, trickster, swindler, cheat, mountebank, quack, sharper. —**Syn. Study.** See KNAVE.

roil, *v.* **1.** muddy, foul, dirty, pollute, befoul, contaminate. **2.** disturb, agitate, perturbate, stir, stir up, churn, whip, whip up. **3.** rile, anger, irritate, irk, vex, peeve, provoke, gripe. —**Ant.** clarify, calm.

roll, *v.* **1.** turn, revolve, rotate, wheel, gyrate, spin, whirl, bowl. **2.** wave, undulate. **3.** sway, rock, swing, list, tilt. **4.** wrap, enfold, envelop, cover. —*n.* **5.** scroll, document. **6.** register, list, inventory, catalogue, roster. **7.** cylinder, roller, spindle. —**Syn. Study.** See LIST.

roly-poly, *adj.* fat, plump, rotund, five-by-five, pudgy. —**Ant.** scrawny, gaunt, skinny.

romance, *n.* **1.** novel, *roman,* tale, story, fiction, (*slang*) bodice ripper. **2.** fancy, extravagance, exaggeration; falsehood, fable, fiction, lie. **3.** love affair, amour.

romantic, *adj.* **1.** fanciful, unpractical, quixotic, extravagant, exaggerated, wild, imaginative, unrealistic, fantastic. **2.** improbable, imaginary, fantastic, chimerical, fictitious, fabulous, unreal. **3.** picturesque. —**Ant.** practical, realistic; probable.

romp, *v.* **1.** play, frolic, gambol, frisk, cavort, caper, rollick, revel, roister, lark about, kick up one's heels. —*n.* **2.** gambol, frolic, caper, revel, escapade. **3.** triumph, easy victory, walkover, walkaway, runaway, pushover.

rook, *n.* **1.** crow, raven. **2.** castle. **3.** sharper, cardsharp, cheat, swindler. —*v.* **4.** cheat, swindle, rob, fleece, defraud.

rosy, *adj.* **1.** pink, reddish, roseate. **2.** red, rubicund, flushed, blooming, ruddy, healthy. **3.** bright, promising, cheerful, optimistic. —**Ant.** dark, dim, cheerless, pessimistic.

rot, *v.* **1.** decompose, decay, mold, molder, putrefy, spoil, corrupt. **2.** corrupt, degenerate. —*n.* **3.** decay, putrefaction, decomposition, corruption, mold. —**Ant.** purify. —**Syn. Study.** See DECAY.

rotate, *v.* turn, spin, revolve, wheel, whirl. —**Syn. Study.** See TURN.

rotten, *adj.* **1.** decomposed, decayed, putrefied, putrescent, putrid, tainted, foul, miasmatic, noxious, ill-smelling, fetid, rank. **2.** corrupt, offensive, amoral, immoral. **3.** contemptible, disgusting, unwholesome, treacherous, dishonest, deceitful, corrupt. **4.** soft, yielding, friable; unsound, defective. —**Ant.** pure; moral; wholesome, honest; hard, inflexible; sound.

roué, *n.* debauchee, rake, profligate.

rough, *adj.* **1.** uneven, bumpy, irregular, rugged, jagged, scabrous, craggy. **2.** shaggy, coarse, hairy, bristly, hirsute. **3.** violent, disorderly, wild, boisterous, turbulent, riotous; sharp, severe, harsh. **4.** disturbed, stormy, agitated, tempestuous, inclement. **5.** harsh, grating, jarring, noisy, cacophonous, inharmonious, discordant, flat, raucous. **6.** uncultured, indelicate, unrefined, impolite, uncivil, unpolished, rude, inconvenient, uncomfortable, crude, coarse. **7.** plain, imperfect, unpolished, uncorrected, unfinished. **8.** vague, inexact, incomplete. **9.**

crude, unwrought,
undressed, unpolished,
unprepared, unset, uncut.
—**Ant.** even, regular; bald,
hairless, smooth; orderly;
fair; harmonious; cultured,
refined; finished, polished;
precise, exact; dressed,
polished.

round, *adj.* **1.** circular,
disklike. **2.** ring-shaped,
hooplike, annular. **3.**
curved, arched. **4.**
cylindrical. **5.** spherical,
globular, rotund, orbed. **6.**
full, complete, entire,
whole, unbroken. **7.** full,
sonorous. **8.** vigorous,
brisk, smart, quick. **9.**
plain, honest,
straightforward, candid,
outspoken, frank, open,
upright, fair. **10.**
unmodified, positive,
unqualified. —*n.* **11.** circle,
ring, curve. **12.** cylinder,
rung. **13.** course, cycle,
revolution, period, series,
succession. —**Ant.**
angular, square,
rectangular, polygonal.

rouse, *v.* **1.** stir, excite,
animate, kindle, fire,
inflame, stimulate,
awaken, provoke. **2.**

anger, provoke, incite, ire.
—**Ant.** calm; pacify.
—**Syn. Study.** See INCITE.

rove, *v.* roam, wander,
range, ramble, stroll,
amble, stray.

row, *n.* **1.** argument,
disagreement, quarrel,
dispute, altercation,
squabble, fight, set-to,
donnybrook, scrap,
knock-down-drag-out. —*v.*
2. argue, quarrel,
squabble, fight,

rowdy, *adj.* **1.** boisterous,
noisy, raucous, rackety,
rambunctious, disorderly,
unruly, brawling,
roistering, obstreperous,
rip-roaring, riotous,
ruffian, ruffianly,
rough-and-tumble. —*n.* **2.**
mischief-maker, ruffian,
hooligan, brawler, street
fighter, tough,
street-tough, hood,
hoodlum, hooligan, thug,
bullyboy, (*Brit.*) teddy
boy, yob, yobbo.

royal, *adj.* regal, majestic,
kingly, imperial, princely.
—**Ant.** servile.

ruckus, *n.* commotion,
disturbance, fuss, row,

to-do, hubbub, ruction, rumpus, uproar, racket, turmoil, brouhaha, foofaraw.

ruddy, *adj.* **1.** red, reddish, rose-colored, rosy, rufous, rubicund. **2.** rosy-cheeked, rosy, glowing, florid, flushed, high-colored, blushing.

rude, *adj.* **1.** discourteous, unmannerly, ill-mannered, impolite, unrefined, uncivil, coarse, curt, brusque, saucy, pert, impertinent, impudent, fresh. **2.** unlearned, untutored, uneducated, untaught, ignorant, uncultured, unrefined, untrained, uncivilized, coarse, uncouth, vulgar, boorish. **3.** rough, harsh, ungentle, coarse, rugged, crude. **4.** unwrought, raw, crude, rough, shapeless, amorphous. **5.** inartistic, inelegant, primitive, rustic, artless, simple, unadorned, unpolished, undecorated. **6.** violent, tempestuous, stormy, fierce, tumultuous, turbulent. **7.** robust, sturdy, vigorous. **—Ant.** courteous, mannerly;

learned; gentle; artistic, elegant; calm. **—Syn. Study.** See RAW.

rudimentary, *adj.* **1.** rudimental, elementary, fundamental, primary, initial. **2.** undeveloped, embryonic, elementary, imperfect. **3.** vestigial, abortive. **—Ant.** advanced; mature, perfect; complete.

ruffle, *v.* **1.** disarrange, rearrange, disorder, rumple, wrinkle, damage, derange. **2.** disturb, discompose, irritate, vex, annoy, upset, agitate, trouble, torment, plague, harry, harass, worry, molest. **—*n.* 3.** disturbance, perturbation, annoyance, vexation, confusion, commotion, flurry, tumult, bustle, agitation. **4.** frill, trimming; ruff. **5.** drumbeat. **—Ant.** arrange, order; compose; composure, peace.

rugged, *adj.* **1.** broken, uneven, rocky, hilly, craggy, irregular. **2.** wrinkled, furrowed. **3.** rough, harsh, stern, severe, hard, stormy, austere. **4.** severe, hard, trying, difficult. **5.** tempestuous, stormy, rough. **6.** harsh, grating, inharmonious, cacophonous, scabrous. **7.** rude, uncultivated, unrefined, unpolished, crude. **8.** homely, plain, ugly. —**Ant.** even, smooth, regular; easy, flexible; fair; harmonious; cultivated, refined; pretty, lovely, beautiful.

ruin, *n.* **1.** decay, dilapidation, ruination, perdition, destruction, havoc, damage, disintegration, devastation, spoliation. **2.** downfall, destruction, decay, fall, overthrow, defeat, undoing, subversion, wreck. —*v.* **3.** spoil, demolish, destroy, damage, reduce to ruin. —**Ant.** construction; creation; create, build.

rule, *n.* **1.** principle, regulation, standard, law, canon, ruling, guide, precept, order, ukase. **2.** control, government, dominion, command, domination, mastery,

sway, authority, direction. —*v.* **3.** administer, command, govern, manage, control, handle, lead, direct, guide, conduct. **4.** decree, decide, deem, judge, settle, establish, order, demand.

ruminate, *v.* **1.** chew cud. **2.** ponder, muse, think, meditate, reflect.

rumor, *n.* story, talk, gossip, hearsay, bruit, news, report.

run, *v.* **1.** race, hasten, hurry, hie, scud, speed, scamper. **2.** flow, pour, stream; go, move, proceed. **3.** melt, fuse, liquefy. **4.** leak, overflow, flood, spread. **5.** creep, trail, climb. **6.** operate, continue. **7.** extend, stretch, reach, spread. **8.** contend, compete, challenge. **9.** pursue, hunt, chase. **10.** convey, transport, ferry, carry. **11.** pierce, stab, thrust, force, drive. **12.** operate, carry on, conduct, manage. **13.** melt, fuse, smelt, liquefy. —*n.* **14.** period, spell, interval. **15.** series, set, course, passage, motion, extent, progress. **16.** stream, rivulet, rill, runnel, brook, channel, burn. **17.** ordinary, standard, average, regular. **18.** way, track. **19.** herd, school, pack, bevy, covey, brood, flock, gaggle, pride; group, company, crowd.

rupture, *n.* **1.** breaking, bursting; breach, fracture, break, split, burst, disruption. **2.** hernia. —*v.* **3.** break, fracture, split, burst, disrupt, separate. —**Ant.** seam, union; unite, organize.

rural, *adj.* rustic, unsophisticated, rugged, rough; crude, boorish. —**Ant.** urban. —**Syn. Study.** RURAL and RUSTIC are terms that refer to the country. RURAL is the neutral term: *rural education.* It is also used subjectively, usu. in a favorable sense: *the charm of rural life.* RUSTIC, however, may have either favorable or unfavorable connotations. In a derogatory sense, it means provincial, boorish, or crude; in a favorable sense, it may suggest a homelike simplicity and lack of sophistication: *rustic manners.*

ruse, See Syn. study at TRICK.

rush, *v.* **1.** dash, hasten, run. **2.** attack, overcome. —*v.* **3.** busyness, haste, hurry. **4.** straw, reeds, fiber. —**Ant.** sloth, lethargy.

rustic, *adj.* rural. —**Ant.** urban. —**Syn. Study.** See RURAL.

ruthless, *adj.* pitiless, merciless, unpitying, unmerciful, cruel, hard, harsh, severe, hard-hearted, uncompassionate, unrelenting, adamant, relentless, inexorable, fell, truculent, inhuman, ferocious, savage, barbarous. —**Ant.** merciful, compassionate, humane.

S

Sabbath, *n.* Lord's day, Sunday, day of rest.
—**Syn. Study.** See SUNDAY.

sabotage, *n.* **1.** subversion, subversiveness, damage, injury, undermining, weakening. —*v.* **2.** undermine, subvert, damage, hurt, disable, weaken, incapacitate, wreck.

saccharine, *adj.* **1.** oversweet, sickly-sweet, cloying, treacly, sugary. **2.** mawkish, oversentimental, maudlin, bathetic, sticky, treacly, cloying, mushy, soppy, sappy, icky. **3.** ingratiating, fawning, obsequious, insinuating, silken, silky, suave, sycophantic. —**Ant.** astringent, bracing.

sack, *n.* **1.** bag, pouch. **2.** pillaging, looting, plundering, pillage, destruction, devastation, desolation, spoliation, ruin, ruination, waste, ravage, rapine. —*v.* **3.** pillage, loot, rob, spoil, despoil, ruin, lay waste, plunder, devastate, demolish, destroy, ravage, rape.

sacred, *adj.* **1.** consecrated, holy, sainted, venerable, hallowed, divine, worshipful. **2.** dedicated, consecrated, revered. **3.** secure, protected, sacrosanct, immune, inviolate, inviolable.
—**Ant.** blasphemous.
—**Syn. Study.** See HOLY.

sacrilege, *n.* blasphemy, impiety, irreverence, profanity, desecration, profanation, heresy, sin, offense, abomination, violation, crime, infamy, disgrace, scandal.

sacrosanct, *adj.* sacred, holy, sanctified, hallowed, blessed, venerable, inviolate, inviolable, untouchable, taboo, tabu.

sad, *adj.* **1.** sorrowful,

mournful, unhappy, despondent, disconsolate, depressed, dejected, melancholy, discouraged, gloomy, downcast, downhearted. **2.** somber, dark, dull. **3.** grievous, deplorable, disastrous, dire, calamitous. **—Ant.** happy.

safe, *adj.* **1.** secure, protected, sound, guarded. **2.** dependable, trustworthy, sure, reliable. **3.** cautious, wary, careful. **—n. 4.** repository, strongbox, coffer, chest, safe deposit box. **—Ant.** unsafe.

safeguard, *n.* **1.** defense, guard, protection, precaution, palladium, bulwark, shield, aegis, armor, armament, cushion, security, insurance. **—v. 2.** defend, guard, protect, shield, secure, bulwark, preserve.

saga, *n.* edda, epic, tale, tradition, legend, history.

sagacious, *adj.* wise, sage, shrewd, discerning, clever, intelligent, judicious, rational, acute, sharp, keen, perspicacious, sharp-witted. **—Ant.** unwise, irrational.

sage, *n.* **1.** wise man, philosopher. **—adj. 2.** prudent, sagacious. **—Ant.** dolt; imprudent.

sailor, *n.* mariner, salt, tar, seaman, seafarer, seafaring man. **—Ant.** landlubber. **—Syn. Study.** SAILOR, SEAMAN, MARINER, SALT are terms for a person who leads a seafaring life. A SAILOR or SEAMAN is one whose occupation is on board a ship at sea, esp. a member of a ship's crew below the rank of petty officer: *a sailor before the mast; an able-bodied seaman.* MARINER is a term found in certain technical expressions: *mariner's compass* (ordinary compass as used on ships); the word now seems elevated or quaint: *The Rime of the Ancient Mariner.* SALT is an informal term for an experienced sailor: *an old salt.*

sake, *n.* **1.** cause, account, interest, score, regard, consideration, respect, reason. **2.** purpose, end, reason.

salacious, *adj.* lustry, lecherous, rakish, lewd, carnal, wanton, lascivious, libidinous, concupiscent; obscene, pornographic, prurient. —**Ant.** modest, prudish.

salient, *adj.* prominent, conspicuous, important, remarkable, striking. —**Ant.** inconspicuous; unimportant.

sallow, *adj.* pallid, washed-out, wan, waxen, sickly, bloodless, anemic, pasty, pasty-faced, whey-faced, greenish, green around the gills, yellowish, jaundiced.

salt, See Syn. study at SAILOR.

salutary, *adj.* healthy, health-giving, salubrious, wholesome. —**Ant.** unwholesome.

salvage, *v.* rescue, redeem, deliver, save, recover, regain, retrieve, recoup, ransom, recycle. —**Ant.** discard.

same, *adj.* **1.** identical; similar, like, corresponding, interchangeable, equal. **2.** agreeing; unchanging. —**Ant.** different; disagreeing.

sameness, *n.* identity, uniformity, monotony. —**Ant.** difference.

sample, *n.* specimen, example, illustration, pattern, model.

sanctify, *v.* bless, consecrate, dedicate, hallow, purify, beatify, enshrine. —**Ant.** desecrate.

sanctimonious, *adj.* hypocritical, unctuous, pious, canting, pietistic, pharisaical, holier-than-thou, smug, Tartuffian, Pecksniffian, simon-pure, self-righteous, goody-goody, goody-two-shoes. —**Ant.** sincere.

sanction, *n.* **1.** authority, permission, countenance, support, ratification, solemnification, authorization. —*v.* **2.** authorize, countenance, approve, confirm, ratify, support, allow, bind.

—**Ant.** disapproval; disallow, disapprove.

sanctuary, *n.* church, temple, shrine, altar, sanctum, adytum.

sane, *adj.* rational, reasoning, reasonable, lucid, clear-headed, clear-thinking, lucid, sound, normal, all there, compos mentis, wise, judicious, sapient, sagacious, sage, prudent, sensible. —**Ant.** insane, foolish.

sanguinary, *adj.* bloody, murderous, bloodthirsty, cruel, savage, fell, ruthless, truculent, pitiless, unmerciful, merciless. —**Ant.** merciful, kind.

sanguine, *adj.* cheerful, hopeful, confident, enthusiastic, buoyant, animated, lively, spirited. —**Ant.** morose, dispirited.

sanitary, *adj.* hygienic, unpolluted, clean, germfree; healthy, salutary. —**Ant.** polluted; unhealthy, unwholesome.

sapient, *adj.* wise, sage, sagacious. —**Ant.** stupid, dull, unwise.

sarcasm, *n.* irony, derision, bitterness, ridicule; taunt, gibe, jeer. —**Syn. Study.** See IRONY.

sarcastic, *adj.* cynical, biting, cutting, mordant, bitter, derisive, ironical, sardonic, satirical. —**Syn. Study.** See CYNICAL.

sardonic, *adj.* sarcastic, bitter, ironical, sneering, malignant, malicious.

satanic, *adj.* evil, wicked, diabolical, devilish, infernal, hellish, malicious, fiendish. —**Ant.** godly, angelic, benevolent.

satiate, *v.* cloy, glut, stuff, gorge, sate, surfeit; gall, disgust, weary.

satire, *n.* irony, sarcasm, ridicule, lampoon, pasquinade, burlesque, exposure, denunciation. —**Syn. Study.** See IRONY.

satirical, *adj.* cynical, sarcastic, sardonic, ironical, taunting, biting, keen, sharp, cutting, severe, mordant, mordacious, bitter, acid.

satisfaction, *n.* **1.** gratification, enjoyment, pleasure, contentment, ease, comfort. **2.** reparation, restitution, amends, expiation, atonement, compensation, indemnification, remuneration, recompense, requital, *Wiedergutmachung*. **3.** payment, discharge, repayment. —**Ant.** dissatisfaction, displeasure, discomfort.

satisfy, *v.* **1.** gratify, meet, appease, pacify, content, please. **2.** fulfill, fill, satiate, sate, suffice, surfeit. **3.** assure, convince, persuade. —**Ant.** dissatisfy, displease.

saturate, *v.* soak, impregnate, imbue, wet, ret, drench. —**Ant.** ted, dry.

saucy, *adj.* impudent, pert, cheeky, flippant, irrepressible, forward, impertinent, cocky, sassy, fresh, flip.

saunter, *v.* stroll, walk, ramble, amble.

savage, *adj.* **1.** wild, rugged, uncultivated, sylvan, rough. **2.** barbarous, uncivilized, rude, unpolished, wild. **3.** fierce, ferocious, wild, untamed, feral, ravenous. **4.** enraged, furious, angry, irate, infuriated. **5.** cruel, brutal, beastly; inhuman, fell, merciless, unmerciful, pitiless, ruthless, bloodthirsty, truculent, sanguinary. —**Ant.** cultivated, cultured; tame; calm; merciful.

savant, *n.* scholar, sage, intellectual, polymath, expert, authority, pundit, egghead, wonk, brain, rocket scientist, maven, (*Brit.*) boffin.

save, *v.* **1.** rescue, salvage, preserve. **2.** safeguard, keep. **3.** set apart, reserve, lay by, economize, hoard, store up, husband. —*prep., conj.* **4.** except, but.

savior, *n.* rescuer, deliverer, saver, lifesaver, safekeeper, preserver, liberator, redeemer, emancipator.

savor, *n.* **1.** taste, flavor, relish; odor, scent, fragrance. —*v.* **2.** flavor, season, spice.

savory, See Syn. study at PALATABLE.

say, *v.* **1.** utter, pronounce, speak, remark, affirm, allege. **2.** express, state, word, declare, tell, argue. **3.** recite, repeat, iterate, reiterate, rehearse. **4.** report, allege, maintain, hold.

scale, *n.* **1.** plate, lamina, flake, peel. **2.** coating, crust, incrustation. **3.** pan, dish. **4.** *(plural)* balance. **5.** steps, degrees, series, gradation, progression. —*v.* **6.** skip, play at ducks and drakes. **7.** weigh, balance. **8.** climb, ascend, mount. **9.** progress, gradate.

scamp, *n.* rascal, imp, mischief-maker, rapscallion, cutup, rogue, little devil, scalawag, scapegrace. —**Ant.** goody two-shoes.

scandal, *n.* **1.** disgrace, damage, discredit, dishonor, offense, shame, disrepute, opprobrium, odium, ignominy. **2.** defamation, gossip, slander, character assassination, aspersion, detraction, calumny, obloquy. —**Ant.** honor, repute; praise, kudos.

scanty, *adj.* meager, sparse, insufficient, inadequate, deficient, thin, spare, small, paltry, poor, stinted, gaunt, lean. —**Ant.** abundant, adequate. —**Syn. Study.** SCANTY, MEAGER, SPARSE refer to insufficiency or deficiency in quantity, number, etc. SCANTY denotes smallness or insufficiency of quantity, number, supply, etc.: *a scanty supply of food.* MEAGER indicates that something is poor, stinted, or inadequate: *meager fare; a meager income.* SPARSE applies particularly to that which grows thinly or is thinly distributed: *sparse vegetation; a sparse population.*

scapegoat, *n.* patsy, goat, fall guy, whipping boy, sacrifice, offering, victim, target, stooge.

scarce, *adj.* rare, insufficient, deficient; uncommon, infrequent.

—**Ant.** abundant, sufficient.

scarcely, *adv.* hardly, barely, not quite, scantly. —**Ant.** definitely, full. —**Syn. Study.** See HARDLY.

scare, *v.* **1.** terrify, alarm, startle, frighten, shock, intimidate. —*n.* **2.** fright, terror, alarm, panic.

scatter, *v.* **1.** sprinkle, broadcast, strew. **2.** dispel, disperse, dissipate, separate, drive away. —**Ant.** gather. —**Syn. Study.** SCATTER, DISPEL, DISPERSE, DISSIPATE imply separating and driving something away so that its original form disappears. To SCATTER is to separate something tangible into parts at random and drive these in different directions: *The wind scattered leaves all over the lawn.* To DISPEL is to drive away or scatter usu. intangible things so that they vanish: *Your explanation has dispelled my doubts.* To DISPERSE is usu. to cause a compact or organized tangible body to separate or scatter in different directions, to be reassembled if desired: *Tear gas dispersed the mob.* To DISSIPATE is usu. to scatter by dissolving or reducing to small atoms or parts that cannot be reunited: *He dissipated his money and his energy in useless activities.*

scene, *n.* **1.** arena, stage, theater. **2.** view, picture, prospect, landscape. **3.** incident, episode, situation. **4.** exhibition, demonstration, spectacle, show, display.

scent, *n.* **1.** odor, aroma, fragrance, smell, savor, redolence, perfume. **2.** track, trail, spoor. —*v.* **3.** detect, perceive, smell. —**Syn. Study.** See ODOR.

schedule, *n.* **1.** roll, catalogue, table, list, inventory, register. **2.** timetable. —*v.* **3.** enter, register, list, enroll, tabulate, classify.

scheme, *n.* **1.** plan, design, program, project, system. **2.** plot, intrigue, stratagem, cabal, conspiracy, contrivance, machination. **3.** system, pattern, diagram, schema, arrangement. —*v.* **4.** plan, plot, contrive, project, devise, design.

schmaltz, *n.* sentimentality, sentimentalism, emotionalism, schwarmerei, mawkishness, bathos, mush, mushiness. —**Ant.** realism, hardheadedness.

scholar, *n.* **1.** savant, wise man, sage. **2.** student, pupil, disciple, learner. —**Ant.** teacher.

scholarship, *n.* learning, knowledge, erudition, wisdom. —**Ant.** stupidity. —**Syn. Study.** See LEARNING.

schooling, *n.* education, training, instruction, tuition, tutelage, learning.

scion, *n.* offspring, child, descendant, fruit, heir, heiress.

scoff, *n., v.* mock, scorn, jeer, gibe, sneer, taunt, ridicule. —**Ant.** envy, praise, exalt. —**Syn. Study.** SCOFF, JEER, SNEER imply behaving with scornful disapproval toward someone or about something. To SCOFF is to express insolent doubt or derision, openly and emphatically: *to scoff at a new invention.* To JEER suggests expressing disapproval and scorn more loudly, coarsely, and unintelligently than in scoffing: *The crowd jeered at the pitcher.* To SNEER is to show by facial expression or tone of voice ill-natured contempt or disparagement: *He sneered unpleasantly in referring to his opponent's misfortunes.*

scold, *v.* **1.** chide, reprove, reproach, rate, berate, censure, rail at, reprimand, blame, rebuke. —*n.* **2.** nag, shrew, virago, termagant, maenad, bacchante. —**Ant.** praise, honor.

scope, *n.* range, extent, space, opportunity, margin, room, latitude, liberty; tract, area, length. —**Syn. Study.** See RANGE.

scorch, *v.* **1.** burn, singe, char, blister, parch, shrivel. **2.** criticize, excoriate, condemn. —**Ant.** praise, laud.

score, *n.* **1.** record, account, reckoning. **2.** notch, scratch, stroke, line, mark. **3.** twenty. **4.** account, reason, ground, consideration, motive, purpose. —*v.* **5.** record, reckon, tabulate, count. **6.** notch, mark, scratch, cut. **7.** gain, win.

scorn, *n.* **1.** contempt, disdain, contumely. **2.** mockery, derision, scoff, sneer. —*v.* **3.** disdain, contemn, despise, detest. —**Ant.** affection, pleasure. —**Syn. Study.** See CONTEMPT.

scoundrel, *n.* villain, knave, rogue, poltroon, scamp, cad, rascal, rapscallion, miscreant, trickster, sharper, cheat, mountebank, wretch. —**Ant.** hero, protagonist. —**Syn. Study.** See KNAVE.

scourge, *n.* **1.** whip, lash, strap, thong. **2.** flogging, punishment. **3.** affliction, calamity, plague, band, pest, nuisance. —*v.* **4.** lash, whip. **5.** punish, chastise, chasten, correct, castigate, afflict, torment.

scramble, *v.* **1.** hasten, rush, scurry, scamper, scuttle, bustle, hustle. **2.** clamber, creep, scrabble, claw, crawl, go on all fours. **3.** vie, compete, contend, jostle, struggle, strive. **4.** mix, intermix, blend, mix up, mingle, jumble. **5.** confuse, mix up, muddle, garble. —*n.* **6.** bustle, rush, hurry, flurry, flutter, commotion. **7.** clutter, jumble, mix, mishmash.

scrap, *n.* **1.** fragment, piece, portion; morsel, crumb, bit, bite. —*adj.* **2.** fragmentary, piecemeal; waste. —*v.* **3.** break up, demolish. **4.** throw away, discard. —**Ant.** whole.

scrappy, *adj.* contentious, disputatious, argumentative, spirited, mettlesome, hot-tempered, hotheaded, feisty, spunky, pugnacious, combative.

scream, *v.* **1.** shriek, screech, cry, screak. —*n.* **2.** outcry, cry, shriek, screech, screak.

screen, *n.* **1.** partition, shelter, cover, protection, guard, shield, defense. **2.** sieve, riddle, grating. —*v.* **3.** shelter, protect, veil, defend, shield, conceal, hide, cover, cloak, mask, shroud. **4.** sift.

screwball, *adj.* **1.** eccentric, off-center, whimsical, capricious, zany, kooky, oddball, madcap, nutty, goofy, wacky. —*n.* **2.** oddity, character, oddball, zany, kook, nut, nutcase.

scrumptious, *adj.* delicious, tasty, savory, palatable, sapid, flavorful, flavorsome, succulent, luscious, ambrosial, delectable, toothsome, mouth-watering, yummy. —**Ant.** tasteless, insipid.

scruple, *n.* **1.** hesitation, reluctance, conscience, restraint, compunction, qualm. —*v.* **2.** hesitate, waver, doubt.

scrupulous, *adj.* **1.** conscientious, reluctant, hesitant, cautious, wary, careful, circumspect. **2.** punctilious, minute, careful, exacting, exact, precise, demanding, rigorous. —**Ant.**

unscrupulous; careless. —**Syn. Study.** SCRUPULOUS, PUNCTILIOUS imply being very careful to do the right or proper thing. SCRUPULOUS implies conscientious care in attending to details: *The scientist described his observations with scrupulous accuracy.* PUNCTILIOUS suggests strictness and rigidity, esp. in observance of social conventions: *punctilious adherence to the rules of etiquette.*

scrutinize, *v.* examine, investigate, dissect, study, sift. —**Ant.** neglect, overlook.

scrutiny, *n.* examination, investigation, dissection, study, inquiry, inspection, inquisition, search. —**Syn. Study.** See EXAMINATION.

scurrilous, *adj.* **1.** gross, indecent, abusive, opprobrious, vituperative, reproachful, insolent, insulting, offensive, ribald. **2.** coarse, jocular, derisive, vulgar, obscene. —**Ant.** decent, polite; proper.

scurvy, *adj.* low, mean, base, contemptible, vile, despicable, worthless. —**Ant.** honorable, dignified, noble.

scuttlebutt, *n.* rumor, gossip, hearsay, report, item, whisper, talk, on-dit, bruit, buzz, dish, talk of the town.

seaman, See Syn. study at SAILOR.

sear, *v.* **1.** burn, char, singe, scorch. **2.** brand, cauterize. **3.** dry up, wither. **4.** harden, callus.

search, *v.* **1.** look for, seek, explore, investigate, examine, scrutinize, inspect. **2.** probe; pierce, penetrate. —*n.* **3.** exploration, examination, investigation, inspection, scrutiny, searching, inquiry, inquisition, pursuit, quest.

seasonable, *adj.* suitable, timely, opportune, fit, convenient, appropriate. —**Ant.** unseasonable, unsuitable, untimely, inopportune.

seasoning, *n.* **1.** flavoring, flavor, seasoner, condiment, spice, herb. **2.** experience, practice, maturation, development, mellowing, tempering, hardening, strengthening, toughening.

seat, *n.* **1.** chair, bench, banquette, easy chair, throne, stool. **2.** bottom, base, fundament. **3.** site, situation, location, locality, locale.

secede, *v.* abdicate, withdraw, retire, separate, resign. —**Ant.** join.

secluded, *adj.* withdrawn, isolated, retired, sequestered, private. —**Ant.** public.

secret, *adj.* **1.** clandestine, hidden, concealed, covert, private, privy, unrevealed, mysterious, unknown, cabalistic, cryptic. **2.** reticent, close-mouthed, secretive. **3.** retired, secluded, private. **4.** occult, obscure, mysterious, latent, abstruse, recondite. —*n.* **5.** mystery. —**Ant.** open, manifest, obvious, apparent.

secrete, *v.* hide, conceal,

cover, shroud, disguise.
—**Ant.** open, manifest.
—**Syn. Study.** See HIDE.

secular, *adj.* worldly,
temporal, mundane,
earthly, earthy, lay,
nonclerical, material,
unspiritual, profane.
—**Ant.** religious, spiritual,
ecclesiastical.

secure, *adj.* **1.** safe,
protected. **2.** fixed, stable,
fast, fastened. **3.** sure,
certain, confident, assured.
—*v.* **4.** obtain, procure,
get, acquire, gain. **5.**
protect, guard, safeguard.
6. make certain, ensure,
assure, guarantee. **7.** make
firm, fasten. —**Ant.**
insecure; unstable; unsure;
lose; unloose, loosen.
—**Syn. Study.** See GET.

sedate, *adj.* calm, quiet,
composed, sober,
undisturbed, unexcited,
staid, cool, collected,
serene, placid, tranquil,
unruffled, unperturbed,
imperturbable, serious,
settled, demure, grave,
thoughtful, contemplative.
—**Ant.** disturbed,
perturbed, excited,
nervous.

sedative, *n.* **1.** soporific,
tranquilizer, opiate, drug,
narcotic, calmative,
barbiturate, antispasmodic,
hypnotic, quieter,
quietener, soother, pacifier,
anodyne. —*adj.* **2.**
soothing, sleep-inducing,
tranquilizing, narcotic,
calmative, somniferous,
soporific, palliative.
—**Ant.** stimulant.

sediment, *n.* lees, dregs,
grounds, precipitate.

sedition, *n.* treason,
mutiny, rebellion, revolt,
revolution, riot,
insurrection, uprising.
—**Ant.** allegiance,
patriotism. —**Syn. Study.**
See TREASON.

seduce, *v.* tempt, lead
astray, corrupt, entice,
beguile, inveigle, decoy,
allure, lure, deceive.
—**Ant.** repel, disgust.
—**Syn. Study.** See TEMPT.

seductive, *adj.* tempting,
captivating, alluring,
enticing, attractive,
beguiling; deceptive.
—**Ant.** repulsive, repellent,
abhorrent.

sedulous, *adj.* diligent,

industrious, assiduous, busy, hardworking, zealous, tireless, painstaking, meticulous, thoroughgoing, persevering, steadfast. —**Ant.** careless, lazy.

see, *v.* **1.** perceive, look at, spy, espy, notice, discern, observe, distinguish, behold, regard. **2.** view, visit, watch. **3.** perceive, discern, penetrate, understand, comprehend, remark. **4.** learn, ascertain, find out, determine. **5.** experience, live through, know, feel, meet with, suffer, undergo. **6.** receive, entertain, visit with. **7.** attend, escort, accompany. **8.** consider, think, deliberate. —*n.* **9.** diocese, bishopric. —**Syn. Study.** See WATCH.

seedy, *adj.* **1.** shabby, run-down, dilapidated, ramshackle, ragged, shoddy, shopworn, scruffy, tatty, ratty, down-at-heel, fly-blown, moth-eaten. **2.** unwell, ailing, ill, sick, sickish, under the weather, run-down, exhausted, beat. —**Ant.** spruce, trim, smart.

seek, *v.* **1.** search for, look for. **2.** pursue, follow, solicit, go after. **3.** ask for, request, inquire after.

seem, *v.* appear, look; pretend, assume. —**Syn. Study.** SEEM, APPEAR, LOOK refer to an outward aspect that may or may not be contrary to reality. SEEM is applied to something that has an aspect of truth and probability: *It seems warmer today.* APPEAR suggests the giving of an impression that may be superficial or illusory: *The house appears to be deserted.* LOOK more vividly suggests the use of the eye (literally or figuratively) or the aspect as perceived by the eye: *She looked frightened.*

seemly, *adj.* fitting, becoming, suited, well-suited, suitable, appropriate, proper, befitting, meet; decent, decorous, right. —**Ant.** unseemly.

seep, *v.* ooze, osmose. —**Ant.** pour.

seethe, *v.* **1.** soak, steep,

ret, saturate. **2.** boil; surge, foam, froth. —**Syn. Study.** See BOIL.

segregate, *v.* isolate, separate, set apart, dissociate. —**Ant.** unite, associate, blend; desegregate.

seize, *v.* **1.** grasp, grab, clutch. **2.** capture, take into custody, arrest, apprehend, catch, take. —**Ant.** loose.

seldom, *adv.* rarely, infrequently, not often. —**Ant.** often, frequently.

select, *v.* **1.** choose, prefer, pick, pick out. —*adj.* **2.** selected, chosen, preferred, choice, special, picked, valuable, excellent. **3.** careful, fastidious, exclusive, selective.

selective, *adj.* discriminating, choosy, scrupulous, particular, discerning, eclectic, fastidious, picky, fussy, finicky. —**Ant.** undiscriminating.

self-evident, *adj.* evident, obvious, axiomatic, self-explanatory, clear. —**Ant.** mysterious.

self-governed, *adj.* self-governing, autonomous, independent. —**Ant.** dependent.

selfish, *adj.* self-interested, self-seeking, egoistic, illiberal, parsimonious, stingy, mean. —**Ant.** unselfish.

self-satisfied, *adj.* self-complacent, complacent, smug, satisfied. —**Ant.** dissatisfied.

sell, *v.* trade, barter, vend, exchange, deal in. —**Ant.** buy.

semblance, *n.* **1.** appearance, aspect, form, show, exterior, mien, bearing, air. **2.** likeness, similarity, resemblance. —**Ant.** dissimilarity, difference.

seminal, *adj.* original, progenitive, creative, primary, primal, basic, fundamental, basal, founding, germinal, germinative, generative. —**Ant.** derivative, imitative.

send, *v.* **1.** transmit, dispatch, forward, convey.

2. impel, throw, cast, hurl, toss, propel, fling, project. —**Ant.** receive.

senile, *adj.* senescent, decrepit, feeble, geriatric, doddering, doddery, rickety, fogyish, old-fogyish, forgetful, absentminded, oblivious, simple-minded, childish. —**Ant.** youthful, alert.

sensation, *n.* **1.** sense, feeling, perception. **2.** excitement, stimulation, animation; agitation, commotion, perturbation.

sensational, *adj.* startling, thrilling, exciting, stimulating. —**Ant.** prosaic, dull.

sense, *n.* **1.** feeling, perception, sensation. **2.** awareness, recognition, realization, apprehension, appreciation, understanding, consciousness. **3.** perception, estimation, appreciation, discernment. **4.** meaning, signification, signficance, import, interpretation, denotation, connotation. **5.** opinion, judgment, feeling, idea, notion, sentiment. —*v.* **6.** perceive, become aware of, discern, appreciate, recognize. —**Syn. Study.** See MEANING.

senseless, *adj.* **1.** insensate, unconscious, insensible, inert, knocked out, cold. **2.** unperceiving, undiscerning, unappreciative, unfeeling, apathetic, uninterested. **3.** stupid, foolish, silly, idiotic, inane, simple, weak-minded, witless; nonsensical, meaningless, asinine. —**Ant.** sensitive; intelligent.

sensibility, *n.* **1.** responsiveness, alertness, awareness, susceptibility, impressibility. **2.** quickness, keenness, acuteness, sensitivity, sensitiveness. **3.** consciousness, appreciation, understanding, rapport. **4.** delicacy, sensitiveness, perceptiveness. —**Ant.** insensibility; dullness; boorishness.

sensible, *adj.* **1.** judicious, intelligent, sagacious, sage, wise, rational, sound, sober, reasonable. **2.** cognizant, aware, conscious, understanding, observant. **3.** appreciable, considerable. **4.** perceptible, discernible, identifiable. **—Ant.** insensible, irrational, unsound; unaware; trifling. **—Syn. Study.** See PRACTICAL.

sensitive, *adj.* **1.** impressionable, susceptible, easily affected. **2.** sensate. **3.** delicate. **—Ant.** insensitive; hard, obdurate, indelicate.

sensitivity, *n.* sensibility.

sensual, *adj.* **1.** voluptuous, sensuous, luxurious. **2.** lewd, unchaste, gross, licentious, lascivious, dissolute. **—Ant.** modest, prudish. **—Syn. Study.** SENSUAL, SENSUOUS both refer to experience through the senses. SENSUAL refers to the enjoyments derived from the senses, esp. to the gratification or indulgence of physical appetites: *sensual pleasures.* SENSUOUS refers to that which is aesthetically pleasing to the senses:

sensuous poetry. See also CARNAL.

sensuous, *adj.* sentient, feeling, sensible. **—Ant.** insensible. **—Syn. Study.** See SENSUAL.

sententious, *adj.* **1.** pithy, concise, laconic, epigrammatic, terse, succinct, didactic. **2.** judicial, magisterial. **—Ant.** prosaic, prosy, long-drawn.

sentient, *adj.* aware, alive, conscious, awake, cognizant, sensitive, sensible, witting, susceptible, susceptive, feeling, perceptive, responsive, receptive, impressionable, sensate, reactive, discriminative, discriminatory. **—Ant.** dulled, insensible.

sentiment, *n.* **1.** attitude, disposition, opinion, feeling, judgment, thought. **2.** emotion, sentimentality, sensitiveness, sensibility, tenderness. **—Ant.** coolness. **—Syn. Study.** See FEELING.

sentimentality, *n.* sentiment.

separate, *v.* **1.** keep apart, divide, part, put apart, disjoin, disconnect, dissever, sever, disunite, sunder, disengage, dissociate, split, break up. **2.** withdraw, cleave. —*adj.* **3.** separated, disjoined, disunited, unattached, apart, divided, severed, detached, distinct, discrete, dissociate; apart, withdrawn, sequestered, alone, isolated. **4.** independent, individual, particular. —**Ant.** unite, connect; together, indistinct, conglomerate; dependent, general.

sepulcher, *n.* **1.** tomb, grave, burial vault, ossuary. —*v.* **2.** bury, entomb, inter. —**Ant.** cradle, womb; unearth, disinter.

sequence, *n.* **1.** following, succession, order, arrangement, series. **2.** outcome, sequel, consequence, result. —**Syn. Study.** See SERIES.

seraglio, *n.* harem.

serendipity, *n.* luck, chance, happenstance, fortuity, fortuitousness, adventitiousness, randomness, fortune, fluke, flukiness, dumb luck.

serene, *adj.* **1.** calm, peaceful, tranquil, unruffled, undisturbed, imperturbable, unperturbed, placid, composed, sedate, staid, collected, cool. **2.** fair, clear, unclouded, bright. —**Ant.** active, disturbed, upset; clouded, inclement. —**Syn. Study.** See PEACEFUL.

serenity, *n.* calmness, composure, tranquillity, peacefulness, calm, sereneness, peace. —**Ant.** perturbation, disturbance.

serf, *n.* slave, esne, ryot, bondman, villein, thrall. —**Ant.** master.

series, *n.* sequence, succession, set, line; order, arrangement. —**Syn. Study.** SERIES, SEQUENCE, SUCCESSION are terms for an orderly following of things one after another. SERIES is applied to a number of things of the same kind, usu. related to each other, arranged or happening in order: *a series of baseball games.* SEQUENCE stresses the continuity in time, thought, cause and effect, etc.: *The scenes came in a definite sequence.* SUCCESSION implies that one thing is followed by another or others in turn, usu. though not necessarily with a relation or connection between them: *a succession of calamities.*

serious, *adj.* **1.** thoughtful, grave, solemn, sober, sedate, staid, earnest. **2.** weighty, important, momentous, grave, critical. —**Ant.** jocular; trivial. —**Syn. Study.** See EARNEST.

sermonize, *v.* preach, evangelize, homilize, preachify, prelect, lecture, hold forth, discourse, dilate, expatiate, dogmatize, moralize.

servant, *n.* domestic, maidservant, servant-girl, employee, maid, menial, servitor, attendant, retainer, butler, footman. —**Ant.** master.

serve, *v.* **1.** wait on, attend. **2.** assist, help, aid, succor. **3.** function, answer, do, suffice. **4.** promote, contribute, forward, advance, assist. **5.** provide, cater, satisfy, purvey.

serviceable, *adj.* **1.** helpful, useful, handy, utile, aidful, employable, utilitarian, convenient, available, effective, valuable. **2.** adequate, tolerable, passable, fair, fairish, unexceptional, middling, so-so, decent, respectable, acceptable, satisfactory.

servile, *adj.* submissive, obsequious, menial, slavish, cringing, low, fawning, abject, mean, base, sycophantic, groveling. —**Ant.** aggressive, overbearing, dignified. —**Syn. Study.** SERVILE, OBSEQUIOUS, SLAVISH describe the submissive or compliant behavior of a slave or an inferior. SERVILE suggests cringing, fawning, and abject submission: *servile responses to questions.* OBSEQUIOUS implies the ostentatious subordination of oneself to the wishes of another, either from fear or from hope of gain: *an obsequious waiter*. SLAVISH stresses the dependence and laborious toil of one who follows or obeys without question: *slavish attentiveness to orders.*

servitude, *n.* slavery, bondage, serfdom, thralldom. —**Syn. Study.** See SLAVERY.

set, *v.* **1.** put, place, position, pose, locate, situate, post, appoint, station, plant. **2.** value, price, rate, prize, evaluate, estimate. **3.** fix, appoint, ordain, settle, establish, determine. **4.** prescribe, assign, predetermine. **5.** adjust, arrange, order, dispose, place, regulate. **6.** frame, mount. **7.** calibrate, regulate. **8.** decline, sink, wane, go down. **9.** solidify, congeal, harden. —*n.* **10.** assortment, outfit, collection, series. **11.** group, clique, coterie, company, circle, class, sect. **12.** direction, bent, inclination, disposition, attitude. **13.** bearing, carriage, mien, posture, appearance, aspect. **14.** stage, scene, secenery, decoration, setting. —*adj.* **15.** fixed, prefixed, predetermined. **16.** prescribed, foreordained. **17.** customary, usual. **18.** fixed, rigid, immovable. **19.** resolved, determined, habitual, stubborn, fixed, obstinate, stiff, unyielding.

settle, *v.* **1.** fix, agree upon, set, establish. **2.** pay, discharge, repay, liquidate. **3.** locate in, people, colonize. **4.** quiet, tranquilize, calm, compose, still, pacify. **5.** stabilize, establish, confirm. **6.** decide, arrange, agree, adjust. **7.** calm down, rest. **8.** sink down, decline, subside, sink, fall.

sever, *v.* separate, divide, put *or* cut apart, part, cut, cleave, sunder, break off, disunite, disjoin, detach, disconnect. —**Ant.** unite.

severe, *adj.* **1.** harsh, extreme, trenchant, biting, acerb, bitter, caustic, satirical, keen, stinging, mordant, mordacious, sharp, cutting. **2.** serious, grave, stern, austere, rigid, rigorous, strict, strait-laced, relentless, hard, unrelenting, inexorable, abrupt, peremptory, curt, short. **3.** rigid, restrained, plain, simple, unadorned, unornamented, chaste. **4.** uncomfortable, distressing, unpleasant, acute, afflictive, violent, intense. **5.** rigid, exact, critical, demanding, accurate, methodical, systematic, exacting. **—Ant.** mild; gradual; flexible; comfortable; inaccurate. **—Syn. Study.** See STERN.

shabby, *adj.* **1.** threadbare, worn, ragged, bedraggled, shopworn, moth-eaten, tattered, scruffy, tatty, out-at-the-elbows. **2.** shoddy, ramshackle, run-down, neglected, decrepit, seedy, squalid, sordid, slummy, wretched. **3.** mean, mean-spirited, base, contemptible, deplorable, egregious, scurvy. **4.** disreputable, discreditable, dishonorable, shameful, ignominious, shady. **5.** unfair,

inequitable, unjust, unsporting, unsportsmanlike, discriminatory.

shack, *n.* shanty, hut, shed, hutch, hovel, cabin, crib, outbuilding, outhouse, lean-to, dump.

shackle, *n.* **1.** fetter, chain, anklet, handcuff, manacle, gyve, hobble. **2.** impediment, obstacle, obstruction, encumbrance. —*v.* **3.** confine, restrain, restrict, fetter, chain, handcuff, hobble. **4.** restrict, trammel, impede, slow, stultify, dull. **—Ant.** liberate, free.

shade, *n.* **1.** darkness, shadow, obscurity, gloom, gloominess, dusk, umbrage. **2.** specter, ghost, apparition, spirit, phantom. **3.** variation, amount, degree, hair, trace, hint, suggestion. **4.** veil, curtain, screen. —*v.* **5.** obscure, dim, darken, cloud, blur, obfuscate. **6.** screen, hide, protect, conceal, cover, shelter. **—Ant.** light.

shake, *v.* **1.** sway, vibrate,

oscillate, quiver, waver, tremble, agitate, shudder, shiver, totter. **2.** brandish, flourish. **3.** agitate, disturb, move, intimidate, frighten, daunt. **4.** unsettle, weaken, enfeeble. —*n.* **5.** tremor, blow, disturbance, shock.

shaky, *adj.* **1.** unsteady, unstable, rickety, unbalanced, teetery, teetering, tottery, tottering, wobbly, doddering, fragile, spindly. **2.** tremulous, trembly, shivery, quivering, quivery, tremulant, jittery, jumpy, skittish. **3.** uncertain, unsure, doubtful, dubious, precarious, problematic, risky, ticklish, dicey, iffy, (*Brit.*) dodgy. **—Ant.** steady, solid.

sham, *n.* **1.** imitation, pretense. —*adj.* **2.** pretended, counterfeit, false, spurious, mock. —*v.* **3.** pretend; imitate, deceive, feign, defraud, impose. **—Ant.** genuine. **—Syn. Study.** See FALSE.

shamble, *v.* shuffle, scuff, scuffle, plod, trudge, tramp, plug, lumber, stumble, stump, clump, slog, schlep, drag one's feet. **—Ant.** swagger, strut.

shambles, *n.* **1.** destruction, ruin, wreckage, ruination, devastation, holocaust, carnage, slaughter. **2.** mess, disorder, confusion, chaos, turmoil, jumble.

shame, *n.* **1.** humiliation, mortification, abashment, chagrin. **2.** disgrace, derision, ignominy, dishonor, reproach, obloquy, opprobrium, odium, infamy, contempt. **3.** scandal. —*v.* **4.** abash, humiliate, mortify, humble, confuse, disconcert. **5.** disgrace, reproach, dishonor, scandalize, debase, tarnish, stain, taint, sully, soil. **—Ant.** honor. **—Syn. Study.** SHAME, EMBARRASSMENT, HUMILIATION, CHAGRIN designate different kinds or degrees of painful feeling caused by injury to one's pride or self-respect. SHAME is a painful feeling caused by the consciousness or exposure of unworthy or indecent conduct or circumstances: *One feels shame at being caught in a lie.* It is similar to guilt in the nature and origin of the feeling. EMBARRASSMENT usu. refers to a less painful feeling, one associated with less serious situations, often of a social nature: *embarrassment over breaking a vase at a party.* HUMILIATION is a feeling of embarrassment at being humbled in the estimation of others: *Being ignored gave him a sense of humiliation.* CHAGRIN is humiliation mingled with vexation or anger: *She felt chagrin at her failure to do well on the test.*

shameful, *adj.* disgraceful, scandalous, mortifying, humiliating, dishonorable, ignominious, disreputable, outrageous, infamous, vile, base, low. —**Ant.** honorable.

shameless, *adj.* **1.** immodest, audacious, unblushing, brazen, indecent, impudent, bold, insolent, indelicate,

unabashed, unashamed. **2.** corrupt, sinful, unprincipled, depraved, profligate, piacular, dissolute, reprobate, vicious, hard, hardened, stony, obdurate, adamant, incorrigible, lost. —**Ant.** modest, proper, principled, flexible.

shanty, *n.* cottage, shack, cot, hut, hovel, cabin, house. —**Ant.** castle, palace.

shape, *n.* **1.** outline, silhouette, form, figure, appearance, aspect. **2.** phantom, specter, manifestation. **3.** guise, disguise. **4.** arrangement, order, pattern. **5.** condition, situation, order. **6.** mold, cast, pattern, form. —*v.* **7.** form, fashion, mold, model. **8.** word, express, term. **9.** adjust, adapt, regulate, frame.

share, *n.* **1.** portion, part, allotment, contribution, quota, lot, proportion. **2.** dividend, stock. —*v.* **3.** divide, apportion, allot, portion, parcel out, deal out, dole, mete out. **4.** partake, participate.

sharp, *adj.* **1.** keen, acute, trenchant. **2.** pointed, peaked. **3.** abrupt, sudden. **4.** distinct, marked, clear. **5.** pungent, biting, acrid, spicy, burning, hot, mordacious, bitter, piquant, sour. **6.** shrill, piercing, loud, high. **7.** cold, piercing, freezing, nipping, biting. **8.** painful, distressing, intense, severe, sore, excruciating, agonizing. **9.** harsh, merciless, unmerciful, severe, acute, cutting, caustic, acid, sarcastic, sardonic, acrimonious, pointed, biting, poignant. **10.** fierce, violent, intense. **11.** keen, eager, hungry. **12.** quick, brisk. **13.** vigilant, alert, awake, on the qui vive, attentive. **14.** acute, shrewd, astute, clever, penetrating, discerning, perspicacious, ingenious, discriminating, ready, smart, cunning, intelligent, bright, quick, sensitive, alert, observant, incisive, vigorous, understanding, active,

reasoning. **15.** dishonest, shady, unlawful, deceitful, cheating. —**Ant.** dull; blunt; unclear; mild; soft; warm; merciful. —**Syn. Study.** SHARP, KEEN, INTELLIGENT, QUICK may all be applied to mental qualities and abilities. SHARP means mentally alert or acute; it implies a clever and astute quality: *a sharp mind.* KEEN suggests an incisive, observant, or penetrating nature: *a keen observer.* INTELLIGENT means not only acute, alert, and active, but also able to reason and understand: *an intelligent reader.* QUICK suggests lively and rapid comprehension, prompt response to instruction, and the like: *quick at figures.*

shatter, *v.* break, crush, shiver, split, crack; explode.

sheen, See Syn. study at POLISH.

sheer, *adj.* **1.** transparent, diaphanous, thin, clear. **2.** unmixed, mere, simple, pure, downright, unadulterated, unqualified, utter. **3.** steep, precipitous, abrupt, perpendicular. —*adv.* **4.** clear, quite, completely, totally, entirely. —*n.* **5.** chiffon, voile. —*v.* **6.** swerve, deviate, turn aside. —**Ant.** opaque; gradual.

shelter, *n.* **1.** protection, refuge, retreat, asylum, cover, screen, sanctuary, shield, haven, harbor. —*v.* **2.** protect, guard, cover, safeguard, shield, hide, shroud, house, harbor, defend. —**Ant.** open.

shiftless, *adj.* **1.** lazy, indolent, slothful, unambitious, slack, dilatory, time-wasting, clock-watching, goldbricking, good-for-nothing, **2.** improvident, inefficient, unresourceful. —**Ant.** vigorous, practical.

shimmer, *v., n.* glisten, shine, gleam, glimmer.

shine, *v.* **1.** beam, glare, gleam, glisten, glimmer, shimmer, sparkle, glow, radiate. —*n.* **2.** radiance,

light. **3.** polish, luster, gloss.

shining, *adj.* **1.** radiant, gleaming, bright, brilliant, resplendent, glistening, effulgent, lustrous. **2.** conspicuous, fine, outstanding, distinguished, eminent, prime, splendid, choice, excellent, select.

shipment, *n.* freight, consignment, cargo, lading.

shirk, *v.* evade, avoid, dodge, shun, duck, elude, escape, sidestep, burke, malinger, goldbrick, slack off, goof off.

shiver, *v., n.* tremble, quake, shudder, shake.

shock, *n.* **1.** blow, impact, collision, encounter, concussion, clash. **2.** disturbance, commotion, agitation. —*v.* **3.** startle, stagger, surprise, stun, astound, paralyze, stupefy, bewilder, dumfound. **4.** horrify, disgust, outrage, nauseate, offend, sicken, revolt. **5.** collide, strike, meet.

shore, *n.* **1.** beach, coast, bank, seashore, riverbank, margin, strand. **2.** support, prop, brace, buttress, stay, post, beam, strut.

short, *adj.* **1.** brief; low. **2.** concise, brief, terse, succinct, laconic, condensed, curt, sententious. **3.** abrupt, curt, sharp, petulant, short-tempered, testy, uncivil, rude. **4.** scanty, poor, insufficient, deficient, inadequate, wanting, lacking. **5.** substandard, inferior, unacceptable, below. **6.** friable, brittle, crumbly. **7.** brachycephalic. —*adv.* **8.** suddenly, abruptly, without notice *or* warning. **9.** briefly, curtly. —**Ant.** long. —**Syn. Study.** SHORT, BRIEF are opposed to *long,* and indicate slight extent or duration. SHORT may imply duration but is also applied to physical distance and certain purely spatial relations: *a short journey.* BRIEF refers esp. to duration of time: *brief intervals.*

shorten, *v.* **1.** curtail, abbreviate, abridge, condense, lessen, limit, restrict, reduce. **2.** take in, reduce, diminish, lessen, contract. —**Ant.** lengthen. —**Syn. Study.** SHORTEN, ABBREVIATE, ABRIDGE, CURTAIL mean to make shorter or briefer. SHORTEN is a general word meaning to make less in extent or duration: *to shorten a dress; to shorten a prison sentence.* The other three terms suggest methods of shortening. ABBREVIATE usu. means to shorten a word or group of words, as by omission of letters: *to abbreviate a name.* To ABRIDGE is to reduce in length or size by condensing, summarizing, and the like: *to abridge a document.* CURTAIL suggests a lack of completeness due to the omission of some part: *to curtail an explanation.*

short-sighted, *adj.* **1.** myopic, near-sighted. **2.** indiscreet, unthinking, thoughtless, imprudent, inconsiderate, tactless. —**Ant.** presbyopic, far-sighted; discreet, thoughtful, prudent.

shout, *v.* cry out, hoot, exclaim, vociferate. —**Ant.** whisper.

shove, *v.* **1.** push, propel. **2.** jostle.

show, *v.* **1.** exhibit, display, demonstrate. **2.** point out, indicate. **3.** guide, accompany, lead, usher, conduct. **4.** interpret, make clear *or* known, clarify, elucidate, explain, discover, reveal, disclose, divulge, publish, proclaim. **5.** prove, demonstrate, evidence. **6.** allege, assert, asseverate; plead. **7.** accord, grant, bestow, confer. **8.** look, appear, seem. —*n.* **9.** display, ostentation, pomp, exhibition, flourish, dash, pageantry, ceremony. **10.** showing, spectacle, appearance. **11.** deception, pretense, pretext, simulation, illusion. **12.** trace, indication. **13.** sight, spectacle, exhibition. —**Ant.** hide, conceal.

showy, *adj.* ostentatious, gaudy, flashy, garish, loud. —**Ant.** humble, quiet.

shrew, *n.* termagant, virago, hussy, nag, scold, bacchante, maenad.

shrewd, *adj.* astute, sharp, acute, quick, discerning, discriminating, perceptive, perspicuous, perspicacious, keen, intelligent, penetrating, ingenious, sagacious. —**Ant.** dull, stupid.

shriek, *n., v.* cry, scream, screech, yell.

shrink, *v.* **1.** retreat, withdraw, avoid, recoil, flinch, retire. **2.** contract, wither, shrivel, lessen, diminish, decrease, dwindle, wane, peter out. —**Ant.** advance; inflate, dilate, increase. —**Syn. Study.** See DECREASE.

shrivel, *v.* wither, wrinkle, decrease, contract, shrink. —**Ant.** blossom.

shroud, *v.* cover, veil, cloak, shield, curtain, hide, conceal, obscure, cloud, becloud. —**Ant.** reveal.

shudder, *v., n.* tremble, shiver, quiver, shake.

shun, *v.* elude, avoid, evade, eschew. —**Ant.** seek.

shut, *v.* **1.** close; slam. **2.** confine, enclose, jail, imprison. **3.** bar, exclude, prohibit, preclude. —*adj.* **4.** closed, fastened. —**Ant.** open.

shy, *adj.* **1.** bashful, diffident, retiring, timid, coy. **2.** suspicious, distrustful, wary, heedful, cautious, careful, chary, reluctant. **3.** short. —*v.* **4.** recoil, draw back, shrink. **5.** throw, toss, hurl, pitch, cast, fling. —**Ant.** forward; trusting; incautious, careless; advance.

sick, *adj.* **1.** ill, unwell, ailing, infirm, indisposed. **2.** (*Brit.*) nauseous, vomiting, nauseated. **3.** pale, wan, white, sickly. **4.** impaired, unsound, out of order. —**Ant.** well, hale, healthy. —**Syn. Study.** See ILL.

sickly, *adj.* **1.** unhealthy, ailing, sick, unwell, puny, weak, frail, feeble, infirm, weakly. **2.** weak, mawkish, sentimental, faint. —**Ant.** strong, healthy.

sidekick, *n.* partner, associate, confederate, cohort, henchman, subordinate, assistant, right hand, man Friday, girl Friday, gal Friday.

siege, *n.* blockade, besieging, attack.

sign, *n.* **1.** token, indication, trace, vestige, hint, suggestion. **2.** mark, symbol; abbreviation. **3.** omen, presage, portent, augury, foreboding. —*v.* **4.** signify, betoken, indicate, mean, signal. **5.** affix a signature to. —**Syn. Study.** SIGN, OMEN, PORTENT refer to something that gives evidence of a future event. SIGN is a general word for a visible trace or indication of an event, either past, present, or future: *Dark clouds are a sign of rain.* An OMEN is a happening or phenomenon that serves as a warning of things to come; it may foreshadow good or evil: *She believed it was a bad omen if a black cat crossed her path.* PORTENT also refers to an indication of future events, usu. ones that are momentous or of ominous significance: *the portents of war.*

significance, *n.* **1.** importance, consequence, moment, weight. **2.** import, meaning, sense, purport. **3.** meaningfulness, expressiveness. **—Ant.** triviality. **—Syn. Study.** See IMPORTANCE. See also MEANING.

significant, *adj.* **1.** important, consequential, momentous, weighty, critical, crucial, vital. **2.** meaningful, expressive, signifying, indicative *or* suggestive of. **—Ant.** insignificant.

signify, *v.* **1.** signal, make known, express, indicate, communicate. **2.** mean, portend, represent, denote, indicate, betoken, purport, imply.

silent, *adj.* **1.** quiet, still, noiseless, soundless. **2.** speechless, dumb, mute; close-mouthed, taciturn, tacit. **3.** inactive, dormant, quiescent. **—Ant.** noisy, clamorous; voluble, talkative; active, kinetic.

silhouette, *n.* **1.** outline, profile, contour, delineation, lineation, lineaments, shape, configuration, shadow, gestalt. **—***v.* **2.** outline, profile, delineate, contour, limn.

silly, *adj.* **1.** foolish, stupid, dull-witted, dim-witted, witless, senseless. **2.** absurd, ridiculous, inane, asinine, frivolous, nonsensical, preposterous, idiotic. **—Ant.** sensible.

similar, *adj.* like, resembling. **—Ant.** unlike, dissimilar, different.

similarity, *n.* likeness, resemblance, similitude, correspondence, parallelism. **—Ant.** difference.

simmer, *v.* seethe, bubble, boil. **—Syn. Study.** See BOIL.

simple, *adj.* **1.** clear, intelligible, understandable, unmistakable, lucid. **2.** plain, unadorned, natural, unaffected, unembellished, neat. **3.** unaffected, unassuming, homely, unpretentious. **4.** mere, bare, elementary, simplex, uncomplicated. **5.** sincere, innocent, artless, naive, guileless, ingenuous, unsophisticated. **6.** humble, lowly. **7.** unimportant, insignificant, trifling, trivial, nonessential, unnecessary, immaterial, inconsequential. **8.** common, ordinary, usual, customary. **9.** unlearned, ignorant, uneducated, untutored, stupid, dense, silly, follish, credulous, shallow. **—Ant.** complicated, complex.

simulate, *v.* imitate, mimic, pretend, feign, parrot, assume, affect, counterfeit, act, fake, sham, play-act, put on.

sin, *n.* **1.** transgression, trespass, violation, crime, offense, wrong, wickedness. —*v.* **2.** transgress, trespass, do wrong, offend. **—Syn. Study.** See CRIME.

since, *adv.* **1.** subsequently. **2.** ago, before now. —*conj.* **3.** because, inasmuch as.

sincere, *adj.* candid, honest, open, earnest, guileless, artless, plain, simple; genuine, true, unaffected, real, unfeigned. **—Ant.** insincere. **—Syn. Study.** See EARNEST.

sincerity, *n.* honesty, candor, frankness, probity, genuineness, artlessness, ingenuousness, guilelessness. **—Ant.** insincerity. **—Syn. Study.** See HONOR.

sinful, *adj.* wicked, iniquitous, depraved, evil, immoral, amoral, bad, mischievous, piacular.

singe, *v.* char, burn, scorch.

single, *adj.* **1.** separate, only, individual, sole, distinct, particular. **2.** alone, solitary, isolated. **3.** unmarried, unwed, spinsterish, old-maid. **4.** sincere, honest, whole-hearted, concentrated, unbiased. **5.** simple, unmixed, pure, uncompounded, unadulterated. —*v.* **6.** pick, choose, select, single out. —*n.* **7.** one,

individual, singleton.
—**Ant.** conglomerate;
married, wed; insincere,
biased; adulterated, mixed.

single-minded, *adj.*
resolute, resolved,
determined, dedicated,
uncompromising,
unswerving, unfaltering,
persistent, relentless,
purposeful, committed,
obstinate, dogged,
tenacious. —**Ant.**
uncertain, distracted.

singular, *adj.* **1.**
extraordinary, remarkable,
unusual, uncommon, rare,
strange, peculiar. **2.**
strange, odd, bizarre,
fantastic, peculiar,
unusual, eccentric, queer,
curious, unaccountable,
exceptional, unparalleled,
unprecedented. **3.** unique.
4. separate, individual,
single. —**Ant.** plural;
common.

sinister, *adj.* **1.** threatening,
portending, portentous,
ominous, inauspicious,
unlucky, unfavorable,
unfortunate, disastrous. **2.**
bad, evil, base, wicked,
sinful, piacular, depraved,
corrupt, perverse,

dishonest, crooked.
—**Ant.** benign, favorable,
fortunate; good, honest.

sinuous, *adj.* **1.** winding,
sinuate, curved, crooked,
serpentine. **2.** indirect,
devious, roundabout.
—**Ant.** straight; direct.

sip, *v.* **1.** drink; absorb;
extract. **2.** savor, taste.
—*n.* **3.** drink. **4.** taste,
savor, sapor.

siren, *n.* seductress,
temptress, Circe, vampire,
vamp, mermaid.

sirocco, *n.* simoom,
cyclone, windstorm, dust
storm.

sit, *v.* **1.** be seated, roost,
perch. **2.** be situated,
dwell, settle, lie, rest,
remain, abide, repose,
stay. **3.** meet, convene.
—**Ant.** stand, lie.

situation, *n.* **1.** location,
position, site, place,
locality, locale, spot. **2.**
condition, case, plight,
state, circumstances,
predicament. **3.** position,
post, job.

size, *n.* **1.** dimensions,
proportions, magnitude,
extent; volume, bulk,

mass. **2.** amount, extent, range. **3.** glue, glaze, coating. —*v.* **4.** sort, catalogue; measure.

skeptic, *n.* **1.** disbeliever, agnostic, atheist, doubter, cynic, infidel, heathen, nullifidian. —*adj.* **2.** skeptical, cynical. —**Ant.** believer, theist.

skeptical, *adj.* skeptic, doubtful, dubious, incredulous, unbelieving. —**Ant.** confident. —**Syn. Study.** See DOUBTFUL.

sketch, *n.* **1.** drawing, outline, draft, design, delineation. **2.** skit, play, act, routine, stint. —*v.* **3.** depict, draw, outline, design, rough out, delineate, portray, represent.

sketchy, *adj.* hasty, imperfect, slight, superficial. —**Ant.** careful, perfect.

skew, *v.* **1.** angle, slant, twist, turn, veer, sideslip, sheer, slew, slue, diverge, divagate. **2.** distort, twist, alter, change, unbalance, upset. —**Ant.** straighten, align.

skilled, *adj.* skillful. —**Ant.** unskilled. —**Syn. Study.** See SKILLFUL.

skillful, *adj.* skilled, expert, ready, adroit, deft, adept, proficient, dexterous, competent, qualified, practiced, accomplished, apt, clever, ingenious, intelligent, learned, knowledgeable. —**Ant.** unskillful, inexpert, maladroit, unqualified. —**Syn. Study.** SKILLFUL, SKILLED, EXPERT refer to ability or competence in an occupation, craft, or art. SKILLFUL suggests adroitness and dexterity: *a skillful watchmaker.* SKILLED implies having had long experience and thus having acquired a high degree of proficiency: *not an amateur but a skilled worker.* EXPERT means having the highest degree of proficiency; it may mean much the same as SKILLFUL or SKILLED, or both: *expert workmanship.*

skin, *n.* **1.** hide, pelt, fur. **2.** integument, covering, peel, rind, hull, shell, husk, crust, coating, outside, film, membrane. —*v.* **3.**

flay, peel, pare, strip, husk, excoriate.

skip, *v.* **1.** spring, jump, gambol, leap, bound, caper, hop. **2.** disregard, skip over, skim over. **3.** ricochet, rebound, bounce. —*n.* **4.** leap, jump, spring, bound, caper, hop.

skirmish, *n.* encounter, battle, fight, conflict, combat, brush.

skittish, *adj.* **1.** sensitive, nervous, anxious, skittery, jumpy, quivery, flighty, fidgety, edgy, fluttery, excitable, high-strung. **2.** shy, timid, bashful, timorous, coy. **3.** frisky, lively, giddy, frivolous, whimsical, capricious. **4.** unpredictable, uncertain, fluctuant, unstable. **5.** cautious, wary, chary, hesitant. —**Ant.** down-to-earth, stolid.

skulk, *v.* **1.** lurk, slink, sneak, hide, lie in wait. **2.** shirk, malinger. —**Syn. Study.** See LURK.

slack, *adj.* **1.** loose, relaxed. **2.** indolent, negligent, lazy, remiss, weak. **3.** slow, sluggish, dilatory, tardy, late, lingering. **4.** dull, inactive, blunted, idle, quiet. —*n.* **5.** decrease, slowing, loosening, relaxation, indolence, negligence, laziness, remissness, weakness. —*v.* **6.** shirk, neglect, skulk, malinger. **7.** relax, abate, reduce, slacken, moderate, mitigate. —**Ant.** tight, tense, taut.

slacken, *v.* **1.** deactivate, relax, slack, abate. **2.** loosen, relax, relieve, abate, mitigate, remit, lessen, diminish. **3.** fail, neglect, defer. **4.** restrain, check, curb, bridle, repress, subdue, control. —**Ant.** tighten; increase.

slang, *n.* argot, jargon, patois, dialect, cant, colloquialism.

slant, *v.* **1.** slope, lean, incline. —*n.* **2.** incline, inclination, pitch, slope, obliquity, obliqueness. **3.** bent, leaning, prejudice, bias, inclination.

slapdash, *adj.* careless, slipshod, sloppy, haphazard, any which

way, hit-or-miss,
hit-and-miss, hasty,
superficial, cursory,
lick-and-a-promise,
quick-and-dirty,
once-over-lightly. **—Ant.**
careful, meticulous.

slash, *v.* **1.** cut, lash, slit,
slice. **2.** cut, reduce, alter,
abridge, abbreviate. —*n.* **3.**
stroke, cut, wound, gash,
slit.

slaughter, *n.* **1.** killing,
butchering. **2.** massacre,
carnage, homicide, murder,
butchery, slaying, killing,
bloodshed, genocide. —*v.*
3. butcher, massacre,
murder, slay, kill, wipe
out, devastate, decimate.
—Syn. Study. SLAUGHTER,
BUTCHER, MASSACRE all
imply violent and bloody
methods of killing when
applied to human beings.
SLAUGHTER and BUTCHER
emphasize brutal or
indiscriminate killing: *to
slaughter enemy soldiers in
battle; to butcher tribal
peoples.* MASSACRE indicates
a wholesale destruction of
helpless or unresisting
victims: *to massacre an
entire village.*

slave, *n.* bond servant,
esne, thrall, ryot, villein,
serf, drudge, vassal,
bondman. **—Ant.** master.

slavery, *n.* **1.** bondage,
servitude, subjection,
thralldom, captivity,
enthrallment. **2.** toil,
drudgery, moil, labor.
—Syn. Study. SLAVERY,
BONDAGE, SERVITUDE refer to
involuntary subjection to
another or others. SLAVERY
emphasizes the idea of
complete ownership and
control by a master: *to be
sold into slavery.* BONDAGE
indicates a state of
subjugation or captivity
often involving
burdensome and degrading
labor: *in bondage to a
cruel master.* SERVITUDE is
compulsory service, often
such as is required by a
legal penalty: *penal
servitude.*

slavish, *adj.* **1.** submissive,
abject, servile, groveling,
menial, drudging. **2.** base,
mean, ignoble, low,
obsequious, fawning,
sycophantic, sneaking,
cringing. **3.** imitative,
emulative. **—Ant.**

independent; elevated, exalted. —**Syn. Study.** See SERVILE.

slay, *v.* **1.** murder, kill, slaughter, massacre, butcher, assassinate. **2.** destroy, extinguish, annihilate, ruin.

sleek, *adj.* smooth, glossy, polished, groomed, slick, elegant, trim, clean, streamlined, svelte. —**Ant.** lumpish.

sleep, *v.* **1.** rest, repose, slumber, nap, drowse, doze. —*n.* **2.** dormancy, inactivity, slumber, rest, repose, nap.

slender, *adj.* **1.** slight, slim, thin, spare, narrow. **2.** small, trivial, few, meager, trifling, insignificant, inadequate, insufficient. **3.** thin, weak, fragile, feeble, fine, delicate, flimsy, frangible, breakable. —**Ant.** large, fat, obese, corpulent. —**Syn. Study.** SLENDER, SLIGHT, SLIM imply a tendency toward thinness. As applied to the human body, SLENDER implies a generally attractive and pleasing thinness: *slender hands.* SLIGHT often adds the idea of frailness to that of thinness: *a slight, almost fragile, figure.* SLIM implies a lithe or delicate thinness: *a slim and athletic figure.*

slide, *v.* slip, slither, glide.

slight, *adj.* **1.** small, insignificant, superficial, shallow, trivial, nugatory, paltry, unimportant. **2.** slender, slim. **3.** frail, flimsy, weak, feeble, delicate, fragile. **4.** unsubstantial, inconsiderable. —*v.* **5.** ignore, disregard, disrespect, neglect, disdain, overlook, scorn, (*slang*) dis. —*n.* **6.** neglect, disregard, disdain, indifference, scorn, contumely, contempt, inattention. **7.** affront, insult, disrespect. —**Ant.** considerable; compliment. —**Syn. Study.** SLIGHT, DISREGARD, NEGLECT, OVERLOOK mean to pay no attention or too little attention to someone or something. To SLIGHT is to ignore or treat as unimportant: *to slight* *one's neighbors.* To DISREGARD is to ignore or treat without due respect: *to disregard the rules.* To NEGLECT is to fail in one's duty toward a person or thing: *to neglect one's correspondence.* To OVERLOOK is to fail to notice or consider someone or something, possibly because of carelessness: *to overlook a bill that is due.* See INSULT. See also SLENDER.

slim, *adj.* **1.** slender, thin, slight. **2.** small, poor, insignificant, trifling, trivial, nugatory, unimportant, paltry, inconsiderable, scanty, weak, unsubstantial. —**Ant.** fat; important. —**Syn. Study.** See SLENDER.

slip, *v.* **1.** slide, slither, glide. **2.** be mistaken, err, blunder, mistake. —*n.* **3.** mistake, error, blunder, fault, oversight; faux pas, indiscretion, backsliding. **4.** scion, cutting, strip. —**Syn. Study.** See MISTAKE.

slippery, *adj.* **1.** slick, smooth, lubricious, slithery, oily, lubricated, greased. **2.** risky, precarious, hazardous, unsafe, ticklish. **3.** changeable, mutable, unstable, shifting, uncertain. **4.** untrustworthy, shifty, tricky, deceitful, devious, evasive, wily, cagey, (*Brit.*) dodgy.

slope, *v., n.* slant, incline.

slothful, *adj.* idle, sluggardly, indolent, lazy, sluggish, inactive, inert, torpid, slack, supine. —**Ant.** industrious, active, energetic. —**Syn. Study.** See IDLE.

slovenly, *adj.* untidy, careless, loose, disorderly, slipshod. —**Ant.** careful, tidy, neat.

slow, *adj.* **1.** deliberate, gradual, moderate, leisurely, unhurried. **2.** sluggish, sluggardly, dilatory, indolent, lazy, slothful. **3.** dull, dense, stupid. **4.** slack. **5.** dragging, late, tardy, behindhand. **6.** tedious, humdrum, dull, boring. —*v.* **7.** retard, hinder, impede, obstruct. —**Ant.**

fast; advance. **—Syn. Study.** SLOW, DELIBERATE, GRADUAL, LEISURELY mean unhurried or not happening rapidly. SLOW means acting or moving without haste: *a slow procession of cars.* DELIBERATE implies the slowness that marks careful consideration: *a deliberate and calculating manner.* GRADUAL suggests the slowness of something that advances one step at a time: *a gradual improvement.* LEISURELY means moving with the slowness allowed by ample time or the absence of pressure: *a leisurely stroll.*

sluggish, *adj.* inactive, slow, lazy, slothful, indolent, dull, inert, dronish, phlegmatic. **—Ant.** quick, active, energetic.

slumber, *v., n.* sleep.

slur, *v.* **1.** slight, disregard, pass over, ignore, overlook. **2.** calumniate, disparage, slander, depreciate, asperse. *—n.* **3.** slight, innuendo, insult, affront. **4.** blot, stain,

stigma, brand, mark, disgrace. **—Ant.** compliment.

sly, *adj.* **1.** cunning, wily, artful, subtle, foxy, crafty. **2.** stealthy, surreptitious, furtive, insidious, secret, underhanded, clandestine. **3.** mischievous, roguish, shrewd, astute, cautious. **—Ant.** direct, obvious.

small, *adj.* **1.** little, tiny, diminutive. **2.** slender, thin, slight, narrow. **3.** unimportant, trivial, minor, secondary, trifling, nugatory, inconsequential, petty, paltry, insignificant. **4.** humble, modest, unpretentious. **5.** mean-spirited, mean, stingy, ungenerous, parsimonious, niggardly, selfish, tight, illiberal, narrow. **6.** ashamed, mortified, abashed. **7.** weak, feeble, faint, diluted. **8.** gentle, soft, low. **—Ant.** large.

small-minded, *adj.* **1.** narrow-minded, narrow, small, illiberal, mean, petty, close-minded, bigoted, intolerant. **2.** provincial, parochial,

insular, limited, confined.
—**Ant.** liberal, eclectic.

smarmy, *adj.* **1.** insincere, false, disingenuous, hypocritical, mealymouthed, sanctimonious **2.** suave, sleek, smug, insinuating, unctuous, fulsome, oily, buttery. **3.** obsequious, flattering, sycophantic, ingratiating.

smart, *v.* **1.** pain, hurt, sting. **2.** wound, insult, affront. —*adj.* **3.** sharp, keen, stinging, poignant, penetrating, painful, severe. **4.** brisk, vigorous, active, energetic, effective, lively, quick. **5.** quick, prompt, nimble, agile, alert, active. **6.** intelligent, bright, sharp, clever, expert, adroit. **7.** shrewd, cunning, adept, quick. **8.** neat, trim, dashing, spruce, pretentious, showy. **9.** elegant, chic, fashionable, voguish, à la mode. —**Ant.** pleasure; dull, stupid.

smash, *v.* **1.** break, shatter, crush, crash. **2.** defeat, overthrow, destroy. **3.** ruin, bankrupt. —*n.* **4.**

smashing, shattering, crash. **5.** collision, destruction, ruin; collapse.

smell, See Syn. study at ODOR.

smirch, *v.* **1.** besmirch, discolor, soil, smear, smudge, smut, smutch, dirty. **2.** sully, tarnish, disgrace, taint, blot, smear. —*n.* **3.** smear, mark, smudge, smut, smutch, dirt. **4.** stain, blot, taint. —**Ant.** clean; honor.

smitten, *adj.* enamored, captivated, charmed, infatuated, bewitched, beguiled, lovestruck, moonstruck, besotted, doting, gaga. —**Ant.** repelled, antipathetic.

smooth, *adj.* **1.** level, even, plain, flat. **2.** bald, hairless, glossy, polished, sleek. **3.** flat, unruffled, calm, undisturbed. **4.** regular, even, easy, fluent. **5.** unruffled, undisturbed, calm, peaceful, tranquil, equable, pacific, peaceable. **6.** elegant, polished, flowing, glib, voluble, soft-spoken, suave, unctuous, oily, bland. **7.**

pleasant, agreeable, polite, courtly, courteous. —*v.* **8.** plane, stroke, scrape, level, press, flatten, iron, roll. **9.** polish, refine. **10.** tranquilize, calm, soothe, assuage, mollify, better. **11.** gloss over, palliate, soften, soothe. —**Ant.** rough, uneven, irregular.

smug, *adj.* **1.** complacent, self-satisfied, self-complacent, satisfied, conceited, self-sufficient, self-confident, self-important, egoistic, self-opinionated, self-reliant. **2.** trim, spruce, neat, smooth, sleek. —**Ant.** dissatisfied.

snare, *n.* **1.** trap, noose, net, seine. —*v.* **2.** trap, entrap, entangle, catch.

snarl, *v.* **1.** growl, grumble, complain, murmur. **2.** entangle, tangle, mat, complicate, confuse, ravel, involve, knot. —*n.* **3.** growl, grumble. **4.** tangle, entanglement, complication, knot, confusion, involvement, intricacy, difficulty.

sneak, *v.* **1.** slink, lurk, skulk, steal. —*n.* **2.** sneaker, lurker. —**Syn. Study.** See LURK.

sneer, *v.* **1.** scorn, jeer, gibe, scoff, disdain, deride, ridicule, criticize, contemn. —*n.* **2.** scoff, gibe, jeer, derision, disdain. —**Syn. Study.** See SCOFF.

sneeze, *v.* sternutate.

snide, *adj.* derogatory, nasty, insinuating, vicious, slanderous, libelous. —**Ant.** complimentary, favorable.

snub, *v.* **1.** disdain, contemn, mortify, humiliate, abash, humble, slight, discomfit. **2.** check, rebuke, stop, reprove, reprimand. —*n.* **3.** rebuke, slight, affront, insult. —**Ant.** accept.

soak, *v.* **1.** steep, drench, wet, sop, saturate. **2.** permeate, osmose, penetrate. —**Ant.** dry.

soar, *v.* **1.** fly, glide. **2.** tower, rise, ascend, mount.

sober, *adj.* **1.** unintoxicated; temperate, abstinent, abstemious. **2.** serious, grave, solemn, quiet, sedate, subdued, staid. **3.** calm, serene, tranquil, peaceful, cool, moderate, composed, unexcited, unimpassioned, unruffled, collected, dispassionate, unconcerned, reasonable, rational, controlled, sane, sound. **4.** somber, dull, neutral, dark. —**Ant.** drunk; wild; immoderate. —**Syn. Study.** See GRAVE.

sociable, *adj.* social. —**Ant.** unfriendly.

social, *adj.* friendly, sociable, amiable, companionable, genial, affable, familiar. —**Ant.** unfriendly.

society, *n.* **1.** organization, association, circle, fellowship, club, fraternity, brotherhood, company, partnership, corporation. **2.** community. **3.** companionship, company, fellowship, sodality.

soft, *adj.* **1.** yielding, pliable, plastic, moldable, malleable, impressible. **2.** smooth, agreeable, delicate. **3.** gentle, low, subdued, melodious, mellifluous, dulcet, sweet,

pleasing, pleasant, flowing. **4.** gentle, mild, balmy, genial. **5.** gentle, mild, lenient, compassionate, tender, bland, sympathetic. **6.** smooth, soothing, ingratiating, mollifying. **7.** impressionable, yielding, affected, compliant, flexible, irresolute, submissive, undecided, weak, delicate, sensitive. **8.** sentimental, weak, feeble, poor, wishy-washy. —**Ant.** hard, inflexible, unyielding.

soften, *v.* **1.** melt, tenderize. **2.** appease, assuage, mollify, moderate, mitigate, modify, soothe, alleviate, calm, quell, still, quiet, ease, allay, abate, qualify, temper, blunt, dull. —**Ant.** harden.

soi-disant, *adj.* self-styled, so-called, pretended. —**Ant.** genuine, real.

solace, *n.* **1.** comfort, alleviation, cheer, consolation, relief. —*v.* **2.** comfort, console, cheer, soothe. **3.** relieve, alleviate, soothe, mitigate, assuage, allay, soften.

sole, *adj.* only, single, solitary, alone, individual, unattended, unique.

solemn, *adj.* **1.** grave, sober, mirthless, unsmiling, serious. **2.** impressive, awe-inspiring, august, imposing, venerable, grand, majestic, stately. **3.** earnest, serious. **4.** formal, dignified, serious, ceremonious, ritual, ceremonial. **5.** religious, reverential, devotional, sacred, ritual. —**Ant.** obstreperous; jovial; unimpressive; insincere; informal. —**Syn. Study.** See GRAVE.

solicit, *v.* **1.** seek, entreat, ask for, request, apply for, beseech, pray, beg, importune, urge, implore, crave, supplicate, sue, petition, appeal to. **2.** influence, incite, activate, urge, impel, excite, arouse, awaken, stimulate.

solicitous, *adj.* **1.** anxious, concerned, apprehensive, uneasy, troubled, disturbed, restless, restive, worried. **2.** desirous, anxious to please. **3.** eager. **4.** careful,

particular. —**Ant.** unconcerned, undisturbed; careless.

solid, *adj.* **1.** three-dimensional, cubic. **2.** dense, compact, firm, hard. **3.** unbroken, continuous, undivided, whole, entire, uniform. **4.** firm, cohesive, compact. **5.** dense, thick, heavy, substantial, sound, stable, stout. **6.** real, genuine, complete, sound, good. **7.** sober-minded, sober, sensible. **8.** thorough, vigorous, strong, solid, big, great, stout. **9.** united, consolidated, unanimous. **10.** successful, solvent, wealthy, rich, reliable, honorable, established, well-established, sound, trustworthy, honest, safe. —**Ant.** flat, two-dimensional; loose; divided; sparse; counterfeit; weak; separate; unsuccessful.

solitary, *adj.* **1.** unattended, alone, lone, lonely. **2.** isolated, retired, lonely, deserted, unfrequented, remote, secluded. —*n.* **3.** hermit, eremite, recluse.

solitude, *n.* **1.** seclusion, isolation, remoteness, loneliness, retirement, privacy. **2.** desert, waste, wilderness.

somber, *adj.* **1.** gloomy, dark, shadowy, dim, unlighted, dusky, murky, cloudy, dull, sunless, dismal. **2.** depressing, dismal, lugubrious, mournful, doleful, funereal, melancholy. **—Ant.** cheerful.

some, *adj.* **1.** any, one, anyone, unspecified. **2.** certain, specific, special, particular. **—Ant.** none.

soothe, *v.* **1.** tranquilize, calm, relieve, comfort, refresh. **2.** allay, mitigate, assuage, alleviate, appease, mollify, soften, lull, balm. **—Ant.** upset, disturb. **—Syn. Study.** See COMFORT.

sophisticated, *adj.* **1.** artificial, changed, mundane, worldly. **2.** deceptive, misleading. **—Ant.** unsophisticated.

sorcery, *n.* magic, witchery, enchantment, witchcraft, spell, necromancy, divination, charm.

sordid, *adj.* **1.** dirty, filthy, soiled, unclean, foul, squalid. **2.** mean, ignoble, amoral, degraded, depraved, low, base. **3.** selfish, self-seeking, mercenary, avaricious, stingy, tight, close, close-fisted, parsimonious, penurious, miserly, niggardly. **—Ant.** clean; honorable; generous.

sore, *adj.* **1.** painful, sensitive, tender, irritated. **2.** grieved, distressed, aggrieved, sorrowful, hurt, pained, depressed, vexed. **3.** grievous, distressing, painful, depressing, severe, sharp, afflictive. **—n. 4.** infection, abscess, wound, ulcer, pustule, boil, cancer, canker. **—Ant.** tough.

sorrow, *n.* **1.** distress, anxiety, anguish, grief, sadness, woe, suffering, misery, wretchedness, regret. **2.** affliction, adversity, trouble, misfortune. **—v. 3.** grieve, mourn, bemoan, bewail, lament. **—Ant.** joy, gladness, delight.

sorrowful, *adj.* **1.** grieved, sad, unhappy, melancholy, depressed, dejected, aggrieved, afflicted, mournful, plaintive, grievous, lamentable. **2.** distressing, dismal, dreary, doleful, sorry, lugubrious, piteous. **—Ant.** happy.

sorry, *adj.* **1.** regretful, sorrowing, sympathetic, pitying. **2.** pitiable, miserable, deplorable. **3.** sorrowful, grieved, sad, unhappy, melancholy, depressed. **4.** grievous, melancholy, dismal, mournful, painful. **5.** wretched, poor, mean, pitiful, base, low, vile, abject, contemptible, bad, despicable, paltry, worthless, shabby. **—Ant.** happy. **—Syn. Study.** See MISERABLE.

sort, *n.* **1.** kind, species, phylum, genera, variety, class, group, family, description, order, race, rank, character, nature, type. **2.** character, quality, nature. **3.** example, pattern, sample, exemplar. **4.** manner, fashion, way, method, means, style. **—v.** **5.** arrange, order, classify, class, separate, divide,

assort, distribute. **6.** assign, join, unite.

sound, *n.* **1.** noise, tone. **2.** strait, channel. **—v. 3.** resound, echo. **4.** utter, pronounce, express. **5.** plumb, probe; dive, plunge. **6.** examine, inspect, investigate, fathom, ascertain, determine. **—adj. 7.** uninjured, unharmed, unbroken, whole, entire, complete, unimpaired, healthy, hale, hearty, robust, hardy, vigorous. **8.** solvent, secure, well-established. **9.** reliable, trustworthy, honest, honorable. **10.** true, truthful, just, fair, judicious, reasonable, rational, sane, sensible, wholesome. **11.** enduring, substantial. **12.** correct, orthodox, right, proper. **13.** upright, honest, good, honorable, loyal, true, virtuous. **14.** unbroken, deep, profound, fast, undisturbed. **15.** vigorous, hearty, thorough, complete. **—Ant.** unsound.

soupçon, *n.* hint, trace,

suggestion, suspicion, flavor, taste, sip. —**Ant.** plethora.

sour, *adj.* **1.** acid, tart. **2.** fermented. **3.** distasteful, disagreeable, unpleasant, bitter. **4.** harsh, ill-tempered, bad-tempered, austere, severe, morose, peevish, testy, short-tempered, hot-tempered, touchy, acrimonious, cross, petulant, crabbed, snappish, waspish, uncivil, rude, crude, rough. —**Ant.** sweet.

sovereign, *n.* **1.** monarch, king, queen, emperor, empress, prince, lord, ruler, potentate. **2.** senate, government. —*adj.* **3.** regal, royal, majestic, princely, imperial, monarchical, kingly. **4.** supreme, chief, paramount, principal, predominant. **5.** utmost, extreme, greatest. **6.** potent, effective, efficacious, effectual.

spacious, *adj.* **1.** ample, large, capacious, roomy, wide. **2.** extensive, vast, huge, extended, tremendous, trackless. —**Ant.** small, cramped, crowded.

span, *n.* **1.** distance, amount, piece, length, extent; nine inches. **2.** extension, reach, extent, stretch. **3.** period, spell. **4.** pair, team, yoke, couple, brace. —*v.* **5.** measure; extend over, reach, pass over, stretch across, cross, compass.

spare, *v.* **1.** forbear, omit, refrain from, withhold, keep from. **2.** save, lay away *or* aside, reserve, set aside *or* apart. —*adj.* **3.** reserved, extra, reserve. **4.** restricted, meager, frugal, sparing, scanty, parsimonious. **5.** lean, thin, slender, slight, gaunt, lank, skinny, raw-boned, emaciated. **6.** economical, temperate, careful.

sparkle, *v.* **1.** glisten, glitter, shine, twinkle, gleam, coruscate, scintillate. **2.** effervesce, bubble. —*n.* **3.** luster, spark, scintillation, glister, glitter, twinkle, twinkling, coruscation. **4.** brilliance, liveliness, vivacity, spirit, glow, piquancy.

sparse, *adj.* **1.** thin, scattered, here and there. **2.** scanty, meager, spare, restricted. **—Ant.** abundant. **—Syn. Study.** See SCANTY.

speak, *v.* utter, talk, voice, converse, communicate, disclose, reveal, pronounce, say, articulate, significate.

special, *adj.* **1.** distinct, distinguished, different, particular, especial, peculiar, singular, specific, plain, unambiguous, certain, individual, single, unusual, uncommon. **2.** extraordinary, exceptional. **—Ant.** unparticular, common; ordinary.

specific, *adj.* special. **—Ant.** unspecific, nonspecific.

specimen, *n.* type, example, sample, model, pattern.

specious, *adj.* plausible, ostensible, feasible; deceptive, false, misleading. **—Ant.** implausible; genuine.

specter, *n.* ghost, phantom, spirit, apparition, shade, shadow. **—Ant.** reality.

speculation, *n.* **1.** contemplation, consideration. **2.** conclusion, supposition, conjecture, surmise, view, hypothesis, theory.

speech, *n.* **1.** utterance, remark, observation, declaration, assertion, asseveration, averral, comment, mention, talk. **2.** talk, oration, address, discourse, harangue. **3.** language, words, lingo, tongue, dialect, patois. **4.** parlance, conversation, parley, communication. **—Syn. Study.** SPEECH, ADDRESS, ORATION, HARANGUE are terms for a communication to an audience. SPEECH is the general word, with no implication of kind or length, or whether planned or not. An ADDRESS is a rather formal, planned speech, appropriate to a particular subject or occasion. An ORATION is a polished, rhetorical address, given usu. on a notable occasion, that employs eloquence and studied methods of delivery. A HARANGUE is an impassioned, vehement speech intended to arouse strong feeling and sometimes to lead to mob action.

speechless, *adj.* **1.** dumb, dumfounded, shocked, mute. **2.** silent, dumb, mute. —**Ant.** loquacious, voluble, talkative.

speed, *n.* **1.** rapidity, alacrity, celerity, quickness, fleetness, velocity, swiftness, dispatch, expedition, haste, hurry. —*v.* **2.** promote, advance, further, forward, expedite, favor. **3.** direct, guide. **4.** accelerate. —**Ant.** sloth. —**Syn. Study.** SPEED, VELOCITY, CELERITY refer to swift or energetic movement or operation. SPEED may apply to human or nonhuman activity; it emphasizes the rate in time at which something travels or operates: *the speed of an automobile; the speed of thought.* VELOCITY, a more technical term, is commonly used to refer to high rates of speed: *the velocity of a projectile.* CELERITY, a somewhat literary term, usu. refers to human movement or operation, and emphasizes dispatch or economy in an activity: *the celerity of his response.*

spellbound, *adj.* rapt, held, gripped, enthralled, fascinated, intrigued, mesmerized, hypnotized, caught, stunned, transfixed. —**Ant.** uninterested, detached.

spend, *v.* **1.** disburse, expend, pay out, dispose of, squander, throw out, waste, lavish, dissipate. **2.** exhaust, use up, consume. **3.** employ, use, apply, devote. —**Ant.** earn.

sphere, *n.* **1.** ball, orb, globe. **2.** shell, ball. **3.** planet, star. **4.** environment, orbit, area, place, province, circle, compass, coterie, set, realm, domain, quarter. **5.** stratum, walk of life, rank.

spin, *v.* **1.** draw out, twist, wind. **2.** twirl, whirl, turn, rotate, gyrate. **3.** produce, fabricate, evolve, develop. **4.** tell, narrate, relate. **5.** draw out, extend, protract, prolong, lengthen. —*n.* **6.** run, ride, drive. —**Syn. Study.** See TURN.

spindly, *adj.* **1.** gaunt, bony, thin, lean, spare, skeletal, scrawny, skinny, lanky, gangly, gangling. **2.** unsteady, shaky, rickety, teetery, teetering, tottery, tottering, wobbly, doddering, fragile. —**Ant.** robust, sturdy.

spineless, *adj.* limp, weak, feeble, irresolute, undetermined, thewless. —**Ant.** strong.

spirit, *n.* **1.** animation, vitality, soul, essence, life, mind, consciousness. **2.** goblin, sprite, elf, fairy, hobgoblin; angel, genius, demon, *prāna.* **3.** ghost, specter, apparition, phantom, shade, shadow. **4.** God, The Holy Ghost, The Holy Spirit, The Comforter, The Spirit of God. **5.** mettle, vigor, liveliness, enthusiasm, energy, zeal, zealousness, ardor, fire, vivacity,

enterprise, resourcefulness. **6.** temper, disposition, attitude, mood, humor, sorts, frame of mind. **7.** character, nature, drift, tenor, gist, sense, complexion, quintessence, essence. **8.** meaning, intent, intention, significance, purport. —*v.* **9.** inspirit, vitalize, animate, instill, encourage, excite.

spirited, *adj.* excited, animated, vivacious, ardent, active, agog, energetic, lively, vigorous, courageous, mettlesome, bold. —**Ant.** dispirited, inactive, indolent.

spite, *n.* **1.** ill will, malevolence, maliciousness, malice, rancor, gall, malignity, venom, spleen. **2.** grudge, hate, pique, hatred. —*v.* **3.** annoy, thwart, injure, hurt, harm.

spiteful, *adj.* malicious, venomous, malevolent, revengeful, vindictive, mean, cruel, hateful, rancorous. —**Ant.** benevolent, friendly.

splendid, *adj.* **1.** gorgeous, magnificent, sumptuous, luxurious, superb, dazzling, imposing. **2.** grand, beautiful, impressive. **3.** glorious, renowned, famed, famous, illustrious, eminent, conspicuous, distinguished, remarkable, celebrated, brilliant, noble. **4.** fine, striking, admirable. —**Ant.** sordid, squalid; ignoble.

splendor, *n.* **1.** magnificence, brilliance, grandeur, pomp, show, display, dash, élan, éclat. **2.** distinction, glory, brillance, fame, eminence, renown, celebrity. **3.** brightness, brilliance, light, luster, dazzle, refulgence. —**Ant.** squalor.

splenetic, *adj.* spleenish, spleeny, irritable, peevish, spiteful, vexatious, irascible, testy, fretful, touchy, edgy, petulant, snappish, waspish, cross, choleric. —**Ant.** moderate, temperate.

spoil, *v.* **1.** damage, impair, ruin, wreck, disfigure, destroy, demolish, mar, harm. **2.** corrupt, vitiate. **3.** plunder, pillage, rob, rape, despoil, ravage, waste. —*n.* **4.** (*often plural*) booty, plunder, loot, pillage. —**Syn. Study.** SPOIL, HUMOR, INDULGE imply attempting to satisfy the wishes or whims of oneself or others. SPOIL implies being so lenient or permissive as to cause harm to a person's character: *to spoil a grandchild.* To HUMOR is to comply with a mood, fancy, or caprice, as in order to satisfy, soothe, or manage: *to humor an invalid.* INDULGE suggests a yielding, though temporary or infrequent, to wishes that perhaps should not be satisfied: *to indulge an irresponsible son.*

spontaneous, *adj.* unpremeditated, natural, unconstrained, voluntary, gratuitous, free, unselfish. —**Ant.** premeditated.

sporadic, *adj.* scattered, occasional, isolated, unconnected, separate. —**Ant.** continuous.

sport, *n.* **1.** pastime, game,

athletics, amusement, diversion, fun, entertainment, frolic, recreation, play. **2.** derision, jesting, ridicule, mockery. **3.** laughingstock. **4.** toy, plaything. —*v.* **5.** play, frolic, gambol, romp, caper, skip. **6.** trifle, deal lightly, discount. **7.** ridicule, make fun.

sportive, *adj.* **1.** playful, frolicsome, jesting, jocose, merry, jocular, gay, sprightly, frisky. **2.** joking, prankish, facetious. —**Ant.** sober, serious.

spot, *n.* **1.** mark, stain, blot, speck. **2.** blemish, flaw, stain, taint, stigma. **3.** place, locality, locale, site, situation. —*v.* **4.** stain, mark, blot, speckle. **5.** sully, blemish, stain, taint, stigmatize, soil, tarnish.

spout, *v.* **1.** spurt, squirt, flow, stream, pour. —*n.* **2.** pipe, tube, nozzle, nose.

sprain, *v.* strain, overstrain, wrench, injure, twist.

spread, *v.* **1.** unroll, unfold, open, expand, stretch out, draw out. **2.** extend, stretch, expand, dilate. **3.** display, set forth. **4.** dispose, distribute, scatter, disperse, ted. **5.** overlay, cover, coat. **6.** emit, scatter, diffuse, radiate. **7.** shed, scatter, diffuse, disseminate, broadcast, publish, circulate, divulge, promulgate, propagate, disperse. —*n.* **8.** expansion, extension, diffusion. **9.** extent, reach, compass; stretch, expanse. **10.** bedspread, cloth, cover, tablecloth. **11.** preserve, jam, jelly, peanut butter.

spring, *v.* **1.** leap, jump, bound, hop, vault. **2.** recoil, fly back, rebound. **3.** shoot, dart, fly. **4.** arise, start, originate, rise, issue, emanate, flow. **5.** grow, develop, increase, wax, thrive. **6.** emerge, emanate, issue, flow, proceed. **7.** bend, warp. **8.** explode. **9.** split, crack. —*n.* **10.** leap, jump, hop, bound, vault. **11.** elasticity, springiness, resiliency, buoyancy, vigor. **12.** split, crack, fissure; bend, warp. **13.** source, origin, mouth, fountainhead, head. —*adj.* **14.** vernal, springtime.

sprinkle, *v.* **1.** scatter, strew, spread, disperse, fling, distribute, rain. **2.** diversify, intersperse.

sprite, See Syn. study at FAIRY.

spry, *adj.* active, nimble, agile, brisk, lively, energetic, animated, quick, smart, alert, ready, prompt. —**Ant.** inactive.

spur, *n.* **1.** goad, prick, rowel. **2.** whip, goad, incitement, stimulus, incentive, inducement, provocation, impulse, instigation. —*v.* **3.** urge, goad, prick, whip, incite, provoke, stimulate, induce, instigate. —**Ant.** discourage.

spurious, *adj.* **1.** counterfeit, sham, false, pretended, unauthentic, bogus, phony, mock, feigned; meretricious, deceitful, fictitious. **2.** illegitimate, bastard. —**Ant.** genuine.

spurn, *v.* reject, disdain, scorn, despise, refuse, contemn. —**Ant.** accept. —**Syn. Study.** See REFUSE.

spurt, *v.* **1.** gush, spout, flow, issue, stream, jet, well, spring. —*n.* **2.** outburst, jet, spout. —**Ant.** drip, ooze.

squalid, *adj.* **1.** foul, repulsive, unclean, dirty, filthy, nasty. **2.** wretched, miserable, degraded. —**Ant.** splendid.

squalor, *n.* squalidness, filth, misery, foulness. —**Ant.** splendor.

squander, *v.* spend, waste, dissipate, throw away, lavish, misuse, expend. —**Ant.** save.

squeamish, *adj.* **1.** modest, prudish; blue. **2.** moral, particular, scrupulous, fastidious, finical, finicky, dainty, delicate, hypercritical, nice. —**Ant.** bold.

stab, *v.* **1.** pierce, wound, gore, spear, penetrate, pin, transfix. **2.** thrust, plunge. —*n.* **3.** thrust, blow, wound.

stability, *n.* firmness, continuance, permanence, constancy, steadiness, steadfastness, strength, immovability, fixedness. —**Ant.** instability.

stable, *n.* **1.** barn, mews. —*adj.* **2.** firm, steady, rigid, fixed, strong, sturdy, established, immovable, permanent, invariable, unvarying, steadfast, unchangeable, unchanging. **3.** enduring, permanent, constant, perdurable, lasting, abiding, secure, fast, perpetual, eternal, everlasting. **4.** unwavering, steadfast, staunch, constant, reliable, steady, solid. —**Ant.** unstable.

stagger, *v.* **1.** sway, reel, totter, waver, falter, vacillate. **2.** hesitate, doubt. **3.** shock, astound, astonish, confound, amaze, nonplus, dumfound, surprise. **4.** alternate, zigzag, rearrange, reorder, overlap.

staid, *adj.* sedate, settled, sober, serious, proper, decorous, correct, quiet, composed, serene, calm, solemn, grave. —**Ant.** wild, indecorous.

stain, *n.* **1.** discoloration, spot, blemish, mark, imperfection, blot. **2.** stigma, disgrace, dishonor, taint, blot, tarnish. **3.** dye, reagent, tint. —*v.* **4.** discolor, taint, spot, streak, soil, dirty, blemish, blot. **5.** blemish, sully, spot, taint, soil, tarnish, disgrace, dishonor, stigmatize, corrupt, debase, defile, contaminate, pollute. **6.** tint, dye, tinge, color.

stake, *n.* **1.** stick, post, pale, picket, pike. **2.** wager, bet. **3.** (*often plural*) prize, winnings, purse. **4.** risk, jeopardy, hazard. —*v.* **5.** risk, hazard, jeopardize, wager, venture, bet, imperil.

stale, *adj.* **1.** vapid, flat, dry, hardened, hard, tasteless, sour, insipid. **2.** uninteresting, hackneyed, trite, stereotyped, old hat, old, common, commonplace. —**Ant.** fresh, modern.

stalemate, *n.* impasse, deadlock, standstill.

stalwart, *adj.* **1.** strong, stout, well-developed,

robust, sturdy, brawny, sinewy, muscular, athletic, strapping, vigorous. **2.** strong, brave, valiant, bold, valorous, intrepid, daring, fearless, firm, resolute, indomitable, gallant. **3.** firm, steadfast, resolute, uncompromising, redoubtable, formidable. —**Ant.** weak, feeble; fearful; infirm, unsteady.

stamina, *n.* strength, vigor, resistance, power, health, robustness. —**Ant.** weakness.

stammer, *v.* stutter, pause, hesitate, falter.

stamp, *v.* **1.** strike, beat, trample, crush, pound. **2.** eliminate, abolish, squash, quash, eradicate. **3.** impress, mark, label, brand, imprint. **4.** characterize, distinguish, reveal. —*n.* **5.** die, block, cut, engraving, brand, branding iron. **6.** impression, design, pattern, brand, mark, print, seal. **7.** character, kind, type, sort, description, cut, style, cast, mold, fashion, form, make.

stand, *v.* **1.** halt, stop, pause. **2.** remain, continue, persist, stay, abide, be firm *or* resolute *or* steadfast *or* steady. **3.** set, erect, place, put, fix. **4.** face, meet, encounter, resist, oppose. **5.** endure, undergo, submit to, bear, sustain, weather, outlast. **6.** tolerate, abide, stomach, endure, suffer, bear, admit, allow. —*n.* **7.** halt, stop, rest, stay. **8.** position, effort, determination, attitude. **9.** station, post, place, position, spot. **10.** platform, dais, grandstand. **11.** stall, booth, table, case, counter. **12.** copse, grove, forest, wood; growth, crop. —**Syn. Study.** See BEAR.

standard, *n.* **1.** criterion, measure, gauge, test, model, example, exemplar, sample, basis, pattern, guide, rule. **2.** grade, level. **3.** emblem, flag, symbol, ensign, banner, pennant, pennon, streamer. **4.** upright, support; bar, rod, timber. —*adj.* **5.** basic, exemplary, guiding, sample, typical. —**Syn.**

Study. STANDARD, CRITERION refer to the basis for making a judgment. A STANDARD is an authoritative principle or rule that usu. implies a model or pattern for guidance, by comparison with which the quantity, excellence, correctness, etc., of other things may be determined: *She could serve as the standard of good breeding.* A CRITERION is a rule or principle used to judge the value, suitability, probability, etc., of something, without necessarily implying any comparison: *Wealth is no criterion of a person's worth.*

standing, *n.* **1.** position, status, rank, credit, reputation, condition. **2.** existence, continuation, duration, residence, membership, experience. **3.** station, booth. —*adj.* **4.** still, stationary, stagnant, unmoving, motionless. **5.** continuing, continuous, unceasing, constant, permanent, unchanging, steady, lasting, durable. **6.**

idle, out of use, unused. **7.** operative, in force, effective, in effect, established, settled.

stanza, *n.* quatrain, stave, poem, staff.

stare, *v., n.* gaze.

stark, *adj.* **1.** sheer, utter, downright, arrant, simple, mere, pure, absolute, entire, unmistakable. **2.** stiff, rigid. **3.** harsh, grim, desolate, dreary, drear. —*adv.* **4.** utterly, absolutely, completely, quite, irrevocable. —**Ant.** vague.

start, *v.* **1.** begin, set out *or* forth, commence, depart. **2.** issue, come up, come, arise. **3.** jump, jerk, twitch, spring. **4.** set up, begin, establish, found, institute, initiate. —*n.* **5.** beginning, outset, initiation, commencement, onset. **6.** impulse, signal, go-ahead, starting gun. **7.** jerk, spasm, fit, twitch, jump. **8.** headstart, lead. **9.** chance, opportunity. —**Ant.** end, terminate. —**Syn. Study.** See BEGIN.

startle, *v.* **1.** disturb, shock,

agitate, surprise, alarm, amaze, astound, astonish, scare, frighten. —*n.* **2.** shock, surprise, alarm. —**Ant.** calm.

state, *n.* **1.** condition, case, circumstances, predicament, pass, plight, situation, status, surroundings, environment, rank, position, standing, stage. **2.** constitution, structure, form, phase. **3.** estate, station, rank, position, standing. **4.** dignity, pomp, display, grandeur, glory, magnificence. **5.** sovereign government, government, federation, commonwealth, community, territory. —*adj.* **6.** public, national, government, federal. **7.** ceremonial, ceremonious, pompous, stately, imposing, sumptuous, dignified. —*v.* **8.** declare, aver, assert, asseverate, set forth, express, affirm, specify. **9.** say. **10.** fix, settle, determine, authorize.

stately, *adj.* imposing, grand, dignified, majestic, elegant, magnificent, state. —**Ant.** base, mean, vile.

statement, *n.* declaration, communication, report, announcement, proclamation.

statesman, See Syn. study at POLITICIAN.

station, *n.* **1.** position, post, place, situation, location. **2.** depot, terminal, way-station, whistle-stop. **3.** standing, rank, dignity. **4.** position, office, rank, calling, occupation, metier, trade, business, employment, office, appointment. —*v.* **5.** assign, place, post, position, locate, establish, set, fix.

status, *n.* **1.** condition, state. **2.** condition, position, standing, rank.

staunch, *adj.* firm, steadfast, stable, steady, constant, resolute, true, faithful, principled, loyal, substantial, strong, sound, stout. —**Ant.** unsteady, disloyal. —**Syn. Study.** See STEADFAST.

stay, *v.* **1.** remain, dwell, reside, abide, sojourn, tarry, rest, lodge. **2.** continue, remain. **3.** stop, halt. **4.** pause, wait, delay, linger. **5.** hold back, detain, restrain, obstruct, arrest, check, hinder, delay, hold, curb, prevent. **6.** suspend, delay, adjourn. **7.** suppress, quell. **8.** appease, satisfy, curb, allay. **9.** wait out. **10.** support, prop, brace, buttress. **11.** rest, rely *or* depend on, confide *or* trust in, lean on. **12.** sustain, bolster, strengthen, uphold. —*n.* **13.** stop, halt, pause, delay, standstill; interruption, break, hiatus, lacuna. **14.** sojourn, rest, repose. **15.** prop, brace, support; crutch. **16.** rope, guy, guy wire. —**Ant.** leave.

steadfast, *adj.* **1.** fixed, directed, fast, firm, established, stable. **2.** stanch, steady, sure, dependable, reliable, resolute, constant, strong, firm, loyal, regular, purposeful, faithful, unwavering. —**Ant.** unsteady; weak; sporadic,

unfaithful. —**Syn. Study.** STEADFAST, STAUNCH, STEADY imply a sureness and continuousness that may be depended upon. STEADFAST literally means fixed in place, but is chiefly used figuratively to indicate undeviating constancy or resolution: *steadfast in one's faith.* STAUNCH literally means watertight, as of a vessel, and therefore strong and firm; figuratively, it is used of loyal support that will endure strain: *a staunch advocate of free trade.* Literally, STEADY is applied to that which is relatively firm in position or continuous in movement or duration: *a steady flow;* figuratively, it implies sober regularity or persistence: *a steady worker.*

steady, *adj.* **1.** firm, fixed, steadfast, stable, balanced, even, regular. **2.** undeviating, invariable, unvarying, regular, constant, unchanging, uninterrupted, uniform, unremitting, continuous.

3. habitual, regular, constant, unchangeable. **4.** firm, unwavering, steadfast. **5.** settled, staid, sedate, sober. —*v.* **6.** stabilize. —**Ant.** unsteady. —**Syn. Study.** See STEADFAST.

steal, *v.* **1.** take, pilfer, purloin, filch, embezzle, peculate, swindle. **2.** win, gain, draw, lure, allure. —**Ant.** provide.

stealthy, *adj.* furtive, surreptitious, secret, clandestine, sly. —**Ant.** obvious, open, manifest.

stem, *n.* **1.** axis, stalk, trunk, petiole, peduncle, pedicel. **2.** stock, family, descent, pedigree, ancestry, lineage, race. —*v.* **3.** rise, arise, originate. **4.** stop, check, dam up, obstruct, hinder, stay. **5.** tamp, plug, tighten. **6.** progress against, oppose, breast, make headway against, withstand.

stench, See Syn. study at ODOR.

stereotyped, *adj.* fixed, settled, conventional, hackneyed, overused, commonplace, trite, banal, dull, ordinary, lifeless, uninteresting, stale, boring, worn, pointless, insipid, inane. —**Ant.** rare, uncommon, unusual; interesting, fresh, sensible.

sterile, *adj.* **1.** uncontaminated, unpolluted, uncorrupted, antiseptic. **2.** barren, unproductive, fruitless, infecund. —**Ant.** fertile.

stern, *adj.* **1.** firm, strict, adamant, unrelenting, uncomprising, severe, harsh, hard, inflexible, forbidding, unsympathetic, rough, cruel, unfeeling. **2.** rigorous, austere, steadfast, rigid. —**Ant.** lenient, flexible. —**Syn. Study.** STERN, SEVERE, HARSH mean strict or firm and can be applied to methods, aspects, manners, or facial expressions. STERN implies uncompromising, inflexible firmness, and sometimes a forbidding aspect or nature: *a stern parent.* SEVERE implies strictness, lack of sympathy, and a tendency to discipline others: *a severe judge.*

HARSH suggests a great severity and roughness, and cruel, unfeeling treatment of others: *a harsh critic.*

stew, *v.* **1.** simmer, boil, seethe. —*n.* **2.** ragout. —**Syn. Study.** See BOIL.

stick, *n.* **1.** branch, shoot, switch. **2.** rod, wand, baton. **3.** club, cudgel; bat. **4.** thrust, stab. **5.** interrruption. —*v.* **6.** pierce, puncture, stab, penetrate, spear, transfix, pin, gore. **7.** impale. **8.** fasten, attach, glue, cement, paste. **9.** adhere, cohere, cling, cleave, hold. **10.** remain, stay, persist, abide. **11.** hesitate, scruple, stickle, waver, doubt. —**Syn. Study.** STICK, ADHERE, COHERE mean to be fastened or attached to something. STICK is the general term; it means to be fastened with glue, pins, nails, etc.: *A gummed label will stick to a package.* Used figuratively, STICK means to hold faithfully or keep steadily to something: *to stick to a promise.* ADHERE is a more

formal term meaning to cling or to stay firmly attached: *Wallpaper will not adhere to a rough surface.* Used figuratively, ADHERE means to be attached as a follower: *to adhere to religious beliefs.* COHERE means to hold fast to something similar to itself: *The particles of sealing wax cohered into a ball.* Used figuratively, COHERE means to be logically connected or attached: *The pieces of evidence did not cohere.*

stiff, *adj.* **1.** rigid, firm, solid, unflexible, unbendable, unbending, unyielding. **2.** violent, strong, steady, unremitting, fresh. **3.** firm, purposive, unrelenting, unyielding, resolved, obstinate, stubborn, pertinacious. **4.** graceless, awkward, clumsy, inelegant, crude, harsh, abrupt. **5.** formal, ceremonious, punctilious, constrained, starched, prim, priggish. **6.** laborious, difficult. **7.** severe, rigorous, straitlaced, austere, strict, dogmatic, uncompromising, positive, absolute, inexorable. **8.** great, high. **9.** taut, tight, tense. **10.** dense, compact, tenacious. —*n.* **11.** prude, prig. —**Ant.** flexible.

stifle, *v.* **1.** smother, suffocate, strangle, garrote, choke. **2.** keep back, repress, check, stop, suppress. **3.** crush, stop, obviate, prevent, preclude, put down, destroy, suppress. —**Ant.** encourage, further, foster.

stigma, *n.* **1.** mark, stain, reproach, taint, blot, spot, tarnish, disgrace, infamy, disrepute. **2.** brand.

still, *adj.* **1.** in place, at rest, motionless, stationary, unmoving, inert, quiescent. **2.** soundless, quiet, hushed, noiseless, silent, mute. **3.** tranquil, calm, peaceful, peaceable, pacific, placid, serene. —*conj.* **4.** but, nevertheless, and yet. —*v.* **5.** silence, hush, quiet, mute, stifle, muffle, smother. **6.** calm, appease, allay, soothe, compose,

pacify, smooth, tranquilize. —*n.* **7.** stillness, quiet, hush, calm. **8.** distillery. —**Ant.** mobile, moving; noisy, clamorous; noise. —**Syn. Study.** See BUT.

stimulate, *v.* **1.** rouse, arouse, activate, incite, animate, excite, urge, provoke, instigate, goad, spur, prod, prick, inflame, fire. **2.** invigorate. —**Ant.** discourage.

stimulus, *n.* incentive, incitement, enticement, stimulation, motive, provocation; stimulant. —**Ant.** discouragement; wet blanket; soporific.

stingy, *adj.* niggardly, penurious, parsimonious, miserly, mean, close, tight, avaricious. —**Ant.** generous. —**Syn. Study.** STINGY, PARSIMONIOUS, MISERLY mean reluctant to part with money, possessions, or other things. STINGY means unwilling to give, share, or spend anything of value: *a stingy employer; an expert stingy with advice.* PARSIMONIOUS describes a stinginess arising from excessive frugality or unwillingness to spend money: *a parsimonious family.* MISERLY implies a pathological pleasure in acquiring and hoarding money: *a miserly neighbor.*

stint, *v.* **1.** limit, restrict, confine, restrain; pinch, straiten. —*n.* **2.** limit, limitation, restriction, restraint, constraint. **3.** share, rate, allotment, portion. —**Ant.** liberate, free.

stir, *v.* **1.** move, agitate, disturb. **2.** shake. **3.** incite, instigate, prompt, rouse, foment, arouse, provoke, stimulate, animate, urge, goad, spur. **4.** affect, excite, move. —*n.* **5.** movement, bustle, ado, agitation, commotion, disorder, uproar, tumult. **6.** impulse, sensation, feeling, emotion.

stock, *n.* **1.** store, goods, inventory, supplies, supply, provision, reserve, hoard. **2.** livestock, cattle, horses, sheep. **3.** trunk, stem. **4.** race, lineage, family, descent, pedigree, ancestry, line, parentage, house, tribe. **5.** handle, haft. **6.** pillory. —*adj.* **7.** staple, standard, standing, customary, permanent. **8.** common, commonplace, ordinary, usual. —*v.* **9.** supply, store, fill.

stoical, *adj.* stoic, impassive, calm, austere, apathetic, imperturbable, cool, indifferent. —**Ant.** sympathetic, warm.

stony, *adj.* **1.** rocky, pebbly, gritty. **2.** unfeeling, merciless, obdurate, adamant, inflexible, stiff, hard, flinty, pitiless, unbending. **3.** motionless, rigid, stock-still.

stoop, *v.* **1.** bend, lean, bow, crouch. **2.** descend, condescend, deign, lower oneself. **3.** stoop down, descend. —*n.* **4.** descent, indignity, condescension, humiliation.

stop, *v.* **1.** cease, leave off, discontinue, desist *or* refrain from. **2.** interrupt, arrest, check, halt, restrain, intermit, terminate, end. **3.** cut off, intercept, withhold, thwart, interrupt, obstruct, impede, hinder, prevent, preclude, delay, restrain, repress, suppress. **4.** block, obstruct, close, seal off, blockade. **5.** cease, pause, quit. —*n.* **6.** halt, cessation, arrest, end, termination, check. **7.** stay, sojourn, stopover. **8.** station, depot, terminal. **9.** block, obstruction, obstacle, hindrance, impediment; plug, stopper, cork. **10.** check, control, governor. **—Ant.** start. **—Syn. Study.** STOP, ARREST, CHECK, HALT imply causing a cessation of movement or progress (literal or figurative). STOP is the general term for the idea: *to stop a clock.* ARREST usu. refers to stopping by imposing a sudden and complete restraint: *to arrest development.* CHECK implies bringing about an abrupt, partial, or temporary stop: *to check a trotting horse.* To HALT means to make a temporary stop, esp. one resulting from a command:

to halt a company of soldiers.

storm, *n.* **1.** gale, hurricane, tempest, tornado, cyclone, sirocco, simoom, dust storm, squall, northeaster, wind, rainstorm, bise, whirlwind, hailstorm, snowstorm, blizzard, thunderstorm. **2.** assault, siege, attack. **3.** violence, commotion, disturbance, strife. **4.** outburst, outbreak. —*v.* **5.** blow; rain, snow, hail, thunder and lightning. **6.** rage, rant, fume, complain. **7.** rush, attack, assault, besiege.

story, *n.* **1.** narrative, tale, legend, fable, romance, anecdote, record, history, chronicle. **2.** plot, theme, incident. **3.** narration, recital, rehearsal, relation. **4.** report, account, description, statement, allegation. **5.** floor, level.

stout, *adj.* **1.** bulky, thick-set, fat, corpulent, plump, portly, fleshy. **2.** bold, hardy, dauntless, brave, valiant, gallant, intrepid, fearless, indomitable, courageous.

3. firm, stubborn, obstinate, contumacious, resolute. **4.** strong, stalwart, sturdy, sinewy, athletic, brawny, vigorous, able-bodied. **5.** thick, heavy. —**Ant.** slim, slender, thin; fearful; weak; light.

straight, *adj.* **1.** direct, right. **2.** candid, frank, open, honest, direct. **3.** honorable, honest, virtuous, upright, erect, just, fair, equitable, straightforward. **4.** right, correct. **5.** unmodified, unaltered, unchanged. —**Ant.** devious, crooked.

straightforward, *adj.* **1.** direct, straight, undeviating, unwavering, unswerving. **2.** honest, truthful, honorable, just, fair. —**Ant.** devious; dishonest.

strain, *v.* **1.** stretch, tighten, tauten. **2.** exert. **3.** sprain, impair, injure, weaken, wrench, twist, tear, overexert. **4.** filter, sift, sieve, filtrate, purify, percolate, seep through. **5.** clasp, hug, embrace, press. **6.** filter, percolate, ooze, seep. —*n.* **7.** force, pressure, effort, exertion. **8.** sprain, injury, wrench. **9.** family, stock, descent, race, pedigree, lineage, ancestry, extraction. **10.** character, tendency, trait. **11.** streak, trace, hint, suggestion.

strait, *n.* difficulty, distress, need, emergency, exigency, crisis, pinch, dilemma, predicament, plight. —**Ant.** ease.

straitlaced, *adj.* prim, stuffy, hidebound, prudish, moralistic, rigid, priggish, puritanical, bluenosed, prissy, Victorian. —**Ant.** free and easy, relaxed, licentious.

strange, *adj.* **1.** unusual, extraordinary, curious, bizarre, odd, queer, singular, peculiar, unfamiliar, inexplicable, unexplained, irregular, unconventional, rare, mysterious, mystifying, eccentric, abnormal, anomalous, exceptional. **2.** alien, foreign, exotic, outlandish, unfamiliar. **3.** unacquainted, unaccustomed, unused, unfamiliar, unknown, unexperienced. **4.** distant, reserved, aloof, supercilious, superior. —**Ant.** usual, commonplace.

stranger, *n.* alien, foreigner, outsider. —**Ant.** friend, relative, ally. —**Syn. Study.** STRANGER, ALIEN, FOREIGNER all refer to someone regarded as outside of or distinct from a particular group. STRANGER may apply to one who does not belong to some group—social, professional, national, etc. —or may apply to a person with whom one is not acquainted. ALIEN emphasizes a difference in political allegiance and citizenship from that of the country in which one is living. FOREIGNER emphasizes a difference in language, customs, and background.

strangle, *v.* garrote; choke, stifle, suffocate, smother, throttle.

stratagem, *n.* plan, scheme, trick, ruse, deception, artifice, wile, intrigue, device, maneuver, contrivance, machination. —**Syn. Study.** See TRICK.

strategy, *n.* tactics, generalship; skillful management.

stream, *n.* **1.** current, rivulet, rill, streamlet, run, runnel, river. **2.** flow, course, tide. **3.** flow, succession, torrent, rush. —*v.* **4.** pour, flow, run, issue, emit.

street, *n.* way, road, roadway, avenue, boulevard, concourse, highway; path, footpath, alley, alleyway.

strength, *n.* **1.** power, force, vigor, health, might, potency, energy, capacity. **2.** firmness, courage, fortitude, resolution. **3.** effectiveness, efficacy, potency, cogency, soundness, validity. **4.** intensity, brightness, loudness, vividness, pungency. **5.** support, stay, prop, brace. —**Ant.** weakness.

strenuous, *adj.* vigorous, energetic, active, animated, spirited, eager, zealous, ardent, resolute, determined, forceful, earnest. —**Ant.** easy.

stress, *v.* **1.** emphasize, accent. **2.** strain. —*n.* **3.** importance, significance, emphasis, weight, accent, force. —**Ant.** unstress, deemphasize, ease, underplay.

stretch, *v.* **1.** draw out, extend, lengthen, elongate. **2.** hold out, reach forth, reach, extend, stretch forth. **3.** spread. **4.** tighten, tauten, strain. **5.** lengthen, widen, distend, dilate, enlarge, broaden. **6.** strain, exaggerate. **7.** recline, lie down. —*n.* **8.** length, distance, tract, expanse, extent, extension, range, reach, compass. —**Ant.** curtail, abbreviate.

strew, *v.* scatter, sprinkle, overspread, broadcast. —**Ant.** gather, reap.

strict, *adj.* **1.** rigid, rigorous, stringent, inflexible, stiff, severe, unbending, unyielding, exacting, demanding, stern, narrow, illiberal, uncompromising, harsh,

austere, straitlaced. **2.** exact, precise, accurate, scrupulous, particular. **3.** close, careful, minute, critical. **4.** absolute, perfect, complete. —**Ant.** flexible. —**Syn. Study.** STRICT, RIGID, RIGOROUS, STRINGENT imply inflexibility, severity, and an exacting quality. STRICT suggests close conformity to rules, requirements, obligations, or principles: *to maintain strict discipline.* RIGID suggests an inflexible, uncompromising, or unyielding nature or character: *a rigid parent.* RIGOROUS suggests that which is harsh or severe, esp. in action or application: *rigorous self-denial.* STRINGENT refers to something that is vigorously exacting, or absolutely binding: *stringent measures to suppress disorder.*

strife, *n.* **1.** conflict, discord, variance, difference, disagreement, contrariety, opposition. **2.** quarrel, struggle, clash, fight, conflict. —**Ant.** peace.

strike, *v.* **1.** thrust, hit, smite, knock, beat, pound, slap, cuff, buffet. **2.** catch, arrest, impress. **3.** come across, meet with, meet, encounter. **4.** affect, overwhelm, impress. —**Syn. Study.** See BEAT.

stringent, *adj.* **1.** strict. **2.** narrow, binding, restrictive. **3.** urgent, compelling, constraining. **4.** convincing, forceful, powerful, effective, forcible, persuasive. —**Ant.** flexible, mollifying, emollient; ineffective. —**Syn. Study.** See STRICT.

strip, *v.* **1.** uncover, peel, decorticate, denude. **2.** remove. **3.** withhold, deprive, divest, dispossess, dismantle. **4.** rob, plunder, despoil, pillage, sack, devastate, spoil, desolate, lay waste. —*n.* **5.** band, ribbon. —**Ant.** cover.

strive, *v.* **1.** endeavor, try, exert oneself, essay, struggle, toil. **2.** contend, compete, fight, struggle. —**Syn. Study.** See TRY.

stroke, *n.* **1.** striking, blow, hitting, beating, beat, knock, rap, tap, pat, thump. **2.** throb, pulsation, beat; rhythm. **3.** apoplexy, paralysis, shock, attack. **4.** feat, achievement, accomplishment. —*v.* **5.** caress, rub gently, massage.

stroll, *v.* **1.** ramble, saunter, meander. **2.** wander, roam, rove, stray. —*n.* **3.** ramble, saunter, promenade, walk.

strong, *adj.* **1.** powerful, vigorous, hale, hearty, healthy, robust, mighty, sturdy, brawny, athletic, sinewy, hardy, muscular, stout, stalwart, Herculean. **2.** powerful, able, competent, potent, capable, puissant, efficient. **3.** firm, courageous, valiant, brave, valorous, bold, intrepid, fearless. **4.** influential, resourceful, persuasive, cogent, impressive. **5.** clear, firm, loud. **6.** well-supplied, rich, substantial. **7.** cogent, forceful, forcible, effective, efficacious, conclusive, potent, powerful. **8.** resistive, resistant, solid, firm, secure, compact, impregnable, impenetrable. **9.** firm, unfaltering, tenacious, unwavering, resolute, solid, tough, stanch, stout. **10.** intoxicating, alcoholic, potent. **11.** intense, brilliant, glaring, vivid, dazzling. **12.** distinct, marked, sharp, stark, contrasty. **13.** strenuous, energetic, forceful, vigorous, zealous, eager, earnest, ardent. **14.** hearty, fervent, fervid, thoroughgoing, vehement, stubborn. **15.** pungent, racy, olent, aromatic, odoriferous; sharp, piquant, spicy, hot, biting. **16.** smelly, rank. **—Ant.** weak.

structure, *n.* **1.** construction, organization, system, arrangement, form, configuration, shape. **2.** building, edifice, bridge, dam, framework. **3.** composition, arrangement.

struggle, *v.* **1.** contend, strive, oppose, contest, fight, conflict. —*n.* **2.** brush, clash, encounter, skirmish, fight, battle, conflict, strife. **3.** effort, strive, endeavor, exertion, labor, pains.

strut, *v.* **1.** swagger, parade. —*n.* **2.** brace, support, prop, stretcher. **—Syn. Study.** STRUT and SWAGGER refer esp. to carriage in walking. STRUT implies swelling pride or pompousness; it means to walk with a stiff, seemingly affected or self-conscious gait: *A turkey struts about the barnyard.* SWAGGER implies a domineering, sometimes jaunty, superiority or challenge and a self-important manner: *to swagger down the street.*

stubborn, *adj.* **1.** obstinate, perverse, contrary, dogged, persistent, intractable, refractory, inflexible, unyielding, unbending, rigid, stiff, contumacious, headstrong, pigheaded, obdurate. **2.** fixed, set, opinionated, resolute, persevering. **3.** hard, tough, stiff, strong, stony.

—**Ant.** tractable, flexible; irresolute. —**Syn. Study.** STUBBORN, OBSTINATE, DOGGED, PERSISTENT imply fixity of purpose or condition and resistance to change. STUBBORN and OBSTINATE both imply resistance to advice, entreaty, protest, or force; but STUBBORN implies an innate characteristic and is the term usu. used when referring to inanimate things: *a stubborn child; a stubborn lock; an obstinate customer.* DOGGED implies willfulness and tenacity, esp. in the face of obstacles: *dogged determination.* PERSISTENT implies having staying or lasting qualities, resoluteness, and perseverance: *persistent questioning.*

student, *n.* pupil, scholar; observer. —**Ant.** teacher.

studied, *adj.* deliberate, premeditated, predetermined, willful, considered, elaborate. —**Ant.** unpremeditated.

study, *n.* **1.** attention, application, investigation, inquiry, research, reading, reflection, meditation, cogitation, thought, consideration, contemplation. **2.** field, area, subject. **3.** zealousness, endeavor, effort, assiduity, sedulousness, assiduousness. **4.** thought, reverie, abstraction. **5.** library, den. —*v.* **6.** read, investigate, practice. **7.** think, reflect, consider, ponder, weigh, estimate, examine, contemplate, scrutinize, turn over. —**Syn. Study.** STUDY, CONSIDER, REFLECT, WEIGH imply fixing the mind upon something, generally doing so with a view to some decision or action. STUDY implies an attempt to obtain a grasp of something by methodical or exhaustive thought: *to study a problem.* CONSIDER implies fixing the mind on something and giving it close attention before making a decision or taking action: *to consider the alternatives.* REFLECT implies looking back quietly over past experience and giving it consideration: *to reflect on similar cases in the past.* WEIGH implies a deliberate and judicial estimate, as by a balance: *to weigh a decision.*

stuff, *n.* **1.** material, substance, matter. **2.** character, qualities, capabilities. **3.** rubbish, trash, waste, nonsense, twaddle, balderdash, inanity, absurdity. —*v.* **4.** fill, cram, pack, crowd, press, stow. **5.** stop up, choke, plug, obstruct. —**Syn. Study.** See MATTER.

stun, *v.* **1.** knock out, shock, dizzy. **2.** astound, stupefy, daze, astonish, amaze, overcome, bewilder, overwhelm, confound.

stupid, *adj.* **1.** dull, vapid, pointless, prosaic, tedious, uninteresting, boring, insipid, flat, humdrum, tiresome, heavy. **2.** foolish, inane, asinine, senseless, simple, half-witted, witless, obtuse, stolid, dumb. —**Ant.** bright, intelligent, clever, shrewd.

sturdy, *adj.* **1.** well-built, strong, robust, stalwart, hardy, muscular, brawny, sinewy, stout, powerful. **2.** firm, stout, indomitable, unbeatable, unconquerable, persevering, resolute, vigorous, determined. —**Ant.** weak.

style, *n.* **1.** kind, sort, type, form, appearance, character. **2.** mode, manner, method, approach, system. **3.** fashion, elegance, smartness, chic, élan, éclat. **4.** touch, characteristic, mark. **5.** stylus. **6.** etching, point *or* needle, graver. **7.** gnomon. —*v.* **8.** call, denominate, name, designate, address, entitle, title, christen, dub, characterize, term.

suave, *adj.* smooth, agreeable, polite, bland, urbane, sophisticated, worldly, mundane. —**Ant.** boorish.

subdue, *v.* **1.** conquer, defeat, suppress, subjugate, vanquish, overcome, overpower, subject. **2.** repress, reduce, overcome.

3. tame, break, discipline, domesticate. **4.** tone down, soften, mollify. —**Syn. Study.** See DEFEAT.

subject, *n.* **1.** theme, topic, conception, point, thesis, object, subject matter. **2.** ground, motive, reason, rationale, cause. **3.** minion, dependent, subordinate. —*adj.* **4.** subordinate, subjacent, subservient, subjected, inferior. **5.** obedient, submissive. **6.** open, exposed, prone, liable. **7.** dependent, conditional, contingent. —*v.* **8.** dominate, control, influence. **9.** make liable, lay open, expose. —**Syn. Study.** SUBJECT, TOPIC, THEME refer to the central idea or matter considered in speech or writing. SUBJECT refers to the broad or general matter treated in a discussion, literary work, etc.: *The subject of the novel was a poor Southern family.* TOPIC often applies to one specific part of a general subject; it may also apply to a limited and well-defined subject: *We covered many topics at the meeting.* The topic of the news story was an escaped prisoner. THEME usu. refers to the underlying idea of a discourse or composition, perhaps not clearly stated but easily recognizable: *The theme of social reform runs throughout her work.*

subjective, *adj.* **1.** mental, unreal, imaginary, illusory, fancied, imagined. **2.** personal, individual. **3.** introspective, contemplative, introversive. **4.** substantial, essential, inherent. —**Ant.** objective.

submerge, *v.* submerse, dip, sink, plunge, immerse.

submissive, *adj.* **1.** unresisting, humble, obedient, tractable, compliant, pliant, yielding, amenable, agreeable. **2.** passive, resigned, patient, docile, tame, long-suffering, subdued.

submit, *v.* yield, surrender, bow, comply, obey, agree, resign. —**Ant.** fight. —**Syn. Study.** See YIELD.

subordinate, *adj.* **1.** lower, inferior. **2.** secondary, unimportant, ancillary. **3.** subservient; dependent. —*n.* **4.** inferior, subject. —*v.* **5.** lower, subject, reduce. —**Ant.** superior; primary.

subside, *v.* **1.** sink, lower, decline, precipitate, descend, settle. **2.** quiet, abate, decrease, diminish, lessen, wane, ebb. —**Ant.** rise; increase.

subsidiary, *adj.* supplementary, auxiliary, tributary, subordinate, secondary, ancillary. —**Ant.** primary, principal.

subsidy, *n.* aid, grant, subvention, support, tribute.

substance, *n.* **1.** matter, material, stuff. **2.** essence, subject matter, theme, subject. **3.** meaning, gist, significance, import, pith, essence. —**Syn. Study.** See MATTER.

substantial, *adj.* **1.** real, actual, material, corporeal. **2.** ample, considerable, sizable. **3.** solid, stout, firm, strong, resolute, stable, sound. **4.** wealthy, influential, responsible. **5.** worthy, valuable. **6.** material, essential, important. —**Ant.** insubstantial, immaterial: trivial; unstable, unsound; poor; unworthy; unimportant.

subtract, *v.* withdraw, take away, deduct, diminish, detract, lessen, lower. —**Ant.** add.

subvention, *n.* subsidy.

succeed, *v.* **1.** flourish, prosper, thrive, go well, make a hit, go swimmingly, prevail. **2.** follow, replace. —**Ant.** fail; precede. —**Syn. Study.** SUCCEED, FLOURISH, PROSPER, THRIVE mean to do well. To SUCCEED is to turn out well or do well; it may also mean to attain a goal: *The strategy succeeded. She succeeded in school.* To FLOURISH is to grow well or fare well: *The plants flourished in the sun. The business flourished under new management.* To PROSPER is to do well, esp. materially or financially: *They worked hard and* *prospered.* To THRIVE is to do well, esp. to achieve wealth; it may also mean to grow or develop vigorously: *The shopping center thrived. The dog thrived on the new diet.* See also FOLLOW.

succession, *n.* **1.** order, sequence, course, series. **2.** descent, transmission, lineage, race. —**Syn. Study.** See SERIES.

successive, *adj.* consecutive, following, sequential, ordered.

succinct, See Syn. study at CONCISE.

succor, *n.* **1.** help, relief, aid, support, assistance. —*v.* **2.** aid, assist, relieve, help, support. —**Syn. Study.** See HELP.

sudden, *adj.* unexpected, abrupt, unlooked for, unforeseen, quick, unanticipated. —**Ant.** deliberate, premeditated, foreseen.

suffer, *v.* undergo, feel, experience, sustain, bear, tolerate, allow, permit, stomach, stand, meet with.

sufficient, *adj.* enough,

adequate, ample, satisfactory, competent. —**Ant.** insufficient.

suggest, *v.* propose, recommend, indicate, hint, insinuate, intimate, prompt, advise. —**Syn. Study.** See HINT.

suggestive, *adj.* expressive.

sulky, *adj.* sullen, ill-humored, resentful, aloof, moody, surly, morose, cross, splenetic, churlish. —**Ant.** temperate, good-natured.

sullen, *adj.* **1.** silent, reserved, sulky, morose, moody. **2.** ill-humored, sour, vexatious, splenetic, bad-tempered. **3.** gloomy, dismal, cheerless, clouded, overcast, somber, mournful, dark. **4.** slow, sluggish, dull, stagnant. —**Ant.** cheerful. —**Syn. Study.** See GLUM.

sully, *v.* **1.** soil, stain, tarnish, taint, blemish, disgrace, dishonor. **2.** dirty, contaminate, corrupt, pollute. —**Ant.** honor.

summary, *n.* **1.** digest, extract, abstract, brief,

synopsis, compendium, epitome, essence, outline, précis, abridgment. —*adj.* **2.** brief, comprehensive, concise, short, condensed, compact, succinct, pithy. **3.** curt, terse, peremptory, laconic. —**Syn. Study.** SUMMARY, BRIEF, DIGEST, SYNOPSIS are terms for a short version of a longer work. A SUMMARY is a brief statement or restatement of main points, esp. as a conclusion to a work: *a summary of a chapter.* A BRIEF is a concise statement, usu. of the main points of a legal case: *The attorney filed a brief.* A DIGEST is a condensed and systematically arranged collection of literary, legal, or scientific matter: *a digest of Roman law.* A SYNOPSIS is a condensed statement giving a general overview of a subject or a brief summary of a plot: *a synopsis of a play.*

summit, *n.* top, peak, apex, pinnacle, acme, vertex, culmination, zenith. —**Ant.** base, bottom.

summon, *v.* **1.** call, invite, bid; convene, convoke. **2.** call forth, rouse, arouse, activate, incite.

superannuated, *adj.* old, aged, decrepit, obsolete, antiquated, antique, anile, senile, passé. —**Ant.** young, youthful, new, voguish.

superb, *adj.* stately, majestic, grand, magnificent, admirable, fine, excellent, exquisite, elegant, splendid, sumptuous, rich, luxurious, gorgeous. —**Ant.** inferior.

supercilious, *adj.* haughty, disdainful, contemptuous, arrogant, scornful, contumelious. —**Ant.** humble.

superficial, *adj.* shallow, external, outward, exterior, slight. —**Ant.** basic, profound.

superfluous, *adj.* unnecessary, extra, needless, *de trop*, redundant, excessive, superabundant. —**Ant.** essential.

superintend, *v.* oversee,

supervise, manage, direct, control, conduct, run.

supernatural, *adj.* **1.** unnatural, superhuman, miraculous, preternatural. **2.** extraordinary, abnormal. **—Syn. Study.** See MIRACULOUS.

supersede, *v.* **1.** replace, displace, supplant, succeed, remove. **2.** void, overrule, annul, neutralize, revoke, rescind. **—Syn. Study.** See REPLACE.

supplant, *v.* displace, supersede, replace, succeed, remove. **—Syn. Study.** See REPLACE.

supple, *adj.* **1.** flexible, pliant, pliable, lithe, limber, lissome, elastic. **2.** compliant, yielding, agreeable, submissive. **3.** obsequious, servile, sycophantic, groveling, slavish, cringing, fawning. **—Ant.** rigid, inflexible.

supplement, *n.* **1.** reinforcement, extension, addition, complement, addendum, appendix, epilogue, postscript. **—v. 2.** complete, add to,

complement. **—Syn. Study.** See COMPLEMENT.

supplicate, *v.* pray, entreat, petition, appeal to, beg, implore, crave, importune, sue, solicit, beseech. **—Ant.** order, command.

supply, *v.* **1.** furnish, provide, replenish, stock, fill. **2.** make up, make up for, satisfy, fulfill. **3.** fill, substitute for, occupy. **—n. 4.** stock, store, inventory, hoard, reserve.

support, *v.* **1.** bear, hold up, sustain, uphold. **2.** undergo, endure, suffer, submit to, tolerate, bear, stand, stomach, go through, put up with. **3.** sustain, keep up, maintain, provide for, nourish, nurture. **4.** back, uphold, second, further, advocate, endorse, forward, defend. **5.** aid, countenance, maintain, help, assist, advocate, succor, abet, relieve, patronize. **6.** corroborate, confirm. **—n. 7.** maintenance, sustenance, living, livelihood, subsistence, keep. **8.** help, aid, succor, assistance, relief. **9.** prop, brace, stay. —**Ant.** fail.

suppose, *v.* **1.** assume, presume, infer, presuppose, take for granted. **2.** believe, think, consider, judge, deem, conclude.

sure, *adj.* **1.** undoubted, indubitable, indisputable. **2.** confident, certain, positive, assured, convinced. **3.** reliable, certain, trusty, trustworthy, honest, infallible, unfailing. **4.** firm, stable, solid, safe, secure, steady. **5.** unerring, accurate, precise, certain, infallible. **6.** inevitable, unavoidable, destined. —**Ant.** unsure, uncertain.

surfeit, *n.* **1.** excess, superabundance, superfluity. **2.** disgust, satiety, nausea. —*v.* **3.** supply, satiate, fill, stuff, gorge, overfeed. —**Ant.** insufficiency.

surmise, *v.* **1.** think, infer, conjecture, guess, imagine, suppose, suspect. —*n.* **2.** conjecture, idea, thought, possibility, likelihood. —**Syn. Study.** See GUESS.

surpass, *v.* exceed, excel, transcend, outdo, beat, outstrip.

surplus, *n.* remainder, excess, surfeit, superabundance, residue. —**Ant.** insufficiency, inadequacy.

surprise, *v.* **1.** astonish, amaze, astound, take unawares, startle, disconcert, bewilder, confuse. —*n.* **2.** assault, attack. **3.** amazement, astonishment, wonder.

surrender, *v.* **1.** yield, give *or* deliver up, cede. **2.** give up, abandon, relinquish, renounce, resign, waive, forgo. **3.** submit, yield, capitulate, give up. —*n.* **4.** resignation, capitulation, relinquishment. —**Syn. Study.** See YIELD.

surreptitious, *adj.* secret, unauthorized, stealthy, clandestine, subrepitious. —**Ant.** open.

surrogate, *n.* **1.** substitute, replacement, stand-in, fill-in, alternate, backup, locum tenens, deputy, agent, relief, proxy, pinch hitter, understudy. —*adj.*

2. substitute, alternate, alternative, backup.
—**Ant.** original, prototype.

surveillance, *n.* watch, care, control, management, supervision.

survey, *v.* **1.** view, scan, observe, watch, inspect, examine, scrutinize. —*n.* **2.** examination, inspection. **3.** poll.

survive, *v.* continue, persist, live, remain, succeed, outlive. —**Ant.** languish, die, fail. —**Syn. Study.** SURVIVE, OUTLIVE refer to remaining alive longer than someone else or after some event. SURVIVE usu. means to succeed in staying alive against odds, to live after some event that has threatened one: *to survive an automobile accident.* It also means to live longer than another person (usu. a relative), but, today, it is used mainly in the passive, as in the fixed expression: *The deceased is survived by his wife and children.* OUTLIVE stresses capacity for endurance, the time element, and sometimes a sense of competition: *She outlived all her enemies.* It is also used, however, of a person or thing that has lived or lasted beyond a certain point: *The machine has outlived its usefulness.*

susceptibility, *n.* sensibility, sensitivity, sensitiveness, susceptiveness, susceptibleness, impressibility. —**Ant.** insusceptibility.

suspect, *v.* **1.** distrust, mistrust, doubt. **2.** imagine, believe, surmise, consider, suppose, guess, conjecture. —*n.* **3.** defendant. —*adj.* **4.** suspected, suspicious. —**Ant.** trust.

suspend, *v.* **1.** hang, attach. **2.** defer, postpone, delay, withhold. **3.** stop, cease, desist, hold up, hold off, discontinue, intermit, interrupt, arrest, debar.

suspense, *n.* **1.** uncertainty, doubt, unsureness, incertitude, indetermination. **2.** indecision, vacillation, hesitation, hesitancy, wavering, irresolution, scruple, misgiving. **3.** suspension, intermission, pause, interruption, cessation, stop, remission, surcease, relief, respite, stay, rest, quiescence. —**Ant.** certainty; decision.

suspicion, *n.* **1.** doubt, mistrust, misgiving, distrust. **2.** imagination, notion, idea, supposition, conjecture, guess. **3.** trace, hint, suggestion. —**Ant.** trust. —**Syn. Study.** SUSPICION, DISTRUST are terms for a feeling that appearances are not reliable. SUSPICION is the positive tendency to doubt the trustworthiness of appearances and therefore to believe that one has detected possibilities of something unreliable, unfavorable, menacing, or the like: *to feel suspicion about the honesty of a prominent man.* DISTRUST may be a passive want of trust, faith, or reliance in a person or thing: *to feel distrust of one's own ability.*

sustain, *v.* **1.** hold *or* bear up, bear, carry, support,

uphold. **2.** undergo, support, suffer, endure, bear. **3.** maintain, support, subsist, nourish, nurture. **4.** purvey, supply, cater, furnish, support, aid, countenance, help. **5.** uphold, confirm, establish, approve. **6.** confirm, ratify, corroborate, justify. —**Ant.** fail; disapprove.

swagger, *v.* **1.** strut, parade. **2.** boast, brag, bluster, blow. —*n.* **3.** boasting, bragging, arrogance, affectation, braggadocio. —**Syn. Study.** See STRUT.

swallow, *v.* **1.** eat, gorge, gulp, engorge, imbibe, drink. **2.** consume, assimilate, absorb, engulf, devour. **3.** accept, receive. —*n.* **4.** mouthful, gulp, draught, drink.

swap, *v., n.* trade, barter, exchange.

swarm, *n.* **1.** horde, bevy, crowd, multitude, throng, mass, host, flock, shoal. —*v.* **2.** crowd, throng. **3.** abound, teem. —**Syn. Study.** See CROWD.

swarthy, *adj.* dark, dusky,

brown, dark-skinned, tawny, swart. —**Ant.** pale.

sway, *v.* **1.** swing, wave, brandish. **2.** incline, lean, bend, tend. **3.** fluctuate, vacillate. **4.** rule, reign, govern, prevail. **5.** direct, dominate, control, influence. —*n.* **6.** rule, dominion, control, power, sovereignty, government, authority, mastery, predominance, ascendency. **7.** influence, power, authority, bias.

swear, *v.* **1.** declare, affirm, avow, depose, state, vow, testify. **2.** promise. **3.** curse, imprecate, blaspheme.

sweat, *v.* **1.** perspire. —*n.* **2.** perspiration. —**Syn. Study.** See PERSPIRATION.

sweeping, *adj.* **1.** broad, wide, extensive, comprehensive, wholesale, vast. **2.** exaggerated, overstated, extravagant, unqualified, hasty. —**Ant.** narrow; qualified.

sweet, *adj.* **1.** sugary, honeyed, syrupy, saccharine. **2.** fresh, pure, clean, new. **3.** musical, melodious, mellifluous, harmonious, tuneful, in tune, dulcet, tuneful, mellow. **4.** fragrant, redolent, aromatic, perfumed, scented. **5.** pleasing, pleasant, agreeable, pleasurable, enjoyable, delightful, charming, lovable, kind, amiable, gracious, engaging, winning, winsome, attractive, gentle. **6.** dear, beloved, precious. **7.** manageable, tractable, easygoing. —**Ant.** sour, bitter.

swell, *v.* **1.** inflate, dilate, distend, grow, expand, blow up. **2.** bulge, protrude. **3.** grow, increase, augment, enlarge. **4.** arise, grow, well up, glow, warm, thrill, heave, expand. **5.** bloat, strut, swagger. —*n.* **6.** bulkiness, distention, inflation, swelling. **7.** bulge, protuberance, augmentation, growth. **8.** wave, sea, billow. **9.** (*slang*) fop, dandy, coxcomb, popinjay, blade, buck. —*adj.* **10.** stylish, elegant, fashionable, grand. **11.** grand, fine, first-rate. **—Ant.** decrease, diminish.

swerve, *v.* deviate, diverge, depart.

swift, *adj.* **1.** speedy, quick, fleet, rapid, fast, expeditious. **2.** quick, prompt, ready, eager, alert, zealous. **—n. 3.** swallow. **—Ant.** slow, slothful. **—Syn. Study.** See QUICK.

swindle, *v.* **1.** cheat, cozen, defraud, dupe, trick, gull, victimize, deceive, con. **—n. 2.** fraud, trickery, confidence game, thimblerig, shell game, deception, knavery.

swindler, *n.* confidence man, cheat, deceiver, charlatan, mountebank, rogue, rascal, knave, sharper, trickster.

swing, *v.* **1.** sway, oscillate, rock, wave, vibrate. **2.** suspend, hang. **—n. 3.** sway, vibration, oscillation. **4.** freedom, margin, range, scope, play, sweep. **5.** jazz, ragtime.

sybarite, *n.* voluptuary, epicurean, sensualist.

sycophant, *n.* flatterer, toady, fawner, parasite, boot-licker, yes-man.

sylph, *n.* salamander, undine, nymph, gnome.

symbiotic, *adj.* mutual, reciprocal, commensal, cooperative, cooperating, synergistic, interacting, interactive, interrelating, **—Ant.** independent, isolated.

symmetry, *n.* balance, proportion, equilibrium, regularity, harmony. **—Syn. Study.** SYMMETRY, BALANCE, PROPORTION, HARMONY all denote qualities based on a correspondence or agreement, usu. pleasing, among the parts of a whole. SYMMETRY implies a regularity in form and arrangement of corresponding parts: *the perfect symmetry of pairs of matched columns.* BALANCE implies equilibrium of dissimilar parts, often as a means of emphasis: *a balance of humor and seriousness.* PROPORTION implies a proper relation among parts: *His long arms were not in proportion to his body.* HARMONY suggests a consistent, pleasing, or orderly combination of parts: *harmony of color.*

sympathetic, *adj.* **1.** sympathizing, compassionate, commiserating, kind, tender, affectionate. **2.** congenial, attached, affected *or* touched by. —**Ant.** unsympathetic.

sympathy, *n.* compassion, pity, empathy, understanding, compassionateness, fellow feeling, concern, support —**Syn. Study.** SYMPATHY, COMPASSION, PITY, EMPATHY denote the tendency or capacity to share the feelings of others. SYMPATHY signifies a general kinship with another's feelings, no matter of what kind: *sympathy with their yearning for freedom; sympathy for the bereaved.* COMPASSION implies a deep sympathy for the sorrows or troubles of another,

and a powerful urge to alleviate distress: *compassion for homeless refugees.* PITY suggests a kindly, but sometimes condescending, sorrow aroused by the suffering or misfortune of others: *Mere pity for the flood victims is no help.* EMPATHY refers to a vicarious participation in the emotions of another, or to the ability to imagine oneself in someone else's predicament: *to feel empathy with a character in a play.*

synopsis, *n.* compendium, condensation, summary, brief, digest, epitome, abstract, abridgment, précis, outline, syllabus. —**Syn. Study.** See SUMMARY.

system, *n.* **1.** assemblage, combination, complex, correlation. **2.** plan, scheme, procedure, arrangement, classification. **3.** world, universe, cosmos. **4.** taxonomy, order.

systematic, See Syn. study at ORDERLY.

T

taboo, *adj.* **1.** forbidden, interdicted, prohibited, banned, sacred, unclean. —*n.* **2.** prohibition, interdiction, exclusion, ostracism. —**Ant.** allowed, sanctioned, approved; permission, approval.

tacit, *adj.* silent, unexpressed, unspoken, unsaid, implied, implicit, understood, inferred. —**Ant.** expressed.

taciturn, *adj.* silent, reserved, uncommunicative, reticent, quiet. —**Ant.** voluble, talkative.

tacky, *adj.* **1.** inferior, tinny, junky, second-hand, shoddy, broken-down, shabby, run-down, ramshackle, seedy, tatty, threadbare. **2.** unfashionable, unstylish, dowdy, frumpy, frumpish, frowzy, drab, stale, old-fashioned, outmoded, stodgy, colorless. **3.** tasteless, gaudy, vulgar, chintzy, cheap, tawdry, cheesy, glitzy, sleazy, loud, garish, low-class, low-rent. —**Ant.** elegant, classy.

tactful, *adj.* diplomatic, adroit, skillful, clever, perceptive, sensitive. —**Ant.** tactless, maladroit. —**Syn. Study.** See DIPLOMATIC.

tactics, *n.* strategy, generalship, maneuvering; maneuvers, procedure.

taint, *n.* **1.** fault, defect, blemish, spot, stain, blot, flaw. **2.** infection, contamination, corruption, defilement. **3.** dishonor, discredit, disgrace. —*v.* **4.** infect, contaminate, defile, poison, corrupt, pollute. **5.** sully, tarnish, blemish, stain, blot.

take, *v.* **1.** get, acquire, procure, obtain, secure. **2.** seize, catch, capture, grasp. **3.** grasp, grip, embrace. **4.** receive,

tale to talkative

8**596**

accept. **5.** pick, select, choose, elect. **6.** subtract, deduct. **7.** carry, convey, transfer. **8.** conduct, escort, lead. **9.** obtain, exact, demand. **10.** occupy, use up, consume. **11.** attract, hold, draw. **12.** captivate, charm, delight, attract, interest, engage, bewitch, fascinate, allure, enchant. **13.** assume, adopt, accept. **14.** ascertain, determine, fix. **15.** experience, feel, perceive. **16.** regard, consider, suppose, assume, presume, hold. **17.** perform, discharge, assume, adopt, appropriate. **18.** grasp, apprehend, comprehend, understand. **19.** do, perform, execute. **20.** suffer, undergo, experience, bear, stand, tolerate, submit to, endure. **21.** employ, use, make use of. **22.** require, need, demand. **23.** deceive, cheat, trick, defraud. **24.** catch, engage, fix. —**Ant.** give.

tale, *n.* **1.** story, narrative, fairy tale, account, fiction. **2.** lie, fib, falsehood, fable.

talent, *n.* ability, aptitude, capacity, capability, gift, genius, faculty, forte. —**Ant.** inability, incapability, weakness. —**Syn. Study.** See ABILITY.

talisman, *n.* fetish, charm, amulet, mascot, lucky-piece, good-luck charm, periapt, phylactery, juju, rabbit's foot, four-leaf clover.

talk, *v.* **1.** speak, converse. **2.** consult, confer, discuss; gossip. **3.** chatter, prattle, prate. **4.** communicate. **5.** utter, speak, mention. —*n.* **6.** speech, talking, conversation, colloquy, discourse, dialogue, chat, communication, parley, conference, confabulation. **7.** report, rumor, gossip, bruit. **8.** prattle, empty words, words. **9.** language, dialect, lingo.

talkative, *adj.* garrulous, loquacious, wordy, verbose, prolix, long-drawn. —**Ant.** taciturn, silent. —**Syn. Study.** TALKATIVE,

GARRULOUS, LOQUACIOUS characterize a person who talks a great deal. TALKATIVE is a neutral or mildly unfavorable word for a person who is much inclined to talk, sometimes without significance: *a talkative child.* The GARRULOUS person talks with wearisome persistence, usu. about trivial things: *a garrulous cab driver.* A LOQUACIOUS person, intending to be sociable, talks continuously and at length: *a loquacious host.*

tall, *adj.* high, elevated, towering, lofty. —**Ant.** short.

tame, *adj.* **1.** domesticated, mild, docile, gentle. **2.** gentle, fearless. **3.** tractable, docile, submissive, meek, subdued, crushed, suppressed. **4.** dull, insipid, unanimated, spiritless, flat, empty, vapid, vacuous, jejune, prosaic, boring, uninteresting, tedious. **5.** spiritless, cowardly, pusillanimous, dastardly. **6.** cultivated. —*v.* **7.** domesticate, break, subdued, make tractable. **8.** soften, tone down, calm, repress, subjugate, enslave. —**Ant.** wild.

tamper, *v.* **1.** meddle, interfere, damage, misuse, alter. **2.** bribe, suborn, seduce, lead astray, corrupt. —**Ant.** neglect, ignore.

tangible, *adj.* **1.** touchable, discernible, material, substantial, palpable, corporeal. **2.** real, actual, genuine, certain, open, plain, positive, obvious, evident, in evidence, perceptible. **3.** definite, specific, ineluctable. —**Ant.** intangible; unreal, imperceptible.

tantalize, *v.* torment, tease, torture, irritate, vex, provoke.

tantamount, *adj.* equal, equivalent. —**Ant.** unequal.

tar, *n.* **1.** pitch, creosote, asphalt. **2.** sailor, seaman, seafaring man, gob, mariner, swabby, seafarer.

tardy, *adj.* **1.** late,

behindhand, slack, dilatory, slow, backward. **2.** slow, sluggish; reluctant. —**Ant.** early, punctual.

tarnish, *v.* **1.** dull, discolor. **2.** sully, stain, taint, blemish, soil. —*n.* **3.** stain, blot, blemish, taint. —**Ant.** brighten.

tarry, *v.* **1.** remain, stay, sojourn, rest, lodge, stop, abide. **2.** delay, linger, loiter; wait. —**Ant.** leave, depart.

tart, *adj.* **1.** sour, sourish, acidic, acerbic, sharp, piquant, bitter. **2.** caustic, sarcastic, mordent, acrimonious, cutting, biting, stinging. —**Ant.** sweet, mellow.

task, *n.* duty, job, chore, assignment, work, labor, drudgery, toil. —**Syn. Study.** TASK, CHORE, ASSIGNMENT, JOB refer to a specific instance or act of work. TASK refers to a clearly defined piece of work, usu. of short or limited duration, assigned to or expected of a person: *the task of collecting dues.* A CHORE is a minor, usu.

routine task, often more tedious than difficult: *the chore of taking out the garbage.* ASSIGNMENT usu. refers to a specific task assigned by someone in authority: *a homework assignment.* JOB is the most general of these terms, referring to almost any work or duty, including one's livelihood: *the job of washing the windows; a well-paid job in advertising.*

taste, *v.* **1.** try, sip, savor. **2.** undergo, experience, feel. **3.** smack, savor. —*n.* **4.** sensation, flavor, savor, scent. **5.** morsel, bit, sip. **6.** relish, liking, fondness, predilection, disposition, partiality, preference, predisposition. **7.** discernment, perception, sense, judgment. **8.** manner, style, character.

tasteless, *adj.* **1.** flavorless, insipid, bland, dull, savorless, flat, watery, uninteresting, wishy-washy, vapid, blah. **2.** inconsiderate, thoughtless, careless, unthinking, unfeeling, hurtful. **3.** inappropriate, unseemly, unsuitable, inapt, improper, ill-chosen, infelicitous. **4.** indelicate, offensive, objectionable, coarse, crass, crude, tacky, vulgar. **—Ant.** tasteful.

tasty, See Syn. study at PALATABLE.

taunt, *v.* **1.** reproach, insult, censure, upbraid, sneer at, flout, revile. **2.** ridicule, mock, jeer, scoff at, make fun of, twit, provoke. *—n.* **3.** gibe, jeer, sarcasm, scorn, contumely, reproach, challenge, scoff, derision, insult, reproach, censure, ridicule. **—Syn. Study.** See RIDICULE.

taut, *adj.* tense, stretched, rigid, unrelaxed, inelastic, tight, drawn, stiff, high-strung, strained. **—Ant.** loose, relaxed.

tavern, *v.* **1.** bar, cafe; pub. **2.** inn, hotel, public house, hostelry.

tawdry, *adj.* cheap, gaudy, showy, ostentatious, flashy, meretricious. **—Ant.** expensive, elegant.

teach, *v.* instruct, educate, inform, enlighten, discipline, train, drill, tutor, school, indoctrinate. **—Ant.** learn. **—Syn. Study.** TEACH, INSTRUCT, TUTOR, TRAIN, EDUCATE share the meaning of imparting information, understanding, or skill. TEACH is the most general of these terms, referring to any practice that furnishes a person with skill or knowledge: *to teach children to write.* INSTRUCT usu. implies a systematic, structured method of teaching: *to instruct paramedics in first aid.* TUTOR means to give private instruction, focusing on an individual's difficulties in a specific subject: *to tutor him in geometry every Thursday afternoon.* TRAIN stresses the development of a desired proficiency or behavior through practice, discipline, and instruction: *to train military recruits.* EDUCATE stresses the development of reasoning and judgment; it often involves preparing a person for an occupation or for mature life: *to educate the young.*

teacher, *n.* instructor, tutor, lecturer, professor, don. —**Ant.** student, pupil.

tear, *n.* **1.** (*plural*) grief, sorrow, regret, affliction, misery. **2.** rip, rent, fissure. **3.** rage, passion, flurry, outburst. —*v.* **4.** pull apart, rend, rip, sunder, sever. **5.** distress, shatter, afflict, affect. **6.** rend, split, divide. **7.** cut, lacerate, wound, injure, mangle.

tease, *adj.* **1.** worry, irritate, bother, trouble, provoke, disturb, annoy, rail at, vex, plague, molest, harry, harass, chafe, hector. **2.** separate, comb, card, shred. **3.** raise a nap, teasel, dress. —**Ant.** calm, assuage, mollify; unite; smooth.

technique, *n.* method, system, apparatus, procedure, practice, mechanism, routine, modus operandi, way, manner, fashion, style, mode.

tedious, *adj.* long, tiresome, irksome, wearisome, prolix, labored, wearing, exhausting, tiring, fatiguing, monotonous, dull, boring. —**Ant.** interesting.

teem, *v.* **1.** abound, swarm, be prolific *or* fertile. **2.** empty, pour out, discharge.

tell, *v.* **1.** narrate, relate, give an account of, recount, describe, report. **2.** communicate, make known, apprise, acquaint, inform, teach, impart, explain. **3.** announce, proclaim, publish, publicize. **4.** utter, express, word, mouth, mention, speak. **5.** reveal, divulge, disclose, betray, declare; acknowledge, own, confess. **6.** say, make plain. **7.** discern, identify, describe, distinguish, discover, make out. **8.** bid, order, command, urge. **9.** mention, enumerate, count, reckon, number, compute, calculate. **10.** operate, have force *or* effect.

temper, *n.* **1.** temperament,

constitution, make-up, nature. **2.** disposition, mood, humor. **3.** passion, irritation, anger, resentment. **4.** calmness, aloofness, moderation, coolness, equanimity, tranquillity, composure. **5.** hardness, elasticity. —*v.* **6.** moderate, mitigate, assuage, mollify, tone down, soften, soothe, calm, pacify, tranquilize, restrain. **7.** suit, adapt, fit, accommodate, adjust. **8.** moisten, mix, blend, work, knead. **9.** modify, qualify.

temperament, *n.* disposition, make-up, temper, constitution, nature.

temperamental, *adj.* moody, irritable, sensitive, hypersensitive, touchy, testy, hot-tempered, bad-tempered, short-tempered. —**Ant.** serene, composed.

temperate, *adj.* moderate, self-restrained, continent; sober, calm, cool, detached, dispassionate. —**Ant.** intemperate, immoderate. —**Syn. Study.** See MODERATE.

tempestuous, *adj.* turbulent, tumultuous, violent, stormy, impetuous. —**Ant.** peaceful, pacific, serene, calm.

temporary, *adj.* transient, transitory, impermanent, discontinuous, fleeting, passing, evanescent, short-lived, ephemeral. —**Ant.** permanent, infinite. —**Syn. Study.** TEMPORARY, TRANSIENT, TRANSITORY agree in referring to that which is not lasting or permanent. TEMPORARY implies an arrangement established with no thought of continuance but with the idea of being changed soon: *a temporary structure.* TRANSIENT describes that which is in the process of passing by, and which will therefore last or stay only a short time: *a transient condition.* TRANSITORY describes an innate characteristic by which a thing, by its very nature, lasts only a short time: *Life is transitory.*

tempt, *v.* **1.** induce, persuade, entice, allure,

seduce, attract, lead astray, invite, inveigle, decoy, lure. **2.** provoke, test, try, prove. —**Syn. Study.** TEMPT, SEDUCE both mean to allure or entice someone into an unwise, wrong, or wicked action. To TEMPT is to attract by holding out the probability of gratification or advantage, often in regard to what is wrong or unwise: *to tempt a high official with a bribe.* To SEDUCE is to lead astray, as from duty or principles, but more often from moral rectitude, chastity, etc.: *to seduce a soldier from loyalty.*

tempting, *adj.* enticing, inviting, seductive, attractive, alluring. —**Ant.** repulsive, repellent.

tenable, *adj.* defensible, defendable, supportable, admissible, viable, reasonable, believable, plausible, credible. —**Ant.** indefensible, unbelievable.

tenacious, *adj.* **1.** retentive. **2.** pertinacious, persistent, stubborn, obstinate, opinionated, sure, positive, certain. **3.** adhesive, sticky, viscous, glutinous. **4.** cohesive, clinging, tough. —**Ant.** unsure, uncertain.

tenacity, *n.* perseverance, persistency, pertinacity, obstinacy. —**Ant.** transitoriness. —**Syn. Study.** See PERSEVERANCE.

tendency, *n.* direction, trend, disposition, predisposition, proneness, proclivity, inclination, leaning, bias, prejudice, drift, bent; movement. —**Ant.** failure, disinclination.

tender, *adj.* **1.** soft, delicate. **2.** weak, delicate, feeble. **3.** young, immature, youthful. **4.** gentle, delicate, soft, lenient, mild. **5.** soft-hearted, sympathetic, tender-hearted, compassionate, pitiful, kind, merciful, affectionate. **6.** affectionate, loving, sentimental, amatory. **7.** considerate, careful, chary, reluctant. **8.** acute, painful, sore, sensitive. **9.** fragile, breakable, frangible, friable. **10.**

ticklish, delicate, sensitive. —v. **11.** offer, proffer, present. —n. **12.** offer, offering, proposal, proffer. **13.** dinghy, skiff, rowboat, lifeboat, motorboat, boat, pinnace, gig. **14.** coal car, coaler. —**Ant.** coarse, rough; strong; mature, adult; merciless, ruthless; apathetic; inconsiderate; tough; accept. —**Syn. Study.** See OFFER.

tenet, *n.* belief, principle, doctrine, dogma, opinion, notion, position, creed.

tense, *adj.* **1.** tight, taut, stretched, rigid, strained. **2.** nervous, neurotic, excited, strained. —**Ant.** lax; relaxed.

tentative, *adj.* experimental, trial, probationary, indefinite. —**Ant.** definite, confirmed.

tenuous, *adj.* **1.** thin, slender, small, attenuated, minute. **2.** rare, thin, rarefied. **3.** unimportant, insignificant, trivial, trifling, nugatory, unsubstantial. —**Ant.** thick; substantial, significant.

termagant, *n.* shrew, maenad, bacchante, virago, nag, beldam, Xantippe, vixen.

terminate, *v.* **1.** end, finish, conclude, close, complete. **2.** bound, limit. **3.** issue, result, turn out, eventuate, prove. —**Ant.** begin, open.

terminology, *n.* language, nomenclature, vocabulary, vernacular, lexicon, verbiage, speech, jargon, dialect, lingo.

terrain, *n.* **1.** land, topography, geography, territory, region. **2.** arena, area, field, bailiwick, sphere, province, domain, specialty.

terrestrial, *adj.* earthly, mundane, worldly, terrene. —**Ant.** celestial. —**Syn. Study.** See EARTHLY.

terrible, *adj.* **1.** dreadful, awful, fearful, frightful, appalling, dire, horrible, horrifying, terrifying, terrific, horrendous, horrid, gruesome, hideous, monstrous. **2.** distressing, severe, extreme, excessive.

—**Ant.** delightful, pleasant; moderate.

terror, *n.* horror, fear, panic, fright, alarm, dismay, consternation. —**Ant.** security, calm.

terrorize, *v.* dominate, coerce, intimidate. —**Ant.** ameliorate, mollify.

terse, *adj.* brief, concise, pithy, neat, compact, succinct, curt, sententious, concentrated. —**Ant.** attenuated. —**Syn. Study.** See CONCISE.

test, *n.* **1.** trial, proof, assay. **2.** examination, quiz, exam. —*v.* **3.** try, essay, prove, examine; refine, assay.

testimony, *n.* evidence, deposition, attestation, declaration, affirmation, corroboration.

testy, *adj.* irritable, impatient, touchy, tetchy, petulant, edgy, short-tempered, peevish, vexatious, choleric, snappish, waspish, splenetic, cross, cranky, irascible, fretful. —**Ant.** composed, calm.

thankful, *adj.* grateful,

indebted, beholden, obliged. —**Ant.** thankless, ungrateful.

thaw, *v.* melt, liquefy, dissolve; warm. —**Ant.** freeze, solidify, sublimate, cool.

theatrical, *adj.* dramatic, histrionic, melodramatic, stagy, operatic, exaggerated, ostentatious, sensational, artificial, mannered, actorish, actressy. —**Ant.** modest, low-key.

theme, *n.* **1.** subject, topic, thesis, point, text. **2.** composition, essay, paper. **3.** motif, thread, tenor, ideas; trend. —**Syn. Study.** See SUBJECT.

theory, *n.* **1.** assumption, hypothesis, rationale, explanation, system, conjecture, guess, plan, scheme, proposal. **2.** view, contemplation, conception. —**Syn. Study.** THEORY, HYPOTHESIS are used in non-technical contexts to mean an untested idea or opinion. A THEORY in technical use is a more or less verified or established explanation accounting for known facts or phenomena: *Einstein's theory of relativity.* A HYPOTHESIS is a conjecture put forth as a possible explanation of phenomena or relations, which serves as a basis of argument or experimentation to reach the truth: *This idea is only a hypothesis.*

therapeutic, *adj.* healing, curative, remedial, corrective, restorative, theriacal, adjuvant, alleviative, palliative, helpful, beneficial, salutary. —**Ant.** harmful, toxic.

therefore, *adv.* hence, whence, wherefore, accordingly, consequently, so, then.

thersitical, *adj.* scurrilous, foul-mouthed, abusive, vindictive, impudent. —**Ant.** honorable, polite, discreet.

thesaurus, *n.* storehouse, repository, treasury; dictionary, encyclopedia.

thick-skinned, *adj.* pachydermatous;

insensitive, dull, obtuse, callous. —**Ant.** thin-skinned, sensitive.

thief, *n.* **1.** robber; pickpocket, mugger. **2.** burglar, cracksman, second-story man, housebreaker, safecracker. —**Syn. Study.** THIEF, ROBBER refer to one who steals. A THIEF takes the goods or property of another by stealth without the latter's knowledge: *like a thief in the night.* A ROBBER trespasses upon the house, property, or person of another, and makes away with things of value, even at the cost of violence: *An armed robber held up the store owner.*

thin, *adj.* **1.** slim, slender, lean, skinny, poor, lank, gaunt, scrawny, emaciated. **2.** sparse, scanty, meager. **3.** fluid, rare, rarefied, tenuous. **4.** unsubstantial, slight, flimsy. **5.** transparent, weak. **6.** faint, slight, poor, feeble. —*v.* **7.** rarefy, dilute, reduce, diminish. —**Ant.** thick, fat, obese;

think to threaten

think to threaten

think to threaten

think to threaten

abundant; substantial; opaque, strong; increase.

think, *v.* **1.** conceive, imagine, picture. **2.** mediate, ponder, consider, regard, suppose, look upon, judge, deem, esteem, count, account. **3.** bear in mind, recollect, recall, remember. **4.** intend, mean, design, purpose. **5.** believe, suppose. **6.** anticipate, expect. **7.** cogitate, meditate, reflect, muse, ponder, ruminate, contemplate.

thirst, *n.* desire, craving, eagerness, hankering, yearning, hunger, appetite. —**Ant.** distaste, apathy.

thorough, *adj.* complete, entire, thoroughgoing, unqualified, perfect, done, finished, completed, total. —**Ant.** incomplete, unfinished.

thought, *n.* **1.** concept, conception, opinion, judgment, belief, idea, notion, tenet, conviction, speculation, consideration, contemplation. **2.** meditation, reflection, musing, cogitation, thinking. **3.** intention, design, purpose, intent. **4.** anticipation, expectation. **5.** consideration, attention, care, regard. **6.** trifle, mote. —**Syn. Study.** See IDEA.

thoughtful, *adj.* **1.** contemplative, meditative, reflective, pensive, deliberative. **2.** careful, heedful, mindful, regardful, considerate, attentive, discreet, prudent, wary, circumspect. —**Ant.** thoughtless.

thoughtless, *adj.* unthinking, careless, heedless, inattentive, inconsiderate, negligent, neglectful, remiss, unmindful, unobservant, unwatchful, reckless, flighty, scatter-brained, light-headed, giddy. —**Ant.** thoughtful.

thrash, *v.* beat, defeat, punish, flog, wallop, maul, drub. —**Syn. Study.** See BEAT.

threaten, *v.* menace, endanger, indicate, presage, impend, portend, augur, forebode, foreshadow, prognosticate. —**Ant.** protect, defend.

threatening, See Syn. study at OMINOUS.

thrifty, *adj.* **1.** frugal, provident, economical, sparing, saving. **2.** thriving, prosperous, successful. **3.** growing, flourishing, vigorous. —**Ant.** wasteful, prodigal, improvident; poor, unsuccessful; stunted. —**Syn. Study.** See ECONOMICAL.

thrive, *v.* prosper, succeed, flourish, increase, advance, luxuriate. —**Ant.** languish, die. —**Syn. Study.** See SUCCEED.

throb, *v.* pulse, beat, drum, pulsate, palpitate, thump, pound, thrum, resonate, vibrate, flutter, quake.

throe, *n.* **1.** seizure, attack, fit, pang, pain, spasm, paroxysm, access, turn, spell. **2.** struggle, distress, stress, strife, difficulty.

throng, *n.* **1.** multitude, crowd, assemblage, swarm, horde, host. —*v.* **2.** swarm, assemble, crowd, press,

jostle; herd. —**Syn. Study.** See CROWD.

throw, *v.* **1.** project, propel, cast, hurl, pitch, toss, fling, launch, send, let fly. —*n.* **2.** cast, fling. **3.** venture, chance. **4.** scarf, boa, stole. **5.** blanket, afghan, robe.

thrust, *v.* **1.** push, force, shove, drive. **2.** stab, pierce, puncture, penetrate. —*n.* **3.** lunge, stab, push, drive, tilt, shove.

thwart, *v.* **1.** frustrate, baffle, oppose, prevent, hinder, obstruct, defeat. —*n.* **2.** seat. —*adj.* **3.** cross, transverse. **4.** adverse, unfavorable. —**Ant.** favor, encourage, support, help.

tidy, *adj.* neat, trim, orderly. —**Ant.** messy, sloppy, untidy.

tie, *v.* **1.** bind, fasten. **2.** knot. **3.** fasten, join, unite, connect, link, knit, yoke, lock. **4.** confine, restrict, limit, obligate, constrain. **5.** equal. —*n.* **6.** cord, string, rope, band, ligature. **7.** necktie, cravat. **8.** knot; link, connection, bond. —**Ant.** loose, loosen, release.

tiff, *n.* quarrel, dispute, disagreement, altercation, spat, argument, bickering, falling out, scrap, dustup, run-in.

time, *n.* **1.** duration. **2.** period, interval, term, spell, span, space. **3.** epoch, era, period, season, age, date. **4.** tempo, rhythm, measure. —*v.* **5.** regulate, gauge.

timely, *adj.* seasonable, opportune, well-timed, prompt, punctual. —**Ant.** untimely, inappropriate, inopportune.

timid, *adj.* fearful, shy, diffident, bashful, retiring, coy, blushing, shrinking, timorous, fainthearted, tremulous, cowardly, dastardly, pusillanimous. —**Ant.** bold, fearless, intrepid.

tinny, *adj.* **1.** unresonant, reedy, thin, hollow, weak, feeble. **2.** inferior, cheap, low-grade, insubstantial, flimsy, cheapjack. —**Ant.** hearty, sturdy.

tint, *n.* **1.** color, hue, tinge,

dye, stain, tincture; rinse; pastel. —*v.* **2.** color, tinge, stain.

tirade, *n.* denunciation, outburst, harangue, declamation.

tire, *v.* **1.** exhaust, weary, fatigue, jade. **2.** exasperate, bore, weary, irk.

tired, *adj.* exhausted, fatigued, weary, wearied, enervated. —**Ant.** energetic, fiery, tireless.

tireless, *adj.* untiring, indefatigable, energetic, active. —**Ant.** tired, tiresome.

tiresome, *adj.* **1.** wearisome, tedious, dull, fatiguing, humdrum. **2.** annoying, vexatious. —**Ant.** interesting, enchanting.

title, *n.* **1.** name, designation, epithet, appellation, denomination, cognomen. **2.** championship. **3.** right, claim. —*v.* **4.** designate, entitle, denominate, term, call, style.

toady, *n.* sycophant, fawner, flatterer, yes-man.

toil, *n.* **1.** work, labor, effort, drudgery, exertion, travail, pains. —*v.* **2.** labor, work, strive, moil, exert. —**Ant.** indolence, sloth. —**Syn. Study.** See WORK.

tolerance, *n.* **1.** toleration, patience, sufferance, forbearance, endurance. **2.** liberality, catholicity, impartiality, magnanimity, open-mindedness. **3.** allowance, variation. —**Ant.** intolerance.

tool, *n.* instrument, implement, utensil, contrivance, device. —**Syn. Study.** TOOL, IMPLEMENT, INSTRUMENT, UTENSIL refer to contrivances for doing work. A TOOL is a contrivance held in and worked by the hand and used for cutting, digging, etc.: *a carpenter's tools.* An IMPLEMENT is any tool or contrivance designed or used for a particular purpose: *agricultural implements.* An INSTRUMENT is anything used in doing certain work or producing a certain result, esp. such as requires delicacy, accuracy, or precision: *surgical or musical instruments.* A UTENSIL is usu. an article for domestic use: *kitchen utensils.* When used figuratively of human agency, TOOL is generally used in a contemptuous sense; INSTRUMENT, in a neutral or good sense: *a tool of unscrupulous men; an instrument of Providence.*

top, *n.* **1.** apex, zenith, acme, peak, summit, pinnacle, vertex, culmination. **2.** best, chief. —*adj.* **3.** highest, uppermost, upper, greatest. **4.** foremost, chief, principal. —*v.* **5.** surpass, excel, outdo. **6.** crop, prune, lop. —**Ant.** bottom, foot; worst; lowest; least.

topic, *n.* subject, theme, thesis, subject matter. —**Syn. Study.** See SUBJECT.

top-notch, *adj.* excellent, fine, superlative, capital, superior, peerless, splendid, matchless, A1, first-rate, first-class,

top-shelf, top-drawer,
blue-chip, gilt-edge,
sterling, five-star,
world-class. —**Ant.**
third-rate, third-string,
inferior.

torment, *v.* **1.** afflict, pain,
rack, torture, harass,
harry, hector, vex, annoy,
irritate, agonize, distress,
excruciate. **2.** plague,
worry, annoy, pester,
tease, provoke, needle,
nettle, trouble, tantalize,
fret. —*n.* **3.** agony, torture,
misery, distress, anguish.
—**Ant.** please.

torpid, *adj.* **1.** inactive,
sluggish, slow, dull,
apathetic, lethargic,
motionless, inert, indolent.
2. dormant, hibernating,
estivating. —**Ant.** active,
energetic. —**Syn. Study.**
See INACTIVE.

torrent, *n.* stream, flow,
downpour. —**Ant.** drop,
drip, dribble.

torrid, *adj.* **1.** hot, tropical,
burning, scorching, fiery,
parching. **2.** ardent,
passionate. —**Ant.** arctic,
frigid, cold; dispassionate,
cool.

tortuous, *adj.* **1.** twisted,
crooked, winding, curved,
twisting, bent, sinuous,
serpentine, sinuate. **2.**
evasive, roundabout,
circuitous, indirect,
deceitful, ambiguous,
crooked, dishonest.
—**Ant.** straight.

torture, *n., v.* torment.

toss, *v., n.* throw.

total, *adj.* **1.** whole, entire,
complete, finished, final,
full, absolute, utter,
unqualified. —*n.* **2.** sum,
whole, entirety, totality,
aggregate, gross. —*v.* **3.**
add up, amount to.

totality, *n.* total, all, sum
total, grand total,
everything, entirety, all
and sundry, kit and
caboodle, whole nine
yards, whole bit, whole
schmear, whole shebang,
whole shooting match,
whole ball of wax, the
works, the lot.

totter, *v.* **1.** stagger, falter,
reel. **2.** sway, rock, waver.
3. shake, tremble, oscillate,
quiver.

touch, *v.* **1.** handle, feel. **2.**
tap, pat, strike, hit. **3.**

come up to, attain, reach, arrive at. **4.** modify, improve. **5.** play, perform. **6.** treat, affect, impress, move, strike, stir, melt, soften. **7.** deal with, treat. **8.** pertain *or* relate to, concern, regard, affect. —*n.* **9.** contact; contiguity. **10.** stroke, pat, tap, blow. **11.** hint, trace, suggestion. **12.** characteristic, trait, style. **13.** quality, kind.

touchy, *adj.* **1.** sensitive, hypersensitive, thin-skinned, temperamental, volatile. **2.** irritable, irascible, cranky, cross, cantankerous, testy, tetchy. **3.** delicate, ticklish, difficult, tricky, sticky, precarious, slippery. —**Syn. Study.** See IRRITABLE.

tough, *adj.* **1.** firm, strong, hard, hardy. **2.** sturdy, hardy, durable. **3.** hardened, incorrigible, troublesome, inflexible, rigid. **4.** vigorous, severe, violent. —**Ant.** weak, feeble, sickly; flexible, soft; slight.

tour, *v.* **1.** travel, visit. —*n.*

2. excursion, trip, journey, expedition.

towering, *adj.* tall, lofty, high, great, elevated. —**Ant.** short, low.

town, *n.* city, metropolis, borough, community, village, burgh, dorp, thorp, hamlet. —**Ant.** country.

toxic, *adj.* harmful, injurious, damaging, deleterious, poisonous, venomous, virulent, malignant, mephitic, deadly, lethal. —**Ant.** beneficial, healthful.

toxin, *n.* poison, venom, virus. —**Ant.** serum, antitoxin. —**Syn. Study.** See POISON.

trace, *n.* **1.** vestige, mark, sign, track, spoor, footprint, trail, record. **2.** mark, indication, evidence. **3.** hint, suggestion, touch, taste, soupçon. —*v.* **4.** track, follow, trail. **5.** ascertain, find out, discover. **6.** draw, delineate, outline, diagram. **7.** copy. —**Ant.** abundance, plethora. —**Syn. Study.** TRACE, VESTIGE agree in denoting marks or signs of something, usu. of the past. TRACE, the broader term, denotes any mark or slight indication of something past or present: *a trace of ammonia in water.* VESTIGE is more limited and refers to some slight, though actual, remains of something that no longer exists: *vestiges of one's former wealth.*

tract, *n.* **1.** stretch, extent, district, territory, region. **2.** space, period. **3.** treatise, pamphlet, essay, sermon, homily, dissertation, disquisition.

tractable, *adj.* docile, malleable, manageable, willing, governable. —**Ant.** intractable.

trade, *n.* **1.** commrce, traffic, business, dealing, exchange, barter. **2.** purchase, sale, exchange, swap. **3.** occupation, vocation, metier, livelihood, living, employment, pursuit, business, profession, craft, calling, avocation. —*v.* **4.** barter, traffic *or* deal in, exchange. **5.** barter, interchange, bargain, deal.

traduce, *v.* slander, calumniate, malign, defame, vilify, abuse, revile, asperse, depreciate, blemish, decry, disparage. —**Ant.** praise, honor.

traffic, *n., v.* trade.

tragic, *adj.* mournful, melancholy, pathetic, distressing, pitiful, calamitous, sorrowful, disastrous, fatal, dreadful. —**Ant.** comic.

trail, *v.* **1.** drag, draw. **2.** track, trace, hunt down. —*n.* **3.** path, track; scent, spoor.

train, See Syn. study at TEACH.

trance, *n.* daze, daydream, reverie, brown study, stupor, coma, swoon, rapture, ecstasy, fugue.

tranquil, See Syn. study at PEACEFUL.

transact, *v.* carry on, enact, conclude, settle, perform, manage, negotiate, conduct.

transform, *v.* change, alter, metamorphose, convert,

transfigure, transmute. —**Ant.** retain. —**Syn. Study.** TRANSFORM, CONVERT mean to change one thing into another. TRANSFORM means to radically change the outward form or inner character: *a frog transformed into a prince; delinquents transformed into responsible citizens.* CONVERT usually means to modify or adapt so as to serve a new or different use or function: *to convert a barn into a house.*

transgress, *v.* **1.** violate, break, contravene, disobey, infringe. **2.** offend, sin, err, trespass. —**Ant.** obey.

transient, *adj.* transitory, temporary, fleeting, passing, flitting, flying, brief, fugitive. —**Ant.** permanent. —**Syn. Study.** See TEMPORARY.

transitory, *adj.* transient. —**Ant.** permanent. —**Syn. Study.** See TEMPORARY.

translation, *n.* paraphrase, version, interpretation, rendering, treatment.

translucent, *adj.*

semitransparent, translucid; transparent. —**Ant.** opaque, dense, solid. —**Syn. Study.** See TRANSPARENT.

transmit, *v.* send, forward, dispatch, convey, transport, carry, transfer, bear, remit.

transparent, *adj.* **1.** transpicuous, diaphanous, clear, pellucid, lucid, limpid, crystalline; translucent. **2.** open, frank, candid. **3.** manifest, obvious. —**Ant.** opaque; clandestine, secretive; concealed. —**Syn. Study.** TRANSPARENT, TRANSLUCENT agree in describing material that light rays can pass through. That which is TRANSPARENT allows objects to be seen clearly through it: *Clear water is transparent.* That which is TRANSLUCENT allows light to pass through, diffusing it, however, so that objects beyond are not distinctly seen: *Ground glass is translucent.*

transport, *v.* **1.** carry, convey. **2.** banish, exile. —*n.* **3.** conveyance, transportation. **4.** freighter, troopship, tanker, oiler. **5.** joy, bliss, rapture, ecstasy, happiness. —**Syn. Study.** See ECSTASY.

trap, *n.* **1.** pitfall, snare, springe. **2.** ambush, pitfall, artifice, stratagem. —*v.* **3.** ensnare, entrap, spring. **4.** ambush.

traumatic, *adj.* injurious, harmful, acute, upsetting, wrenching, painful, shocking, stunning, devastating, excruciating.

traverse, *v.* **1.** go counter to, obstruct, thwart, frustrate, contravene. **2.** contradict, deny. **3.** pass *or* go across, cross, cross over. —*n.* **4.** obstruction, bar, obstacle. **5.** crosspiece, crossbar, barrier, railing, lattice, screen. —*adj.* **6.** transverse, cross.

travesty, *n., v.* burlesque, parody, lampoon, caricature, take-off. —**Syn. Study.** See BURLESQUE.

treacherous, *adj.* **1.** traitorous, unfaithful, faithless, untrustworthy, treasonable, treasonous, perfidious, disloyal. **2.** deceptive, unreliable, insidious, recreant, deceitful. **3.** unstable, insecure. —**Ant.** faithful, trustworthy, loyal; reliable; stable, secure.

treachery, *n.* betrayal, treason, disloyalty, faithlessness, perfidy. —**Ant.** loyalty, fealty.

treason, *n.* sedition, disloyalty, treachery, disaffection, lese majesty. —**Ant.** loyalty, allegiance. —**Syn. Study.** TREASON, SEDITION mean disloyalty or treachery to one's country or its government. TREASON is any attempt to overthrow the government or impair the well-being of a state to which one owes allegiance. According to the U.S. Constitution, it is the crime of levying war against the U.S. or giving aid and comfort to its enemies. SEDITION is any act, writing, speech, etc., directed unlawfully against state authority, the government, or the constitution, or calculated to bring it into contempt or to incite others to hostility or disaffection; it does not amount to treason and therefore is not a capital offense.

treasure, *n.* **1.** wealth, riches, hoard, funds; valuables, jewels. —*v.* **2.** lay away, store, stock, husband, save, garner. **3.** prize, cherish.

treat, *v.* **1.** act *or* behave toward. **2.** look upon, consider, regard, deal with. **3.** discuss, deal with, handle. **4.** entertain, regale, feast. **5.** negotiate, settle, bargain, come to terms. —*n.* **6.** feast, fête, entertainment, banquet.

tremble, *v.* **1.** shake, quiver, quaver, quake, shiver, shudder. **2.** vibrate, oscillate, totter. —*n.* **3.** trembling, shaking, quivering.

tremendous, *adj.* **1.** huge, gigantic, colossal. **2.** dreadful, awful, horrid, horrendous, terrible, terrific, terrifying, horrifying, appalling. —**Ant.** small, tiny,

microscopic. —**Syn. Study.** See HUGE.

tremor, *n.* **1.** trembling, shaking, vibration, oscillation, shivering, quivering, quaking. **2.** quake, earthquake, temblor.

tremulous, *adj.* **1.** fearful, timorous, timid, frightened, afraid. **2.** vibratory, vibrating, quivering, shaking, trembling, shivering. —**Ant.** fearless, intrepid; solid, firm.

trenchant, *adj.* **1.** incisive, keen, sharp, cutting, bitting, sarcastic, sardonic, acute, pointed, caustic, piquant. **2.** thoroughgoing, vigorous, effective. —**Ant.** weak, mollifying; ineffective.

trend, *n.* **1.** course, drift, tendency, direction, inclination. —*v.* **2.** tend, extend, stretch, run, incline.

trespass, *n.* **1.** invasion, encroachment, intrusion, infringement. **2.** offense, sin, wrong, transgression, crime, misdemeanor,

misdeed, error, fault. —*v.*
3. encroach, infringe,
intrude, invade. **4.**
transgress, offend, sin.
—**Syn. Study.** TRESPASS,
ENCROACH, INFRINGE imply
overstepping boundaries or
violating the rights of
others. To TRESPASS is to
invade the property or
rights of another, esp. to
pass unlawfully within the
boundaries of private land:
*The hunters trespassed on
the farmer's fields.* To
ENCROACH is to intrude,
gradually and often
stealthily, on the territory,
rights, or privileges of
another, so that a footing
is imperceptibly
established: *The sea slowly
encroached on the land.* To
INFRINGE is to break in
upon or invade another's
rights, customs, or the
like, by violating or
disregarding them: *to
infringe on a patent.*
trial, *n.* **1.** test, proof,
experiment, examination,
testing. **2.** attempt, effort,
endeavor, struggle, essay.
3. test, assay, criterion,
proof, touchstone,

standard. **4.** probation. **5.**
affliction, suffering,
tribulation, distress,
sorrow, grief, trouble,
misery, woe, hardship.
trick, *n.* **1.** device,
expedient, artifice, wile,
stratagem, ruse, deception,
fraud, trickery, cheating,
deceit, duplicity. **2.**
semblance, appearance. **3.**
prank, joke, practical joke.
4. shift, dodge, swindle,
maneuver, hoax,
confidence game. **5.**
jugglery, sleight-of-hand,
legerdemain,
prestidigitation. —*v.* **6.**
cheat, swindle, beguile,
dupe, fool, deceive,
defraud, delude, cozen. **7.**
dress, array, deck. —**Syn.
Study.** TRICK, ARTIFICE, RUSE,
STRATAGEM are terms for
crafty or cunning devices
intended to deceive. TRICK,
the general term, refers
usu. to an underhanded
act designed to cheat
someone, but it sometimes
refers merely to a
pleasurable deceiving of
the senses: *to win by a
trick.* Like TRICK, but to a
greater degree, ARTIFICE

emphasizes the cleverness or cunning with which the proceeding is devised: *an artifice of diabolical ingenuity.* RUSE and STRATAGEM emphasize the purpose for which the trick is designed; RUSE is the more general term, and STRATAGEM sometimes implies a more elaborate procedure or a military application: *We gained entrance by a ruse. His stratagem gave the army command of the hill.* See also CHEAT.

trickery, *n.* artifice, trick, stratagem, fraud, deception, deceit, chicanery, knavery. —**Ant.** honesty.

trifling, *adj.* **1.** trivial, insignificant, unimportant, petty, paltry, negligible, nugatory, slight, worthless, piddling, immaterial. **2.** frivolous, shallow, light, empty. —**Ant.** important, significant, worthy; profound. —**Syn. Study.** See PETTY.

trim, *v.* **1.** reduce, pare, clip, prune, shave, shear, cut, lop, curtail. **2.**

modify, adjust, prepare, arrange. **3.** dress, array, deck, bedeck, ornament, decorate, adorn, embellish, garnish, trick out. —*n.* **4.** condition, order, case, plight, situation, state. **5.** dress, array, equipment, gear, trappings, trimmings. **6.** trimming, embellishment, decoration; cutting, clipping, priming, reduction. —*adj.* **7.** neat, smart, compact, tidy, well-ordered, ordered. **8.** prepared, well-equipped. —**Ant.** augment, increase.

trip, *n.* **1.** journey, voyage, excursion, pilgrimage, travel, tour, jaunt, junket. **2.** stumble, misstep. **3.** slip, mistake, error, blunder, erratum, lapse, oversight, miss. —*v.* **4.** stumble. **5.** bungle, blunder, err, slip, miss, overlook. **6.** hop, skip, dance. **7.** tip, tilt. —**Syn. Study.** TRIP, EXPEDITION, JOURNEY, PILGRIMAGE, VOYAGE are terms for a course of travel made to a particular place, usu. for some specific purpose. TRIP is the general word, indicating going any distance and returning, for either business or pleasure, and in either a hurried or a leisurely manner: *a trip to Europe; a bus trip.* An EXPEDITION, made often by an organized group, is designed for a specific purpose: *an archaeological expedition.* JOURNEY indicates a trip of considerable length, mainly by land, and is usu. applied to travel that is more fatiguing than a trip: *an arduous journey to Tibet.* A PILGRIMAGE is made as to a shrine, from motives of piety or veneration: *a pilgrimage to Lourdes.* A VOYAGE usu. indicates leisurely travel by water to a distant place: *a voyage around the world.*

trite, *adj.* commonplace, ordinary, common, hackneyed, stereotyped, stale. —**Ant.** original, uncommon, unusual, extraordinary. —**Syn. Study.** See COMMONPLACE.

triumph, *n.* **1.** victory, conquest, success. **2.** joy, exultation, ecstasy, jubilation, celebration. —*v.* **3.** win, succeed, prevail. **4.** rejoice, exult, celebrate. **5.** glory, be elated *or* glad, rejoice. —**Ant.** defeat, loss. —**Syn. Study.** See VICTORY.

trivial, *adj.* trifling, petty, unimportant, insignificant, nugatory, paltry, slight, immaterial, frivolous, small. —**Ant.** important, significant, material. —**Syn. Study.** See PETTY.

troop, *n.* **1.** assemblage, crowd, band, squad, party, body, unit, company, group, troupe. **2.** herd, flock, swarm, throng. —*v.* **3.** gather, flock together, swarm, throng, collect. **4.** associate, consort. **5.** assemble, group, convene.

trophy, *n.* **1.** token, remembrance, memento, souvenir, keepsake, commemoration, memorial. **2.** prize, reward, laurel, laurels, garland, award.

trouble, *v.* **1.** disturb, distress, worry, concern, agitate, upset, disorder, disarrange, confuse, derange. **2.** inconvenience, put out, discommode, incommode. **3.** annoy, vex, bother, irritate, irk, pester, plague, fret, torment, torture, harry, hector, harass, badger, disquiet, molest, perturb. —*n.* **4.** molestation, harassment, annoyance, difficulty, embarrassment. **5.** misery, distress, affliction, concern, worry, grief, agitation, care, suffering, calamity, dolor, adversity, tribulation, trial, misfortune, woe, pain, sorrow. **6.** disturbance, disorder. **7.** inconvenience, exertion, pains, effort. —**Ant.** calm, mollify; convenience, encourage, accommodate; happiness, fortune.

troublesome, *adj.* **1.** annoying, vexatious, perplexing, galling, harassing. **2.** laborious, difficult, arduous, hard, burdensome, wearisome. —**Ant.** simple, easy; trouble-free.

troupe, *n.* troop.

truculent, *adj.* fierce, brutal, savage, harsh, threatening, bullying, overbearing, ferocious, cruel, malevolent. —**Ant.** affable, amiable. —**Syn. Study.** See FIERCE.

trudge, *v.* walk, pace, tramp, plod. —**Syn. Study.** See PACE.

true, *adj.* **1.** factual, actual, real, authentic, genuine, veracious, truthful, veritable. **2.** sincere, honest, honorable, just, faithful, equitable, fair. **3.** loyal, faithful, trusty, trustworthy, staunch, constant, steady, steadfast, unwavering, unfaltering. **4.** accurate, exact, faithful, correct, precise; agreeing. **5.** right, proper. **6.** legitimate, rightful. **7.** reliable, sure, unfailing, persevering. —*adv.* **8.** truly, truthfully. **9.** exactly, accurately, precisely. —*v.* **10.** shape, adjust, place. —**Ant.** untrue.

trust, *n.* **1.** reliance, confidence, assurance, security, certainty, belief, faith. **2.** expectation, hope, faith. **3.** credit. **4.** obligation, responsibility, charge. **5.** commitment, office, duty, charge. —*v.* **6.** rely on, confide in, have confidence in, depend upon. **7.** believe, credit. **8.** expect, hope. **9.** entrust, commit, consign. **—Ant.** mistrust, distrust.

trustworthy, *adj.* reliable, true, honest, honorable, faithful, staunch, loyal, steadfast, steady, straightforward.

truth, *n.* **1.** fact, reality, verity, veracity. **2.** genuineness, reality, actuality. **3.** honesty, uprightness, integrity, sincerity, candor, frankness, openness, ingenuousness, probity, fidelity, virtue. **4.** accuracy, precision, exactness, nicety. **—Ant.** lie, fiction, fabrication, untruth; fraudulence; dishonesty; inaccuracy.

try, *v.* **1.** attempt, essay, endeavor, strive, put forth effort. **2.** test, prove, examine, investigate. **3.** melt, render; extract, refine, distill. **—Syn. Study.** TRY, ATTEMPT, ENDEAVOR, STRIVE all mean to put forth an effort toward a specific end. TRY is the most often used and most general term: *to try to decipher a message; to try hard to succeed.* ATTEMPT, often interchangeable with TRY, sometimes suggests the possibility of failure and is often used in reference to more serious or important matters: *to attempt to formulate a new theory of motion.* ENDEAVOR emphasizes serious and continued exertion of effort, sometimes aimed at dutiful or socially appropriate behavior: *to endeavor to fulfill one's obligations.* STRIVE stresses persistent, vigorous, even strenuous effort, often in the face of obstacles: *to strive to overcome a handicap.*

tryst, *n.* appointment, meeting, rendezvous, assignation.

tumid, *adj.* **1.** swollen, distended, dilated, enlarged, turgid. **2.** pompous, turgid, bombastic, inflated, grandiloquent, grandiose, rhetorical, declamatory. —**Ant.** deflated, self-effacing.

tumult, *n.* **1.** commotion, disturbance, disorder, turbulence, uproar, hubbub, fracas, agitation, affray, melee; riot, outbreak, uprising, revolt, revolution, mutiny. **2.** agitation, perturbation, excitement, ferment. —**Ant.** peace, order; calm, serenity.

tumultuous, *adj.* **1.** uproarious, turbulent, riotous, violent. **2.** noisy, disorderly, irregular, boisterous, obstreperous. **3.** disturbed, agitated, unquiet, restive, restless, nervous, uneasy. —**Ant.** calm, peaceful, pacific; regular, orderly; quiet, restful.

tuneful, *adj.* musical, melodious, harmonious, dulcet, sweet. —**Ant.** discordant, sour, flat.

turbid, *adj.* muddy, foul, polluted, murky, mucky, cloudy, clouded, beclouded, dark, smoky,

roiled, roily, thick, opaque. —**Ant.** clear, pellucid.

turgid, *adj.* **1.** swollen, distended, tumid. **2.** pompous, bombastic. —**Ant.** humble.

turmoil, *n.* commotion, disturbance, tumult, agitation, disquiet, turbulence, confusion, disorder, bustle, trouble, uproar. —**Ant.** quiet, serenity, order, peace.

turn, *v.* **1.** rotate, spin, revolve. **2.** change, reverse, divert, deflect, transfer. **3.** change, alter, metamorphose, transmute, transform, convert. **4.** direct, aim. **5.** shape, form, fashion, mold. **6.** send, drive. **7.** curve, bend, twist. **8.** disturb, derange, infuriate, infatuate, distract. **9.** sour, ferment. —*n.* **10.** rotation, spin, gyration, revolution. **11.** change, reversal. **12.** direction, drift, trend. **13.** change, deviation, twist, bend, turning, vicissitude, variation. **14.** shape, form, mold, cast, fashion, manner. **15.** inclination, bent, tendency, aptitude, talent, proclivity, propensity. **16.** need, exigency, requirement, necessity. **—Syn. Study.** TURN, REVOLVE, ROTATE, SPIN indicate moving in a more or less rotary, circular fashion. TURN is the general and popular word for motion on an axis or around a center, but it is used also of motion that is less than a complete circle: *A gate turns on its hinges.* REVOLVE refers esp. to movement in an orbit around a center, but is sometimes exchangeable with ROTATE, which refers only to the motion of a body around its own center or axis: *The moon revolves about the earth. The earth rotates on its axis.* To SPIN is to rotate very rapidly: *A top spins.*

tussle, *v.* **1.** struggle, fight, wrestle, scuffle. —*n.* **2.** struggle, fight, scuffle, conflict.

tutor, See Syn. study at TEACH.

twilight, *n.* **1.** evening, dusk, eventide, gloaming, sunset, sundown, nightfall, crepuscule, (*Brit. dial.*) cockshut. **2.** decline, diminution, close, end, ending, finish, conclusion.

twist, *v.* **1.** intertwine, braid, plait. **2.** combine, associate. **3.** contort, distort. **4.** change, alter, pervert. **5.** wind, coil, curve, bend, roll. **6.** writhe, squirm, wriggle. **7.** turn, spin, rotate, revolve. —*n.* **8.** curve, bend, turn. **9.** turning, turn, rotation, rotating, spin. **10.** spiral, helix, coil. **11.** turn, bent, bias, proclivity, propensity. **12.** torsion, torque.

twit, *v.* **1.** taunt, gibe at, banter, tease. **2.** deride, reproach, upbraid.

tycoon, *n.* magnate, leader, top executive, baron, personage, mogul, panjandrum, nabob, VIP, worthy, big shot, wheel, big wheel, bigwig, brass hat, big-time operator. **—Ant.** nobody, nonentity, cipher.

type, *n.* **1.** kind, sort, class, classification, group, family, genus, phylum, form, stamp. **2.** sample, specimen, example, representative, prototype, pattern, model, exemplar, original, archetype. **3.** form, character, stamp. **4.** image, figure, device, sign, symbol.

tyrannical, *adj.* arbitary, despotic, dictatorial, cruel, harsh, severe, oppressive, unjust, imperious, domineering, inhuman. —**Ant.** judicious, unbiased, just, humane.

tyrant, *n.* despot, autocrat, dictator, oppressor. —**Ant.** slave, serf.

tyro, *n.* beginner, neophyte, novice, greenhorn; learner, student. —**Ant.** expert.

U

ubiquitous, *adj.* omnipresent, being, everywhere, present. —**Ant.** absent, missing.

ugly, *adj.* **1.** repulsive, offensive, displeasing, ill-favored, hard-featured, unlovely, unsightly, homely. **2.** revolting, terrible, base, vile, monstrous, corrupt, heinous, amoral. **3.** disagreeable, unpleasant, objectionable. **4.** troublesome, disadvantageous, threatening, dangerous, ominous. **5.** rough, stormy, tempestuous. **6.** surly, spiteful, ill-natured, quarrelsome, vicious, bad-tempered. —**Ant.** beautiful.

ulterior, *adj.* **1.** unacknowledged, unavowed, unexpressed, hidden, concealed, covert, secret, latent, obscure, ambiguous, cryptic, enigmatic. **2.** further, farther, distant, thither, yon, yonder, remoter. —**Ant.** open, explicit; close, present.

ultimate, *adj.* final, decisive, last, extreme, furthest, farthest, remotest. —**Ant.** prime, primary.

ultimatum, *n.* warning, notice, threat, demand, insistence, final offer.

umbrage, *n.* offense, pique, resentment, displeasure, grudge. —**Ant.** pleasure.

umpire, *n.* **1.** referee, arbitrator, arbiter, judge. —*v.* **2.** arbitrate, referee, judge; decide, settle. —**Syn. Study.** See JUDGE.

unabashed, *adj.* **1.** bold, brazen, undaunted, fearless, doughty, confident, sure. **2.** shameless, brazen-faced, forward, immodest, unblushing. —**Ant.** timid, retiring; modest, prim.

unaccountable, *adj.* **1.** unanswerable, irresponsible. **2.** inexplicable, inscrutable, strange, unexplainable, incomprehensible, unintelligible. —**Ant.** accountable.

unaccustomed, *adj.* **1.** unusual, unfamiliar, new. **2.** unused. —**Ant.** accustomed.

unaffected, *adj.* **1.** sincere, genuine, honest, real, unfeigned, natural, plain, naive, simple, guileless, artless. **2.** unmoved, untouched, unimpressed, unstirred. —**Ant.** affected.

unanimity, *n.* accord, agreement, unanimousness, harmony, unity, unison, concert. —**Ant.** discord, disagreement.

unapt, *adj.* **1.** unfitted, unsuited, unsuitable, unfit, inappropriate, inapplicable, irrelevant. **2.** unlikely, indisposed. **3.** slow, inapt, unskillful, inept, incompetent, unqualified. —**Ant.** apt.

unassuming, *adj.* modest, unpretending, unpretentious, humble, unostentatious. —**Ant.** immodest, pretentious.

unbearable, *adj.* unendurable, intolerable, insufferable, insupportable. —**Ant.** bearable.

unbecoming, *adj.* **1.** inappropriate, unsuited, unapt, unsuitable, unfitted, unfit. **2.** unseemly, improper, indecent. —**Ant.** becoming, appropriate; seemly, proper. —**Syn. Study.** See IMPROPER.

unbiased, *adj.* fair, equitable, impartial, tolerant, unprejudiced, neutral, disinterested. —**Ant.** biased, prejudiced.

unbounded, *adj.* **1.** unlimited, boundless, limitless, immense, vast, infinite, immeasurable, endless, interminable, illimitable. **2.** unrestrained, unconfined, unfettered, unchained, uncontrolled, unbridled, immoderate. —**Ant.** bounded, limited; restrained.

unbroken, *adj.* **1.** whole, intact, complete, entire. **2.** uninterrupted, continuous, deep, sound, fast, profound, undisturbed. **3.** undisturbed, unimpaired. —**Ant.** broken, incomplete; interrupted, discontinuous; impaired.

unburden, *v.* **1.** disburden, unload, relieve. **2.** disclose, reveal; confess. —**Ant.** burden.

uncalled-for, *adj.* unnecessary, improper, unwarranted. —**Ant.**

necessary, essential, proper.

uncanny, *adj.* strange, preternatural, supernatural, weird, odd. —**Ant.** common, usual, natural. —**Syn. Study.** See WEIRD.

uncertain, *adj.* **1.** insecure, precarious, unsure, doubtful, unpredictable, problematical, unstable, unreliable, unsafe, fallible, perilous, dangerous. **2.** unassured, undecided, indeterminate, undetermined, unfixed, unsettled, indefinite, ambiguous, questionable, dubious. **3.** doubtful, vague, indistinct. **4.** undependable, changeable, variable, capricious, unsteady, irregular, fitful, desultory, chance. —**Ant.** certain.

uncivil, *adj.* **1.** ill-mannered, unmannerly, rude, impolite, discourteous, disrespectful, uncouth, boorish, brusque, curt, impudent. **2.** uncivilized. —**Ant.** civil.

unclean, *adj.* **1.** dirty,

soiled, filthy, nasty, foul.
2. evil, vile, base, impure,
unvirtuous, unchaste,
sinful, corrupt, polluted.
—**Ant.** clean.

uncomfortable, *adj.* **1.**
disquieting, discomforting.
2. uneasy, ill at ease,
unhappy, miserable,
cheerless. —**Ant.**
comfortable.

uncommon, *adj.* unusual,
rare, scarce, infrequent,
odd, singular, strange,
peculiar, remarkable,
queer, extraordinary,
exceptional. —**Ant.**
common.

uncommunicative, *adj.*
reserved, taciturn,
close-mouthed, reticent.
—**Ant.** communicative,
talkative, voluble.

uncompromising, *adj.*
unyielding, inflexible, rigid,
firm, steadfast, obstinate.
—**Ant.** compromising,
yielding, flexible.

unconcern, *n.* indifference,
nonchalance, insouciance.
—**Ant.** concern.

unconditional, *adj.*
unrestricted, absolute,
complete, unqualified,

unconditioned, unreserved,
categorical. —**Ant.**
conditional, restricted,
qualified.

unconscionable, *adj.* **1.**
unscrupulous, shady,
dishonest, unlawful. **2.**
unreasonable, excessive,
extravagant, exorbitant.
—**Ant.** scrupulous;
reasonable.

uncouth, *adj.* **1.** awkward,
clumsy, unmannerly,
discourteous, rude,
ill-mannered, uncivil. **2.**
unusual, strange, odd,
unknown, unfamiliar.
—**Ant.** courteous; natural,
usual.

uncover, *v.* lay bare,
disclose, reveal, expose,
open, strip. —**Ant.** cover,
conceal.

unctuous, *adj.* **1.** fatty, oily,
greasy, oleaginous,
unguent, lardaceous. **2.**
insinuating, smarmy,
obsequious, flattering,
sycophantic, ingratiating,
Pecksniffian.

undaunted, *adj.*
undiscouraged, fearless,
brave, intrepid,

undismayed. **—Ant.** daunted, discouraged.

undeniable, *adj.* **1.** irrefutable, indisputable, indubitable, incontrovertible, incontestable, unquestionable; obvious, evident, clear, certain, sure, unimpeachable, unassailable. **2.** good, unexceptionable. **—Ant.** doubtful, dubitable, questionable; poor.

undergo, *v.* experience, suffer, bear, tolerate, sustain, endure. **—Ant.** avoid.

underground, *adj.* **1.** subterranean, subterrestrial, subsurface, belowground, underearth, buried. **2.** secret, clandestine, hidden, undercover, cabalistic, surreptitious. **3.** avant-garde, experimental, antiestablishment, revolutionary, radical, subversive.

underhand, *adj.* secret, stealthy, sly, crafty, dishonorable, clandestine,

surreptitious. **—Ant.** open, candid.

understand, *v.* **1.** perceive, grasp, realize, comprehend, interpret, conceive, know, see, apprehend, discern. **2.** learn, hear. **3.** accept, believe. **—Ant.** misunderstand. **—Syn. Study.** See KNOW.

undertow, *n.* underset, undercurrent, riptide, cross-current.

undine, *n.* sprite, water nymph, sylph.

undying, *adj.* immortal, deathless, unending, eternal, everlasting, permanent. **—Ant.** dying, mortal, temporary.

unearthly, *adj.* weird, ultramundane, supernatural, preternatural, ghostly, spectral, unnatural, strange. **—Ant.** earthly, terrestrial.

uneducated, *adj.* untutored, unschooled, unenlightened, uninstructed, uncultivated, untaught, uninformed, unlettered, illiterate, ignorant. **—Ant.**

cultivated, cultured,
literate.

unemployed, *adj.*
unoccupied, idle, at
liberty, jobless, between
engagements. **—Ant.**
employed, occupied.

unequaled, *adj.*
unparalleled, matchless,
unmatched, unrivaled,
peerless, inimitable,
incomparable. **—Ant.**
parallel, rival, comparable.

unequivocal, *adj.* clear,
plain, simple, direct,
unambiguous, certain,
obvious, evident,
incontestable, absolute,
explicit, unmistakable.
—Ant. equivocal,
ambiguous.

unerring, *adj.* unfailing,
right, correct, exact,
precise, sure, infallible,
certain, accurate, definite.
—Ant. errant, failing,
fallible.

unessential, *adj.*
nonessential, unimportant,
dispensable, immaterial,
unnecessary. **—Ant.**
essential.

unexpected, *adj.*
unforeseen, unanticipated,

sudden, abrupt; surprising.
—Ant. expected, foreseen,
anticipated, gradual.

unfair, *adj.* biased, partial,
prejudiced, unjust,
inequitable. **—Ant.** fair.

unfaithful, *adj.* **1.** false,
disloyal, perfidious,
faithless, treacherous,
traitorous, deceitful,
recreant, untrustworthy. **2.**
dishonest, crooked,
unlawful. **3.** inaccurate,
inexact, imprecise. **4.**
fickle, untrue, inconstant;
adulterous. **—Ant.**
faithful.

unfavorable, *adj.*
disadvantageous,
unpropitious, adverse,
inimical. **—Ant.**
favorable.

unfeeling, *adj.* insensible,
insensate, numb, callous,
unsympathetic, hard,
hard-hearted. **—Ant.**
feeling, sympathetic.

unfit, *adj.* **1.** unfitted,
unsuited, unsuitable,
inappropriate, inapt,
unapt. **2.** unqualified,
incompetent, incapable.
—v. 3. disqualify. **—Ant.**
fit.

unfortunate, *adj.* unlucky, unhappy, luckless, unsuccessful, hapless, star-crossed, ill-starred. —**Ant.** fortunate.

unfriendly, *adj.* inimical, unkindly, hostile, unkind. —**Ant.** friendly.

unfruitful, *adj.* unproductive, barren, sterile, fruitless. —**Ant.** fruitful.

ungainly, *adj.* awkward, clumsy, ungraceful, uncouth. —**Ant.** graceful.

ungodly, *adj.* irreligious, impious, sinful, piacular, profane, wicked, depraved, polluted, corrupted, base, vile, evil. —**Ant.** godly.

unguarded, *adj.* **1.** unprotected, undefended, open, naked, defenseless. **2.** incautious, imprudent, thoughtless, careless. —**Ant.** guarded, protected; cautious, careful.

unhappy, *adj.* **1.** sad, miserable, wretched, sorrowful, downcast, cheerless, disconsolate, inconsolable, distressed, afflicted. **2.** unlucky, unfortunate, hapless. **3.** unfavorable, inauspicious, unpropitious. **4.** infelicitous, inappropriate, inapt, unapt. —**Ant.** happy.

unhealthful, *adj.* **1.** insalubrious, unwholesome, unhealthy, noxious, poisonous, harmful. **2.** ill, unhealthy, sick. —**Ant.** healthy, healthful, hale, hearty.

unhealthy, *adj.* **1.** sickly, delicate, frail, weak, feeble, enfeebled, ill, diseased, afflicted. **2.** unwholesome, unhealthful, unsanitary, unhygienic, insalubrious, deleterious, poisonous, noxious. —**Ant.** healthy.

uniform, *adj.* **1.** invariable, unchanging, unwavering, unvarying, unvaried, unchanged, constant, regular. **2.** undiversified, unvariegated, dun, solid, plain. **3.** regular, even. **4.** consistent, regular, constant. **5.** agreeing, alike, similar. —*n.* **6.** livery. —**Ant.** irregular, wavering; diversified; uneven; inconsistent.

unimpeachable, *adj.*

irreproachable, unassailable, blameless, unexceptionable. —**Ant.** reproachable, censurable.

unimportant, *adj.* trivial, trifling, paltry, nugatory, secondary, insignificant, petty, slight. —**Ant.** important.

uninterested, *adj.* indifferent, unconcerned. —**Ant.** interested.

union, *n.* **1.** junction, combination, unity, coalition. **2.** society, association, league, confederacy, alliance. **3.** marriage, matrimony, wedlock. **4.** brotherhood. —**Ant.** separation, fissure. —**Syn. Study.** See ALLIANCE.

unique, *adj.* **1.** sole, only, single. **2.** unequaled, alone, peerless. **3.** rare, unusual, singular, odd, peculiar, strange, uncommon. —**Ant.** common, usual.

unite, *v.* **1.** join, combine, incorporate, connect, conjoin, couple, link, yoke, associate. **2.** combine, amalgamate, compound,

blend, coalesce, fuse, weld, consolidate. **3.** marry, wed. —**Ant.** separate, sever. —**Syn. Study.** See JOIN.

unity, *n.* **1.** oneness, union, singleness, singularity, individuality. **2.** concord, harmony, agreement, unison, concert, unanimity, uniformity. —**Ant.** disunity; disharmony.

universal, *adj.* **1.** general, whole, total, entire; ecumenical. —*n.* **2.** concept. —**Ant.** local; special. —**Syn. Study.** See GENERAL.

unjust, *adj.* **1.** inequitable, partial, unfair, prejudiced, biased. **2.** undeserved, unjustified, unjustifiable, unmerited. —**Ant.** just.

unkind, *adj.* harsh, cruel, unmerciful, unfeeling, distressing. —**Ant.** kind.

unlawful, *adj.* illegal, illicit, illegitimate; bastard, spurious, natural. —**Ant.** lawful, legal. —**Syn. Study.** See ILLEGAL.

unlike, *adj.* different, dissimilar, diverse, variant,

heterogeneous. **—Ant.** like.

unlimited, *adj.* unrestricted, unconstrained, unrestrained, boundless, unfettered, limitless, unbounded, vast, extensive, infinite. **—Ant.** limited.

unlucky, *adj.* unfortunate, hapless, ill-fated, unsuccessful, ill-omened. **—Ant.** lucky.

unmeasured, *adj.* **1.** unlimited, measureless, immense, vast, infinite. **2.** unrestrained, intemperate, unconstrained; unstinting, lavish. **—Ant.** measured, finite; temperate, constrained.

unmerciful, *adj.* merciless, pitiless, unpitying, relentless, cruel, unsparing; unconscionable. **—Ant.** merciful.

unmindful, *adj.* heedless, regardless, careless, inattentive, neglectful, negligent, unobservant, forgetful. **—Ant.** mindful, aware.

unmistakable, *adj.* clear, plain, evident, obvious,

palpable, patent. **—Ant.** unclear, dim.

unmitigated, *adj.* unqualified, absolute, complete, consummate. **—Ant.** mitigated.

unmixed, *adj.* pure, unalloyed, unmingled, unadulterated. **—Ant.** mixed, impure, mongrel.

unnatural, *adj.* **1.** affected, forced, strained, out of character. **2.** unusual, strange, abnormal, irregular, anomalous, aberrant. **3.** cruel, evil, inhuman, heartless, hard-hearted, brutal. **—Ant.** natural; humane.

unnecessary, *adj.* needless, superfluous, *de trop.* **—Ant.** necessary.

unnerve, *v.* discourage, disarm, shake, fluster, disconcert, upset. **—Ant.** steel, encourage.

unparalleled, *adj.* matchless, unmatched, unequaled, unrivaled, peerless. **—Ant.** equaled.

unpleasant, *adj.* unpleasing, disagreeable, unpalatable, unappetizing, offensive, obnoxious, noisome, repulsive, repellent; noxious. —**Ant.** pleasant.

unpractical, *adj.* impractical, visionary, speculative, theoretical. —**Ant.** practical.

unprejudiced, *adj.* unbiased, impartial, fair. —**Ant.** prejudiced, biased.

unpretentious, *adj.* modest, unassuming, shy, abashed, bashful, self-effacing, unpretending, retiring, unobtrusive. —**Ant.** pretentious.

unprincipled, *adj.* unscrupulous, tricky, shrewd, dishonest, cagey, wicked, bad, evil, amoral. —**Ant.** principled; scrupulous. —**Syn. Study.** See UNSCRUPULOUS.

unqualified, *adj.* **1.** unfit, incompetent. **2.** absolute, unmitigated, out-and-out, thorough, complete, direct, unrestricted, downright. —**Ant.** qualified.

unquestionable, *adj.* indisputable, indubitable, incontrovertible, undeniable, irrefutable, incontestable; unexceptionable. —**Ant.** questionable.

unquiet, *adj.* restless, restive, turbulent, tumultuous, disturbed, agitated, upset, uneasy, nervous, perturbed, fidgety. —**Ant.** quiet.

unreal, *adj.* imaginary, artificial, unpractical, visionary, sham, spurious, fictitious, illusive, illusory, vague, theoretical, impractical. —**Ant.** real.

unreasonable, *adj.* **1.** irrational, senseless, foolish, silly, preposterous, absurd, stupid, nonsensical, idiotic. **2.** immoderate, exorbitant, excessive, unjust, unfair, extravagant. —**Ant.** reasonable.

unreconstructed, *adj.* unapologetic, impenitent, unrepenting, stubborn, defiant, obdurate, die-hard, standpat.

unrefined, *adj.* **1.** unpurified, coarse, harsh, crude. **2.** unpolished, uncultured, ill-bred, rude, boorish, vulgar, gross. —**Ant.** refined.

unrelenting, *adj.* unabating, relentless, unremitting, implacable, inexorable, merciless, unmerciful, ruthless, pitiless, unpitying, uncompassionate, cruel, hard, bitter, harsh, stern, remorseless, austere. —**Ant.** relenting.

unreserved, *adj.* **1.** full, entire, complete, unlimited. **2.** frank, open, ingenuous, candid, naive, artless, guileless, undesigning, sincere. —**Ant.** reserved, incomplete; artful.

unruffled, *adj.* smooth, calm, unperturbed, tranquil, serene, collected, imperturbable, cool, composed, peaceful, controlled, undisturbed. —**Ant.** ruffled.

unruly, *adj.* ungovernable, disobedient, insubordinate, unmanageable, uncontrollable, refractory, stubborn, lawless; turbulent, tumultuous, disorderly, riotous. —**Ant.** obedient, subordinate. —**Syn. Study.** UNRULY, INTRACTABLE, RECALCITRANT, REFRACTORY describe persons or things that resist management or control. UNRULY suggests constant disorderly behavior or character: *an unruly child; unruly hair.* INTRACTABLE suggests in persons a determined resistance to all attempts to guide or direct them, and in things a resistance to attempts to shape, improve, or modify them: *an intractable social rebel; an intractable problem.* RECALCITRANT implies a stubborn rebellion against authority or direction: *a recalcitrant prisoner.* REFRACTORY also implies a mulish disobedience, but leaves open the possibility of eventual compliance: *The refractory youth needs more understanding.*

unsatisfactory, *adj.* disappointing, inadequate, insufficient. —**Ant.** satisfactory.

unsavory, *adj.* tasteless, insipid; unpleasant, offensive, distasteful. —**Ant.** savory, tasteful.

unscrupulous, *adj.* unrestrained, unrestricted, conscienceless,

unprincipled, unethical.
—**Ant.** scrupulous,
restrained. —**Syn. Study.**
UNSCRUPULOUS, UNPRINCIPLED
refer to a lack of moral or
ethical standards.
UNSCRUPULOUS means not
controlled by one's
conscience and
contemptuous of what one
knows to be right or
honorable: *an unscrupulous
landlord.* UNPRINCIPLED
means lacking or not
aware of moral standards
that should restrain one's
actions: *an unprincipled
rogue.*

unseasonable, *adj.*
inopportune, ill-timed,
untimely, inappropriate.
—**Ant.** seasonable,
opportune.

unseat, *v.* displace, depose;
throw. —**Ant.** place.

unseemly, *adj.* unfitting,
unbecoming, improper,
indecorous, indecent,
unbefitting, inappropriate.
—**Ant.** seemly, fitting,
becoming. —**Syn. Study.**
See IMPROPER.

unsettled, *adj.* unstable,
unsteady, shaky,

undependable, unsure,
unfixed, undetermined,
indeterminate, changeable,
wavering, vacillating,
infirm, fickle, faltering,
irresolute. —**Ant.** settled,
stable, steady.

unsightly, *adj.* unpleasant,
unattractive, ugly,
disagreeable, hideous.
—**Ant.** beautiful.

unskillful, *adj.* untrained,
inexpert, awkward,
bungling, clumsy, inapt,
maladroit. —**Ant.** skillful.

unsophisticated, *adj.* **1.**
simple, artless, ingenuous,
guileless, naive. **2.**
unadulterated, pure,
genuine. —**Ant.**
sophisticated.

unsound, *adj.* **1.** diseased,
defective, impaired,
decayed, rotten, sickly,
sick, ill, infirm, unhealthy,
unwholesome. **2.**
fallacious, unfounded,
invalid, false, erroneous,
untenable, faulty. **3.**
fragile, breakable,
frangible. **4.** unreliable,
unsubstantial. —**Ant.**
sound.

unsparing, *adj.* liberal,

profuse, generous, lavish, bountiful; unmerciful, merciless, ruthless, pitiless, unsympathetic, severe, unforgiving, harsh, inexorable, unrelenting, relentless, uncompromising. —**Ant.** illiberal, sparing, penurious.

unspeakable, *adj.* unutterable, inexpressible, ineffable, indescribable.

unstable, *adj.* **1.** infirm, unsteady, precarious. **2.** unsteadfast, inconstant, wavering, vacillating, undecided, unsettled. —**Ant.** stable.

unsteady, *adj.* **1.** unfixed, infirm, faltering. **2.** fluctuating, wavering, unsettled, vacillating, fickle, changeable, unstable. **3.** irregular, unreliable. —**Ant.** steady.

unsuitable, *adj.* inappropriate, unfitting, unbefitting, unbecoming. —**Ant.** suitable.

untangle, *v.* unravel, unsnarl, disentangle. —**Ant.** tangle, snarl, entangle.

unthinkable, *adj.* inconceivable. —**Ant.** conceivable.

untidy, *adj.* slovenly, disordered; sloppy. —**Ant.** tidy.

untie, *v.* unfasten, loose, unknot, undo, unbind. —**Ant.** tie.

untimely, *adj.* unpropitious, unseasonable, inappropriate. —**Ant.** timely.

untruth, *n.* falsehood, fib, lie, fiction, story, tale, tall tale, fabrication, fable, forgery, invention. —**Ant.** truth.

unusual, *adj.* uncommon, extraordinary, exceptional, rare, strange, remarkable, singular, curious, queer, odd. —**Ant.** usual.

unvarnished, *adj.* plain, unembellished, unexaggerated. —**Ant.** embellished, exaggerated.

unwary, *adj.* incautious, unguarded, imprudent, indiscreet, hasty, careless, rash, heedless, precipitous, headlong. —**Ant.** wary.

unwholesome, *adj.*

unhealthy, insalubrious, unhealthful, deleterious, noxious, noisome, poisonous, baneful, pernicious; corrupt. —**Ant.** wholesome.

unwieldy, *adj.* bulky, unmanageable, clumsy, ponderous, heavy. —**Ant.** manageable, light.

unwise, *adj.* foolish, imprudent, injudicious, ill-advised, indiscreet. —**Ant.** wise.

unwitting, *adj.* unaware, unknowing, unconscious, inadvertent, unintentional, ignorant. —**Ant.** intentional, aware.

unworthy, *adj.* inadequate, undeserving; worthless, base. —**Ant.** worthy.

unyielding, *adj.* **1.** inflexible, firm, stanch, steadfast, adamant, resolute, indomitable, pertinacious, determined. **2.** stubborn, obstinate, stiff, intractable, perverse, headstrong, willful. —**Ant.** flexible.

upbraid, *v.* reproach, chide, reprove, blame, censure, condemn. —**Ant.** praise, laud. —**Syn. Study.** See REPRIMAND.

uphold, *v.* **1.** support, sustain, maintain, countenance. **2.** raise, elevate. —**Ant.** attack.

uplifting, *adj.* edifying, improving, bettering, educational, informative, informational, instructive, enlightening. —**Ant.** debasing, corruptive.

uppermost, *adj.* highest, topmost, predominant, supreme. —**Ant.** lowermost, lowest.

uppity, *adj.* arrogant, haughty, disdainful, scornful, presumptuous, cocky, supercilious, snobbish, snobby, stuck-up, snooty, (*Brit.*) toffee-nosed. —**Ant.** modest, unassuming, down-to-earth.

upright, *adj.* **1.** erect, vertical, perpendicular, plumb. **2.** honest, just, righteous, honorable, straightforward, virtuous, true, good, pure, conscientious. —*n.* **3.** pole, prop, support, pile, pier,

column, Lally column.
—**Ant.** horizontal, prone.

uprising, *n.* insurrection, revolt, revolution, rebellion.

uproar, *n.* disturbance, tumult, disorder, turbulence, commotion, hubbub, furor, din, clamor, noise; fracas, melee, riot. —**Ant.** peace.

upset, *v.* **1.** overturn, capsize. **2.** overthrow, defeat, depose, displace. **3.** disturb, derange, unnerve, disconcert, agitate, perturb, fluster. —*n.* **4.** overturn, overthrow, defeat. **5.** nervousness, perturbation, disturbance. **6.** disorder, mess. —*adj.* **7.** overturned, capsized. **8.** disordered, messy; sloppy. **9.** worried, concerned, disconcerted, agitated, disturbed, perturbed, irritated. —**Ant.** steady, stabilize.

urbane, *adj.* courteous, polite, refined, elegant, polished, smooth, suave. —**Ant.** discourteous, impolite.

urge, *v.* **1.** push, force, impel, drive. **2.** press, push, hasten. **3.** impel, constrain, move, activate, animate, incite, instigate, goad, stimulate, spur. **4.** induce, persuade, solicit, beg, beseech, importune, entreat, implore. **5.** insist upon, allege, assert, aver, declare, asseverate. **6.** recommend, advocate, advise. —*n.* **7.** impulse, influence, force, drive, push. **8.** reflex. —**Ant.** deter, discourage.

urgent, *adj.* **1.** pressing, compelling, forcing, driving, imperative, requiring, immediate. **2.** insistent, importunate, earnest, eager. —**Ant.** unimportant.

use, *v.* **1.** employ, utilize, make use of, apply, avail oneself of. **2.** expend, consume, use up, waste, exhaust. **3.** practice, put to use, exercise. **4.** act *or* behave toward, treat, deal with. **5.** accustom, habituate, familiarize, inure. —*n.* **6.** employment, utilization, application, exercise. **7.** utility, usefulness, service, advantage, profit, benefit, avail. **8.** help, profit, good. **9.** custom, practice, usage, habit. **10.** occasion, need. **11.** treatment, handling. —**Ant.** disuse. —**Syn. Study.** USE, UTILIZE mean to put something into action or service. USE is a general word referring to the application of something to a given purpose: *to use a telephone.* USE may also imply that the thing is consumed or diminished in the process: *I used all the butter.* When applied to persons, USE implies a selfish or sinister purpose: *He used his friend to advance himself.* UTILIZE, a more formal word, implies practical, profitable, or creative use: *to utilize solar energy to run a machine.*

useful, *adj.* **1.** serviceable, advantageous, profitable, helpful, effectual, effective, efficacious, beneficial, salutary. **2.** practical, practicable, workable. —**Ant.** useless.

useless, *adj.* **1.** unavailing, futile, inutile, fruitless, vain, ineffectual, profitless, bootless, valueless, worthless, hopeless. **2.** unserviceable, unusable. —**Ant.** useful. —**Syn. Study.** USELESS, FUTILE, VAIN refer to something that is of no use, value, profit, or advantage. USELESS refers to something of no avail because of the circumstances or because of some inherent defect: *It is useless to reason with him.* FUTILE suggests wasted or ill-advised effort and complete failure to achieve a desired end: *Their attempts to save the business were futile.* VAIN describes something that is fruitless or unsuccessful in spite of all possible effort: *It is vain to keep on hoping.*

usual, *adj.* habitual, accustomed, customary; common, ordinary, familiar, prevailing, prevalent, everyday, general, frequent, regular, expected, predictable, settled, constant, fixed. —**Ant.** unusual. —**Syn. Study.** USUAL, CUSTOMARY,

HABITUAL refer to something that is familiar because it is commonly met with or observed. USUAL indicates something that is to be expected by reason of previous experience, which shows it to occur more often than not: *There were the usual crowds at the monument.* CUSTOMARY refers to something that accords with prevailing usage or individual practice: *customary courtesies; a customary afternoon nap.* HABITUAL refers to a practice that has become fixed by regular repetition: *a clerk's habitual sales pitch.*

utensil, See Syn. study at TOOL.

utilitarian, *adj.* useful, practical, serviceable, helpful, functional, pragmatical, workaday, handy, utile, aidful, convenient, effective, valuable. —**Ant.** impractical, useless.

utilize, *v.* use. —**Syn. Study.** See USE.

utter, *v.* **1.** express, speak, pronounce, say, voice. **2.** publish, proclaim, announce, promulgate. **3.** circulate. —*adj.* **4.** complete, total, absolute, unconditional, unqualified, entire. —**Ant.** partial, incomplete, relative.

V

vacant, *adj.* **1.** empty, void. **2.** devoid *or* destitute of, lacking, wanting. **3.** untenanted, unoccupied, empty. **4.** free, unoccupied, unemployed, leisure, unencumbered. **5.** unthinking, thoughtless. **6.** vacuous, blank, inane. —**Ant.** full; occupied; encumbered; thoughtful.

vacate, *v.* quit, abandon, leave, evacuate, desert, forsake, withdraw from,

relinquish, clear, move.
—**Ant.** occupy.

vacillate, *v.* **1.** sway, waver, reel, stagger. **2.** fluctuate, waver, hesitate. —**Syn. Study.** See WAVER.

vacuous, *adj.* vacant, empty, hollow, void, bland, blank, insipid, fatuous, inane, empty-headed, airheaded, vapid, bubbleheaded, bubblebrained, out to lunch, nobody home, foolish, silly, asinine —**Ant.** serious, lofty,

vagabond, *adj.* **1.** wandering, nomadic, homeless, vagrant. **2.** good-for-nothing, worthless. —*n.* **3.** tramp, vagrant, hobo, gypsy, outcast, loafer. **4.** scamp, rascal, knave, idler, vagrant.

vagary, *n.* whim, whimsy, fancy, twist, turn, conceit, caprice, crotchet, quirk, kink, megrim, peculiarity, oddity, notion, inspiration, brainstorm.

vagrant, *adj., n.* vagabond.

vague, *adj.* **1.** indefinite, unspecific, imprecise, obscure, dim, uncertain, unsure, indistinct, undetermined, indeterminate, unsettled. **2.** unclear, unknown, unfixed, lax, loose. —**Ant.** definite, specific.

vain, *adj.* **1.** useless, hollow, idle, worthless, unimportant, nugatory, trifling, trivial, inefficient, unavailing, unfruitful, futile, vapid. **2.** conceited, egotistical, self-complacent, proud, vainglorious, arrogant, overweening, inflated. —**Ant.** useful; humble. —**Syn. Study.** See USELESS.

vainglory, *n.* **1.** egotism, vanity, conceit. **2.** pomp, show, ostentation. —**Ant.** humility.

valiant, *adj.* brave, bold, courageous, stout, stouthearted, intrepid. —**Ant.** cowardly. —**Syn. Study.** See BRAVE.

valid, *adj.* just, well-founded, sound, substantial, logical, good, cogent, authoritative, effectual, efficient, efficacious, effective, binding, legal. **—Ant.** invalid, unjust.

valor, *n.* courage, boldness, firmness, bravery, intrepidity, spirit. **—Ant.** cowardice.

valuable, *adj.* **1.** costly, expensive, rare, precious, dear. **2.** useful, serviceable, important, estimable, worthy. **—Ant.** worthless.

value, *n.* **1.** worth, merit, desirability, usefulness, utility, importance. **2.** cost, price. **3.** valuation, evaluation, estimation. **4.** force, import, significance. **—v. 5.** estimate, rate, price, appraise. **6.** regard, esteem, appreciate, prize. **—Syn. Study.** VALUE, WORTH both imply excellence and merit. VALUE is excellence based on desirability, usefulness, or importance; it may be measured in terms of its equivalent in money, goods, or services: *the value of sunlight; the value of a painting.* WORTH usu. implies inherent excellence based on spiritual and moral qualities that command esteem: *Few*

knew her true worth. See also APPRECIATE.

vanish, *v.* **1.** disappear, evanesce. **2.** end, cease, fade. **—Ant.** appear; begin. **—Syn. Study.** See DISAPPEAR.

vanity, *n.* **1.** pride, conceit, self-esteem, egotism, self-complacency, self-admiration. **2.** hollowness, emptiness, sham, unreality, folly, triviality, futility. **—Ant.** humility. **—Syn. Study.** See PRIDE.

vanquish, *v.* conquer, defeat, overcome, overpower, subjugate, suppress, subdue, crush, quell, rout. **—Ant.** lose.

vapid, *adj.* **1.** lifeless, dull, flavorless, insipid, flat. **2.** spiritless, unanimated, dull, uninteresting, tedious, tiresome, prosaic. **—Ant.** spirited, animated.

variable, *adj.* **1.** changeable, alterable. **2.** inconstant, fickle, vacillating, wavering, fluctuating, unsteady. **—Ant.** invariable; constant.

variance, *n.* **1.** divergence, discrepancy, difference. **2.** disagreement, dispute, quarrel, controversy, dissension, discord, strife. —**Ant.** invariance, similitude, sameness.

variation, *n.* **1.** change, mutation, vicissitude, alteration, modification. **2.** deviation, divergence, difference, discrepancy; diversity. —**Ant.** sameness.

variety, *n.* **1.** diversity, difference, discrepancy, divergence. **2.** diversity, multiplicity. **3.** assortment, collection, group. **4.** kind, sort, class, species. —**Ant.** sameness.

various, *adj.* differing, different, divers, distinct, several, many, diverse, sundry, diversified, variegated, varied. —**Ant.** same, similar. —**Syn. Study.** VARIOUS, DIVERSE, DIFFERENT, DISTINCT describe things that are not identical. VARIOUS stresses the multiplicity and variety of sorts or instances of a thing or class of things: *various kinds of seaweed.*

DIVERSE suggests an even wider variety or disparity: *diverse opinions.* DIFFERENT points to a separate identity, or a dissimilarity in quality or character: *two different versions of the same story.* DISTINCT implies a uniqueness and lack of connection between things that may possibly be alike: *plans similar in objective but distinct in method.*

vary, *v.* **1.** change, alter, diversify, modify. **2.** transform, metamorphose, transmute, change. **3.** differ, deviate. **4.** alternate.

vast, *adj.* extensive, immense, huge, enormous, gigantic, colossal, measureless, boundless, unlimited, prodigious, stupendous. —**Ant.** limited, small.

vault, *n.* **1.** arch, ceiling, roof. **2.** cellar, catacomb, crypt, tomb. **3.** safe, safety deposit box. —*v.* **4.** arch. **5.** leap, spring, jump.

vaunt, *v.* boast, brag, crow, trumpet, gloat, exult,

flaunt, parade, gasconade, show off, grandstand, hotdog.

vehemence, *n.* eagerness, impetuosity, verve, fire, ardor, violence, fervor, zeal, passion, enthusiasm, fervency, fury. —**Ant.** coolness, apathy, antipathy.

vehement, *adj.* eager, impetuous, impassioned, passionate, violent, ardent, zealous, earnest, fervent, fervid, burning, fiery, afire, ablaze. —**Ant.** cool, dispassionate.

velleity, *n.* wish, preference, choice, inclination, tendency, predilection, desire, whim, fancy.

velocity, *n.* rapidity, swiftness, quickness, speed, alacrity, celerity. —**Syn. Study.** See SPEED.

venal, *adj.* corrupt, bribable, unscrupulous, mercenary, purchasable, sordid. —**Ant.** pure, scrupulous.

veneration, *n.* respect, reverence, awe. —**Ant.**

disrespect, irreverence. —**Syn. Study.** See RESPECT.

vengeance, *n.* avenging, revenge, retribution, requital, retaliation. —**Ant.** forgiveness, pardon. —**Syn. Study.** See REVENGE.

venial, *adj.* excusable, forgivable, pardonable. —**Ant.** inexcusable, unforgivable, mortal.

venom, *n.* **1.** poison, virus. **2.** spite, malice, malignity, maliciousness, spitefulness, acrimony, bitterness, acerbity, malevolence, gall, spleen, hate, contempt. —**Syn. Study.** See POISON.

ventilate, *v.* **1.** air, air out, cross-ventilate, freshen, refresh, aerate. **2.** tell, relate, disclose, reveal, divulge, lay open, express, air, vent, make known, make public, discuss. —**Ant.** seal; repress, suppress, clam up, keep mum.

venture, *n.* **1.** hazard, danger, jeopardy, risk, peril. **2.** speculation. —*v.* **3.** endanger, imperil, risk, jeopardize, hazard. **4.** dare, presume, make bold.

venturous, *adj.* **1.** bold, daring, adventurous, venturesome, daring, rash, intrepid, fearless, enterprising. **2.** hazardous, dangerous, risky, perilous. **—Ant.** fearful, cowardly; secure, safe.

verbal, *adj.* oral, nuncupative, spoken, worded. **—Ant.** mental, physical.

verbose, See Syn. study at WORDY.

verge, *n.* **1.** edge, rim, margin, brim, lip. **2.** brink, limit. **3.** belt, strip, border. **4.** room, area, scope. **5.** rod, wand, mace, staff. **—***v.* **6.** border, tend, lean, incline.

vernacular, *adj.* **1.** ordinary, colloquial, informal, conversational, spoken, nonliterary, vulgate, vulgar, demotic, general, popular, everyday, commonplace, household, down-to-earth. **2.** local, localized, regional, areal, parochial, provincial, limited, confined. **—***n.* **3.**

terminology, language, nomenclature, vocabulary, lexicon, verbiage, tongue, speech, jargon, dialect, lingo. **—Syn. Study.** See LANGUAGE.

verse, *n.* **1.** stich. **2.** poetry, meter, poesy, versification, numbers. **3.** stanza, strophe, stave, section.

versed, *adj.* experienced, practiced, skilled. **—Ant.** inexperienced, unskilled.

version, *n.* **1.** translation, rendering, interpretation. **2.** variant, form, rendition.

vertical, *adj.* upright, plumb, zenithal, erect, perpendicular. **—Ant.** horizontal.

verve, *n.* spirit, spiritedness, buoyancy, dash, stylishness, animation, joie de vivre, brio, élan, gusto, panache, fire, esprit, vivacity, zest, oomph, zing.

vestige, *n.* trace, hint, suggestion, mark, evidence, token. **—Syn. Study.** See TRACE.

vex, *v.* **1.** irritate, annoy, pester, provoke, anger, irk, fret, nettle. **2.** torment, plague, worry, hector, harry, harass, torture, persecute. **3.** agitate, discuss, debate. —**Ant.** delight.

vexatious, *adj.* disturbing, annoying, vexing, troublesome, irritating. —**Ant.** delightful, pleasant.

vexed, *adj.* **1.** disturbed, troubled, annoyed. **2.** disputed, discussed. —**Ant.** delighted.

viable, *adj.* workable, doable, achievable, tenable, supportable, operable, manageable, feasible, practicable. —**Ant.** impractical, unworkable, unachievable.

vibrant, *adj.* **1.** vibrating, shaking, oscillating; resonant. **2.** pulsating, energetic, powerful, vigorous; exciting, thrilling.

vibrate, *v.* **1.** oscillate; shake, tremble, quiver, shiver. **2.** resound, echo.

vicarious, *adj.* substituted; delegated, deputed. —**Ant.** real, actual.

vice, *n.* **1.** fault, sin, depravity, iniquity, wickedness, corruption. **2.** blemish, blot, imperfection, defect. —**Ant.** virtue. —**Syn. Study.** See FAULT.

vicinity, *n.* **1.** area, neighborhood, environs, precincts, purlieus, vicinage, district, surroundings, environment, milieu. **2.** proximity, nearness, closeness, propinquity.

vicious, *adj.* **1.** immoral, depraved, profligate, sinful, corrupt, bad, abandoned, iniquitous. **2.** reprehensible, blameworthy, censurable, wrong, improper. **3.** spiteful, malignant, malicious, malevolent. **4.** faulty, defective. **5.** ill-tempered, bad-tempered, refractory. —**Ant.** moral; commendatory; benevolent; temperate.

victimize, *v.* dupe, swindle, cheat, deceive, trick, defraud, cozen, fool, hoodwink, beguile. —**Syn. Study.** See CHEAT.

victory, *n.* conquest,

triumph, success. —**Ant.** defeat. —**Syn. Study.** VICTORY, CONQUEST, TRIUMPH refer to a successful outcome of a struggle. VICTORY suggests the decisive defeat of an opponent in a contest of any kind: *victory in battle; a football victory.* CONQUEST implies the taking over of control by the victor, and the obedience of the conquered: *a war of conquest; the conquest of Peru.* TRIUMPH implies a particularly outstanding victory: *the triumph of a righteous cause; the triumph of justice.*

vie, *v.* compete, rival, contend, strive.

view, *n.* **1.** sight, vision. **2.** prospect, scene, vista. **3.** aspect, appearance. **4.** contemplation, examination, survey, inspection. **5.** aim, intention, purpose, reason, end, design, intent, object. **6.** consideration, regard. **7.** account, description. **8.** conception, idea, notion, opinion, theory, belief, judgment, estimation, assessment, impression, valuation. —*v.* **9.** see, behold, witness, contemplate, regard, look at, survey, inspect, examine. —**Syn. Study.** VIEW, PROSPECT, SCENE, VISTA refer to whatever lies open to sight. VIEW is the general word: *a fine view of the surrounding countryside.* PROSPECT suggests a sweeping and often distant view, as from a vantage point: *The prospect from the mountaintop was breathtaking.* SCENE suggests an organic unity in the details, as is found in a picture: *a woodland scene.* VISTA suggests a long narrow view, as along an avenue between rows of trees: *a pleasant vista.* See OPINION.

vigilant, *adj.* attentive, wary, alert, awake, sleepless, watchful. —**Ant.** inattentive, unwary.

vigorous, *adj.* strong, active, robust, sturdy, sound, healthy, hale, energetic, forcible, powerful, effective, forceful. —**Ant.** weak, inactive.

vile, *adj.* **1.** wretched, bad; base, low, vicious, evil, depraved, iniquitous. **2.** offensive, obnoxious, objectionable, repulsive, disgusting, despicable, revolting, repellent, nauseous, nauseating. **3.** foul, vulgar, obscene. **4.** poor, wretched, mean, menial, low, degraded, ignominious, contemptible. **5.** valueless, paltry, trivial, trifling, niggling, nugatory. —**Ant.** good, elevated.

vilify, *v.* defame, traduce, depreciate, slander, disparage, malign, calumniate, revile, abuse, blacken, asperse, slur, decry. —**Ant.** commend, honor, praise.

village, *n.* town, hamlet, municipality, community.

villain, *n.* scoundrel, cad, bounder, knave, rascal, rapscallion, scamp, rogue, scapegrace, miscreant, reprobate. —**Ant.** hero, protagonist.

vindicate, *v.* **1.** clear, exonerate. **2.** uphold, justify, maintain, defend, assert, support. —**Ant.** convict, blame.

vindictive, *adj.* revengeful, vengeful, spiteful, unforgiving, rancorous, unrelenting. —**Ant.** forgiving.

violation, *n.* **1.** breach, infringement, transgression. **2.** desecration, defilement. **3.** ravishment, rape, defloration, debauchment. —**Ant.** obedience. —**Syn. Study.** See BREACH.

violence, *n.* **1.** injury, wrong, outrage, injustice. **2.** vehemence, impetuosity, fury, intensity, severity, acuteness. **3.** energy, force.

virgin, *n.* **1.** maiden, maid, ingenue. —*adj.* **2.** pure, unsullied, undefiled, chaste, unpolluted. **3.** unmixed, unalloyed, pure, unadulterated. **4.** untouched, untried, unused, fresh, new, maiden. —**Ant.** defiled, polluted, impure, unchaste; adulterated.

virile, *adj.* masculine, manly, vigorous, male.

—**Ant.** effeminate. —**Syn. Study.** See MALE.

virtue, *n.* **1.** goodness, uprightness, morality, probity, rectitude, integrity. **2.** chastity, virginity, purity. **3.** justice, prudence, temperance, fortitude; faith, hope, charity. **4.** excellence, merit, quality, asset. **5.** effectiveness, efficacy, force, power, potency. —**Ant.** vice. —**Syn. Study.** See GOODNESS.

virtuous, *adj.* right, upright, moral, righteous, good, chaste, pure. —**Ant.** vicious.

virulent, *adj.* **1.** poisonous, malignant, deadly, venomous. **2.** hostile, bitter, acrimonious, acerb, spiteful, vicious. —**Ant.** harmless.

virus, *n.* poison, venom, toxin.

visage, *n.* **1.** face, countenance, physiognomy. **2.** aspect, appearance. —**Syn. Study.** See FACE.

viscous, *adj.* sticky, adhesive, glutinous, ropy, thick.

visible, *adj.* **1.** perceptible, discernible, open. **2.** understandable, discernible. **3.** apparent, manifest, obvious, evident, open, clear, patent, palpable, conspicuous, observable, unmistakable. —**Ant.** invisible.

vision, *n.* **1.** sight. **2.** perception, discernment. **3.** view, image, conception, idea, anticipation. **4.** apparition, specter, ghost, phantom, phantasm, illusion, chimera.

visionary, *adj.* **1.** fanciful, unpractical, impractical, impracticable, fancied, unreal, ideal, imaginary, speculative, illusory, chimerical, romantic. —*n.* **2.** romantic, dreamer, idealist, theorist, enthusiast. —**Ant.** practical, practicable.

visitor, *n.* caller, guest, visitant. —**Ant.** host, hostess.

vista, *n.* view. —**Syn. Study.** See VIEW.

vital, *adj.* indispensable,

essential, necessary, important, critical. —**Ant.** dispensable, secondary, unimportant.

vitriolic, *adj.* acid, bitter, caustic, scathing. —**Ant.** bland, mild, sweet.

vituperate, *v.* abuse, revile, objurgate, censure, vilify, reproach, upbraid, berate, scold. —**Ant.** praise, commend.

vivacious, *adj.* lively, animated, sprightly, spirited, brisk, sportive. —**Ant.** inanimate, dull, inactive.

vivid, *adj.* **1.** bright, brilliant, intense, clear, lucid. **2.** animated, spirited, vivacious, lively, intense. **3.** vigorous, energetic. **4.** picturesque, lifelike, realistic. **5.** perceptible, clear, discernible, apparent. **6.** strong, distinct, striking. —**Ant.** dull.

vocation, *n.* business, occupation, profession, calling, trade, métier, employment, pursuit.

vociferous, *adj.* clamorous, noisy, loud, obstreperous,

uproarious. —**Ant.** quiet, pacific, peaceful.

vogue, *n.* fashion, style, mode; currency, acceptance, favor, usage, custom, practice.

void, *adj.* **1.** useless, ineffectual, vain, ineffective, nugatory. **2.** empty, devoid, destitute, vacant. **3.** unoccupied, vacated, unfilled. —*n.* **4.** space, vacuum; gap, opening. —*v.* **5.** invalidate, nullify, annul. **6.** empty, discharge, evacuate, vacate, emit. —**Ant.** useful; full; occupied; validate; fill.

volition, *n.* will, will-power, determination, preference, discretion, choice, option.

voluble, *adj.* fluent, glib, talkative, loquacious. —**Ant.** taciturn, quiet, silent. —**Syn. Study.** See FLUENT.

volume, *n.* **1.** book, tome; scroll, manuscript, codex, papyrus. **2.** size, measure, amount, magnitude. **3.** mass, quantity, amount. **4.** loudness, softness.

voluntary, *adj.* **1.** deliberate,

considered, purposeful, willful, intentional, intended, designed, planned. **2.** spontaneous, impulsive, free, unforced, natural, unconstrained. —**Ant.** involuntary. —**Syn. Study.** See DELIBERATE.

voluptuous, *adj.* sensual, luxurious, epicurean. —**Ant.** intellectual.

voracious, *adj.* ravenous, greedy, hungry, rapacious. —**Ant.** apathetic.

vouchsafe, *v.* give, grant, bestow, confer, accord, award, concede, allow, permit, condescend, stoop, deign. —**Ant.** deny, refuse.

vow, *n., v.* pledge, promise.

voyage, *n.* trip, flight, cruise, sailing. —**Syn. Study.** See TRIP.

vulgar, *adj.* **1.** coarse, inelegant, ribald. **2.** underbred, unrefined, boorish, common, mean, ignoble, plebeian, crude, rude. **3.** vernacular, colloquial. —**Ant.** elegant; refined; standard. —**Syn. Study.** See COMMON.

vulnerable, *adj.* **1.** defenseless, exposed, unprotected, unguarded, helpless, penetrable, woundable, damageable, assailable, attackable, vincible. **2.** liable, open, susceptible, prone, at risk. —**Ant.** invulnerable, impregnable, invincible, impervious.

vying, *adj.* competing, competitive.

W

wacky, *adj.* eccentric, irrational, whimsical, knockabout, zany, madcap, foolish, silly, crazy, screwball, goofy, oddball. —**Ant.** serious, sobersided.

waffle, *v.* **1.** vacillate, dither, equivocate, hesitate, tergiversate, waver, seesaw, fluctuate, hem and haw, back and fill, yo-yo, (*Brit.*) haver. **2.** blather, babble, prattle, gabble, prate.

wage, *n.* **1.** (*usually plural*) hire, pay, salary, stipend, earnings, emolument, compensation, remuneration, allowance. **2.** recompense, return, reward. —*v.* **3.** carry on, undertake, engage in.

wager, *n.* **1.** stake, hazard, bet, risk, venture, pledge. —*v.* **2.** stake, bet, hazard, risk, lay a wager.

waggish, *adj.* roguish, jocular, humorous, mischievous, tricky, sportive, merry, jocose, droll, comical, funny.

wagon, *n.* cart, van, truck, dray; lorry, wain; buckboard, dogcart.

wait, *v.* **1.** stay, rest, expect, await, remain, be inactive *or* quiescent, linger, abide, tarry, pause, delay. —*n.* **2.** delay, halt, waiting, tarrying, lingering, pause, stop. **3.** ambushment, ambush. —**Ant.** proceed.

waive, *v.* **1.** relinquish, forgo, resign, demit, surrender, renounce, give up, remit. **2.** defer, put off *or* aside. —**Ant.** require, demand.

wake, *v.* **1.** awake, rise, arise, get up. **2.** rouse, waken, arouse, awaken. **3.** stimulate, activate, animate, kindle, provoke, motivate. —*n.* **4.** vigil, deathwatch. **5.** track, path, course, trail. —**Ant.** sleep.

wakeful, *adj.* **1.** sleepless, awake, insomnious, restless. **2.** watchful, vigilant, wary, alert, observant, on the qui vive. —**Ant.** sleepy.

waken, *v.* wake.

walk, *v.* **1.** step, stride, stroll, saunter, ambulate, perambulate, promenade, pace, march, tramp, hike, tread. —*n.* **2.** stroll, promenade, march, tramp, hike, constitutional. **3.** gait, pace, step, carriage. **4.** beat, sphere, area, field, course, career; conduct, behavior. **5.** sidewalk,

path, lane, passage,
footpath, alley, avenue.

wall, *n.* **1.** battlement,
breastwork, bulwark,
barrier, bunker, rampart,
bastion. **2.** barrier,
obstruction. **3.**
embankment, dike. —*v.* **4.**
enclose, shut off, divide,
protect; immure.

wallow, *v.* welter, flounder,
roll.

wan, *adj.* pale, pallid,
sickly, ashen. —**Ant.**
ruddy, robust. —**Syn.
Study.** See PALE.

wander, *v.* **1.** ramble, rove,
roam, stray, range, stroll,
meander, saunter. **2.**
move, pass, extend. **3.**
deviate, err, go astray,
digress, swerve, veer. **4.**
rave, be delirious.

wane, *v.* **1.** decrease,
decline, diminish, fail,
sink. —*n.* **2.** decrease,
decline, diminution;
failure, decay. —**Ant.**
wax.

wangle, *v.* manipulate,
maneuver, finagle,
connive, machinate,
scheme, plot, intrigue,

connive, con, talk into,
angle, (*Brit.*) nobble.

wannabe, *n.* aspirant,
aspirer, emulator, hopeful,
seeker, wisher, wanter,
imitator, candidate,
postulant, applicant,
solicitant.

want, *v.* **1.** need, desire,
wish, require, lack. —*n.* **2.**
necessity, need,
requirement, desideratum.
3. lack, dearth, scarcity,
scarceness, inadequacy,
insufficiency, scantiness,
paucity, meagerness,
deficiency, defectiveness.
4. destitution, poverty,
privation, penury,
indigence, straits. —**Ant.**
relinquish. —**Syn. Study.**
See LACK.

wanton, *adj.* **1.** reckless,
malicious, unjustifiable,
careless, heedless, willful,
inconsiderate, groundless.
2. deliberate, calculated,
uncalled-for. **3.** unruly,
wild, reckless. **4.** lawless,
unbridled, loose,
lascivious, lewd, licentious,
dissolute, lustful, prurient,
lecherous, salacious,
incontinent, concupiscent,
libidinous. **5.** luxurious,

magnificent, elegant, lavish. —*v.* **6.** squander, waste. —**Ant.** justifiable, careful; lawful; prudish; inelegant; save.

warble, *v.* sing, trill, vocalize, carol, lilt, give voice, descant, croon, chant, intone, pipe, belt.

warden, *n.* warder, guardian, guard, custodian, keeper, caretaker, superintendent.

wardrobe, *n.* furnishings, apparel, wear, clothing, clothes, garb, attire, garments, habiliment, dress, haberdashery, raiment, gear, duds, togs, threads.

warlike, *adj.* martial, military; bellicose, belligerent, hostile, inimical, unfriendly. —**Ant.** peaceful.

warm, *adj.* **1.** lukewarm, tepid, heated. **2.** hearty, enthusiastic, emotional, zealous, fervent, fervid, ardent, excited, eager. **3.** cordial, hearty, glowing. **4.** attached, friendly, amiable, amicable, close, inimate.

5. heated, irritated, annoyed, vexed, angry, irate, furious. **6.** animated, lively, brisk, vigorous, vehement. **7.** strong, fresh. —*v.* **8.** warm up, heat up, heat, make warm. **9.** animate, excite, waken, stir, stir up, rouse, arouse. —**Ant.** cool.

warn, *v.* **1.** caution, admonish, forewarn. **2.** notify, apprise, inform. —**Syn. Study.** WARN, CAUTION, ADMONISH imply attempting to prevent someone from running into danger or unpleasant circumstances. To WARN is to inform plainly and strongly of possible or imminent trouble, or to advise that doing or not doing something will have dangerous consequences: *The scout warned the fort of the attack. I warned them not to travel to that country.* To CAUTION is to advise to be careful and to take necessary precautions: *Tourists were cautioned to watch their belongings.* To ADMONISH is to advise of negligence or a fault in an earnest, authoritative, but friendly way, so that corrective action can be taken: *to admonish a student for constant lateness.*

warning, *n.* caution, admonition, advice; omen, sign, augury, presage, portent.

warp, *v.* **1.** bend, twist, turn, contort, distort, spring. **2.** swerve, deviate. **3.** distort, bias, pervert. —**Ant.** straighten.

warrant, *n.* **1.** authorization, sanction, justification, commission. **2.** pledge, guarantee, assurance, security, surety, warranty. **3.** certificate, license, receipt, commission, permit, voucher, writ, order, chit. —*v.* **4.** authorize, sanction, approve, justify, guarantee, vouch for. **5.** assure, promise, guarantee, secure, affirm, vouch for, attest.

wary, *adj.* alert, cautious, vigilant, careful, circumspect, watchful, scrupulous, discreet.

—**Ant.** unwary. —**Syn. Study.** See CAREFUL.

wash, *v.* **1.** cleanse, clean, lave, launder, scrub, mob, swab, rub. **2.** wet, bedew, moisten. **3.** bathe. —*n.* **4.** washing, ablution, cleansing, bathing. **5.** fen, marsh, bog, swamp, morass, slough.

washout, *n.* failure, loss, flop, fiasco, botch, fizzle, clinker, nonstarter, loser, dud, bust, turkey, also-ran. —**Ant.** success, win, triumph.

waspish, *adj.* **1.** resentful, snappish. **2.** irascible, petulant, testy.

waste, *v.* **1.** consume, spend, throw out, expend, squander, misspend, dissipate. **2.** destroy, consume, wear away, erode, eat away, reduce, wear down, emaciate, enfeeble. **3.** lay waste, devastate, ruin, ravage, pillage, plunder, desolate, sack, spoil, despoil. **4.** diminish, dwindle, perish, wane, decay. —*n.* **5.** consumption, expenditure, dissipation, diminution, decline, emaciation, loss, destruction, decay, impairment. **6.** ruin, devastation, spoliation, desolation, plunder, pillage. **7.** desert, wilderness, wild. **8.** refuse, rubbish, trash, garbage. —*adj.* **9.** unused, useless, superfluous, extra, *de trop.* **10.** uninhabited, desert, deserted, wild, desolate, barren. **11.** decayed, ghost; devastated, laid waste, ruined, ravaged, sacked, destroyed. **12.** rejected, refuse. —**Ant.** save.

watch, *v.* **1.** look, see, observe. **2.** contemplate, regard, mark, view, look upon. **3.** wait for, await, expect. **4.** guard, protect, tend. —*n.* **5.** observation, inspection, attention. **6.** lookout, sentinel, sentry, watchman, guard; vigil, watchfulness, alertness. **7.** timepiece.

watchful, *adj.* vigilant, alert, observant, attentive, heedful, careful, circumspect, cautious, wary, wakeful, awake. —**Ant.** unwary, inattentive, incautious.

watchword, *n.* **1.** password, countersign, shibboleth. **2.** slogan, motto.

watery, *adj.* **1.** wet, fluid, liquid, flowing, runny, liquidy, aqueous, serous, hydrous, hydrated, teary. **2.** dilute, diluted, watered, watered-down, weak, thin, feeble, wishy-washy, tasteless, bland. —**Ant.** dry, sere, parched, arid; strong, potent, full-strength.

wave, *n.* **1.** ridge, swell, undulation, ripple, breaker, surf, sea. —*v.* **2.** undulate, fluctuate, oscillate; flutter, float, sway, rock. —**Ant.** hollow.

waver, *v.* **1.** sway, flutter. **2.** thicker, quiver. **3.** shake, tremble, quiver, shiver. **4.** vacillate, fluctuate, alternate, hesitate. —**Syn. Study.** WAVER, VACILLATE refer to an inability to decide or to stick to a decision. WAVER usu. implies a state of doubt, uncertainty, or fear that prevents one from pursuing a chosen course: *He made plans to move,* *but wavered at the last minute.* VACILLATE means to go back and forth between choices without reaching a decision, or to make up one's mind and change it again suddenly: *Stop vacillating and set a day.*

wax, *v.* **1.** increase, extend, grow, lengthen, enlarge, dilate. **2.** grow, become, come *or* get to be. —**Ant.** wane.

way, *n.* **1.** manner, mode, fashion, method. **2.** habit, custom, usage, practice, wont. **3.** means, course, plan, method, scheme, device. **4.** respect, particular, detail, part. **5.** direction. **6.** passage, progress, extent. **7.** distance, space, interval. **8.** path, course, passage, channel, road, route, track, avenue, highroad, highway, freeway, throughway. —**Syn. Study.** See METHOD.

wayward, *adj.* **1.** contrary, headstrong, stubborn, capricious, captious, obstinate, disobedient, unruly, refractory, intractable, willful,

perverse. **2.** irregular, unsteady, inconstant, changeable. —**Ant.** agreeable, obedient, tractable; regular, constant. —**Syn. Study.** See WILLFUL.

weak, *adj.* **1.** fragile, frail, breakable, delicate. **2.** feeble, senile, anile, old, infirm, decrepit, weakly, sickly, unhealthy, unwell, debilitated, invalid. **3.** impotent, ineffectual, ineffective, inefficient, inadequate, inefficacious. **4.** unconvincing, inconclusive, lame, illogical, unsatisfactory, vague. **5.** unintelligent, simple, foolish, stupid, senseless, silly. **6.** irresolute, vacillating, unstable, unsteady, wavering, weak-kneed, fluctuating, undecided. **7.** faint, slight, slender, slim, inconsiderable, flimsy, poor, trifling, trivial. **8.** deficient, wanting, short, lacking, insufficient. —**Ant.** strong.

weaken, *v.* enfeeble, debilitate, enervate, undermine, sap, exhaust, deplete, diminish, lessen, lower, reduce, impair, minimize, invalidate. —**Ant.** strengthen.

weakling, *n.* coward, craven, recreant, dastard, poltroon, caitiff, milksop, baby, doormat, yes-man, Milquetoast, mollycoddle, jellyfish, weak sister, empty suit, invertebrate, wuss, wimp, crybaby, mama's boy, pantywaist, sissy, nebbish, gutless wonder, chicken, quitter.

weakly, *adj.* weak, feeble, sickly. —**Ant.** strong.

weakness, *n.* **1.** feebleness, fragility. **2.** flaw, defect, fault. **3.** tenderness, liking, inclination. —**Ant.** strength. —**Syn. Study.** See FAULT.

wealth, *n.* **1.** property, riches. **2.** abundance, profusion. **3.** assets, possessions, goods, property. **4.** affluence, opulence, fortune, treasure, funds, cash, pelf. —**Ant.** poverty.

wealthy, *adj.* **1.** rich, affluent, opulent,

prosperous, well-to-do, moneyed. **2.** abundant, ample, copious. —**Ant.** poor, poverty-stricken; scanty, scarce.

wearisome, *adj.* **1.** fatiguing, tiring. **2.** tiresome, boring, tedious, irksome, monotonous, humdrum, dull, prosy, prosaic, vexatious, trying. —**Ant.** energetic; interesting.

weary, *adj.* **1.** exhausted, tired, wearied, fatigued, spent. **2.** impatient, dissatisfied. **3.** tiresome, tedious, irksome, wearisome. —*v.* **4.** fatigue, tire, exhaust, tire *or* wear out, jade. **5.** harass, harry, irk. —**Ant.** energetic; patient; interesting; interest, captivate.

weather-beaten, *adj.* **1.** weathered, weather-scarred, roughened, storm-tossed, battered, run-down, worn-down, faded, worn, washed-out, bleached, damaged, eroded, etiolated. **2.** tanned, bronzed, darkened, toughened, roughened.

weave, *v.* **1.** interlace, intertwine, braid, plait. **2.** contrive, fabricate, construct, compose. **3.** introduce, insert, intermix, intermingle.

weep, *v.* shed tears, cry, sob, lament, bewail, bemoan. —**Ant.** laugh, rejoice.

weigh, *v.* consider, balance, ponder, contemplate, study. —**Syn. Study.** See STUDY.

weight, *n.* influence, importance, power, moment, efficacy, import, consequence, significance.

weighty, *adj.* **1.** heavy, ponderous. **2.** burdensome, onerous. **3.** important, momentous, significant, serious, grave, consequential. —**Ant.** light; unimportant, insignificant.

weird, *adj.* eerie, ghostly, unearthly, ultramundane, uncanny, mysterious, unnatural, supernatural, preternatural. —**Ant.** natural. —**Syn. Study.** WEIRD, EERIE, UNCANNY refer to that which is mysterious and apparently outside natural law. WEIRD suggests the intervention of supernatural influences in human affairs: *weird doings in the haunted house; a weird coincidence.* EERIE refers to something ghostly that makes one's flesh creep: *eerie moans from a deserted house.* UNCANNY refers to an extraordinary or remarkable thing that seems to defy the laws established by experience: *an uncanny ability to recall numbers.*

welfare, *n.* well-being, prosperity, success, happiness, weal, benefit, profit, advantage.

well, *adv.* **1.** satisfactorily, favorable, advantageously, fortunately, happily. **2.** commendably, meritoriously, excellently. **3.** properly, correctly, skillfully, adeptly, efficiently, accurately. **4.** judiciously, reasonably, suitably, properly. **5.** adequately, sufficiently, satisfactorily. **6.** thoroughly, soundly,

abundantly, amply, fully.
7. considerably, rather,
quite, fairly. **8.** personally,
intimately. —*adj.* **9.** sound,
healthy, healthful, hale,
hearty. **10.** satisfactory,
good, fine. **11.** proper,
fitting, suitable, befitting,
appropriate. **12.** fortunate,
successful, well-off, happy.
—**Ant.** poorly, badly; ill,
sick.

well-built, *adj.* **1.**
able-bodied, well-knit,
well-proportioned,
muscular, well-muscled,
athletic, brawny, burly,
thickset, stacked, hunky.
2. sturdy, strong, durable,
solid, rugged,
well-constructed,
well-made, well-finished.
—**Ant.** scrawny, fragile.

wet, *adj.* **1.** soaked,
drenched, dampened,
moistened. **2.** damp,
moist, dank, humid. **3.**
humid, misty, drizzling,
rainy. —*n.* **4.** moisture,
wetness, rain, humidity,
drizzle, dampness,
dankness. —*v.* **5.** drench,
saturate, soak, ret. —**Ant.**
dry.

wherewithal, *n.* means,
resources, resorts,
recourses, money, cash,
funds, capital, bankroll,
finances, purse, assets.

whim, *n.* fancy, notion,
caprice, whimsy, humor,
vagary, quirk, crotchet,
chimera. —**Ant.**
consideration.

whimsical, *adj.* capricious,
notional, changeable,
crotchety, freakish,
fanciful, odd, peculiar,
curious, singular, queer,
quaint.

whine, *v.* complain,
grumble; moan, cry.
—**Syn. Study.** See
COMPLAIN.

whip, *v.* **1.** lash, beat; flog,
thrash, scourge, beat,
switch, punish, flagellate,
chastise; castigate. **2.** pull,
jerk, snatch, seize, whisk.
—*n.* **3.** switch, leash,
scourge.

whirl, *v.* **1.** gyrate,
pirouette, spin, rotate,
revolve, twirl, wheel. —*n.*
2. rotation, gyration, spin,
revolution.

whiten, *v.* blanch, bleach,

etiolate. —**Ant.** blacken, darken.

whitewash, *v.* **1.** gloss over, cover up, hide, conceal, disguise, camouflage, paper over, mask. **2.** justify, excuse, alibi, exculpate, palter, extenuate, explain away, vindicate.

whole, *adj.* **1.** entire, full, total, undiminished, undivided, integral, complete, unbroken, unimpaired, perfect, uninjured, faultless, undamaged, sound, intact. —*n.* **2.** totality, total, sum, entirety, aggregate, sum total. —**Ant.** partial; part.

wholesome, *adj.* **1.** salutary, beneficial, helpful, good. **2.** healthful, salubrious, nourishing, nutritious, healthy, salutary, invigorating. —**Ant.** unwholesome. —**Syn. Study.** See HEALTHY.

wicked, *adj.* evil, bad, immoral, amoral, unprincipled, sinful, piacular, unrighteous, ungodly, godless, impious, profane, blasphemous;

profligate, corrupt, depraved, dissolute, heinous, vicious, vile, iniquitous, abandoned, flagitious, nefarious, treacherous, villainous, atrocious. —**Ant.** good.

wide, *adj.* **1.** broad. **2.** extensive, vast, spacious, ample, comprehensive, large, expanded, distended. —**Ant.** narrow.

wild, *adj.* **1.** untamed, undomesticated, feral, ferine, savage, unbroken, ferocious. **2.** uncultivated, uninhabited. **3.** uncivilized, barbarous, barbarian. **4.** violent, furious, boisterous, tempestuous, stormy, disorderly, frenzied, turbulent, impetuous. **5.** frantic, mad, distracted, crazy, insane. **6.** enthusiastic, eager, anxious. **7.** excited. **8.** undisciplined, unruly, lawless, turbulent, self-willed, ungoverned, unrestrained, riotous, wayward, outrageous. **9.** unrestrained, unbridled, uncontrolled, untrammeled. **10.** reckless, rash, fantastic,

extravagant, impracticable.
11. queer, grotesque, bizarre, strange, imaginary, fanciful, visionary. **12.** disorderly, disheveled, unkempt. —*n.* **13.** waste, wilderness, desert. —**Ant.** tame, domesticated.

wilderness, *n.* wild.

wild-eyed, *adj.* **1.** wild, manic, maniacal, rabid, frantic, frenzied, raving, amok, mad, crazy, berserk. **2.** visionary, quixotic, unrealistic, extreme, fanatical, fanatic, far-out, off-the-wall, harebrained. —**Ant.** calm, composed; sensible, practical.

wile, *n.* **1.** trick, artifice, stratagem, ruse, deception, contrivance, maneuver, device. **2.** deceit, cunning, trickery, chicanery, fraud, cheating, defrauding, imposture, imposition.

will, *n.* **1.** determination, resolution, resoluteness, decision, forcefulness. **2.** volition, choice. **3.** wish, desire, pleasure, disposition, inclination. **4.** purpose, determination. **5.** order, direction, command, behest, bidding. —*v.* **6.** decide, decree, determine, direct, command, bid. **7.** bequeath, devise, leave.

willful, *adj.* **1.** willed, voluntary, intentional, volitional. **2.** self-willed, headstrong, perverse, obstinate, intractable, wayward, stubborn, intransigent, persistent, contrary, contumacious, refractory, disagreeable, pigheaded, cantankerous, unruly, inflexible, obdurate, adamant. —**Ant.** unintentional, involuntary; tractable. —**Syn. Study.** WILLFUL, HEADSTRONG, PERVERSE, WAYWARD refer to a person who stubbornly persists in doing as he or she pleases. WILLFUL implies opposition to those whose wishes, suggestions, or commands ought to be respected or obeyed: *a willful son who ignored his parents' advice.* HEADSTRONG is used in a similar way, but implies foolish and sometimes reckless behavior: *headstrong teens who could* *not be restrained.* PERVERSE implies stubborn persistence in opposing what is right or acceptable, often with the express intention of being contrary or disagreeable: *taking a perverse delight in arguing with others.* WAYWARD suggests stubborn disobedience that gets one into trouble: *a reform school for wayward youths.*

wily, *adj.* crafty, cunning, artful, sly, foxy, tricky, intriguing, arch, designing, deceitful, treacherous, crooked, seditious. **—Ant.** dull, stupid.

win, *v.* **1.** succeed, advance, win out. **2.** obtain, gain, procure, secure, earn, acquire, achieve, attain, reach. **3.** win over, persuade, convince. **—Ant.** lose. **—Syn. Study.** See GAIN.

wince, *v.* recoil, shrink, quail, cringe, flinch, draw back **—Syn. Study.** WINCE, RECOIL, SHRINK, QUAIL all mean to draw back from what is dangerous, fearsome, difficult, or unpleasant. WINCE suggests an involuntary contraction of the facial features triggered by pain, embarrassment, or revulsion: *to wince as a needle pierces the skin; to wince at coarse language.* RECOIL denotes a physical movement away from something disgusting or shocking, or a similar psychological shutting out or avoidance: *to recoil at the sight of a dead body; to recoil from the idea of retiring.* SHRINK may imply a fastidious and scrupulous avoidance of the distasteful, or a cowardly withdrawal from what is feared: *to shrink from mentioning a shameful act; to shrink from asking for a raise.* QUAIL often suggests trembling or other physical manifestations of fear: *to quail before an angry mob.*

wind, *n.* **1.** air, blast, breeze, gust, zephyr, draught. **2.** hint, intimation, suggestion. **3.** vanity, conceitedness, flatulence, emptiness. **4.**

winding, bend, turn, curve, twist, twisting. —*v.* **5.** bend, turn, meander, curve, be devious. **6.** coil, twine, twist, encircle, wreathe. —**Syn. Study.** WIND, BREEZE, ZEPHYR, GUST, BLAST refer to a current of air set in motion naturally. WIND applies to air in motion, blowing with any degree of gentleness or violence: *a strong wind; a westerly wind.* A BREEZE is usu. a cool, light wind; technically, it is a wind of 4–31 mph: *a refreshing breeze.* ZEPHYR, a literary word, refers to a soft, mild breeze: *a zephyr whispering through palm trees.* A GUST is a sudden, brief rush of air: *A gust of wind scattered the leaves.* A BLAST is a brief but more violent rush of air, usu. a cold one: *a wintry blast.*

wink, *v.* **1.** blink, nictitate. **2.** twinkle, sparkle.

winning, *adj.* taking, engaging, charming, captivating, attractive, winsome. —**Ant.** losing, repulsive.

wisdom, *n.* **1.** discretion, judgment, discernment, sense, common sense, sagacity, insight, understanding, prudence. **2.** knowledge, information, learning, sapience, erudition, enlightenment. —**Ant.** stupidity.

wise, *adj.* **1.** discerning, judicious, sage, sensible, penetrating, sagacious, intelligent, perspicacious, profound, rational, prudent, reasonable. **2.** learned, erudite, schooled. —*n.* **3.** manner, fashion; respect, degree. —**Ant.** unwise.

wish, *v.* **1.** want, crave, desire, long for; need, lack. **2.** bid, direct, command, order. —*n.* **3.** desire, will, want, inclination.

wit, *n.* **1.** drollery, facetiousness, repartee, humor. **2.** understanding, intelligence, sagacity, wisdom, intellect, mind, sense. —**Syn. Study.** See HUMOR.

withdraw, *v.* **1.** draw back *or* away, take back, subtract, remove; retract, recall, disavow, recant, revoke, rescind. **2.** depart, retire, retreat, secede. —**Ant.** advance.

wither, *v.* shrivel, fade, decay, wrinkle, shrink, dry, decline, wilt, languish, droop, waste, waste away. —**Ant.** flourish, thrive.

withhold, *v.* hold back, restrain, check, keep back, suppress, repress. —**Ant.** promote, advance. —**Syn. Study.** See KEEP.

withstand, *v.* resist, oppose, confront, face, face up to, hold out against. —**Ant.** fail. —**Syn. Study.** See OPPOSE.

witness, *v.* **1.** see, perceive, observe, watch, look at, mark, notice, note. **2.** testify, bear witness. —*n.* **3.** beholder, spectator, eyewitness. **4.** testimony, evidence.

witty, *adj.* facetious, droll, humorous, funny, clever, original, sparkling, brilliant, jocose, jocular. —**Ant.** silly, stupid.

wizard, *n.* enchanter, magician, sorcerer, necromancer, conjurer, charmer, diviner, seer, soothsayer.

woe, *n.* distress, affliction, trouble, sorrow, grief, misery, anguish, tribulation, trial, agony, wretchedness, disconsolateness, depression, melancholy. —**Ant.** joy, happiness.

woman, *n.* female, lady. —**Ant.** man. —**Syn. Study.** WOMAN, FEMALE, LADY are nouns referring to adult human beings who are biologically female, that is, capable of bearing offspring. WOMAN is the general, neutral term: *a wealthy woman.* In scientific, statistical, and other objective use FEMALE is the neutral contrastive term to MALE: *104 females to every 100 males.* FEMALE is sometimes used disparagingly: *a gossipy female.* LADY in the sense "polite, refined woman" is a term of approval: *We know you will always behave like a lady.*

womanish, See Syn. study at WOMANLY.

womanlike, See Syn. study at WOMANLY.

womanly, *adj.* womanlike, womanish; feminine, female; attractive, mature, motherly, fully developed, ripe —**Syn. Study.** WOMANLY, WOMANLIKE, WOMANISH mean having traits or qualities considered typical of or appropriate to adult human females. WOMANLY, a term of approval, suggests such admirable traits as self-possession, modesty, and motherliness: *a womanly consideration for others.* WOMANLIKE may be a neutral synonym for WOMANLY, or it may convey mild disapproval: *womanlike tears and reproaches.* WOMANISH is usually disparaging. Applied to women, it suggests traits not socially approved: *a womanish petulance;* applied to men, it suggests traits not culturally acceptable for men but (in what is regarded as a sexist notion) typical of women:

a womanish shrillness in his speech. See also FEMALE.

wonder, *v.* **1.** think, speculate, conjecture, mediate, ponder, question. **2.** marvel, be astonished *or* astounded. —*n.* **3.** surprise, astonishment, amazement, awe, bewilderment, puzzlement; admiration.

wonderful, *adj.* marvelous, extraordinary, remarkable, awesome, startling, wondrous, miraculous, prodigious, astonishing, amazing, astounding, phenomenal, unique, curious, strange, odd, peculiar, (*slang*) phat. —**Ant.** usual, ordinary, common.

wont, *adj.* **1.** accustomed, used, habituated, wonted. —*n.* **2.** custom, habit, practice, use. —**Ant.** unaccustomed.

word, *n.* **1.** expression, utterance; assertion, affirmation, declaration, statement, asseveration. **2.** warrant, assurance, promise, pledge. **3.** intelligence, tidings, news, report, account, advice, information. **4.** signal, catchword, password, watchword, shibboleth, countersign. **5.** order, command, bidding. —*v.* **6.** express, style, phrase.

wording, *n.* diction, phrasing, expressing.

wordy, *adj.* prolix, redundant, verbose, pleonastic, tedious, superfluous —**Syn. Study.** WORDY, PROLIX, REDUNDANT, VERBOSE all mean using more words than necessary to convey the desired meaning. WORDY, the broadest of these terms, may merely refer to the use of many words but usu. implies that the speech or writing is wearisome or ineffectual: *a wordy review that obscured the main point.* PROLIX refers to speech or writing extended to tedious length by the inclusion of inconsequential details: *a prolix style that robs the story of all its excitement.* REDUNDANT refers to unnecessary repetition by using different words or

expressions to convey the same idea: *The editor cut four redundant paragraphs from the article.* VERBOSE adds the idea of pompous or bombastic speech or writing that has little substance: *a verbose speech that put everyone to sleep.*

work, *n.* **1.** exertion, labor, toil, drudgery, moil. **2.** undertaking, task, enterprise, project, responsibility. **3.** employment, industry, occupation, business, profession, trade, calling, vocation, metier. **4.** deed, performance, fruit, fruition, feat, achievement. —*v.* **5.** labor, toil, moil, drudge. **6.** act, operate. **7.** operate, use, manipulate, manage, handle. **8.** bring about, perform, produce, cause, do, execute, finish, effect, originate, accomplish, achieve. **9.** make, fashion, execute, finish. **10.** move, persuade, influence. —**Ant.** leisure, indolence, idleness, sloth. —**Syn. Study.** WORK, DRUDGERY, LABOR, TOIL refer to exertion of body or mind in performing or accomplishing something. WORK is a general word that refers to exertion that is either easy or hard: *pleasurable work; backbreaking work.* DRUDGERY suggests continuous, dreary, and dispiriting work, esp. of a menial or servile kind: *Cleaning these blinds is sheer drudgery.* LABOR denotes hard manual work, esp. for wages: *Repairing the bridge will require months of labor.* TOIL suggests wearying or exhausting labor: *The farmer's health was failing from constant toil.*

worked, *adj.* wrought, formed, fashioned, forged, crafted, devised —**Syn. Study.** WORKED, WROUGHT both apply to something on which effort has been applied. WORKED implies expended effort of almost any kind: *a worked silver mine.* WROUGHT implies fashioning, molding, or making, esp. of metals: *wrought iron.*

worldly, *adj.* **1.** secular, earthly, mundane, temporal, terrestrial, common. **2.** mundane, urbane, cosmopolitan, suave. —**Ant.** spiritual; naive. —**Syn. Study.** See EARTHLY.

world-weary, *adj.* apathetic, depressed, anomic, jaded, indifferent, uncaring, blasé, impassive, detached, listless, burned-out, downbeat, pessimistic, cynical. —**Ant.** optimistic, cheerful, hopeful.

worry, *v.* **1.** fret, torment oneself, chafe, be troubled *or* vexed, fidget. **2.** trouble, torment, annoy, plague, pester, bother, vex, tease, harry, hector, harass, molest, persecute, badger, irritate, disquiet, disturb. —*n.* **3.** uneasiness, anxiety, apprehension, solicitude, concern, disquiet, fear, misgiving, care. —**Syn. Study.** See CONCERN.

worship, *n.* **1.** reverence, homage, adoration, honor. **2.** regard, idolizing, idolatry, deification. —*v.* **3.** revere, respect, venerate, reverence, honor, glorify, adore. **4.** adore, adulate, idolize, deify, love, like. —**Ant.** detest.

worth, *adj.* **1.** deserving, meriting, justifying. —*n.* **2.** usefulness, value, importance, merit, worthiness, credit, excellence. —**Ant.** uselessness. —**Syn. Study.** See VALUE.

worthy, *adj.* commendable, meritorious, worthwhile, deserving, estimable, excellent, exemplary, righteous, upright, honest. —**Ant.** unworthy.

wound, *n.* **1.** injury, hurt, cut, stab, laceration, lesion, damage. **2.** harm, insult, pain, grief, anguish. —*v.* **3.** injure, hurt, harm, damage, cut, stab, lacerate.

wrath, *n.* anger, ire, rage, resentment, indignation, dudgeon, irritation, fury, choler, exasperation, passion. —**Ant.** equanimity, pleasure, delight.

wrathful, *adj.* angry, ireful, irate, furious, enraged, raging, incensed, resentful,

indignant. —**Ant.** equable, pleased.

wreck, *n.* **1.** ruin, destruction, devastation, desolation. **2.** shipwreck. —*v.* **3.** shipwreck, spoil, destroy, devastate, ruin, shatter. —**Ant.** create.

wrest, *v.* extract, take. —**Ant.** give, yield.

wretched, *adj.* **1.** miserable, pitiable, dejected, distressed, woeful, afflicted, woebegone, forlorn, unhappy, depressed. **2.** sorry, miserable, despicable, mean, base, vile, bad, contemptible, poor, pitiful, worthless. —**Ant.** happy. —**Syn. Study.** See MISERABLE.

wrong, *adj.* **1.** bad, evil, wicked, sinful, immoral, piacular, iniquitous, reprehensible, unjust, crooked, dishonest. **2.** erroneous, inaccurate, incorrect, false, untrue, mistaken. **3.** improper, inappropriate, unfit, unsuitable. **4.** awry, amiss, out of order. —*n.* **5.** evil, wickedness, misdoing, misdeed, sin, vice, immorality, iniquity. —*v.* **6.** injure, harm, maltreat, abuse, oppress, cheat, defraud, dishonor. —**Ant.** right.

wrongheaded, *adj.* perverse, stubborn, contrary, ornery, balky, wayward, obstinate, unreasonable, froward, difficult, mulish. —**Ant.** reasonable, compliant.

wrought, See Syn. study at WORKED.

wry, *adj.* **1.** bent, twisted, crooked, distorted, awry, askew. **2.** devious, misdirected, perverted. —**Ant.** straight; pointed.

X Y Z

xanthous, *adj.* yellow.

xenophobic, *adj.* restrictive, exclusive, exclusionary, prohibitionary, closed-door, selective, restricted, restrictive, chauvinist, chauvinistic, jingoistic, insular, separatist, segregationist, discriminatory, intolerant, biased, bigoted, racist, ethnocentric. —**Ant.** inclusive, welcoming.

x-rated, *adj.* erotic, sexy, sexual, adult, salacious, lewd, bawdy, ribald, obscene, pornographic. —**Ant.** clean, wholesome, innocuous.

x-ray, *v.* **1.** roentgenize. —*n.* **2.** roentgenogram.

xylograph, *n.* wood engraving.

xyloid, *adj.* woodlike, ligneous.

yahoo, *n.* **1.** boor, vulgarian, churl, lout, barbarian, know-nothing, ignoramus, redneck, ruffian, Neanderthal, slob. **2.** rube, yokel, hayseed, hick, groundling. **3.** dullard, dope, dunce, buffoon, clown, dimwit, bozo.

yawn, *v.* **1.** gape. —*n.* **2.** opening, space, chasm.

yearn, *v.* long, hanker,

pine, yen, crave, hunger, covet. —**Syn. Study.** YEARN, LONG, HANKER, PINE all mean to feel a strong desire for something. YEARN stresses the depth and power of the desire: *to yearn to begin a new life.* LONG implies a wholehearted desire for something that is or seems unattainable: *to long to relive one's childhood.* HANKER suggests a restless or incessant craving: *to hanker after fame and fortune.* PINE adds the notion of physical or emotional suffering due to the real or apparent hopelessness of one's desire: *to pine for a lost love.*

yearning, *n.* longing, craving, desire. —**Syn. Study.** See DESIRE.

yes-man, *n.* flatterer, sycophant, toady, apple-polisher, stooge, boot-licker, flunky, lackey, rubber stamp, minion, myrmidon.

yield, *v.* **1.** give forth, produce, furnish, supply, render, bear, impart, afford, bestow. **2.** give up, cede, surrender, submit, give way, concede, relinquish, abandon, abdicate, resign, waive, forgo. **3.** relax, bend, bow. —*n.* **4.** produce, harvest, fruit, crop. —**Syn. Study.** YIELD, SUBMIT, SURRENDER mean to give way or give up to a person or thing. To YIELD is to relinquish or concede under some degree of pressure, either from a position of weakness or from one of advantage: *to yield ground to an enemy; to yield the right of way.* To SUBMIT is to give up more completely to authority or superior force and to cease opposition, usu. with reluctance: *The mutineers finally submitted to the captain's orders.* To SURRENDER is to give up complete possession of and claim to, usu. after resistance: *to surrender a fortress; to surrender one's rights.*

young, *adj.* **1.** youthful, juvenile, immature. —*n.* **2.** offspring. —**Ant.** old, ancient; progenitors, parents.

youngster, *n.* youth, lad, stripling, child, boy. —**Ant.** oldster.

youth, *n.* **1.** youngness, minority, adolescence, teens, immaturity. **2.** young man, youngster, teen-ager, adolescent, stripling, lad, boy, juvenile. —**Ant.** maturity; man, adult.

youthful, *adj.* young. —**Ant.** old.

yo-yo, *v.* vacillate, fluctuate, vary, shift, dither, equivocate, waffle, hesitate, tergiversate, waver, seesaw, fluctuate, hem and haw, come and go, (*Brit.*) haver. —**Ant.** stabilize.

Yule, *n.* Christmas, Christmastide.

zaftig, *adj.* rounded, Rubenesque, full, plump, pleasingly plump, curvaceous, curvy, buxom, voluptuous, pneumatic, built for comfort. —**Ant.** gaunt, skinny, emaciated, shapeless.

zany, *adj.* **1.** comic, comical, farcical, funny, droll, whimsical, waggish, prankish, lunatic, ludicrous, hilarious, crazy, off-the-wall, loopy. —*n.* **2.** comic, clown, comedian, joker, jokester, cutup, prankster, merry-andrew, madcap, buffoon, kook, nut, weirdo.

zap, *v.* eliminate, annihilate, terminate, take out, waste, nuke, cancel, stop, undo, do in, finish, finish off, knock out, abort, scrub, censor, censor out, edit out, delete, erase.

zeal, *n.* ardor, enthusiasm, diligence, eagerness, fervor, desire, endeavor, fervency, warmth, earnestness, intensity, intenseness, passion, spirit. —**Ant.** apathy, coolness.

zealot, *n.* bigot, fanatic, maniac. —**Syn. Study.** See FANATIC.

zealous, *adj.* ardent, enthusiastic, eager, earnest, fervid, fervent, warm, intense, passionate, spirited. —**Ant.** apathetic, uninterested, dispassionate, cool.

zephyr, *n.* breeze. —**Syn. Study.** See WIND.

zest, *n.* piquancy, interest, charm; relish, gusto, heartiness, enjoyment, spice, tang. —**Ant.** dullness.

zilch, *n.* nothing, zero, nil, naught, aught, zip, nada, nix, goose egg, diddly, diddly-squat, squat.

zone, *n.* **1.** belt, tract, area, region, district, section, girth. **2.** region, climate, clime. —*v.* **3.** encircle, gird, girdle, band.

zymosis, *n.* fermentation; germination; decomposition; decay.

THESE GREAT TITLES ARE ALSO AVAILABLE IN LARGE PRINT:

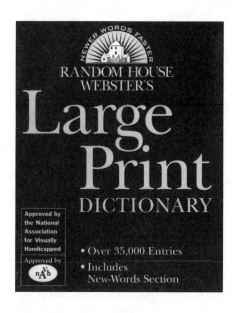

HARDCOVER: 0-375-40114-8
PAPERBACK: 0-375-70106-0
Complete Your Large Print
Reference Set!

0-679-77450-5
The #1 Bestseller That Will
Bring Health and Wellness
Into Your Life

0-679-77452-1
The National Bestseller from
Mystery Writer P. D. James